Bible Readings
for the Home

STUDYING THE WORD OF GOD

"Search the scriptures; for in them ye think ye have eternal life: and they are they which testify of me." John 5:39

Bible Readings
for the Home

A Study of 200 Vital Scripture Topics
in Question-and-Answer Form
Contributed by a Large
Number of Bible
Scholars

Revised and Newly Illustrated
Sixteen Full Pages in Color

REVIEW AND HERALD PUBLISHING ASSOCIATION

Washington, D.C.

1958

COPYRIGHTED MCMXIV, MCMXXXV, MCMXLII,
MCMXLIX, AND MCMLVIII BY THE
REVIEW AND HERALD PUBLISHING ASSOCIATION
COPYRIGHTED IN LONDON, ENGLAND
ALL RIGHTS RESERVED

OFFSET IN THE U.S.A.

Table of Contents

	PAGE
THE BIBLE—ITS ORIGIN, HISTORY, AND PLACE IN THE WORLD	13
THE VALUE OF BIBLE STUDY	19

PART I—The Bible; How to Study and Understand It

THE SACRED SCRIPTURES	25
HOW TO UNDERSTAND THE BIBLE	28
POWER IN THE WORD OF GOD	33
THE LIFE-GIVING WORD	36
CHRIST IN ALL THE BIBLE	39

PART II—Sin; Its Origin, Results, and Remedy

CREATION AND THE CREATOR	45
THE ORIGIN OF EVIL	48
THE FALL AND REDEMPTION OF MAN	50
CREATION AND REDEMPTION	55
THE CHARACTER AND ATTRIBUTES OF GOD	59
THE LOVE OF GOD	61
THE DEITY OF CHRIST	64
PROPHECIES RELATING TO CHRIST	67
CHRIST THE WAY OF LIFE	72
SALVATION ONLY THROUGH CHRIST	75

PART III—The Way to Christ

VICTORIOUS FAITH	79
HOPE IN GOD	82
REPENTANCE	85
CONFESSION AND FORGIVENESS	88
CONVERSION, OR THE NEW BIRTH	93
CHRISTIAN BAPTISM	97
RECONCILED TO GOD	101
ACCEPTANCE WITH GOD	103
JUSTIFICATION BY FAITH	106
RIGHTEOUSNESS AND LIFE	111

Consecration	113
Bible Election	116
Bible Sanctification	119
Importance of Sound Doctrine	123
Present Truth	127
The Obedience of Faith	133

PART IV—The Life and Teachings of Christ

Birth, Childhood, and Early Life of Christ	139
A Sinless Life	143
Our Pattern	145
Our Helper and Friend	147
Christ's Ministry	149
Christ the Great Teacher	153
Miracles of Christ	156
Sufferings of Christ	161
The Resurrection of Christ	166

PART V—The Holy Spirit

The Holy Spirit and His Work	171
Fruit of the Spirit	174
Gifts of the Spirit	177
The Gift of Prophecy	179
The Outpouring of the Spirit	185

PART VI—The Sure Word of Prophecy

Prophecy, Why Given	191
Nebuchadnezzar's Dream	195
The Kingdoms of Grace and Glory	200
Four Great Monarchies	205
The Kingdom and Work of Antichrist	211
The Prophetic Symbols of Daniel 8	219
The Hour of God's Judgment	226
The Atonement in Type and Antitype	234
The Judgment	240
The Judgment-Hour Message	245
The Fall of Modern Babylon	249
The Closing Gospel Message	257
Satan's Warfare Against the Church	261
A Great Persecuting Power	266
Making an Image to the Beast	271

CONTENTS

A Prophetic History of the Church	281
The Book With Seven Seals	286
The Seven Last Plagues	292
The Mystery of God Finished	298

PART VII—Coming Events and Signs of the Times

Our Lord's Great Prophecy	301
Increase of Knowledge	309
The Conflict Between Capital and Labor	313
The Atomic Age—What Next?	316
The World's Conversion	323
Christ's Second Coming	328
Manner of Christ's Coming	334
Object of Christ's Coming	336
The Resurrection of the Just	339
The Gathering of Israel	342
The Millennium	345
The Day of the Lord	350
Elijah the Prophet	352

PART VIII—The Law of God

The Law of God	357
The Perpetuity of the Law	363
Why Was the Law Given at Sinai?	368
Penalty for Transgression	373
The Law of God in the Patriarchal Age	375
The Law of God in the New Testament	378
The Moral and Ceremonial Laws	381
The Two Covenants	387
What Was Abolished by Christ?	394
The Law and the Gospel	398

PART IX—The Sabbath

Institution of the Sabbath	405
God's Memorial	409
Reasons for Sabbathkeeping	413
Manner of Observing the Sabbath	417
Christ and the Sabbath	423
The Sabbath in the New Testament	427
The Change of the Sabbath	430
The Seal of God and the Mark of Apostasy	442

THE LORD'S DAY	447
THE SABBATH IN HISTORY	453
SABBATH REFORM	460

PART X—*Christian Liberty*

THE AUTHOR OF LIBERTY	465
THE POWERS THAT BE	469
INDIVIDUAL ACCOUNTABILITY	475
UNION OF CHURCH AND STATE	477
SABBATH LEGISLATION	483
WHO PERSECUTE AND WHY	487

PART XI—*Life Only in Christ*

ORIGIN, HISTORY, AND DESTINY OF SATAN	495
WHAT IS MAN?	500
LIFE ONLY IN CHRIST	505
THE INTERMEDIATE STATE	506
THE TWO RESURRECTIONS	509
FATE OF THE TRANSGRESSOR	514
THE MINISTRATION OF GOOD ANGELS	518
THE DARK MINISTRY OF EVIL ANGELS	524
SPIRITUALISM	527

PART XII—*Christian Growth and Experience*

GROWTH IN GRACE	535
THE CHRISTIAN ARMOR	537
WALKING IN THE LIGHT	540
SAVING FAITH	543
TRIALS AND THEIR OBJECT	547
OVERCOMING	550
THE MINISTRY OF SORROW	552
COMFORT IN AFFLICTION	555
TRUSTING IN JESUS	560
PATIENT ENDURANCE	562
CONTENTMENT	564
CHEERFULNESS	567
CHRISTIAN COURTESY	570
CONFESSING FAULTS AND FORGIVING ONE ANOTHER	571
THE DUTY OF ENCOURAGEMENT	575
UNITY OF BELIEVERS	577
MEEKNESS AND HUMILITY	580

CONTENTS

SOBRIETY AND DIGNITY	583
TRUE WISDOM	585
DILIGENCE IN LABOR	589
PERFECTION OF CHARACTER	591
SOWING AND REAPING	593

PART XIII—Prayer and Public Worship

IMPORTANCE OF PRAYER	597
MEDITATION AND PRAYER	601
WATCHING UNTO PRAYER	604
ANSWERS TO PRAYER	606
PUBLIC WORSHIP	609
REVERENCE FOR THE HOUSE OF GOD	613
CHRISTIAN COMMUNION	617
PRAISE AND THANKSGIVING	619
THE VALUE OF SONG	621

PART XIV—Christian Service

THE GIFT OF GIVING	624
THE SHEPHERD AND HIS WORK	627
PREACHING THE GOSPEL	629
MISSIONARY WORK	632
THE POOR, AND OUR DUTY TOWARD THEM	635
CHRISTIAN HELP WORK	637
VISITING THE SICK	641
HEALING THE SICK	643
ORDER AND ORGANIZATION	646
SUPPORT OF THE MINISTRY	649
FREEWILL OFFERINGS	651
WHO IS THE GREATEST?	654

PART XV—Admonitions and Warnings

SINFUL PRIDE	659
SELFISHNESS	660
COVETOUSNESS	661
DANGER OF DEBT	666
RESPECT OF PERSONS	669
BACKSLIDING	672
UNBELIEF AND DOUBT	675
JUDGING AND CRITICIZING	678
GOSSIPING AND BACKBITING	681

PART XVI—The Home

The Marriage Institution	691
A Happy Home	695
Religion in the Home	699
Honor Due to Parents	703
Child Training	706
Promises for the Children	709
Teaching the Children	711
The Mother	715
Evils of City Life	717
Purity of Heart	720

PART XVII—Health and Temperance

Good Health	725
Christian Temperance	727
Evils of Intemperance	729
Sacred Admonitions	734
True Temperance Reform	735

PART XVIII—The Kingdom Restored

Promises to the Overcomer	738
The Subjects of the Kingdom	740
Eternal Life	744
The Home of the Saved	747
The New Jerusalem	752
The Conflict Ended	755

The Game of Life	759
Authorities Quoted in Bible Readings for the Home	760
Index	762

Hypocrisy and Dissimulation 685
The Just Recompense 687

List of Illustrations

The Guest Divine (In color)	Frontispiece
Studying the Word of God	2
God's Unchanging Word	14
The Holy Book	24
Jesus at the Home of Martha and Mary	32
Our Blessed Redeemer	44
Man's First Home (In color) Facing page	49
Christ Bruises the Serpent's Head	54
The Crucifixion (In color) Facing page	65
Abraham Called of God	78
Return of the Prodigal Son	86
Nicodemus Learns a Vital Lesson	92
Baptism of Christ	96
The Friend of Sinners (In color) Facing page	113
Searching the Scriptures	122
Samuel Reproves Saul	134
The Visit of the Shepherds	138
Jesus Stills the Tempest (In color) Facing page	145
Christ Teaching the Multitude	152
On the Way to Calvary	160
The Holy Spirit Bestowed at Pentecost	170
Paul, a Prophet of the New Testament	180
Prophecy Lifts the Curtain	190
Daniel, the Prophetic Interpreter	194
The Four Beasts of Daniel 7	206
The Vision of Daniel 8	218
The Last Judgment (In color) Facing page	225
2300 Days (Diagram)	230
Heaven's Last Appeal	246
Time Running Out	256
A Refuge in the Wilderness	262
The Declaration of Independence	270
The Falling Stars of November 13, 1833	300
Symbols of Our Modern Times	310
Capital and Labor in Conflict	314
A Startled World (In color) Facing page	321
Christ Answering His Disciples' Questions	330
The Millennium (Diagram)	346
The Second Coming of Christ (In color) Facing page	353
God Writes His Law	356
Judgment Is Sure	372
The Moral Law Stands Forever	382
The Ceremonial Law Ended at the Cross	382
The First Sabbath in Eden	404

Sabbath Morning	412
Gathering the Manna	418
Healing the Blind Man on the Sabbath	422
Christ and the Law	436
Jesus Teaching in the Synagogue at Nazareth	452
Christ and the Tribute Money	464
Constantine Issues the First Sunday Law	482
The Pride of Lucifer	494
The Resurrection of the Just	510
The Resurrection of Jesus (In color) _____ Facing page	513
The Guardian Angel	520
Christ or Diana?	534
The Precious Word (In color) _____ Facing page	545
Christ the Consoler	558
A Happy Family	566
Be Not Dismayed	574
Diligence Is the Enemy of Poverty	588
In the House of Prayer and Praise	596
Never Man Prayed as He Prayed (In color) _____ Facing page	609
Light From the Sacred Page	602
The Christ	612
The Lord's Supper	616
Called to Service (In color) _____ Facing page	625
The Good Shepherd	626
The Good Samaritan	638
The Great Physician	642
The Widow's Two Mites	652
The Chase of Fortune	658
"Come Unto Me"	670
The Divine Counselor (In color) _____ Facing page	673
Mark Your Words	682
Marriage Is Honorable	690
The Home Circle	696
Jesus and His Mother	702
Christ Blessing Little Children (In color) _____ Facing page	705
The First Teacher	714
In the Out-of-Doors	724
Death on the Highway	730
Paradise Lost to Paradise Restored (In color) _____ Facing page	737
"A Little Child Shall Lead Them"	746
Home at Last	748
Peace Forevermore (In color) _____ Facing page	753
The Game of Life	758

The Bible—Its Origin, History, and Place in the World

THE Bible contains proof in itself of its divine origin. No other book can answer the questionings of the mind or satisfy the longings of the heart as does the Bible. It is adapted to every age and condition of life, and is full of that knowledge which enlightens the mind and sanctifies the soul.

In the Bible we have a revelation of the living God. Received by faith, it has power to transform the life. During all its history a divine Hand has been over it, and preserved it for the world.

How, When, and Why Written

Centuries after the Flood, as men became numerous and darkness was again settling over the world, holy men wrote as they were moved by the Spirit of God. Thus God spoke to His people, and through them to the world, that a knowledge of God and of His will might not perish from the earth.

For centuries this work went on, until Christ, the promised Seed, came. With Him, and the blessed message of light and salvation proclaimed by Him and by His apostles, the Scripture record closed, and the word of God was complete.

Original Writings and Translations

For the most part the Old Testament Scriptures were first written in Hebrew, upon scrolls, or rolls of parchment, linen, or papyrus. These were later translated into Greek, the oldest translation being known as the Septuagint, or "Version of the Seventy," which was made at Alexandria for the Alexandrian Library. The work of translation was begun under the patronage of Ptolemy Philadelphus, about 285 B.C. The original order for this translation is said to have been given by Alexander the Great, who previously, upon visiting Jerusalem in 332 B.C., had learned from the prophecy of Daniel that Grecia was to overthrow the Persian kingdom. See Josephus, *Antiquities of the*

GOD'S UNCHANGING WORD

"All scripture is given by inspiration of God." 2 Timothy 3:16.

Jews, book 11, chap. 8, par. 5. This was the version in common use in the time of Christ.

The New Testament is accepted by scholars as being originally written in Greek (although Matthew is thought by some to have been first written in Hebrew, and later translated into Greek).

At an early date Latin translations, both of the Septuagint and of the Greek New Testament, were made by different individuals. A more carefully prepared Latin version of the whole Bible, the Vulgate of Jerome, was made A.D. 383-405. It was called the Vulgate, or "common" version, because it was that in common use among Latin-speaking people.

PRINTING AND THE BIBLE

Printing, however, being yet unknown, copies of the Bible could be produced only by the slow, laborious, and expensive process of handwriting. This necessarily greatly limited its circulation. Worse still, its illuminating and saving truths were largely hidden for centuries by the errors, superstitions, and apostasy of the Dark Ages. During this time the common people knew little of its contents.

But with the invention of the art of printing about the middle of the fifteenth century, and with the dawn of the great Reformation in the century following, the Bible entered upon a new era, preparatory to the final proclamation of the gospel throughout the world.

Not a little significant is the fact that the first important book printed in Europe from movable type was the Bible in Latin, printed by Johann Gutenberg, issued at Mainz, Germany, about 1456. The copy of the Gutenberg Bible owned by the Library of Congress is perhaps the most valuable printed book in the world.

THE BIBLE IN NATIVE TONGUES

Thus far, however, the Bible had been printed only in an ancient tongue, not understood by the common people, and without the word of God in their hands, the good seed sown among them was easily destroyed. "Oh," said the advocates of its pure teachings, "if the people only had the word of God in their own language, this would not happen! Without this it will be impossible to establish the laity in the truth."

And why should they not have it in their own tongue? they reasoned. Moses wrote in the language of the people of his time; the prophets spoke in the tongue familiar to the men whom they addressed; and the New Testament was written in the language then current throughout the Roman world.

The translation of the Bible into English by John Wyclif and his associates, about 1380, was one of the chief events leading to the Reformation. It also prepared the way for the revival of Christianity in England, and the multiplying there of the word by the millions, for all the world, that has followed.

To make such a translation at that time, says Neander, "required a bold spirit which no danger could appal." For making it Wyclif was attacked from various quarters, because, it was claimed, "he was introducing among the multitude a book reserved exclusively for the use of the priests." In the general denunciation it was declared that "thus was the gospel by him laid more open to the laity, and to women who could read, than it had formerly been to the most learned of the clergy; and in this way the gospel pearl is cast abroad, and trodden underfoot of swine." In the preface to his translation, Wyclif exhorted all the people to read the Scriptures.

A sense of awe and a thrill of joy filled the heart of the great German Reformer when, at the age of twenty, while examining the volumes in the library of the University of Urfurt, he held in his hands, for the first time in his life, a complete copy of the Bible. "O God," he murmured, "could I but have one of these books, I would ask no other treasure." A little later he found in a convent a chained Bible. To this he had constant recourse.

But all these Bibles here, as elsewhere, save in England, were in an ancient tongue, and could be read only by the educated. Why, thought Luther, should the living word be confined to dead languages? Like Wyclif, therefore, he resolved to give his countrymen the Bible in their own tongue. This he did, the New Testament in 1522, and the Bible complete, the crowning work of his life, in 1534.

Impressed with the idea that the people should read the Scriptures in their mother tongue, William Tyndale, likewise, in 1525, gave to the English people his translation of the New Testament, and later, of portions of the Old Testament Scriptures. His ardent desire that they should know the Bible was well expressed in the statement that if God spared his life he would cause the boy that drives the plow to know more of the Scriptures than was commonly known by the divines of his day.

The first complete printed English Bible was that of Miles Coverdale, printed at Zurich, Switzerland, in 1535. Matthew's Bible, Taverner's Bible, and The Great Bible prepared at the suggestion of Thomas Cromwell, Earl of Essex, appeared soon after. Thus the light of truth began to shine forth once more, but not without opposition.

Burning of Bibles

As Jehoiakim, king of Judah, and the princes under King Zedekiah showed their contempt for God by burning the writings of Jeremiah, and confining the prophet in a dungeon (Jeremiah 36:20-23; 38:1-6), so now men sought to stem the rising tide of reform by burning the Bible and its translators.

Bible burning was inaugurated in England by the destruction of copies of the Antwerp edition of Tyndale's New Testament, at St. Paul's Cross, London, in 1527, followed by the burning of a second edition in 1530. A little later the writings and translations of Wyclif, Tyndale, Basil, Barnes, Coverdale, and others, were banned and in some cases burned.

Forty-three years after the death of Wyclif, or in A.D. 1428, by order of the Council of Constance his bones were dug up and burned. October 6, 1536, by order of Charles V of Germany, Tyndale was strangled and burned at the stake at Vilvorde, near Brussels. "If Luther will not retract," wrote Henry VIII of England, "let himself and his writings be committed to the flames."

Such, under the spiritual tyranny that ruled in those times, was the fate of many who stood for God and His word.

The Word Not Bound

But the word of God could not be forever bound. In attempting to prevent its circulation men soon discovered that they were undertaking a work beyond their strength.

The Bible had taken deep root in the hearts of the people. What kings and prelates had sought to suppress and destroy, kings and prelates now began to foster and supply.

In his *Stories From English History,* pages 196, 197, Henry P. Warren says: "Henry, by Cromwell's advice, ordered a translation of the Bible to be made in English, and a copy to be placed in every church. There had been English translations before, but they had not been in the hands of the people generally, and had only been read secretly and in fear. . . . Cromwell then appointed Cranmer and the bishops to revise the Bible, and publish it without note or comment; and in the year 1539 a copy of the English Bible was chained to the reading-desk of every parish church. From that time the Bible has never ceased to be printed and sold freely."

Says Charles C. Coffin, in his *Story of Liberty,* chapter 2, page 44: "The people listen to the reading with wonder and delight. They begin to think; and when men begin to think, they take a step toward freedom. They see that the Bible gives them rights which hitherto have been denied them—the right to read, to acquire knowledge. Schools are started. Men and women, who till now have not known a letter of the alphabet, learn to read: children teach their parents. It is the beginning of a new life—a new order of things in the community—the beginning of liberty."

THE BIBLE TO ALL THE WORLD

Finally, great Bible societies were organized in England, America, and many of the countries of Europe, for the purpose of giving the Bible to the world—to every nation, kindred, tongue, and people in its own language. Chief among these are the British and Foreign Bible Society, founded in 1804, and the American Bible Society, founded in 1816. These and like organizations have circulated literally hundreds of millions of copies of the Bible in a vast number of languages.

Thus is the world being provided with the word of God, preparatory to the giving of the closing gospel message to all mankind, the ending of the reign of sin, and the advent of the Lord in glory. "And this gospel of the kingdom shall be preached in all the world for a witness unto all nations; and then shall the end come." Matthew 24:14.

The Value of Bible Study

The Bible is God's great textbook for man. It is His lamp to our feet and light to our path in this world of sin. The value of Bible study cannot therefore be overestimated.

Considered from a literary standpoint alone, the Bible stands pre-eminent. Its terse, chaste style; its beautiful and impressive imagery; its interesting stories and well-told narratives; its deep wisdom and its sound logic; its dignified language and its elevated themes, all make it worthy of universal reading and careful study.

As an educating power, the Bible has no equal. Nothing so broadens the vision, strengthens the mind, elevates the thoughts, and ennobles the affections as does the study of the sublime and stupendous truths of revelation. A knowledge of its principles is an essential preparation to every calling. To the extent that it is studied and its teachings are received, it gives strength of character, noble ambition, keenness of perception, and sound judgment. Of all the books ever written, none contains lessons so instructive, precepts so pure, or promises so great as the Bible.

There is nothing that so convinces the mind of the inspiration of the Bible as does the reading of the Bible itself, and especially those portions known as the prophecies. After the resurrection of Christ, when everything else seemed to have failed to convince the disciples that He had risen from the dead, He appealed to the inspired word, and "expounded unto them in all the scriptures [the Old Testament] the things concerning himself" (Luke 24:25-27), and they believed. On another occasion He said, "If they hear not Moses and the prophets, neither will they be persuaded, though one rose from the dead." Luke 16:31.

As a guide, the Bible is without a rival. It gives a calm peace in believing, and a firm hope of the future. It solves the great problems of life and destiny, and inspires to a life of purity, patience, and well-doing. It fills the heart with love for God and a desire to do good to others, and thus prepares for usefulness here and for a home in heaven. It teaches the value of the soul, by revealing the price that has been paid to redeem it. It makes known the only antidote for sin, and presents the only perfect code of morals ever given. It tells of the future and the preparation necessary to meet it. It makes us bold for the right, and sustains the soul in adversity and affliction. It lights up the dark valley of death, and points to a life unending. It leads to God, and to Christ, whom to know is life eternal. In short, it is the one book to live by and die by.

As the king of Israel was instructed to reproduce a copy of the law, and to read therein "all the days of his life," that he might "fear the Lord," keep His word, and thus prolong his days and the days of his children (Deuteronomy 17:18-20), so ought men now to study the Bible, and from it learn that fear which is the beginning of wisdom, and that knowledge which is unto salvation. As an aid and incentive to this, *Bible Readings for the Home* has been prepared and published.

Bible Readings; Their Value and Use

Briefly stated, a Bible reading consists of questions asked concerning some subject, and answers to them from the Bible. In other words, a Bible reading is a topical study of the Bible by means of questions and answers.

In either receiving or imparting knowledge, there is nothing like the interrogation point. Nothing so readily quickens thought or awakens interest as a question. Children would learn little if they asked no questions, and he would indeed be a poor teacher who asked and answered none.

Knowing the value of this means of awakening thought, arousing interest, and imparting information, God, in His wisdom, inspired those who wrote the Bible to ask many questions, that He might set us to thinking and studying about the great themes with which it deals. (See Job 38:4, 7; 14:14; Psalm 8:4; Malachi 3:1, 2, 8; Exodus 32:26; 1 Chronicles 29:5.)

But God not only asks questions; He answers them. The following may be cited as a few short Bible readings, taken, both questions and answers, directly from the Bible itself:

"What man is he that desireth life, and loveth many days, that he may see good?

"Keep thy tongue from evil, and thy lips from speaking guile. Depart from evil, and do good; seek peace, and pursue it." Psalm 34:12-14.

"Who hath woe? who hath sorrow? who hath contentions? who hath babbling? who hath wounds without cause? who hath redness of eyes?

"They that tarry long at the wine; they that go to seek mixed wine." Proverbs 23:29, 30.

"Who shall ascend into the hill of the Lord? or who shall stand in his holy place?

"He that hath clean hands, and a pure heart; who hath not lifted up his soul unto vanity, nor sworn deceitfully. He shall receive the blessing from the Lord, and righteousness from the God of his salvation." Psalm 24:3-5. (See also Psalm 15 and Isaiah 33:14-17.)

The Bible itself, therefore, sets the example of giving instruction and of imparting most valuable information by means of asking questions and answering them.

The readings in this book as originally prepared were contributed by a large number of Bible instructors, whose experience in giving Bible readings had taught them the most effective methods of presenting the different subjects treated. More than a million copies of the book as thus prepared have been sold.

The work has recently been revised and new illustrations have been added. The readings have been classified and carefully arranged according to topics. Thus prepared, it is once more sent forth on its mission of light and blessing.

As a help in enabling the reader quickly to discover the words which most directly answer the question asked, they are generally printed in italic, unless the entire scripture quoted is required for the purpose. Important words in quotations from other works have been printed in italic in order to call attention to significant points in the quotations.

Bible Readings will be found an excellent aid to private, family, and public study of the word of God.

GOD'S HOLY WORD

By WILLIAM WALSHAM HOW

O word of God incarnate,
  O wisdom from on high,
O truth unchanged, unchanging,
  O light of our dark sky!
We praise thee for the radiance
  That from the hallowed page,
A lamp to guide our footsteps,
  Shines on from age to age.

The church from her dear Master
  Received the gift divine,
And still that light she lifteth
  O'er all the earth to shine.
It is the golden casket
  Where gems of truth are stored,
It is the heaven-drawn picture
  Of Christ the living Word.

It floateth like a banner
  Before God's host unfurled,
It shineth like a beacon
  Above the stormy world;
It is the chart and compass
  That o'er life's raging sea,
'Mid mists and rocks and quicksands,
  Still guides, O Christ, to thee!

Part One

The Bible; How to Study and Understand It

	PAGE
The Sacred Scriptures	25
How to Understand the Bible	28
Power in the Word of God	33
The Life-giving Word	36
Christ in All the Bible	39

CHARLES CAREY

THE HOLY BOOK

"Thy word is a lamp unto my feet, and a light unto my path." Psalm 119:105

The Sacred Scriptures

By what name did Jesus refer to the sacred writings of the Old Testament, the Bible of His day?

"Jesus saith unto them, Did ye never read in *the scriptures,* The stone which the builders rejected, the same is become the head of the corner?" Matthew 21:42.

What other title is given the revelation of God to man?

"And he answered and said unto them, My mother and my brethren are these which hear *the word of God,* and do it." Luke 8:21.

Note.—It is interesting to note that the word *Bible* does not occur in the Bible itself. It is derived from the Latin *biblia,* which came from the Greek *biblos,* meaning "book." The Greek word *biblos* in turn is derived from *byblos,* meaning "papyrus," the name of the material upon which ancient books were written. The Greeks called this writing material *byblos* because they obtained it from the Phoenician port of Byblos.

The Bible has 66 books and was written by 35 or 40 men over a period of some 1,500 years. The books are called the "word of God," or the "Scriptures." "Scriptures" means "writings."

The Manner in Which the Scriptures Were Given

How were the Scriptures given?

"All scripture is given *by inspiration of God.*" 2 Timothy 3:16.

Note.—When New Testament writers speak of "scripture" they refer to the Old Testament Scriptures. But inasmuch as the same God who inspired the writers of the Old Testament also inspired the writers of the New Testament, what the latter declare concerning the inspiration and value of the earlier writings is equally true of the New Testament.

By whom were the men directed who thus spoke for God?

"For the prophecy came not in old time by the will of man: but holy men of God spake as they were moved *by the Holy Ghost.*" 2 Peter 1:21.

What specific instance is mentioned by Peter?

"Men and brethren, this scripture must needs have been fulfilled, *which the Holy Ghost by the mouth of David spake before concerning Judas,* which was guide to them that took Jesus." Acts 1:16.

Who, therefore, did the speaking through these men?

"*God,* who at sundry times and in divers manners spake in time past unto the fathers by the prophets." Hebrews 1:1.

THE PURPOSE OF THE SCRIPTURES

For what purpose were the Scriptures written?

"For whatsoever things were written aforetime were written *for our learning,* that we through patience and comfort of the scriptures might have hope." Romans 15:4.

For what is all scripture profitable?

"All scripture is given by inspiration of God, and is profitable *for doctrine, for reproof, for correction, for instruction in righteousness.*" 2 Timothy 3:16.

What was God's design in thus giving the Scriptures?

"That the man of God may be *perfect, throughly furnished unto all good works.*" Verse 17.

What does God design that His word shall be to us in this world of darkness, sin, and death?

"Thy word is *a lamp* unto my feet, and *a light* unto my path." Psalm 119:105.

THE DIVISIONS OF THE SCRIPTURES

What three general divisions did Jesus refer to in the writings of the Old Testament?

"And he said unto them, These are the words which I spake unto you, while I was yet with you, that all things must be fulfilled, which were written in *the law of Moses,* and in *the prophets,* and in *the psalms,* concerning me." Luke 24:44.

NOTE.—"The law of Moses" was a common Jewish term for the first five books of the Old Testament. In "the prophets" they included Isaiah, Jeremiah, Ezekiel, and the twelve Minor Prophets; also Joshua, Judges, 1 and 2 Samuel, and 1 and 2 Kings. "The psalms" included all the remaining books.

Upon what evidence did Jesus base His Messiahship?

"And beginning at *Moses* and all the *prophets,* he expounded unto them *in all the scriptures* the things concerning himself." Verse 27.

Note.—Jesus referred particularly to the Old Testament prophecies as proof of His Messiahship. When Christ spoke of the Scriptures He meant the Old Testament, for the New Testament had not yet been written.

The Character of God and His Word

What is God called in the Scriptures?

"He is the Rock, his work is perfect: for all his ways are judgment: *a God of truth* and without iniquity, just and right is he." Deuteronomy 32:4.

What, therefore, must be the character of His word?

"Sanctify them through thy truth: *thy word is truth.*" John 17:17.

To what extent has God magnified His word?

"Thou hast magnified thy word *above all thy name.*" Psalm 138:2.

Note.—A man's name stands for his character. It is the same with God. When God places His word above His name, His character becomes the foundation of His word and the pledge that His word will be fulfilled. (Hebrews 6:13, 14.)

The Testimony of Job and Isaiah

What estimate did Job place upon the words of God?

"Neither have I gone back from the commandment of his lips; *I have esteemed the words of his mouth more than my necessary food.*" Job 23:12.

How firm was the faith of the great Isaiah in God's word?

"The grass withereth, the flower fadeth: but *the word of our God shall stand for ever.*" Isaiah 40:8.

How to Understand the Bible

BIBLE APPROVAL OF PERSONAL STUDY

What did Christ say concerning the study of the Scriptures?

"*Search the scriptures;* for in them ye think ye have eternal life: and they are they which testify of me." John 5:39.

NOTE.—Christ here refers to the Old Testament Scriptures, the "Bible" of His day. However, His statement is equally true of the New Testament. The same is generally true of the term "scriptures" throughout the New Testament.

For what were the Bereans commended?

"These were more noble than those in Thessalonica, in that they received the word with all readiness of mind, and *searched the scriptures daily, whether those things were so.*" Acts 17:11.

NOTE.—"If God's Word were studied as it should be," says a modern Bible student, "men would have a breadth of mind, a nobility of character, and a stability of purpose that is rarely seen in these times. But there is but little profit derived from a hasty reading of the Scriptures. One may read the whole Bible through, and yet fail to see its beauty or comprehend its deep and hidden meaning. One passage studied until its significance is clear to the mind, and its relation to the plan of salvation is evident, is of more value than the perusal of many chapters with no definite purpose in view and no positive instruction gained."

EASY AND MORE DIFFICULT PORTIONS

By what comparison is it indicated that some portions of God's word are more difficult to understand than others?

"For when for the time ye ought to be teachers, ye have need that one teach you again which be *the first principles of the oracles of God;* and are become such as have need of *milk,* and not of *strong meat.*" Hebrews 5:12.

In what way is this comparison further explained?

"For every one that useth milk is unskilful in the word of

righteousness: for he is a *babe*. But strong meat belongeth to them that are of *full age,* even those who by reason of use have their senses exercised to discern both good and evil." Verses 13, 14.

What writings are specifically mentioned as containing some things difficult to understand?

"And account that the longsuffering of our Lord is salvation; even as our beloved brother *Paul* also according to the wisdom given unto him hath written unto you; as also in all *his epistles,* speaking in them of these things; *in which are some things hard to be understood,* which they that are unlearned and unstable wrest, as they do also the other scriptures, unto their own destruction." 2 Peter 3:15, 16.

NOTE.—Some scriptures are too plain to be misunderstood, while the meaning of others cannot so readily be discerned. To obtain a comprehensive knowledge of any Bible truth, scripture must be compared with scripture, and there should be "careful research and prayerful reflection." But all such study will be richly rewarded.

What did Christ say concerning the book of Daniel?

"When ye therefore shall see the abomination of desolation, spoken of by Daniel the prophet, stand in the holy place, (*whoso readeth, let him understand*)." Matthew 24:15.

What other book of the Bible is especially commended for our study?

"Blessed is he that readeth, and they that hear *the words of this prophecy* [the book of Revelation], and keep those things which are written therein: for the time is at hand." Revelation 1:3.

THE SPIRIT OF GOD AND THE BIBLE

Who alone comprehends the things of God?

"For what man knoweth the things of a man, save the spirit of man which is in him? even so the things of God knoweth no man, but *the Spirit of God.*" 1 Corinthians 2:11.

How thoroughly does the Spirit search out the hidden treasures of truth?

"But God hath revealed them unto us by his Spirit: for *the*

Spirit *searcheth all things, yea, the deep things of God."* Verse 10.

What is one purpose for which the Holy Spirit was sent?

"But the Comforter, which is the Holy Ghost, whom the Father will send in my name, *he shall teach you all things, and bring all things to your remembrance, whatsoever I have said unto you."* John 14:26.

Why cannot the natural man receive the things of the Spirit?

"But the natural man receiveth not the things of the Spirit of God: for they are foolishness unto him: neither can he know them *because they are spiritually discerned."* 1 Corinthians 2:14.

PLACE OF PRAYER IN BIBLE STUDY

For what spiritual enlightenment should everyone pray?

"Open thou mine eyes, that I may behold wondrous things out of thy law." Psalm 119:18.

For what spiritual gift did the apostle Paul pray?

"That the God of our Lord Jesus Christ, the Father of glory, may give unto you *the spirit of wisdom and revelation in the knowledge of him."* Ephesians 1:17.

Upon what conditions is an understanding of divine things promised?

"Yea, *if thou criest after knowledge, and liftest up thy voice for understanding; if thou seekest her as silver, and searchest for her as for hid treasures;* then shalt thou understand the fear of the Lord, and find the knowledge of God." Proverbs 2:3-5.

ANOTHER CONDITION OF RECEIVING LIGHT

What is promised him who wills to do God's will?

"If any man will [literally, "desires" or "wills"] do his will, *he shall know of the doctrine,* whether it be of God, or whether I speak of myself." John 7:17.

NOTE.—It is proper to repeat again and again the eternal truth that if *any* man will search the word of God for light, with a heart fully submitted to do the will of God as it is revealed to him, that man will receive light. It is the seed of the word of God that falls into an *honest* heart that brings forth fruit unto everlasting life. (Luke 8:11-15.)

When asked by the rich young man the conditions of eternal life, to what did Jesus direct his attention?

"He said unto him, *What is written in the law? how readest thou?*" Luke 10:26.

NOTE.—The Jews of Christ's day called the first five books of the Bible, which were written by Moses, "the law."

RESULTS OF SINCERE BIBLE STUDY

What are the Scriptures able to do for one who believes them?

"And that from a child thou hast known the holy scriptures, *which are able to make thee wise unto salvation through faith which is in Christ Jesus.*" 2 Timothy 3:15.

What great blessing did Christ confer upon His disciples after His resurrection?

"*Then opened he their understanding,* that they might understand the scriptures." Luke 24:45.

How did Christ reprove those who, though familiar with the letter of the Scriptures, failed to understand them?

"Jesus answered and said unto them, *Ye do err, not knowing the scriptures, nor the power of God.*" Matthew 22:29.

Whom did Jesus pronounce blessed?

"But he said, Yea, rather, *blessed are they that hear the word of God, and keep it.*" Luke 11:28.

JESUS AT THE HOME OF MARTHA AND MARY

HEINRICH HOFMANN, ARTIST

"Mary hath chosen that good part, which shall not be taken from her." Luke 10:42.

Power in the Word of God

THE POWER OF GOD'S WORD IN NATURE

THROUGH what agency did God create the heavens?

"*By the word of the Lord* were the heavens made; and all the host of them *by the breath of his mouth.* . . . For *he spake,* and it was done; *he commanded,* and it stood fast." Psalm 33:6-9.

By what does Christ uphold all things?

"Upholding all things *by the word of his power.*" Hebrews 1:3.

Of what are some willingly ignorant?

"For this they willingly are ignorant of, that *by the word of God the heavens were of old,* and the earth standing out of the water and in the water: *whereby the world that then was, being overflowed with water, perished.*" 2 Peter 3:5, 6.

By what are the present heavens and earth reserved for a similar fate?

"But the heavens and the earth, which are now, *by the same word* are kept in store, reserved unto fire against the day of judgment and perdition of ungodly men." Verse 7.

In what other scripture is it shown that creative power is exercised through the word of God?

"Let them praise the name of the Lord: *for he commanded, and they were created.*" Psalm 148:5.

POWER OF GOD'S WORD IN REDEMPTION

What change is wrought in one who is in Christ?

"Therefore if any man be in Christ, *he is a new creature* [literally, *"a new creation"*]: old things are passed away; behold, *all things are become new.*" 2 Corinthians 5:17.

In what other words is this experience described?

"Jesus answered and said unto him, Verily, verily, I say

unto thee, Except a man be *born again,* he cannot see the kingdom of God." John 3:3.

Through what agency is this new creation, or new birth, accomplished?

"Being born again, not of corruptible seed, but of incorruptible, *by the word of God,* which liveth and abideth for ever." 1 Peter 1:23.

Natural and Spiritual Light Compared

What is the first creative commandment recorded in the Bible? and what was the result of it?

"And God said, *Let there be light:* and *there was light."* Genesis 1:3.

What connection is there between the creation of light in the beginning, and the light of the gospel?

"For God, who commanded the light to shine out of darkness, hath shined in our hearts, to give *the light of the knowledge of the glory of God in the face of Jesus Christ."* 2 Corinthians 4:6.

Amazing Power of the Word Spoken

Why were the people astonished at Christ's teaching?

"And they were astonished at his doctrine: *for his word was with power."* Luke 4:32.

What testified to the power of the word of Christ?

"And they were all amazed, and spake among themselves, saying, What a word is this! for *with authority and power he commandeth the unclean spirits, and they come out."* Verse 36.

How did God heal His people anciently?

"He sent his word, and healed them, and delivered them from their destructions." Psalm 107:20.

How did the centurion show his faith in Christ?

"The centurion answered and said, Lord, I am not worthy that thou shouldest come under my roof: but *speak the word only, and my servant shall be healed."* Matthew 8:8.

The Seed of God's Word Working in Us

What did Christ say is the seed of the kingdom of God?

"The seed is *the word of God.*" Luke 8:11.

Where should the word of Christ dwell?

"Let the word of Christ *dwell in you* richly in all wisdom." Colossians 3:16.

What did Christ say of the unbelieving Jews respecting the word of God?

"Ye have not his word abiding in you: for whom he hath sent, him ye believe not." John 5:38.

How does the word of God work in the believer?

"For this cause also thank we God without ceasing, because, when ye received the word of God which ye heard of us, ye received it not as the word of men, but as it is in truth, the word of God, *which effectually worketh also in you that believe.*" 1 Thessalonians 2:13.

Heart Results of God's Word

What nature is imparted through the promises of God?

"Whereby are given unto us exceeding great and precious promises: *that by these ye might be partakers of the divine nature,* having escaped the corruption that is in the world through lust." 2 Peter 1:4.

By what are believers made clean?

"Now ye are clean *through the word which I have spoken unto you.*" John 15:3.

How may a young man cleanse his way?

"Wherewithal shall a young man cleanse his way? *by taking heed thereto according to thy word.*" Psalm 119:9.

What power has the word when hidden in the heart?

"Thy word have I hid in mine heart, *that I might not sin against thee.*" Psalm 119:11. (See also Psalm 17:4.)

The Life-giving Word

THE WORD OF GOD A LIVING WORD

WHAT is the nature of the word of God?

"For the word of God is *quick* [literally, *"living"*], and *powerful,* and *sharper than any twoedged sword,* piercing even to the dividing asunder of soul and spirit, and of the joints and marrow, and is *a discerner of the thoughts and intents of the heart."* Hebrews 4:12.

How are the oracles of God described?

"This is he, that was in the church in the wilderness with the angel which spake to him in the mount Sina, and with our fathers: who received *the lively oracles* to give unto us." Acts 7:38.

What was Peter's testimony concerning Christ's words?

"Then Simon Peter answered him, Lord, to whom shall we go? *thou hast the words of eternal life."* John 6:68.

What did the Saviour declare His Father's commandment to be?

"And I know that his commandment is *life everlasting."* John 12:50.

THE WORD COMPARED TO FOOD

What lesson was intended by feeding the children of Israel with the manna?

"And he humbled thee, and suffered thee to hunger, and fed thee with manna, which thou knewest not, neither did thy fathers know; *that he might make thee know that man doth not live by bread only, but by every word that proceedeth out of the mouth of the Lord doth man live."* Deuteronomy 8:3.

What instance is recorded of one who fed upon the true manna?

"Thy words were found, and I did eat them; and thy word

was unto me the joy and rejoicing of mine heart: for I am called by thy name, O Lord God of hosts." Jeremiah 15:16.

What reference did Jesus make to this same manna of life?

"But he answered and said, It is written, Man shall not live by *bread alone, but by every word* that proceedeth out of the mouth of God." Matthew 4:4.

How did the word of God become food to Jesus?

"Jesus saith unto them, *My meat is to do the will of him* that sent me, and to *finish his work.*" John 4:34.

Jesus as the Living Word

What name is applied to Jesus as the revelation of the thought of God in the flesh?

"In the beginning was *the Word*, and the Word was with God, and the Word was God." John 1:1. "And he was clothed with a vesture dipped in blood: and his name is called *The Word of God.*" Revelation 19:13.

What did this Word become?

"And the Word was made *flesh,* and dwelt among us." John 1:14.

What was in the Word?

"In him was *life;* and the life was the light of men." John 1:4.

What is Jesus therefore also called?

"That which was from the beginning, which we have heard, which we have seen with our eyes, which we have looked upon, and our hands have handled, of *the Word of life.*" 1 John 1:1.

Jesus as the Living Bread

What did Jesus declare Himself to be?

"And Jesus said unto them, *I am the bread of life:* he that cometh to me shall never hunger; and he that believeth on me shall never thirst." John 6:35.

What did He suggest that men should do with Him, the bread of life?

"As the living Father hath sent me, and I live by the Father: *so he that eateth me, even he shall live by me.* This is that bread which came down from heaven: not as your fathers did eat manna, and are dead: *he that eateth of this bread shall live for ever.*" John 6:57, 58.

What did Jesus really mean by our eating His flesh?

"It is the spirit that quickeneth; the flesh profiteth nothing: the words that I speak unto you, they are *spirit,* and they are *life.*" Verse 63.

Note.—Thus we clearly understand that to eat the flesh of the Son of God is to live by His words. As one has said, "He who by faith receives the word is receiving the very life and character of God."—*Christ's Object Lessons,* p. 38.

The Table of the Lord

What grand privilege do we have?

"And have *tasted the good word of God,* and the powers of the world to come." Hebrews 6:5. (See Jeremiah 15:16.)

What glorious invitation is extended to all?

"O *taste* and see that the Lord is good: blessed is the man that trusteth in him." Psalm 34:8.

How are we instructed to pray for both physical and spiritual nourishment?

"Give us this day our daily bread." Matthew 6:11.

Note.—When "the Word became flesh, and dwelt among us," the thought of God was revealed in human flesh. When holy men of God "spake as they were moved by the Holy Ghost," the thought of God was revealed in human language. The union of the divine and the human in the manifestation of God's thought in the flesh is declared to be "the mystery of godliness"; and there is the same mystery in the union of the divine thought and human language. The two revelations of God, in human flesh and in human speech, are both called the *Word of God,* and both are the *Word of life.* He who fails to find Christ thus in the Scriptures will not be able to feed upon the Word as the life-giving Word.

Christ in All the Bible

GENERAL REFERENCES TO CHRIST

Of whom did Christ say the Scriptures testify?

"Search the scriptures; for in them ye think ye have eternal life: and *they are they which testify of me.*" John 5:39.

NOTE.—"Search the Old Testament Scriptures: for they are they that testify of Christ. To find Him in them is the true and legitimate end of their study. To be able to interpret them as He interpreted them is the best result of all Biblical learning."—DEAN ALFORD.

Of whom did Moses and the prophets write?

"Philip findeth Nathanael, and saith unto him, We have found him, of whom Moses in the law, and the prophets, did write, *Jesus of Nazareth,* the son of Joseph." John 1:45.

NOTE.—In her translation of the Old Testament Scriptures, Helen Spurrell expressed the following wish for all who should read her translation: "May very many exclaim, as the translator has often done when studying numerous passages in the original, *I have found the Messiah!*"

From whose words did Christ say the disciples ought to have learned of His death and resurrection?

"O fools, and slow of heart to believe all that *the prophets* have spoken: ought not Christ to have suffered these things, and to enter into his glory?" Luke 24:25, 26.

How did Christ make it clear to them that the Scriptures testify of Him?

"And beginning at Moses and all the prophets, *he expounded unto them in all the scriptures the things concerning himself.*" Verse 27.

CHRIST THE SEED

Where do we find the first promise of a Redeemer?

"And the Lord God said unto the serpent, . . . I will put enmity between thee and the woman, and between thy seed and *her seed;* it shall bruise thy head, and thou shalt bruise his heel." Genesis 3:14, 15.

In what words was this promise renewed to Abraham?

"In thy seed shall all the nations of the earth be blessed." Genesis 22:18. (See also Genesis 26:4; 28:14.)

To whom did this promised seed refer?

"Now to Abraham and his seed were the promises made. He saith not, And to seeds, as of many; but as of one, And to thy seed, *which is Christ."* Galatians 3:16.

The Angel and the Rock

Whom did God promise to send with Israel to guide them into the Promised Land?

"Behold, I send *an Angel* before thee, to keep thee in the way, and to bring thee into the place which I have prepared." Exodus 23:20.

Who was the Rock that went with them?

"And did all drink the same spiritual drink: for they drank of that spiritual Rock that followed [literally, "went with"] them: and *that Rock was Christ."* 1 Corinthians 10:4.

Birth, Life, Suffering, Death, Resurrection

Where was the Saviour to be born?

"But thou, *Bethlehem* Ephratah, though thou be little among the thousands of Judah, *yet out of thee shall he come forth* unto me that is to be ruler in Israel; whose goings forth have been from of old, from everlasting." Micah 5:2.

In what prophecy are Christ's life, suffering, and death touchingly foretold?

In the fifty-third chapter of Isaiah.

Where is the price of Christ's betrayal foretold?

"So they weighed for my price *thirty pieces of silver."* Zechariah 11:12. (See Matthew 26:15.)

Where in the Psalms are Christ's dying words recorded?

"My God, my God, why hast thou forsaken me?" Psalm 22:1. (See Matthew 27:46.) "Into thine hand I commit my spirit." Psalm 31:5. (See Luke 23:46.)

How is Christ's resurrection foretold in the Psalms?

"For *thou wilt not leave my soul in hell;* neither wilt thou suffer thine Holy One to see *corruption."* Psalm 16:10. (See Acts 2:25-31.)

CHRIST'S SECOND COMING AND KINGDOM

In what words does Daniel foretell Christ's receiving His kingdom?

"I saw in the night visions, and, behold, one like *the Son of man* came with the clouds of heaven, and came to the Ancient of days, and they brought him near before him. And *there was given him dominion, and glory, and a kingdom,* that all people, nations, and languages, should serve him: his dominion is an everlasting dominion, which shall not pass away, and his kingdom that which shall not be destroyed." Daniel 7:13, 14. (See also Luke 1:32, 33; 19:11, 12; Revelation 11:15.)

How is Christ's second coming described in the Psalms?

"Let the floods clap their hands: let the hills be joyful together before the Lord; *for he cometh to judge the earth:* with righteousness shall he judge the world, and the people with equity." Psalm 98:8, 9. *"Our God shall come, and shall not keep silence:* a fire shall devour before him, and it shall be very tempestuous round about him. He shall call to the heavens from above, and to the earth, that he may judge his people." Psalm 50:3, 4.

THE FACE IN THE PUZZLE PICTURE

Did you ever see one of those puzzle pictures on which you were told to discover the face of a man, or some object? You turned it this way and that, and finally, there you suddenly saw it, just as plain as day, and wondered why you had not seen it before! The great face in the Bible is that of Jesus. He is the supreme object of the Scriptures. "Search the scriptures; . . . they . . . testify of me." John 5:39.

Like the scarlet thread that runs through every inch of rope in the British Navy, like the melody of a beautiful song, like the theme of a great masterpiece, so is Jesus in the Scriptures. He is the author and the hero, the beginning and the ending of your Holy Bible.

TITLES GIVEN TO CHRIST IN THE BIBLE

IN THE OLD TESTAMENT

Seed of the woman. Genesis 3:15.
Mine Angel. Exodus 23:23.
A Star out of Jacob. Numbers 24:17.
A Prophet. Deuteronomy 18:15, 18.
Captain of the host of the Lord. Joshua 5:14.
A Friend that sticketh closer than a brother. Proverbs 18:24.
Chiefest among ten thousand. Song of Solomon 5:10.
(One) altogether lovely. Song of Solomon 5:16.
The Mighty God. Isaiah 9:6.
The Everlasting Father. Isaiah 9:6.
The Prince of Peace. Isaiah 9:6.
The Lord Our Righteousness. Jeremiah 23:5, 6.
The Son of God. Daniel 3:25.
The Son of man. Daniel 7:13.
Michael, . . . the Great Prince. Daniel 12:1.
The Branch. Zechariah 6:12, 13.
The Messenger of the covenant. Malachi 3:1.
The Sun of Righteousness. Malachi 4:2.

IN THE NEW TESTAMENT

The Word. John 1:1.
The Lamb of God. John 1:29.
The Bread of Life. John 6:35.
The Light of the world. John 8:12.
The Door of the sheep. John 10:7.
The Good Shepherd. John 10:11.
The Resurrection and the Life. John 11:25.
The Way, the Truth, and the Life. John 14:6.
The True Vine. John 15:1.
That Rock. 1 Corinthians 10:4.
The last Adam. 1 Corinthians 15:45.
The Chief Cornerstone. Ephesians 2:20.
The Man Christ Jesus. 1 Timothy 2:5.
A Great High Priest. Hebrews 4:14.
The Author and Finisher of our faith. Hebrews 12:2.
The Chief Shepherd. 1 Peter 5:4.
An Advocate. 1 John 2:1.
Michael, the Archangel. Jude 9.
The Lion of the tribe of Judah. Revelation 5:5.
The Morning Star. Revelation 22:16.
King of kings, and Lord of lords. Revelation 19:16.

NOTE.—Christ is referred to in the Bible under something like three hundred different titles and figures, of which the above are only examples.

Part Two

Sin; Its Origin, Results, and Remedy

	PAGE
Creation and the Creator	45
The Origin of Evil	48
The Fall and Redemption of Man	50
Creation and Redemption	55
The Character and Attributes of God	59
The Love of God	61
The Deity of Christ	64
Prophecies Relating to Christ	67
Christ the Way of Life	72
Salvation Only Through Christ	75

OUR BLESSED REDEEMER

W. EBBINGHAUS, ARTIST

"Thou shalt call his name Jesus: for he shall save his people from their sins." Matthew 1:21.

Creation and the Creator

THE STORY OF CREATION AND CONTROL

BY WHOM were the heavens and the earth created?

"In the beginning *God* created the heaven and the earth." Genesis 1:1.

NOTE.—Here is the Bible's challenge to every form of error, from the infidel who says there is no God to the polytheist who says there are many gods. The Bible is the book of *God*.

By what means did God bring the heavens and earth into existence?

"By the word of the Lord were the heavens made; and all the host of them by the breath of his mouth. . . . For he *spake,* and it was done; he *commanded,* and it stood fast." Psalm 33:6-9.

Through whom did God create all things?

"For *by him* [the Son] were all things created, that are in heaven, and that are in earth, visible and invisible, whether they be thrones, or dominions, or principalities, or powers: *all things were created by him, and for him."* Colossians 1:16. "All things were made *by him* [literally, *"through him"*]; and without him was not any thing made that was made." John 1:3. (See also Hebrews 1:1, 2.)

What was God's object in making the earth?

"For thus saith the Lord that created the heavens; God himself that formed the earth and made it; he hath established it, he created it not in vain, *he formed it to be inhabited."* Isaiah 45:18.

How did God provide inhabitants for the world He had created?

"And the Lord God formed man of the dust of the ground, and breathed into his nostrils the breath of life; and man became a living soul." "And the Lord God caused a deep sleep to fall upon Adam, and he slept: and he took one of his ribs, and closed up the flesh instead thereof; and the rib, which the Lord

God had taken from man, made he a woman, and brought her unto the man." Genesis 2:7, 21, 22.

In whose image was man created?

"So God created man *in his own image,* in the image of God created he him; male and female created he them." Genesis 1:27.

To what glorious position did God assign man?

"Let them have dominion over the fish of the sea, and over the fowl of the air, and over the cattle, and *over all the earth."* Verse 26.

"What is man, that thou art mindful of him? and the son of man, that thou visitest him? For thou hast made him a little lower than the angels, and hast *crowned him with glory and honour. Thou madest him to have dominion over the works of thy hands;* thou hast put all things under his feet." Psalm 8:4-6.

What home did God make for man in the beginning?

"And the Lord God planted *a garden* eastward in Eden; and there he put the man whom he had formed." "And the Lord God took the man, and put him into *the garden of Eden* to dress it and to keep it." Genesis 2:8, 15.

How did God provide for the perpetuation of life?

"And out of the ground made the Lord God to grow every tree that is pleasant to the sight, and good for food; *the tree of life* also in the midst of the garden, and the tree of knowledge of good and evil." Genesis 2:9.

What simple plan did God devise to test man's loyalty and obedience?

"And the Lord God commanded the man, saying, Of every tree of the garden thou mayest freely eat: but *of the tree of the knowledge of good and evil, thou shalt not eat of it:* for in the day that thou eatest thereof thou shalt surely die." Verses 16, 17.

By what power are all things upheld?

"Upholding all things *by the word of his power."* Hebrews 1:3.

The Speech of Nature

What do the heavens declare?

"The heavens *declare the glory of God*. . . . Day unto day uttereth speech." Psalm 19:1, 2.

What may be perceived through the things that are made?

"For *the invisible things of him* from the creation of the world are clearly seen, being understood by the things that are made, even *his eternal power and Godhead; so that they are without excuse.*" Romans 1:20.

The New Creation

Whose workmanship is the Christian?

"For we are *his workmanship,* created in Christ Jesus unto good works, which God hath before ordained that we should walk in them." Ephesians 2:10.

In view of the curse upon the earthly creation, what has God promised?

"For, behold, *I create new heavens and a new earth*: and the former shall not be remembered, nor come into mind." Isaiah 65:17. (See Revelation 21:1.)

The Instinct of Worship and Brotherhood

What contrast is drawn in the Scriptures between the Creator and false gods?

"Thus shall ye say unto them, *The gods that have not made the heavens and the earth,* even they shall perish from the earth, and from under these heavens." Jeremiah 10:11.

To whom is our worship justly due?

"O come, let us worship and bow down: let us kneel before *the Lord our maker*." Psalm 95:6.

What is the true basis of the brotherhood of man?

"*Have we not all one Father? hath not one God created us?* why do we deal treacherously every man against his brother, by profaning the covenant of our fathers?" Malachi 2:10.

The Origin of Evil

THE BEING WHO FIRST SINNED

With whom did sin originate?

"He that committeth sin is of the devil; for *the devil sinneth from the beginning.*" 1 John 3:8.

NOTE.—Without the Bible, the question of the origin of evil would remain unexplained.

From what time has the devil been a murderer?

"Ye are of your father the devil, and the lusts of your father ye will do. *He was a murderer from the beginning,* and abode not in the truth, because there is no truth in him." John 8:44.

What is the devil's relationship to lying?

"When he speaketh a lie, he speaketh of his own: for *he is a liar, and the father of it.*" Same verse.

Was Satan created sinful?

"Thou wast *perfect* in thy ways from the day that thou wast created, *till iniquity was found in thee.*" Ezekiel 28:15.

NOTE.—Ezekiel here refers to Satan under the figure "king of Tyrus." (See verse 12.) This, and the statement in John 8:44, that he *"abode* not in the truth," show that Satan was once *perfect,* and *in the truth.* Peter speaks of "the angels that *sinned*" (2 Peter 2:4); and Jude refers to "the angels which *kept not their first estate*" (Jude 6). These angels were once in a state of sinlessness.

What further statement of Christ seems to lay the responsibility for the origin of sin upon Satan and his angels?

"Then shall he say also unto them on the left hand, Depart from me, ye cursed, into everlasting fire, *prepared for the devil and his angels.*" Matthew 25:41.

SATAN AND CHRIST CONTRASTED

What led to Satan's sin, rebellion, and downfall?

"*Thine heart was lifted up because of thy beauty,* thou hast corrupted thy wisdom by reason of thy *brightness.*" Ezekiel 28:17. "Thou hast said in thine heart, *I will ascend into heaven, I will exalt my throne above the stars of God: I will sit also upon the mount of the congregation, in the sides of the north: . . . I will be like the most High.*" Isaiah 14:13, 14.

Note.—In a word, pride and self-exaltation led to Satan's downfall, and for these there is no justification or adequate excuse. "Pride goeth before destruction, and a haughty spirit before a fall." Proverbs 16:18. Hence, while we may know of the origin, cause, character, and results of evil, no good or sufficient reason or excuse can be given for it. To excuse it is to justify it; and the moment it is justified it ceases to be sin. All sin is a manifestation of selfishness in some form, and its results are the opposite of those prompted by love. The experiment of sin will result finally in its utter abandonment and banishment forever, by all created intelligences, throughout the entire universe of God. Only those who stubbornly cling to sin will be destroyed with it. The wicked will then be destroyed, root and branch (Malachi 4:1), and the righteous shall "shine as the brightness of the firmament," and "as the stars for ever and ever." Daniel 12:3. See reading on "Origin, History, and Destiny of Satan," page 495.

In contrast with the pride and self-exaltation exhibited by Satan, what spirit did Christ manifest?

"Who, being in the form of God, thought it not robbery to be equal with God: but *made himself of no reputation,* and took upon him the form of a *servant,* and was made in the likeness of *men:* and being found in fashion as a man, *he humbled himself,* and became obedient unto *death,* even *the death of the cross.*" Philippians 2:6-8.

After man had sinned, how did God show His love, and His willingness to forgive?

"For God so loved the world, that he gave his only begotten Son, that whosoever believeth in him should not perish, but have everlasting life." John 3:16.

Up and Down

In heaven Satan sought to lift himself up above God. He was cast down to earth. On earth Jesus humbled Himself and was then exalted to the right hand of the Majesty in the heavens. We who would go up to heaven must first go down to the cross—that old rugged cross, where Jesus died for sin and where we die to sin.

The Fall and Redemption of Man

DEFINITION AND NATURE OF SIN

What is sin declared to be?

"Whosoever committeth sin transgresseth also the law: for *sin is the transgression of the law.*" 1 John 3:4.

What precedes the manifestation of sin?

"Then when *lust* hath conceived, it bringeth forth sin." James 1:15.

THE RESULTS OF SIN

What is the final result, or fruit, of sin?

"And sin, when it is finished, bringeth forth *death.*" Same verse. "The wages of sin is *death.*" Romans 6:23.

Upon how many of the human race did death pass as the result of Adam's transgression?

"By one man sin entered into the world, and death by sin; and so *death passed upon all men,* for that all have sinned." Romans 5:12. "In Adam *all die.*" 1 Corinthians 15:22.

How were the earth itself and its vegetation affected by Adam's sin?

"Cursed is the ground for thy sake; in sorrow shalt thou eat of it all the days of thy life; *thorns also and thistles shall it bring forth to thee."* Genesis 3:17, 18.

What additional curse came as the result of the first murder?

"And the Lord said unto Cain, . . . And *now art thou cursed from the earth,* which hath opened her mouth to receive thy brother's blood from thy hand; *when thou tillest the ground, it shall not henceforth yield unto thee her strength."* Genesis 4:9-12.

What terrible judgment came in consequence of continued sin and transgression against God?

THE FALL AND REDEMPTION OF MAN

"And the Lord said, I will destroy man whom I have created from the face of the earth." "The end of all flesh is come before me; for the earth is filled with violence." "And Noah was six hundred years old when the *flood of waters* was upon the earth." "The same day were *all the fountains of the great deep broken up, and the windows of heaven were opened.*" Genesis 6:7, 13; 7:6, 11.

After the Flood, what came in consequence of further apostasy from God?

"And the Lord came down to see the city and the tower, which the children of men builded. And the Lord said, Behold, the people is one, and they have all one language; and this they begin to do: and now nothing will be restrained from them, which they have imagined to do. Go to, let us go down, and there *confound their language, that they may not understand one another's speech.* So the Lord scattered them abroad from thence upon the face of all the earth: and they left off to build the city." Genesis 11:5-8.

Into what condition has sin brought the entire creation?

"For we know that the whole creation *groaneth* and *travaileth in pain together* until now." Romans 8:22.

GOD'S DELAY IN DESTROYING SIN

What explains God's apparent delay in dealing with sin?

"The Lord is not slack concerning his promise, as some men count slackness; but is *longsuffering to us-ward,* not willing that any should perish, but that all should come to repentance." 2 Peter 3:9.

What is God's attitude toward the sinner?

"For *I have no pleasure in the death of him that dieth,* saith the Lord God: wherefore turn yourselves, and live ye." Ezekiel 18:32.

Can man free himself from the dominion of sin?

"Can the Ethiopian change his skin, or the leopard his spots? *then may ye also do good, that are accustomed to do evil.*" Jeremiah 13:23.

What place has the will in determining whether man shall have life?

"And the Spirit and the bride say, Come. And let him that heareth say, Come. And let him that is athirst come. And *whosoever will, let him take the water of life freely.*" Revelation 22:17.

Christ, the Sinner, and Satan

To what extent has Christ suffered for sinners?

"He was *wounded* for our transgressions, he was *bruised* for our iniquities: the *chastisement* of our peace was upon him; and with his *stripes* we are healed." Isaiah 53:5.

For what purpose was Christ manifested?

"And ye know that *he was manifested to take away our sins;* and in him is no sin. . . . He that committeth sin is of the devil; for the devil sinneth from the beginning. For this purpose the Son of God was manifested, *that he might destroy the works of the devil.*" 1 John 3:5-8.

What was one direct purpose of the incarnation of Christ?

"Forasmuch then as the children are partakers of flesh and blood, he also himself likewise took part of the same; *that through death he might destroy him that had the power of death, that is, the devil.*" Hebrews 2:14.

The End of Sin and Sorrow

What triumphant chorus will mark the end of the reign of sin?

"And every creature which is in heaven, and on the earth, and under the earth, and such as are in the sea, and all that are in them, heard I saying, *Blessing, and honour, and glory, and power, be unto him that sitteth upon the throne, and unto the Lamb for ever and ever.*" Revelation 5:13.

When and by what means will the effects of sin be removed?

"But the day of the Lord will come as a thief in the night; in the which the heavens shall pass away with a great noise, and *the elements shall melt with fervent heat, the earth also and the works that are therein shall be burned up."* 2 Peter 3:10.

How thoroughly will the effects of sin be removed?

"And God *wipe away all tears* from their eyes; and there shall be *no more death, neither sorrow, nor crying, neither shall there be any more pain: for the former things are passed away.*" Revelation 21:4. "*And there shall be no more curse:* but the throne of God and of the Lamb shall be in it [the Holy City]; and his servants shall serve him." Revelation 22:3.

Will sin and its evil results ever appear again?

"There shall be *no more death.*" "And there shall be *no more curse.*" Revelation 21:4; 22:3.

THE POET WHO DECIDED TO DROWN HIMSELF

That sin exists none can deny. Why it was permitted has perplexed many minds. But He who can bring light out of darkness (2 Corinthians 4:6), make the wrath of man to praise Him (Psalm 76:10), and turn a curse into a blessing (Deuteronomy 23:5), can bring good out of evil, and turn mistakes and downfalls into steppingstones to higher ground. Heaven will be happier for the sorrows of earth. "Sorrows remembered sweeten present joy," says Robert Pollok in The Course of Time, *book 1. In the final outcome it will be seen that all things have worked together for good to them that love God. (See Romans 8:28.) Cowper, despondent and about to drown himself, was carried the wrong way by his driver, and went home to write the inspiring hymn below.*

~~~~~~~~~~

> God moves in a mysterious way
>   His wonders to perform;
> He plants His footsteps in the sea,
>   And rides upon the storm.
>
> . . . . .
>
> Ye fearful saints fresh courage take;
>   The clouds ye so much dread
> Are big with mercy, and shall break
>   In blessings on your head.
>
> . . . . .
>
> Blind unbelief is sure to err,
>   And scan His work in vain:
> God is His own interpreter,
>   And He will make it plain.
>
> —WILLIAM COWPER

CHRIST BRUISES THE SERPENT'S HEAD

"For this purpose the Son of God was manifested, that he might destroy the works of the devil." 1 John 3

Creation and Redemption

CHRIST IN CREATION

WHAT is revealed concerning God in the first verse of the Bible?

"In the beginning *God created the heaven and the earth.*" Genesis 1:1.

What contrast is repeatedly drawn in the Scriptures between the true God and false gods?

"Thus shall ye say unto them, *The gods that have not made the heavens and the earth,* even they shall perish from the earth, and from under these heavens. . . . The portion of Jacob is not like them: for *he is the former of all things;* and Israel is the rod of his inheritance: The Lord of hosts is his name." Jeremiah 10:11-16. (See Jeremiah 14:22; Acts 17:22-29; Revelation 14:6-10.)

Through whom did God work in creating all things?

"In the beginning was *the Word,* and the Word was with God, and the Word was God. The same was in the beginning with God. *All things were made by him;* and without him was not any thing made that was made." John 1:1-3.

CHRIST THE CREATOR REDEEMS

Through whom is redemption wrought?

"But God commendeth his love toward us, in that, while we were yet sinners, *Christ died for us.* Much more then, being now justified by his blood, we shall be saved from wrath through him." Romans 5:8, 9.

What scripture speaks of the Creator as Redeemer?

"But now thus saith *the Lord that created thee, O Jacob,* and he that formed thee, O Israel, Fear not: for *I have redeemed thee,* I have called thee by thy name; thou art mine." Isaiah 43:1.

What prayer of David shows that he regarded redemption as a creative work?

"Create in me a clean heart, O God; and renew a right spirit within me." Psalm 51:10.

In what scripture do we learn that Christ, the active agent in creation, is also the head of the church?

"For by him were all things created, that are in heaven, and that are in earth, visible and invisible, whether they be thrones, or dominions, or principalities, or powers: *all things were created by him,* and for him: and he is before all things, and *by him all things consist.* And *he is the head of the body, the church:* who is the beginning, the firstborn from the dead; that in all things he might have the preeminence." Colossians 1:16-18.

What scripture plainly states that it is creative power which transforms the believer?

"For we are his workmanship, *created in Christ Jesus unto good works,* which God hath before ordained that we should walk in them." Ephesians 2:10.

The Creator's Upholding, Sustaining Power

Who keeps the heavenly bodies in their places?

"To whom then will ye liken me, or shall I be equal? saith *the Holy One.* Lift up your eyes on high, and behold who hath created these things, *that bringeth out their host by number:* he calleth them all by names by the greatness of his might, for that he is strong in power; not one faileth." Isaiah 40:25, 26.

What can the same Holy One do for the believer?

"Now unto him that is able to *keep you from falling,* and to present you faultless before the presence of his glory with exceeding joy, to the only wise God our Saviour, be glory and majesty, dominion and power, both now and ever. Amen." Jude 24, 25.

What is the measure of the power which is available for the help of the believer?

"That the God of our Lord Jesus Christ, the Father of glory, may give unto you the spirit of wisdom and revelation in the knowledge of him: the eyes of your understanding being enlightened; that ye may know what is the hope of his calling, and what the riches of the glory of his inheritance in the saints, and what is the exceeding greatness of his power to us-ward who believe, *according to the working of his mighty power, which he wrought in Christ, when he raised him from the dead, and set him at his own right hand in the heavenly places.*" Ephesians 1:17-20.

Who is declared to be the source of power to the weak?

"Hast thou not known? hast thou not heard, that the everlasting God, the Lord, *the Creator* of the ends of the earth, fainteth not, neither is weary? there is no searching of his understanding. *He giveth power to the faint;* and to them that have no might he increaseth strength." Isaiah 40:28, 29.

Through whose agency is the material universe sustained?

"And he [Christ] is before all things, and in him all things *hold together.*" Colossians 1:17, R.V., margin.

What statement shows that all things, both material and spiritual, are sustained by the same personal agency?

"But to us there is . . . one Lord Jesus Christ, *by whom are all things, and we by him.*" 1 Corinthians 8:6.

God's Memorial and Sign

Of what great work is the Sabbath both a memorial and a sign?

"*Remember the sabbath day,* to keep it holy. Six days shalt thou labour, and do all thy work: but the seventh day is the sabbath of the Lord thy God: in it thou shalt not do any work, thou, nor thy son, nor thy daughter, thy man servant, nor thy maid servant, nor thy cattle, nor thy stranger that is within thy gates: *for in six days the Lord made heaven and earth, the sea, and all that in them is,* and rested the seventh day: wherefore the Lord blessed the sabbath day, and hallowed it." Exodus 20:8-11. "It is a *sign* between me and the children of Israel for ever: *for in six days the Lord made heaven and earth,* and on the seventh day he rested, and was refreshed." Exodus 31:17.

Inasmuch as creation and redemption are both wrought by the same creative power, of what besides the original creation was the Sabbath given to be a sign?

"Moreover also I gave them my sabbaths, to be a sign between me and them, *that they might know that I am the Lord that sanctify them.*" Ezekiel 20:12.

The Reason for Worship

Why is God worthy to receive glory and honor?

"Thou art worthy, O Lord, to receive glory and honour and power: *for thou hast created all things,* and for thy pleasure they are and were created." Revelation 4:11.

Note.—That comparatively modern view of creation known as evolution, which rests upon human research rather than upon divine revelation, and which substitutes an impersonal force for a personal Creator, overthrows the very foundation of the gospel. Redemption is simply the new creation, and the Creator is the Redeemer. The Head of the original creation is the Head of the new creation. The original creation was wrought through Christ by the power of the word; the new creation, or redemption, is wrought in exactly the same way. The evolution theory of creation inevitably involves an evolution theory of the gospel, and sets aside the truth concerning sin, the atoning sacrifice of Christ, and the necessity of becoming new creatures through faith in the saving power of Christ.

About the Ape Man

For a long time now men have been seeking to find a missing link —a creature about half man and half beast. They cannot produce him in the laboratory of breeding. They have never found a single bone or fossil of this so-called original ancestor, *the supposed common ancestor of the gorilla, orangutan, gibbon, and chimpanzee, and of man.*

Posing specimens are mere pretensions. Great scientists know it and say it. It is a pitiful fact that millions believe in the missing-link phantom, and the religious faith of many has been thrust through by the prongs of this fallacy.

What man needs today is not to discover a missing link to connect him with beasts, but to find in glorious experience that great connecting link between man and God, even our Lord Jesus Christ, who came and lived and died that we might be restored to fellowship with the Creator of all things.

"Frail children of dust, and feeble as frail,
In Thee do we trust, nor find Thee to fail;
Thy mercies, how tender! how firm to the end!
Our Maker, Defender, Redeemer, and Friend!"

The Character and Attributes of God

God's Justice, Holiness, and Righteousness

What two basic characteristics are part of God's nature?

"The Lord is *righteous* in all his ways, and *holy* in all his works." Psalm 145:17.

Does Christ possess these same attributes?

"By his knowledge shall *my righteous servant* [Christ] justify many." Isaiah 53:11. "Neither wilt thou suffer *thine Holy One* to see corruption." Acts 2:27.

In what language is the justice of God described?

"He is the Rock, his work is perfect: for *all his ways are judgment:* a God of truth and without iniquity, *just and right is he.*" Deuteronomy 32:4.

His Strength, Wisdom, and Faithfulness

What is said of the strength and wisdom of God?

"Behold, God is *mighty,* and despiseth not any: he is *mighty in strength and wisdom.*" Job 36:5.

What treasures are hid in Christ?

"In whom are hid all the treasures of *wisdom* and *knowledge.*" Colossians 2:3.

What is said of God's faithfulness in keeping His promises?

"Know therefore that the Lord thy God, he is God, *the faithful God,* which keepeth covenant and mercy with them that love him and keep his commandments to a thousand generations." Deuteronomy 7:9.

The Love and Compassion of God

In what one word is the character of God expressed?

"He that loveth not knoweth not God; for God is *love.*" 1 John 4:8.

What is said of the tender compassion of God?

"But thou, O Lord, art a God *full of compassion*, and gracious, longsuffering, and plenteous in mercy and truth." Psalm 86:15.

HIS GRACIOUS IMPARTIALITY

In what words is His impartiality proclaimed?

"For the Lord your God is God of gods, and Lord of lords, a great God, a mighty, and a terrible, *which regardeth not persons, nor taketh reward.*" Deuteronomy 10:17. "Then Peter opened his mouth, and said, Of a truth I perceive that *God is no respecter of persons:* but in every nation he that feareth him, and worketh righteousness, is accepted with him." Acts 10:34, 35.

To how many is the Lord good?

"The Lord is *good to all:* and his tender mercies are over all his works." Psalm 145:9.

Why did Christ tell us to love our enemies?

"But I say unto you, Love your enemies, bless them that curse you, do good to them that hate you, and pray for them which despitefully use you, and persecute you; *that ye may be the children of your Father which is in heaven: for he maketh his sun to rise on the evil and on the good, and sendeth rain on the just and on the unjust."* Matthew 5:44, 45.

CHRIST'S CALL TO HIS PEOPLE

How perfect does Christ tell His followers to be?

"Be ye therefore perfect, *even as your Father which is in heaven is perfect."* Verse 48.

THE SEEING EYE

In the great La Salle Hotel fire at Chicago a blind lecturer was trapped on the eleventh floor; but she followed her Seeing Eye dog, Fawn, to safety while scores of people with eyes perished. For all spiritually blind persons, faith is the seeing eye. It comes by hearing, and hearing by the word of God. (Romans 10:17.) "Have faith in God." Mark 11:22.

The Love of God

WHAT is God declared to be?

"God is love." 1 John 4:16.

How great is God's love for the world?

"For God so loved the world, that he gave his only begotten Son, that whosoever believeth in him should not perish, but have everlasting life." John 3:16.

In what act especially has God's infinite love been manifested?

"In this was manifested the love of God toward us, because that *God sent his only begotten Son into the world, that we might live through him."* 1 John 4:9.

God's Delight

In what does God delight?

"Who is a God like unto thee, that pardoneth iniquity, and passeth by the transgression of the remnant of his heritage? he retaineth not his anger for ever, because *he delighteth in mercy."* Micah 7:18.

How are the mercies of Heaven continually manifested to the sons of men?

"It is of the Lord's mercies that we are not consumed, because his compassions fail not. *They are new every morning:* great is thy faithfulness." Lamentations 3:22, 23.

Upon how many does God bestow His blessings?

"He maketh his sun to rise on the evil and on the good, and sendeth rain on the just and on the unjust." Matthew 5:45.

In view of God's great love, what may we confidently expect?

"He that spared not his own Son, but delivered him up for us all, how shall he not with him also freely *give us all things?* Romans 8:32.

Fellowship, Sonship, and Trust

What did Jesus say of the one who loves Him?

"He that loveth me shall be loved of my Father, and I will love him, and will manifest myself to him." John 14:21.

Into what relationship to God does His love bring us?

"Behold, what manner of love the Father hath bestowed upon us, that we should be called *the sons of God."* 1 John 3:1.

As sons of God to what will we submit? How may we know that we are the sons of God?

"For *as many as are led by the Spirit of God,* they are the sons of God.... *The Spirit itself beareth witness with our spirit,* that we are the children of God." Romans 8:14-16.

How is the love of God supplied to the believer?

"And hope maketh not ashamed; because the love of God is shed abroad in our hearts *by the Holy Ghost* which is given unto us." Romans 5:5.

When men appreciate God's love, what will they do?

"How excellent is thy lovingkindness, O God! therefore the children of men *put their trust under the shadow of thy wings."* Psalm 36:7.

Fellowship of Believers

In view of God's great love to us, what attitude should we take toward one another?

"Beloved, if God so loved us, *we ought also to love one another."* 1 John 4:11.

With what measure of love should we serve others?

"Hereby perceive we the love of God, because he laid down his life for us: and *we ought to lay down our lives for the brethren."* 1 John 3:16.

What exhortation is based upon Christ's love for us?

"And *walk in love,* as Christ also hath loved us, and hath given himself for us an offering and a sacrifice to God for a sweet-smelling savour." Ephesians 5:2.

Love's Wise Way

Upon what ground does God's work for sinners rest?

"But God, who is rich in mercy, *for his great love wherewith he loved us,* even when we were dead in sins, hath quickened us together with Christ, (by grace ye are saved;) and hath raised *us up together, and made us sit together* in heavenly places in Christ Jesus." Ephesians 2:4-6. (See Titus 3:5, 6.)

What is God's love able to do for His children?

"Nevertheless the Lord thy God would not hearken unto Balaam; but the Lord thy God *turned the curse into a blessing* unto thee, because the Lord thy God loved thee." Deuteronomy 23:5.

In what other way is God's love sometimes shown?

"For whom the Lord loveth he *chasteneth,* and *scourgeth* every son whom he receiveth." Hebrews 12:6.

Love Everlasting

How enduring is God's love for us?

"The Lord hath appeared of old unto me, saying, Yea, *I have loved thee with an everlasting love:* therefore with lovingkindness have I drawn thee." Jeremiah 31:3.

Can anything separate the true child of God from the love of God?

"For I am persuaded, that neither death, nor life, nor angels, nor principalities, nor powers, nor things present, nor things to come, nor height, nor depth, nor any other creature, shall be able to separate us from the love of God, which is in Christ Jesus our Lord." Romans 8:38, 39.

Unto whom will the saints forever ascribe praise?

"*Unto him that loved us, and washed us from our sins* in his own blood, ... to him be glory and dominion for ever and ever." Revelation 1:5, 6.

The Deity of Christ

THE FATHER'S TESTIMONY

How has the Father shown that His Son is one person of the Godhead?

"But *unto the Son he saith,* Thy throne, *O God,* is for ever and ever: a sceptre of righteousness is the sceptre of thy kingdom." Hebrews 1:8.

How was He recognized by the Father while on earth?

"And lo a voice from heaven, saying, *This is my beloved Son,* in whom I am well pleased." Matthew 3:17.

CHRIST'S TESTIMONY

In what way did Christ refer to the eternity of His being?

"And now, O Father, glorify thou me with thine own self with the glory which I had with thee *before the world was.*" John 17:5. "But thou, Bethlehem Ephratah, though thou be little among the thousands of Judah, yet out of thee shall he come forth unto me that is to be ruler in Israel; whose goings forth have been from of old, *from everlasting.*" Micah 5:2. (See margin, and Matthew 2:6; John 8:58; Exodus 3:13, 14.)

What does Christ say is His relation to the Father?

"I and my Father are *one.*" John 10:30.

How did Christ assert an equal proprietorship with His Father in the kingdom?

"The Son of man shall send forth his angels, and they shall gather out of *his kingdom* all things that offend, and them which do iniquity." Matthew 13:41.

To whom do the elect equally belong?

"And shall not God avenge *his own elect,* which cry day and night unto him, though he bear long with them?" Luke 18:7. "And he [the Son of man] shall send his angels with a great sound of a trumpet, and they shall gather together *his elect* from the four winds, from one end of heaven to the other." Matthew 24:31.

Who are equally joined in bestowing the final rewards?

"But without faith it is impossible to please him [God, the Father]: for he that cometh to God must believe that he is, and that *he is a rewarder of them that diligently seek him.*" Hebrews 11:6. "For the Son of man shall come in the glory of his Father with his angels; and *then he shall reward every man according to his works.*" Matthew 16:27.

NOTE.—In the texts (Matthew 16:27; 13:41; 24:31) in which Christ refers to the angels as "his angels" and to the kingdom as "his kingdom" and to the elect as "his elect," He refers to Himself as "the Son of man." It thus appears that while He was on earth as a man, He recognized His essential deity and His equality with His Father in heaven.

What does God declare Himself to be?

"Thus saith the Lord the King of Israel, and his redeemer the Lord of hosts; I am the *first,* and I am the *last;* and beside me there is no God." Isaiah 44:6.

In what scripture does Christ adopt the same expression?

"And, behold, I come quickly; and my reward is with me, to give every man according as his work shall be. I am Alpha and Omega, the beginning and the end, the *first* and the *last.*" Revelation 22:12, 13.

APOSTLES JOHN AND PAUL SPEAK

What scripture states that the Son of God was God manifested in the flesh?

"In the beginning was the Word, and the Word was with God, and *the Word was God.*" "And *the Word was made flesh,* and dwelt among us, (and we beheld his glory, the glory as of the only begotten of the Father,) full of grace and truth." John 1:1, 14.

What fullness dwells in Christ?

"For in him dwelleth *all the fulness of the Godhead bodily.*" Colossians 2:9.

Christ the Saviour

How was He manifested on earth as a Saviour?

"For unto you is *born* this day in the city of David a Saviour, which is Christ the Lord." Luke 2:11.

How was Christ begotten in the flesh?

"And the angel answered and said unto her, *The Holy Ghost* shall come upon thee, and *the power of the Highest* shall overshadow thee: therefore also that holy thing which shall be born of thee shall be called the Son of God." Luke 1:35.

Why was it necessary that He should be born thus, and partake of human nature?

"Wherefore in all things it behoved him to be made like unto his brethren, *that he might be a merciful and faithful high priest in things pertaining to God,* to make reconciliation for the sins of the people." Hebrews 2:17.

Having such a wonderful Saviour, what are we exhorted to do?

"Seeing then that we have a great high priest, that is passed into the heavens, Jesus the Son of God, *let us hold fast our profession*. For we have not an high priest which cannot be touched with the feeling of our infirmities; but was in all points tempted like as we are, yet without sin." Hebrews 4:14, 15.

The King Came Down

The King of glory stooped low to take humanity. Rude and forbidding were His earthly surroundings. His glory was veiled, that the majesty of His outward form might not become an object of attraction. He shunned all outward display. Riches, worldly honor, and human greatness can never save a soul from death; Jesus purposed that no attraction of an earthly nature should call men to His side. Only the beauty of heavenly truth must draw those who would follow Him. The character of the Messiah had long been foretold in prophecy, and He desired men to accept Him upon the testimony of the word of God.—The Desire of Ages, p. 39.

Prophecies Relating to Christ

PREDICTIONS AND WRITINGS OF MOSES

WHOM did Moses say the Lord would raise up?

"The Lord thy God will raise up unto thee *a Prophet* from the midst of thee, of thy brethren, like unto me; unto him ye shall hearken." Deuteronomy 18:15. (See also verse 18.)

What use of this prophecy by the apostle Peter shows that it referred to Christ?

"For Moses truly said unto the fathers, *A prophet* shall the Lord your God raise up unto you of your brethren, like unto me. . . . Yea, and all the prophets from Samuel and those that follow after, as many as have spoken, have likewise foretold of *these days*." Acts 3:22-24.

Under what striking emblem was He prophesied of by Balaam?

"There shall come *a Star* out of Jacob, and a Sceptre shall rise out of Israel." Numbers 24:17.

In what scripture does Christ apply the same emblem to Himself?

"I am the root and the offspring of David, and *the bright and morning star*." Revelation 22:16. (See also 2 Peter 1:19; Revelation 2:28.)

PROPHECIES OF HIS BIRTH

In what language did Isaiah foretell Christ's birth?

"Behold, *a virgin shall conceive, and bear a son,* and shall call his name Immanuel." Isaiah 7:14.

In what event was this prophecy fulfilled?

"Now *all this was done* [the birth of Jesus of the virgin Mary], that it might be fulfilled which was spoken of the Lord by the prophet, saying, Behold, a virgin shall be with child, and shall bring forth a son, and they shall call his name

Emmanuel, which being interpreted is, God with us." Matthew 1:22, 23.

Where was the Messiah to be born?

"But thou, *Bethlehem Ephratah,* though thou be little among the thousands of Judah, yet out of thee shall he come forth unto me that is to be ruler in Israel." Micah 5:2.

When was Jesus born?

"Jesus was born in Bethlehem of Judaea *in the days of Herod the king."* Matthew 2:1.

What prophecy was fulfilled in the slaughter of the children of Bethlehem?

"Then Herod, when he saw that he was mocked of the wise men, was exceeding wroth, and sent forth, and *slew all the children that were in Bethlehem,* and in all the coasts thereof, from two years old and under, according to the time which he had diligently inquired of the wise men. Then was fulfilled *that which was spoken by Jeremy the prophet,* saying, In Rama was there a voice heard, lamentation, and weeping, and great mourning, Rachel weeping for her children, and would not be comforted, because they are not." Matthew 2:16-18.

The Great Announcer

How was Christ's first advent to be heralded?

"The voice of him that crieth in the wilderness, Prepare ye the way of the Lord, make straight in the desert a highway for our God." Isaiah 40:3.

By whom was this fulfilled?

"And this is the record of *John,* when the Jews sent priests and Levites from Jerusalem to ask him, Who art thou?" "He said, *I am the voice of one crying in the wilderness,* Make straight the way of the Lord." John 1:19, 23.

Christ's Preaching and Reception

What prediction did the prophet Isaiah make concerning Christ's preaching?

"The Spirit of the Lord God is upon me; because *the Lord hath anointed me to preach good tidings unto the meek;* he hath sent me to bind up the brokenhearted, to proclaim liberty to the captives, and the opening of the prison to them that are bound." Isaiah 61:1.

What application did Jesus make of this prophecy?

"And he came to Nazareth, where he had been brought up: and, as his custom was, he went into the synagogue on the sabbath day, and stood up for to read. And there was delivered unto him the book of the prophet Esaias. And when he had opened the book, he found the place where it was written, The Spirit of the Lord is upon me, because he hath anointed me to preach the gospel to the poor; he hath sent me to heal the brokenhearted, to preach deliverance to the captives, and recovering of sight to the blind, to set at liberty them that are bruised. . . . And he began to say unto them, *This day is this scripture fulfilled in your ears.*" Luke 4:16-21. (See Luke 7:19-22.)

How was Christ to be received by His own people?

"He is *despised* and *rejected* of men; a man of sorrows, and acquainted with grief: and we hid as it were our faces from him; he was *despised,* and *we esteemed him not.*" Isaiah 53:3.

How is the fulfillment of this prophecy recorded?

"He was in the world, and the world was made by him, and the world knew him not. *He came unto his own, and his own received him not.*" John 1:10, 11.

His Trial and Crucifixion

How, according to prophecy, was Christ to conduct Himself when on trial?

"He was oppressed, and he was afflicted, *yet he opened not his mouth:* he is brought as a lamb to the slaughter, and as a sheep before her shearers is dumb, *so he openeth not his mouth.*" Isaiah 53:7.

When accused by His enemies before Pilate, how did Christ treat these accusations?

"Then said Pilate unto him, Hearest thou not how many things they witness against thee? And *he answered him to never a word;* insomuch that the governor marvelled greatly." Matthew 27:13, 14.

What prophecy foretold of the disposal of Christ's garments at the crucifixion?

"They *part my garments* among them, and *cast lots* upon my vesture." Psalm 22:18.

What record answers to this prophecy?

"And they crucified him, and *parted his garments, casting lots:* that it might be fulfilled which was spoken by the prophet, They parted my garments among them, and upon my vesture did they cast lots." Matthew 27:35.

What was foretold of His treatment while on the cross?

"They gave me also *gall* for my meat; and in my thirst they gave me *vinegar* to drink." Psalm 69:21.

What was offered Christ at His crucifixion?

"They gave him *vinegar* to drink mingled with *gall:* and when he had tasted thereof, he would not drink." Matthew 27:34. (See also John 19:28-30, and page 165 of this work.)

With whom did the prophet Isaiah say Christ would make His grave?

"And he made his grave with the *wicked,* and with the *rich* in his death." Isaiah 53:9.

With whom was Christ crucified?

"Then were there *two thieves* crucified with him, one on the right hand, and another on the left." Matthew 27:38.

Burial and Resurrection

Who took charge of Christ's body after it was taken down from the cross?

"*A rich man of Arimathaea, named Joseph,* . . . went to Pilate, and begged the body of Jesus. . . . He wrapped it in a clean linen cloth, and laid it in his own new tomb, which he had hewn out in the rock." Verses 57-60.

PROPHECIES RELATING TO CHRIST

To what experience in the life of a noted prophet did Christ refer when speaking of the length of His stay in the grave?

"But he answered and said unto them, An evil and adulterous generation seeketh after a sign; and there shall no sign be given to it, but the sign of the prophet Jonas: for *as Jonas was three days and three nights in the whale's belly;* so shall the Son of man be three days and three nights in the heart of the earth." Matthew 12:39, 40.

What prophecy foretold Christ's triumph over death?

"For *thou wilt not leave my soul in hell;* neither wilt thou suffer thine Holy One to see corruption." Psalm 16:10. (See Acts 2:24-27.)

Look upon Jesus, sinless is He;
Father, impute His life unto me.
My life of scarlet, my sin and woe,
Cover with His life, whiter than snow.

Deep are the wounds transgression has made;
Red are the stains; my soul is afraid.
O to be covered, Jesus, with Thee,
Safe from the law that now judgeth me!

Longing the joy of pardon to know;
Jesus holds out a robe white as snow;
"Lord, I accept it! leaving my own,
Gladly I wear Thy pure life alone."

Reconciled by His death for my sin,
Justified by His life pure and clean,
Sanctified by obeying His word,
Glorified when returneth my Lord.

—F. E. Belden

Christ the Way of Life

WHAT does Jesus declare Himself to be?

"Jesus saith unto him, *I am the way, the truth, and the life:* no man cometh unto the Father, but by me." John 14:6.

MAN'S SITUATION

In what condition are all men?

"But the scripture hath concluded all *under sin.*" Galatians 3:22. "For *all have sinned,* and come short of the glory of God." Romans 3:23.

What are the wages of sin?

"The wages of sin is *death.*" Romans 6:23.

How many are affected by Adam's transgression?

"Wherefore, as by one man sin entered into the world, and death by sin; and so *death passed upon all men.*" Romans 5:12.

When man first transgressed, what was done to prevent him from living forever in sin?

"And now, lest he put forth his hand, and take also of the tree of life, and eat, and live for ever. . . . So *he drove out the man;* and he placed at the east of the garden of Eden Cherubims, and a flaming sword which turned every way, to keep the way of the tree of life." Genesis 3:22-24.

GOD'S GIFT AND REMEDY

To counteract the effect of sin, what gift has God provided?

"The wages of sin is death; but the gift of God is *eternal life.*" Romans 6:23.

How many may receive this gift?

"And the Spirit and the bride say, Come. And let him that heareth say, Come. And let him that is athirst come. And *whosoever will,* let him take the water of life freely." Revelation 22:17.

CHRIST THE WAY OF LIFE

In whom is the gift?

"This is the record, that God hath given to us eternal life, and *this life is in his Son.*" 1 John 5:11.

In receiving the Son, what do we have in Him?

"He that hath the Son hath *life.*" Verse 12.

What loss do those sustain who do not accept Him?

"And he that hath not the Son of God *hath not life.*" Same verse.

In what other way is this same truth stated?

"He that believeth on the Son hath everlasting life: and he that believeth not the Son shall not see life; but the wrath of God abideth on him." John 3:36.

After one truly receives Christ, whose life will be manifested in him?

"I am crucified with Christ: nevertheless I live; yet not I, but *Christ liveth in me:* and the life which I now live in the flesh I live by the faith of the Son of God, who loved me, and gave himself for me." Galatians 2:20.

Spiritual Death and Rebirth

In what condition are all before they are quickened with Christ?

"God, who is rich in mercy, for his great love wherewith he loved us, even when we were *dead in sins,* hath quickened us together with Christ." Ephesians 2:4, 5.

What is this change from death to life called?

"Being *born again,* not of corruptible seed, but of incorruptible, by the word of God, which liveth and abideth for ever." 1 Peter 1:23.

Salvation Through Faith

What is declared to be one purpose of Christ's death?

"Forasmuch then as the children are partakers of flesh and blood, he also himself likewise took part of the same; *that through death he might destroy him that had the power of death, that is, the devil.*" Hebrews 2:14.

Why have all been reckoned under sin?

"But the scripture hath concluded all under sin, *that the promise by faith of Jesus Christ might be given to them that believe.*" Galatians 3:22.

How then do all become children of God?

"For ye are all the children of God *by faith in Christ Jesus.*" Verse 26.

With whom are the children of God joint heirs?

"If children, then heirs; heirs of God, and *joint-heirs with Christ.*" Romans 8:17.

The Prince of Orange Makes a Pledge

When William, Prince of Orange, handed a chosen man a written pledge for a high position in his kingdom if the man would support him, the man declined it, saying, "Your Majesty's word is sufficient. I would not serve a king if I could not trust his word."

"Then answered Peter and said unto him, Behold, we have forsaken all, and followed thee; what shall we have therefore? And Jesus said unto them, Verily I say unto you, . . . ye also shall sit upon twelve thrones, judging the twelve tribes of Israel. And every one that hath forsaken houses, or brethren, or sisters, or father, or mother, or wife, or children, or lands, for my name's sake . . . shall inherit everlasting life." Matthew 19:27-29.

Jesus wrote no pledge. He pledged His word, and we may rely upon it. His word is good, and will be fulfilled. The question is, "Shall we follow Him?"

"Thou art the Way, the Truth, the Life;
　Grant us that way to know,
The truth to keep, that life to win,
　Whose joys eternal flow."

Salvation Only Through Christ

For what purpose did Christ come into the world?

"This is a faithful saying, and worthy of all acceptation, that Christ Jesus came into the world *to save sinners.*" 1 Timothy 1:15.

Why was He to be named "Jesus"?

"Thou shalt call his name Jesus: *for he shall save his people from their sins.*" Matthew 1:21.

Is there salvation through any other?

"Neither is there salvation in any other: for *there is none other name* under heaven given among men, *whereby we must be saved.*" Acts 4:12.

Through whom only may we come to God?

"There is one God, and *one mediator between God and men, the man Christ Jesus;* who gave himself a ransom for all, to be testified in due time. . . . I will therefore that men pray every where, lifting up holy hands, without wrath and doubting." 1 Timothy 2:5-8.

What has Christ been made for us, and for what purpose?

"For he hath made him to be *sin* for us, who knew no sin; *that we might be made the righteousness of God in him.*" 2 Corinthians 5:21.

How dependent are we upon Christ for salvation?

"Without me ye can do nothing." John 15:5.

The Divine-Human Christ

What three essentials for a Saviour are found in Christ?

Deity. "But unto the Son he saith, Thy throne, *O God,* is for ever and ever." Hebrews 1:8.

Humanity. "When the fulness of the time was come, God sent forth his Son, *made of a woman,* made under the law." Galatians 4:4.

Sinlessness. "*Who did no sin,* neither was guile found in his mouth." 1 Peter 2:22.

How did Christ show from the Scriptures that the promised Saviour of the world must be both human and divine?

"While the Pharisees were gathered together, Jesus asked them, saying, What think ye of Christ? whose son is he? They say unto him, *The son of David.* He saith unto them, *How then doth David in spirit call him Lord,* saying, The Lord said unto my Lord, Sit thou on my right hand, till I make thine enemies thy footstool? *If David then call him Lord, how is he his son?*" Matthew 22:41-45.

Note.—Another has aptly put this important truth concerning the union of the human and divine Christ thus: "Divinity needed humanity that humanity might afford a channel of communication between God and man. Man needs a power out of and above himself to restore him to the likeness of God. There must be a power working from within, a new life from above, before men can be changed from sin to holiness. That power is Christ."

What two facts testify to the union of divinity and humanity in Christ?

"Concerning his Son Jesus Christ our Lord, which was *made of the seed of David according to the flesh; and declared to be the Son of God with power, according to the spirit of holiness, by the resurrection from the dead.*" Romans 1:3, 4.

Complete Victory

How complete was Christ's victory over death?

"I am the first and the last: *I am he that liveth, and was dead; and, behold, I am alive for evermore,* Amen; and have the keys of *hell and of death.*" Revelation 1:17, 18. (See Acts 2:24.)

How complete is the salvation obtained in Christ?

"Wherefore *he is able also to save them to the uttermost* that come unto God by him, seeing he ever liveth to make intercession for them." Hebrews 7:25.

What should we say for such a Saviour?

"Thanks be unto God for his unspeakable gift." 2 Corinthians 9:15.

Part Three

The Way to Christ

	PAGE
Victorious Faith	79
Hope in God	82
Repentance	85
Confession and Forgiveness	88
Conversion, or the New Birth	93
Christian Baptism	97
Reconciled to God	101
Acceptance With God	103
Justification by Faith	106
Righteousness and Life	111
Consecration	113
Bible Election	116
Bible Sanctification	119
Importance of Sound Doctrine	123
Present Truth	127
The Obedience of Faith	133

ABRAHAM CALLED OF GOD

"By faith Abraham, when he was called to go out . . . , obeyed; . . . not knowing whither he went." Hebrews 11:8

Victorious Faith

NATURE AND NECESSITY OF TRUE FAITH

WHAT is faith declared to be?

"Faith is *the substance of things hoped for, the evidence of things not seen.*" Hebrews 11:1.

How necessary is faith?

"Without faith it is impossible to please him." Verse 6.

Is mere assent to divine truth sufficient?

"Thou believest that there is one God; thou doest well: *the devils also believe, and tremble.*" James 2:19.

What is required besides a belief in the existence of God?

"For he that cometh to God must believe that he is, and *that he is a rewarder of them that diligently seek him.*" Hebrews 11:6, last part.

What is necessary in order that the preaching of the gospel may be profitable?

"For unto us was the gospel preached, as well as unto them: but the word preached did not profit them, not being *mixed with faith* in them that heard it." Hebrews 4:2.

What is the character of any act or service not performed in faith?

"Whatsoever is not of faith is *sin*." Romans 14:23.

SOURCE, CENTER, AND BASIS OF FAITH

From whom does faith come?

"*God* hath dealt to every man the measure of faith." Romans 12:3.

Why did God raise Christ from the dead?

"Who by him do believe in God, that raised him up from the dead, and gave him glory; *that your faith and hope might be in God.*" 1 Peter 1:21.

What is Christ's relation to this faith?

"Looking unto Jesus the *author* and *finisher* of our faith." Hebrews 12:2.

What is the basis of faith?

"So then faith cometh by hearing, and hearing by *the word of God*." Romans 10:17.

By what principle is genuine faith actuated?

"In Jesus Christ neither circumcision availeth any thing, nor uncircumcision; but faith which worketh by *love*." Galatians 5:6.

Of what is faith a fruit?

"But *the fruit of the Spirit* is love, joy, peace, longsuffering, gentleness, goodness, *faith*." Verse 22.

FRUITS OF FAITH

What relation does faith bear to knowledge?

"Through faith we understand that the worlds were framed by the word of God." Hebrews 11:3.

What in the early church showed living faith?

"Remembering without ceasing your *work of faith*, and labour of love." 1 Thessalonians 1:3.

How does Abraham's experience show that obedience and faith are inseparable?

"By faith Abraham, when he was called to go out into a place which he should after receive for an inheritance, *obeyed;* and he went out, not knowing whither he went." Hebrews 11:8.

With what, therefore, is the faith of Jesus joined?

"Here is the patience of the saints: here are they that keep *the commandments of God,* and *the faith of Jesus.*" Revelation 14:12.

In what other statement is the same truth emphasized?

"But wilt thou know, O vain man, that *faith without works is dead?*" James 2:20.

VICTORIOUS FAITH

How is faith brought to perfection?

"Seest thou how faith wrought with his works, and *by works was faith made perfect?*" Verse 22.

OTHER OBSERVATIONS

What is the result of faith's being put to the test?

"The trying of your faith *worketh patience.*" James 1:3.

What relationship to God is established by faith?

"For ye are all the *children of God by faith* in Christ Jesus." Galatians 3:26.

How do the children of God walk?

"For *we walk by faith,* not by sight." 2 Corinthians 5:7.

Upon what condition may one expect answers to prayer?

"But *let him ask in faith,* nothing wavering. For he that wavereth is like a wave of the sea driven with the wind and tossed." James 1:6.

To what parts of the ancient armor is faith compared?

"Above all, taking the *shield* of faith, wherewith ye shall be able to quench all the fiery darts of the wicked." Ephesians 6:16. "Putting on the *breastplate* of faith and love." 1 Thessalonians 5:8.

What chapter in the Bible is devoted to faith?

The eleventh chapter of Hebrews. In verses 33-38 are summarized the victories of the heroes of faith.

What gives victory in our conflicts with the world?

"This is the victory that overcometh the world, *even our faith.*" 1 John 5:4.

What is the ultimate purpose of faith?

"Receiving the end of your faith, even *the salvation of your souls.*" 1 Peter 1:9.

Hope in God

WHAT is the relation between faith and hope?

"Now faith is the *substance* of things *hoped for,* the evidence of things not seen." Hebrews 11:1.

Why were the Scriptures written?

"For whatsoever things were written aforetime were written for our learning, *that we through patience and comfort of the scriptures might have hope."* Romans 15:4.

Why should God's wonderful works be rehearsed to the children?

"We will not hide them from their children, shewing to the generation to come the praises of the Lord, and his strength, and his wonderful works that he hath done.... *That they might set their hope in God,* and not forget the works of God, but keep his commandments." Psalm 78:4-7.

FROM DESPAIR TO LIVING HOPE

In what condition are those who are without Christ?

"Wherefore remember, that ye being in time past Gentiles in the flesh, . . . that at that time ye were without Christ, being aliens from the commonwealth of Israel, and strangers from the covenants of promise, *having no hope,* and without God in the world." Ephesians 2:11, 12.

What does hope become to the Christian?

"Which hope we have as *an anchor of the soul,* both sure and stedfast, and which entereth into that within the veil." Hebrews 6:19.

Who have hope in their death?

"The wicked is driven away in his wickedness: but *the righteous hath hope in his death."* Proverbs 14:32.

In bereavement, from what hopeless sorrow are Christians delivered?

"But I would not have you to be ignorant, brethren, concerning them which are asleep, *that ye sorrow not, even as others which have no hope.*" 1 Thessalonians 4:13.

Unto what has the resurrection of Christ begotten us?

"Blessed be the God and Father of our Lord Jesus Christ, which according to his abundant mercy hath *begotten us again unto a lively hope* by the resurrection of Jesus Christ from the dead." 1 Peter 1:3.

What is the Christian's hope called?

"Looking for *that blessed hope,* and the glorious appearing of the great God and our Saviour Jesus Christ." Titus 2:13.

At what time did Paul expect to realize his hope?

"Henceforth there is laid up for me a crown of righteousness, which the Lord, the righteous judge, shall give me *at that day:* and not to me only, but unto all them also that love *his appearing.*" 2 Timothy 4:8.

What does the prophet Jeremiah say is a good thing for a man to do?

"It is good *that a man should both hope and quietly wait for the salvation of the Lord.*" Lamentations 3:26.

Purifying, Abounding, Enduring Hope

What will this hope lead one to do?

"And every man that hath this hope in him *purifieth himself,* even as he is pure." 1 John 3:3.

What is said of the hope of the hypocrite?

"So are the paths of all that forget God; and *the hypocrite's hope shall perish:* whose hope shall be cut off, and whose trust shall be a spider's web." Job 8:13, 14.

What is the condition of one whose hope is in God?

"*Happy* is he that hath the God of Jacob for his help, whose hope is in the Lord his God." Psalm 146:5. "*Blessed* is the man that trusteth in the Lord, and whose hope the Lord is." Jeremiah 17:7.

In what may the child of God abound?

"Now the God of hope fill you with all joy and peace in believing, that ye may *abound in hope,* through the power of the Holy Ghost." Romans 15:13.

In what do Christians rejoice?

"By whom also we have access by faith into this grace wherein we stand, and *rejoice in hope of the glory of God.*" Romans 5:2.

What will prevent us from being put to shame?

"And *hope maketh not ashamed;* because the love of God is shed abroad in our hearts by the Holy Ghost which is given unto us." Verse 5.

In the time of trouble, who will be the hope of God's people?

"The Lord also shall roar out of Zion, and utter his voice from Jerusalem; and the heavens and the earth shall shake: but *the Lord will be the hope of his people,* and the strength of the children of Israel." Joel 3:16.

What inspiring words are spoken to such as hope in God?

"Be of good courage, and he shall strengthen your heart, all ye that hope in the Lord." Psalm 31:24.

How long should our hope endure?

"We desire that every one of you do shew the same diligence to the full assurance of *hope unto the end.*" Hebrews 6:11.

"How cheering is the Christian's hope
  While toiling here below!
It buoys us up while passing through
  This wilderness of woe.

"It points us to a land of rest
  Where saints with Christ will reign;
Where we shall meet the loved of earth,
  And never part again;

"A land where sin can never come,
  Temptations ne'er annoy,
Where happiness will ever dwell,
  And that without alloy."

Repentance

Sin and Repentance

Who are called to repentance?

"I came not to call the righteous, but *sinners* to repentance." Luke 5:32.

What accompanies repentance?

"And that repentance and *remission of sins* should be preached in his name among all nations." Luke 24:47.

By what means is sin made known?

"By the law is the knowledge of sin." Romans 3:20.

How many are sinners?

"We have before proved *both Jews and Gentiles,* that *they are all under sin."* Verse 9.

What do transgressors bring upon themselves?

"Let no man deceive you with vain words: for because of these things cometh *the wrath of God* upon the children of disobedience." Ephesians 5:6.

Sensing Sin and Experiencing Salvation

Who awakens the soul to a sense of its sinful condition?

"When *he* [*the Comforter*] *is come, he will reprove* [literally, *"convince"*] *the world of sin."* John 16:8.

What are fitting inquiries for those convicted of sin?

"Men and brethren, *what shall we do?"* "Sirs, *what must I do to be saved?"* Acts 2:37; 16:30.

What replies does Inspiration return to these inquiries?

"Repent, and be baptized every one of you in the name of Jesus Christ for the remission of sins." *"Believe on the Lord Jesus Christ,* and thou shalt be saved." Acts 2:38; 16:31.

RETURN OF THE PRODIGAL SON

"Father, I have sinned against heaven, and before thee." Luke 15:18.

Fruits of True Repentance

What will the truly repentant sinner be constrained to do?

"I will *declare mine iniquity;* I will be *sorry* for my sin." Psalm 38:18.

What is the result of godly sorrow?

"For godly sorrow *worketh repentance to salvation.*" 2 Corinthians 7:10.

What does the sorrow of the world do?

"The sorrow of the world *worketh death.*" Same verse.

How does godly sorrow for sin manifest itself?

"For behold this selfsame thing, that ye sorrowed after a godly sort, what *carefulness* it wrought in you, yea, what *clearing of yourselves,* yea, what indignation, yea, what fear, yea, what vehement desire, yea, what zeal, yea, what revenge! In all things ye have approved yourselves to be clear in this matter." Verse 11.

What did John the Baptist say to the Pharisees and Sadducees when he saw them come to his baptism?

"O generation of vipers, who hath warned you to flee from the wrath to come?" Matthew 3:7.

What did he tell them to do?

"Bring forth therefore fruits meet for repentance." Verse 8.

Note.—There can be no true repentance without reformation. Repentance is a change of mind; reformation is a corresponding change of life.

When God sent the Ninevites a warning message, how did they show their repentance, and what was the result?

"And God saw their works, that *they turned from their evil way; and God repented of the evil, that he had said that he would do unto them;* and he did it not." Jonah 3:10.

What leads sinners to repentance?

"Or despisest thou the riches of his goodness and forbearance and longsuffering; not knowing that *the goodness of God leadeth thee to repentance?*" Romans 2:4.

Confession and Forgiveness

WHAT instruction is given concerning confession of sin?

"Speak unto the children of Israel, When a man or woman shall commit any sin that men commit, to do a trespass against the Lord, and that person be guilty; *then they shall confess their sin which they have done.*" Numbers 5:6, 7.

How futile is it to attempt to hide sin from God?

"But if ye will not do so, behold, ye have sinned against the Lord: and *be sure your sin will find you out.*" Numbers 32:23. "Thou hast set our iniquities before thee, our secret sins in the light of thy countenance." Psalm 90:8. "All things are naked and opened unto the eyes of him with whom we have to do." Hebrews 4:13.

What promise is made to those who confess their sins?

"If we confess our sins, *he is faithful and just to forgive us our sins,* and to cleanse us from all unrighteousness." 1 John 1:9.

What different results attend the covering and the confessing of sins?

"He that covereth his sins *shall not prosper:* but whoso confesseth and forsaketh them *shall have mercy.*" Proverbs 28:13.

BEING DEFINITE IN CONFESSION

How definite should we be in confessing our sins?

"And it shall be, when he shall be guilty in one of these things, that he shall confess that he hath sinned *in that thing.*" Leviticus 5:5.

NOTE.—"True confession is always of a specific character, and acknowledges particular sins. They may be of such a nature as to be brought before God only; they may be wrongs that should be confessed to individuals who have suffered injury through them; or they may be of a public character, and should then be as publicly confessed. But all confession should be definite and to the point, acknowledging the very sins of which you are guilty."—*Steps to Christ,* p. 43.

How fully did Israel once acknowledge their wrongdoing?

"And all the people said unto Samuel, Pray for thy servants unto the Lord thy God, that we die not: for *we have added unto all our sins this evil, to ask us a king."* 1 Samuel 12:19.

When David confessed his sin, what did he say God did?

"I acknowledged my sin unto thee, and mine iniquity have I not hid. I said, I will confess my transgressions unto the Lord; and *thou forgavest the iniquity of my sin."* Psalm 32:5.

God's Delight in Forgiving

What is God ready to do for all who seek for forgiveness?

"For thou, Lord, art good, and *ready to forgive;* and plenteous in mercy unto all them that call upon thee." Psalm 86:5.

Upon what did David rest his hope of forgiveness?

"Have mercy upon me, O God, according to thy lovingkindness: *according unto the multitude of thy tender mercies* blot out my transgressions." Psalm 51:1.

What is the measure of the greatness of God's mercy?

"For *as the heaven is high above the earth,* so great is his mercy toward them that fear him." Psalm 103:11.

How fully does the Lord pardon when one repents?

"Let the wicked forsake his way, and the unrighteous man his thoughts: and let him return unto the Lord, and he will have mercy upon him; and to our God, for *he will abundantly pardon."* Isaiah 55:7.

What reason is given for God's readiness to forgive sin?

"Who is a God like unto thee, that pardoneth iniquity, and passeth by the transgression of the remnant of his heritage? He retaineth not his anger for ever, *because he delighteth in mercy."* Micah 7:18. (See Psalm 78:38.)

Why does God manifest such mercy and long-suffering toward men?

"The Lord is not slack concerning his promise, as some men count slackness; but is longsuffering to us-ward, *not willing that any should perish,* but that all should come to repentance." 2 Peter 3:9.

Specific Examples

When the prodigal son, in the parable, repented and turned toward home, what did his father do?

"When he was yet a great way off, his father saw him, and *had compassion,* and ran, and fell on his neck, and kissed him." Luke 15:20.

How did the father show his joy at his son's return?

"The father said to his servants, *Bring forth the best robe, and put it on him;* and put a ring on his hand, and shoes on his feet: and *bring hither the fatted calf, and kill it;* and let us eat, and be merry: for this my son was dead, and is alive again; he was lost, and is found." Verses 22-24.

What is felt in heaven when a sinner repents?

"Likewise, I say unto you, *there is joy in the presence of the angels of God* over one sinner that repenteth." Verse 10.

What did Hezekiah say God had done with his sins?

"Behold, for peace I had great bitterness: but thou hast in love to my soul delivered it from the pit of corruption: for *thou hast cast all my sins behind thy back.*" Isaiah 38:17.

How completely does God wish to separate sin from us?

"Thou wilt cast all their sins into the depths of the sea." Micah 7:19. "As far as the east is from the west, so far hath he removed our transgressions from us." Psalm 103:12.

How did the people respond to the preaching of John?

"Then went out to him Jerusalem, and all Judaea, and all the region round about Jordan, and were baptized of him in Jordan, *confessing their sins.*" Matthew 3:5, 6.

How did some of the believers at Ephesus testify to the sincerity of the confession of their sins?

"And many that believed came, and *confessed, and shewed their deeds.* Many of them also which used curious arts *brought their books together, and burned them before all men:* and they counted the price of them, and found it fifty thousand pieces of silver." Acts 19:18, 19.

Conditions of Forgiveness

Upon what basis has Christ taught us to ask forgiveness?

"And forgive us our debts, *as we forgive our debtors.*" Matthew 6:12.

What spirit must those cherish whom God forgives?

"For *if ye forgive men their trespasses,* your heavenly Father will also forgive you: but if ye forgive not men their trespasses, neither will your Father forgive your trespasses." Verses 14, 15.

What exhortation is based on the fact that God has forgiven us?

"And be ye kind one to another, tenderhearted, *forgiving one another,* even as God for Christ's sake hath forgiven you." Ephesians 4:32.

The Blessed Giver and Receiver

Through whom are repentance and forgiveness granted?

"The God of our fathers raised up *Jesus,* whom ye slew and hanged on a tree. Him hath God exalted with his right hand to be a Prince and a Saviour, for *to give repentance* to Israel, and *forgiveness of sins.*" Acts 5:30, 31.

In what condition is one whose sins are forgiven?

"*Blessed* is he whose transgression is forgiven, whose sin is covered. Blessed is the man unto whom the Lord imputeth not iniquity, and in whose spirit there is no guile." Psalm 32:1, 2.

NICODEMUS LEARNS A VITAL LESSON

"Except a man be born again, he cannot see the kingdom of God." John 3:3.

Conversion, or the New Birth

NECESSITY OF CONVERSION

How did Jesus emphasize the necessity of conversion?

"Verily I say unto you, *Except ye be converted,* and become as little children, *ye shall not enter into the kingdom of heaven.*" Matthew 18:3.

In what other statement did He teach the same truth?

"Verily, verily, I say unto thee, *Except a man be born again,* he cannot see the kingdom of God." John 3:3.

How did He further explain the new birth?

"Jesus answered, Verily, verily, I say unto thee, *Except a man be born of water and of the Spirit,* he cannot enter into the kingdom of God." Verse 5.

With what comparison did He illustrate the subject?

"The wind bloweth where it listeth, and thou hearest the sound thereof, but canst not tell whence it cometh, and whither it goeth: *so is every one that is born of the Spirit."* Verse 8.

AGENCY OF THE NEW CREATION

What takes place when one is converted to Christ?

"Wherefore if any man is in Christ, *he is a new creation:* the old things are passed away; behold, they are become new." 2 Corinthians 5:17, R.V., margin. (See Acts 9:1-22; 22:1-21; 26:1-23.)

What is the value of merely outward forms?

"For in Christ Jesus *neither circumcision availeth any thing, nor uncircumcision,* but a new creature." Galatians 6:15.

Through what was the original creation wrought?

"By the word of the Lord were the heavens made; and all the host of them by the breath of his mouth." Psalm 33:6.

Through what instrumentality is conversion wrought?

"Being born again, not of corruptible seed, but of incorruptible, *by the word of God,* which liveth and abideth for ever." 1 Peter 1:23.

Results of True Conversion

What change is wrought in conversion, or the new birth?

"Even when we were dead in sins, hath *quickened* us [made us alive] together with Christ, (by grace ye are saved;)." Ephesians 2:5.

What is one evidence of this change from death to life?

"We know that we have passed from death unto life, because *we love the brethren*. He that loveth not his brother abideth in death." 1 John 3:14.

From what is a converted sinner saved?

"Let him know, that he which converteth the sinner from the error of his way, shall save a soul from *death,* and shall hide a multitude of sins." James 5:20. (See Acts 26:14-18.)

To whom are sinners brought by conversion?

"Create in me a clean heart, O God; and renew a right spirit within me. Cast me not away from thy presence. . . . Then will I teach transgressors thy ways; and sinners shall be *converted unto thee.*" Psalm 51:10-13.

In what words to Peter did Jesus indicate the kind of service a converted person should render to his brethren?

"And the Lord said, Simon, Simon, behold, Satan hath desired to have you, that he may sift you as wheat: but I have prayed for thee, that thy faith fail not: and *when thou art converted, strengthen thy brethren.*" Luke 22:31, 32.

What other experience is associated with conversion?

"For this people's heart is waxed gross, and their ears are dull of hearing, and their eyes they have closed; lest at any time they should see with their eyes, and hear with their ears, and should understand with their heart, and should be *converted,* and I should *heal them.*" Matthew 13:15.

What gracious promise does God make to His people?

"I will heal their backsliding, I will love them freely: for mine anger is turned away from him." Hosea 14:4.

By what means is this healing accomplished?

"He [Christ] was wounded for our transgressions, he was bruised for our iniquities: the chastisement of our peace was upon him; and *with his stripes we are healed.*" Isaiah 53:5.

What are the evidences that one has been born of God?

"If ye know that he is righteous, ye know that *every one that doeth righteousness is born of him.*" "Beloved, let us love one another: for love is of God; and *every one that loveth is born of God,* and knoweth God." 1 John 2:29; 4:7.

What indwelling power keeps such from sinning?

"Whosoever is born of God doth not commit sin; for *his* [God's] *seed remaineth in him:* and he cannot sin, because he is born of God." 1 John 3:9. (See 1 John 5:4; Genesis 39:9.)

What will be the experience of those born of the Spirit?

"There is therefore now *no condemnation* to them which are in Christ Jesus, who walk not after the flesh, but after the Spirit." Romans 8:1.

BELIEVING AND BEHOLDING JESUS

What is true of everyone who believes in Jesus?

"Whosoever believeth that Jesus is the Christ is *born of God.*" 1 John 5:1.

What change is wrought by beholding Jesus?

"But we all, with open face beholding as in a glass the glory of the Lord, are *changed into the same image* from glory to glory even as by the Spirit of the Lord." 2 Corinthians 3:18.

NOTE.—We were slaves to sin. Jesus came down and suffered with us, and for us, and delivered us. As we behold Him in His word, and in prayer and meditation, and serve Him in the person of others, we may be changed more and more into the glory of His likeness; then, if faithful, we shall someday see Him "face to face."

BAPTISM OF CHRIST

"This is my beloved Son, in whom I am well pleased." Matthew 3:1

Christian Baptism

Belief, Repentance, and Baptism

What ordinance is closely associated with believing the gospel?

"And he said unto them, Go ye into all the world, and preach the gospel to every creature. He that believeth and is *baptized* shall be saved; but he that believeth not shall be damned." Mark 16:15, 16.

What did the apostle Peter associate with baptism in his instruction on the day of Pentecost?

"Then Peter said unto them, *Repent,* and be baptized every one of you in the name of Jesus Christ for the remission of sins." Acts 2:38.

In reply to his inquiry concerning salvation, what was the Philippian jailer told to do?

"And they said, *Believe on the Lord Jesus Christ,* and thou shalt be saved, and thy house." Acts 16:31.

What followed immediately after the jailer and his family had accepted Christ as their Saviour?

"And he took them [Paul and Silas] the same hour of the night, and washed their stripes; and was *baptized,* he and all his, straightway." Verse 33.

Spiritual Significance of Baptism

In connection with Christian baptism, what is washed away?

"And now why tarriest thou? arise, and be baptized, and *wash away thy sins,* calling on the name of the Lord." Acts 22:16. (See Titus 3:5; 1 Peter 3:21.)

By what means are sins washed away?

"Unto him that loved us, and washed us from our sins *in his own blood."* Revelation 1:5.

Union With Christ in Baptism

Into whose name are believers to be baptized?

"Go ye therefore, and make disciples of all the nations, baptizing them into the name of the *Father* and of the *Son* and of the *Holy Ghost*." Matthew 28:19, R.V.

When believers are baptized into Christ, whom do they put on?

"For as many of you as have been baptized into Christ have *put on Christ*." Galatians 3:27.

Into what experience are those baptized who are baptized into Christ?

"Know ye not, that so many of us as were baptized into Jesus Christ were *baptized into his death?*" Romans 6:3.

Note.—Baptism is a gospel ordinance commemorating the *death, burial,* and *resurrection* of Christ. In baptism public testimony is given to the effect that the one baptized has been crucified with Christ, buried with Him, and is raised with Him to walk in newness of life. Only one mode of baptism can rightly represent these facts of experience, and that is immersion—the mode followed by Christ and the primitive church.

How is such a baptism described?

"Therefore we are *buried with him* by baptism into death: that like as Christ was raised up from the dead by the glory of the Father, even so we also should walk in newness of life." Verse 4.

How fully are we thus united with Christ in His experience of death and resurrection?

"For if we have been *planted together* in the likeness of his *death*, we shall be also in the likeness of *his resurrection*." Verse 5.

What will follow this union with Christ in His death and resurrection?

"Now if we be dead with Christ, we believe that we shall also *live with him*." Verse 8.

In what working of God is faith to be exercised in connection with baptism?

"Buried with him in baptism, wherein also ye are risen with him *through the faith of the operation of God, who hath raised him from the dead.*" Colossians 2:12.

BAPTISM AND THE HOLY SPIRIT

At the beginning of His ministry, what example did Jesus set for the benefit of His followers?

"Then cometh Jesus from Galilee to Jordan unto John, to be *baptized* of him." Matthew 3:13.

What remarkable experience attended the baptism of Jesus?

"And Jesus, when he was baptized, went up straightway out of the water: and, lo, the heavens were opened unto him, and he saw *the Spirit of God descending like a dove, and lighting upon him:* and lo a voice from heaven, saying, *This is my beloved Son, in whom I am well pleased.*" Verses 16, 17.

What promise is made to those who repent and are baptized?

"Then Peter said unto them, Repent, and be baptized every one of you in the name of Jesus Christ for the remission of sins, and *ye shall receive the gift of the Holy Ghost.*" Acts 2:38.

What instruction did the apostle Peter give concerning the Gentiles who had believed?

"Can any man forbid water, that these should not be baptized, which have received the Holy Ghost as well as we? *And he commanded them to be baptized in the name of the Lord.*" Acts 10:47, 48.

PHILIP BAPTIZES AN ETHIOPIAN AND SAMARITANS

What question did the eunuch ask after Philip had preached Jesus unto him?

"And as they went on their way, they came unto a certain water: and the eunuch said, See, here is water; *what doth hinder me to be baptized?*" Acts 8:36.

In order to baptize the eunuch, where did Philip take him?

"And he commanded the chariot to stand still: and *they*

went down both into the water, both Philip and the eunuch; and he baptized him." Verse 38.

How did the people of Samaria publicly testify to their faith in the preaching of Philip?

"But when they believed Philip preaching the things concerning the kingdom of God, and the name of Jesus Christ, *they were baptized,* both men and women." Verse 12.

Unity and Heavenly Purpose

How perfect is the unity into which believers are brought by being baptized into Christ?

"For as the body is one, and hath many members, and all the members of that one body, being many, are one body: so also is Christ. For by one Spirit are we all *baptized into one body,* whether we be Jews or Gentiles, whether we be bond or free; and have been all *made to drink into one Spirit.*" 1 Corinthians 12:12, 13.

After being united with Christ in the likeness of His death and resurrection, what should the believer do?

"If ye then be risen with Christ, *seek those things which are above,* where Christ sitteth on the right hand of God." Colossians 3:1.

~~~~~~~~~~

> Lord, in humble, sweet submission,
>   Here we meet to follow Thee,
> Trusting in Thy great salvation,
>   Which alone can make us free.
>
> Naught have we to claim as merit,
>   All the duties we can do
> Can no crown of life inherit;
>   All the praise to Thee is due.
>
> Yet we come in Christian duty,
>   Down beneath the wave to go;
> O the bliss! the heavenly beauty!
>   Christ the Lord was buried so.
>
> —Robert T. Daniel

Reconciled to God

IN WHAT prophecy was the work of reconciliation foretold?

"Seventy weeks are determined upon thy people and upon thy holy city, to finish the transgression, and to make an end of sins, and *to make reconciliation for iniquity.*" Daniel 9:24.

What message of entreaty has God sent to us through His appointed messengers?

"Now then we are ambassadors for Christ, as though God did beseech you by us: we pray you in Christ's stead, *be ye reconciled to God.*" 2 Corinthians 5:20.

Through whom is this reconciliation made?

"All things are of God, who hath reconciled us to himself *by Jesus Christ,* and hath given to us the ministry of reconciliation." Verse 18.

THE PRICE OF RECONCILIATION

What was required in order to effect this reconciliation?

"For if, when we were enemies, we were reconciled to God by *the death of his Son,* much more, being reconciled, we shall be saved by his life." Romans 5:10.

What basis for reconciliation was made by Christ's death?

"Having made *peace* through the blood of his cross, by him to reconcile all things unto himself." Colossians 1:20.

How was He treated?

"But he was *wounded* for our transgressions, he was *bruised* for our iniquities: the *chastisement* of our peace was upon him; and with his *stripes* we are healed." Isaiah 53:5.

What did John declare concerning Him?

"Behold the Lamb of God, *which taketh away the sin of the world.*" John 1:29.

To what place did Christ carry these sins?

"Who his own self bare our sins in his own body *on the tree,* that we, being dead to sins, should live unto righteousness: by whose stripes ye were healed." 1 Peter 2:24.

THE FATHER SUFFERS WITH CHRIST

In thus reconciling the world unto Himself, what attitude did God take toward men?

"God was in Christ, reconciling the world unto himself, *not imputing their trespasses unto them.*" 2 Corinthians 5:19.

What rendered it possible for God to treat sinners thus?

"All we like sheep have gone astray; we have turned every one to his own way; and *the Lord hath laid on him the iniquity of us all.*" Isaiah 53:6.

UNITY, PURPOSE, AND JOY OF RECONCILIATION

How did Christ reconcile all men to God through the cross?

"And that he might reconcile both unto God *in one body* by the cross, having slain the enmity thereby." Ephesians 2:16.

What is the great purpose of the work of reconciliation?

"And you, that were sometime alienated and enemies in your mind by wicked works, yet now hath he reconciled in the body of his flesh through death, *to present you holy and unblameable and unreproveable in his sight.*" Colossians 1:21, 22.

Through whom is the reconciliation received?

"We also joy in God *through our Lord Jesus Christ,* by whom we have now received the atonement [literally, "reconciliation"]." Romans 5:11.

ONE CHOICE OF THREE

For holy heaven and sinful earth to be reconciled and come to peaceful relations, one of three things was necessary. Heaven must take up earthly ways, or earth must turn to heavenly ways, or both must be merged. In the nature of the case there was only one real way —earth must be reconciled to God. To open the door of heaven to man meant Calvary. There every sinner may find the peace of reconciliation, fellowship with God, and hope of everlasting life.

Acceptance With God

IN WHOM has God made us accepted?

"Blessed be the God and Father of our Lord Jesus Christ, who hath blessed us with all spiritual blessings . . . in Christ: according as he hath chosen us in him . . . to the praise of the glory of his grace, wherein he hath made us *accepted in the beloved.*" Ephesians 1:3-6.

What great gift comes with our acceptance of Christ?

"And this is the will of him that sent me, that every one which seeth the Son, and believeth on him, may have *everlasting life:* and I will raise him up at the last day." John 6:40. (See also John 17:2.)

GOD'S WORD AS EVIDENCE OF ACCEPTANCE

What is the foundation of faith?

"Faith cometh by hearing, and hearing *by the word of God.*" Romans 10:17.

What is the first and primary evidence of our acceptance with God?

"If we receive the witness of men, *the witness of God is greater:* for this is the witness of God *which he hath testified of his Son.* . . . And this is the record, *that God hath given to us eternal life, and this life is in his Son.*" 1 John 5:9-11.

NOTE.—The primary basis of all faith and acceptance is the word of God—that which God Himself has *said.* To receive and believe this is the first essential to salvation—the first evidence of acceptance.

Why did John write his testimony concerning God's love and purpose in giving Christ?

"These things have I written unto you that believe on the name of the Son of God; *that ye may know that ye have eternal life, and that ye may believe on the name of the Son of God.*" Verse 13. "These are written, *that ye might believe that Jesus is the Christ, the Son of God; and that believing ye might have life through his name.*" John 20:31.

Evidence Within Us

What witness does the true believer in Christ have that he is accepted of God?

"He that believeth on the Son of God *hath the witness in himself: he that believeth not God hath made him a liar;* because he believeth not the *record* that God gave of his Son." 1 John 5:10.

Note.—Faith and feeling should not be confounded. Faith is ours to exercise in the word of God, regardless of our feelings, and often in opposition even to our feelings. Many fail to accept the pardon and assurance of the acceptance of Heaven, because they do not take God at His word, but instead turn their attention to their changeable moods and feelings. *Faith* always precedes the *joyful feelings* which naturally result from the assurance of forgiveness and acceptance. This order is never reversed.

What is another evidence of divine acceptance?

"We know that we have passed from death unto life, *because we love the brethren.*" 1 John 3:14.

Three Witnesses of Acceptance

What three definite witnesses of acceptance are mentioned by John?

"There are three that bear witness in earth, the *Spirit,* and the *water,* and the *blood:* and these three agree in one." 1 John 5:8.

How does the Spirit witness to our acceptance with God?

"Because ye are sons, God hath sent forth the Spirit of his Son into your hearts, crying, *Abba, Father.*" Galatians 4:6. "The Spirit itself beareth witness with our spirit, that we are the children of God." Romans 8:16.

Of what is Christian baptism an evidence?

"As many of you as have been baptized into Christ have *put on Christ.*" Galatians 3:27.

Note.—In baptism, the water and the Spirit both bear witness of God's acceptance. The same Spirit which, at Christ's baptism, said, "This is my beloved Son, in whom I am well pleased," witnesses to the acceptance of every sincere believer at his baptism.

To what does the blood of Christ witness?

"These things write we unto you, that your joy may be full. ... If we walk in the light, as he is in the light, we have fellowship one with another, and the blood of Jesus Christ his Son *cleanseth us from all sin.*" 1 John 1:4-7. "In whom we have redemption through his blood, *the forgiveness of sins.*" Ephesians 1:7. (See also Revelation 1:5, 6.)

JESUS AND ACCEPTANCE

How only do any become children of God?

"Ye are all the children of God *by faith in Christ Jesus.*" Galatians 3:26.

When may we find acceptance with God through Christ?

"I have heard thee *in a time accepted,* and *in the day of salvation* have I succoured thee: behold, *now is the accepted time;* behold, *now is the day of salvation.*" 2 Corinthians 6:2.

To whom, therefore, should we ascribe glory and honor?

"*Unto him that loved us, and washed us from our sins in his own blood,* and hath made us kings and priests unto God and his Father; to him be glory and dominion for ever and ever. Amen." Revelation 1:5, 6.

THE MAN WITH THE STEAMER TICKET

There is a story told of a man who purchased a steamer ticket to Europe, and then proceeded to get together a supply of food to last him for the trip. He had a somewhat miserable time of it, until one day someone found him eating cheese and crackers in a secluded corner. He was informed that his ticket entitled him to fine, appetizing meals at the dining table. Thereafter he was well fed.

God has provided salvation through Jesus Christ. Many promises are given to us. Faith accepts the blessings Heaven proffers. "Have faith in God." Mark 11:22.

Justification by Faith

What is the ground of justification on God's part?

"That being justified *by his grace*, we should be made heirs according to the hope of eternal life." Titus 3:7.

What is the means through which this justifying grace is made available to the sinner?

"Much more then, being now justified *by his [Christ's] blood*, we shall be saved from wrath through him." Romans 5:9.

How is justification laid hold upon?

"Therefore we conclude that a man is justified *by faith* without the deeds of the law." Romans 3:28.

What is the only way sinners may be justified, or made righteous?

"Knowing that a man is not justified by the works of the law, but *by the faith of Jesus Christ*, even we have believed in Jesus Christ, that we might be justified by the faith of Christ, and not by the works of the law." Galatians 2:16.

What concrete example makes clear the meaning of this doctrine?

"And he brought him [Abraham] forth abroad, and said, Look now toward heaven, and tell the stars, if thou be able to number them: and he said unto him, So shall thy seed be. And *he believed in the Lord; and he counted it to him for righteousness.*" Genesis 15:5, 6.

How is the righteousness thus obtained described?

"And be found in him, not having mine own righteousness, which is of the law, but that which is through the faith of Christ, *the righteousness which is of God by faith.*" Philippians 3:9.

Upon what basis is justification granted?

"And not as it was by one that sinned, so is the *gift:* for the judgment was by one to condemnation, but *the free gift* is of many offences unto justification." Romans 5:16.

JUSTIFICATION BY FAITH

Upon what basis does the reward come to one who works?

"Now to him that worketh is the reward not reckoned of grace, but of *debt*." Romans 4:4.

Upon what condition is faith reckoned for righteousness?

"But to him that worketh not, but *believeth on him that justifieth the ungodly,* his faith is counted for righteousness." Verse 5.

How does grace, as the ground of justification, exclude righteousness by works?

"And *if by grace, then is it no more of works: otherwise grace is no more grace.* But if it be of works, then is it no more grace: otherwise work is no more work." Romans 11:6.

In what way are both Jews and Gentiles to be justified?

"Is he the God of the Jews only? is he not also of the Gentiles? Yes, of the Gentiles also: seeing it is one God, which shall justify the circumcision *by faith,* and uncircumcision *through faith.*" Romans 3:29, 30.

What statement testifies to Abraham's faith in God?

"He staggered not at the promise of God through unbelief; but was strong in faith, giving glory to God; and *being fully persuaded that, what he had promised, he was able also to perform.*" Romans 4:20, 21.

What did this bring to him?

"And therefore *it was imputed to him for righteousness.*" Verse 22.

How may we receive this same imputed righteousness?

"Now it was not written for his sake alone, that it was imputed to him; but for us also, to whom it shall be imputed, *if we believe on him that raised up Jesus our Lord from the dead.*" Verses 23, 24.

Why must justifying faith lay hold upon both the death and the resurrection of Christ?

"Who was *delivered for our offences,* and was *raised again for our justification.*" Verse 25. (See 1 Corinthians 15:17.)

Note.—The resurrection of Christ, the promised Seed (Galatians 3:16), was necessary in order to fulfill to Abraham the promise of an innumerable seed; and therefore Abraham's faith in the promise of God which included the resurrection, was reckoned to him for righteousness. His faith laid hold upon that which made imputed righteousness possible. (See Hebrews 11:17-19.)

What is inseparable from the experience of justification by faith?

"Be it known unto you therefore, men and brethren, that through this man is preached unto you *the forgiveness of sins:* and by him all that believe are *justified from all things,* from which ye could not be justified by the law of Moses." Acts 13: 38, 39.

How has Christ made it possible for righteousness to be imputed to the believer?

"For as by one man's disobedience many are made sinners, so *by the obedience of one* shall many be made righteous." Romans 5:19.

What prophetic declaration foretold this truth?

"In the Lord shall all the seed of Israel be *justified,* and shall glory." Isaiah 45:25.

What other prediction asserts the same great truth?

"By his knowledge shall my righteous servant justify many; for he shall bear their iniquities." Isaiah 53:11.

What does the imputed righteousness of Christ enable God to do, and still be just?

"To declare, I say, at this time his righteousness: *that he might be just, and the justifier of him which believeth in Jesus."* Romans 3:26.

By what name is Christ appropriately called?

"Behold, the days come, saith the Lord, that I will raise unto David a righteous Branch, and a King shall reign and prosper, and shall execute judgment and justice in the earth. In his days Judah shall be saved, and Israel shall dwell safely: and this is his name whereby he shall be called, THE LORD OUR RIGHTEOUSNESS." Jeremiah 23:5, 6.

What blessed experience follows upon the acceptance of Christ as our righteousness?

JUSTIFICATION BY FAITH

"Therefore being justified by faith, *we have peace with God* through our Lord Jesus Christ." Romans 5:1.

What does Christ thus become to the believer?

"For *he is our peace,* who hath made both one, and hath broken down the middle wall of partition between us." Ephesians 2:14.

On what basis is there no possibility of justification for the sinner?

"Therefore by the deeds of the law there shall no flesh be justified in his sight: for by the law is the knowledge of sin." Romans 3:20.

How does the death of Christ bear testimony to this?

"I do not frustrate the grace of God: for *if righteousness come by the law, then Christ is dead in vain."* Galatians 2:21.

NOTE.—In the book of Galatians, and often elsewhere in the New Testament, the word "law" denotes the Jewish system of legal righteousness, that is, righteousness presumably attained through the mechanical performance of prescribed religious acts.

What is proved by any attempt to be justified by the law?

"Christ is become of no effect unto you, whosoever of you are justified by the law; *ye are fallen from grace."* Galatians 5:4.

Why did Israel fail to attain unto righteousness?

"But Israel, which followed after the law of righteousness, hath not attained to the law of righteousness. Wherefore? *Because they sought it not by faith, but as it were by the works of the law.* For they stumbled at that stumblingstone." Romans 9:31, 32.

What is revealed by the law?

"By the law is *the knowledge of sin."* Romans 3:20.

What bears witness to the genuineness of the righteousness obtained by faith, apart from the deeds of the law?

"But now the righteousness of God without the law is manifested, *being witnessed by the law and the prophets."* Verse 21.

NOTE.—Here, the word "law" denotes the first five books of the Bible.

Does faith set aside the law of God?

"Do we then make void the law through faith? *God forbid:* yea, we *establish* the law." Verse 31.

What scripture shows that the righteousness which is received by grace through faith must not be made an excuse for continuing in sin?

"What shall we say then? *Shall we continue in sin, that grace may abound? God forbid.* How shall we, that are dead to sin, live any longer therein?" Romans 6:1, 2.

Does faith exclude works?

"But wilt thou know, O vain man, that *faith without works is dead?*" James 2:20.

What is the evidence of genuine, living faith?

"Shew me thy faith without thy works, and *I will shew thee my faith by my works.*" Verse 18.

What, then, are the visible proofs of genuine justification by faith?

"Ye see then how that by *works* a man is justified, and not by faith only." Verse 24. (See also verse 22.)

What great exchange has been wrought for us in Christ?

"For he hath made him to be sin for us, who knew no sin; that we might be made the righteousness of God in him." 2 Corinthians 5:21.

NOTE.—Said Luther: "Learn to know Christ and Him crucified. Learn to sing unto Him a new song; to despair of thyself, and say, Thou, O Lord Jesus! Thou art my righteousness, and I am Thy sin! Thou hast taken what is mine, and given me what is Thine. What Thou wert not Thou hast become, in order that what I was not I might become."—Letter to Spenlein (1516), LUTHER's *Sammtliche Schriften* (Walch ed.), vol. 21a, col. 21, as translated by MERLE D'AUBIGNE, *History of the Reformation,* book 2, chap. 8.

Righteousness and Life

WHAT is assured to the believer in Christ?

"For God so loved the world, that he gave his only begotten Son, that whosoever believeth in him should not perish, but have *everlasting life.*" John 3:16.

What is revealed in the gospel?

"For therein is *the righteousness of God* revealed from faith to faith: as it is written, The just shall live by faith." Romans 1:17.

What has Christ brought to light through the gospel?

"Who hath abolished death, and hath brought *life and immortality* to light through the gospel." 2 Timothy 1:10.

How closely are righteousness and life thus united?

"In the way of *righteousness* is *life;* and in the pathway thereof there is no death." Proverbs 12:28.

What does he find who follows after righteousness?

"He that followeth after righteousness and mercy findeth *life, righteousness,* and *honour.*" Proverbs 21:21.

GRACE, THE SPIRIT, AND RIGHTEOUSNESS

Through what does grace reign unto eternal life?

"That as sin hath reigned unto death, even so might grace reign *through righteousness* unto eternal life by Jesus Christ our Lord." Romans 5:21.

What is the very life of the Spirit?

"And if Christ be in you, the body is dead because of sin; but the Spirit is life because of *righteousness.*" Romans 8:10.

GOD'S COMMANDMENTS AND RIGHTEOUSNESS

What are the commandments of God declared to be?

"All thy commandments are *righteousness.*" Psalm 119:172.

What did Jesus declare God's commandment to be?

"And I know that his commandment is *life everlasting.*" John 12:50.

Christ, Life, and Righteousness

What does the prophet Jeremiah declare Christ to be?

"And this is his name whereby he shall be called, THE LORD OUR RIGHTEOUSNESS." Jeremiah 23:6.

What does Christ declare Himself to be?

"I am the way, the truth, and the *life.*" John 14:6.

What did Christ indicate as essential to eternal life?

"And he said unto him, Why callest thou me good? there is none good but one, that is, God: but *if thou wilt enter into life, keep the commandments.*" Matthew 19:17.

Note.—The righteousness of God, which is obtained by faith in Christ, brings with it the life of God, which is inseparably connected with righteousness; and the life of God, which is bestowed upon man as a gift through his faith in Christ, is a life of righteousness— the righteousness, or rightdoing, of Christ.

How Life and Righteousness Are Received

How is righteousness received?

"For if by one man's offence death reigned by one; much more they which receive abundance of grace and of *the gift of righteousness* shall reign in life by one, Jesus Christ." Romans 5:17.

How is eternal life bestowed?

"For the wages of sin is death; but the *gift* of God is eternal life through Jesus Christ our Lord." Romans 6:23.

Both or Neither

He who would receive the free gift of God by which he may live forever, must of necessity receive into his life the righteousness of God whereby he is made fit to live evermore. Man cannot receive eternal life without receiving righteousness. He cannot accept one or the other, but rather both or neither.

Consecration

WHAT offering did King Hezekiah command to be made when he re-established the worship of the Temple, following a period of apostasy?

"And Hezekiah commanded to offer the *burnt offering* upon the altar. And when the burnt offering began, the song of the Lord began also with the trumpets, and with the instruments ordained by David king of Israel." 2 Chronicles 29:27.

How did Hezekiah interpret the meaning of this service to the people of Judah?

"Then Hezekiah answered and said, *Now ye have consecrated yourselves unto the Lord,* come near and bring sacrifices and thank offerings into the house of the Lord. And the congregation brought in sacrifices and thank offerings; and as many as were of a free heart burnt offerings." Verse 31.

NOTE.—The morning and the evening burnt offering (Exodus 29:38-41) symbolized the daily consecration of the chosen people to the Lord.

CALL TO CONTINUAL CONSECRATION

How does the apostle Paul urge this consecration upon all Christians?

"I beseech you therefore, brethren, by the mercies of God, that ye present your bodies a living sacrifice, holy, acceptable unto God, which is your reasonable service." Romans 12:1.

What is the sacrifice of praise declared to be?

"Through him then let us offer up a sacrifice of praise to God continually, that is, the fruit of lips which make confession to his name." Hebrews 13:15, R.V.

How is the service of consecration to be carried forward by the Christian church?

"Ye also, as lively stones, are built up a spiritual house, an holy priesthood, *to offer up spiritual sacrifices,* acceptable to God by Jesus Christ." 1 Peter 2:5.

The Example of Jesus

Who has set the example of complete consecration?

"And whosoever will be chief among you, let him be your servant: even as *the Son of man* came not to be ministered unto, but to minister, and to give his life a ransom for many." Matthew 20:27, 28.

What position has Jesus taken among His brethren?

"For whether is greater, he that sitteth at meat, or he that serveth? is not he that sitteth at meat? but *I am among you as he that serveth.*" Luke 22:27.

In what does likeness to Christ consist?

"Let this *mind* be in you, which was also in Christ Jesus." Philippians 2:5.

What did Christ's spirit of meekness and consecration lead Him to do?

"But made himself of no reputation, and *took upon him the form of a servant,* and was made in the likeness of men." Verse 7.

To what extent did Christ humble Himself?

"And being found in fashion as a man, he humbled himself, and became obedient *unto death, even the death of the cross.*" Verse 8.

Call to Complete Consecration

How does He exhort us to the same consecration?

"*Take my yoke upon you, and learn of me;* for I am meek and lowly in heart: and ye shall find rest unto your souls." Matthew 11:29.

What does He make the condition of discipleship?

"So likewise, whosoever he be of you that forsaketh not all that he hath, he cannot be my disciple." Luke 14:33.

What is proof that one does not belong to Christ?

"If any man have not the Spirit of Christ, he is none of his." Romans 8:9.

How should he walk who professes to abide in Christ?

"He that saith he abideth in him *ought himself also so to walk, even as he walked.*" 1 John 2:6.

Do we belong to ourselves?

"Know ye not that . . . *ye are not your own?* for ye are bought with a price." 1 Corinthians 6:19, 20.

What are we therefore exhorted to do?

"Therefore *glorify God in your body, and in your spirit,* which are God's." Verse 20.

NOTE.—Our time, strength, and means are God's, and should be given to His service.

Of what are the bodies of Christians the temple?

"What? know ye not that your body is *the temple of the Holy Ghost* which is in you, which ye have of God?" Verse 19.

When truly consecrated, for what is one ready?

"Also I heard the voice of the Lord, saying, Whom shall I send, and who will go for us? *Then said I, Here am I; send me.*" Isaiah 6:8.

How is this willingness for service otherwise expressed?

"Behold, as the eyes of servants look unto the hand of their masters, and as the eyes of a maiden unto the hand of her mistress; *so our eyes wait upon the Lord our God.*" Psalm 123:2.

DOWN ON ONE KNEE

A story is told that illustrates how one must get down to a full and complete surrender. A small boy attended a Methodist revival with his mother. On returning home he said, "Mother, Mr. So-and-So is under conviction, but he will not find peace tonight." "Why not?" asked his mother. In simplicity the boy answered, "Because he was down on only one knee, and he will never find peace until he gets down on both knees." Nothing short of complete, unreserved surrender to the whole will of God will be acceptable either to God or to ourselves in the long run. But, thanks be to God, such a wholehearted consecration will be acceptable and fruitful unto life eternal.

Bible Election

THE CALL, THE CROWN, AND THE CONDITION

WHAT does the apostle Peter admonish us to do?

"Wherefore . . . brethren, *give diligence to make your calling and election sure.*" 2 Peter 1:10.

NOTE.—This text at once reveals the fact that our salvation, so far as our own individual cases are concerned, is dependent upon our own action. We are elected to be saved; but we are to give diligence to make this election *sure*. If we do not, it will not meet its purpose in our case, and we shall be lost.

What admonition given by Christ teaches the same truth?

"Behold, I come quickly: *hold that fast which thou hast, that no man take thy crown.*" Revelation 3:11.

NOTE.—A crown has been prepared for each of the finally redeemed. Every soul is a candidate in the race for eternal life, and hence for a crown. Faith in Jesus and perseverance to the end will make our election sure.

Upon what condition is the crown of life promised?

"*Be thou faithful unto death,* and I will give thee a crown of life." Revelation 2:10.

GOD'S CALL IN CHRIST TO HOLINESS

In whom, and from what time, have we been chosen unto holiness and salvation?

"According as he hath chosen us *in him* [*Christ*] *before the foundation of the world*." Ephesians 1:4, first part.

What is the character of those thus chosen before the foundation of the world?

"That we should be *holy* and *without blemish* before him in love." Same verse, last part, R.V.

To what has God foreordained those who attain to this character?

"Having foreordained us *unto adoption as sons* through Jesus Christ unto himself." Verse 5, R.V.

According to what does God call us?

"And we know that all things work together for good to them that love God, to them who are the called *according to his purpose.*" Romans 8:28.

According to what have we been predestinated?

"Being predestinated *according to the purpose of him who worketh all things after the counsel of his own will.*" Ephesians 1:11.

ENDURING FAITH AND SALVATION

Upon what condition is salvation offered?

"Believe on the Lord Jesus Christ, and thou shalt be saved." Acts 16:31.

For how long must this faith be preserved in order to bring final salvation?

"He that shall endure unto the end, the same shall be saved." Matthew 24:13. (See James 1:12; Revelation 2:10.)

In what fact may every believer rejoice?

"But rejoice *that your names are written in heaven.*" Luke 10:20, R.V.

Whose names are to be retained in the book of life?

"He that overcometh, . . . I will not blot out his name out of the book of life." Revelation 3:5.

GOD'S CHOICE AND MAN'S CHOICE

What scripture is sometimes cited as evidence that God is arbitrary in His dealings with men?

"Therefore hath he mercy on whom he *will* have mercy, and whom he *will* he hardeneth." Romans 9:18.

But what other scripture shows with whom God *wills* to be merciful, and with whom otherwise?

"With the *merciful* thou wilt shew thyself *merciful;* with an *upright* man thou wilt shew thyself *upright;* with the *pure* thou wilt shew thyself *pure;* and with the *froward* thou wilt shew thyself *froward*." Psalm 18:25, 26. (See also Isaiah 55:7.)

Note.—God wills that men shall be saved. He has foreordained the characters that will entitle men to salvation, but He does not *compel* anyone to receive Christ, possess this character, and be saved. This is a matter of individual choice. By His mighty acts and judgments in Egypt, God "hardened Pharaoh's heart." Exodus 7:3, 13, 22. But the same manifestations *softened* the hearts of others. The difference was in the *hearts,* and in the way God's message and dealings were received; not in God. The same sun which melts the wax hardens the clay. Exodus 8:32 says that Pharaoh hardened his own heart.

How many does God desire to be saved?

"Who will have all men to be saved, and to come unto the knowledge of the truth." 1 Timothy 2:4.

What, on man's part, is essential to salvation?

"Choose you this day whom ye will serve." Joshua 24:15. "If any man *willeth to do his will,* he shall know of the teaching." John 7:17, R.V. *"Believe* on the Lord Jesus Christ, and thou shalt be saved." Acts 16:31. "Whosoever *will,* let him take the water of life freely." Revelation 22:17.

Deciding the Election

A man once wished to join a certain church, but said he could not do so on account of the views this church held on the subject of "election." The minister to whom he was sent for help and enlightenment failing to make the matter clear, an old colored man, a layman, came to the rescue, and said, "Brother, this is the very easiest thing in the church. You see, it is like this: The votin' is goin' on all the time; and God, He is votin' for you; and the devil, he is votin' agin you; and whichever way you *vote, that is the way the* election *goes." Commenting upon this incident, Rev. Wilbur Chapman, the noted evangelist says, "I have studied theology some myself, and graduated at a theological seminary; but I never got anything quite so good as that."*

Bible Sanctification

THE CALL TO SANCTIFICATION

What inspired prayer sets the standard of Christian experience?

"And the very God of peace *sanctify you wholly;* and I pray God your whole *spirit* and *soul* and *body* be preserved *blameless* unto the coming of our Lord Jesus Christ." 1 Thessalonians 5:23.

How necessary is the experience of sanctification?

"Follow after peace with all men, and the sanctification *without which no man shall see the Lord.*" Hebrews 12:14, R.V.

What distinct purpose did Christ have in giving Himself for the church?

"Husbands, love your wives, even as Christ also loved the church, and gave himself for it; *that he might sanctify and cleanse it* with the washing of water by the word." Ephesians 5:25, 26.

What kind of church would He thus be able to present to Himself?

"That he might present it to himself *a glorious church, not having spot, or wrinkle, or any such thing;* but that it should be holy and without blemish." Verse 27.

CHRIST'S BLOOD AND TRANSFORMATION

By what is this cleansing from sin and fitting for God's service accomplished?

"For if the blood of bulls and of goats, and the ashes of an heifer sprinkling the unclean, sanctifieth to the purifying of the flesh: how much more shall the *blood of Christ,* who through the eternal Spirit offered himself without spot to God, *purge your conscience from dead works to serve the living God?*" Hebrews 9:13, 14. (See also chapter 10:29.)

What change is thus brought about?

"And be not conformed to this world: but *be ye transformed by the renewing of your mind,* that ye may prove what is that good, and acceptable, and perfect, will of God." Romans 12:2.

What encouragement is held out as an aid in attaining this experience?

"For *this is the will of God,* even your sanctification." 1 Thessalonians 4:3.

Sanctification a Growth in Grace

In the experience of sanctification, what attitude must one assume toward the truth?

"God hath from the beginning chosen you to salvation through sanctification of the Spirit and *belief of the truth.*" 2 Thessalonians 2:13.

What instruction shows that sanctification is a progressive work?

"But *grow* in grace, and in the knowledge of our Lord and Saviour Jesus Christ." 2 Peter 3:18. (See chapter 1:5-7.)

What experience of Paul is in harmony with this?

"Brethren, *I count not myself to have apprehended:* but this one thing I do, forgetting those things which are behind, and reaching forth unto those things which are before, *I press toward the mark* for the prize of the high calling of God in Christ Jesus." Philippians 3:13, 14.

Can anyone boast of sinlessness?

"If we say that we have no sin, we deceive ourselves, and the truth is not in us." 1 John 1:8.

What are we exhorted by the prophet to seek?

"Seek ye the Lord, all ye meek of the earth, which have wrought his judgment; *seek righteousness, seek meekness:* it may be ye shall be hid in the day of the Lord's anger." Zephaniah 2:3.

In whose name should everything be done?

"And whatsoever ye do in word or deed, *do all in the name of the Lord Jesus.*" Colossians 3:17.

In all we do, whose glory should we have in view?

"Whether therefore ye eat, or drink, or whatsoever ye do, *do all to the glory of God.*" 1 Corinthians 10:31.

Shut Out or Shut In

What classes of persons are necessarily shut out of the kingdom of God?

"For this ye know, that no whoremonger, nor unclean person, nor covetous man, who is an idolater, hath any inheritance in the kingdom of Christ and of God." Ephesians 5:5. "Know ye not that the unrighteous shall not inherit the kingdom of God? Be not deceived: neither fornicators, nor idolaters, nor adulterers, nor effeminate, nor abusers of themselves with mankind, nor thieves, nor covetous, nor drunkards, nor revilers, nor extortioners, shall inherit the kingdom of God." 1 Corinthians 6:9, 10.

What must be crucified and eliminated from our lives if we would be holy?

"Mortify therefore your members which are upon the earth; fornication, uncleanness, inordinate affection, evil concupiscence, and covetousness, which is idolatry: for which things' sake the wrath of God cometh on the children of disobedience." Colossians 3:5, 6.

When purged from these sins, in what condition is a man, and for what is he prepared?

"If a man therefore purge himself from these, *he shall be a vessel unto honour, sanctified, and meet for the Master's use, and prepared unto every good work.*" 2 Timothy 2:21.

An Anglican Minister Speaks

"Sanctification is the term used to describe the work of God the Holy Ghost upon the character of those who are justified. We are justified in order that we may be sanctified, and we are sanctified in order that we may be glorified. 'Whom He justified, them He also glorified.' Romans 8:30. The grace of God is given to make us holy, and so to fit us for God's presence in eternity; for 'without holiness no man shall see the Lord.' Hebrews 12:14."—Rev. Vernon Staley, *The Catholic Religion* (Anglican), p. 327.

COPYRIGHT, 1949, BY REVIEW AND HERALD

CHARLES CAREY

SEARCHING THE SCRIPTURES

"Study to shew thyself approve
unto God." 2 Timothy 2:1

Importance of Sound Doctrine

WHAT DIFFERENCE DOES IT MAKE?

Does it matter what one believes, so long as he is sincere?

"God hath from the beginning chosen you to salvation through sanctification of the Spirit *and belief of the truth.*" 2 Thessalonians 2:13.

NOTE.—Doctrine affects the *life*. Truth leads to life and God; error to death and destruction. No one would think of saying it matters not what *god* one worships, so long as he is sincere, any more than he would think of saying it matters not what one *eats* or *drinks*, so long as he *relishes* what he eats and drinks; or what *road* he travels, so long as he *thinks* he is on the right road. Sincerity is a virtue; but it is not the test of sound doctrine. God wills that we shall know the *truth*, and He has made provision whereby we may *know what is truth*.

Did Joshua think it immaterial what god Israel served?

"Now therefore fear the Lord, and serve him in sincerity and in truth: and *put away the gods which your fathers served on the other side of the flood and in Egypt; and serve ye the Lord.* And if it seem evil unto you to serve the Lord, choose you this day whom ye will serve; whether the gods which your fathers served that were on the other side of the flood, or the gods of the Amorites, in whose land ye dwell: but *as for me and my house, we will serve the Lord.*" Joshua 24:14, 15.

NOTE.—The influence of all idolatrous worship is degrading. (See Romans 1:21-32; Numbers 15; 1 Corinthians 10:20; 1 John 5:21.)

What advice was given to Timothy while preparing for the gospel ministry?

"Till I come, give attendance to reading, to exhortation, to *doctrine*. . . . Take heed unto thyself, and unto the *doctrine*." 1 Timothy 4:13-16.

What solemn charge was given him concerning his public work?

"I charge thee therefore before God, and the Lord Jesus Christ, who shall judge the quick and the dead at his appearing and his kingdom; *Preach the word; . . . reprove, rebuke, exhort with all longsuffering and doctrine."* 2 Timothy 4:1, 2.

What similar instruction was given to Titus?

"But speak thou the things which become *sound doctrine:*" "in all things shewing thyself a pattern of good works: *in doctrine shewing uncorruptness,* gravity, sincerity." Titus 2:1, 7.

Warning Against False Doctrines

Of what kind of doctrines should we beware?

"That we henceforth be no more children, tossed to and fro, and carried about with every *wind of doctrine."* Ephesians 4:14. (See also Hebrews 13:9.)

What is a "wind of doctrine"?

"And the prophets shall become *wind,* and *the word is not in them."* Jeremiah 5:13.

Note.—Calling a doctrine a wind of doctrine does not make it such. That is a wind of doctrine which is not sustained by the Word of God.

What danger attends the teaching of false doctrine?

"Who concerning the truth have erred, saying that the resurrection is past already; and *overthrow the faith of some."* 2 Timothy 2:18.

What kind of worship results from false teaching?

"But in vain they do worship me, teaching for doctrines the commandments of men." Matthew 15:9.

By what doctrines are some to be misled in the last days?

"Now the Spirit speaketh expressly, that in the latter times some shall depart from the faith, giving heed to seducing spirits, and *doctrines of devils."* 1 Timothy 4:1. (See 2 Peter 2:1.)

To what would men turn their ears?

"For the time will come when they will not endure sound doctrine; but after their own lusts shall they heap to themselves teachers, having itching ears; *and they shall turn away their ears from the truth, and shall be turned unto fables."* 2 Timothy 4: 3, 4.

IMPORTANCE OF SOUND DOCTRINE

THE TEST OF TRUE AND FALSE

How may we determine the truthfulness of any doctrine?

"Prove all things; hold fast that which is good." 1 Thessalonians 5:21.

NOTE.—The Bible is the test of all doctrine. Whatever does not harmonize and square with this, is not to be received. "There is but one standard of the everlastingly right and the everlastingly wrong, and that is the Bible."—T. DE WITT TALMAGE.

For what is all scripture profitable?

"All scripture is given by inspiration of God, and is *profitable for doctrine.*" 2 Timothy 3:16.

What will sound doctrine enable the faithful teacher to do?

"Holding fast the faithful word as he hath been taught, that he may be able *by sound doctrine both to exhort and to convince the gainsayers.*" Titus 1:9.

OUR PERSONAL ATTITUDE TOWARD TRUTH

Who are the disciples of Jesus, and what gracious work does the truth do for those who receive it?

"If ye continue in my word, then are ye my disciples indeed; and *ye shall know the truth, and the truth shall make you free.*" John 8:31, 32.

Through what are they to be sanctified?

"Sanctify them through *thy truth:* thy word is truth." John 17:17.

Can we close our ears to truth and remain innocent before God?

"He that turneth away his ear from hearing the law, *even his prayer shall be abomination.*" Proverbs 28:9.

What did Christ say of those who will to do God's will?

"If any man willeth to do his will, *he shall know of the teaching,* whether it be of God, or whether I speak from myself." John 7:17, R.V. (See also Psalm 25:9; John 8:12.)

Results of Our Choice

What will God allow to come to those who reject truth?

"Because they received not the love of the truth, that they might be saved. And for this cause God shall send them *strong delusion*, that they should believe a lie: that they all might be damned who believed not the truth, but had pleasure in unrighteousness." 2 Thessalonians 2:10-12.

What fate awaits blind teachers and their followers?

"Let them alone: they be blind leaders of the blind. And if the blind lead the blind, *both shall fall into the ditch*." Matthew 15:14.

To whom will the gates of the heavenly city finally be opened?

"Open ye the gates, that *the righteous nation which keepeth the truth* may enter in." Isaiah 26:2. (See also Revelation 22:14.)

~~~~~~~~

Truth is the gem for which we seek,
O tell us where shall it be found!
For this we search, and pray, and weep,
That truth may in our hearts abound.

We want the truth on every point.
We want it all to practice by;
Do thou, O Lord, our eyes anoint
With a fresh unction from on high.

—Charlotte Haskins

Present Truth

By what are men sanctified?

"Sanctify them *through thy truth:* thy word is truth." John 17:17.

To what knowledge would God have all men come?

"Who will have all men to be saved, and *to come unto the knowledge of the truth.*" 1 Timothy 2:4.

After receiving a knowledge of the truth, what must one do in order to be sanctified by it?

"God hath from the beginning chosen you to salvation through sanctification of the Spirit and *belief of the truth.*" 2 Thessalonians 2:13.

And what besides a mere belief in the truth is necessary?

"Elect according to the foreknowledge of God the Father, through sanctification of the Spirit, *unto obedience.*" 1 Peter 1:2.

What effect does obedience to the truth have?

"Seeing *ye have purified your souls in obeying the truth* through the Spirit." Verse 22.

How should the truth ever be cherished?

"Buy the truth, and *sell it not.*" Proverbs 23:23.

Note.—That is, buy the truth at whatever sacrifice or cost, and sell it under no consideration.

Special Messages for Special Times

Does the Bible recognize what may be called "present truth"?

"Wherefore I will not be negligent to put you always in remembrance of these things, though ye know them, and be established in the *present truth.*" 2 Peter 1:12.

Note.—Some truths are applicable in all ages, and are therefore *present* truth for every generation; others are of a special character, and are applicable to only one generation. They are none the less important, however, because of this; for upon their acceptance or rejection depends the salvation or loss of the people for that generation. Of this kind was Noah's message of a coming Flood. To the generation to whom it was preached that message was *present truth;* to later generations it has been *past truth,* and not a present, testing message. Similarly, had the first advent message of John the Baptist, of the Messiah at hand, been proclaimed in the generation either before or after John's time, it would not have been applicable—would not have been *present truth.* The people of the generation before would not have lived to see it fulfilled, and to those living after, it would have been wrongly timed. Not so with general truths, such as love, faith, hope, repentance, obedience, justice, and mercy. These are always in season, and of a saving nature at all times. Present truths, however, always include all these.

What was the special message for Noah's day?

"And God said unto Noah, *The end of all flesh is come* before me; for the earth is filled with violence through them; and, behold, *I will destroy them with the earth. Make thee an ark of gopher wood.*" Genesis 6:13, 14.

How did Noah show his faith in this message?

"*By faith Noah, being warned of God of things not seen as yet, moved with fear, prepared an ark* to the saving of his house; by the which he condemned the world, and became heir of the righteousness which is by faith." Hebrews 11:7.

How many were saved in the ark?

"The longsuffering of God waited in the days of Noah, while the ark was a preparing, wherein few, that is, *eight souls were saved by water.*" 1 Peter 3:20.

NOTE.—Doubtless many who were lost in the Flood held, in a nominal way, to faith in God; but the test as to the genuineness of this came with Noah's special message; and the difference between their faith and his was made plain when they rejected the saving truth for that time—the warning message concerning the coming Flood.

JONAH AND NINEVEH

What special message was given to Jonah for Nineveh?

"So Jonah arose, and went unto Nineveh, according to the word of the Lord. . . . And Jonah began to enter into the city a day's journey, and he cried, and said, *Yet forty days, and Nineveh shall be overthrown.*" Jonah 3:3, 4.

What saved the people from the predicted overthrow?

"So the people of Nineveh *believed God,* and proclaimed a fast, and put on sackcloth, from the greatest of them even to the least of them." "And God saw their works, that *they turned from their evil way;* and God repented of the evil, that he had said that he would do unto them; and he did it not." Verses 5, 10. (See Jeremiah 18:7-10.)

NOTE.—So likewise would God have spared the antediluvian world had they received Noah's message, and turned from their evil ways.

THE PREACHING OF JOHN THE BAPTIST

What was the special mission of John the Baptist?

"There was a man sent from God, whose name was John. The same came for a witness, *to bear witness of the Light,* that all men through him might believe." John 1:6, 7.

What answer did he return when asked concerning his mission?

"He said, *I am the voice of one crying in the wilderness, Make straight the way of the Lord, as said the prophet Esaias.*" Verse 23.

What did Christ say of those who rejected John's message?

"But the Pharisees and lawyers *rejected the counsel of God against themselves,* being not baptized of him." Luke 7:30.

What did those do who were baptized of John?

"And all the people that heard him [Jesus], and the publicans, *justified God,* being baptized with the baptism of John." Verse 29.

NOTE.—That is, they honored God by this act of faith.

CHRIST AND HIS RECEPTION

Did God's chosen people receive the promised Messiah when He came?

"He came unto his own, and *his own received him not.*" John 1:11.

What reason did they give for not receiving Him?

"We know that God spake unto Moses: *as for this fellow, we know not from whence he is.*" John 9:29.

Note.—That was the trouble; they had no faith in anything new. They *knew* that God spoke by Moses: it required little faith to believe that. They felt perfectly safe in accepting him, for everything had demonstrated that he was sent of God. All could see that. But here was One whom, although He had come in fulfillment of the prophecies of Moses and the prophets as their long-looked-for Messiah, they felt there was a risk in accepting, because they did not understand the prophecies relating to Him, and time had not worked out to their satisfaction the truthfulness of His claims. It required too much *faith,* as against their desire to walk by *sight,* to accept Christ. It also called for a change of views in some things, and a reformation in life. So they rejected Him. They believed in the Flood, faith in which had saved Noah; they believed in Elijah also, and professed faith in all the prophets; but when it came to this special truth for their time, they refused to accept it. Thus it has been in all ages, and thus we may expect it to continue to be to the end.

How did Christ say those who rejected Him reasoned?

"Ye build the tombs of the prophets, and garnish the sepulchres of the righteous, and say, If we had been in the days of our fathers, we would not have been partakers with them in the blood of the prophets." Matthew 23:29, 30.

Note.—While they condemned the action of their fathers in slaying the prophets whom God had sent with messages of reproof and warning applicable to those times, they soon filled up the measure of the iniquity of their fathers by putting to death the Son of God. This showed that they would have done as did their fathers had they lived in their day. Thus we see that present truths are testing truths.

What was the result of the Jews' not accepting Christ?

"And when he was come near, he beheld the city, and wept over it, saying, If thou hadst known, even thou, at least in this thy day, the things which belong unto thy peace! but *now they are hid from thine eyes.*" Luke 19:41, 42. "Behold, your house is left unto you *desolate.*" Matthew 23:38.

Special Message for the Last Days

Is there to be a special message for the last days?

"Therefore be ye also ready: for in such an hour as ye think not the Son of man cometh. *Who then is a faithful and wise servant,* whom his lord hath made ruler over his household, *to give them meat in due season?*" Matthew 24:44, 45.

Note.—In the last days a message will go forth which will be "meat in due season" to the people. This must be the warning concerning the Lord's soon coming, and the preparation necessary to meet Him. Because such a message was not always preached is no evidence that it is not now to be proclaimed. In his farewell address to the Pilgrim Fathers on their departure from Holland for America, John Robinson said: "The Lord knoweth whether I shall live ever to see your faces more. But whether the Lord hath appointed it or not, I charge you before God and His blessed angels to follow me no farther than I have followed Christ. If God should reveal anything to you by any other instrument of His, be as ready to receive it as ever you were to receive any truth of my ministry; for I am very confident the Lord hath more truth and light yet to break forth out of His holy word. For my part, I cannot sufficiently bewail the condition of the reformed churches, who are come to a period in religion, and will go at present no farther than the instruments of their reformation. The Lutherans cannot be drawn to go beyond what Luther saw; . . . and the Calvinists, you see, stick fast where they were left by that great man of God, who yet saw not all things. This is a misery much to be lamented; for though they were burning and shining lights in their time, yet they penetrated not into the whole counsel of God, but were they now living, would be as willing to embrace further light as that which they first received."

What does Christ say of that servant who, when He comes, is found giving "meat in due season"?

"*Blessed* is that servant, whom his lord when he cometh shall find so doing." Verse 46.

Note.—The coming of Christ in glory has been the hope of the faithful in all ages.

Luther declared: "I persuade myself verily, that the day of judgment will not be absent full three hundred years. God will not, can not, suffer this wicked world much longer."

Said Knox, the Scottish Reformer: "Has not our Lord Jesus carried up our flesh into heaven and shall He not return? We know that He shall return, and that with expedition."

Ridley and Latimer, who laid down their lives for the truth, looked in faith for the Lord's coming. Ridley wrote: "The world without doubt—this I do believe, and therefore I say it—draws to an end."

Said Baxter: "The thoughts of the coming of the Lord are most sweet and joyful to me. It is the work of faith and the character of His saints to love His appearing and to look for that blessed hope."

What will be the burden of the closing gospel message?

"Fear God, and give glory to him; for the hour of his judgment is come: and worship him that made heaven, and earth, and the sea, and the fountains of waters. . . . Babylon is fallen, is fallen. . . . If any man worship the beast and his image, and receive his mark in his forehead, or in his hand, the same shall drink of the wine of the wrath of God." Revelation 14:7-10.

How are those described who accept this message?

"Here is the patience of the saints: here are they that keep the commandments of God, and the faith of Jesus." Verse 12.

How earnestly is this work to be prosecuted?

"And the lord said unto the servant, Go out into the highways and hedges, *and compel them to come in,* that my house may be filled." Luke 14:23.

NOTE.—This work is now going on. In every part of the world the sound of this closing gospel message is being heard, and the people are being urged to accept it, and to prepare for Christ's coming and kingdom. See readings on pages 245-260.

The Obedience of Faith

What did the Lord command Abraham to do?

"Now the Lord had said unto Abram, *Get thee out of thy country,* and from thy kindred, and from thy father's house, *unto a land that I will shew thee.*" Genesis 12:1.

How did Abraham respond to this command?

"*So Abram departed,* as the Lord had spoken unto him; and Lot went with him: and Abram was seventy and five years old when he departed out of Haran." Verse 4.

Of what was Abraham's obedience the fruit?

"By *faith* Abraham, when he was called, obeyed to go out unto a place which he was to receive for an inheritance; and he went out, not knowing whither he went." Hebrews 11:8, R.V.

Abraham's Supreme Test

What command did the Lord later give to Abraham?

"And he said, *Take now thy son, thine only son Isaac, whom thou lovest,* and get thee into the land of Moriah; *and offer him there for a burnt offering* upon one of the mountains which I will tell thee of." Genesis 22:2.

Upon what ground were the previous promises then renewed to Abraham?

"And said, By myself have I sworn, saith the Lord, for *because thou hast done this thing, and hast not withheld thy son, thine only son:* that in blessing I will bless thee, and in multiplying I will multiply thy seed as the stars of the heaven, and as the sand which is upon the sea shore; and thy seed shall possess the gate of his enemies; and in thy seed shall all the nations of the earth be blessed; *because thou hast obeyed my voice.*" Verses 16-18.

What enabled Abraham to endure the test?

"By *faith* Abraham, when he was tried, offered up Isaac: and

SAMUEL REPROVES SAUL

"To obey is better than sacrifice, and hearken than the fat of rams." 1 Samuel 15:2

he that had received the promises offered up his only begotten son." Hebrews 11:17.

Of what were the works of Abraham an evidence?

"Was not Abraham our father *justified* by works, when he had offered Isaac his son upon the altar?" James 2:21.

By his works what was shown to be perfect?

"Seest thou how faith wrought with his works, and *by works was faith made perfect?*" Verse 22.

Genuine Faith

What kind of faith avails with God?

"In Jesus Christ neither circumcision availeth any thing, nor uncircumcision; but *faith which worketh by love.*" Galatians 5:6.

Note.—The faith which justifies is the faith which works. Those who say, and do not, are not men of faith. The obedience which is pleasing to God is the fruit of that faith which takes God at His word, and submits to the working of His power, being fully assured that what He has promised He is able also to perform. This is the faith which is reckoned for righteousness. (See Romans 4:21, 22.)

For what purpose is the grace of Christ received?

"Through whom we received grace and apostleship, *unto obedience of faith* among all nations, for his name's sake." Romans 1:5, R.V.

What effect did the preaching of the apostles have upon the hearers?

"And the word of God increased; and *the number of the disciples multiplied* in Jerusalem greatly; *and a great company of the priests were obedient to the faith.*" Acts 6:7.

How highly does God regard obedience?

"And Samuel said, Hath the Lord as great delight in burnt offerings and sacrifices, as in obeying the voice of the Lord? Behold, *to obey is better than sacrifice, and to hearken than the fat of rams.*" 1 Samuel 15:22.

The Example of Jesus

What example of obedience to the will of the Father has Christ set for us?

"And being found in fashion as a man, he humbled himself, and *became obedient unto death,* even the death of the cross." Philippians 2:8.

At what cost did even He learn the lesson of obedience?

"Though he were a Son, yet *learned he obedience by the things which he suffered.*" Hebrews 5:8.

To whom did Christ become the author of salvation?

"And being made perfect, he became the author of eternal salvation *unto all them that obey him.*" Verse 9.

How complete should this obedience be?

"Casting down imaginations, and every high thing that exalteth itself against the knowledge of God, and *bringing into captivity every thought to the obedience of Christ.*" 2 Corinthians 10:5.

What charge did Jesus bring against the Pharisees?

"And he said unto them, Full well *ye reject the commandment of God, that ye may keep your own tradition.*" Mark 7:9.

NOTE.—Human tradition is simply the voice of man preserved in the church. To follow the traditions of men instead of obeying the commandments of God is to repeat the sin of Saul.

FATE AND DESTINY

What will be the fate of those who do not obey the gospel of Christ?

"And to you who are troubled rest with us, when the Lord Jesus shall be revealed from heaven with his mighty angels, in flaming fire *taking vengeance on them that know not God, and that obey not the gospel of our Lord Jesus Christ.*" 2 Thessalonians 1:7, 8.

What condition is attained in obeying the truth?

"Seeing ye have *purified your souls in obeying the truth* through the Spirit unto unfeigned love of the brethren, see that ye love one another with a pure heart fervently." 1 Peter 1:22.

What promise is made to the obedient?

"If ye be willing and obedient, *ye shall eat the good of the land.*" Isaiah 1:19.

Part Four

The Life and Teachings of Christ

	PAGE
Birth, Childhood, and Early Life of Christ	139
A Sinless Life	143
Our Pattern	145
Our Helper and Friend	147
Christ's Ministry	149
Christ the Great Teacher	153
Miracles of Christ	156
Sufferings of Christ	161
The Resurrection of Christ	166

STENDERS, ARTIST

THE VISIT OF THE SHEPHERDS

"They came with haste, and found . . . the babe lying in a manger." Luke 2:16.

Birth, Childhood, and Early Life of Christ

ANCIENT PROMISES OF DELIVERANCE

IN WHAT promise was a Saviour from sin first revealed?

"And the Lord said unto the serpent, . . . I will put enmity between thee and the woman, and between thy seed and *her seed;* it shall bruise thy head, and thou shalt bruise his heel." Genesis 3:14, 15.

Through whom was a restoration of the lost dominion promised to Abraham?

"To thee will I give it, and to *thy seed* for ever." Genesis 13:15.

Who was this promised seed?

"He saith not, And to seeds, as of many; but as of one, And to thy seed, which is *Christ.*" Galatians 3:16.

THE BIRTH OF JESUS

Where was Christ to be born?

"And . . . he [Herod] demanded of them where Christ should be born. And they said unto him, *In Bethlehem of Judaea.*" Matthew 2:4-6. (See Micah 5:2.)

Of whom was Christ to be born?

"Behold, *a virgin* shall conceive, and bear a son, and shall call his name Immanuel." Isaiah 7:14.

NOTE.—Immanuel means "God with us." (See Matthew 1:23.)

Before His birth, what did the angel say to Joseph concerning the naming of the child?

"And she shall bring forth a son, and *thou shalt call his name Jesus:* for he shall save his people from their sins." Matthew 1:21.

At His birth, what message did the angel bring to the shepherds abiding in the field?

139

"And the angel said unto them, Fear not: for, behold, *I bring you good tidings of great joy,* which shall be to all people. For unto you is born this day in the city of David a Saviour, which is Christ the Lord." Luke 2:10, 11.

In what song of praise did a host of angels join?

"And suddenly there was with the angel a multitude of the heavenly host praising God, and saying, *Glory to God in the highest, and on earth peace, good will toward men.*" Verses 13, 14.

What prophecy of Isaiah was fulfilled at Christ's birth?

"For unto us a child is born, unto us a son is given: and the government shall be upon his shoulder." Isaiah 9:6.

What did the prophet say His name should be called?

"And his name shall be called Wonderful, Counsellor, The mighty God, The everlasting Father, The Prince of Peace. Of the increase of his government and peace there shall be no end." Verses 6, 7.

What did the devout Simeon say when he saw Jesus?

"And when the parents brought in the child Jesus, to do for him after the custom of the law, then took he him up in his arms, and blessed God, and said, Lord, now lettest thou thy servant depart in peace, according to thy word: for mine eyes have seen thy salvation, which thou hast prepared before the face of all people; a light to lighten the Gentiles, and the glory of thy people Israel." Luke 2:27-32.

How did the aged prophetess Anna express herself at the sight of Jesus?

"And she coming in that instant *gave thanks likewise unto the Lord,* and spake of him to all them that looked for redemption in Jerusalem." Verse 38.

What did the wise men of the East do when they had found Jesus?

"When they were come into the house, they saw the young child with Mary his mother, and *fell down, and worshipped him:* and when they had opened their treasures, they *presented unto him gifts; gold, and frankincense, and myrrh.*" Matthew 2:11.

Into and Out of Egypt

How did Jesus come to live for a time in Egypt?

"And when they were departed, behold, the angel of the Lord appeareth to Joseph in a dream, saying, Arise, and take the young child and his mother, and flee into Egypt, and be thou there until I bring thee word: for Herod will seek the young child to destroy him." Verse 13.

How does the revelator describe this satanic desire to destroy Christ?

"And the dragon stood before the woman which was ready to be delivered, for to devour her child as soon as it was born." Revelation 12:4.

By what means did Herod seek to destroy Christ?

"Then Herod, when he saw that he was mocked of the wise men, was exceeding wroth, and sent forth, and *slew all the children that were in Bethlehem,* and in all the coasts thereof, from two years old and under." Matthew 2:16.

After Herod's death, where did Joseph and his family live?

"*And he came and dwelt in a city called Nazareth:* that it might be fulfilled which was spoken by the prophets, He shall be called a Nazarene." Verse 23.

At Nazareth and Jerusalem

What is said of Christ's childhood and early life?

"And the child *grew,* and *waxed strong in spirit, filled with wisdom:* and *the grace of God was upon him.*" "And he went down with them, and came to Nazareth, and *was subject unto them.*" Luke 2:40, 51.

Upon returning from a feast at Jerusalem, how did Joseph and Mary lose Jesus when He was twelve years old?

"But *they, supposing him to have been in the company,* went a day's journey; and they sought him among their kinsfolk and acquaintance. And when they found him not, they turned back again to Jerusalem, seeking him." Verses 44, 45.

NOTE.—This is how many lose Jesus today. They suppose He is in their *company,* but do not see to it that He is with them *personally.*

Through carelessness it takes but a day to lose Him; but, when once lost, it sometimes takes days of sorrowful searching, as it did Joseph and Mary, to find Him again.

What was Jesus doing when they found Him?

"And it came to pass, that after three days they found him in the temple, *sitting in the midst of the doctors, both hearing them, and asking them questions.*" Verse 46.

How did His questions and answers impress those who heard Him?

"And all that heard him *were astonished at his understanding and answers.*" Verse 47.

With what words do the Scriptures conclude the record of Christ's early life?

"And Jesus increased in wisdom and stature, and in favour with God and man." Verse 52.

Heaven's Pattern for Earth's Youth

Christ's early life is a pattern for all children and youth. It was marked by respect and love for His mother. He was obedient to His parents, and kind to all. He hated sin, and to every temptation turned a deaf ear. He sought to understand the reason of things, and so increased in knowledge and wisdom. He was sympathetic and tenderhearted, and ever ready to relieve the oppressed, the sorrowing, and the suffering. If we love Christ, we shall love to talk of Him; our sweetest thoughts will be of Him; and by beholding Him we shall be changed into the same image.

~~~~~~~

A LITTLE child, Thou art our guest,
That weary ones in Thee may rest;
Forlorn and lowly is Thy birth,
That we may rise to heaven from earth.

Thou comest in the darksome night,
To make us children of the light;
To make us, in the realms divine,
Like Thine own angels round Thee shine.

—MARTIN LUTHER

A Sinless Life

Personal Testimony

What testimony is borne concerning Christ's life on earth?

"*Who did no sin*, neither was guile found in his mouth." 1 Peter 2:22.

What is true of all other members of the human family?

"*For all have sinned*, and come short of the glory of God." Romans 3:23.

With what question did Christ challenge His enemies?

"Which of you convinceth me of sin?" John 8:46.

Christ's Humanity and Temptation

To what extent was Christ tempted?

"[He] was *in all points tempted like as we are*, yet without sin." Hebrews 4:15.

In His humanity, of what nature did Christ partake?

"Forasmuch then as the children are partakers of flesh and blood, *he also himself likewise took part of the same;* that through death he might destroy him that had the power of death, that is, the devil." Hebrews 2:14.

How fully did Christ share our common humanity?

"Wherefore *in all things it behoved him to be made like unto his brethren*, that he might be a merciful and faithful high priest in things pertaining to God, to make reconciliation for the sins of the people." Verse 17.

Note.—Jesus Christ is both Son of God and Son of man. As a member of the human family "it behoved him to be made like unto his brethren"—"in the likeness of sinful flesh." Just how far that "likeness" goes is a mystery of the incarnation which men have never been able to solve. The Bible clearly teaches that Christ was tempted just as other men are tempted—"in all points . . . like as we are." Such temptation must necessarily include the possibility of sinning;

but Christ was without sin. There is no Bible support for the teaching that the mother of Christ, by an immaculate conception, was cut off from the sinful inheritance of the race, and therefore her divine Son was incapable of sinning. Concerning this false doctrine Dean F. W. Farrar has well said:

"Some, in a zeal at once intemperate and ignorant, have claimed for Him not only an actual sinlessness but a nature to which sin was divinely and miraculously impossible. What then? If His great conflict were a mere deceptive phantasmagoria, how can the narrative of it profit us? If *we* have to fight the battle clad in that armour of human free-will, . . . what comfort is it to us if our great Captain fought not only victoriously, but without real danger; not only uninjured, but without even the possibility of a wound? . . . Let us beware of contradicting the express teaching of the Scriptures, . . . by a supposition that He was not liable to real temptation."—*The Life of Christ* (1883 ed.), vol. 1, p. 57.

God's Demonstration of Victory

Where did God, in Christ, condemn sin, and gain the victory for us over temptation and sin?

"For what the law could not do, in that it was weak through the flesh, God sending his own Son in the likeness of sinful flesh, and for sin, *condemned sin in the flesh*." Romans 8:3.

Note.—God, in Christ, condemned sin, not by pronouncing against it merely as a judge sitting on the judgment seat, but by coming and living *in the flesh,* and yet without sinning. In Christ, He demonstrated that it is possible, by His grace and power, to resist temptation, overcome sin, and *live a sinless life in the flesh*.

By whose power did Christ live the perfect life?

"The words that I speak unto you I speak not of myself: but *the Father that dwelleth in me, he doeth the works.*" John 14:10.

Note.—In His humanity Christ was as dependent upon divine power to do the works of God as is any man to do the same thing. He employed no means to live a holy life that are not available to every human being. Through Him, every one may have God dwelling in him and working in him "to *will* and to *do* of his good pleasure." (1 John 4:15; Philippians 2:13.)

What unselfish purpose did Jesus ever have before Him?

"For I came down from heaven, *not to do mine own will, but the will of him that sent me.*" John 6:38.

Our Pattern

In Thoughts and Actions

How should the Christian walk?

"He that saith he abideth in him ought himself also so to walk, even *as he walked*." 1 John 2:6. (See Colossians 2:6.)

What mind should be in us?

"Let this mind be in you, which was also in Christ Jesus." Philippians 2:5.

Note.—The mind of Christ was characterized by humility (verses 6-8); dependence upon God (John 5:19, 30); a determination to do only the Father's will (John 5:30; 6:38); thoughtfulness of others (Acts 10:38); and a willingness to sacrifice and suffer, and even to die, for the good of others (2 Corinthians 8:9; Romans 5:6-8; 1 Peter 2:24).

In Childhood and Youth

As a child, what example did Christ set in the matter of obeying His parents?

"And he went down with them, and came to Nazareth, and *was subject unto them*." Luke 2:51.

How are His childhood and youth described?

"And Jesus *increased in wisdom* and *stature,* and *in favour with God and man*." Verse 52.

Devotion and Ceremony

What example did He set concerning baptism?

"Then cometh Jesus from Galilee to Jordan unto John, *to be baptized of him*. But John forbad him, saying, I have need to be baptized of thee, and comest thou to me? And Jesus answering said unto him, Suffer it to be so now: for *thus it becometh us to fulfil all righteousness*. Then he suffered him." Matthew 3:13-15.

How did Christ teach the prayerful life?

"He went out into a mountain to pray, and continued all night in prayer to God." Luke 6:12. "He took Peter and John and James, and went up into a mountain to pray." Luke 9:28.

Pattern of Love

To what kind of work did Jesus devote His life?

"Who went about *doing good*." Acts 10:38.

For whom and why did Christ leave the riches of heaven?

"For ye know the grace of our Lord Jesus Christ, that, though he was rich, *yet for your sakes he became poor, that ye through his poverty might be rich.*" 2 Corinthians 8:9.

When reviled and mistreated, what did He do?

"Who, when he was reviled, *reviled not again;* when he suffered, *he threatened not;* but committed himself to him that judgeth righteously." 1 Peter 2:23.

How did He pray for those who crucified Him?

"Then said Jesus, *Father, forgive them; for they know not what they do.*" Luke 23:34. (See Acts 3:17.)

What is the inspired testimony concerning Him?

"*Thou hast loved righteousness, and hated iniquity;* therefore God, even thy God, hath anointed thee with the oil of gladness above thy fellows." Hebrews 1:9.

Like the Pattern

"Lord, teach me how to preach Thee, too,
In everything I say and do,
Till others learn to follow Thee
Because you loved and guided me."

Our Helper and Friend

The Perfect Helper

Through Christ, what has been opened to the house of David?

"In that day there shall be *a fountain* opened to the house of David and to the inhabitants of Jerusalem *for sin and for uncleanness.*" Zechariah 13:1.

Who has borne our sins, and stands ready to help us?

"I that speak in righteousness, *mighty to save.*" Isaiah 63:1, last part.

For what purpose did Christ come to this world?

"For the Son of man is come *to seek and to save that which was lost.*" Luke 19:10.

Through what was Christ made a complete and perfect Saviour?

"For it became him, for whom are all things, and by whom are all things, in bringing many sons unto glory, to make the captain of their salvation perfect *through sufferings.*" Hebrews 2:10.

His Perfect Salvation

Because of this, what is Christ able to do?

"For in that he himself hath suffered being tempted, *he is able to succour them that are tempted.*" Verse 18.

How complete a Saviour is He?

"Wherefore *he is able also to save them to the uttermost that come unto God by him,* seeing he ever liveth to make intercession for them." Hebrews 7:25.

From what is He able to keep us?

"Now unto him that is able *to keep you from falling,* and to present you faultless before the presence of his glory with exceeding joy, to the only wise God our Saviour, be glory and majesty, dominion and power, both now and ever. Amen." Jude 24, 25.

The Perfect Friend

What does He call those who accept Him?

"Henceforth I call you not servants; . . . I have called you *friends*." John 15:15.

What kind of friend is He?

"There is *a friend that sticketh closer than a brother*." Proverbs 18:24.

What is the mark of a true friend?

"*A friend loveth at all times,* and a brother is born for adversity." Proverbs 17:17.

The Rock

Unchanging as the Sphinx that stands
Amid the desert's beating sands—
A grand old stone that moveth not
Though winds may blow and suns beat hot,
Its visage scarred by sandstorm blast,
Its head unbowed, its calmness vast—
So would I meet the adverse days
And fortune's strange, untempered ways.

But I, alas, am not of stone.
I have no strength to stand alone.
A bit of vine, my body bends
With every breeze that toward me wends.
I droop beneath the sun's hot glow;
I quail 'neath winter's frost and snow.
I would not be a thing so weak!
Oh, where is strength? For this I seek!

Thou Mighty Rock, from Zion's hill
I see Thy beacon shining still.
O Tower of strength, to Thee I cling!
Away my fears and weakness fling.
Thy peace and power shall make me stand
Unfaltering 'mid life's beating sand.

—Ethel M. Hartzell

Christ's Ministry

PREDICTION AND PREPARATION

With what words had John the Baptist announced Christ's ministry?

"He that cometh after me is mightier than I, whose shoes I am not worthy to bear: he shall baptize you with the Holy Ghost, and with fire." Matthew 3:11.

About how old was Jesus when He began His ministry?

"And Jesus himself began to be *about thirty years of age.*" Luke 3:23.

By what act and what miraculous manifestations was His ministry opened?

"And it came to pass in those days, that Jesus came from Nazareth of Galilee, and was *baptized of John in Jordan*. And straightway coming up out of the water, he saw the heavens opened, and *the Spirit like a dove descending upon him: and there came a voice from heaven, saying, Thou art my beloved Son, in whom I am well pleased.*" Mark 1:9-11.

Before entering upon His ministry, through what experience did Jesus pass?

"And immediately the Spirit driveth him into the wilderness. *And he was there in the wilderness forty days, tempted of Satan;* and was with the wild beasts; and the angels ministered unto him." Verses 12, 13. (See also Matthew 4:1-11; Luke 4:1-13.)

With what was Jesus anointed for His work?

"How God anointed Jesus of Nazareth *with the Holy Ghost and with power:* who went about doing good, and healing all that were oppressed of the devil; for God was with him." Acts 10:38.

ANNOUNCEMENT AT NAZARETH

Where did Jesus conduct much of His ministry?

"And Jesus returned in the power of the Spirit into *Galilee:*

and there went out a fame of him through all the region round about. And he taught in their synagogues, being glorified of all." Luke 4:14, 15.

How did He announce His mission while at Nazareth?

"And he came to Nazareth, where he had been brought up: and, as his custom was, he went into the synagogue on the sabbath day, and stood up for to read. And there was delivered unto him the book of the prophet Esaias. And when he had opened the book, he found the place where it was written, The Spirit of the Lord is upon me, because he hath anointed me to preach the gospel to the poor; he hath sent me *to heal the brokenhearted, to preach deliverance to the captives, and recovering of sight to the blind, to set at liberty them that are bruised, to preach the acceptable year of the Lord.* . . . And he began to say unto them, *This day is this scripture fulfilled in your ears.*" Verses 16-21.

How were the people impressed with His preaching?

"And all bare him witness, and *wondered at the gracious words which proceeded out of his mouth.*" Verse 22.

Why were the people at Capernaum astonished at His teaching?

"And [He] came down to Capernaum, a city of Galilee, and taught them on the sabbath days. And they were astonished at his doctrine: *for his word was with power.*" Verses 31, 32.

Wherein did His teaching differ from that of the scribes?

"And it came to pass, when Jesus had ended these sayings, the people were astonished at his doctrine: *for he taught them as one having authority, and not as the scribes.*" Matthew 7:28, 29.

How did the common people receive Christ?

"And the common people heard him *gladly.*" Mark 12:37.

COMPASSIONATE PHYSICIAN

In His ministry, what work was closely associated with His preaching?

"And Jesus went about all Galilee, teaching in their synagogues, and preaching the gospel of the kingdom, and *healing all manner of sickness and all manner of disease among the people."* Matthew 4:23.

NOTE.—In His ministry, Christ combined plain, practical teaching with practical, helpful relief work.

How extensive was His fame, and how many were attracted to Him?

"And his fame went throughout all Syria: and they brought unto him all sick people that were taken with divers diseases and torments, and those which were possessed with devils, and those which were lunatick, and those that had the palsy; and he healed them. And there followed him *great multitudes* of people from *Galilee,* and from *Decapolis,* and from *Jerusalem,* and from *Judaea,* and from *beyond Jordan."* Verses 24, 25.

What expression used frequently in narrating His ministry shows Christ's deep sympathy with mankind?

"But when he saw the multitudes, *he was moved with compassion* on them, because they fainted, and were scattered abroad, as sheep having no shepherd." "And Jesus went forth, and saw a great multitude, and was *moved with compassion* toward them, and he healed their sick." Matthew 9:36; 14:14.

THE BURDEN OF JESUS

In what few words did Christ sum up the object of His ministry?

"For the Son of man is come *to seek and to save that which was lost."* Luke 19:10.

How did Christ feel over the impenitence of Jerusalem?

"And when he was come near, he beheld the city, and *wept over it."* Verse 41.

A REFORMER AT HEADQUARTERS

In no other place did Christ appear so much a reformer as in Jerusalem, the headquarters of the Jewish religion, which religion, though having come from Christ Himself, had degenerated into mere formalism and a round of ceremony. Both the beginning and the close of His ministry here were marked by a cleansing of the Temple. (John 2:13-18 and Matthew 21:12-16.)

CHRIST TEACHING THE MULTITUDE

HEINRICH HOFMANN, ARTIST

"Never man spake like this man." "All bare him witness, and wondered at the gracious words which proceeded out of his mouth." John 7:46, Luke 4:22.

Christ the Great Teacher

His Reputation and Power

What report did the officers bring who were sent out by the chief priests and Pharisees to take Jesus?

"Never man spake like this man." John 7:46.

How did Christ teach the people?

"He taught them *as one having authority*, and not as the scribes." Matthew 7:29.

Note.—"The teaching of the scribes and elders was cold and formal, like a lesson learned by rote. To them the Word of God possessed no vital power. Their own ideas and traditions were substituted for its teaching. In the accustomed round of service they professed to explain the law, but no inspiration from God stirred their own hearts or the hearts of their hearers."

Why was Christ's preaching so impressive?

"For *his word was with power*." Luke 4:32.

With what was He filled?

"And Jesus being *full of the Holy Ghost* returned from Jordan, and was led by the Spirit into the wilderness." Verse 1.

How freely was the Holy Spirit bestowed upon Him?

"For he whom God hath sent speaketh the words of God: *for God giveth not the Spirit by measure unto him*." John 3:34.

Predicted Parables Astonish Men

How had Christ's teaching by parables been foretold?

"I will open my mouth *in a parable:* I will utter dark sayings of old." Psalm 78:2.

How was this fulfilled?

"Without a parable spake he not unto them." Matthew 13:34.

What question did Christ's wonderful teaching call forth?

"And when he was come into his own country, he taught

153

them in their synagogue, insomuch that they were astonished, and said, *Whence hath this man this wisdom,* and these mighty works?" Verse 54.

Jesus Exalts the Law

What did Isaiah say Christ would do with the law?

"He will *magnify* the law, and make it *honourable*." Isaiah 42:21.

Because some thought He had come to destroy the law, what did Christ say?

"Think not that I am come to destroy the law, or the prophets: I am not come to destroy, but to fulfil. For verily I say unto you, Till heaven and earth pass, one jot or one tittle shall in no wise pass from the law, till all be fulfilled. Whosoever therefore shall break one of these least commandments, and shall teach men so, he shall be called the least in the kingdom of heaven: but whosoever shall do and teach them, the same shall be called great in the kingdom of heaven. For I say unto you, That except your righteousness shall exceed the righteousness of the scribes and Pharisees, ye shall in no case enter into the kingdom of heaven." Matthew 5:17-20.

His Burning Testimony

What testimony did Nicodemus bear concerning Him?

"Rabbi, *we know that thou art a teacher come from God:* for no man can do these miracles that thou doest, except God be with him." John 3:2.

What did Christ's words at Jacob's well lead the woman of Samaria to ask?

"The woman then left her waterpot, and went her way into the city, and saith to the men, Come, see a man which told me all things that ever I did: *is not this the Christ?*" John 4:28, 29.

How were the two on the way to Emmaus affected by Christ's conversation with them?

"And they said one to another, *Did not our heart burn within us, while he talked with us by the way,* and while he opened to us the scriptures?" Luke 24:32.

In His teaching, to what did Christ direct attention?

"And beginning at Moses and all the prophets, he expounded unto them in all the scriptures the things concerning himself." "And he said unto them, These are the words which I spake unto you, while I was yet with you, that all things must be fulfilled, which were written in the *law of Moses,* and in the *prophets,* and in the *psalms,* concerning me. Then opened he their understanding, that they might understand *the scriptures."* Verses 27, 44, 45.

How did He encourage His disciples to look for the fulfillment of prophecy?

"When ye therefore shall see the abomination of desolation, spoken of by Daniel the prophet, stand in the holy place, (*whoso readeth, let him understand:*) then let them which be in Judaea flee into the mountains." Matthew 24:15, 16.

"Blest *they who seek*
While in their youth,
With spirit meek,
The way of truth.
To them the Sacred Scriptures now display
Christ as the only true and living way;
His precious blood on Calvary was given
To make them heirs of bliss in heaven.
And e'en on earth the child of God can trace
The blessings of his Saviour's grace.
For them He bore
His Father's frown,
For them He wore
The thorny crown;
Nailed to the cross,
Endured its pain,
That His life's loss
Might be their gain.
Then haste to choose
That better part,
Nor e'en refuse
The Lord thy heart,
Lest He declare,
'I know you not,'
And deep despair
Should be your lot.
Now look to Jesus, who on Calvary died,
And trust on Him who there was crucified."

Miracles of Christ

Miraculous Power Admitted

What testimony did the chief priests and Pharisees bear concerning Christ's work?

"Then gathered the chief priests and the Pharisees a council, and said, What do we? for *this man doeth many miracles.*" John 11:47.

By what did Peter, on the day of Pentecost, say that Christ had been approved by God?

"Ye men of Israel, hear these words; Jesus of Nazareth, a man approved of God among you *by miracles and wonders and signs, which God did by him in the midst of you,* as ye yourselves also know." Acts 2:22.

By what means did Christ claim to cast out devils?

"But if I *with the finger of God* cast out devils, no doubt the kingdom of God is come upon you." Luke 11:20. Matthew 12:28 says "by the *Spirit* of God."

Note.—Under the third plague in Egypt—that of turning the dust into lice—the magicians, failing to duplicate it, said to Pharaoh, "This is the finger of God." (Exodus 8:18, 19.)

Upon what ground did Nicodemus rest his belief that Christ was a teacher from God?

"Rabbi, we know that thou art a teacher come from God: *for no man can do these miracles that thou doest, except God be with him.*" John 3:2.

Opposition Arises

After the healing of the blind man, upon what charge did some of the Pharisees seek to prove that Christ was not of God?

"Therefore said some of the Pharisees, This man is not of God, *because he keepeth not the sabbath day.*" John 9:16, first part.

NOTE.—This was a false charge. Christ did keep the Sabbath, but not according to the Pharisees' idea of Sabbathkeeping. (See reading on "Christ and the Sabbath," page 423.)

What question did others raise in opposition to this view?

"Others said, *How can a man that is a sinner do such miracles?* And there was a division among them." Same verse, last part.

THE FAITH OF MANY

What was the result of Christ's working miracles at His first Passover?

"Now when he was in Jerusalem at the Passover, in the feast day, *many believed in his name, when they saw the miracles which he did.*" John 2:23.

What question did the performing of these miracles lead many to ask?

"And many of the people believed on him, and said, *When Christ cometh, will he do more miracles than these which this man hath done?*" John 7:31.

Why were many attracted to Christ?

"A great multitude followed him, *because they saw his miracles which he did on them that were diseased.*" John 6:2.

NOTE.—A miracle is the display of divine or superhuman power in some unusual or extraordinary manner; hence its nature to attract attention. Christ fed the five thousand with the multiplied loaves and fishes, and all men wondered. Every day God feeds millions of humanity with the multiplied fruits of the earth, and no one marvels. Christ, by a shortened process, changed water into wine, and everybody was astonished; but every year God does this in the usual way—through the vine—in almost limitless quantities, and no one is astonished. A divine miracle, therefore, whenever performed, is wrought to heal and to save, and to call attention to the source of divine power.

What did the people say when they saw these things?

"*He hath done all things well:* he maketh both the deaf to hear, and the dumb to speak." Mark 7:37.

What kinds of disease and sickness did Jesus cure?

"And Jesus went about all Galilee, teaching in their synagogues, and preaching the gospel of the kingdom, and *healing all manner of sickness and all manner of disease among the people.*" "Great multitudes followed him, and *he healed them all.*" Matthew 4:23; 12:15.

Who were brought to Him for healing?

"And they brought unto him *all sick people that were taken with divers diseases and torments,* and those which were *possessed with devils,* and those which were *lunatick,* and those that had the palsy; and he healed them." Matthew 4:24.

To the woman who had been healed by touching His garment, what did Christ say made her whole?

"*Thy faith* hath made thee whole." Matthew 9:22.

What did He say to the two blind men as He healed them?

"According to your *faith* be it unto you." Verse 29.

To another whose sight He had restored, what did Christ say?

"*Thy faith* hath saved thee." Luke 18:42.

Why did not Christ work many miracles in His own country?

"And he did not many mighty works there *because of their unbelief.*" Matthew 13:58.

What lesson did Christ design to teach in healing the man sick of the palsy?

"But *that ye may know that the Son of man hath power upon earth to forgive sins,* (he said unto the sick of the palsy,) I say unto thee, Arise, and take up thy couch, and go into thine house." Luke 5:24.

NOTE.—By His miracles, therefore, Christ designed to teach faith in the power of God not only to *restore the body* but to *heal the soul.*

What effect did Christ's miracles have upon the individuals restored, and the people who witnessed them?

"And immediately he received his sight, and followed him, *glorifying God: and all the people, when they saw it, gave praise unto God.*" "And all the people *rejoiced* for all the glorious things that were done by him." Luke 18:43; 13:17.

What message did Christ send to John the Baptist while John was in prison, to strengthen his wavering faith?

"Go and shew John again those things which ye do hear and see: *The blind receive their sight, and the lame walk, the lepers are cleansed, and the deaf hear, the dead are raised up, and the poor have the gospel preached to them.* And blessed is he, whosoever shall not be offended in me." Matthew 11:4-6.

The Climax of His Miracles

In what miracle did Christ bring to a climax His works on earth?

"And when he thus had spoken, he cried with a loud voice, *Lazarus, come forth.* And he that was dead came forth, bound hand and foot with graveclothes: and his face was bound about with a napkin. Jesus saith unto them, Loose him, and let him go." John 11:43, 44.

What was the result of this great miracle?

"Then *many of the Jews* which came to Mary, and had seen the things which Jesus did, *believed on him.*" Verse 45.

Because of the interest in Him, which this miracle created, what did the Pharisees say?

"Behold, *the world is gone after him.*" John 12:19.

What did Jesus present to the people as a basis of confidence in Him?

"If I do not the works of my Father, believe me not. But if I do, though ye believe not me, *believe the works:* that ye may know, and believe, that the Father is in me, and I in him." "Believe me that I am in the Father, and the Father in me: or else *believe me for the very works' sake.*" John 10:37, 38; 14:11.

Why were the miracles of Christ recorded by the inspired writers?

"And many other signs truly did Jesus in the presence of his disciples, which are not written in this book: but *these are written, that ye might believe that Jesus is the Christ, the Son of God; and that believing ye might have life through his name.*" John 20:30, 31.

ON THE WAY TO CALVARY

L. THIERSCH, ARTIST

"When they had mocked him, they took off the purple from him, and put

Sufferings of Christ

For what purpose did Christ come into the world?

"This is a faithful saying, and worthy of all acceptation, that Christ Jesus came into the world *to save sinners;* of whom I am chief." 1 Timothy 1:15.

What constrained God to give His Son to die for man?

"For *God so loved the world,* that he gave his only begotten Son, that whosoever believeth in him should not perish, but have everlasting life." John 3:16. (See 1 John 4:9, 10; Romans 5:8.)

What did the prophet say Christ would be called to endure?

"He was *oppressed,* and he was *afflicted,* yet he opened not his mouth: he is brought as a lamb to the slaughter, and as a sheep before her shearers is dumb, so he openeth not his mouth. He was taken from prison and from judgment: and who shall declare his generation? for he was *cut off out of the land of the living:* for the transgression of my people was he stricken." Isaiah 53:7, 8.

Did Christ know beforehand the treatment He was to receive?

"Then he took unto him the twelve, and said unto them, *Behold, we go up to Jerusalem, and all things that are written by the prophets concerning the Son of man shall be accomplished.* For he shall be delivered unto the Gentiles, and shall *be mocked,* and *spitefully entreated,* and *spitted on:* and they shall *scourge him,* and *put him to death.*" Luke 18:31-33.

Agony in the Garden

How heavy was the burden which rested on His soul on the night of His betrayal?

"And he took with him Peter and the two sons of Zebedee, and began to be sorrowful and very heavy. Then saith he unto them, *My soul is exceeding sorrowful, even unto death:* tarry ye here, and watch with me." Matthew 26:37, 38.

What prayer of Christ shows that the redemption of a lost world trembled in the balance in that terrible hour?

"And he went a little farther, and fell on his face, and prayed, saying, *O my Father, if it be possible, let this cup pass from me:* nevertheless not as I will, but as thou wilt." Verse 39.

How great was the agony of His soul?

"And being in an agony he prayed more earnestly: and his sweat was as it were great drops of blood falling down to the ground." Luke 22:44.

After He had prayed this remarkable prayer three times, what occurred?

"And while he yet spake, behold a multitude, and he that was called Judas, one of the twelve, went before them, and drew near unto Jesus to kiss him. But Jesus said unto him, Judas, *betrayest thou the Son of man with a kiss?"* Verses 47, 48.

BEFORE PRIESTS AND COUNCIL

To what place was Christ taken?

"Then took they him, and led him, and brought him *into the high priest's house.* And Peter *followed afar off."* Verse 54.

While at the high priest's house, how did Peter deny Him?

"Another confidently affirmed, saying, Of a truth this fellow also was with him: for he is a Galilaean. And Peter said, *Man, I know not what thou sayest.* And immediately, while he yet spake, the cock crew. And the Lord turned, and looked upon Peter." Verses 59-61.

To what insults was Christ subjected at the house of the high priest?

"And *the men that held Jesus mocked him, and smote him.* And when they had blindfolded him, *they struck him on the face,* and asked him, saying, Prophesy, who is it that smote thee?" Verses 63, 64.

Where was Christ next taken?

"And as soon as it was day, the elders of the people and the chief priests and the scribes came together, and *led him into their council*." Verse 66.

What admission did they secure from Him as the basis of condemning Him?

"Then said they all, Art thou then the Son of God? And he said unto them, *Ye say that I am*. And they said, What need we any further witness? for we ourselves have heard of his own mouth." Verses 70, 71.

To Pilate and Herod

What was the next step in their plan to secure lawful authority to carry out their unlawful purpose?

"And the whole multitude of them arose, and *led him unto Pilate.*" Luke 23:1.

When Pilate desired Christ released, how did they remonstrate?

"And *they were the more fierce*, saying, *He stirreth up the people*, teaching throughout all Jewry, beginning from Galilee to this place." Verse 5.

NOTE.—This has ever been a favorite accusation of the enemies of truth against the work of true reformers. The Romans at this very time had a law forbidding the teaching of any new religion "whereby the minds of men may be *disturbed.*"

When Pilate heard that Christ was from Galilee, what did he do?

"And as soon as he knew that he belonged unto Herod's jurisdiction, *he sent him to Herod*, who himself also was at Jerusalem at that time." Verse 7.

Who appeared to accuse Christ before Herod?

"And *the chief priests and scribes* stood and vehemently accused him." Verse 10.

To what indignities did Herod subject the Saviour?

"And Herod with his men of war *set him at nought*, and *mocked him*, and *arrayed him in a gorgeous robe*, and sent him again to Pilate." Verse 11.

What did Pilate propose to do when Christ was again brought before him?

"I have found no cause of death in him: *I will therefore chastise him, and let him go.*" Verse 22.

Instead of consenting to His release, what did Christ's accusers now demand?

"And *they were instant* [literally, *"were urgent"*] *with loud voices, requiring that he might be crucified.* And the voices of them and of the chief priests prevailed." Verse 23.

Although Pilate had declared his belief in Christ's innocence, yet what cruel punishment did he inflict upon him?

"Then Pilate therefore took Jesus, and *scourged him.*" John 19:1.

What shameful treatment did Christ receive from the soldiers?

"And *when they had platted a crown of thorns, they put it upon his head,* and a reed in his right hand: and they bowed the knee before him, and mocked him, saying, Hail, King of the Jews! *And they spit upon him, and took the reed, and smote him on the head.*" Matthew 27:29, 30.

To Calvary

After He had been brought to the place of crucifixion, what drink was offered Christ to stupefy Him?

"They gave him *vinegar to drink mingled with gall:* and when he had tasted thereof, he would not drink." Verse 34.

In what prayer for those who crucified Him did Christ manifest the true spirit of the gospel—love for sinners?

"Then said Jesus, *Father, forgive them; for they know not what they do.*" Luke 23:34.

With what words did the chief priests and others mock Jesus while on the cross?

"Likewise also the chief priests mocking him, with the scribes and elders, said, *He saved others; himself he cannot save.* If he be the King of Israel, let him now come down from the cross, and we will believe him." Matthew 27:41, 42.

Note.—In their blindness they could not see that Christ could not save others and save Himself at the same time.

As He cried out in agony on the cross, and said, "I thirst," what was given Him?

"And straightway one of them ran, and *took a spunge, and filled it with vinegar,* and put it on a reed, and *gave him to drink.*" Verse 48. (See John 19:28, 29.)

What closed this terrible scene?

"When Jesus therefore had received the vinegar, he said, It is finished: *and he bowed his head, and gave up the ghost.*" John 19:30.

By what miracle and phenomenon in nature did God indicate the character of the deed which was being committed?

"And it was about the sixth hour [noon], and *there was a darkness over all the earth* until the ninth hour. And *the sun was darkened,* and *the veil of the temple was rent in the midst.*" Luke 23:44, 45.

The Divine Purpose

What divine purpose was wrought out in the sufferings of Christ?

"For it became him, for whom are all things, and by whom are all things, in bringing many sons unto glory, *to make the captain of their salvation perfect through sufferings.*" Hebrews 2:10.

For whom did Christ suffer all these things?

"He was *wounded for our transgressions,* he was *bruised for our iniquities: the chastisement of our peace was upon him; and with his stripes we are healed.*" Isaiah 53:5.

How much was included in the gift of Christ for the salvation of man?

"He that spared not his own Son, but delivered him up for us all, *how shall he not with him also freely give us all things?*" Romans 8:32.

The Resurrection of Christ

IN WHAT psalm was the resurrection of Christ foretold?

"For thou wilt not leave my soul in hell [Heb., *she'ol,* "the realm of the dead"]: neither wilt thou suffer thine Holy One to see corruption." Psalm 16:10.

In what way was Jonah a type of Christ?

"For as Jonas was three days and three nights in the whale's belly; so shall the Son of man be three days and three nights in the heart of the earth." Matthew 12:40.

In what plain words did Christ foretell His resurrection?

"From that time forth began Jesus to shew unto his disciples, how that he must go unto Jerusalem, and suffer many things of the elders and chief priests and scribes, and be killed, *and be raised again the third day.*" Matthew 16:21. "And while they abode in Galilee, Jesus said unto them, The Son of man shall be betrayed into the hands of men: and they shall kill him, *and the third day he shall be raised again.*" Matthew 17:22, 23.

NOTE.—According to Jewish reckoning, one full day together with any portion of the preceding day and of the day following would be considered "three days."

When asked by the Jews for a sign of His Messiahship, what did Jesus say?

"Jesus answered and said unto them, *Destroy this temple, and in three days I will raise it up.*" John 2:19.

To what temple did He refer?

"Then said the Jews, Forty and six years was this temple in building, and wilt thou rear it up in three days? But *he spake of the temple of his body.*" Verses 20, 21.

AFTER THE RESURRECTION

After His resurrection, what effect had this prediction upon His disciples?

"When therefore he was risen from the dead, his disciples remembered that he had said this unto them; and *they believed the scripture, and the word which Jesus had said."* Verse 22.

How did the chief priests and Pharisees seek to prevent the fulfillment of Christ's words concerning His resurrection?

"Now the next day, that followed the day of the preparation, the chief priests and Pharisees came together unto Pilate, saying, Sir, we remember that that deceiver said, while he was yet alive, After three days I will rise again. *Command therefore that the sepulchre be made sure until the third day,* lest his disciples come by night, and steal him away, and say unto the people, He is risen from the dead: so the last error shall be worse than the first." Matthew 27:62-64.

How did Pilate comply with their request?

"Pilate said unto them, Ye have a watch: go your way, *make it as sure as ye can.* So they went, and made the sepulchre sure, sealing the stone, and setting a watch." Verses 65, 66.

How futile was all this?

"In the end of the sabbath, as it began to dawn toward the first day of the week, came Mary Magdalene and the other Mary to see the sepulchre. And, behold, there was a great earthquake: for the angel of the Lord descended from heaven, and came and rolled back the stone from the door, and sat upon it. His countenance was like lightning, and his raiment white as snow: and for fear of him the keepers did shake, and became as dead men. And the angel answered and said unto the women, Fear not ye: for I know that ye seek Jesus, which was crucified. He is not here: for *he is risen, as he said."* Matthew 28:1-6.

Was it possible for Christ to "be holden of death"?

"Him, being delivered by the determinate counsel and foreknowledge of God, ye have taken, and by wicked hands have crucified and slain: whom God hath raised up, having loosed the pains of death: *because it was not possible that he should be holden of it."* Acts 2:23, 24.

Divine Comments on the Resurrection

In what language does the apostle Paul speak of the resurrection of Christ?

"For I delivered unto you first of all that which I also received, how that Christ died for our sins according to the scriptures; and that he was buried, and that *he rose again the third day according to the scriptures.*" 1 Corinthians 15:3, 4.

Who does the apostle say saw Christ after He was risen?

"He was seen of *Cephas,* then of *the twelve:* after that, he was seen of *above five hundred brethren at once.* . . . After that, he was seen of *James;* then of *all the apostles.* And last of all he was seen of *me* also, as of one born out of due time." Verses 5-8.

What importance is attached to Christ's resurrection?

"If Christ be not risen, then is our preaching vain, and your faith is also vain. . . . Ye are yet in your sins. Then they also which are fallen asleep in Christ are perished." Verses 14-18.

What positive assurance of the resurrection is given?

"But *now is Christ risen from the dead,* and become the firstfruits of them that slept." Verse 20.

What great truth therefore follows?

"As in Adam all die, even so in Christ shall all be made alive." Verse 22.

What cheering message has Christ sent to His people touching His resurrection?

"I am he that liveth, and was dead; and, behold, *I am alive for evermore,* Amen; *and have the keys of hell and of death.*" Revelation 1:18.

What is the measure of the power of God which believers may experience in their daily lives?

"That ye may know . . . the exceeding greatness of his power to us-ward who believe, *according to the working of his mighty power, which he wrought in Christ, when he raised him from the dead.*" Ephesians 1:18-20.

What Christian ordinance has been given as a memorial of Christ's burial and resurrection?

Baptism, the symbol of the new birth. Romans 6:3-5.

Part Five

The Holy Spirit

	PAGE
The Holy Spirit and His Work	171
Fruit of the Spirit	174
Gifts of the Spirit	177
The Gift of Prophecy	179
The Outpouring of the Spirit	185

THE HOLY SPIRIT BESTOWED AT PENTECOST

"It shall come to pass in the last days . . . I will pour out of my Spirit upon all flesh." Acts 2:17

The Holy Spirit and His Work

THE COMFORTER

What precious promise did Jesus make to His disciples shortly before His crucifixion?

"I will pray the Father, and *he shall give you another Comforter*, that he may abide with you for ever." John 14:16.

Why was it necessary for Christ to go away?

"Nevertheless I tell you the truth; It is expedient for you that I go away: for *if I go not away, the Comforter will not come unto you;* but if I depart, I will send him unto you." John 16:7.

Who is the Comforter, and what was He to do?

"But the Comforter, even the Holy Spirit, whom the Father will send in my name, *he shall teach you all things,* and bring to your remembrance all that I said unto you." John 14:26, R.V.

What other work was the Comforter to do?

"And when he is come, he will *reprove* [literally, "*convince*"] the world of *sin,* and of *righteousness,* and of *judgment.*" John 16:8.

THE SPIRIT OF TRUTH

By what other title is the Comforter designated?

"But when the Comforter is come, whom I will send unto you from the Father, even *the Spirit of truth,* which proceedeth from the Father, he shall testify of me." John 15:26.

What did Jesus say the Spirit of truth would do?

"Howbeit when he, the Spirit of truth, is come, *he will guide you into all truth:* for he shall not speak of himself; but whatsoever he shall hear, that shall he speak: and *he will shew you things to come.*" John 16:13.

NOTE.—The Spirit *speaks* (1 Timothy 4:1); *teaches* (1 Corinthians 2:3); *bears witness* (Romans 8:16); *makes intercession* (Romans 8:26); *distributes the gifts* (1 Corinthians 12:11); and *invites the sinner* (Revelation 22:17).

Why cannot the world receive Him?

"Even the Spirit of truth; whom the world cannot receive, *because it seeth him not, neither knoweth him.*" John 14:17.

What did Christ say the Holy Spirit would reveal?

"He shall glorify *me:* for he shall *receive of mine,* and shall shew it unto you." John 16:14.

NOTE.—It is plain from these scriptures that the Holy Spirit is the personal representative of Christ upon the earth, abiding in the church by dwelling in the hearts of the believers. It follows that any attempt to make a man the vicegerent of Christ in the place of the third person of the Godhead is an attempt to put man in the place of God. Thus does the fundamental principle of the Papacy set aside the person and the work of the Holy Spirit.

How has God revealed the hidden things of the kingdom?

"But God hath revealed them unto us *by his Spirit:* for the Spirit searcheth all things, yea, the deep things of God." 1 Corinthians 2:10.

Who moved upon the prophets to give their messages?

"For the prophecy came not in old time by the will of man: but holy men of God spake as they were moved by *the Holy Ghost.*" 2 Peter 1:21.

After Pentecost, how was the gospel preached?

"With the Holy Ghost sent down from heaven." 1 Peter 1:12.

HEAVEN'S UNION WITH BELIEVERS

How intimate is His union with believers?

"But ye know him; for *he dwelleth with you,* and shall be *in you.*" John 14:17.

Whose presence does the Holy Spirit bring to the believers?

"I will not leave you comfortless: *I will come to you.*" Verse 18.

What promise is thus fulfilled?

"Lo, *I am with you alway*, even unto the end of the world." Matthew 28:20. (See also John 14:21-23.)

What threefold union is thus established?

"At that day ye shall know that *I am in my Father*, and *ye in me*, and *I in you*." John 14:20.

Note.—Romans 8:9 shows the spirit of each of the three persons of the Godhead to be one and the same spirit.

Warning

What warning is therefore given?

"Grieve not the holy Spirit of God, whereby ye are sealed unto the day of redemption." Ephesians 4:30.

Is there a limit to the strivings of God's Spirit?

"And the Lord said, My spirit shall not always strive with man." Genesis 6:3.

Note.—The limit is determined by the creature rather than by the Creator. It is when there is an utter abandonment to evil, and further appeals would be without avail. God, foreknowing all things, may designate a definite period of probation for man, as in the case of the one hundred and twenty years before the Flood (Genesis 6:3); but His Spirit never ceases to strive with man as long as there is hope of his salvation.

For what did David pray?

"Cast me not away from thy presence; and *take not thy holy spirit from me.*" Psalm 51:11.

Heaven's Willingness and Invitation

How willing is God to give to us the Holy Spirit?

"If ye then, being evil, know how to give good gifts unto your children: how much more shall your heavenly Father give the Holy Spirit to them that ask him?" Luke 11:13.

How does Jesus, through the Spirit, seek an entrance to every heart?

"Behold, *I stand at the door, and knock:* if any man hear my voice, and open the door, I will come in to him, and will sup with him, and he with me." Revelation 3:20.

Fruit of the Spirit

WHAT is the fruit of the Spirit?

"The fruit of the Spirit is love, joy, peace, longsuffering, gentleness, goodness, faith, meekness, temperance." Galatians 5: 22, 23.

What are the works of the flesh?

"Now the works of the flesh are manifest, which are these; Adultery, fornication, uncleanness, lasciviousness, idolatry, witchcraft, hatred, variance, emulations, wrath, strife, seditions, heresies, envyings, murders, drunkenness, revellings, and such like." Verses 19-21.

NOTE.—The evils here mentioned are a close parallel to the lists found in Matthew 15:18, 19; Mark 7:20-23; Romans 1:29-31; and 2 Timothy 3:1-5.

How may the works of the flesh be avoided?

"*Walk in the Spirit,* and ye shall not fulfil the lust of the flesh." Galatians 5:16.

THE FRUIT OF LOVE

By what is the love of God shed abroad in the heart?

"The love of God is shed abroad in our hearts *by the Holy Ghost* which is given unto us." Romans 5:5.

What is love declared to be?

"And above all these things put on love, which is *the bond of perfectness.*" Colossians 3:14, R.V.

By what does genuine faith work?

"For in Jesus Christ neither circumcision availeth any thing, nor uncircumcision; but *faith which worketh by love.*" Galatians 5:6.

What does love do?

"Hatred stirreth up strifes: but *love covereth all sins.*" Proverbs 10:12. "Have fervent charity among yourselves: for *charity shall cover the multitude of sins*." 1 Peter 4:8.

In what way does love manifest itself?

"Love suffereth long, and is kind; love envieth not; love vaunteth not itself, is not puffed up, doth not behave itself unseemly, seeketh not its own, is not provoked, taketh not account of evil." 1 Corinthians 13:4, 5, R.V.

The Kingdom of God

Of what does the kingdom of God consist?

"For the kingdom of God is not meat and drink; but *righteousness*, and *peace*, and *joy* in the Holy Ghost." Romans 14:17.

Note.—It is the Christian's privilege to have righteousness, peace, and joy—a righteousness which is of God by faith (Romans 3:21, 22); a peace that passeth understanding (Philippians 4:7), which the world can neither give nor take away; and a joy that rejoices evermore (1 Thessalonians 5:16; Philippians 4:4).

Gentleness, Goodness, Faith

What does God's gentleness do for us?

"Thy gentleness hath *made me great*." Psalm 18:35.

What spirit should we show toward others?

"And the servant of the Lord must not strive; but *be gentle unto all men*." 2 Timothy 2:24.

What does the goodness of God do?

"Or despisest thou the riches of his goodness and forbearance and longsuffering; not knowing that *the goodness of God leadeth thee to repentance?*" Romans 2:4.

How should we treat those who have wronged us?

"Dearly beloved, *avenge not yourselves*, but rather give place unto wrath: for it is written, Vengeance is mine; I will repay, saith the Lord. Therefore *if thine enemy hunger, feed him; if he thirst, give him drink: for in so doing thou shalt heap coals of fire on his head*." Romans 12:19, 20.

How does faith determine our standing with God?

"But *without faith it is impossible to please him:* for he that cometh to God must believe that he is, and that he is a rewarder of them that diligently seek him." Hebrews 11:6.

MEEKNESS AND TEMPERANCE

How does God regard the meek and quiet spirit?

"Whose adorning . . . let it be the hidden man of the heart, . . . even the ornament of *a meek and quiet spirit, which is in the sight of God of great price."* 1 Peter 3:3, 4.

In our Christian growth and experience, what is to accompany faith, courage, and knowledge?

"Add to your faith virtue; and to virtue knowledge; and to knowledge *temperance."* 2 Peter 1:5, 6.

NOTE.—One of the briefest and best definitions of temperance is *self-control.* The word in the text means much more than mere abstinence from intoxicating drinks—the limited sense now frequently given to it. It means control, strength, power, or ascendancy over exciting and evil passions of all kinds. It denotes the self-rule which the overcomer or converted man has over the evil propensities of his nature. Commenting on this passage, Dr. Albert Barnes says: "The influences of the Holy Spirit on the heart make a man *moderate* in all indulgences; teach him to restrain his passions, and to govern himself."

How highly is he commended who controls his spirit?

"He that is slow to anger is better than the mighty; and *he that ruleth his spirit than he that taketh a city."* Proverbs 16:32.

FROM CONDEMNATION TO PEACE

What is said of all these different virtues?

"Against such there is no law." Galatians 5:23, last clause.

NOTE.—The law condemns sin. But all these things, being virtues, are in harmony with the law. They are produced by the Spirit; and the law, which is spiritual, cannot, therefore, condemn them.

To what unity are Christians exhorted?

"Endeavouring to keep *the unity of the Spirit* in the bond of peace." Ephesians 4:3.

Gifts of the Spirit

GIFTS FROM THE GODHEAD

Concerning what subject ought we to be informed?

"Now *concerning spiritual gifts,* brethren, I would not have you ignorant." 1 Corinthians 12:1.

When Christ ascended, what did He give to men?

"Wherefore he saith, When he ascended up on high, he led captivity captive [literally, "he led captives captive"], and *gave gifts unto men.*" Ephesians 4:8.

What were these gifts that Christ gave to men?

"And he gave some, *apostles;* and some, *prophets;* and some, *evangelists;* and some, *pastors* and *teachers.*" Verse 11.

How are these gifts elsewhere spoken of?

"And God hath set some in the church, first *apostles,* secondarily *prophets,* thirdly *teachers,* after that *miracles,* then *gifts of healings, helps, governments, diversities of tongues.*" 1 Corinthians 12:28.

PURPOSE OF THE GIFTS

For what purpose were these gifts bestowed upon the church?

"*For the perfecting of the saints, for the work of the ministry, for the edifying of the body of Christ:* . . . that we henceforth be no more children, tossed to and fro, and carried about with every wind of doctrine, by the sleight of men, and cunning craftiness, whereby they lie in wait to deceive; but speaking the truth in love, may grow up into him in all things, which is the head, even Christ." Ephesians 4:12-15.

What result is to be obtained by the exercise of the gifts in the church?

"*Till we all come in* [literally, "*into*"] *the unity of the faith, and of the knowledge of the Son of God, unto a perfect man,* unto the measure of the stature of the fulness of Christ." Verse 13.

How is unity preserved in the diversities of gifts?

"Now there are diversities of gifts, but *the same Spirit.*" 1 Corinthians 12:4.

For what purpose is the manifestation of this one Spirit given?

"But the manifestation of the Spirit is given to every man *to profit withal*. For to one is given by the Spirit the word of *wisdom;* to another the word of *knowledge* by the same Spirit; to another *faith* by the same Spirit; to another the gifts of *healing* by the same Spirit; to another the *working of miracles;* to another *prophecy;* to another *discerning of spirits;* to another *divers kinds of tongues;* to another the *interpretation of tongues.*" Verses 7-10.

Who controls the distribution of the gifts of the Spirit?

"But all these worketh that one and *the selfsame Spirit,* dividing to every man severally *as he will.*" Verse 11.

Was it God's design that all should possess the same gifts?

"Are all apostles? are all prophets? are all teachers? are all workers of miracles? have all the gifts of healing? do all speak with tongues? do all interpret?" Verses 29, 30.

Period of the Gifts

Were the gifts of the Spirit to continue forever?

"Whether there be prophecies, *they shall be done away;* whether there be tongues, *they shall cease;* whether there be knowledge, *it shall be done away.*" 1 Corinthians 13:8, R.V.

When will the gifts of the Spirit be no longer needed?

"*When that which is perfect is come,* then that which is in part shall be done away." Verse 10.

The Gift of Prophecy

AVENUES OF COMMUNICATION

How did God communicate with man in Eden?

"And the Lord God *called unto Adam, and said unto him,* Where art thou?" Genesis 3:9.

Since the Fall, by what means has God generally made known His will to man?

"I have also spoken *by the prophets,* and I have multiplied visions, and used similitudes, *by the ministry of the prophets.*" Hosea 12:10.

What things belong to God, and what to us?

"The secret things belong unto the Lord our God: but *those things which are revealed* belong unto us and to our children for ever." Deuteronomy 29:29.

How fully and to whom does God reveal His purposes?

"Surely the Lord God will do *nothing,* but *he revealeth his secret unto his servants the prophets.*" Amos 3:7.

How does the Lord reveal Himself to His prophets?

"If there be a prophet among you, I the Lord will make myself known unto him in a *vision,* and will speak unto him in a *dream.*" Numbers 12:6.

Under what influence did the prophets of old speak?

"For the prophecy came not in old time by the will of man: but holy men of God spake *as they were moved by the Holy Ghost.*" 2 Peter 1:21. (See 2 Samuel 23:2.)

How are both the origin of prophecy and the means of communicating it still further shown?

"The Revelation of Jesus Christ, *which God gave unto him,* to shew unto his servants things which must shortly come to pass; and *he sent and signified it by his angel unto his servant John.*" Revelation 1:1.

PAUL, A PROPHET OF THE NEW TESTAMENT

"Prophecy came not in old time by the will of man: but holy men of God spake as they were moved by the Holy Ghost." 2 Peter 1:21

THE GIFT OF PROPHECY

What angel revealed to Daniel his visions and dreams?

"Whiles I was speaking in prayer, even the man *Gabriel,* whom I had seen in the vision at the beginning, being caused to fly swiftly, touched me about the time of the evening oblation. And *he informed me, and talked with me, and said,* O Daniel, I am now come forth to give thee skill and understanding." Daniel 9:21, 22. (See also chapter 10, and Revelation 22:9, 10.)

What Spirit was in the prophets inditing their utterances?

"Of which salvation the prophets have enquired and searched diligently, who prophesied of the grace that should come unto you: searching what, or what manner of time *the Spirit of Christ which was in them,* did signify, when it testified beforehand the sufferings of Christ, and the glory that should follow." 1 Peter 1:10, 11.

How were the Lord's words to the prophets preserved?

"Daniel had a dream and visions of his head upon his bed: then *he wrote the dream,* and told the sum of the matters." Daniel 7:1. (See Jeremiah 51:60; Revelation 1:10, 11.)

By whom has God spoken to us in these last days?

"God, who at sundry times and in divers manners spake in time past unto the fathers by the prophets, hath in these last days spoken unto us *by his Son.*" Hebrews 1:1, 2.

What was one of the offices to be filled by the Messiah?

"The Lord thy God will raise up unto thee *a Prophet* from the midst of thee, of thy brethren, like unto me; unto him ye shall hearken." Deuteronomy 18:15.

FORETELLING THE FUTURE

Can the wise men of the world foretell the future?

"Daniel answered before the king, and said, The secret which the king hath demanded can neither wise men, enchanters, magicians, nor soothsayers, shew unto the king." Daniel 2:27, R.V.

Who did Daniel say could reveal secrets?

"But *there is a God in heaven that revealeth secrets,* and

maketh known to the king Nebuchadnezzar what shall be in the latter days." Verse 28.

How did the prophet Daniel acknowledge the insufficiency of human wisdom?

"As for me, this secret is not revealed to me for any wisdom that I have more than any living, but for their sakes that shall make known the interpretation to the king, and that thou mightest know the thoughts of thy heart." Verse 30.

After revealing and interpreting the dream, what did Daniel say?

"The great God hath made known to the king what shall come to pass *hereafter.*" Verse 45.

How does God show His foreknowledge?

"Behold, the former things are come to pass, and *new things do I declare: before they spring forth I tell you of them.*" Isaiah 42:9.

What was foretold through the prophet Joel?

"And it shall come to pass afterward, that I will pour out my spirit upon all flesh; and *your sons and your daughters shall prophesy, your old men shall dream dreams, your young men shall see visions.*" Joel 2:28.

When did this prediction begin to be fulfilled?

"But this is that which was spoken by the prophet Joel; And it shall come to pass in the last days, saith God, I will pour out of my Spirit upon all flesh: and your sons and your daughters shall prophesy, and your young men shall see visions, and your old men shall dream dreams." Acts 2:16, 17.

Prophetic Leadership

What were some of the gifts Christ gave to His church?

"When he ascended up on high, he led captivity captive, and gave gifts unto men. . . . And he gave some, *apostles;* and some, *prophets;* and some, *evangelists;* and some, *pastors* and *teachers.*" Ephesians 4:8-11.

By what means did God deliver and preserve Israel?

THE GIFT OF PROPHECY

"*By a prophet* the Lord brought Israel out of Egypt, and *by a prophet* was he preserved." Hosea 12:13.

When Moses complained of his slowness of speech, what did God say Aaron should be to him?

"And he shall be thy *spokesman* unto the people: and he shall be, even he shall be to thee instead of *a mouth,* and thou shalt be to him instead of God." Exodus 4:16.

What did God afterward call Aaron?

"And the Lord said unto Moses, See, I have made thee a god to Pharaoh: and Aaron thy brother shall be *thy prophet.*" Exodus 7:1.

TESTS OF TRUE AND FALSE PROPHETS

What is one test by which to detect false prophets?

"When a prophet speaketh in the name of the Lord, *if the thing follow not, nor come to pass,* that is the thing which the Lord hath not spoken, but the prophet hath spoken it presumptuously: thou shalt not be afraid of him." Deuteronomy 18:22.

What other test should be applied in determining the validity of the claims of a prophet?

"If there arise among you a prophet, or a dreamer of dreams, and giveth thee a sign or a wonder, and the sign or the wonder come to pass, whereof he spake unto thee, saying, *Let us go after other gods,* which thou hast not known, and *let us serve them;* thou shalt not hearken unto the words of that prophet, or that dreamer of dreams: for the Lord your God proveth you, to know whether ye love the Lord your God with all your heart and with all your soul. *Ye shall walk after the Lord your God, and fear him, and keep his commandments, and obey his voice,* and ye shall serve him, and cleave unto him." Deuteronomy 13:1-4.

NOTE.—From these scriptures it will be seen that, in the first place, if a prophet's words do not prove to be true, it is evidence that God has not sent that prophet. On the other hand, even though the thing predicted comes to pass, if the pretended prophet seeks to lead others to break God's commandments, this, regardless of all signs, should be positive evidence that he is not a true prophet.

What rule did Christ give for distinguishing between true and false prophets?

"*By their fruits* ye shall know them." Matthew 7:20.

Attitude Toward God's Prophets

How did God's prophets anciently use the words of former prophets in exhorting the people to obedience?

"*Should ye not hear the words which the Lord hath cried by the former prophets,* when Jerusalem was inhabited and in prosperity?" Zechariah 7:7.

What is the promised result of believing God's prophets?

"Believe in the Lord your God, so shall ye be established; *believe his prophets, so shall ye prosper.*" 2 Chronicles 20:20.

What admonition is given regarding the gift of prophecy?

"*Despise not prophesyings.* Prove all things; hold fast that which is good." 1 Thessalonians 5:20, 21.

What will characterize the last, or remnant, church?

"And the dragon was wroth with the woman, and went to make war with the remnant of her seed, *which keep the commandments of God, and have the testimony of Jesus Christ.*" Revelation 12:17.

What is the "testimony of Jesus"?

"The testimony of Jesus is *the spirit of prophecy.*" Revelation 19:10. (See Revelation 1:9.)

What results when this gift is absent?

"Where there is no vision, *the people perish:* but he that keepeth the law, happy is he." Proverbs 29:18. (See also Psalm 74:9.)

Come, Holy Spirit, come,
   Let Thy bright beams arise,
Dispel the sorrow from our minds,
   The darkness from our eyes.

Convince us all of sin,
   Then lead to Jesus' blood,
And to our wondering view reveal
   The mercies of our God.

—Joseph Hart

The Outpouring of the Spirit

Promise and Preparation of Pentecost

For what did Christ, just before His ascension, tell His disciples to wait?

"And, behold, I send the promise of my Father upon you: but tarry ye in the city of Jerusalem, *until ye be endued with power from on high.*" Luke 24:49.

With what did He say they would be baptized?

"Ye shall be baptized *with the Holy Ghost* not many days hence." Acts 1:5.

Note.—John the Baptist had foretold this baptism. He said, "I indeed baptize you with water unto repentance: but he that cometh after me is mightier than I, whose shoes I am not worthy to bear: he shall baptize you with the Holy Ghost, and with fire." Matthew 3:11.

For what work was this baptism to prepare them?

"But ye shall receive power, after that the Holy Ghost is come upon you: and *ye shall be witnesses unto me* both in Jerusalem, and in all Judaea, and in Samaria, and unto the uttermost part of the earth." Acts 1:8.

Results of Pentecost

What were some of the results of the preaching of the gospel under the outpouring of the Spirit?

"Now when they heard this, *they were pricked in their heart,* and said, . . . Men and brethren, what shall we do? Then Peter said unto them, Repent, and be baptized every one of you in the name of Jesus Christ for the remission of sins, and ye shall receive the gift of the Holy Ghost. . . . Then they that gladly received his word were baptized: *and the same day there were added unto them about three thousand souls.*" Acts 2:37-41. "And by the hands of the apostles were many signs and wonders wrought among the people; . . . *and believers were the more added to the Lord,* multitudes both of men and women." Acts

5:12-14. "And the word of God increased; and *the number of the disciples multiplied in Jerusalem greatly;* and a great company of the priests were obedient to the faith." Acts 6:7.

How did persecution affect the preaching of the gospel?

"And at that time there was a great persecution against the church which was at Jerusalem; and they were all scattered abroad throughout the regions of Judaea and Samaria, except the apostles. . . . Therefore *they that were scattered abroad went every where preaching the word.*" Acts 8:1-4.

Note.—"Persecution has only had a tendency to extend and establish the faith which it was designed to destroy. . . . There is no lesson which men have been so slow to learn as that to oppose and persecute men is the very way to confirm them in their opinions, and to spread their doctrines."—Dr. Albert Barnes, on Acts 4:4.

A Latter-Day Outpouring

What prophecy was fulfilled in the Pentecostal outpouring of the Spirit in the time of the apostles?

"But Peter, standing up with the eleven, lifted up his voice, and said, . . . These are not drunken, as ye suppose. . . . But *this is that which was spoken by the prophet Joel;* And it shall come to pass in the last days, saith God, I will pour out of my Spirit upon all flesh: and your sons and your daughters shall prophesy, and your young men shall see visions, and your old men shall dream dreams: and on my servants and on my handmaidens I will pour out in those days of my Spirit; and they shall prophesy." Acts 2:14-18. (See Joel 2:28, 29.)

What expressions in the prophecy of Joel seem to imply a double fulfillment of this outpouring of the Spirit?

"Be glad then, ye children of Zion, and rejoice in the Lord your God: for he hath given you the *former rain* moderately, and he will cause to come down for you the rain, the *former rain,* and the *latter rain* in the first month." Joel 2:23. (See also Hosea 6:3.)

Note.—In Palestine the early rains prepare the soil for the seed sowing, and the latter rains ripen the grain for the harvest. So the early outpouring of the Spirit prepared the world for the extensive sowing of the gospel seed, and the final outpouring will come to ripen

THE OUTPOURING OF THE SPIRIT

the golden grain for the harvest of the earth, which Christ says is "the end of the world." Matthew 13:37-39; Revelation 14:14, 15.

For what are we told to pray in the time of the "latter rain"?

"Ask ye of the Lord rain in the time of the latter rain; so the Lord shall make bright clouds, and give them showers of rain, to every one grass in the field." Zechariah 10:1.

NOTE.—Before the apostles received the baptism of the Spirit in the early rain on the day of Pentecost, they all "continued with one accord in prayer and supplication." Acts 1:14. During this time they confessed their faults, put away their differences, ceased their selfish ambitions and contentions for place and power, so that when the time for the outpouring came, "they were all *with one accord* in one place," ready for its reception. To be prepared for the final outpouring of the Spirit, all sin and selfish ambition must again be put away, and a like work of grace wrought upon the hearts of God's people.

THE CALL OF REVELATION'S ANGEL

How is the closing work of the gospel under the outpouring of the Spirit described by the revelator?

"After these things I saw another angel come down from heaven, having great power; and *the earth was lightened with his glory."* Revelation 18:1.

What does this angel say?

"And he cried mightily with a strong voice, saying, *Babylon the great is fallen, is fallen,* and is become the habitation of devils, and the hold of every foul spirit, and a cage of every unclean and hateful bird." Verse 2.

NOTE.—The religious world will then be in much the same condition as was the Jewish nation after it had rejected Christ at His first advent. (See 2 Timothy 3:1-5.)

What did Peter on the day of Pentecost tell his hearers to do?

"And with many other words did he testify and exhort, saying, *Save yourselves from this untoward generation."* Acts 2:40.

What similar call and appeal will be made under the final outpouring of the Spirit?

"And I heard another voice from heaven, saying, *Come out*

of her, my people, that ye be not partakers of her sins, and that ye receive not of her plagues. For her sins have reached unto heaven, and God hath remembered her iniquities." Revelation 18:4, 5.

Note.—A great work will be accomplished in a short time under the final outpouring of the Spirit. Many voices all over the earth will sound the warning cry. Signs and wonders will be wrought by the believers, and, as at Pentecost, thousands will be converted in a day.

Those who fail to heed this final gospel call, like the unbelieving Jews, will be doomed to destruction. The seven last plagues will overtake them, as war, famine, death, and destruction overtook the Jews, who, not believing in Christ, failed to heed His call to flee, and shut themselves up in Jerusalem to their doom. Those who heed the call, and separate themselves from sin and from sinners, will be saved.

~~~~~~~~~~

"What poor, despised company
　　Of travelers are these,
Who walk in yonder narrow way,
　　Along the rugged maze?

"Ah! these are of a royal line,
　　All children of a King,
Heirs of immortal crowns divine;
　　And lo! for joy they sing.

"Why do they, then, appear so mean,
　　And why so much despised?
Because of their rich robes unseen
　　The world is not apprized.

"But why keep they that narrow road—
　　That rugged, thorny maze?
Why, that's the way their Leader trod,
　　They love and keep His ways.

"Why do they shun the pleasing path
　　That worldlings love so well?
Because that is the road to death,
　　The open road to hell.

"What! is there then no other road
　　To Salem's happy ground?
Christ is the only way to God,
　　No other can be found."

Part Six

The Sure Word of Prophecy

	PAGE
Prophecy, Why Given	191
Nebuchadnezzar's Dream	195
The Kingdoms of Grace and Glory	200
Four Great Monarchies	205
The Kingdom and Work of Antichrist	211
The Prophetic Symbols of Daniel 8	219
The Hour of God's Judgment	226
The Atonement in Type and Antitype	234
The Judgment	240
The Judgment-Hour Message	245
The Fall of Modern Babylon	249
The Closing Gospel Message	257
Satan's Warfare Against the Church	261
A Great Persecuting Power	266
Making an Image to the Beast	271
A Prophetic History of the Church	281
The Book With Seven Seals	286
The Seven Last Plagues	292
The Mystery of God Finished	298

PROPHECY LIFTS THE CURTAIN

"I have told you before it come to pass, that, when it is come to pass, ye might believe." John 14:2

Prophecy, Why Given

THE GIVING OF PROPHECY

Why were the Sacred Writings given?

"For whatsoever things were written aforetime were written *for our learning, that we through patience and comfort of the scriptures might have hope.*" Romans 15:4.

By what means is all scripture given?

"All scripture is given *by inspiration of God.*" 2 Timothy 3:16, first part.

For what is it profitable?

"And is profitable for *doctrine,* for *reproof,* for *correction,* for *instruction in righteousness.*" Same verse, last part.

How was the prophecy given?

"For the prophecy came not in old time by the will of man: but *holy men of God spake as they were moved by the Holy Ghost.*" 2 Peter 1:21.

SECRETS OF THE FUTURE

What is the Lord able to do regarding the future?

"Behold, the former things are come to pass, and new things do I declare: *before they spring forth I tell you of them.*" Isaiah 42:9.

How far-reaching is God's ability to reveal the future?

"Remember the former things of old: for I am God, . . . and there is none like me, *declaring the end from the beginning,* and from ancient times the things that are not yet done." Isaiah 46: 9, 10.

NOTE.—Since He knows all things, the future is present with God. More, perhaps, than any other one thing, the prophecies of the Bible and their fulfillment bear witness to its divine inspiration.

To whom does God reveal the secrets of the future?

"Surely the Lord God will do nothing, but he revealeth his secret unto his servants *the prophets.*" Amos 3:7.

To whom do the things which have been revealed belong?

"The secret things belong unto the Lord our God: but those things which are revealed belong *unto us and to our children for ever.*" Deuteronomy 29:29.

More Certain Than Sight

What testimony did the apostle Peter bear concerning his experience on the mount of transfiguration?

"For we have not followed cunningly devised fables, when we made known unto you the power and coming of our Lord Jesus Christ, *but were eyewitnesses of his majesty.*" 2 Peter 1:16.

When did he say he saw the majesty of Christ, and heard the voice from heaven?

"And this voice which came from heaven we heard, *when we were with him in the holy mount.*" Verse 18.

How does he emphasize the reliability of prophecy?

"And we have the word of prophecy *made more sure.*" Verse 19, R.V.

Note.—Every fulfillment of prophecy is a confirmation of the truthfulness and reliability of prophecy.

What admonition is therefore given?

"Whereunto ye do well that ye *take heed,* as unto a lamp shining in a dark place, until the day dawn, and the day-star arise in your hearts." Verse 19, last part, R.V.

Jesus and the Theme of Prophecy

What has ever been the theme of God's prophets?

"Receiving the end of your faith, even *the salvation of your souls.* Of which salvation the prophets have enquired and searched diligently, who prophesied of the grace that should come unto you." 1 Peter 1:9, 10.

Whose spirit inspired their utterances?

"Searching what, or what manner of time *the Spirit of Christ which was in them* did signify, when it testified beforehand the sufferings of Christ, and the glory that should follow." Verse 11.

In what prophecy did Christ recognize Daniel as a prophet?

"When ye therefore shall see the abomination of desolation, spoken of by *Daniel the prophet,* stand in the holy place, (whoso readeth, let him understand)." Matthew 24:15.

To what time were the prophecies of Daniel, as a whole, to be sealed?

"But thou, O Daniel, shut up the words, and seal the book, even to *the time of the end:* many shall run to and fro, and knowledge shall be increased." Daniel 12:4.

What assurance was given by the angel that these prophecies would be understood in the last days?

"And he said, Go thy way, Daniel: for the words are closed up and sealed till the time of the end. Many shall be purified, and made white, and tried; but the wicked shall do wickedly: and none of the wicked shall understand; *but the wise shall understand."* Verses 9, 10.

What is the last book of the Bible called?

"*The Revelation of Jesus Christ,* which God gave unto him." Revelation 1:1.

What is said of those who read, hear, and keep the things contained in this book?

"*Blessed* is he that readeth, and they that hear the words of this prophecy, and keep those things which are written therein." Verse 3.

DANIEL, THE PROPHETIC INTERPRETER

"This great image, whose brightness wa[s] excellent, stood before thee; and th[e] form thereof was terrible." Daniel 2:3[1]

Nebuchadnezzar's Dream

(The Great Image of Daniel 2)

WHAT statement did Nebuchadnezzar, king of Babylon, make to his wise men whom he had assembled?

"And the king said unto them, *I have dreamed a dream, and my spirit was troubled to know the dream.*" Daniel 2:3.

After being threatened with death if they did not make known the dream and the interpretation, what did the wise men say to the king?

"The Chaldeans answered before the king, and said, *There is not a man upon the earth that can shew the king's matter:* therefore there is no king, lord, nor ruler, that asked such things at any magician, or astrologer, or Chaldean. And it is a rare thing that the king requireth, and *there is none other that can shew it before the king, except the gods, whose dwelling is not with flesh.*" Verses 10, 11.

DANIEL AND THE DREAM

After the wise men had thus confessed their inability to do what the king required, who offered to interpret the dream?

"Then *Daniel* went in, and desired of the king that he would give him time, and that he would shew the king the interpretation." Verse 16.

After Daniel and his fellows had sought God earnestly, how were the dream and its interpretation revealed to Daniel?

"Then was the secret revealed unto Daniel *in a night vision*. Then Daniel blessed the God of heaven." Verse 19.

When brought before the king, what did Daniel say?

"Daniel answered in the presence of the king, and said, The secret which the king hath demanded cannot the wise men, the astrologers, the magicians, the soothsayers, shew unto the king; but *there is a God in heaven that revealeth secrets,* and maketh known to the king Nebuchadnezzar what shall be in the latter days. Thy dream, and the visions of thy head upon thy bed, are these." Verses 27, 28.

What did Daniel say the king had seen in his dream?

"Thy dream, and the visions of thy head upon thy bed, are these; ... Thou, O king, sawest, and behold *a great image*. This great image, whose brightness was excellent, stood before thee; and the form thereof was terrible." Verses 28-31.

Of what were the different parts of the image composed?

"This image's head was of fine *gold*, his breast and his arms of *silver*, his belly and his thighs of *brass*, his legs of *iron*, his feet *part of iron and part of clay*." Verses 32, 33.

By what means was the image broken to pieces?

"Thou sawest till that *a stone* was cut out without hands, which smote the image upon his feet that were of iron and clay, and brake them to pieces." Verse 34.

What became of the various parts of the image?

"Then was the iron, the clay, the brass, the silver, and the gold, broken to pieces together, and *became like the chaff of the summer threshingfloors; and the wind carried them away*, that no place was found for them: and the stone that smote the image became a great mountain, and filled the whole earth." Verse 35.

DANIEL AND THE INTERPRETATION

With what words did Daniel begin the interpretation of the dream?

"Thou, O king, art a king of kings: for the God of heaven hath given thee a kingdom, power, and strength, and glory. And wheresoever the children of men dwell, the beasts of the field and the fowls of the heaven hath he given into thine hand, and hath made thee ruler over them all. *Thou art this head of gold.*" Verses 37, 38.

NOTE.—The character of the Neo-Babylonian Empire is fittingly indicated by the nature of the material composing that portion of the image by which it was symbolized—the head of gold. It was "the golden kingdom of a golden age." The metropolis, Babylon, reached a height of unrivaled magnificence.

NEBUCHADNEZZAR'S DREAM

What was to be the nature of the next kingdom?

"After thee shall arise another kingdom *inferior to thee.*" Verse 39, first part.

Who was the last Babylonian king?

"In that night was *Belshazzar* the king of the Chaldeans slain. And Darius the Median took the kingdom, being about threescore and two years old." Daniel 5:30, 31.

To whom was Belshazzar's kingdom given?

"Thy kingdom is divided, and given to *the Medes and Persians.*" Verse 28.

By what is this kingdom of the Medes and Persians—the Persian Empire—represented in the great image?

The breast and arms of silver. (Daniel 2:32.)

By what is the Greek, or Macedonian, Empire, which succeeded the kingdom of the Medes and Persians, represented in the image?

"His belly and his thighs of *brass.*" Daniel 2:32. "And another *third kingdom of brass,* which shall bear rule over all the earth." Verse 39.

NOTE.—That the empire which replaced the Persian was the Greek is clearly stated in Daniel 8:5-8, 20, 21. Concerning the two stages of the Greco-Macedonian Empire—first united under Alexander the Great and then divided under his successors—see pp. 222, 223.

What is said of the fourth kingdom?

"And the fourth kingdom *shall be strong as iron:* forasmuch as iron breaketh in pieces and subdueth all things: and as iron that breaketh all these, *shall it break in pieces and bruise.*" Verse 40.

NOTE.—It is well known that the great world power that absorbed the fragments of the empire of Alexander the Great was Rome.

What scripture refers to Roman emperors as ruling the world?

"And it came to pass in those days, that *there went out a decree from Caesar Augustus, that all the world should be taxed.*" Luke 2:1.

NOTE.—Describing the Roman conquests, Gibbon uses the very

imagery employed in the vision of Daniel 2. He says: "The arms of the republic, sometimes vanquished in battle, always victorious in war, advanced with rapid steps to the Euphrates, the Danube, the Rhine, and the ocean; and the images of *gold* or *silver*, or *brass*, that might serve to represent the nations and their kings, were successively broken by the *iron* monarchy of Rome."—*The History of the Decline and Fall of the Roman Empire*, chap. 38, par. 1, under "General Observations," at the close of the chapter.

Man's Failure to Unite Nations

What was indicated by the mixture of clay and iron in the feet and toes of the image?

"And whereas thou sawest the feet and toes, part of potters' clay, and part of iron, *the kingdom shall be divided.*" Daniel 2:41.

Note.—The barbarian tribes that overran the Roman Empire formed the kingdoms which developed into the nations of modern Europe. See p. 209.

In what prophetic language was the varying strength of the ten kingdoms of the divided empire indicated?

"And as the toes of the feet were *part of iron, and part of clay,* so the kingdom shall be *partly strong, and partly broken* [literally, *"brittle"*]." Verse 42.

Were any efforts to be made to reunite the divided empire of Rome?

"And whereas thou sawest iron mixed with miry clay, *they shall mingle themselves with the seed of men:* but they shall not cleave one to another, even as iron is not mixed with clay." Verse 43.

Note.—Charlemagne, Charles V, Louis XIV, Napoleon, Kaiser Wilhelm, and Hitler all tried to reunite the broken fragments of the Roman Empire and failed. By marriage and intermarriage of royalty ties have been formed with a view to strengthening and cementing together the shattered kingdom, but none have succeeded. The element of disunion remains. Many political revolutions and territorial changes have occurred in Europe since the end of the Western Roman Empire in A.D. 476; but its divided state still remains.

This remarkable dream, as interpreted by Daniel, represents in the briefest form, and yet with unmistakable clearness, a series of world empires from the time of Nebuchadnezzar to the close of earthly history and the setting up of the everlasting kingdom of God. History confirms the prophecy. Babylon was the leading world power at the time of this dream, 603 B.C. The succeeding Persian Empire, which included the Medes also, began its first year in 538 B.C. (most historians date the fall of the city in the latter part of the preceding year, 539 B.C.). The victory of the Greek forces at the Battle of Arbela, in 331 B.C., marked the downfall of the Persian Empire, and the Macedonian Greeks then became the undisputed world power of that time. After the battle of Pydna, in Macedonia, in 168 B.C., no power in the world was strong enough to withstand the Romans; and at that time, therefore, world leadership may be said to have passed from the Greeks to the Romans, and the fourth kingdom was fully established. The division of Rome into ten kingdoms, definitely foretold in the vision recorded in the seventh chapter of Daniel, occurred in the century preceding A.D. 476.

What is to take place in the days of these kingdoms?

"And in the days of these kings shall *the God of heaven set up a kingdom, which shall never be destroyed:* . . . but it shall break in pieces and consume all these kingdoms, and it shall stand for ever." Verse 44.

NOTE.—This verse foretells the establishment of another universal kingdom, the kingdom of God. This kingdom is to overthrow and supplant all existing earthly kingdoms, and is to stand forever. The time for the setting up of this kingdom was to be "in the days of these kings." This cannot refer to the four preceding empires, or kingdoms, for they were not contemporaneous, but successive; neither can it refer to an establishment of the kingdom at Christ's first advent, for the ten kingdoms which arose out of the ruins of the Roman Empire were not yet in existence. It must therefore refer to the divided kingdoms, or nations, that succeeded Rome, represented by the present nations of Europe. This final kingdom, then, is yet future.

In what announcement in the New Testament is the establishment of the kingdom of God made known?

"And the seventh angel sounded; and there were great voices in heaven, saying, *The kingdoms of this world are become the kingdoms of our Lord, and of his Christ;* and he shall reign for ever and ever." Revelation 11:15.

For what have we been taught to pray?

"*Thy kingdom come.* Thy will be done in earth, as it is in heaven." Matthew 6:10.

The Kingdoms of Grace and Glory

To what throne are we exhorted to come to find mercy?

"Let us therefore come boldly unto the *throne of grace,* that we may obtain mercy, and find grace to help in time of need." Hebrews 4:16.

Note.—It would be useless to come before any throne for a favor if that throne had no occupant. The throne of grace, therefore, supposes the King of grace. If there is a King, He must have subjects, and laws to govern those subjects. Then, while in this state, and receiving grace, or favor, from God, one must be in the kingdom of grace.

Kingdom of Glory Future

To what other kingdom do the Scriptures call our attention, and when is it to be set up?

"When the Son of man shall come in his glory, and all the holy angels with him, then shall he sit upon the *throne of his glory.*" Matthew 25:31.

Note.—The kingdom of glory is to be established at the second coming of Christ. Christ said to Pilate, "My kingdom is not of this world." John 18:36.

How did Jesus seek to correct the false idea of the disciples and the Jews that He was then to set up His kingdom of glory?

"He added and *spake a parable,* because he was nigh to Jerusalem, and because they thought that the kingdom of God should immediately appear." Luke 19:11.

In this parable what did Jesus teach?

"A certain *nobleman* went into a far country to receive for himself a kingdom, and to return." Verse 12.

Who is the nobleman?

"I go to prepare a place for you. And if I go and prepare a

place for you, I will come again, and receive you unto myself; that where I am, there ye may be also." John 14:2, 3.

Note.—The nobleman is Christ Jesus. When He ascended to His Father He was seated upon His Father's throne, which, while probation lingers, is the throne of grace. Soon He is to receive His kingdom of glory. He has not yet returned, but when He comes it will be to claim His subjects, and to take them to be with Him where He is. The kingdom of glory will be set up at the second coming of Christ, but not on this earth until the close of the one thousand years. (See Revelation 20:6; 15:2, 3, and reading on "The Millennium," page 345.)

Kingdom of Grace Present

In what words did Jesus make it clear that the only kingdom God now has on the earth is the kingdom of grace?

"When he was demanded of the Pharisees, when the kingdom of God should come, he answered them and said, The kingdom of God cometh not with observation: neither shall they say, Lo here! or, lo there! for, behold, the kingdom of God *is within you*." Luke 17:20, 21.

Note.—Christ reigns only over willing subjects. His reign now is wholly spiritual. Not until His second coming will He set up His kingdom of glory.

By what are men saved from sin?

"By *grace* are ye saved through *faith;* and that not of yourselves: it is the gift of God." Ephesians 2:8. (See Romans 6:23.)

Note.—It follows, then, that only through the grace, or favor, of God can those be saved who have been sinners. There is no other way. Abraham, Moses, and David, as well as Peter, Paul, and John, were saved by grace. These all, therefore, were in the kingdom of grace, which must have been in existence as early as there was a lost man who needed grace.

When Christ sent out His disciples, what did He tell them to preach?

"He sent them to preach the *kingdom of God,* and to heal the sick." Luke 9:2.

In carrying out their commission what did they preach?

"They departed, and went through the towns, preaching the *gospel,* and healing every where." Verse 6.

Note.—Theirs was not a gospel of compulsion, but of persuasion; not a gospel of the sword, but of the love of God; not a political gospel, but the gospel of the Gift of God.

In the parable of the wheat and tares what does the good seed represent?

"The field is the world; the good seed are the *children of the kingdom;* but the tares are the children of the wicked one." Matthew 13:38.

Who sowed the tares in the kingdom?

"The enemy that sowed them is the *devil.*" Verse 39.

Note.—Satan first sowed the tares of sin in Eden. Hence the kingdom of God was in existence at that time. The earth was a part of God's kingdom, and was designed to be under His rule forever.

To whom did God entrust His kingdom on this earth?

"God said, Let us make *man* in our image, after our likeness: and *let them have dominion* over the fish of the sea, and over the fowl of the air, and over the cattle, and over all the earth, and over every creeping thing that creepeth upon the earth." Genesis 1:26.

What did man do with this trust?

"By one man *sin* entered into the world, and death by sin." "By one man's *disobedience* many were made sinners." Romans 5:12, 19.

Note.—Man fell, and the world became the abode of sin. Satan will continue his reign until sin is blotted out. Whoever would become a subject of God's kingdom must now separate from the kingdom that has been usurped by Satan. The sinner must yield obedience to God's laws. Those who do this enter into an arrangement made by God, by which they become His subjects, and renounce the service of Satan. They are then in God's kingdom, His kingdom of grace, because they are the subjects of God's favor, or grace.

The Throne of Glory

What did God promise to David, king of Israel?

"Thy seed will I establish for ever, and *build up thy throne to all generations.*" Psalm 89:4.

Through whom was his throne to be perpetuated?

"Unto us a child is born, unto us a son is given: and the *government shall be upon his shoulder:* and his name shall be called Wonderful, Counsellor, The mighty God, The everlasting Father, The Prince of Peace. Of the increase of his government and peace there shall be no end, upon the throne of David." Isaiah 9:6, 7.

Who is this seed of David, the heir to his throne?

"Thou shalt . . . bring forth a son, and shalt call his name Jesus. He shall be great, and shall be called the Son of the Highest: and the Lord God shall give *unto him the throne of his father David."* Luke 1:31, 32.

What did God, through the prophet, say concerning Israel?

"Thou, profane wicked prince of Israel, whose day is come, when iniquity shall have an end, thus saith the Lord God; Remove the diadem, and take off the crown. . . . I will overturn, overturn, overturn, it: and it shall be no more, until he come whose right it is; and I will give it him." Ezekiel 21:25-27.

NOTE.—This threefold overturning was accomplished in the successive overthrow of the Babylonian, Persian, and Greek empires. The Jews were under the rule of each of these dynasties. The last overturning may be identified generally with the Roman succession to the territories of the Macedonian empires, but the league between the Romans and the Jews, made in 161 B.C., brought the latter people more particularly under the protectorate of that iron power, and in 63 B.C. Pompey annexed Judea as part of a province. With the establishment of Christ's church the throne of David, the kingdom of Israel, was to be no more till He should come to whom it belongs.

While on earth Jesus did not take the throne. Did He, upon ascending to heaven, take His throne, or did He occupy His Father's throne with Him?

"To him that overcometh will I grant to sit with me in my throne, even as I also overcame, and am set down with my Father *in his throne."* Revelation 3:21. "The Lord said unto my Lord, Sit thou at my right hand, until I make thine enemies thy footstool." Psalm 110:1.

What is He doing at the Father's right hand?

"The Lord hath sworn, and will not repent, Thou art a

priest for ever after the order of Melchizedek." Psalm 110:4. (See Hebrews 10:12, 13.)

When His priestly work is finished, what will Christ receive?

"I saw in the night visions, and, behold, one like the Son of man came with the clouds of heaven, and came to the Ancient of days, and they brought him near before him. And there was given him *dominion, and glory, and a kingdom,* that all people, nations, and languages, should serve him: his dominion is an everlasting dominion, which shall not pass away, and his kingdom that which shall not be destroyed." Daniel 7: 13, 14.

When He comes in the clouds of glory, on whose throne will He sit?

"When the Son of man shall come in his glory, and all the holy angels with him, then shall he sit upon the *throne of his glory*." Matthew 25:31. (See Revelation 11:15.)

What will He then say to the redeemed?

"Come, ye blessed of my Father, inherit the kingdom prepared for you from the foundation of the world." Matthew 25:34.

O for that flame of living fire
  Which shone so bright in saints of old;
Which bade their souls to heaven aspire,
  Calm in distress, in danger bold!

Remember, Lord, the ancient days;
  Renew Thy work, Thy grace restore;
And while to Thee our hearts we raise,
  On us Thy Holy Spirit pour.

—WILLIAM H. BATHURST

Four Great Monarchies

Daniel's Dream

At what time was Daniel's second vision given?

"*In the first year of Belshazzar king of Babylon* Daniel had a dream and visions of his head upon his bed: then he wrote the dream, and told the sum of the matters." Daniel 7:1.

What effect did this dream have upon Daniel?

"I Daniel was *grieved in my spirit* in the midst of my body, and the visions of my head *troubled me.*" Verse 15.

Note.—The effect of Daniel's dream upon him, it will be noticed, was similar to the effect of Nebuchadnezzar's dreams upon him; it troubled him. (See Daniel 2:1.)

What did Daniel ask of one of the heavenly attendants who stood by him in his dream?

"I came near unto one of them that stood by, *and asked him the truth of all this.* So he told me, and made me know the interpretation of the things." Verse 16.

What did the prophet see in this vision?

"Daniel spake and said, I saw in my vision by night, and, behold, *the four winds of the heaven strove upon the great sea.*" Verse 2.

What was the result of this strife?

"And *four great beasts came up from the sea,* diverse one from another." Verse 3.

The Meaning of the Beast Symbols

What did these four beasts represent?

"These great beasts, which are four, are *four kings, which shall arise out of the earth.*" Verse 17.

Note.—The word *kings* here, as in Daniel 2:44, denotes kingdoms, as explained in verses 23 and 24 of the seventh chapter, the two words being used interchangeably in this prophecy.

THE FOUR BEASTS OF DANIEL 7

"These great beasts, which are four, are four kings which shall arise out of the earth." Daniel 7:17

FOUR GREAT MONARCHIES

In symbolic language, what is represented by winds?

Strife, war, commotion. (See Jeremiah 25:31-33; 49:36, 37.)

Note.—That winds denote strife and war is evident from the vision itself. As a result of the striving of the winds, kingdoms rise and fall.

What, in prophecy, is symbolized by waters?

"And he saith unto me, The waters which thou sawest . . . are *peoples,* and *multitudes,* and *nations,* and *tongues.*" Revelation 17:15.

Note.—In the second chapter of Daniel, under the figure of an image of man, the mere political outline of the rise and fall of earthly kingdoms is given, preceding the setting up of God's everlasting kingdom. In the seventh chapter earthly governments are represented as viewed in the light of Heaven—under the symbols of wild and ferocious beasts—the last, in particular, oppressing and persecuting the saints of the Most High. Hence the change in the symbols used to represent these kingdoms.

What was the first beast like?

"The first was like a lion, and had eagle's wings: I beheld till the wings thereof were plucked, and it was lifted up from the earth, and made to stand upon the feet as a man, and a man's heart was given to it." Daniel 7:4.

Note.—The lion, the first of these four great beasts, like the golden head of Nebuchadnezzar's dream, represents the Babylonian monarchy; the lion, the king of beasts, standing at the head of his kind, as gold does of metals. The eagle's wings doubtless denote the rapidity with which Babylon rose to its peak of power under Nebuchadnezzar, who reigned from 605 b.c. to 562 b.c. (605 b.c. was his accession year, and the following year was counted his first official year.)

By what was the second kingdom symbolized?

"And behold another beast, *a second, like to a bear,* and it raised up itself on one side, and it had three ribs in the mouth of it between the teeth of it: and they said thus unto it, Arise, devour much flesh." Verse 5.

Note.—"This was the *Medo-Persian* empire, represented here under the symbol of the *bear.* . . . The Medes and Persians are compared to a *bear* on account of their *cruelty* and *thirst after blood,* a bear being a most voracious and cruel animal."—ADAM CLARKE, *Commentary*, on Daniel 7:5.

The first year of this kingdom of the Medes and Persians is dated from 538 B.C.

By what was the third universal empire symbolized?

"After this I beheld, and lo another, *like a leopard,* which had upon the back of it four wings of a fowl; the beast had also four heads; and dominion was given to it." Verse 6.

NOTE.—If the wings of an eagle on the back of a lion denoted rapidity of movement in the Babylonian Empire (Habakkuk 1:6-8), four wings on the leopard must denote unparalleled celerity of movement in the Grecian Empire. A study of Alexander's campaigns proves this to be historically true.

"In the spring of 334 B.C. Alexander crossed over to Asia Minor at the head of an army of some thirty-five thousand Macedonians and Greeks. . . . Four years later—he had overthrown the Persian empire founded by Cyrus the Great, and set himself up as its ruler by right of conquest. Another four years were spent in the subjugation of the wild tribes of the Iranian Plateau and the more civilized peoples of the Indus Valley. In this short space of eight years Alexander had annexed an area of little less than two million square miles, containing a population of more than twenty million persons. The amazing rapidity of his conquest, a feat all the more remarkable in view of the small force at his disposal, was due in large part to the superior organization of the Macedonian army, the excellence of Alexander's generals, trained in the school of his father, Philip, and his own superlative qualities as a general and a leader of men."—A. E. R. BOAK, ALBERT HYMA, and PRESTON SLOSSON, *The Growth of European Civilization* (1938), vol. 1, pp. 59, 60. Copyright, 1938, by F. S. Crofts & Co., Inc. Used by permission of Appleton-Century-Crofts, Inc.

"The beast had also four heads." The Grecian Empire maintained its unity but a short time after the death of Alexander, which occurred in 323 B.C. Within twenty-two years after the close of his brilliant career, or by 301 B.C., the empire was divided among four of his leading generals. (See page 222.)

How was the fourth kingdom represented?

"After this I saw in the night visions, and behold *a fourth beast, dreadful and terrible, and strong exceedingly; and it had great iron teeth:* it devoured and brake in pieces, and stamped the residue with the feet of it: and it was diverse from all the beasts that were before it; *and it had ten horns.*" Verse 7.

FOUR GREAT MONARCHIES

What was the fourth beast declared to be?

"Thus he said, *The fourth beast shall be the fourth kingdom upon earth,* which shall be diverse from all kingdoms, and shall devour the whole earth, and shall tread it down, and break it in pieces." Verse 23.

NOTE.—"This is allowed, on all hands, to be the Roman empire. It was *dreadful, terrible,* and *exceeding strong:* . . . and became, in effect, what the Roman writers delight to call it, *the empire of the whole world.*"—ADAM CLARKE, *Commentary,* on Daniel 7:7.

World power may be said to have passed from the Greeks to the Romans at the Battle of Pydna, in 168 B.C.

"Finally, in 168, the Romans . . . won a complete victory over Perseus [of Macedonia] in the battle of Pydna. The Macedonian kingdom was at an end. . . . Having disposed of Macedonia the Romans turned their attention to other Greek states with the intention of rewarding their friends and punishing their enemies. . . . Henceforth it was clear that Rome was the real sovereign in the eastern Mediterranean and that her friends and allies only enjoyed local autonomy, while they were expected to be obedient to the orders of Rome."—A. E. R. BOAK, *A History of Rome to 565 A.D.* (1938 ed.), p. 109. Copyright, 1921, 1929, 1943, by the Macmillan Company. Used by permission.

What was denoted by the ten horns?

"And the ten horns out of this kingdom are *ten kings that shall arise.*" Verse 24.

NOTE.—The Roman Empire was broken up into ten kingdoms in the century preceding A.D. 476. Because of the uncertainties of the times, religious writers have differed in the enumeration of the exact kingdoms intended by the prophecy. Says one writer on Bible prophecy:

"The ten horns may not be strictly permanent, but admit of partial change. Some may perhaps fall, or be blended, and then replaced by others. The tenfold character may thus be dominant through the whole, and appear distinctly at the beginning and close of their history, though not strictly maintained every moment."

"A tenfold division, such as some have looked for, mathematical and unvaried, would frustrate one-half of the prediction; and would deprive the rest of all its freedom and moral grandeur. But now every part is alike accomplished. At the same time, by these partial changes in the list of the doomed kingdoms, the reproach of a stern fatalism, which otherwise would cloud the equity of divine Providence, is rolled away."—T. R. BIRKS, *The Four Prophetic Empires, and the*

Kingdom of Messiah: Being an Exposition of the First Two Visions of Daniel (1845 ed.), pp. 143, 144, 152.

What change did Daniel see take place in these horns?

"I considered the horns, and, behold, *there came up among them another little horn, before whom there were three of the first horns plucked up by the roots:* and, behold, in this horn were eyes like the eyes of man, and a mouth speaking great things." Verse 8.

What inquiry on the part of Daniel shows that the fourth beast, and especially the little-horn phase of it, constitutes the leading feature of this vision?

"Then *I would know the truth of the fourth beast,* which was diverse from all the others, exceeding dreadful, whose teeth were of iron, and his nails of brass; which devoured, brake in pieces, and stamped the residue with his feet; *and of the ten horns* that were in his head, and *of the other which came up,* and *before whom three fell;* even of that horn that had eyes, and a mouth that spake very great things, whose look was more stout than his fellows." Verses 19, 20.

When was the little horn to arise?

"And another shall rise *after them.*" Verse 24.

NOTE.—The ten horns, as already shown, arose when Rome, the fourth kingdom, was divided into ten kingdoms. This division was completed by A.D. 476. The little-horn power which was to arise after them and before whom three of the other kings—the Heruli, the Vandals, and the Ostrogoths—fell, was the papacy.

"Out of the ruins of political Rome, arose the great moral Empire in the 'giant form' of the Roman Church."—A. C. FLICK, *The Rise of the Mediaeval Church* (New York: G. P. Putnam's Sons, 1909), p. 150.

"Under the Roman Empire the popes had no temporal powers. But when the Roman Empire had disintegrated and its place had been taken by a number of rude, barbarous kingdoms, the Roman Catholic church not only became independent of the states in religious affairs but dominated secular affairs as well."—CARL CONRAD ECKHARDT, *The Papacy and World-Affairs* (Chicago: University of Chicago Press, 1937), p. 1.

With the place and the time of the kingdom of the little horn identified, the study of its character and work will be considered in the readings which follow.

The Kingdom and Work of Antichrist

What is said of the little horn as compared with the ten horns of the fourth beast of Daniel 7?

"He shall be *diverse* from the first, and he shall subdue three kings." Daniel 7:24.

Note.—The papacy, which arose on the ruins of the Roman Empire, differed from all previous forms of Roman power in that it was an ecclesiastical despotism claiming universal dominion over both spiritual and temporal affairs, especially the former. It was a union of church and state, frequently with the church dominant. (See page 210.)

"Whatever Roman elements the barbarians and Arians left . . . [came] under the protection of the Bishop of Rome, who was the chief person there after the Emperor's disappearance. . . . *The Roman Church in this way privily pushed itself into the place of the Roman World-Empire, of which it is the actual continuation;* the empire has not perished, but has only undergone a transformation. . . . That is no mere 'clever remark,' but the recognition of the true state of the matter historically, and the most appropriate and fruitful way of describing the character of this Church. It still governs the nations. . . . It is a political creation, and as imposing as a World-Empire, because the continuation of the Roman Empire. The Pope, who calls himself 'King' and 'Pontifex Maximus,' is Caesar's successor."—Adolf Harnack, *What Is Christianity?* (New York: G. P. Putnam's Sons, 1903), pp. 269, 270.

"No, the Church will not descend into the tomb. It will survive the Empire. . . . At length a second empire will arise, and of this empire the Pope will be the master—more than this, he will be the master of Europe. He will dictate his orders to kings who will obey them."—Joseph Turmel (under the pseudonym Andre Lagarde), *The Latin Church in the Middle Ages* (New York: Charles Scribner's Sons, 1915), preface, p. vi.

The Papacy and God

What attitude of rivalry was the papacy, represented by the little horn, to assume toward the Most High?

"And he shall *speak great words against the most High.*" Verse 25, first clause.

How does Paul, speaking of the man of sin, describe this same power?

"Who opposeth and exalteth himself above all that is called God, or that is worshipped; so that he as God sitteth in the temple of God, shewing himself that he is God." 2 Thessalonians 2:4.

NOTE.—The following extracts from authoritative works, most of them by Roman Catholic writers, will indicate to what extent the papacy has done this:

"All names which in the Scriptures are applied to Christ, by virtue of which it is established that he is over the church, all the same names are applied to the Pope."—ROBERT BELLARMINE, *Disputationes de Controversiis,* Tom. 2, "Controversia Prima," Book 2 ("De Conciliorum Auctoritate" [On the Authority of Councils]), chap. 17 (1628 ed., vol. 1, p. 266), translated.

"For thou art the shepherd, thou art the physician, thou art the director, thou art the husbandman; finally, thou art another God on earth."—Christopher Marcellus' Oration in the Fifth Lateran Council, 4th session, in J. D. Mansi, *Sacrorum Conciliorum . . . Collectio,* vol. 32, col. 761, translated.

"For not man, but God separates those whom the Roman Pontiff (who exercises the functions, not of mere man, but of the true God), having weighed the necessity or benefit of the churches, dissolves, not by human but rather by divine authority."—"The Decretals of Gregory IX," book 1, title 7, chap. 3, in *Corpus Juris Canonici* (1555-56 ed.), vol. 2, col. 203, translated.

"The pope is the supreme judge of the law of the land. . . . He is the vicegerent of Christ, who is not only a Priest forever, but also King of kings and Lord of lords."—*La Civilta Cattolica,* March 18, 1871, quoted in LEONARD WOOLSEY BACON, *An Inside View of the Vatican Council* (American Tract Society ed.), p. 229, n.

"Christ entrusted His office to the chief pontiff; . . . but all power in heaven and in earth has been given to Christ; . . . therefore the chief pontiff, who is His vicar, will have this power."—*Corpus Juris Canonici* (1555-56 ed.), vol. 3, *Extravagantes Communes,* book 1, chap. 1, col. 29, translated from a gloss on the words *Porro Subesse Romano Pontiff.*

"Hence the Pope is crowned with a triple crown, as king of heaven and of earth and of the lower regions (*infernorum*)."—LUCIUS FERRARIS, *Prompta Bibliotheca,* "Papa" (the Pope), art. 2 (1772-77 ed., vol. 6, p. 26), translated.

"All the faithful of Christ must believe that the holy Apostolic See and the Roman Pontiff possesses the primacy over the whole world, and that the Roman Pontiff is the successor of blessed Peter, Prince of the Apostles, and is true vicar of Christ, and head of the whole Church, and father and teacher of all Christians; and that full power was given to him in blessed Peter to rule, feed, and govern the universal Church by Jesus Christ our Lord."—First Dogmatic Constitution on the Church of Christ (*Pastor Aeternus,* published in the fourth session of the Vatican Council, 1870), chap. 3, in PHILIP SCHAFF, *Creeds of Christendom* (New York: Harper), vol. 2, p. 262.

"We teach and define that it is a dogma divinely revealed: that the Roman Pontiff, when he speaks *ex cathedra,* that is, when in discharge of the office of pastor and doctor of all Christians, by virtue of his supreme Apostolic authority, he defines a doctrine regarding faith or morals to be held by the universal Church, by the divine assistance promised to him in blessed Peter, is possessed of that infallibility with which the divine Redeemer willed that his Church should be endowed for defining doctrine regarding faith or morals; and that therefore such definitions of the Roman Pontiff are irreformable of themselves, and not from the consent of the Church."—*Ibid.,* chap. 4, pp. 270, 271.

Among the twenty-seven propositions known as the "Dictates of Hildebrand," who, under the name of Gregory VII, was Pope from 1073 to 1087, occur the following:

"2. That the Roman pontiff alone is justly styled universal.

"6. That no person . . . may live under the same roof with one excommunicated by the Pope.

"9. That all princes should kiss his feet only.

"12. That it is lawful for him to depose emperors.

"18. That his sentence is not to be reviewed by any one; while he alone can review the decisions of all others.

"19. That he can be judged by no one.

"22. That the Roman Church never erred, nor will it, according to the Scriptures, ever err.

"26. That no one is to be accounted a Catholic who does not harmonize with the Roman Church.

"27. That he can absolve subjects from their allegiance to unrighteous rulers."—CESARE BARONIUS, *Annales,* year 1076, secs. 31-33, vol. 17 (1869 ed.), pp. 405, 406, translated.

"They have assumed infallibility, which belongs only to God. They profess to forgive sins, which belongs only to God. They profess to open and shut heaven, which belongs only to God. They profess to be higher than all the kings of the earth, which belongs only to God. And they go beyond God in pretending to loose whole nations from their oath of allegiance to their kings, when such kings do not please them. And they go *against* God, when they give *indulgences for sin.* This is the *worst* of all blasphemies."—ADAM CLARKE, *Commentary,* on Daniel 7:25.

THE PAPACY AND GOD'S PEOPLE

How was the little horn to treat God's people?

"And shall *wear out the saints* of the most High." Daniel 7:25.

NOTE.—"Under these bloody maxims [previously mentioned] those persecutions were carried on, from the eleventh and twelfth centuries almost to the present day, which stand out on the page of history. After the signal of open martyrdom had been given in the canons of Orleans, there followed the extirpation of the Albigenses, under the form of a crusade, the establishment of the inquisition, the cruel attempts to extinguish the Waldenses, the martyrdoms of the Lollards, the cruel wars to exterminate the Bohemians, the burning of Huss and Jerome, and multitudes of other confessors, before the Reformation; and afterwards, the ferocious cruelties practised in the Netherlands, the martyrdoms of queen Mary's reign, the extinction, by fire and sword, of the reformation in Spain and Italy, by fraud and open persecution in Poland, the massacre of Bartholomew, the persecution of the Huguenots by the League, . . . and all the cruelties and perjuries connected with the revocation of the edict of Nantz [Nantes]. These are the more open and conspicuous facts which explain the prophecy, besides the slow and secret murders of the holy tribunal of the inquisition."—T. R. BIRKS, *The Four Prophetic Empires, and the Kingdom of Messiah* (1845 ed.), pp. 248, 249.

The number of the victims of the Inquisition in Spain is given in *The History of the Inquisition in Spain,* by Llorente, formerly secretary of the Inquisition (1827 ed.), page 583. This authority acknowledges that more than 300,000 suffered persecution in Spain alone, of whom 31,912 died in the flames. Millions more were slain for their faith throughout Europe.

"That the Church of Rome has shed more innocent blood than any other institution that has ever existed among mankind, will be questioned by no Protestant who has a competent knowledge of history. The memorials, indeed, of many of her persecutions are now so scanty that it is impossible to form a complete conception of the multitude of her victims, and it is quite certain that no powers of imagination can adequately realise their sufferings."—W. E. H. LECKY, *History of the Rise and Influence of the Spirit of Rational-*

The Papacy and God's Law

What else does the prophecy say the little horn would do?

"And he shall *think to change the times and the law.*" Daniel 7:25, third clause, R.V.

NOTE.—Of the power of the pope to alter divine laws a Catholic writer has the following to say:

"The pope is of so great authority and power that he can modify, explain, or interpret even divine laws. . . . The pope can modify divine law, since his power is not of man, but of God, and he acts as vicegerent of God upon earth."—LUCIUS FERRARIS, *Prompta Bibliotheca,* "Papa," art. 2, translated.

Although the Ten Commandments, the law of God, are found in the Roman Catholic versions of the Scriptures, as they were originally given, yet the faithful are instructed from the catechisms of the church, and not directly from the Bible. As it appears in these, the law of God has been changed and virtually re-enacted by the papacy. Furthermore, communicants not only receive the law from the church but deal with the church concerning any alleged infractions of that law, and when they have satisfied the ecclesiastical authorities the whole matter is settled.

The second commandment, which forbids the making of, and bowing down to, images, is omitted in Catholic catechisms, and the tenth, which forbids coveting, is divided into two.

As evidence of the change which has been made in the law of God by the papal power, and that it acknowledges the change and claims the authority to make it, note the following from Roman Catholic publications:

"Q. *Have you any other way of proving that the Church has power to institute festivals of precept?*

"A. Had she not such power, she could not have done that in which all modern religionists agree with her;—she could not have substituted the observance of Sunday the first day of the week, for the observance of Saturday the seventh day, a change for which there is no Scriptural authority."—STEPHEN KEENAN, *A Doctrinal Catechism,* "On the Obedience Due to the Church," chap. 2, p. 174. (Imprimatur, John Cardinal McCloskey, archbishop of New York.)

"Q. *How prove you that the Church hath power to command feasts and holydays?*

"A. By the very act of changing the Sabbath into *Sunday,* which

Protestants allow of; and therefore they fondly contradict themselves, by keeping *Sunday* strictly, and breaking most other feasts commanded by the same church.

"Q. *How prove you that?*

"A. Because by keeping *Sunday,* they acknowledge the Church's power to ordain feasts, and to command them under sin: and by not keeping the rest by her commanded, they again deny, in fact, the same power."—Henry Tuberville, *An Abridgment of the Christian Doctrine,* p. 58.

"You may read the Bible from Genesis to Revelation, and you will not find a single line authorizing the sanctification of Sunday. The Scriptures enforce the religious observance of Saturday, a day which we never sanctify."—James Cardinal Gibbons, *The Faith of Our Fathers* (1917 ed.), pp. 72, 73.

God's Judgment and Kingdom

Until what time were the saints, times, and laws of the Most High to be given into the hands of the little horn?

"And they shall be given into his hand *until a time and times and the dividing of time."* Daniel 7:25, last clause.

In what other prophecies is this same period mentioned?

"And to the woman were given two wings of a great eagle, that she might fly into the wilderness, into her place, where she is nourished for *a time, and times, and half a time,* from the face of the serpent." Revelation 12:14. "And there was given unto him a mouth speaking great things and blasphemies; and power was given unto him to continue *forty and two months."* Revelation 13:5. (See also Revelation 11:2.) "And the woman fled into the wilderness, where she hath a place prepared of God, that they should feed her there *a thousand two hundred and threescore days."* Revelation 12:6.

In symbolic prophecy what length of time is represented by a day?

Answer: A year of literal time.

Note.—In prophecies such as those of Daniel 2, 7, and 8 and most of the book of Revelation, the persons, animals, objects, and actions described are symbolic. That is, they are not reality itself, but figurative representations of real persons, things, and events. Accordingly, it is reasonable to suppose that the time periods specified in such prophetic passages are also symbolic. An instance of such usage occurs in Ezekiel 4:6, where the prophet was to perform a symbolic act for 40 days, each day being representative of a literal year.

The additional fact that the time periods of Daniel 7 and 8—the 1260 days and the 2300 days—do not correspond meaningfully with any known historical periods of the lengths of time thus specified in "days" confirms the conclusion that these figures must be representative of symbolic rather than literal time. Also, when the 2300 days is recognized as representing the whole, of which the 490 years of Daniel 9 constitutes a part (see page 228), it is evident that the 2300 days must be considered in a symbolic sense.

A "time" in prophecy being the same as a year (Daniel 11:13, margin and R.V.), three and one-half times would be three and a half years. This is obviously the same as 42 months. And as both these periods are identified by the above texts as equivalent to a thousand two hundred and threescore days, it is evident that a prophetic year is composed of 360 days, or 12 months of 30 days each. Since in Bible prophecy a day represents a year, the period, then, which was to mark the time of the supremacy of the little horn—the papacy—over the saints, times, and law of God, would therefore be 1260 years.

The decree of the emperor Justinian, issued in A.D. 533, recognized the pope as "head of all the holy churches." (Justinian's Code, book 1, title 1, sec. 4, in *The Civil Law,* translated by S. P. Scott, vol. 12, p. 12.) The overwhelming defeat of the Ostrogoths in the siege of Rome, five years later, A.D. 538, was a death blow to the independence of the Arian power then ruling Italy, and marks that year as notable in the development of papal supremacy. The year 538, then, may be taken as marking the beginning of the 1260 years of this prophecy, which would extend to the year 1798. As a direct result of the revolt against papal authority in the French Revolution, the French army, under Berthier, entered Rome, and the pope was taken prisoner in February, 1798, dying in exile at Valence, France, the following year. The year 1798, during which this death stroke was inflicted upon the papacy, may thus be taken as marking the close of the long prophetic period mentioned in this prophecy.

What fate will eventually befall the little horn?

"But the judgment shall sit, and they shall *take away his dominion, to consume and to destroy it unto the end."* Daniel 7:26.

To whom will the dominion finally be given?

"And the kingdom and dominion, and the greatness of the kingdom under the whole heaven, shall be given *to the people of the saints of the most High."* Verse 27.

COPYRIGHT, 1949, BY REVIEW AND HERALD
HARRY BAERG, ARTIST

THE VISION OF DANIEL 8

The conflict between the Grecian and Medo-Persian empires

The Prophetic Symbols of Daniel 8

THE VISION OF DANIEL

Where was Daniel at the time of this vision?

"I saw in a vision; and it came to pass, when I saw, that I was at Shushan in the palace, which is in the province of Elam; and I saw in a vision, and I was by the river of Ulai." Daniel 8:2.

What first appeared to the prophet?

"Then I lifted up mine eyes, and saw, and, behold, there stood before the river a ram which had two horns." Verse 3.

What next appeared upon the scene?

"As I was considering, behold, an he goat came from the west on the face of the whole earth, and touched not the ground: and the goat had a notable horn between his eyes. And he came to the ram that had two horns, which I had seen standing before the river, and ran unto him in the fury of his power. And I saw him come close unto the ram, and he was moved with choler against him, and smote the ram, and brake his two horns: and there was no power in the ram to stand before him, but he cast him down to the ground, and stamped upon him; and there was none that could deliver the ram out of his hand. Therefore the he goat waxed very great." Verses 5-8.

When the notable horn was broken, what came up?

"When he was strong, the great horn was broken; and for it came up four notable ones toward the four winds." Verse 8.

What came out of one of these horns?

"Out of one of them came forth a little horn, which waxed exceeding great, toward the south, and toward the east, and toward the pleasant land. And it waxed great, even to the host of heaven; and it cast down some of the host and of the stars to the ground, and stamped upon them." Verses 9, 10.

Gabriel Explains the Vision

What command was given to an angel who stood by?

"I heard a man's voice between the banks of Ulai, which called, and said, Gabriel, make this man to understand the vision." Verse 16.

What were the first words that the angel then uttered before the prophet?

"Understand, O son of man: for at the time of the end shall be the vision." Verse 17.

Note.—These words of the angel, "at the time of the end shall be the vision," cannot possibly mean that it would be necessary to wait until the time of the end before the ram and the he-goat appeared upon the stage of action, for the angel said plainly that the ram with the two horns represented the Medo-Persian Empire and that the goat represented Greece (verses 20, 21). And it was in the third year of Belshazzar, before the overthrow of Babylon by the Medes and Persians, that the vision was given.

But a long time period is included in this important prophecy, and the angel informed the prophet that the events of the vision, including those to occur during and at the end of the great time period, would reach far beyond Daniel's time, even into the time of the end; that is, into an epoch which would find its climax in the second coming of Christ.

Some there are who would have us believe that the wonderful prophecies and the grand truths of the book of Daniel cannot be understood, and therefore that it is a waste of time to study them. But while Daniel himself says he was astonished at the vision, "but none understood it," we find the angel saying to him at a later time that the sealing of these prophecies was only "till the time of the end."

"But thou, O Daniel, shut up the words, and seal the book, even to the time of the end: many shall run to and fro, and knowledge shall be increased." "And he said, Go thy way, Daniel: for the words are closed up and sealed till the time of the end. Many shall be purified, and made white, and tried; but the wicked shall do wickedly: and none of the wicked shall understand; but the wise shall understand." Daniel 12:4, 9, 10.

Though some of its prophecies were sealed until the time of the end, there were portions of Daniel's prophecies that were to be understood in Christ's day. In Jesus' wonderful discourse to His disciples regarding the signs of His coming (recorded in Matthew 24), reference is made to Daniel's prophecy, and the exhortation is given, "Whoso readeth, let him understand."

THE PROPHETIC SYMBOLS OF DANIEL 8

The book of Daniel, then, can be understood, and it was written for our special benefit. We may find comfort and hope in its marvelous predictions, so accurately fulfilled, knowing that the sublime events yet future will surely come to pass, as the prophecy has foretold.

In a few words Daniel's prophecy speaks volumes. Into a few short chapters is compressed the history, written in advance, which, as we look back upon it, spans more than twenty-three long centuries. Not having before him the pageant of the centuries which history now brings to view, it was not to be expected that the aged prophet would be able to comprehend all that God through visions and the words of the heavenly messenger revealed to him. The events of his own day and time he could well understand, but though given a bird's-eye view of the sweep of the centuries, the peaks of future history so far distant from him were beyond his ken.

But the angel had been commanded, "Make this man to understand the vision," and he therefore proceeded to explain the meaning of the symbols which the prophet had seen. And looking back upon the prophecy from this distant time, we can see how accurately the divine mind guided the prophet's hand in depicting the startling world events which have taken place from that day to this.

How did the angel then proceed to fulfill his mission to Daniel?

"The ram which thou sawest having two horns are the kings of Media and Persia. And the rough goat is the king of Grecia." Verses 20, 21.

NOTE.—We have already read the words of Scripture prophecy which describe the fury with which the goat would attack the ram.

"The 'goat came from the west on the face of the whole earth.' That is, Greece lay west of Persia and attacked from that direction. The Greek army swept everything on the face of the earth before it.

"The goat 'touched not the ground.' Such was the marvelous celerity of his movements that he seemed to fly from point to point with the swiftness of the wind. The same characteristic of speed is indicated by the four wings of the leopard in the vision of Daniel 7, representing the same nation.

"*Alexander the 'Notable Horn.'*—The notable horn between his eyes is explained in verse 21 to be the first king of the Macedonian Empire. This king was Alexander the Great.

"A concise account of the overthrow of the Persian Empire by Alexander is given in verses 6 and 7. The battles between the Greeks and the Persians are said to have been exceedingly fierce. Some of the scenes recorded in history vividly bring to mind the figure used in the prophecy—a ram standing before the river, and the goat running toward him in 'the fury of his power.' Alexander first vanquished the generals of Darius at the River Granicus in Phrygia. He next attacked and routed Darius at the passes of Issus in Cilicia, and afterward defeated him on the plains of Arbela in Syria. This latter battle occurred in 331 B.C., and marked the fall of the Persian Empire. By this event Alexander became master of the whole country. Concerning verse 6—'He [the goat] came to the ram that had two horns, which I had seen standing before the river, and ran unto him in the fury of his power'—Thomas Newton says: 'One can hardly read these words without having some image of Darius's army standing and guarding the River Granicus, and of Alexander on the other side with his forces plunging in, swimming across the stream, and rushing on the enemy with all the fire and fury that can be imagined.'"—URIAH SMITH, *The Prophecies of Daniel and the Revelation,* pp. 152, 153.

What is represented by the four horns standing up in the place of the one broken?

"Now that being broken, whereas four stood up for it, four kingdoms shall stand up out of the nation, but not in his power." Verse 22.

NOTE.—The ram was said to represent the Persian Empire, the he-goat the Greek or Macedonian Empire, and the great horn that was broken symbolized the first king, Alexander the Great. Alexander died in the prime of life and at the height of his conquests, being only about thirty-three years old at the time of his decease.

It is said that as a result of a drunken debauch he was seized with a violent fever, and from this he died eleven days later, June 13, 323 B.C. Thus it truly came to pass, as Daniel had foretold, that "when he was strong, the great horn was broken; and for it came up four." How accurate the prophecy! How true to the historical facts! Concerning the breakup of Alexander's empire we read:

"The story of the Successors, in the tradition, is the story of a struggle for power among the generals. War went on almost without intermission from 321 to 301 B.C.; and, except for the brief episode of Antipater's regency, the conflict was one between the centrifugal forces within the empire, represented by the satraps (territorial dynasts), and whatever central power stood for unity. The conflict falls into two divisions; in the first the central power represents the kings, but after 316 it means Antigonus, who claimed personally to stand in Alexander's place. But though the actors changed, the issues were the same throughout; the end was complete victory for the dynasts."—*The Cambridge Ancient History* (1928-39 ed.), vol. 6, p. 462. Used by permission of the Cambridge University Press.

"The death of Eumenes left Antigonus in virtual control of Asia. . . . His aim was to obtain the whole empire for himself without reference to the royal house. . . . But he kept up appearances; . . . he claimed to act for Alexander's son, and his army made him regent. . . . The old central power was dead; but it had merely been replaced by another, far more energetic, ambitious, and businesslike, and controlled by a single brain. . . . Seleucus persuaded Ptolemy, Lysimachus, and Cassander, that Antigonus' ambition threatened their very existence, and the three rulers formed a definite alliance. Cassander [held] . . . Macedonia, . . . Ptolemy . . . Egypt; . . . Lysimachus . . . held the Dardanelles crossings. . . . The history of the next four years, 315-312, is that of the first war between Antigonus and the coalition."—*Ibid.*, pp. 482, 483.

"Ptolemy after his victory [over Antigonus] also took the title of king (305), and was followed by Cassander, Lysimachus, and Seleucus. The title affirmed their independent rule in their respective territories; Antigonus of course did not recognize this."—*Ibid.*, pp. 498, 499. "The four kings renewed the coalition of 315, but this time not to bridle Antigonus but to destroy him."—*Ibid.*, p. 502.

"In spring 301 . . . at Ipsus near Synnada the two great armies met in the 'battle of the kings.' . . . Antigonus was defeated and killed. . . . The struggle between the central power and the dynasts was ended, and with Antigonus' death the dismemberment of the Graeco-Macedonian world became inevitable. Demetrius fled to Ephesus, while Lysimachus and Seleucus divided Antigonus' kingdom. Cassander was recognized as king of Macedonia."—*Ibid.*, p. 504.

What is represented by the "little horn" of verse 9?

"In the latter time of their [successors of Alexander] kingdom, when the transgressors are come to the full, a king of fierce countenance, and understanding dark sentences, shall stand up." Verse 23.

NOTE.—"The little horn comes forth from one of the horns of the goat. How, it may be asked, can that be true of Rome? Earthly governments are not introduced into prophecy until they become in some way connected with the people of God. Rome became connected with the Jews, the people of God at that time, by the famous Jewish League in 161 B.C. But seven years before this, that is, in 168 B.C., Rome had conquered Macedonia, and made that country a part of its empire. Rome is therefore introduced into prophecy just as, from the overthrow of the Macedonian horn of the goat, it is going forth to new conquests in other directions. It appeared to the prophet as coming forth from one of the horns of the goat."—URIAH SMITH, *The Prophecies of Daniel and the Revelation*, p. 158.

"From the opening of the historic period the development of Roman civilization was profoundly affected by foreign influences, in particular by Etruscan and Greek. But whereas the influence of the Etruscans virtually ceased with the expulsion of their kings from Rome, that of the Greeks continued with increasing strength throughout the whole of the period of the republic. . . . It was inevitable that the older and more advanced Hellenic civilization should leave an indelible imprint upon the younger and less highly developed culture of Rome. And, in fact, there is hardly a single important aspect of Roman civilization that does not reveal unmistakable traces of imitating or borrowing ideas that originated among the Greeks. With obvious truth the Roman poet Horace could say: 'Captive Greece has captured her rude conqueror.'"—A. E. R. BOAK, ALBERT HYMA, and PRESTON SLOSSON, *The Growth of European Civilization,* vol. 1, p. 84. Copyright, 1938, by F. S. Crofts & Co., Inc. Used by permission of Appleton-Century-Crofts, Inc.

"Contact with the Greeks led to the introduction of Greek divinities and, of much greater importance, to the identification of the native Italian gods with those of the Greek pantheon, with the result that Greek mythology and forms of artistic representation were taken over wholesale by the Romans."—*Ibid.,* p. 93.

As these historical quotations reveal, the pagan Roman Empire may be described as coming out of the Greek Empire. However, as the following question and answer show, the little horn represents more than simply pagan Rome.

What was this little horn to do to God's sanctuary?

"Yea, he magnified himself even to the prince of the host, and by him the daily sacrifice was taken away, and the place of his sanctuary was cast down." Daniel 8:11.

NOTE.—As just explained, the little horn of Daniel 8 represents, first, the ancient Roman Empire. It was pagan Rome that in A.D. 70 laid the Temple in Jerusalem desolate and brought its services to an end, as forcefully described in the prophetic language of verses 9-13. However, as will be seen (see pages 226 to 233), the prophetic time period of verse 14 was to extend almost eighteen centuries beyond A.D. 70. This fact demands that the little horn be viewed not simply as pagan Rome but also as papal Rome, its successor. This relationship between pagan Rome and papal Rome is clearly set forth in the prophecy of Daniel 7 (see page 210).

This fact also demands that the word "sanctuary," as used in verses 11-14, not be understood to refer exclusively to the Jerusalem Temple. There being no such "sanctuary" on earth during the remainder of that long prophetic time period, the term "sanctuary," in

THE PROPHETIC SYMBOLS OF DANIEL 8

verse 14, must refer to the "sanctuary" in heaven, "the true tabernacle, which the Lord pitched, and not man," of which the sanctuary on earth was only a "shadow" (Hebrews 8:2, 5).

As the prophet Daniel beheld the persecuting work of the little horn of Daniel 7, what did he see take place?

"The judgment shall sit, and they shall take away his dominion, to consume and to destroy it unto the end." Daniel 7:26.

NOTE.—In the prophecy of the seventh chapter there is traced the history of the rise and fall of the four great kingdoms, the division of the fourth, as represented by the ten horns, and the establishment of the papacy under the symbol of the little horn, before whom three fell. As the prophet beheld the persecutions of this power, he saw the Ancient of days sit and the judgment begin. Following the judgment, the kingdom was to be given to the saints of the Most High.

The eighth chapter of Daniel reviews briefly the history of the kingdoms, predicts the persecutions of the chosen people by pagan and papal Rome, and gives a remarkable prophecy concerning the sanctuary.

SANCTUARY TO BE CLEANSED

At what time, according to the prophecy, was the sanctuary to be cleansed?

"He said unto me, Unto two thousand and three hundred days; then shall the sanctuary be cleansed." Daniel 8:14.

NOTE.—The Jewish Day of Atonement was on the tenth day of the seventh month, at which time the sanctuary was cleansed. This Day of Atonement was looked upon by the Jews as a day of judgment, and was, in fact, a type of the investigative judgment in heaven. The 2300-day period, representing 2300 years according to symbolic prophecy, reaches to the cleansing of the sanctuary in heaven, or the investigative judgment. A study of the symbols and time period of this chapter, and of their interpretation in this and the ninth chapter, gives a clear understanding of this period. See pp. 226 to 233.

As Daniel saw the chosen people of God persecuted and scattered, as well as the desolation of the Holy City and the sanctuary, how did it affect the prophet?

"I Daniel *fainted*, and *was sick* certain days; afterward I rose up, and did the king's business." Daniel 8:27.

The Hour of God's Judgment

(The 2300 Days of Daniel 8, 9)

What startling message is given in Revelation 14:7?

"Fear God, and give glory to him; for the *hour of his judgment is come:* and worship him that made heaven, and earth, and the sea, and the fountains of waters."

When is the hour of God's judgment?

"He said unto me, Unto two thousand and three hundred days; then shall the sanctuary be cleansed." Daniel 8:14.

Note.—By a study of the succeeding chapters on the sanctuary, it will be seen that the cleansing of the earthly sanctuary on the Day of Atonement included a work of judgment. The Jewish people understood it so. This 2300-day period, being 2300 literal years (see note, page 216), reaches down to the cleansing of the sanctuary in heaven, or, in other words, to the time when the investigative judgment begins, as described in Daniel 7:9, 10.

Why was not this time period fully explained when the angel first appeared to Daniel?

"I Daniel fainted, and was *sick certain days;* afterward I rose up, and did the king's business; and I was astonished at the vision, but none understood it." Verse 27.

Note.—The prophet had been given a vision of the great nations of his and succeeding days and the persecutions of God's people, concluding with the time period pointing to the cleansing of the sanctuary. But the aged Daniel fainted and was sick certain days. Consequently, the interpretation was arrested, and was not completed until after the recovery of the prophet. The vision and its partial explanation were given in the third year of Belshazzar's reign with his father Nabonidus; the interpretation of the time period was given following the fall of Babylon, in the first year of Darius.

At some time subsequent to Daniel's recovery from his illness, to what did he turn his attention?

"In the first year of Darius . . . I Daniel understood by books the number of the years, whereof the word of the Lord came

THE HOUR OF GOD'S JUDGMENT

to Jeremiah the prophet, that he would accomplish seventy years in the desolations of Jerusalem." Daniel 9:1, 2.

NOTE.—Nebuchadnezzar besieged Jerusalem in the third year of Jehoiakim (Daniel 1:1), and Jeremiah announced the seventy-year captivity in the fourth year of Jehoiakim (Jeremiah 25:1, 12). This means that the first deportation of the Jews to Babylon, when Daniel and his companions were carried away, was at that time. The seventy years of Jeremiah's prophecy would expire in 536 B.C. Since the first year of the Persian Empire began in 538 B.C., the restoration period was therefore only two years distant from that time.

What did this nearness of the time of restoration from captivity lead Daniel to do?

"I set my face unto the Lord God, to seek by *prayer and supplications,* with fasting, and sackcloth, and ashes." Verse 3.

In what especially was the prophet interested?

"Now therefore, O our God, hear the prayer of thy servant, and his supplications, and cause thy face to shine upon thy *sanctuary that is desolate,* for the Lord's sake." Verse 17.

GABRIEL AGAIN APPEARS

While Daniel was praying concerning the sanctuary lying desolate at Jerusalem, who appeared on the scene?

"Yea, whiles I was speaking in prayer, even the man *Gabriel,* whom I had seen in the vision at the beginning, being caused to fly swiftly, touched me about the time of the evening oblation." Verse 21.

NOTE.—It was fitting that the angel Gabriel should return to the prophet for the purpose of explaining that portion of the prophecy in Daniel 8 which had not been interpreted, the time period, when Daniel was earnestly praying for the sanctuary made desolate at Jerusalem. The angel not only would tell him of the earthly typical sanctuary and its future, but would give him, for the benefit of those living at the time of the end, a view of the true heavenly service.

What did the angel at once ask the prophet to consider?

"He informed me, and talked with me, and said, O Daniel, I am now come forth to give thee skill and understanding. . . . Therefore understand the matter, and *consider the vision.*" Verses 22, 23.

NOTE.—It is evident that the angel began just where he had left off in explanation of the prophecy of the eighth chapter; for he introduces no new line of prophecy, no new vision. "Consider *the* vision." In the Hebrew the definite article *the* here clearly specifies the vision previously mentioned. This is obviously the vision of the preceding chapter. Since the 2300-day period was the only part of the former vision left unexplained, the angel would naturally begin with an interpretation of that period.

What portion of the 2300 days mentioned in the vision was allotted to the Jews?

"Seventy weeks [literally, *"seventy sevens"*] are determined upon thy people and upon thy holy city." Verse 24, first clause.

NOTE.—The word translated "weeks," literally, "sevens," is used in Jewish literature to refer to periods of seven days and also to periods of seven years. Jewish and Christian scholars, generally, have concluded that the context here requires that "weeks" of years be understood. "Seventy weeks" of seven years each would be 490 years.

In post-Biblical Hebrew the word here translated "determined" had the meaning "to cut," "to cut off," "to determine," "to decree." In view of the fact that the seventy weeks of Daniel 9 are a part of the 2300 days of chapter 8, and were cut off from them and assigned particularly to the Jews, the meaning "to cut" here seems especially appropriate.

The seventy weeks, therefore, were "determined," or cut off. There are two periods of time under consideration, the first the 2300-day period, the second the seventy-week period. They both had to do with the restoration of the Jewish people and the sanctuary, for the Jews were in captivity and the sanctuary was in ruins. The two periods must then begin with the restoration, and thus at the same time. The full restoration of the Jewish laws and government pertaining to the people and their sanctuary took place in 457 B.C., as we shall see later. It is reasonable, then, to say that the seventy weeks were a part of the 2300-year period, and that they were thus "cut off" as a period pertaining to the Jewish people and their sanctuary service.

What was to be accomplished at or near the close of this seventy-week period?

"To finish the transgression, and to make an end of sins, and to make reconciliation for iniquity, and to bring in everlasting righteousness, and to seal up the vision and prophecy, and to anoint the most Holy." Verse 24, last part.

NOTE.—*"To Finish the Transgression."*—The Jews were to fill up the measure of their iniquity by rejecting and crucifying the Messiah; they would then no longer be His peculiar, chosen people. Read Matthew 21:38-43; 23:32-38; 27:25.

"To Make an End of Sins."—The best explanation of this clause is given in Hebrews 9:26: "Now once in the end of the world hath he appeared to put away sin by the sacrifice of himself"; and in Romans 8:3: "What the law could not do, in that it was weak through the flesh, God sending his own Son in the likeness of sinful flesh, and for sin, condemned sin in the flesh."

"To Bring in Everlasting Righteousness."—This must mean the righteousness of Christ—that righteousness by which He was enabled to make an atonement for sin, and which, through faith, may be imputed to the penitent believer.

"To Anoint the Most Holy."—The Hebrew words here used are regularly employed of the sanctuary, but not of persons. The anointing of the "most Holy," then, must refer to the anointing of the heavenly sanctuary, when Christ became the "minister of the sanctuary, and of the true tabernacle, which the Lord pitched, and not man." Hebrews 8:2.

THE BEGINNING OF THE TIME PERIOD

When did the angel say that the seventy weeks were to begin?

"Know therefore and understand, that from the going forth of the commandment to restore and to build Jerusalem unto the Messiah the Prince shall be seven weeks, and threescore and two weeks: the street shall be built again, and the wall, even in troublous times." Daniel 9:25.

NOTE.—Seventy weeks would be a period of 490 literal years (see note, page 216).

Sixty-nine (7 weeks and 62 weeks) of the seventy weeks were to reach "unto the Messiah the Prince." *Messiah* is Christ, "the Anointed." *Messiah* is the Hebrew word, and *Christ* the Greek word, meaning "anointed."

How was Jesus anointed?

"God anointed Jesus of Nazareth with the Holy Ghost and with power." Acts 10:38.

At what time did Jesus receive the special anointing of the Holy Spirit?

2300 DAYS (YEARS)
The Most Significant Prophetic Period in the Bible

The 2300 years was to reach, according to Daniel's prophecy, "from the going forth of the commandment to restore and to build Jerusalem," to the time for the cleansing of the sanctuary.

457 B.C.—Artaxerxes, king of Persia, commanded the restoration and rebuilding of Jerusalem. (Daniel 9:25; Ezra 6:1, 6-12.) Beginning of the 2300 years.

408 B.C.—The reconstruction and restoration of Jerusalem carried to completion during the first 49 years of Daniel's long time prophecy. The work was finished in 408 B.C. (Daniel 9:25.)

A.D. 27—Jesus, anointed with the Holy Spirit at His baptism, began to preach and to teach. (Matthew 3:16; Acts 10:38.) From 457 B.C. to Christ the "anointed," 483 years.

A.D. 31—Messiah "cut off" "in the midst of the week," A.D. 31, after three and one-half years of blessed ministry. (Daniel 9:27; Matthew 27:50, 51.) The remaining three and a half years of the seventieth week bring us to the close of the four-hundred-ninety-year period allotted to the Jewish people.

A.D. 34—Stoning of Stephen. From that time the gospel was preached to the Gentiles. (Daniel 9:24; Acts 7:54-58; 8:1.) From 457 B.C. to "the times of the Gentiles," 490 years.

A.D. 1844—End of the 2300 years. Cleansing of the heavenly sanctuary in the hour of God's judgment. (Daniel 8:14; Revelation 14:7.)

A.D. 1844—The threefold message of Revelation 14:6-12 heralded to all the world, just before Christ's second coming.

THE HOUR OF GOD'S JUDGMENT

"Jesus also being baptized, and praying, the heaven was opened, and the Holy Ghost descended in a bodily shape like a dove upon him, and a voice came from heaven, which said, Thou art my beloved Son." Luke 3:21, 22.

What prophecy did Jesus quote shortly after this as applying to Himself?

"The Spirit of the Lord is upon me, because he hath anointed me to preach the gospel to the poor." Luke 4:18. (See Mark 1:15.)

NOTE.—It is evident that the sixty-nine weeks (483 years) were to reach to the baptism of Christ, as that was the time of His anointing by the Holy Spirit. John the Baptist began his work in the fifteenth year of the reign of Tiberius (Luke 3:1-3), and this would put the anointing of Jesus in A.D. 27, at the time of His baptism.

When was a decree made to restore and build Jerusalem?

"This Ezra went up from Babylon. . . . And there went up some of the children of Israel, and of the priests, and the Levites, and the singers, and the porters, and the Nethinims, unto Jerusalem, in the seventh year of Artaxerxes the king. And he came to Jerusalem in the fifth month, which was in the seventh year of the king." Ezra. 7:6-8.

NOTE.—Three decrees were issued by Persian monarchs for the restoration of the Jews to their homeland. They are mentioned in the book of Ezra: "They builded, and finished it, according to the commandment of the God of Israel, and according to the commandment of Cyrus, and Darius, and Artaxerxes king of Persia." Ezra 6:14.

The decree of Cyrus pertained to the Temple only; the decree of Darius Hystaspes provided for the continuance of that work, hindered by Smerdis; but the decree of Artaxerxes restored the full Jewish government, making provision for the enforcement of their laws. This last decree, therefore, is the one from which we reckon the seventy weeks, as well as the 2300 days.

The letter of Artaxerxes to Ezra, conferring upon him authority to do this work, is found in Ezra 7:11-26.

The decree of Artaxerxes was issued in the seventh year of his reign, and according to ancient methods of chronology, went into effect in Jerusalem in the fall of 457 B.C. Reckoning 483 full years from the first day of 457 B.C. would bring us to the last day of A.D. 26. This is demonstrated from the fact that it requires all of the twenty-six years A.D. and all of the 457 years B.C. to make 483 years, which may be illustrated by the following diagram:

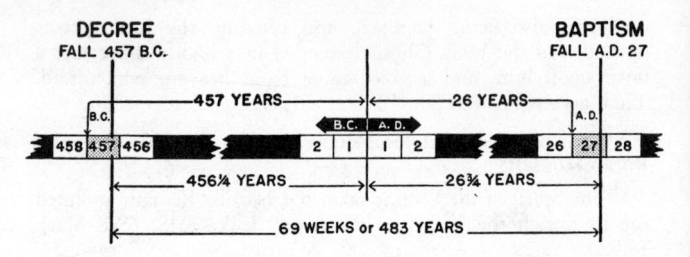

```
DECREE                                              BAPTISM
FALL 457 B.C.                                      FALL A.D. 27

         ←──── 457 YEARS ────→  ←── 26 YEARS ──→
    B.C.                      B.C. A.D.              A.D.
  458 457 456              2   1  1   2           26  27  28
         ←── 456¼ YEARS ──→    ←── 26¾ YEARS ──→
         ←──────── 69 WEEKS or 483 YEARS ────────→
```

The diagram also reveals that if the decree for the complete restoration of Jerusalem did not go into effect until after Ezra reached Jerusalem, that is, until past the middle of the year 457 B.C. (Ezra 7:8), then all the time of the first part of that year not included in the period must be added to the last day of A.D. 26, which would bring us to the latter part of A.D. 27, the time of Christ's baptism. This "seals up," or makes sure, the prophecy.

At the close of 483 years, in A.D. 27, one week, or seven years of the 490, yet remained. What was to be done in the midst of that week?

"He shall confirm the covenant with many for one week: and in the midst of the week he shall cause the sacrifice and the oblation to cease." Daniel 9:27.

NOTE.—As the sixty-nine weeks ended in the fall of A.D. 27, the middle of the seventieth week, or the three and a half years, would end in the spring of A.D. 31, when Christ was crucified, and by His death caused to cease, or brought to an end, the sacrifices and oblations of the earthly sanctuary. Three and a half years more (the last part of the seventieth week) would end in the autumn of A.D. 34. This brings us to the end of the 490 years which were "cut off" from the 2300. There still remain 1810 years, which, if added to A.D. 34, take us to A.D. 1844.

A.D. 1844 AND THE INVESTIGATIVE JUDGMENT

And what did the angel say would then take place?

"He said unto me, Unto two thousand and three hundred days; then shall the sanctuary be cleansed." Daniel 8:14.

NOTE.—In other words, the great closing work of Christ for the world, the investigative judgment, would at that time begin. The typical Day of Atonement for Israel occupied but one day in a year.

This may occupy but a correspondingly short time. Already that work has been going on for more than a century, and must soon close. Who is ready to meet its decisions?

Under what symbol is the importance of the judgment-hour message emphasized?

"I saw another *angel fly in the midst of heaven,* having the everlasting gospel to preach unto them that dwell on the earth, and to every nation, and kindred, and tongue, and people, *saying with a loud voice,* Fear God, and give glory to him; for the hour of his judgment is come." Revelation 14:6, 7.

NOTE.—The symbol of an angel is here used to represent the message of the judgment which is to be preached to every nation. Since angels preach their messages to men through human agencies, it would be understood that this symbol of an angel flying in midheaven represents a great religious movement giving to men the judgment-hour message.

In view of the investigative judgment, what are we admonished to do?

"Fear God, and give glory to him; for the hour of his judgment is come: and *worship him that made heaven and earth, and the sea, and the fountains of waters."* Verse 7.

What earnest admonition is given by the apostle Paul?

"The times of this ignorance God winked at; but now *commandeth all men every where to repent:* because he hath appointed a day, in the which he will judge the world in righteousness by that man whom he hath ordained; whereof he hath given assurance unto all men, in that he hath raised him from the dead." Acts 17:30, 31.

The Atonement in Type and Antitype

THE SANCTUARY AND TWO APARTMENTS

What did God, through Moses, command Israel to make?

"And let them make me *a sanctuary;* that I may dwell among them." Exodus 25:8.

What was offered in this sanctuary?

"In which were offered both gifts and sacrifices." Hebrews 9:9.

Besides the court, how many parts had this sanctuary?

"And the vail shall divide unto you between the *holy place* and the *most holy."* Exodus 26:33.

What was in the first apartment, or holy place?

"For there was a tabernacle made; the first, wherein was the *candlestick,* and the *table,* and the *shewbread;* which is called the sanctuary." Hebrews 9:2. "And he put the golden altar in the tent of the congregation before the vail." Exodus 40:26. (See also Exodus 30:1-6.)

What was contained in the second apartment?

"And after the second veil, the tabernacle which is called the Holiest of all; which had the *golden censer, and the ark of the covenant* overlaid round about with gold." Hebrews 9:3, 4. (See also Exodus 40:20, 21.)

By what name was the cover of the ark known?

"And thou shalt put *the mercy seat* above upon the ark; and in the ark thou shalt put the testimony that I shall give thee." Exodus 25:21.

Where was God to meet with Israel?

"And there I will meet with thee, and I will commune with

THE ATONEMENT IN TYPE AND ANTITYPE 235

thee *from above the mercy seat, from between the two cherubims which are upon the ark of the testimony.*" Verse 22.

What was in the ark, under the mercy seat?

"And he wrote in *the tables,* according to the first writing, *the ten commandments.* . . . And I turned myself and came down from the mount, and *put the tables in the ark* which I had made." Deuteronomy 10:4, 5.

When did the priest minister in the first apartment?

"Now these things having been thus prepared, the priests go in *continually* into the first tabernacle, accomplishing the services." Hebrews 9:6, R.V.

Who went into the second apartment? When and why?

"But into the second went *the high priest alone once every year, not without blood, which he offered for himself, and for the errors of the people.*" Verse 7.

THE DAILY SERVICE

What were sinners desiring pardon instructed to do?

"And if any one of the common people sin through ignorance, while he doeth somewhat against any of the commandments of the Lord . . . : then he shall bring his offering, a kid of the goats, a female without blemish, for his sin which he hath sinned. And *he shall lay his hand upon the head of the sin offering, and slay the sin offering in the place of the burnt offering.*" Leviticus 4:27-29.

NOTE.—According to this, if a man sinned in Israel, he violated one of the Ten Commandments that were in the ark under the mercy seat. These commandments are the foundation of God's government. To violate them is to commit sin, and so become subject to death. (1 John 3:4; Romans 6:23.) But there was a mercy seat reared above these holy and just commandments. In the dispensation of His mercy God grants the sinner the privilege of confessing his sins, and bringing a substitute to meet the demands of the law, and thus of obtaining mercy.

What was done with the blood of the offering?

"And the priest shall take of the blood thereof with his finger, and put it upon the horns of the altar of burnt offering, and *shall pour out all the blood thereof at the bottom of the altar."* Verse 30.

Note.—After a person discovered his sin by the law which demanded the death of the transgressor, he first brought his offering, then he confessed his sin while laying his hands on the head of the victim, thus, in figure, transferring his sin to the victim; the victim was next slain in the court, or outer part of the sanctuary, and its blood put on the horns of the altar and poured at the foot of the altar. In this way sins were pardoned, and, in the typical service, transferred to the sanctuary.

The Day of Atonement

After this accumulation of the sins of the year, what service took place yearly on the tenth day of the seventh month?

"And this shall be a statute for ever unto you: that in the seventh month, on the tenth day of the month, ye shall afflict your souls, . . . for *on that day shall the priest make an atonement for you, to cleanse you, that ye may be clean from all your sins before the Lord."* Leviticus 16:29, 30.

How was the sanctuary itself to be cleansed, and how were the sins of the people to be finally disposed of?

"And he [the high priest] shall take of the congregation of the children of Israel two kids of the goats for a sin offering. . . . And he shall take the two goats, and present them before the Lord at the door of the tabernacle of the congregation. And Aaron shall cast lots upon the two goats, one lot *for the Lord,* and the other lot *for the scapegoat."* Verses 5-8.

Note.—The Hebrew word for scapegoat is *Azazel*. See margin of verse 8. It is used as a proper name, and, according to the opinion of the most ancient Hebrews and Christians, refers to Satan, the angel who revolted and persisted in rebellion and sin.

What was done with the blood of the goat upon which the Lord's lot fell?

"Then shall he kill the goat of the sin offering, that is for the people, and bring his blood within the vail, . . . *and sprinkle it upon the mercy seat,* and before the mercy seat." Verse 15.

Why was it necessary to make this atonement?

"And he shall make an atonement for the holy place, *because*

THE ATONEMENT IN TYPE AND ANTITYPE

of the uncleanness of the children of Israel, and because of their transgressions in all their sins: and so shall he do for the tabernacle of the congregation, that remaineth among them in the midst of their uncleanness." Verse 16.

Note.—Sins were transferred to the sanctuary during the year by the blood and flesh of the sin offerings made daily at the door of the tabernacle. Here they remained until the Day of Atonement, when the high priest went into the most holy place with the blood of the goat on which the Lord's lot fell; and, bearing the accumulated sins of the year and coming before the mercy seat, he there, in type, atoned for them, and so cleansed the sanctuary.

After having made atonement for the people in the most holy place, what did the high priest next do?

"And when he hath made an end of reconciling the holy place, and the tabernacle of the congregation, and the altar, he shall bring the live goat: and Aaron shall lay both his hands upon the head of the live goat, and confess over him all the iniquities of the children of Israel, and all their transgressions in all their sins, putting them upon the head of the goat, and shall send him away by the hand of a fit man into the wilderness. And the goat shall bear upon him all their iniquities unto a land not inhabited: and he shall let go the goat in the wilderness." Verses 20-22.

Note.—The offering of the Lord's goat cleansed the sanctuary. By this offering the sins of the people, transferred there during the year, were, in type, atoned for; but they were not by this offering finally disposed of, or destroyed. The scapegoat, symbolizing Satan, the great tempter and originator of sin, was brought to the sanctuary, *and upon his head* were placed these already atoned-for sins. The sending away of the goat into the wilderness separated the sins forever from the sanctuary. (On the scapegoat see M'Clintock and Strong, *Cyclopaedia of Biblical, Theological, and Ecclesiastical Literature*, vol. 9, pp. 397, 398, art. "Scapegoat"; *The Encyclopedic Dictionary*, vol. 1, p. 397; *The New Schaff-Herzog Encyclopedia of Religious Knowledge*, vol. 1, p. 389, art. "Azazel.")

A Type of the Heavenly Sanctuary

What was this earthly sanctuary and its round of service?

"Which was *a figure* for the time then present." Hebrews 9:9.

Of what sanctuary, or tabernacle, is Christ the minister?

"A minister of the sanctuary, and of the true tabernacle, *which the Lord pitched, and not man.*" Hebrews 8:2.

Of what was the blood of all the sacrifices of the former dispensation only a type?

"Neither by the blood of goats and calves, but *by his own blood* he entered in once into the holy place, having obtained eternal redemption for us." Hebrews 9:12. (See Ephesians 5:2.)

NOTE.—Through the sacrifices and offerings brought to the altar of the earthly sanctuary, the penitent believer was to lay hold, by faith, of the merits of Christ, the Saviour to come.

At Christ's death, what miracle signified that the priestly services of the earthly sanctuary were finished?

"Jesus, when he had cried again with a loud voice, yielded up the ghost. And, behold, *the veil of the temple was rent in twain from the top to the bottom.*" Matthew 27:50, 51.

NOTE.—Type had met antitype; the shadow had reached the substance. Christ, the great sacrifice, had been slain, and was now to enter upon His work as our great High Priest in the sanctuary in heaven. The priestly work in the earthly sanctuary was typical of the work of Christ in the heavenly sanctuary.

How are the heavenly and earthly sanctuaries related?

"Who serve unto the *example* and *shadow* of heavenly things, as Moses was admonished of God when he was about to make the tabernacle: for, See, saith he, that thou make all things according to the *pattern* shewed to thee in the mount." Hebrews 8:5.

By what comparison is it shown that the heavenly sanctuary will be cleansed?

"It was therefore necessary that the patterns of things in the heavens should be purified with these; *but the heavenly things themselves with better sacrifices than these.*" Hebrews 9:23.

When Christ has finished His priestly mediatorial work in the heavenly sanctuary, what decree will go forth?

"He that is unjust, let him be unjust still: and he which is filthy, let him be filthy still: and he that is righteous, let him be righteous still: and he that is holy, let him be holy still." Revelation 22:11.

NOTE.—This declaration is made immediately before the coming of Christ in the clouds of heaven.

According to Daniel's vision of the judgment, what is to be given to Christ while still before the Father?

"I saw . . . , and, behold, one like the Son of man came . . . to the Ancient of days, and they brought him near before him. And there was given him *dominion, and glory, and a kingdom,* that all people, nations, and languages, should serve him." Daniel 7:13, 14.

What will occur when the Lord descends from heaven?

"For the Lord himself shall descend from heaven with a shout, with the voice of the archangel, and with the trump of God: and *the dead in Christ shall rise first: then we which are alive and remain shall be caught up together with them in the clouds, to meet the Lord in the air:* and so shall we ever be with the Lord." 1 Thessalonians 4:16, 17.

What statement immediately following the announcement mentioned in Revelation 22:11, indicates that a judgment work had been in progress before Christ comes?

"And, behold, I come quickly; and *my reward is with me, to give every man according as his work shall be."* Revelation 22:12.

NOTE.—The typical sanctuary service is fully met in the work of Christ. As the atonement day of the former dispensation was really a day of judgment, so the atonement work of Christ will include the investigation of the cases of His people prior to His coming the second time to receive them unto Himself.

Is there a specified time for the cleansing of the heavenly sanctuary?

"And he said unto me, *Unto two thousand and three hundred days; then shall the sanctuary be cleansed."* Daniel 8:14.

NOTE.—The prophetic period of 2300 days (years) extends to A.D. 1844, whereas the divinely appointed services of the earthly sanctuary ceased at the cross (Daniel 9:27; Matthew 27:50, 51), and the sanctuary itself was destroyed in A.D. 70, when Titus captured Jerusalem. For explanation of the period here mentioned see the preceding reading.

The Judgment

What assurance have we that there will be a judgment?

"God . . . hath appointed a day, in the which he will judge the world." Acts 17:30, 31.

Was the judgment still future in Paul's day?

"As he reasoned of righteousness, temperance, and *judgment to come,* Felix trembled." Acts 24:25.

How many must meet the test of the judgment?

"I said in mine heart, God shall judge *the righteous and the wicked.*" Ecclesiastes 3:17. "*For we must all appear before the judgment seat of Christ;* that every one may receive the things done in his body, according to that he hath done, whether it be good or bad." 2 Corinthians 5:10.

What reason did Solomon give for urging all to fear God and keep His commandments?

"*For God shall bring every work into judgment,* with every secret thing, whether it be good, or whether it be evil." Ecclesiastes 12:14.

What view of the judgment scene was given Daniel?

"I beheld till the thrones were cast down [literally, "placed"], and the Ancient of days did sit, whose garment was white as snow, and the hair of his head like the pure wool: his throne was like the fiery flame, and his wheels as burning fire. A fiery stream issued and came forth from before him: thousand thousands ministered unto him, and ten thousand times ten thousand stood before him: the judgment was set, and the books were opened." Daniel 7:9, 10.

Out of what will all be judged?

"And *the books were opened:* and another book was opened, which is the book of life: and *the dead were judged out of those things which were written in the books,* according to their works." Revelation 20:12.

THE JUDGMENT

For whom has a book of remembrance been written?

"Then they that feared the Lord spake often one to another: and the Lord hearkened, and heard it, and a book of remembrance was written before him *for them that feared the Lord, and that thought upon his name.*" Malachi 3:16. (See Revelation 20:12.)

THE JUDGMENT SCENE

Who opens the judgment and presides over it?

"I beheld till the thrones were cast down [literally, "placed"], and *the Ancient of days did sit.*" Daniel 7:9.

Who minister to God and assist in the judgment?

"Thousand thousands [of angels] ministered unto him, and ten thousand times ten thousand stood before him." Verse 10. (See Revelation 5:11.)

Who is brought before the Father at this time?

"I saw in the night visions, and, behold, *one like the Son of man* came with the clouds of heaven, and came to the Ancient of days, and they brought him near before him." Verse 13.

What does Christ as the advocate of His people confess before the Father and His angels?

"He that overcometh, the same shall be clothed in white raiment; and I will not blot out his name out of the book of life, but *I will confess his name before my Father, and before his angels.*" Revelation 3:5. (See Matthew 10:32, 33; Mark 8:38.)

NOTE.—During this judgment scene both the righteous and the wicked dead are still in their graves. The record of each one's life, however, is in the books of heaven, and by that record the characters and deeds of all are well known. Christ is there to appear in behalf of those who have chosen Him as their advocate. (1 John 2:1.) He presents His blood as He appeals for their sins to be blotted from the books of record. As the place of judgment is in heaven, where God's throne is, and as Christ is present in person, it follows that the work of judgment is also in heaven. All are judged by the record of their lives, and thus answer for the deeds done in the body. This work will not only decide forever the cases of the dead but also close the probation of all who are living, after which Christ will come to take to Himself those who have been found loyal to Him.

After the subjects of the kingdom have been determined by the investigative judgment, what is given to Christ?

"And there was given him *dominion,* and *glory,* and *a kingdom,* that all people, nations, and languages, should serve him." Daniel 7:14.

Christ's Second Coming

When He comes the second time, what title will He bear?

"And he hath on his vesture and on his thigh a name written, *King of kings,* and *Lord of lords.*" Revelation 19:16.

What will He then do for each one?

"For the Son of man shall come in the glory of his Father with his angels; and *then he shall reward every man according to his works.*" Matthew 16:27. (See Revelation 22:12.)

Where will Christ then take His people?

"In my Father's house are many mansions: if it were not so, I would have told you. I go to prepare a place for you. And if I go and prepare a place for you, *I will come again, and receive you unto myself; that where I am, there ye may be also."* John 14:2, 3.

How many of the dead will be raised?

"For the hour is coming, in the which *all that are in the graves* shall hear his voice, and shall come forth; they that have done good, unto the resurrection of life; and they that have done evil, unto the resurrection of damnation." John 5:28, 29. (See Acts 24:15.)

What time intervenes between the two resurrections?

"And I saw the souls of them that were beheaded for the witness of Jesus, and for the word of God, and which had not worshipped the beast, neither his image, neither had received his mark upon their foreheads, or in their hands; and they lived and reigned with Christ a thousand years. *But the rest of the dead lived not again until the thousand years were finished."* Revelation 20:4, 5.

Note.—The Greek words translated "lived and reigned" may also properly be rendered, "came to life and reigned." In view of the statement of verse 5 that "the *rest* of the dead lived not again until the thousand years were finished" the translation "came to life and reigned" appears preferable.

The Saints in Judgment

What work did Daniel see finally assigned to the saints?

"I beheld, and the same horn made war with the saints, and prevailed against them; until the Ancient of days came, and *judgment was given to the saints of the most High;* and the time came that the saints possessed the kingdom." Daniel 7: 21, 22.

How long will the saints engage in this work of judgment?

"And I saw thrones, and they sat upon them, and *judgment was given unto them: . . . and they lived and reigned with Christ a thousand years."* Revelation 20:4.

Who will thus be judged by the saints?

"Do ye not know that *the saints shall judge the world?* and if the world shall be judged by you, are ye unworthy to judge the smallest matters? Know ye not that *we shall judge angels?* how much more things that pertain to this life?" 1 Corinthians 6:2, 3.

Christ Executes Judgment

How will the decisions of the judgment be executed?

"And out of his [Christ's] mouth goeth a sharp sword, that with it he should smite the nations: and he shall rule them with a rod of iron: and he treadeth the winepress of the fierceness and wrath of Almighty God." Revelation 19:15.

Why is the *execution* of the judgment given to Christ?

"For as the Father hath life in himself; so hath he given to the Son to have life in himself; and hath given him authority to execute judgment also, *because he is the Son of man."* John 5: 26, 27.

How was the opening of the judgment to be made known to the world?

"And I saw another angel fly in the midst of heaven, having the everlasting gospel to preach unto them that dwell on the earth, and to every nation, and kindred, and tongue, and people, saying with a loud voice, *Fear God, and give glory to him; for the hour of his judgment is come.*" Revelation 14:6, 7.

NOTE.—There are three phases of the judgment mentioned in the Scriptures: the investigative judgment, preceding the Second Advent; the judgment of the lost world and wicked angels by Christ and the saints during the one thousand years following the Second Advent; and the executive judgment, or punishment of the wicked at the close of this period. The investigative judgment takes place in heaven before Christ comes, in order to ascertain who are worthy to be raised in the first resurrection, at His coming, and who among the living are to be changed in the twinkling of an eye, at the sound of the last trump. It is necessary for this to take place before the Second Advent, as there will be no time for such a work between the coming of Christ and the raising of the righteous dead. The executive judgment on the wicked occurs after their cases have been examined by the saints during the thousand years. (Revelation 20:4, 5; 1 Corinthians 6:1-3.) The investigative judgment is that which is announced to the world by the angel's message of Revelation 14:6, 7.

REVIVE our drooping faith,
  Our doubts and fears remove,
And kindle in our breasts the flame
  Of never-dying love.

'Tis Thine to cleanse the heart,
  To sanctify the soul,
To pour fresh life in every part,
  And new create the whole.

Come, Holy Spirit, come,
  Our minds from bondage free;
Then shall we know, and praise, and love,
  The Father, Son, and Thee.

—JOSEPH HART

The Judgment-Hour Message

NATURE AND TIME OF THE MESSAGE

What prophetic view of the judgment was given Daniel?

"I beheld till the thrones were cast down [literally, "placed"], and the Ancient of days did sit. . . . Thousand thousands ministered unto him, and ten thousand times ten thousand stood before him: the judgment was set, and the books were opened." Daniel 7:9, 10.

What assurance has God given of the judgment?

"Because *he hath appointed a day, in the which he will judge the world* in righteousness by that man whom he hath ordained; whereof he hath given assurance unto all men, *in that he hath raised him from the dead.*" Acts 17:31.

What message announces that the judgment hour has come?

"And I saw another angel fly in the midst of heaven, having the everlasting gospel to preach unto them that dwell on the earth, and to every nation, and kindred, and tongue, and people, saying with a loud voice, Fear God, and give glory to him; for *the hour of his judgment is come:* and worship him that made heaven, and earth, and the sea, and the fountains of waters." Revelation 14:6, 7.

In view of the judgment hour, what is proclaimed anew?

"The everlasting gospel." Verse 6, first part.

How extensively is this message to be proclaimed?

"To *every nation,* and *kindred,* and *tongue,* and *people.*" Verse 6, last part.

What is the whole world called upon to do?

"Fear God, and give glory to him." Verse 7.

What special reason is given for this?

"For *the hour of his judgment is come.*" Same verse.

Whom are all called upon to worship?

COPYRIGHT, 1949, BY REVIEW AND HERALD

KREIGH COLLINS, ARTIST

HEAVEN'S LAST APPEAL

"Fear God, and give glory to him; for the hour of his judgment is come: and worship him that made heaven, and earth." Revelation 14

"Him that made heaven, and earth." Same verse.

Note.—There is only one gospel (Romans 1:16, 17; Galatians 1:8), first announced in Eden (Genesis 3:15), preached to Abraham (Galatians 3:8) and to the children of Israel (Hebrews 4:1, 2), and proclaimed anew in every generation. In its development the gospel meets the needs of every crisis in the world's history. John the Baptist in his preaching announced the kingdom of heaven at hand (Matthew 3:1, 2), and prepared the way for the first advent. (John 1:22, 23.) So when the time of the judgment comes, and Christ's Second Advent is near, a worldwide announcement of these events is to be made in the preaching of the everlasting gospel adapted to meet the need of the hour.

What prophetic period extends to the time of the cleansing of the sanctuary, or the investigative judgment?

"And he said unto me, Unto *two thousand and three hundred days;* then shall the sanctuary be cleansed." Daniel 8:14.

When did this long period expire?

In A.D. 1844. See reading on page 232.

Note.—The whole period extends to the time of the judgment, just preceding the Second Advent, and at its expiration a special gospel message is sent to all the world, proclaiming the judgment hour at hand and calling upon all to worship the Creator. The facts of history answer to this interpretation of the prophecy, for at this very time (1844) just such a message was being proclaimed in various parts of the world. This was the beginning of the great Second Advent message which is now being proclaimed throughout the world.

CALL TO WORSHIP THE CREATOR

How is the true God distinguished from all false gods?

"Thus shall ye say unto them, *The gods that have not made the heavens and the earth,* even they shall perish from the earth. . . . *He* [*the true God*] *hath made the earth by his power, he hath established the world by his wisdom, and hath stretched out the heavens by his discretion*." Jeremiah 10:11, 12.

For what reason is worship justly due to God?

"For the Lord is a great God, and a great King above all gods. . . . *The sea is his, and he made it: and his hands formed the dry land.* O come, let us worship and bow down: let us kneel before the Lord our *maker*." Psalm 95:3-6.

Why do the inhabitants of heaven worship God?

"The four and twenty elders fall down before him, . . . saying, Thou art worthy, O Lord, to receive glory and honour and power: *for thou hast created all things,* and for thy pleasure they are and were created." Revelation 4:10, 11.

What memorial of His creative power did God establish?

"Remember *the sabbath day,* to keep it holy. . . . *For in six days the Lord made heaven and earth, the sea, and all that in them is,* and rested the seventh day: wherefore the Lord blessed the sabbath day, and hallowed it." Exodus 20:8-11.

What place has the Sabbath in the work of salvation?

"Moreover also I gave them my sabbaths, to be *a sign* between me and them, that they might know that I am the Lord that *sanctify* them." Ezekiel 20:12.

THE STANDARD FOR ALL

How many are concerned in the judgment?

"For we must *all* appear before the judgment seat of Christ; that *every one* may receive the things done in his body, *according to that he hath done, whether it be good or bad.*" 2 Corinthians 5:10.

What will be the standard in the judgment?

"For whosoever shall keep the whole law, and yet offend in one point, he is guilty of all. For he that said, Do not commit adultery, said also, Do not kill. Now if thou commit no adultery, yet if thou kill, thou art become a transgressor of the law. So speak ye, and so do, as they that shall be judged *by the law of liberty.*" James 2:10-12.

In view of the judgment, what exhortation is given?

"Let us hear the conclusion of the whole matter: *Fear God, and keep his commandments:* for this is the whole duty of man. For God shall bring every work into judgment, with every secret thing, whether it be good, or whether it be evil." Ecclesiastes 12:13, 14.

The Fall of Modern Babylon

FOLLOWING the judgment-hour message of Revelation 14:6, 7, what reason is given for Babylon's fall?

"And there followed another angel, saying, *Babylon is fallen, is fallen,* that great city, because *she made all nations drink of the wine of the wrath of her fornication.*" Revelation 14:8.

THE FALL OF ANCIENT BABYLON

What prophetic warning was given of the fall of ancient Babylon?

"Flee out of the midst of Babylon, and deliver every man his soul: be not cut off in her iniquity; for this is the time of the Lord's vengeance; he will render unto her a recompence." Jeremiah 51:6.

At the time of the fall of the Babylonian Empire to the Medes and Persians, how did Belshazzar and his court defy the true God?

"They brought the golden vessels that were taken out of the temple of the house of God which was at Jerusalem; and the king, and his princes, his wives, and his concubines, drank in them. They drank wine, and praised the gods of gold, and of silver, of brass, of iron, of wood, and of stone." Daniel 5:3, 4.

NOTE.—The gospel of the kingdom was preached in Babylon through Daniel, and Nebuchadnezzar was brought to acknowledge and to worship the true God. But after Nebuchadnezzar's death his successors failed to profit by his experience. The climax was reached when Belshazzar used the sacred vessels from the house of God, dedicated to His worship, in which to drink the Babylonian wine of idolatrous worship. Then came the handwriting on the wall, the fall of ancient Babylon, and the death of Belshazzar. See Daniel 5.

Aside from rejecting God's message, what did ancient Babylon do to the nations?

"Babylon hath been a golden cup in the Lord's hand, that *made all the earth drunken:* the nations have drunken of her *wine;* therefore the nations are mad." Jeremiah 51:7.

NOTE.—Through the centuries the astrological beliefs of the Chaldeans of Babylon eventually "penetrated as far as India, China, and Indo-China, where divination by means of the stars is still practised. ... In the opposite direction they spread to Syria, to Egypt, and over the whole Roman world."—FRANZ CUMONT, *Astrology and Religion Among the Greeks and Romans* (Putnam's, 1912 ed.), p. 74.

MODERN BABYLON

In the visions of John what interpretation is given of the impure woman with a golden cup in her hand, seated on a seven-headed beast?

"And the woman which thou sawest is *that great city, which reigneth over the kings of the earth*." Revelation 17:18. (See verses 3, 4, 9.)

NOTE.—The great city which reigned over the kings of the earth in John's time was Rome; and that seven-hilled city has given its name to the power which succeeded to its dominion—the organization which is represented by the woman, the Church of Rome, ruled by the papacy. (See page 210.) In the closing days of earth's history "Babylon the great" includes all apostate forms of Christianity.

In this same prophecy how is this religio-political power, the Roman Church, or the papacy, designated as the counterpart of ancient Babylon?

"And upon her forehead was a name written, MYSTERY, BABYLON THE GREAT." Verse 5.

NOTE.—The parallels between the Roman Church and ancient Babylon are striking, as we view the pagan Babylonian state religion with its wealthy and politically powerful hierarchy, its elaborate temple ritual, its priestly monopoly of learning, its liturgy performed in an ancient language unknown to the common people, its processions of divine images, its great spring festival in which mourning is followed by rejoicing, its ubiquitous virgin mother goddess who intercedes for her worshipers. But there is even more than a parallel; there is a genuine line of inheritance, from Babylon through the Roman Empire to the Roman Church, of many religious elements.

"The mighty Catholic Church was little more than the Roman Empire baptised."—A. C. FLICK, *The Rise of the Mediaeval Church* (Putnam's 1909 ed.), p. 148. Cardinal Newman lists many examples of things admittedly "of pagan origin" which that church introduced "in order to recommend the new religion to the heathen"; "the use of temples, and these dedicated to particular saints, and ornamented on occasions with branches of trees; incense, lamps, and candles; votive offerings on recovery from illness; holy water; asylums; holydays and seasons, use of calendars, processions, blessings on the fields; sacerdotal vestments, the tonsure, the ring in marriage, turning to the East, images at a later date, perhaps the ecclesiastical chant, and the Kyrie Eleison."—J. H. NEWMAN, *An Essay on the Development of Christian Doctrine* (1920 ed.), p. 373. (See *Bible Readings*, page 211.)

The Roman Empire was heir not only to the territories but also to the religions of Greece and the East. Later Roman paganism was orientalized through the adoption of eastern deities, all influenced by astrology and many of them transformed into sun gods, such as, for example, Mithra, who combined Persian and Chaldean elements. (See Franz Cumont, *Astrology and Religion Among the Greeks and Romans* [1912 ed.], pp. 89-91.) "The solar theology of the 'Chaldaeans' [that is, of "the Babylonian priests of the Hellenistic age" and after] had a decisive effect" upon the "final form reached by the religion of the pagan Semites, and, following them, by that of the Romans when Aurelian, the conqueror of Palmyra, had raised *Sol invictus* [the invincible Sun] to the rank of supreme divinity in the Empire."—*The Cambridge Ancient History*, vol. 11, pp. 643, 646, 647. Used by permission of Cambridge University Press. From Palmyra he transferred to the new sanctuary the images of Helios (the sun) and *Bel, the ancient patron god of Babylon*. (See Cumont, *The Oriental Religions in Roman Paganism* [1911], pp. 114, 115, 124.)

Babylon also contributed "the great and ubiquitous cult" of the virgin mother-goddess (actually more important than the highest gods); Babylonian Ishtar is identified with Astarte, Ashtoreth, Persephone, Artemis (Diana) of Ephesus, Venus, perhaps Isis, and others. (See S. H. Langdon, *Semitic Mythology* [1931 ed.], pp. 12, 13, 19, 20, 24, 32, 34, 108, 344, 368, 369.) This multiform goddess was called virgin mother (*ibid.*, pp. 16, 18, 19), merciful mother (p. 111), queen of heaven (p. 25), my lady—compare "Madonna"—or our lady (p. 341), and was often depicted by mother-and-infant images (pp. 34, 111), or as a *mater dolorosa* interceding with a wrathful god in behalf of her worshiper (pp. 151, 188; see also *Encyclopaedia Britannica* [1945 ed.], vol. 2, p. 858, art. "Babylonian and Assyrian Religion"). Today many local virgin cults are evidently continuations of those of ancient goddesses. (See Gordon J. Laing, *Survivals of Roman Religion* [1931 ed.], pp. 92-95, 123, 124, 129-131, 238-241.)

The influence of astrological sun worship can be seen in the idea —if not the mode—of purgatory (Cumont, *Astrology and Religion*, pp. 190, 191), the adoption of December 25, the birthday of the Invincible Sun, and the Mithraic Sunday, also orientation of church buildings and praying toward the east (*ibid.,* pp. 161-163; Laing, *op. cit.,* pp. 148-153, 190-193), and even the nimbus which crowns pictured saints (Laing, *op. cit.,* p. 246). (Laing offers other interesting examples of pagan survivals in Catholicism, especially from Isis worship—holy water, votive offerings, elevation of sacred objects, the priest's bell, the decking of images, and possibly tonsure—also processions, festivals, prayers for the dead, saint cults, relics, and so forth.)

What actions point to this identification?

"With whom the kings of the earth have committed fornication, and the inhabitants of the earth have been made drunk with the wine of her fornication." Verse 2. (See verse 4.)

Note.—Ancient Babylonian religion had immoral features, but modern Babylon commits spiritual fornication, polluting the church with false doctrines and pagan practices, and having illicit connection with the secular powers to enforce her teachings; and like her ancient namesake, Roman Babylon has made many nations drink impure wine from her cup.

The Cup of Christ and the Cup of Babylon

What cup does Jesus offer in the Lord's Supper?

"This cup is the new covenant in my blood." Luke 22:20, R.V.

What is plainly set forth as the essential teaching of the new covenant?

"For this is the covenant that I will make with the house of Israel after those days, saith the Lord; *I will put my laws into their mind, and write them in their hearts:* and I will be to them a God, and they shall be to me a people." Hebrews 8:10.

When Christ thus ministers the law in the heart, what is the result?

"For *the law of the Spirit of life in Christ Jesus* hath made me free from the law of sin and death. For what the law could not do, in that it was weak through the flesh, God sending his own Son in the likeness of sinful flesh, and for sin, condemned sin in the flesh: that the righteousness of the law might be fulfilled in us, who walk not after the flesh, but after the Spirit." Romans 8:2-4.

In what other statement is this same truth expressed?

"It is the spirit that quickeneth; the flesh profiteth nothing: *the words that I speak unto you, they are spirit,* and they are life." John 6:63.

What kind of teaching have men substituted for the words which are spirit and life?

"Howbeit in vain do they worship me, *teaching for doctrines the commandments of men.* . . . And he said unto them, Full well ye reject the commandment of God, that ye may keep your own *tradition.*" Mark 7:7-9.

NOTE.—There are two cups, the cup of the Lord and the cup of Babylon. The Lord's cup contains the living truth "as the truth is in Jesus"; the cup of Babylon, her false doctrines—her human tradition substituted for the living word and law of God, and her unlawful union with the secular power, upon which she depends to enforce her teachings rather than upon the power of God. Thus, while maintaining a form of godliness, she denies the power thereof. (2 Timothy 3:1-5.)

The Roman Church says of the Bible and tradition, "Though these two divine streams are in themselves, on account of their divine origin, of equal sacredness, and are both full of revealed truths, still, of the two, TRADITION is to us more clear and safe."—JOSEPH FAA DI BRUNO, *Catholic Belief* (1884 ed.), p. 45.

"2. Scripture and Tradition of Equal Value.—Since the truths contained in Scripture and those handed down by Tradition both come from God, Scripture and Tradition are of equal value as sources of faith. Both deserve the same reverence and respect. Each alone is sufficient to establish a truth of our holy faith."—JOHN LAUX, *A Course in Religion for Catholic High Schools and Academies* (1936 ed.), vol. 1, p. 50. Imprimatur, Bishop Francis W. Howard, March 25, 1932. Quoted with permission of Benziger Brothers, Inc., proprietors of the copyright.

"4. The Catholic Rule of Faith.—Scripture and Tradition are called the *remote rule of faith,* because the Catholic does not base his faith *directly* on these sources. The *proximate rule of faith* is for him the One, Holy, Catholic, and Apostolic Church, which alone has received from God the authority to interpret infallibly the doctrines He has revealed, whether these be contained in Scripture or in Tradition."—*Ibid.,* p. 51.

The substitution of the law of the church for the law of God, thus fulfilling Daniel 7:25, testifies to the complete subordination of the word of God to the authority of the church. The worldwide teaching of these doctrines in place of the pure gospel has led the world astray, and has made all nations drink of the impure wine from her cup. The Reformation of the sixteenth century, denying the supremacy of the church's authority and tradition over the Bible, was an effort to return to the pure truth of God's word.

How do Babylon's daughters show their mother's characteristics?

"And upon her forehead was a name written, MYSTERY, BABYLON THE GREAT, THE *MOTHER OF HARLOTS* AND ABOMINATIONS OF THE EARTH." Revelation 17:5.

NOTE.—The authoritative Creed of Pope Pius IV says in Article 10: "I acknowledge the Holy Catholic Apostolic Church for the mother and mistress of all churches." When professed Protestant churches repudiate the fundamental principle of Protestantism by accepting human speculation, tradition, or political power in place of the authority and power of God's word, they may be regarded as daughters of Babylon. Their fall is then included in hers, and calls for a proclamation of the fall of modern Babylon.

Many representatives of modernist Protestantism have, in one way or another, rejected fundamental Bible doctrines such as the fall of man, the Bible doctrine of sin, the inspiration of the Scriptures, the sufficiency of Scripture as a rule of faith and practice; the deity of Christ, His virgin birth, His resurrection, His vicarious expiatory and propitiatory atonement, His second coming to establish the kingdom of God, salvation by grace through faith in Christ, regeneration by the power of the Holy Spirit, the efficacy of prayer in the name of Jesus, the ministration of angels, miracles as the direct interposition of God's power. There are many leaders of modern Protestantism who have not adopted the creed of the Roman Church, and have not joined that body, yet who belong to the same class in rejecting God's word for human authority. There is apostasy in both cases, and both classes must be included in Babylon and be involved, in the final analysis, in her fall—for in the largest sense Babylon embraces all false religion, all apostasy.

To what extent is the apostasy, or fall, of modern Babylon, the mother, and of her daughters, to be carried?

"And after these things I saw another angel come down from heaven, having great power; and the earth was lightened with his glory. And he cried mightily with a strong voice, saying, Babylon the great is fallen, is fallen, and *is become the habita-*

tion of devils, and the hold of every foul spirit, and a cage of every unclean and hateful bird. For all nations have drunk of the wine of the wrath of her fornication, and the kings of the earth have committed fornication with her, and the merchants of the earth are waxed rich through the abundance of her delicacies." Revelation 18:1-3.

God's Call to Come Out

What is to be the final fate of modern Babylon?

"And *a mighty angel took up a stone like a great millstone, and cast it into the sea, saying, Thus with violence shall that great city Babylon be thrown down, and shall be found no more at all.* . . . And in her was found the blood of prophets, and of saints, and of all that were slain upon the earth." Verses 21-24.

What final call to come out of Babylon is to go forth?

"And I heard another voice from heaven, saying, *Come out of her, my people, that ye be not partakers of her sins, and that ye receive not of her plagues.* For her sins have reached unto heaven, and God hath remembered her iniquities." Verses 4, 5.

What is the song of those who come out of Babylon?

"Alleluia: for the Lord God omnipotent reigneth. Let us be glad and rejoice, and give honour to him." Revelation 19:6, 7.

Spirit of life, and light, and love,
  Thy heavenly influence give;
Quicken our souls, our guilt remove,
  That we in Christ may live.

His love within us shed abroad,
  Life's ever-springing well;
Till God in us, and we in God,
  In love eternal dwell.

—Thomas Haweis

TIME RUNNING OUT

"We have also a more sure word of prophecy; whereunto ye do well that ye take heed." 2 Peter 1:

The Closing Gospel Message

A Warning Against False Worship

What indicates that the messages of the judgment hour and the fall of Babylon are two parts of a threefold message?

"And *the third angel followed them.*" Revelation 14:9, first clause.

What apostasy from the worship of God is named here?

"If any man *worship the beast and his image, and receive his mark* in his forehead, or in his hand." Same verse, last part.

What is to be the fate of those who, instead of worshiping God, engage in this false worship?

"*The same shall drink of the wine of the wrath of God, which is poured out without mixture into the cup of his indignation;* and he shall be tormented with fire and brimstone in the presence of the holy angels, and in the presence of the Lamb: and the smoke of their torment ascendeth up for ever and ever: and they have no rest day nor night, who worship the beast and his image, and whosoever receiveth the mark of his name." Verses 10, 11. (See Isaiah 33:13; 34:1-10; Hebrews 12:29.)

How are those described who heed this warning?

"Here is the patience of the saints: here are they that keep the commandments of God, and the faith of Jesus." Verse 12.

Who Is the Beast Power?

What description is given of the beast against whose worship this closing warning message is given?

"And I stood upon the sand of the sea, and saw a beast rise up out of the sea, having seven heads and ten horns, and upon his horns ten crowns, and upon his heads the name of blasphemy. And the beast which I saw was like unto a leopard, and his feet were as the feet of a bear, and his mouth as the mouth of a lion: and the dragon gave him his power, and his seat, and great authority." Revelation 13:1, 2.

Note.—In this composite beast from the sea are combined the symbols of the seventh chapter of Daniel, representing the Roman, Greco-Macedonian, Medo-Persian, and Babylonian empires. Its blasphemous words, its persecution of the saints, and its allotted time (verses 5-7) show that this beast, under one of its seven-headed manifestations, is identical with the little horn of the vision of Daniel 7, modern Babylon, the papacy. (See reading on "The Kingdom and Work of Antichrist," page 211.) The worship of the beast is the rendering of that homage to the papacy which is due to God alone. The system of religion enforced by the papacy contains the paganism of Babylon, Persia, Greece, and Rome, indicated by the beast's composite character (verse 2), disguised under the forms and names of Christianity. The Roman Pontifex Maximus, for instance, was continued in the pope, who is the head of the Roman priesthood. But this scripture in Revelation shows that the pope's power and his seat and his great authority do not come from Christ.

What challenge is made by those who worship the beast?

"And they worshipped the dragon which gave power unto the beast: and they worshipped the beast, saying, *Who is like unto the beast? who is able to make war with him?*" Verse 4.

Whose sovereignty is thus challenged?

"Forasmuch as *there is none like unto thee, O Lord;* thou art great, and thy name is great in might." Jeremiah 10:6. (See Psalms 71:19; 86:8; 89:6, 8.)

What specifications of "the man of sin" are thus met?

"Let no man deceive you by any means: for that day shall not come, except there come a falling away first, and that man of sin be revealed, the son of perdition; *who opposeth and exalteth himself above all that is called God, or that is worshipped; so that he as God sitteth in the temple of God, shewing himself that he is God.*" 2 Thessalonians 2:3, 4. (See pages 211-213.)

What did Babylon give the nations to drink?

"She made all nations drink of *the wine of the wrath of her fornication.*" Revelation 14:8, last part. (See pages 250-254.)

What are those to drink who accept the teachings of Babylon, and thus render homage to the beast?

"The same shall drink of *the wine of the wrath of God,*

which is poured out without mixture into the cup of his indignation." Verse 10, first part.

Note.—The cup of the Lord, which contains the new covenant in the blood of Christ, and the cup of the wine of the wrath of Babylon are both offered to the world. To drink of the former, that is, to accept the true gospel, is to receive everlasting life; but to drink of the wine of Babylon, that is, to accept the false gospel taught by the papacy, will result in drinking of the wine of the wrath of God from the cup of His indignation. The true gospel means everlasting life; the false gospel, everlasting death.

False Worship Enforced

Under what threatened penalty is the worship of the image of the beast enforced?

"And he had power to give life unto the image of the beast, that the image of the beast should both speak, and *cause [decree] that as many as would not worship the image of the beast should be killed.*" Revelation 13:15.

Note.—For an explanation of the image of the beast, see reading on "Making an Image to the Beast," page 271.

What universal boycott is to be employed in an attempt to compel all to receive the mark of the beast?

"And he causeth all, both small and great, rich and poor, free and bond, to receive a mark in their right hand, or in their foreheads: and *that no man might buy or sell, save he that had the mark, or the name of the beast, or the number of his name.*" Verses 16, 17.

Note.—Regarding the mark of the beast see reading on "The Seal of God and the Mark of Apostasy," page 442.

Satan, or God?

Who is the real power operating through the beast?

"The *dragon* gave him his power, and his seat, and great authority." Verse 2, last part.

Who is this dragon?

"And the great dragon was cast out, that old serpent, called the *Devil*, and *Satan*, which deceiveth the whole world." Revelation 12:9.

How did the devil seek to induce Jesus to worship him?

"And the devil, taking him up into an high mountain, shewed unto him all the kingdoms of the world in a moment of time. And the devil said unto him, *All this power will I give thee,* and the glory of them: for that is delivered unto me; and to whomsoever I will I give it. *If thou therefore wilt worship me, all shall be thine."* Luke 4:5-7.

How did Jesus show His loyalty to God?

"And Jesus answered and said unto him, *Get thee behind me, Satan: for it is written, Thou shalt worship the Lord thy God, and him only shalt thou serve."* Verse 8.

NOTE.—The threefold message of Revelation 14:6-12 is proclaimed in connection with the closing scenes of the great controversy between Christ and Satan. Lucifer has sought to put himself in the place of God (Isaiah 14:12-14), and to secure to himself the worship that is due God alone. The final test comes over the commandments of God. Those who acknowledge the supremacy of the beast by yielding obedience to the law of God as changed and enforced by the papacy, when the real issue has been clearly defined, will, in so doing, worship the beast and his image, and receive his mark. Such will take the side of Satan in his rebellion against God's authority.

How many will yield to the demand to worship the beast?

"And all that dwell upon the earth shall worship him, whose names are not written in the book of life of the Lamb slain from the foundation of the world." Revelation 13:8.

In the judgment-hour message, whom are all called upon to fear, glorify, and worship?

"Fear God, and give glory to him; for the hour of his judgment is come: and *worship him that made heaven, and earth, and the sea, and the fountains of waters."* Revelation 14:7.

Who will sing the victor's song on the sea of glass?

"And I saw as it were a sea of glass mingled with fire: and *them that had gotten the victory over the beast, and over his image, and over his mark, and over the number of his name,* stand on the sea of glass, having the harps of God. And they sing the song of Moses the servant of God, and the song of the Lamb, saying, Great and marvellous are thy works, Lord God Almighty." Revelation 15:2, 3.

Satan's Warfare Against the Church

A Woman Clothed With the Sun

Under what figure was the Christian church represented to the apostle John?

"And there appeared a great wonder [margin, "sign"] in heaven; *a woman* clothed with the sun, and the moon under her feet, and upon her head a crown of twelve stars." Revelation 12:1.

Note.—Frequently in the Scriptures a woman is used to represent the church. (See Jeremiah 6:2; 2 Corinthians 11:2.) The sun represents the light of the gospel with which the church was clothed at the first advent (1 John 2:8); the moon under her feet, the waning light of the former dispensation; and the twelve stars, the twelve apostles.

How is the church at the first advent described?

"And she being with child cried, travailing in birth, and pained to be delivered." Verse 2.

Note.—The church is in labor and pain while she brings forth Christ and her children, in the midst of afflictions and persecutions. (See Romans 8:19, 22; 1 John 3:1, 2; 2 Timothy 3:12.)

How are the birth, work, and ascension of Christ briefly described?

"And she brought forth a man child, who was to rule all nations with a rod of iron: and her child was caught up unto God, and to his throne." Verse 5.

Note.—That this passage refers to Christ is clearly evident when it is compared with Psalm 2:7-9.

The Great Red Dragon

What other sign, or wonder, appeared in heaven?

"And there appeared another wonder in heaven; and behold *a great red dragon,* having seven heads and ten horns, and

A REFUGE IN THE WILDERNESS

The flight of Bible-loving Christians into mountain fastnesses to escape from their persecutors is symbolized by the dragon pursuing the woman (the church). (Revelation 12:13, 14.)

SATAN'S WARFARE AGAINST THE CHURCH

seven crowns upon his heads. And his tail drew the third part of the stars of heaven, and did cast them to the earth: and the dragon stood before the woman which was ready to be delivered, for to devour her child as soon as it was born." Verses 3, 4.

Who is this dragon said to be?

"And the great dragon was cast out, *that old serpent*, called the *Devil*, and *Satan*, which deceiveth the whole world." Verse 9.

NOTE.—Primarily the dragon represents Satan, the great enemy and persecutor of the church in all ages. But Satan works through principalities and powers in his efforts to destroy the people of God. It was through a Roman king, King Herod, that he sought to destroy Christ as soon as He was born. (Matthew 2:16.) Rome must therefore also be symbolized by the dragon. The seven heads of the dragon are interpreted by some to refer to the "seven hills" upon which the city of Rome is built; by others, to the seven forms of government through which Rome passed; and by still others, and more broadly, to the seven great monarchies which have oppressed the people of God; namely, Egypt, Assyria, Chaldea, Persia, Greece, pagan Rome, and papal Rome, in either of which Rome is represented and included. (See pages 266, 267.) The ten horns, as in the fourth beast of Daniel 7, evidently refer to the kingdoms into which Rome was finally divided, and thus again identify the dragon with the Roman power.

How is the conflict between Christ and Satan described?

"And there was war in heaven: Michael and his angels fought against the dragon; and the dragon fought and his angels, and prevailed not; neither was their place found any more in heaven. And the great dragon was cast out, that old serpent, called the Devil, and Satan, which deceiveth the whole world: he was cast out into the earth, and his angels were cast out with him." Verses 7-9.

NOTE.—This conflict, begun in heaven, continues on earth. Near the close of Christ's ministry He said, "I beheld Satan as lightning *fall from heaven*." Luke 10:18. "Now is the judgment of this world: now shall the prince of this world be *cast out*." John 12:31. From the councils of the representatives of the various worlds to which Satan, as the prince of this world, was formerly admitted (Job 1:6, 7; 2:1, 2), he was cast out when he crucified Christ, the Son of God.

What shout of triumph was heard in heaven following the victory gained by Christ?

"And I heard a loud voice saying in heaven, *Now is come salvation, and strength, and the kingdom of our God, and the power of his Christ:* for the accuser of our brethren is *cast down,* which accused them before our God day and night. . . . Therefore rejoice, ye heavens, and ye that dwell in them." Verses 10-12.

Persecution on Earth

Why was woe at this same time proclaimed to the world?

"Woe to the inhabiters of the earth and of the sea! *for the devil is come down unto you, having great wrath, because he knoweth that he hath but a short time.*" Verse 12, last part.

Note.—This not only shows that, since the crucifixion of Christ, Satan knows that his doom is sealed, and that he has but a limited time in which to work, but that his efforts are largely if not wholly now confined to this world and concentrated upon its inhabitants. Better than many professed Christians, Satan knows that time is short.

What did the dragon do when cast to the earth?

"And when the dragon saw that he was cast unto the earth, *he persecuted the woman* which brought forth the man child." Verse 13.

Note.—The persecution of Christians began under pagan Rome, but was carried on far more extensively under papal Rome. (Matthew 24:21, 22.)

What definite period of time was allotted to this great persecution of God's people under papal Rome?

"And to the woman were given two wings of a great eagle, that she might fly into the wilderness, into her place, where she is nourished for *a time, and times, and half a time,* from the face of the serpent." Verse 14.

Note.—This is the same period as that mentioned in Daniel 7:25, and, like the ten horns, identifies the dragon with the fourth beast of Daniel 7, and its later work with the work of the little horn of that same beast. In Revelation 13:5 this period is referred to as "forty and two months," and in Revelation 12:6 as 1260 days, each representing 1260 literal years, the period allotted to the supremacy of papal Rome. Beginning in A.D. 538, it ended in 1798, when the pope was taken prisoner by the French. (See note on page 217.) The woman fleeing into the wilderness fittingly describes the condition of the church during those times of bitter persecution.

SATAN'S WARFARE AGAINST THE CHURCH

What was Satan's design in thus persecuting the church?

"And the serpent cast out of his mouth water as a flood after the woman, *that he might cause her to be carried away of the flood.*" Verse 15.

How was the flood stayed, and Satan's design defeated?

"*And the earth helped the woman,* and the earth opened her mouth, and swallowed up the flood which the dragon cast out of his mouth." Verse 16.

NOTE.—The mountain fastnesses, quiet retreats, and secluded valleys of Europe for centuries shielded many who refused allegiance to the papacy. Here, too, may be seen the results of the work of the Reformation of the sixteenth century, when some of the governments of Europe came to the help of various reform groups, by staying the hand of persecution and protecting the lives of those who dared to take their stand against the papacy. The discovery of America and the opening up of this country as an asylum for the oppressed of Europe at this time may also be included in the "help" here referred to.

What did Christ say would be the result if the days of persecution were not shortened?

"Except those days should be shortened, *there should no flesh be saved:* but for the elect's sake those days shall be shortened." Matthew 24:22.

Still bent on persecution, how does Satan manifest his enmity against the remnant church?

"And the dragon was wroth with the woman, and *went to make war with the remnant of her seed,* which keep the commandments of God, and have the testimony of Jesus Christ." Revelation 12:17.

NOTE.—To the very end Satan will persecute and seek to destroy the people of God. Against the remnant, or last portion of the church, he is especially to make war. Their obedience to God's commandments and their possession of the testimony of Jesus, or Spirit of prophecy (Revelation 19:10), are especially offensive to him, and excite his intense ire.

A Great Persecuting Power

THE TEN-HORNED BEAST OF REVELATION 13

What is the first symbol of Revelation 13?

"And I stood upon the sand of the sea, and saw *a beast rise up out of the sea, having seven heads and ten horns,* and upon his horns ten crowns, and upon his heads the name of blasphemy." Revelation 13:1.

NOTE.—As already learned from studying the dragon of Daniel, a beast in prophecy represents some great earthly power or kingdom; a head or horn, a governing power; waters, "peoples, and multitudes, and nations, and tongues." Revelation 17:15.

"The beasts of Daniel and John are empires. The ten-horned beast is the Roman power.... The head is the governing power in the body. The heads of this beast represent successive governments."—H. GRATTAN GUINNESS, *Romanism and the Reformation,* pp. 144, 145.

How is this beast further described?

"And the beast which I saw was *like unto a leopard,* and his feet were as *the feet of a bear,* and his mouth *as the mouth of a lion."* Verse 2, first part.

NOTE.—These are the characteristics of the first three symbols of Daniel 7—the *lion, bear,* and *leopard* there representing the kingdoms of *Babylon, Persia,* and *Greece*—and suggest this beast as representing or belonging to the kingdom symbolized by the *fourth beast* of Daniel 7, or *Rome.* Both have ten horns. Like the dragon of Revelation 12, it also has seven heads; but as the dragon symbolized Rome in its entirety, particularly in its pagan phase, this, like the "little horn" coming up among the ten horns of the fourth beast of Daniel 7, represents Rome in its later or papal form. Both it and the little horn have "a mouth" speaking great things; both make war upon the saints; both continue for the same period.

Allowing a very broad meaning to the symbol, the Douay Version, or English Catholic Bible, in a note on Revelation 13:1, explains the seven heads of this beast as follows: "The seven heads are seven kings, that is, seven principal kingdoms or empires, which have exercised, or shall exercise, tyrannical power over the people of God: of these, five were then fallen, viz., the Egyptian, Assyrian, Chaldean, Persian, and Grecian monarchies; one was present, viz., the empire of Rome; and the seventh and chiefest was to come, viz., the great Antichrist and his empire." That the seventh head represents Antichrist, or the papacy, there can be little doubt. (See page 263.)

The Dragon Gives Place to the Beast

What did the dragon give this beast?

"And the dragon gave him his *power,* and his *seat,* and *great authority*." Verse 2, latter part.

Note.—It is an undisputed fact of history that under the later Roman emperors, after Constantine, the religion of the Roman government was changed from pagan to papal; that the bishops of Rome received rich gifts and great authority from Constantine and succeeding emperors; that after A.D. 476 the Bishop of Rome became the most influential power in Western Rome, and by Justinian, in 533, was declared "head of all the holy churches," and "corrector of heretics." (See note on page 217.) "The removal of the capital of the Empire from Rome to Constantinople in 330, left the Western Church, practically free from imperial power, to develop its own form of organisation. The Bishop of Rome, *in the seat of the Caesars,* was now the greatest man in the West, and was soon [when the barbarians overran the empire] forced to become the political as well as the spiritual head."—A. C. Flick, *The Rise of the Mediaeval Church* (Putnam's, 1909 ed.), p. 168.

Thus Rome pagan became Rome papal; church and state were united, and the persecuting power of the dragon was conferred upon the professed head of the church of Christ, or papal Rome. "The Pope, who calls himself 'King' and 'Pontifex Maximus,' is Caesar's successor."—Adolf Harnack, *What Is Christianity?* (Putnam's, 1903 ed.), p. 270. (See pages 210, 211.)

How are the character, work, period of supremacy, and great power of the beast described?

"And there was given unto him a mouth speaking great things and blasphemies; and power was given unto him to continue forty and two months. And he opened his mouth in blasphemy against God, to blaspheme his name, and his tabernacle, and them that dwell in heaven. And it was given unto him to make war with the saints, and to overcome them: and power was given him over all kindreds, and tongues, and nations." Verses 5-7.

Note.—All these specifications have been fully and accurately met in the papacy, and identify this beast as representing the same power as that represented by the little-horn phase of the fourth beast of Daniel 7, and the little horn of Daniel 8, in its chief and essential features and work. (See Daniel 7:25; 8:11, 12, 24, 25, and readings on pages 211, 219. For an explanation of the time period mentioned, see page 217.)

The Beast Is Wounded

What was to happen to one of the heads of this beast?

"And I saw *one of his heads as it were wounded to death; and his deadly wound was healed: and all the world wondered after the beast.*" Verse 3.

Note.—The "deadly wound" to the papal head of this beast was inflicted when the French, in 1798, entered Rome, and took the pope prisoner, eclipsing, for a time, the power of the papacy and depriving it of its temporalities. Again in 1870 temporal dominion was taken from the papacy, and the pope looked upon himself as the prisoner of the Vatican. By 1929 the situation had changed to the extent that Cardinal Gasparri met Premier Mussolini in the historic palace of Saint John Lateran to settle a long quarrel—returning temporal power to the papacy, to "heal a wound of 59 years" (*The Catholic Advocate* [Australia], April 18, 1929, p. 16).

The front page of the San Francisco *Chronicle* of February 12, 1929, carries pictures of Cardinal Gasparri and Mussolini, signers of the Concordat, with the headline "Heal Wound of Many Years." The Associated Press dispatch says: "In affixing the autographs to the memorable document, healing the wound which has festered since 1870, extreme cordiality was displayed on both sides." To such a position of influence over the nations is the papacy finally to attain that just before her complete overthrow and destruction she will say, "I sit a queen, and am no widow, and shall see no sorrow." Revelation 18:7. (See Isaiah 47:7-15; Revelation 17:18.)

What is said of the papacy's captivity and downfall?

"He that leadeth into captivity shall go into captivity: he that killeth with the sword must be killed with the sword." Verse 10.

What questions indicate the high position of this beast-power?

"And they worshipped the dragon which gave power unto the beast: and they worshipped the beast, saying, *Who is like unto the beast? who is able to make war with him?*" Verse 4.

A GREAT PERSECUTING POWER

How universal is the worship of this power to become?

"And all that dwell upon the earth shall worship him, whose names are not written in the book of life of the Lamb slain from the foundation of the world." Verse 8.

THE BEAST DESTROYED

What did John say was to be the end of this beast?

"And the beast was taken, and with him the false prophet that wrought miracles before him. . . . *These both were cast alive into a lake of fire burning with brimstone.*" Revelation 19:20. (See Isaiah 47:7-15; 2 Thessalonians 2:3-8; Revelation 17:16, 17; 18:4-8.)

What is the fate of the fourth beast of Daniel 7?

"I beheld then because of the voice of the great words which the horn spake: I beheld even till the beast was *slain,* and his body *destroyed,* and *given to the burning flame.*" Daniel 7:11.

'Tis midnight; and on Olives' brow
　　The star is dimmed that lately shone:
'Tis midnight; in the garden, now,
　　The suffering Saviour prays alone.

'Tis midnight; and from all removed,
　　The Saviour wrestles lone with fears;
E'en that disciple whom He loved
　　Heeds not His Master's grief and tears.

'Tis midnight; and for others' guilt
　　The Man of Sorrows weeps in blood;
Yet He who hath in anguish knelt,
　　Is not forsaken by His God.

'Tis midnight; and from ether plains
　　Is borne the song that angels know;
Unheard by mortals are the strains
　　That sweetly soothe the Saviour's woe.

—WILLIAM B. TAPPAN

S. DODSON, RUSSELL HARLAN, ARTISTS

THE DECLARATION OF INDEPENDENCE

Founded on principles of liberty, the United States came into being, in prophetic symbol, as an innocent creature among the ferocious beast-nations of earth

Making an Image to the Beast

Another Beast Appears

When was the papal head of the first beast of Revelation 13 wounded?

In 1798, when the papacy was temporarily overthrown by the French, under General Berthier. (See preceding reading.)

What did the prophet see coming up at this time?

"And I beheld *another beast coming up out of the earth;* and he had two horns like a lamb, and he spake as a dragon." Revelation 13:11.

Note.—John Wesley, in his note on Revelation 13:11, written in 1754, says of the two-horned beast: "He is not yet come: tho' he cannot be far off. For he is to appear at the End of the forty-two Months of the first Beast."—*Explanatory Notes Upon the New Testament* (1791 ed.), vol. 3, p. 299.

The previous beast came up out of the "sea," which indicates its rise among the peoples and nations of the world then in existence (Revelation 17:15), whereas this latter power comes up out of the "earth," where there had not before been "peoples, and multitudes, and nations, and tongues." In 1798, when the papal power received its deadly wound, the United States, located in the Western Hemisphere, was the only great world power then coming into prominence in territory not previously occupied by peoples, multitudes, and nations. Only nine years preceding this (in 1789), the United States adopted its national Constitution. It is within the territory of the United States, therefore, that we may look for a fulfillment of this prophecy.

The eminent American preacher De Witt Talmage based a sermon, "America for God," on the text of Revelation 13:11, interpreting the beast with two horns like a lamb as referring to the United States. "Is it reasonable," he said, "to suppose that God would leave out from the prophecies of his Book this whole Western Hemisphere? No, No!" See his *500 Selected Sermons*, vol. 2 (1900), p. 9.

What is the character of this new power?

"He had *two horns like a lamb.*" Verse 11.

Note.—How fittingly is the United States characterized in these words! The nations of the past, pictured in the Bible as beasts of prey, were filled with intolerance, persecution, and oppression. In sharp contrast, the United States was founded on the principles of liberty, equality, and tolerance. The men who had fled the tribulations of the Old World were determined that those trials should not be repeated in the New.

The principles of civil and religious liberty which have made the United States great were incorporated into the fundamental law of the nation at its very founding. We quote from the first amendments to the Constitution, commonly known as the Bill of Rights:

Article I. "Congress shall make no law respecting an establishment of religion, or prohibiting the free exercise thereof; or abridging the freedom of speech or of the press; or the right of the people peaceably to assemble, and to petition the government for a redress of grievances."

Article IV. "The right of the people to be secure in their persons, houses, papers, and effects, against unreasonable searches and seizures, shall not be violated."

Article V. "No person shall be . . . subject for the same offense to be twice put in jeopardy of life or limb, nor shall be compelled in any criminal case to be a witness against himself; nor to be deprived of life, liberty, or property, without due process of law; nor shall private property be taken for public use without just compensation."

For these principles men have fought and died. For them statesmen have valiantly contended throughout the nation's history. For these liberties, millions today are ready to sacrifice even life itself.

The Dragon's Voice Heard Again

Notwithstanding the lamblike appearance of this power, what will ultimately happen?

"And he *spake as a dragon*." Verse 11.

Note.—The voice of the dragon is the voice of intolerance and persecution. It is repugnant to the American mind to think that religious persecution might mar the fair record of the nation founded on liberty to all. But all through the history of the country, from its very founding, farseeing statesmen have recognized that the tendency to enforce religious dogmas by civil law is all too common with mankind, and is liable to break out in active persecution in unexpected places unless specifically guarded against.

Said Thomas Jefferson, at the very beginning of the nation's existence: "The spirit of the times may alter, will alter. Our rulers will become corrupt, our people careless. A single zealot may commence persecution, and better men be his victims."—*Notes on Virginia,* Query XVII, in *The Works of Thomas Jefferson* (Ford ed., 1904-05), vol. 4, pp. 81, 82.

MAKING AN IMAGE TO THE BEAST

In a letter to Rabbi Mordecai M. Noah, this same great American wrote: "Your sect by its sufferings has furnished a remarkable proof of the universal spirit of religious intolerance, inherent in every sect.... Our laws have applied the only antidote to the vice.... But more remains to be done; for although we are free by the law, we are not so in practice; public opinion erects itself into an Inquisition, and exercises its office with as much fanaticism as fans the flames of an auto da fe."—Letter to Mordecai M. Noah, May 28, 1818, *Thomas Jefferson Papers,* vol. 213, p. 37988, in Manuscript Division, Library of Congress.

To the honor of the nation, it should be said that noble statesmen have largely held in check the tendency which Thomas Jefferson foresaw working in the body politic. But no American can shut his eyes to the fact that paralleling these noble efforts, zealous efforts have been made by misguided religious leaders to secure civil enforcement of religious usages.

How much power will this beast exercise?

"And *he exerciseth all the power of the first beast before him,* and causeth the earth and them which dwell therein to worship the first beast, whose deadly wound was healed." Verse 12.

Note.—The "first beast before him"—papal Rome (see preceding reading)—exercised the power of persecuting all who differed with it in religious matters.

What means will be employed to lead the people back into false worship?

"And deceiveth them that dwell on the earth *by the means of those miracles which he had power to do* in the sight of the beast." Verse 14, first part.

What will this power propose that the people shall do?

"Saying to them that dwell on the earth, *that they should make an image to the beast, which had the wound by a sword, and did live."* Verse 14, latter part.

Note.—The beast "which had the wound by a sword, and did live," is the papacy. That was a church dominating the civil power, a union of church and state, enforcing its religious dogmas by the civil power, by confiscation, imprisonment, and death. An image to this beast would be another ecclesiastical organization clothed with civil power—another union of church and state—to enforce religion by law.

Sunday Law Advocates

Does the history of the United States show that religious organizations have attempted to secure legislation involving religion?

Organizations such as the National Reform Association, the International Reform Federation, the Lord's Day Alliance of the United States, and the New York Sabbath Committee have for years worked to secure Sunday legislation. They have often secured the aid of civic groups.

What, according to its constitution, is an avowed object of the National Reform Association?

"To secure such an amendment to the Constitution of the United States as will . . . indicate that this is a Christian nation, and place all the Christian laws, institutions, and usages of our government on an undeniably legal basis in the fundamental law of the land."—David McAllister, *The National Reform Movement . . . a Manual of Christian Civil Government* (1898 ed.), "Article II of Constitution," pp. 15, 16.

Note.—The general superintendent of the National Reform Association and editor of the *Christian Statesman* propounds the following amendment to the First Amendment of the United States Constitution:

"How to take a most dangerous weapon out of the hands of secularists: Amend the highest written law of the land, our Federal Constitution, so that it shall plainly proclaim the will of the Lord of nations as the rule of our national life and the standard of our national conduct in dealing with all our problems—internal and external, national and international. As that Constitution now stands, the secularist is perpetually quoting it on his side, loudly proclaiming that there is in it nothing that warrants the Christian usages, and as loudly and persistently demanding that all these and their like shall go out of the latter that it may be brought into perfect harmony with the former. Our answer should be—Never! But we will instead change the written document that it may be in perfect harmony with the unwritten and so furnish an undeniably legal basis for all we have that is Christian in our national life and character and also for more of its kind that is still needed."—*Christian Statesman*, August, 1921, p. 25.

At first glance, such a statement as this might appear worthy of endorsement. But a closer examination reveals a reasoning basically the same as that employed by religious leaders of past ages, who persecuted all who differed with them. If the laws of the land should reg-

MAKING AN IMAGE TO THE BEAST

ulate religious observances, a man could be forced to attend church, to be baptized, or to pay for the support of the clergy.

What has this association said on this point regarding the Catholic Church?

"We cordially, gladly, recognize the fact that in South American Republics, and in France and other European countries, the Roman Catholics are the recognized advocates of national Christianity, and stand opposed to all the proposals of secularism. . . . *Whenever they are willing to co-operate in resisting the progress of political atheism, we will gladly join hands with them* in a World's Conference for the promotion of National Christianity,—which ought to be held at no distant day—many countries could be represented only by Roman Catholics."—Editorial, *Christian Statesman* (official organ of the National Reform Association), Dec. 11, 1884, p. 2.

What has the pope commanded all Catholics to do in regard to government?

"First and foremost it is the duty of all Catholics worthy of the name and wishful to be known as the most loving children of the Church . . . to endeavor to bring back all civil society to the pattern and form of Christianity which We have described."—*The Great Encyclical Letters of Leo XIII*, "Encyclical Letter *Immortale Dei*, Nov. 1, 1885," p. 132.

NOTE.—On September 7, 1947, Pope Pius XII declared that "'the time for reflection and planning is past' in religious and moral fields and the 'time for action' has arrived." He said that "the battle in religious and moral fields hinged on five points: Religious culture, *the sanctifying of Sunday*, the saving of the Christian family, social justice and loyalty and truthfulness in dealings."—*Evening Star* (Washington, D.C.), Sept. 8, 1947.

What is the object of the International Reform Federation?

"The Reform Bureau [now Federation] is the first 'Christian lobby' established at our national capital to speak to government in behalf of all denominations."—*History of the International Reform Bureau* (1911), p. 2.

NOTE.—The securing of compulsory Sunday legislation is one of the chief objects of this and other like organizations. (See pages 60-62 of the above-named work.)

What is the object of the Lord's Day Alliance?

"This organization proposes in every possible way to aid in preserving Sunday as a *civil institution*. Our national security requires the active support of all good citizens in the maintenance of our American Sabbath. *Sunday laws must be enacted and enforced*."—Quoted as "principles contained in the Constitution" of the original organization (then called the American Sabbath Union); cited in The Lord's Day Alliance, *Twenty-fifth Annual Report* (1913), p. 6.

What was one of the first objectives stated by the Federal Council of the Churches of Christ in America (predecessor of the National Council of the Churches of Christ in the United States of America)?

"That all encroachments upon the claims and the sanctities of the Lord's Day should be *stoutly resisted* through the press, the Lord's Day associations and alliances, *and by such legislation as may be secured to protect and preserve this bulwark of our American Christianity*."—Resolution passed in the first meeting of the Federal Council of the Churches of Christ in America (1908), in its first *Biennial Report*, p. 103.

Note.—Thus it will be seen that the securing of laws for the enforcement of Sunday observance is a prominent feature in all these organizations in their efforts to "Christianize" the nation. In doing this many fail to see that they are repudiating the principles of Christianity, of Protestantism, and of the United States Constitution, and playing directly into the hand of that power which originated the Sunday sabbath—the papacy. (See reading on pages 430-432.)

What arguments have been offered for Sunday laws?

"That the day might be devoted with less interruption to the purposes of devotion." "That the devotion of the faithful might be free from all disturbance."—Augustus Neander, *General History of the Christian Religion and Church,* Torrey translation (3d American ed.), vol. 2, p. 301.

Note.—In the fourth and fifth centuries, Sunday shows and Sunday theaters, it was complained, hindered the "devotion of the faithful," because many of the members attended them in preference to the church services. The church, therefore, demanded that the state should interfere, and promote Sunday observance by law. "In this way," says Neander, "the church received help from the state for the furtherance of her ends."—*Ibid.,* pp. 300, 301. This union of church and state served to establish the papacy in power. A similar course pursued now will produce the same results.

"On the baseless assumption that the seventh day, set apart and established in the law, has been in some way superseded by the first day, recognized in the gospel, a good deal of hurtful legislation has been enacted on the pretext of sanctifying the Sabbath and honoring God. Men who really do know better are willing to wrest the Scriptures and appeal to popular ignorance in order to gain a point. Such conduct is unworthy of any good cause.

"This error had its origin in the iniquitous union of church and state, and is a relic of that oppressive system. . . . In current usage the so-called Sabbath legislation does not apply to the Bible Sabbath at all, but to the first day of the week. The practical effect of such legislation generally is to annul the divine commandment, and to put in its place a human statute. The vicious assumption underlying such legislation is that divine law may be changed or amended by human enactment. In thousands of minds to-day the law of God concerning the Sabbath day is rendered of none effect by the so-called Sabbath legislation enacted by civil governments. Such legislation belittles the authority of Jehovah."—J. J. TAYLOR (Baptist), *The Sabbatic Question* (New York: Fleming H. Revell, 1914), pp. 51, 52, 58. (See pages 433-440, 450, 451, 455, 456, 458 in *Bible Readings* for statements by writers of various denominations.)

EARLY AND MODERN SUNDAY LAWS

Who is responsible for the present State Sunday laws of the United States?

"During nearly all our American history *the churches* have influenced the States to make and improve Sabbath laws."—W. F. CRAFTS in *Christian Statesman*, July 3, 1890, p. 5.

NOTE.—These Sunday laws are a survival of the complete union of church and state which existed at the founding of the colonies. "Such laws [as the Maryland Sunday law of 1723] were the outgrowth of the system of religious intolerance that prevailed in many of the colonies."—Decision of Court of Appeals of the District of Columbia, Jan. 21, 1908, in *Washington Law Reporter*, Feb. 14, 1908, p. 103.

The first Sunday law imposed on an American colony (Virginia, 1610) required church attendance, and prescribed the death penalty for the third offense. (See Peter Force, *Tracts Relating to the Colonies in North America* [1844 ed.], vol. 3, no. 2, p. 11.)

Why is a national Sunday law demanded?

"National Sunday legislation is needed to make the State laws complete and effective," say its advocates.

Note.—The *State* laws enforcing a religious day are relics of a union of church and state in Colonial times. But the *nation* whose foundation principles of civil and religious freedom are aptly symbolized by two lamblike horns does not exercise "all the power of the first beast" and require men "to worship the first beast, whose deadly wound was healed," until it abandons its separation of church and state to the extent of enforcing religious requirements on a national scale, thus constituting an "image," or likeness, to the first beast.

The Mark of Papal Authority

What does the prophet say this second ecclesiastico-political power will attempt to enforce upon all the people?

"And he causeth all, both small and great, rich and poor, free and bond, to receive *a mark* in their right hand, or in their foreheads." Revelation 13:16.

Note.—This mark, called in verse 17 "the mark . . . of the beast," is set over against the seal of God in the book of Revelation. (See Revelation 14:9, 10, and the reading on page 442.)

What means will be employed to compel all to receive this mark?

"And *that no man might buy or sell, save he that had the mark,* or the name of the beast, or the number of his name." Verse 17.

Note.—That is, all who refuse to receive this mark will be boycotted, or denied the rights and privileges of business and trade, or the ordinary means of gaining a livelihood.

What is claimed as the mark of papal authority?

The setting aside of the Sabbath given by God in the fourth commandment—the seventh day—and the substitution of Sunday by the authority of the Catholic Church. (See page 445.)

Note.—"*Ques.*—How prove you that the [Roman Catholic] Church hath power to command feasts and holydays?

"*Ans.*—By the very act of changing the Sabbath into Sunday, which Protestants allow of; and therefore they fondly contradict themselves, by keeping Sunday strictly, and breaking most other feasts commanded by the same church."—Henry Tuberville, *An Abridgment of the Christian Doctrine* (reprint, 1833), p. 58.

MAKING AN IMAGE TO THE BEAST

The mark, then, of the papal power—the beast (see readings on pages 257 and 266)—is the false sabbath in opposition to God's true Sabbath.

Since the Sunday sabbath originated with the Roman power (the first beast), to whom will men yield homage when, knowing the facts, they choose to observe Sunday, instead of the Bible Sabbath, in deference to compulsory Sunday laws?

"Know ye not, that *to whom ye yield yourselves servants to obey, his servants ye are to whom ye obey?*" Romans 6:16.

NOTE.—"The observance of *Sunday* by the Protestants is an homage they pay, in spite of themselves, to the authority of the [Catholic] Church."—LOUIS SEGUR, *Plain Talk About the Protestantism of Today* (1868 ed.), p. 213.

The conscientious observance of Sunday as the Sabbath on the part of those who hitherto have supposed it to be the Sabbath has, without doubt, been accepted of God as Sabbathkeeping. It is only when light comes that sin is imputed. (John 9:41; 15:22; Acts 17:30.)

What does Christ say about our duty to the state?

"Render therefore unto *Caesar* the things which are *Caesar's;* and unto *God* the things that are *God's.*" Matthew 22:21.

NOTE.—The Sabbath belongs to God. Its observance, therefore, should be rendered only to Him.

What special miracle is finally to be performed to deceive men and fasten them in deception?

"And he doeth great wonders, so that *he maketh fire come down from heaven on the earth in the sight of men.*" Revelation 13:13.

NOTE.—In the time of Elijah, in the controversy over Baal worship, this was the test as to who was the true God—the God that answered by *fire.* (1 Kings 18:24.) Now, in earth's last hour, as a counterfeit test, fire will be made to come down from heaven to confirm men in false worship.

To what length will this effort to enforce the worship of the image of the beast be carried?

"And he had power to give life unto the image of the beast, that the image of the beast should both speak, and cause [decree] that as many as would not worship the image of the beast *should be killed.*" Verse 15.

God's People Delivered

What deliverance will God finally bring to His people in this controversy?

"And I saw as it were a sea of glass mingled with fire: and *them that had gotten the victory over the beast, and over his image, and over his mark, and over the number of his name,* stand on the sea of glass, having the harps of God." Revelation 15:2.

What song will they sing?

"And they sing *the song of Moses* the servant of God, and *the song of the Lamb.*" Verse 3.

What was the song of Moses?

A song of deliverance from oppression. (See Exodus 15.)

The Blind Hymn Writer

Fanny Crosby, the noted hymn writer, was blinded at the age of six weeks, apparently by the application of a too strong poultice to her eyes. Frances R. Havergal, of England, wrote of her as follows:

> Sweet blind singer over the sea,
> Tuneful and jubilant, how can it be
> That the notes of gladness that float so far,
> As if they fell from an evening star,
> Are the notes of one who may never see
> Visible music of flower and tree?
>
> How can she sing in the dark like this?
> What is her fountain of joy and bliss?
> Her heart can see. Her heart can see.
> Well may she sing so joyously;
> For the King Himself, in His tender grace,
> Hath shown her the brightness of His face.

A Prophetic History of the Church

THE MESSAGE OF REVELATION

WHAT title is given the last book of the Bible?

"The Revelation of Jesus Christ." Revelation 1:1.

To whom do those things which are revealed belong?

"The secret things belong unto the Lord our God: but *those things which are revealed belong unto us and to our children for ever.*" Deuteronomy 29:29.

For what purpose was the Revelation given?

"The Revelation of Jesus Christ, which God gave unto him, *to shew unto his servants things which must shortly come to pass.*" Revelation 1:1.

What great event, according to this book, is imminent?

"*Behold, he cometh with clouds;* and every eye shall see him, and they also which pierced him: and all kindreds of the earth shall wail because of him." Verse 7.

NOTE.—This book not only opens and closes with the subject of Christ's second coming, but its various prophecies reach down to this as the great culminating event to the church and the world.

What encouragement is given to study this book?

"*Blessed is he that readeth,* and they that *hear* the words of this prophecy, and *keep* those things which are written therein: for the time is at hand." Verse 3.

THE SEVEN CHURCHES

To whom was the book dedicated?

"To the seven churches which are in Asia." Verse 4.

What were the names of these seven churches?

"What thou seest, write in a book, and send it unto the seven churches which are in Asia; unto *Ephesus,* and unto *Smyrna,* and unto *Pergamos,* and unto *Thyatira,* and unto *Sardis,* and unto *Philadelphia,* and unto *Laodicea.*" Verse 11.

NOTE.—John's letters to "the seven churches which are in Asia" were addressed to actual groups of Christian believers in the Roman province of Asia. These messages describe conditions existing in these churches in John's day and provide counsel appropriate to their particular needs. But because there were actually more churches in "Asia" than the seven named, and because the number seven recurs repeatedly in the Revelation in what is evidently a symbolic sense, these seven particular churches are to be understood as representative of the church as a whole and the messages addressed to them as applicable also to seven periods or states of the church reaching from the first advent of Christ to the second. Throughout Scripture the number seven, when used symbolically, is generally understood to indicate completeness. A study of history reveals that these messages are indeed applicable in a special way to seven successive periods that cover the entire history of the Christian church.

Thomas Newton, although not himself holding this view, tells us that "many contend, and among them such learned men as More and Vitringa, that the seven epistles are prophetical of so many successive periods and states of the church from the beginning to the conclusion of all."—*Dissertations on the Prophecies* (1804 ed.), vol. 2, p. 167.

The good qualities and defects of these churches are pointed out, with admonitions, exhortations, and warnings suitable for each, all of which are also applicable to individual Christian experience.

By what title is the first state of the church distinguished?

"Unto the angel of the church of *Ephesus* write." Revelation 2:1.

NOTE.—Ephesus fitly symbolizes the character and condition of the church in its first state, when its members received the doctrine of Christ in its purity, and enjoyed the benefits and blessings of the gifts of the Holy Spirit. This message may be thought of as applicable to the first century, or approximately the lifetime of the apostles. (See Uriah Smith, *The Prophecies of Daniel and the Revelation* [rev. ed.], pp. 361-368.)

After commending this church for their good works, what charge did the Lord bring against them?

"Nevertheless I have somewhat against thee, because *thou hast left thy first love.* Remember therefore from whence thou art fallen, and *repent, and do the first works.*" Verses 4, 5.

A PROPHETIC HISTORY OF THE CHURCH

Note.—The "first love" is the love of the truth, and the desire of making it known to others. The "first works" are the fruit of this love.

What name is given to the second state of the church?

"Unto the angel of the church in *Smyrna* write." Verse 8.

Note.—The name *Smyrna* is thought by some to mean *myrrh*, or *sweet-smelling incense*. The message addressed to Smyrna may be thought of as applicable to the period of time when many of the saints of God suffered martyrdom under pagan Rome during the second, third, and early fourth centuries.

How is the closing period of tribulation of the church during this time referred to?

"Fear none of those things which thou shalt suffer: behold, *the devil shall cast some of you into prison,* that ye may be tried; and *ye shall have tribulation ten days:* be thou faithful unto death, and I will give thee a crown of life." Verse 10.

Note.—The most severe of the persecutions under pagan Rome was under the emperor Diocletian, from A.D. 303 to 313.

What name is given to the third state of the church?

"To the angel of the church in *Pergamos* write." Verse 12.

Note.—Pergamos, which was built on a lofty hill, fitly represents that period following Constantine's conversion to the setting up of the papacy with its seat of authority in Rome. During this period the church, which formerly "had not where to lay its head, is raised to sovereign authority in the state, enters into the prerogatives of the pagan priesthood, grows rich and powerful." But at the same time, "received into her bosom vast deposits of foreign material from the world and from heathenism."—Philip Schaff, *History of the Christian Church,* vol. 3 (Scribners, 1902 ed.), p. 5.

Among the heathen rites and ceremonies previously introduced into the Christian religion was the heathen festival, *Sunday* (sun's day), then established by law, resulting in the first day of the week taking the place of the Sabbath of the Bible.

How was the faithfulness of this church commended?

"I know thy works, and where thou dwellest, even where Satan's seat is: and *thou holdest fast my name, and hast not denied my faith,* even in those days wherein Antipas was my faithful martyr, who was slain among you, where Satan dwelleth." Verse 13.

NOTE.—There is good reason to believe that "Antipas" refers to a class of persons rather than an individual; for no reliable information concerning such a person is now to be found in any authentic early church histories.

What title was given to the fourth state of the church?

"Unto the angel of the church in *Thyatira* write." Verse 18.

NOTE.—Thyatira symbolizes the condition of God's people during the long, dark period of papal supremacy and persecution connected with the 1260-year prophecy. During that time millions of the saints of God were put to death in the most cruel manner that wicked men and demons could invent. Christ referred to this time in His wonderful prophecy recorded in Matthew 24, in these words: "For then shall be great tribulation, such as was not since the beginning of the world to this time, no, nor ever shall be. And except those days should be shortened, there should no flesh be saved: but for the elect's sake those days shall be shortened." The tribulation of the 1260 years was cut short through the influence of the Reformation.

What promise did God leave for these persecuted ones?

"But that which ye have already hold fast till I come. And he that overcometh, and keepeth my works unto the end, *to him will I give power over the nations:* and he shall rule them with a rod of iron; as the vessels of a potter shall they be broken to shivers: even as I received of my Father." Verses 25-27.

By what name is the fifth state of the church addressed?

"Unto the angel of the church in *Sardis* write." Revelation 3:1.

NOTE.—Sardis was admonished to "be watchful, and strengthen the things which remain" (verse 2). At that time the great tribulation of the people of God was at an end, but it was only as a result of the Reformation that any of God's people were left *remaining*. (See Matthew 24:21, 22, and note under Thyatira.) The Sardis church may be thought of as representing the reformed churches during the time of the Reformation and onward.

What endearing title is given the sixth church?

"To the angel of the church in *Philadelphia* write." Verse 7.

NOTE.—Philadelphia means *brotherly love*. The message addressed to it may be thought of as applying to the church during the Advent awakening, from the late eighteenth century to the opening of "the hour of his judgment" in 1844.

A PROPHETIC HISTORY OF THE CHURCH

What words to this church show the Second Advent near?

"*Behold, I come quickly:* hold that fast which thou hast, that no man take thy crown." Verse 11.

What is Christ's message to the last church?

"Unto the angel of the church of the *Laodiceans* write; . . . I know thy works, that thou art neither cold nor hot. . . . Because thou sayest, I am rich, and increased with goods, and have need of nothing; . . . I counsel thee to buy of me gold tried in the fire, that thou mayest be rich; and white raiment, that thou mayest be clothed. . . . As many as I love, I rebuke and chasten: be zealous therefore, and repent." Verses 14-19.

Note.—Some think that the word Laodicea signifies *the judging of the people,* or, according to Cruden, *a just people.* This church exists in the time of the judgment and the proclamation of the final warning messages preceding Christ's second coming. (See Revelation 14:6-16, and reading on pages 245-248.) This is a time of great profession, with but little vital godliness and true piety.

THE SAVIOUR'S INVITATION

What encouragement is given to heed this message?

"Behold, I stand at the door, and knock: if any man hear my voice, and open the door, I will come in to him, and will sup with him, and he with me." Verse 20.

Note.—The pointed, searching messages to the seven churches contain most important lessons of admonition, encouragement, and warning for all Christians in all ages. The seven promises to the overcomer found in this line of prophecy (Revelation 2:7, 11, 17, 26-28; 3:5, 12, 21), with the eighth or universal promise recorded in Revelation 21:7, form a galaxy of promises as precious, as comforting, and as inspiring as any recorded in the Scriptures. (See pages 551, 738, 739.)

The Book With Seven Seals

THE SEALED BOOK

WHAT did John the revelator see in the right hand of Him who sat on the throne?

"And I saw in the right hand of him that sat on the throne *a book written* within and on the backside, *sealed with seven seals.*" Revelation 5:1.

What did the Lamb do with this book?

"And he came and took the book out of the right hand of him that sat upon the throne." Verse 7.

Why was Christ declared worthy to open these seals?

"Thou art worthy to take the book, and to open the seals thereof: *for thou wast slain, and hast redeemed us to God by thy blood* out of every kindred, and tongue, and people, and nation." Verse 9.

OPENING THE SEALS

What was shown upon the opening of the first seal?

"And I saw when the Lamb opened one of the seals . . . *a white horse:* and he that sat on him had a bow; and a crown was given unto him: and he went forth conquering, and to conquer." Revelation 6:1, 2.

NOTE.—The seven seals delineate the experiences through which the church was to pass from the beginning of the Christian Era to the second coming of Christ. The white horse, with his rider going forth to conquer, fitly represents the early Christian church in its purity, going into all the world with the gospel message of salvation, a fit emblem of the church triumphant in the first century.

What appeared upon the opening of the second seal?

"And when he had opened the second seal, . . . there went out *another horse that was red:* and power was given to him that sat thereon to take peace from the earth, and that they should kill one another: and there was given unto him a great sword." Verses 3, 4.

NOTE:—As whiteness in the first horse denoted the purity of the gospel which its rider propagated, so the color of the second horse would show that corruption had begun to creep in when this symbol applies. It is true that such a state of things did succeed the apostolic church. Speaking of the second century, James Wharey says: "Christianity began already to wear the garb of heathenism. The seeds of most of those errors that afterwards so entirely overran the church, marred its beauty, and tarnished its glory, were already beginning to take root."—*Sketches of Church History* (1840 ed.), p. 39.

"The mighty Catholic Church was little more than the Roman Empire baptised. Rome was transformed as well as converted. . . . Christianity could not grow up through Roman civilisation and paganism, however, without in turn being coloured and influenced by the rites, festivities, and ceremonies of old polytheism. Christianity not only conquered Rome, but Rome conquered Christianity. It is not a matter of great surprise, therefore, to find that from the first to the fourth century the Church had undergone many changes."—A. C. FLICK, *The Rise of the Mediaeval Church* (Putnam's, 1909 ed.), pp. 148, 149.

What was the color of the symbol under the third seal?

"When he had opened the third seal, I heard the third beast say, Come and see. And I beheld, and lo *a black horse;* and he that sat on him had a pair of balances in his hand." Verse 5.

NOTE.—The "black" horse fitly represents the spiritual darkness and degeneracy that characterized the church from the time of Constantine till the establishment of papal supremacy in A.D. 538. Of the condition of things in the fourth century, Philip Schaff says: "But the elevation of Christianity as the religion of the state presents also an opposite aspect to our contemplation. It involved great risk of degeneracy to the church. . . . The christianizing of the state amounted therefore in great measure to a paganizing and secularizing of the church. . . . The mass of the Roman empire was baptized only with water, not with the Spirit and fire of the gospel, and it smuggled heathen manners and practices into the sanctuary under a new name."—*History of the Christian Church*, vol. 3 (Scribner's, 1902 ed.), p. 93.

What were the color and character of the fourth symbol?

"And when he had opened the fourth seal, . . . behold *a pale horse:* and his name that sat on him was *Death,* and *Hell* [Greek, *hadēs,* "the *grave*"] *followed with him*. And power was given unto them over the fourth part of the earth, *to kill with sword,* and with *hunger,* and with *death,* and with the *beasts of the earth.*" Verses 7, 8.

NOTE.—The original denotes the *pale* or *yellowish* color of blighted plants, an unnatural color for a horse. The symbol evidently refers to the work of persecution and death carried on by the Roman Church against the people of God from about the time of the beginning of papal supremacy in A.D. 538 to the Reformation.

On opening the fifth seal, what was seen under the altar?

"And when he had opened the fifth seal, I saw under the altar *the souls of them that were slain for the word of God, and for the testimony which they held.*" Verse 9.

NOTE.—This is a view of the martyr victims of papal persecution from the sixteenth century to the time when the persecuting power of the papacy was restrained.

What were these martyrs represented as doing?

"And *they cried with a loud voice,* saying, How long, O Lord, holy and true, dost thou not judge and avenge our blood on them that dwell on the earth?" Verse 10.

NOTE.—Their cruel mistreatment cried for vengeance, just as Abel's blood cried to God from the ground. Genesis 4:10. They were not in heaven, but under the altar, where they had been slain. On this Adam Clarke says: "The altar is upon earth, not in heaven." See next note.

What was given these martyrs?

"And *white robes were given unto every one of them;* and it was said unto them, that they should rest yet for a little season, until their fellowservants also and their brethren, that should be killed as they were, should be fulfilled [or, "were fulfilled"]." Verse 11.

NOTE.—These had been slain during the centuries covered by the preceding seal. Their persecutors, most of them at least, had died. And if they had at death passed to their punishment, as is by some supposed, why should the martyred ones still importune for their punishment? In this, as in other parts of the Bible, the figure of personification is used, in which inanimate objects are represented as alive and speaking, and things that are not as though they were. (See Judges 9:8-15.) These martyrs had gone down as heretics under the darkness and superstition of the preceding seal, covered with ignominy and shame. Now, in the light of the Reformation, their true character appears, and they are seen to have been righteous, and hence are given "white robes." "The fine linen [white robes] is the righteousness of saints." Revelation 19:8. Righteousness is ascribed to them; and when they have rested a little longer where they are—under the altar—till all others who are to die for their faith have followed them, then together they will be raised to immortality.

It should be noted, further, that the first six of the seven seals depict events taking place on earth, not in heaven. The altar at whose base the souls of these martyrs lie is the altar on which they were sacrificed for their faith. It is sufficient to point out that they were slain on earth, not in heaven, and that there is no altar of sacrifice in heaven.

What was first seen on the opening of the sixth seal?

"And I beheld when he had opened the sixth seal, and, lo, there was *a great earthquake*." Verse 12, first part.

NOTE.—Following the events of the fifth seal, and preceding the signs next mentioned, comes a great earthquake, commonly identified as the Lisbon earthquake. "The Lisbon Earthquake, which occurred on November 1, 1755, is the most notable earthquake of history."—*Nelson's New Loose-leaf Encyclopedia* (Book Production Industries Inc.), art. "Earthquake." Says Sir Charles Lyell: "A violent shock threw down the greater part of the city. In the course of about six minutes, 60,000 persons perished. The sea first retired and laid the bar dry; it then rolled in, rising 50 feet or more above its ordinary level. . . . The area over which this convulsion extended is very remarkable."—*Principles of Geology* (11th ed., 1872), vol. 2, pp. 147, 148.

Encyclopaedia Britannica (1945) estimates the deaths at a lower figure, but says that the effects of the quake were felt from Scotland to Asia Minor and that the distinctive feature of the Lisbon earthquake was the agitation of inland lakes and streams far beyond the disturbed area—in Italy, Switzerland, Great Britain, Sweden, and Norway. (Articles "Lisbon" and "Earthquakes.")

What was to follow the great earthquake?

"And *the sun became black* as sackcloth of hair, and *the moon became as blood*." Same verse, latter part.

NOTE.—May 19, 1780, is known in history as the "dark day." The obscuration extended, in varying degrees, over New England and into New York. Newspapers said that a smoky haze from continued forest fires, which had been noticeable for several days, combined with heavy clouds to produce an unaccountable darkness from about 11 A.M. until past midnight, after which time the moon and stars reappeared. "There was the appearance of midnight at noonday," and in the evening, although the moon was just past full, "perhaps it was never darker since the children of Israel left the house of bondage." In connection with this extraordinary phenomenon the moon was reported to appear red. The cause was disputed, for the forest fires seemed insufficient to explain such an extensive darkness, and the exact cause has never been settled. (Letter signed "Viator" in *Independent Chronicle* [Boston], May 25, 1780, p. 2; see also the *Pennsylvania Evening Post* [Philadelphia], June 6, 1780, p. 62.) (For further explanation see page 304.)

What other event is mentioned under this seal?

"And *the stars of heaven fell unto the earth,* even as a fig tree casteth her untimely figs, when she is shaken of a mighty wind." Verse 13.

NOTE.—When the Scripture mentions *stars falling,* it evidently means what even an astronomer refers to as "falling stars," or meteors. Within a little over a half century following the most notable darkening of the sun and moon, a number of star showers occurred, but "probably the most remarkable of all the meteoric showers that have ever occurred was that of the Leonids, on November 12 [12-13], 1833" (Charles A. Young, *Manual of Astronomy* [1902 ed.], sec. 521), when "a tempest of *falling stars* broke over the earth. North America bore the brunt of its pelting" (Agnes M. Clerke, *A Popular History of Astronomy in the Nineteenth Century* [1885 ed.], p. 369).

An eyewitness reported: "This language of the prophet has always been received as metaphorical. Yesterday it was literally fulfilled, . . . as no man before yesterday had conceived to be possible that it should be fulfilled. . . . Were I to hunt through nature for a simile, I could not find one so apt to illustrate the appearance of the heavens as that which St. John uses in the prophecy. . . . They were what the world understands by the name of 'Falling Stars.' . . . The falling stars did not come, as if from *several* trees shaken, but from one: those which appeared in the east fell toward the East; those which appeared in the north fell toward the North; those which appeared in the west fell toward the West; and those which appeared in the south, (for I went out of my residence in the Park,) fell toward the South; and they fell, not as the *ripe* fruit falls. Far from it. But they *flew, they were cast,* like the *unripe* fruit, which at first refuses to leave the branch; and, when it does break its hold, flies swiftly, *strait off,* descending; and in the multitude falling some cross the track of others, as they are thrown with more or less force."—Eyewitness account in the *New York Journal of Commerce,* vol. 8, no. 534, Saturday, Nov. 16, 1833. (See page 306.)

What is the next event mentioned in the prophecy?

"And *the heaven departed as a scroll* when it is rolled to-

THE BOOK WITH SEVEN SEALS

gether; and every mountain and island were moved out of their places." Verse 14.

NOTE.—This event is still future, and will take place in connection with Christ's second coming. We are now standing between the two events—the last of the signs in the heavens, and the parting of the heavens and removal of earthly things out of their places. The great signs here mentioned which mark the approach of Christ's second coming and the dissolution of all earthly things, are all in the past, and the world awaits the sound of the last trump as the closing scene in earth's drama.

How will this great event affect the world?

"And the kings of the earth, and the great men, and the rich men, and the chief captains, and the mighty men, and every bondman, and every free man, hid themselves in the dens and in the rocks of the mountains; and said to the mountains and rocks, Fall on us, and hide us from the face of him that sitteth on the throne, and from the wrath of the Lamb: for the great day of his wrath is come; and who shall be able to stand?" Verses 15-17.

After the sealing work in Revelation 7, which takes place under the sixth seal, how is the seventh seal introduced?

"And when he had opened the seventh seal, *there was silence in heaven* about the space of half an hour." Revelation 8:1.

NOTE.—The sixth seal introduced the events connected with the second coming of Christ. The seventh seal most naturally, therefore, would refer to that event, or to some accompanying result of it. When Christ comes, all the holy angels will accompany Him (Matthew 25:31); and it follows that silence will necessarily, therefore, reign in heaven during their absence. A half hour of prophetic time would be about seven days. The seven seals, therefore, bring us down to the second coming of Christ.

The Seven Last Plagues

God's Warning and Unmixed Wrath

What is God's final warning against false worship?

"If any man worship the beast and his image, and receive his mark in his forehead, or in his hand, *the same shall drink of the wine of the wrath of God, which is poured out without mixture into the cup of his indignation;* and he shall be tormented with fire and brimstone in the presence of the holy angels, and in the presence of the Lamb." Revelation 14:9, 10.

Note.—During probationary time God's wrath is always tempered, or mingled, with mercy. Thus the prophet Habakkuk prays, "In wrath remember mercy." Habakkuk 3:2. God's wrath unmixed with mercy is visited only when mercy has done its final work, and evil has gone to the limit, so that there is "no remedy." (See Genesis 6:3; 15:16; 19:12, 13; 2 Chronicles 36:16; Matthew 23:37, 38; Luke 19:42-44; 2 Peter 2:6; Jude 7.)

In what is the wrath of God filled up?

"And I saw another sign in heaven, great and marvellous, seven angels having *the seven last plagues;* for *in them is filled up the wrath of God.*" Revelation 15:1.

How does Joel describe the day of the Lord?

"Alas for the day! for the day of the Lord is at hand, and as a destruction from the Almighty shall it come." "For the day of the Lord is great and very terrible; and who can abide it?" Joel 1:15; 2:11.

What has Daniel said of this time?

"And there shall be a time of trouble, such as never was since there was a nation even to that same time: and at that time thy people shall be delivered, every one that shall be found written in the book." Daniel 12:1. (See Ezekiel 7:15-19.)

Note.—The seven last plagues will be the most terrible scourges ever visited upon man. As Ahab accused Elijah of being the cause of Israel's calamities (1 Kings 18:17, 18), so, in the time of trouble, the wicked and those who have departed from God will be enraged at the righteous, will accuse them as being the cause of the plagues, and will seek to destroy them as did Haman the Jews. (See Esther 3:8-14). But God will miraculously deliver His people at this time as He did then.

What decree will be issued by God just prior to the "seven last plagues"?

"He that is unjust, let him be unjust still: and *he which is filthy, let him be filthy still:* and *he that is righteous, let him be righteous still:* and *he that is holy, let him be holy still.* And, behold, I come quickly; and my reward is with me, to give every man according as his work shall be." Revelation 22:11, 12.

"Gather yourselves together, yea, gather together, O nation not desired; *before the decree bring forth,* before the day pass as the chaff, before the fierce anger of the Lord come upon you, before the day of the Lord's anger come upon you." Zephaniah 2:1, 2.

NOTE.—Revelation 15:8 reveals that no man can enter the temple in heaven while the plagues are being poured out. All mediation for sin ceases. Revelation 16:11 shows that there is no repentance after the close of probation. The pouring out of the plagues is the beginning of the judgment of God against the wicked. (See Revelation 18:7, 8; 16:5, 6.) The plagues are poured out unmingled with mercy. (See Revelation 14:10.) They are the expression of God's justice upon unrepentant sinners. (Revelation 16:5-7.)

THE SEVEN PLAGUES IN ORDER

What will be the first plague, and upon whom will it fall?

"And the first went, and poured out his vial upon *the earth;* and *there fell a noisome and grievous sore upon the men which had the mark of the beast, and upon them which worshipped his image."* Revelation 16:2.

What will constitute the second plague?

"And the second angel poured out his vial upon *the sea;* and *it became as the blood of a dead man: and every living soul died in the sea."* Verse 3.

What will be the third plague?

"And the third angel poured out his vial upon *the rivers and fountains of waters;* and *they became blood."* Verse 4.

Note.—The second plague affects the sea. The third plague comes closer to the habitations of men, and affects the land. The water supplies are contaminated.

Why, under these plagues, does the Lord give men blood to drink?

"*For they have shed the blood of saints and prophets,* and thou hast given them blood to drink; for they are worthy." Verse 6.

Note.—In this is shown God's abhorrence of oppression and persecution. The plagues are God's rebukes against colossal forms of sin.

What will be the fourth plague?

"And the fourth angel poured out his vial upon *the sun;* and *power was given unto him to scorch men with fire.*" Verse 8. (See Joel 1:16-20.)

Note.—Sun worship is a very ancient and widespread form of idolatry. In this plague God manifests His displeasure at this form of idolatry. That which men have worshiped as a god, becomes a plague and a tormentor. Thus it was in the plagues of Egypt. Those things which the Egyptians had worshiped became scourges to them instead of benefactors and blessings.

Will even this terrible judgment lead men to repent?

"And men were scorched with great heat, and *blasphemed the name of God,* which hath power over these plagues: and *they repented not to give him glory.*" Verse 9.

What will be the fifth plague?

"And the fifth angel poured out his vial upon *the seat of the beast;* and *his kingdom was full of darkness;* and they gnawed their tongues for pain." Verse 10.

Note.—This plague strikes at the very seat of the great apostasy of the latter days, the papacy. It will doubtless be similar in effect to the like plague in Egypt, which was a darkness that could "be felt." (Exodus 10:21-23.) By this plague that iniquitous, haughty, and apostate spiritual despotism which has set itself up as possessing all truth, and as being the light of the world, is enshrouded in midnight darkness.

What takes place under the sixth plague?

"And the sixth angel poured out his vial upon the great river

Euphrates; and the water thereof was dried up, that the way of the kings of the east might be prepared." Verse 12.

What gathers the nations to the battle of Armageddon?

"And I saw *three unclean spirits* like frogs come out of the mouth of the dragon, and out of the mouth of the beast, and out of the mouth of the false prophet. For they are *the spirits of devils,* working miracles, which go forth unto the kings of the earth and of the whole world, to gather them to the battle of that great day of God Almighty. . . . And he gathered them together into a place called in the Hebrew tongue Armageddon." Verses 13-16.

NOTE.—This scripture shows that it is the spirit of Satan which incites men to war. The dragon represents paganism; the beast, the papacy; and the false prophet, apostate Protestantism—the three great religious apostasies since the Flood.

At this time what event is imminent?

"*Behold, I come as a thief.* Blessed is he that watcheth, and keepeth his garments, lest he walk naked, and they see his shame." Verse 15.

What takes place under the seventh plague?

"And the seventh angel poured out his vial into *the air.* . . . And there were *voices,* and *thunders,* and *lightnings;* and *there was a great earthquake,* such as was not since men were upon the earth, so mighty an earthquake, and so great. And the great city was divided into three parts, *and the cities of the nations fell.*" Verses 17-19.

What accompanies the earthquake?

"And there fell upon men *a great hail out of heaven,* every stone about the weight of a talent: and men blasphemed God because of the plague of the hail; for the plague thereof was exceeding great." Verse 21. (See Job 38:22, 23; Psalm 7:11-13.)

What will the Lord be to His people at this time?

"The Lord also shall roar out of Zion, and utter his voice from Jerusalem; and the heavens and the earth shall shake: *but the Lord will be the hope of his people, and the strength of the children of Israel.*" Joel 3:16. (See Jeremiah 25:30, 31; Haggai 2:21; Hebrews 12:26; Psalm 91:5-10.)

NOTE.—To prepare His people and the world for these terrible judgments, the Lord sends a warning message to every nation, kindred, tongue, and people, as He warned the world through Noah. (See Revelation 14:6-10.)

Just before the pouring out of the plagues, what call does God send to His people still in Babylon?

"And I heard another voice from heaven, saying, *Come out of her, my people, that ye be not partakers of her sins, and that ye receive not of her plagues.* For her sins have reached unto heaven, and God hath remembered her iniquities." Revelation 18:4, 5. (See Genesis 19:12-17; Jeremiah 51:6; and page 249.)

How suddenly will the plagues come upon modern Babylon?

"Therefore shall her plagues come *in one day,* death, and mourning, and famine; and she shall be utterly burned with fire: for strong is the Lord God who judgeth her. . . . For in *one hour* is thy judgment come." Revelation 18:8-10.

THE FAMINE AND THE FINISH

What famine will come at this time upon those who have rejected God's messages of mercy?

"Behold, the days comes, saith the Lord God, that *I will send a famine in the land, not a famine of bread, nor a thirst for water, but of hearing the words of the Lord:* and they shall wander from sea to sea, and from the north even to the east, they shall run to and fro to seek the word of the Lord, and shall not find it." Amos 8:11, 12. (See Luke 13:25; Proverbs 1:24-26; Hebrews 12:15-17.)

What announcement is made under the seventh plague?

"And there came a great voice out of the temple of heaven, from the throne, saying, *It is done.*" Revelation 16:17.

NOTE.—God made man to bless him. (Genesis 1:28.) When His blessings are abused, He withholds them, to teach men their source and their proper use. (Haggai 1:7-11.) Judgments are sent that men may "learn righteousness." (Isaiah 25:9; 1 Kings 17:1.) That men do not repent under the plagues is no evidence that God has ceased to be merciful and forgiving. They simply demonstrate that all have determined their destiny, and that even the severest judgments of God will not move the ungodly and impenitent to repentance.

What psalms will prove to be of particular comfort and encouragement to God's people during the time of the seven last plagues?

Psalms 46 and 91. (See also Isaiah 33:13-17.)

How Readest Thou?

"It is one thing to read the Bible through,
Another thing to read to learn and do.
Some read it with design to learn to read,
But to the subject pay but little heed.
Some read it as their duty once a week,
But no instruction from the Bible seek;
While others read it with but little care,
With no regard to how they read, nor where.
Some read to bring themselves into repute,
By showing others how they can dispute;
While others read because their neighbors do,
To see how long 'twill take to read it through.
Some read it for the wonders that are there—
How David killed a lion and a bear;
While others read it with uncommon care,
Hoping to find some contradictions there.
Some read as if it did not speak to them,
But to the people at Jerusalem.
One reads with father's specs upon his head,
And sees the thing just as his father said.
Some read to prove a preadopted creed,
Hence understand but little that they read;
For every passage in the book they bend
To make it suit that all-important end.
Some people read, as I have often thought,
To teach the book instead of being taught;
And some there are who read it out of spite.
I fear there are but few who read it right.
But read it prayerfully, and you will see,
Although men contradict, God's words agree;
For what the early Bible prophets wrote,
We find that Christ and His apostles quote.
So trust no creed that trembles to recall
What has been penned by one and verified by all."

The Mystery of God Finished

Following the sixth trumpet, what did John see?

"And I saw *another mighty angel come down from heaven,* clothed with a cloud: and a rainbow was upon his head, and his face was as it were the sun. . . . And he had in his hand *a little book open.*" Revelation 10:1, 2.

Note.—The book of Daniel, which was "sealed" till the time of the end, is doubtless referred to. (See Daniel 12:4, 9.)

What solemn announcement did this angel make?

"And the angel . . . sware by him that liveth for ever and ever, . . . *that there should be time no longer.*" Revelation 10:5, 6.

Note.—Not literal nor probationary time, but prophetic time. The 2300-day period, which ended in 1844, appears to be alluded to here. (See page 226.) No prophetic period reaches beyond this.

What is finished when the seventh trumpet begins?

"In the days of the voice of the seventh angel, when he shall begin to sound, *the mystery of God* should be finished." Verse 7.

Note.—The mystery of God is the gospel. (Ephesians 3:1-6; Galatians 1:11, 12.)

What was John's experience with the little book?

"And I took the little book out of the angel's hand, and ate it up; and it was in my mouth *sweet as honey:* and as soon as I had eaten it, my belly was *bitter.*" Verses 8-10.

Note.—In this is strikingly foretold the experience of those who proclaimed the Advent and the judgment-hour message of 1843-44. Joyous in the hope that Christ was coming then, they were bitterly disappointed, as were the early disciples regarding the setting up of an earthly kingdom by Christ. (Luke 24:21; Acts 1:6, 7.) They found that there was still a work on earth for them to do, as did the early disciples following the death, resurrection, and ascension of Christ.

What shows that God had a further message for the world?

"And he said unto me, *Thou must prophesy again* before many peoples, and nations, and tongues, and kings." Verse 11.

Part Seven

Coming Events and Signs of the Times

	PAGE
Our Lord's Great Prophecy	301
Increase of Knowledge	309
The Conflict Between Capital and Labor	313
The Atomic Age—What Next?	316
The World's Conversion	323
Christ's Second Coming	328
Manner of Christ's Coming	334
Object of Christ's Coming	336
The Resurrection of the Just	339
The Gathering of Israel	342
The Millennium	345
The Day of the Lord	350
Elijah the Prophet	352

COPYRIGHT, 1949, BY REVIEW AND HERALD

WILLIAM HEASLIP, ARTIST

THE FALLING STARS OF NOVEMBER 13, 1833

"The stars shall fall from heaven, and the powers of the heavens shall be shaken." Matthew 24:29

Our Lord's Great Prophecy

JERUSALEM'S DESTRUCTION AND ITS MEANING

How did Christ feel concerning Jerusalem?

"And when he was come near, he beheld the city, and *wept over it,* saying, If thou hadst known, even thou, at least in this thy day, the things which belong unto thy peace! but now they are hid from thine eyes." Luke 19:41, 42.

In what words did He foretell its destruction?

"Thine enemies shall cast a trench about thee, and compass thee round, and keep thee in on every side, and shall lay thee even with the ground, and thy children within thee; and they shall not leave in thee one stone upon another; because thou knewest not the time of thy visitation." Verses 43, 44.

What pitiful appeal did He make to the impenitent city?

"O Jerusalem, Jerusalem, thou that killest the prophets, and stonest them which are sent unto thee, how often would I have gathered thy children together, even as a hen gathereth her chickens under her wings, and ye would not!" Matthew 23:37.

As He was about to leave the Temple, what did He say?

"Behold, your house is left unto you *desolate.*" Verse 38.

NOTE.—The Jews filled up their cup of iniquity by their final rejection and crucifixion of Christ, and their persecution of His followers after His resurrection. (See Matthew 23:29-35; John 19:15; Acts 4-8.)

Hearing these words, what questions did the disciples ask?

"Tell us, when shall these things be? and what shall be the sign of thy coming, and of the end of the world?" Matthew 24:3.

NOTE.—The overthrow of Jerusalem and of the Jewish nation is a type of the final destruction of all the cities of the world, and of all nations. The descriptions of the two events seem to be blended. Christ's prophetic words reached beyond Jerusalem's destruction to the final conflagration; they were spoken not for the early disciples only but also for those who were to live during the closing scenes of the world's history. Christ gave definite signs, both of the destruction of Jerusalem and of His second coming.

Did Christ indicate that either event was imminent?

"Jesus answered and said unto them, *Take heed that no man deceive you.* For many shall come in my name, saying, I am Christ; and shall deceive many. And ye shall hear of wars and rumours of wars: see that ye be not troubled: *for all these things must come to pass, but the end is not yet."* Verses 4-6.

What did He say of the wars, famines, pestilences, and earthquakes that were to precede these events?

"All these are *the beginning of sorrows."* Verse 8.

NOTE.—These were to precede and culminate in the overthrow, first, of Jerusalem, and finally of the whole world; for, as already noted, the prophecy has a double application, first, to Jerusalem and the Jewish nation, and second, to the whole world. The destruction of Jerusalem for its rejection of Christ at His first coming was a type of the destruction of the world at the end for its rejection of Christ in refusing to heed the closing warning message sent by God to prepare the world for Christ's Second Advent.

What would be the experiences of His people?

"Then shall they deliver you up to be afflicted, and shall kill you: and ye shall be hated of all nations for my name's sake. And then shall many be offended, and shall betray one another, and shall hate one another. And many false prophets shall rise, and shall deceive many. And because iniquity shall abound, the love of many shall wax cold." Verses 9-12.

Who did He say would be saved?

"But *he that shall endure unto the end,* the same shall be saved." Verse 13.

When did Christ say the end would come?

"And *this gospel of the kingdom* shall be *preached in all the world* for a *witness* unto *all nations; and then shall the end come."* Verse 14.

NOTE.—Before the fall of Jerusalem, Paul carried the gospel to Rome—then the capital of the world. He wrote of the saints of "Caesar's household" (Philippians 4:22), and further said that the gospel had been "preached to every creature which is under heaven." Colossians 1:23.

Thus it was respecting the end of the Jewish nation; and thus it will be in the end of the world as a whole. When the gospel, or good news, of Christ's coming kingdom has been preached in all the world for a witness unto all nations, then the end will come. As the end of the Jewish nation came with overwhelming destruction, so will come the end of the world. (See reading on page 292.)

What would be a sign of the fall of Jerusalem?

"And *when ye shall see Jerusalem compassed with armies,* then know that the desolation thereof is nigh." Luke 21:20.

When the sign appeared, what were the disciples to do?

"When ye therefore shall see the abomination of desolation, spoken of by Daniel the prophet, stand in the holy place, (whoso readeth, let him understand:) then let them which be in Judaea *flee into the mountains.*" Matthew 24:15, 16.

NOTE.—In A.D. 66, when Cestius came against the city, but unaccountably withdrew, the Christians discerned in this the sign foretold by Christ, and fled (Eusebius, *Church History,* book 3, chap. 5), while 1,100,000 Jews are said to have been killed in the terrible siege in A.D. 70. Here is a striking lesson on the importance of studying the prophecies and heeding the signs of the times. Those who believed Christ and watched for the sign which He had foretold were saved, while the unbelieving perished. So in the end of the world the watchful and believing will be delivered, while the careless and unbelieving will be snared and taken. (See Matthew 24:36-44; Luke 21:34-36; 1 Thessalonians 5:1-6.)

When the sign appeared, how suddenly were they to flee?

"Let him which is on the housetop not come down to take any thing out of his house: neither let him which is in the field return back to take his clothes." Verses 17, 18.

How did Christ further show His care for His disciples?

"But pray ye that your flight be not in *the winter,* neither on *the sabbath day.*" Verse 20.

NOTE.—Flight in winter would entail discomfort and hardship; an attempt to flee on the Sabbath would doubtless meet with difficulty.

The prayers of Christ's followers were heard. Events were so overruled that neither Jews nor Romans hindered their flight. When Cestius retreated, the Jews pursued his army, and the Christians thus had an opportunity to leave the city. The country was cleared of enemies, for at the time of this siege, the Jews had assembled at Jerusalem for the Feast of Tabernacles. Thus the Christians of Judea were able to escape unmolested, and in the autumn, a most favorable time for flight.

What trying experience did Christ then foretell?

"For *then shall be great tribulation,* such as was not since the beginning of the world to this time, no, nor ever shall be." Verse 21.

NOTE.—In the siege of Jerusalem a prophecy of Moses (Deuteronomy 28:47-53) was literally fulfilled: "Thou shalt eat the fruit of thine own body, the flesh of thy sons and of thy daughters, . . . in the siege, and in the straitness, wherewith thine enemies shall distress thee." For the fulfillment, see Josephus, *Wars of the Jews,* book 6, chap. 3, par. 4.

Following the destruction of Jerusalem came the persecution of the Christians under pagan emperors during the first three centuries of the Christian Era. Later came the greater and more terrible persecution during the long centuries of papal supremacy, foretold in Daniel 7:25 and Revelation 12:6. All these tribulations occurred under either pagan or papal Rome.

For whose sake would the period be shortened?

"And except those days should be shortened, there should no flesh be saved: but *for the elect's sake those days shall be shortened."* Verse 22.

NOTE.—Through the influence of the Reformation of the sixteenth century, and the movements which grew out of it, the power of the papacy to enforce its decrees against those it pronounced heretics was gradually lessened, until general persecution ceased almost wholly by the middle of the eighteenth century, before the 1260 years ended.

Against what deceptions did Christ then warn us?

"Then if any man shall say unto you, Lo, here is Christ, or there; believe it not. For there shall arise false Christs, and false prophets, and shall shew great signs and wonders; insomuch that, if it were possible, they shall deceive the very elect." Verses 23, 24.

SIGNS IN SUN, MOON, AND STARS

What signs of the end would be seen in the heavens?

"There shall be signs in the *sun,* and in the *moon,* and in the *stars."* Luke 21:25.

When were the first of these signs to appear?

"Immediately after the tribulation of those days shall the sun be darkened, and the moon shall not give her light, and the stars shall fall from heaven." Matthew 24:29.

"But *in those days, after that tribulation,* the sun shall be darkened, and the moon shall not give her light, and the stars of heaven shall fall, and the powers that are in heaven shall be shaken." Mark 13:24, 25. Compare Joel 2:30, 31; 3:15; Isaiah 13:10; Amos 8:9.

NOTE.—Within the 1260 years, but after the persecution (about the middle of the eighteenth century), the signs of His coming began to appear.

1. *A wonderful darkening of the sun and moon.* (See also page 289.) The remarkable dark day of May 19, 1780, is described by Samuel Williams of Harvard. The professor relates that the obscuration approached with the clouds from the southwest "between the hours of ten and eleven, A.M. and continued until the middle of the next night," varying in degree and duration in different localities. In some places "persons could not see to read common print in the open air, for several hours," although "this was not generally the case." "Candles were lighted up in the houses;—the birds having sung their evening songs, disappeared, and became silent;—the fowls retired to roost;—the cocks were crowing all around, as at break of day;—objects could not be distinguished but at a very little distance; and everything bore the appearance and gloom of night." (See *Memoirs of the American Academy of Arts and Sciences* [through 1783], vol. 1, pp. 234, 235.)

Since the moon, full the night before, was on the opposite side of the earth, there was no eclipse of the sun—nor could an eclipse last so long. The causes assigned seem inadequate to account for the area covered.

"The darkness of *the following evening* was probably as gross as ever has been observed since the Almighty fiat gave birth to light. It wanted only palpability to render it as extraordinary, as that which overspread the land of Ægypt in the days of Moses. . . . If every luminous body in the universe had been shrouded in impenetrable shades, or struck out of existence, the darkness could not have been more complete. A sheet of white paper held within a few inches of the eyes was equally invisible with the blackest velvet."—SAMUEL TENNEY, Letter (1785) in *Collections of the Massachusetts Historical Society,* part 1, vol. 1 (1792 ed.), pp. 97, 98.

Timothy Dwight, president of Yale, remembered that "a very general opinion prevailed, that the day of judgment was at hand. The

[Connecticut] House of Representatives, being unable to transact their business, adjourned," but the Council lighted candles, preferring, as a member said, to be found at work if the judgment were approaching. (See John W. Barber, *Connecticut Historical Collections* [2d ed., 1836], p. 403.)

There was no agreement among the current writers as to the cause of this unparalleled darkness, but there was entire agreement as to the extraordinary character of it. Any suggestion of a natural cause or causes for the darkness can in no wise militate against the significance of the event. Sixteen and a half centuries before it occurred the Saviour had definitely foretold this twofold sign, saying, "In those days, after that tribulation, the sun shall be darkened, and the moon shall not give her light." Mark 13:24. These signs occurred exactly as predicted, and at the time indicated so long before their occurrence. It is this fact, and not the cause of the darkness, that is significant in this connection. When the Lord would open a path for His people through the sea, He did it by "a strong east wind." Exodus 14:21. Was it for this reason any less miraculous? When the bitter waters were made sweet (Exodus 15:23-25), was the divine interposition any less real because certain natural means were used, having apparently some part, under divine direction, in rendering the water fit for drinking? In like manner, even though it were possible for science to account for the remarkable darkness of May 19, 1780, instead of merely speculating concerning it, the event would not be discredited thereby as a merciful sign of the approaching end of probationary time.

2. *Remarkable display of falling stars.* (See also page 290.)

"The morning of November 13th, 1833," says an eyewitness, a Yale astronomer, "was rendered memorable by an exhibition of the phenomenon called shooting stars, which was probably more extensive and magnificent than any similar one hitherto recorded.... Probably no celestial phenomenon has ever occurred in this country, since its first settlement, which was viewed with so much admiration and delight by one class of spectators, or with so much astonishment and fear by another class."—DENISON OLMSTED in *The American Journal of Science and Arts,* vol. 25 (1834), pp. 363, 364.

"From the Gulf of Mexico to Halifax, until daylight with some difficulty put an end to the display, the sky was scored in every direction with shining tracks and illuminated with majestic fireballs. At Boston, the frequency of meteors was estimated to be about half that of flakes of snow in an average snowstorm.... Traced backwards, their paths were invariably found to converge to a point in the constellation Leo."—AGNES M. CLERKE, *A Popular History of Astronomy* (1885 ed.), pp. 369, 370.

Frederick Douglass, in reminiscing about his early days in slavery, says: "I witnessed this gorgeous spectacle, and was awe-struck. The air seemed filled with bright descending messengers from the sky.... I was not without the suggestion at the moment that it might be *the harbinger of the coming of the Son of Man;* and in my then state of mind I was prepared to hail Him as my friend and deliverer. I had read that 'the stars shall fall from heaven,' and they were now falling."—*Life and Times of Frederick Douglass* (1941 ed.), p. 117.

WORLD CONDITIONS, PREPARATION

What were to be the signs on earth of Christ's coming?

"*Distress of nations,* with perplexity; *the sea and the waves roaring; men's hearts failing them for fear,* and for looking after those things which are coming on the earth." Luke 21:25, 26.

NOTE.—For world conditions see readings on pages 309-327.

What was to be the next great event after these signs?

"And then shall they see *the Son of man coming in a cloud with power and great glory.*" Verse 27. (See Matthew 24:30.)

When these things *begin* to happen, what should we do?

"And when these things begin to come to pass, then *look up, and lift up your heads;* for your redemption draweth nigh." Luke 21:28.

When the trees put forth their leaves, what do we know?

"Now learn a parable of the fig tree; When his branch is yet tender, and putteth forth leaves, *ye know that summer is nigh.*" Matthew 24:32.

What do we likewise know after these signs are seen?

"So likewise ye, when ye shall see all these things, *know that it is near, even at the doors.*" Verse 33. "So likewise ye, when ye see these things come to pass, *know ye that the kingdom of God is nigh at hand.*" Luke 21:31.

What did Christ say of the certainty of this prophecy?

"Verily I say unto you, This generation shall not pass, till all these things be fulfilled. Heaven and earth shall pass away, but my words shall not pass away." Matthew 24:34, 35.

NOTE.—What Christ foretold of the destruction of Jerusalem came true to the very letter. Likewise may we be assured that what

He has said about the end of the world will as certainly and as literally be fulfilled.

Who alone knows the exact day of Christ's coming?

"But of that day and hour *knoweth no man,* no, not the angels of heaven, but *my Father only.*" Verse 36.

What moral conditions would precede Christ's Second Advent?

"But as the days of Noe were, so shall also the coming of the Son of man be. For as in the days that were before the flood they were *eating* and *drinking, marrying* and *giving in marriage,* until the day that Noe entered into the ark, and knew not until the flood came, and took them all away; *so shall also the coming of the Son of man be.*" Verses 37-39.

What important admonition has Christ given us?

"Therefore *be ye also ready:* for in such an hour as ye think not the Son of man cometh." Verse 44.

What will be the experience of those who say in their hearts that the Lord is not soon coming?

"If that evil servant shall say in his heart, My lord delayeth his coming; and shall begin to smite his fellowservants, and to eat and drink with the drunken; the lord of that servant shall come in a day when he looketh not for him, and in an hour that he is not aware of, and shall cut him asunder ["cut him off," margin], and appoint him his portion with the hypocrites: there shall be weeping and gnashing of teeth." Verses 48-51.

Increase of Knowledge

Prophetic Knowledge Increased

When might the world look for an increase of knowledge?

"But thou, O Daniel, shut up the words, and seal the book, *even to the time of the end:* many shall run to and fro, and knowledge shall be increased." Daniel 12:4.

Note.—The book of Daniel was not to be shut up *till the end*—for then there would be no time to develop or utilize knowledge—but until "*the time of the end,*" a period just preceding the end. During this time there was to be a great increase of knowledge concerning the prophecies of Daniel.

Until what time were the saints to be persecuted under the Roman power?

"And some of them of understanding shall fall, to try them, and to purge, and to make them white, *even to the time of the end: because it is yet for a time appointed.*" Daniel 11:35.

Note.—The close of the period allotted for this persecution was to mark the beginning of "the time of the end."

How long were they to be under the power of the little horn, or papal Rome?

"And he shall speak great words against the most High, and shall wear out the saints of the most High, . . . and they shall be given into his hand *until a time and times and the dividing of time.*" Daniel 7:25.

Note.—This verse and the preceding one show that the time of the end begins at the end of the "time and times and the dividing of time," or 1260 years, of the dominance of the little horn. This, then, locates the beginning of "the time of the end" as 1798, as shown on pages 216, 217.

After 1798 was there an unsealing of the book that had been sealed "even to the time of the end"?

At the time of the ending of the 1260 years of the little horn in 1798, there was an awakening of interest in the study of the prophecies in general, and especially of Daniel; further, there was

PHOTOS BY GENDREAU, GALLOWAY, U.S. AIR FORCE, U.S. ARMY AND NAVY, J. C. ALLEN, SEABOARD RAILWAY

SYMBOLS OF OUR MODERN TIMES

"Many shall run to and fro, and knowledge shall be increased." Daniel 12:4.

an unprecedented spreading of the word of God to the far corners of the earth.

NOTE.—The Religious Tract Society of London was organized in 1799, the British and Foreign Bible Society in 1804, the American Bible Society in 1816, and the American Tract Society in 1825. The Bible has been translated into more than 1,000 languages and dialects. To all parts of the globe have gone forth hundreds of millions of copies of the Scriptures, and countless pages of tracts, pamphlets, and religious papers disseminating knowledge of the truths of salvation. It was at this time that Protestant Christians began an era of foreign mission work which has taken missionaries to almost every country in the world. Thus in this "time of the end" the gospel of the kingdom has gone "to every nation, and kindred, and tongue, and people."

PROGRESS OF SCIENTIFIC KNOWLEDGE

How has scientific knowledge increased along with the increase of knowledge about the book of Daniel?

"The technological conditions of human life had changed faster *between 1800 and 1919* than in the preceding 2,000 years—one might perhaps say 3,000 years."—LUCIEN PRICE, "Between Two Wars," chap. 2 in *Religion in the Post-War World,* vol. 2, p. 22. Cambridge, Mass.: Harvard University Press, 1945. Reprinted by permission of the publishers.

NOTE.—"Suddenly, with the utilization of steam and electricity, more changes were made in technology in two generations than in all the thousands of years of previous human history put together. Wheels and machines turned so fast that man could cover more distances in one day than he used to be able to do in a lifetime."—NORMAN COUSINS, *Modern Man Is Obsolete* (1945 ed.), pp. 15, 16. Reprinted by permission of the Viking Press, Inc., New York.

In 1798 steam-powered machinery was a recent development, gas lighting and the cast iron plow had come in the year before, and electricity was an interesting laboratory experiment. Following are some of the principal inventions and discoveries since 1798 (authorities differ on certain dates):

Fulton's first steamboat in 1803.	Photography in 1839.
Power printing press in 1811.	Anesthesia in 1846.
Steam railway in 1825.	Sewing machine in 1846.
Mower and reaper in 1831.	Bessemer steel in 1856.
Electric telegraph in 1836.	Machine gun in 1861.
Vulcanized rubber in 1839.	Ironclad war vessel in 1862.

Typewriter in 1864.
Pasteur's germ theory in 1864.
Telephone in 1876.
Phonograph in 1877.
Electric railway in 1879.
Incandescent electric light in 1879.
Gasoline engine in 1883.
Steam turbine in 1884.
Linotype in 1885.
Automobile in 1892.
Motion pictures in 1893.
X-ray in 1895.

Wireless telegraphy in 1895.
Radium in 1898.
Wireless telephony in 1902.
First piloted airplane in 1903.
Radio broadcasting in 1920.
Insulin in 1922.
Television broadcasting in 1936.
Jet turbine in 1937.
Penicillin in 1938.
Shipboard radar in 1938.
Nuclear weapons in 1945.
Earth satellites in 1957.

What are other marks of a new era in "the time of the end"?

Unprecedented political, religious, and intellectual freedom, education of the masses, movements of population, changing of old ideas.

NOTE.—By 1798 there had already begun a series of revolutions "in Western culture which continued into the nineteenth and twentieth centuries and which partly swept away the existing order and brought in a new era. The French Revolution with its profound repercussions in Europe and the revolutions in the Americas which both preceded and succeeded it ushered in a new political order. Republics were set up which aspired to be democratic and more of popular representation in government was forced upon the remaining monarchs. . . . The Industrial Revolution inaugurated the age of the machine. Wealth and population rapidly mounted. Cities mushroomed almost overnight. . . . The commerce of the Occident penetrated to every inhabited country of the globe."—KENNETH SCOTT LATOURETTE, *The Christian Outlook* (New York: Harper and Brothers, 1948), pp. 55, 56.

For what do all these changes pave the way?

"This gospel of the kingdom shall be preached in all the world for a witness unto all nations; and then shall the end come." Matthew 24:14.

NOTE.—"As never before it is possible to acquaint men the world around with the Gospel. The many means of communication—the radio and the airplane, added to the seemingly more prosaic contributions of earlier days, the printed page, the railway, the steamship, and the automobile—make physically feasible the reaching of all men."—*Ibid.*, pp. 200, 201.

The Conflict Between Capital and Labor

God's Message to the Rich

What are some sins of this last-day industrial age?

"Men shall be *lovers of their own selves, covetous,* boasters, proud, . . . trucebreakers." 2 Timothy 3:2.

When, according to prophecy, were men to amass wealth?

"Go to now, *ye rich men,* weep and howl for your miseries that shall come upon you. Your riches are corrupted, and your garments are motheaten. Your gold and silver is cankered; and the rust of them shall be a witness against you, and shall eat your flesh as it were fire. *Ye have heaped treasure together for the last days."* James 5:1-3.

NOTE.—This age of man's greatest intellectual and material achievement is marked by a race for money, and vast accumulations of wealth contrasted with misery and poverty. Our age most fully fits the prophecy.

Why did Christ, in the parable, reprove the man who hid his talent and failed to put it to good use?

"Thou wicked and slothful servant, . . . *thou oughtest therefore to have put my money to the exchangers, and then at my coming I should have received mine own with usury."* Matthew 25:26, 27.

What did Christ tell the rich young man to do?

"Sell that thou hast, and give to the poor, and thou shalt have treasure in heaven: and come and follow me." Matthew 19:21.

What, in the parable, did God say to the rich man who thought to build larger barns in which to store his goods?

"But God said unto him, *Thou fool, this night thy soul shall be required of thee:* then whose shall those things be, which thou hast provided?" Luke 12:20.

H. A. ROBERTS, S. M. HARLAN

CAPITAL AND LABOR IN CONFLICT

"Be patient therefore, brethren, unto the coming of the Lord." James 5:7.

THE CONFLICT BETWEEN CAPITAL AND LABOR

Who gives men the power to get wealth?

"But thou shalt remember the Lord thy God: for *it is he that giveth thee power to get wealth.*" Deuteronomy 8:18.

How does James condemn greed among the rich?

"*Ye have lived in pleasure on the earth, and been wanton;* ye have nourished your hearts, as in a day of slaughter. *Ye have condemned and killed the just;* and he doth not resist you." James 5:5, 6.

NOTE.—This indicates that they have lived in luxury and for pleasure, heedless of their responsibility to God or to their fellow men. Heartless greed disregards the rights, the welfare, and even the lives of those affected by its merciless schemes and intrigues. The righteous, or just, however, do not make forcible resistance to this unjust treatment.

How have the rich defrauded the laborers?

"*The hire of the labourers who have reaped down your fields, which is of you kept back by fraud,* crieth: and the cries of them which have reaped are entered into the ears of the Lord." Verse 4.

Seeking a fair remuneration, what do many laborers do?

Form labor unions, engage in strikes, boycotts, et cetera.

NOTE.—These means may improve conditions temporarily, but they cannot eradicate the deep-seated evil; it lies in the heart; and nothing but conversion—a change of the heart—can eradicate the sin of selfishness—a failure to love one's neighbor as oneself. The struggle between capital and labor is inevitable as long as sin and selfishness are in the world. And near the end it becomes more intense, because then sin comes to the full.

GOD'S MESSAGE TO THE LABORER

What are God's people told to do at this time?

"*Be patient therefore, brethren, unto the coming of the Lord.* Behold, the husbandman waiteth for the precious fruit of the earth, and hath long patience for it, until he receive the early and latter rain. *Be ye also patient;* stablish your hearts: *for the coming of the Lord draweth nigh.*" James 5:7, 8.

The Atomic Age—What Next?

Signs of the Times

Why did Christ reprove the Pharisees and the Sadducees?

"O ye hypocrites, ye can discern the face of the sky; but *can ye not discern the signs of the times?*" Matthew 16:3.

What are several signs given by the prophets which identified Christ, at His *first* coming, as the Messiah?

"Therefore the Lord himself shall give you a sign; Behold, *a virgin shall conceive, and bear a son, and shall call his name Immanuel.*" Isaiah 7:14. For fulfillment see Matthew 1:22, 23.

"But thou, *Bethlehem* Ephratah, though thou be little among the thousands of Judah, yet out of thee shall he come forth unto me that is to be ruler in Israel." Micah 5:2. For fulfillment see Matthew 2:1.

"Rejoice greatly, O daughter of Zion; shout, O daughter of Jerusalem: behold, thy King cometh unto thee: he is just, and having salvation; *lowly, and riding upon an ass, and upon a colt the foal of an ass.*" Zechariah 9:9. For fulfillment see Matthew 21:4, 5.

What did the disciples ask about Christ's *second* coming?

"And as he sat upon the mount of Olives, the disciples came unto him privately, saying, Tell us, when shall these things be? and *what shall be the sign of thy coming, and of the end of the world?*" Matthew 24:3.

What were to be the signs *on earth* of Christ's coming?

"There shall be . . . upon the earth *distress of nations, with perplexity;* the sea and the waves roaring; *men's hearts failing them for fear,* and for *looking after those things which are coming on the earth:* for the powers of heaven shall be shaken." Luke 21:25, 26.

Distress, Perplexity, Fear

What critical situation was to characterize the nations?

"Distress of nations, with perplexity." Luke 21:25.

NOTE.—Stop for a few minutes of serious reflection. Look at the nations of earth today. Every nation is distressed; even the victors in World War II have been at a loss to know what to do for the world's ills. And "bidden or unbidden, the atomic bomb sits in on all the councils of nations; in its light all other problems of international relations are dwarfed."—HENRY L. STIMSON, former U.S. Secretary of War, in *Harper's Magazine,* March, 1946, p. 204.

James S. Stewart speaks of "this immensely critical hour when millions of human hearts are *besieged by fierce perplexities;* when so many established landmarks of the spirit are gone, old securities wrecked, familiar ways and habits, plans and preconceptions, banished never to return."—*Heralds of God* (New York: Charles Scribner's Sons, 1946), p. 12.

Three years after the war's end the United Nations commission working on international control of atomic energy gave up its frustrated efforts, and the UN organization still seemed to be united in just one thing, namely, distress and perplexity over their inability to unite on anything.

What attitude is manifested among men today?

"Men's hearts failing them for *fear.*" Luke 21:26.

NOTE.—In addition to the accumulated fears resulting from war, destruction, economic troubles, and social revolutions, mankind is now overshadowed by the new fear of atomic power. We find it often repeated: "the menaces to civilization itself before which the thoughtful of our day stand in *palsied and futile fear*" (Latourette, *The Christian Outlook,* Harper, 2d ed., 1948, p. 200); *"despair* is creeping up on us" (editorial, *The Christian Century,* Nov. 19, 1947, p. 1391, reprinted by permission); "a time of confusion and *deep-seated anxiety without parallel* in our experience," and an "almost psychopathic *emphasis on the idea of security*" (Virgil Jordan, *Manifesto for the Atomic Age* [1946 ed.], p. 15).

"Today the world is sick with ... a *many-dimensional fear,*" summarized a noted science editor in the first year of the Atomic Age: "On the surface we find the fear of the old Army men: that the other fellow will get an atom bomb before we can perfect our own defense. *But against the atomic bomb there is no defense.* Just below the surface lurks the Diplomat's fear: if we give away the atomic power secret we will lose our bargaining power. *But there is no atomic power secret.* Again, ... the Industrialist's fear: will this new power source upset the economic structure of the world and my private apple cart? *This new power is a discovery at least as great as man's discovery of fire. Who can predict what will come of it?* ... To the scientist, ... the blackest fear of all [means] not to be allowed to seek the truth wherever it leads him.... Death to science ... means death to our great civilization, whose foundation is knowledge and whose goal is liberty."—HELEN M. DAVIS, editorial in *Chemistry,* November, 1945.

"When the scientist has emerged from his laboratory to prophesy our extinction unless we mend our incorrigible ways, and editors have turned into Jeremiahs, how can any man who reads scramble for a dollar, play bridge, or contemplate his children or others' with any satisfaction? But man lives by hope and is by nature an optimist."—HARRISON SMITH, editorial in *The Saturday Review of Literature,* Aug. 21, 1948, p. 20.

One noted atomic scientist, Harold C. Urey, said, "I am a frightened man, myself. All the scientists I know are frightened—frightened for their lives—and frightened for *your* life."—"I'm a Frightened Man," *The Saturday Review of Literature,* Aug. 7, 1948.

What is it that men fear?

"Men's hearts failing them . . . *for looking after those things which are coming on the earth."* Luke 21:26.

NOTE.—The prophecy specifies *fear for the future.*

"The devastation that could be wrought by an Atomic Age war is too appalling to be fully realized. The vision stuns our imagination. But if present trends continue it is only a question of time before such a war will come." "The time is short. Looking at the destruction already wrought, at the materialism growing on every side, at the increasing bitterness and unrest throughout the world, at the tremendous power of our latest weapons, a realist might well conclude that many of us now living will see the start of a war which will end in more dark ages."—CHARLES A. LINDBERGH in *Reader's Digest,* September, 1948, pp. 134, 138.

The editor of the *Christian Century* observed:

"Despair is creeping up on us—on the best of us most of all. The stars of promise have all but faded from our sky. We are on a road that leads to destruction, and destruction is drawing close."—November 19, 1947, p. 1391. Used by permission.

What declaration of Jeremiah concerning the plans and predictions of many of the great men of his day aptly describes the situation today?

"The wise men are ashamed, they are dismayed and taken: lo, they have rejected the word of the Lord; and what wisdom is in them?" Jeremiah 8:9.

NOTE.—We of the present disillusioned generation have learned that "not much is left of the theory of automatic progress. . . . Indeed, the splitting of the atom, which represented the furthest reach of the new physics into the mysteries of matter, also annihilated the last of the nineteenth-century notions of an inevitable millennium."—*Fortune,* October, 1948, p. 112.

"The tower of Babel," says James S. Stewart, "has crashed, and the world is littered with the wreckage of disillusionment."—*Heralds of God* (Scribners), p. 12.

As early as 1933 Paul Hutchinson spoke of "the final destruction of the illusion of inevitable progress which Herbert Spencer and the Victorian evolutionists fastened upon the pre-war liberalism of the West" (*The Forum,* April, 1933, p. 226); and after World War II Raymond B. Fosdick found this idea of automatic progress "curiously unreal" in the light of man's record in recent decades, which has shown him "apparently closer to barbarism than we fondly believed" (*The New York Times Magazine,* Dec. 30, 1945, p. 5).

What does the Bible point to as the cause of the world's peril?

"In the last days perilous times shall come. *For men shall be lovers of their own selves, covetous,* boasters, *proud,* blasphemers, disobedient to parents, unthankful, unholy, without natural affection, *truce-breakers, false accusers,* incontinent, *fierce,* despisers of those that are good, traitors, heady, highminded, lovers of pleasures more than lovers of God; having a form of godliness, but denying the power thereof." 2 Timothy 3:1-5.

NOTE.—The trouble is with *man himself.* "It is not the weapon so much as *it is the human beings who may wish to use it that constitute the real danger,"* continued Fosdick (*ibid.,* p. 29). "The emergence of the atomic bomb requires an advance in ethical and moral standards far greater and more immediate than the human race seems at this moment capable of making."

And a *Fortune* editorial points out that the problem of atomic fission is a spiritual one—the cure of "the fission that exists in men's minds and in their hearts."—January, 1946, pp. 97, 98.

"Scientists themselves now proclaim that their science has reached the point in its development where it becomes imperative *to do something about man.* They prophesy doomsday unless their warning is heeded. . . .

"When we talk about the nature of man, we are standing on ground that has been pre-empted by Christianity. On this ground, science and Christianity now meet face to face. With one voice they declare that the future is precarious, and with one voice they declare that it is precarious *because of man.* Christianity puts its finger upon that in man's nature which science now gravely fears may cause his destruction and the destruction of the earth with him. Science and

Christianity are now looking at the same thing in man. Science has no word for it, but Christianity has. That word is *sin*. ...

"Sin, says Christianity, is inherent in man's nature. Unless something is done to destroy the power of sin in the heart of man, his existence in a scientific world will always remain under the shadow of imminent self-destruction."—CHARLES CLAYTON MORRISON in *The Christian Century*, March 13, 1946, pp. 330-332. Used by permission.

Of what is all this an evidence?

The nearness of a great change—"perhaps the end."

NOTE.—Early in World War II Pierre van Paassen declared that a civilization was passing (*Days of Our Years* [rev. ed., 1940], p. 557), and Pitirim A. Sorokin, Harvard professor, saw an epochal turning point in the history of the world (*The Crisis of Our Age* [1941], p. 22).

On the day Japan surrendered, Gen. Douglas A. MacArthur spoke these alarming words: "A new era is upon us. ... We have had our last chance. If we do not now devise some greater and more equitable system Armageddon will be at our door."—*The New York Times*, Sept. 2, 1945, p. 3.

The President of the United States in a speech to the Federal Council of Churches of Christ in America in session at Columbus, Ohio, on March 6, 1946, said: "*If the world is long to survive,* the gigantic power which man has acquired through atomic energy must be matched by spiritual strength of greater magnitude. All mankind now stands in the doorway to destruction—or upon the threshold of the greatest age in history."—*Biennial Report*, 1946, pp. 108, 109.

A professor in liberal Andover Newton Theological Seminary was moved to write an article on "Atomic Apocalypse," in which he said, after discussing future possibilities, including "global dissolution": "Perhaps the next few summers may lengthen into a few more summers of opportunity. Again, no man can say. But let men search the Scriptures and ponder the facts of science, the vagaries of world politics, the economic, emotional and industrial condition of the peoples—conditions pointing sharply toward *finis,* soon or a little later."—WESNER FALLAW in *The Christian Century*, Sept. 25, 1946, p. 1148. Used by permission.

What prophetic passage of Scripture once ignored now bursts into prominence and is quoted by men of the world?

"But the day of the Lord will come as a thief in the night; in the which the heavens shall pass away with a great noise, and the elements shall melt with fervent heat, the earth also and the works that are therein shall be burned up, . . . wherein the heavens being on fire shall be dissolved." 2 Peter 3:10-12. (See also Isaiah 13:6-11.)

Note.—"Within the pages of the New Testament," says Winthrop S. Hudson, "one is forever stumbling upon passages, long ignored, which suddenly speak directly to the mood of the hour. From utter irrelevance they become luminous with meaning. The closing lines of II Peter [3:10-13] are a case in point. A year ago they were completely foreign to our thinking, but listen to them today!"—*The Christian Century,* Jan. 9, 1946, p. 46. Used by permission.

"Sir Richard Gregory, at a recent meeting of the British Association for the Advancement of Science, quoted [from the same Scripture]. . . . In this country also there are atomic scientists who regard the destruction of all life on this planet from atomic chain reaction as theoretically possible. . . .

"The believer in providence is, however, not confronted with anything new in principle. The end of human existence on earth was regarded by the early Christians as near at hand; by modern Christians as far in the future. . . . What is new in the present situation is not the possibility of a last generation but the possibility—sobering enough I grant—that *ours may be the last generation!*"—Ernest Fremont Tittle in *The Christian Century,* May 1, 1946, p. 556. Used by permission.

"We are on our way towards removing the last barrier that prevent[s] man from converting the earth into a planetary crematorium."—Norman Cousins, editorial in *The Saturday Review of Literature,* Aug. 7, 1948, pp. 7, 8.

The editors of this book do *not* say that man-made atomic energy will start a chain reaction in the atmosphere and consume man and all his works. Atomic energy may never be used in a world conflict to destroy a large part of the population of the globe. The Bible indicates that God, not man, will destroy the earth, and that He will do it in His own way.

However, when scientists, men of the world, and modernist leaders agree that the wiping out of the world as we know it will happen very soon unless man can be given a new heart, the Christian views that as a commentary on statements in the Bible which were frequently scoffed at in this our day, and as a sign of the nearness of the time when God will step in to "destroy them that destroy the earth."

What do all these admonitions and warnings mean to you and me?

"Since all these things are thus on the verge of dissolution, *what sort of men ought you to be in all holy living and godly conduct,* expecting and helping to hasten the coming of the day of God, by reason of which the heavens, all ablaze, will be dissolved, and the elements will burn and melt?" 2 Peter 3:11, 12, Weymouth.

What may we expect to follow this destruction?

"But in accordance with His promise we expect *new heavens and a new earth,* in which righteousness dwells. Therefore, beloved, as you are expecting this, earnestly *seek to be found by Him, free from blemish or reproach, in peace.*" 2 Peter 3:13, 14, Weymouth.

NOTE.—"A new heaven and a new earth, when all things that are will have passed away and old things will have been made new— these conditions are possible only after world's end. What the nature of this end will be no man can say.

"Christians normally reckon with eschatology [the doctrine of last things]. It was Christian abnormality which ignored eschatology for so long. But August 6, 1945, brought back normality, however much believers may lose themselves in the engulfing fear of unbelievers. The normality which the atomic blasts over Japan brought back to Christian believers consists of the rightness, the correctness, of not only contemplating but also *expecting* world's end."—WESNER FALLAW in *The Christian Century,* Sept. 25, 1946, p. 1148. Used by permission.

To what are many Christians looking forward in this atomic age?

To the coming of Christ.

NOTE.—"In the event that the present turbulent period is prolonged by nations' successfully retaining their tenuous sovereignty, we face increasing tensions, fears and spiritual blight until goaded beyond endurance, . . . others than Christians will also begin to cry, 'O Lord, come quickly!' "—*Ibid.,* p. 1147.

"Three years after the Second World War the course of political and economic events has persuaded vast numbers of people that the doom of mankind is sealed. . . . To the warnings of the fatal result of an atomic and biological war there are added the death knells rung by prophets of man's starvation."—HARRISON SMITH in *The Saturday Review of Literature,* Aug. 21, 1948, p. 20.

The publishers of this book are trying, in these pages, as well as in many other of their publications, to do this very thing—to proclaim the Scripture prophecies and their fulfillments which indicate the nearness of the coming of Christ to end this age of perplexity and trouble, and also to usher in the eternal bliss of God's kingdom.

The World's Conversion

"Either—Or"

What alternatives are foreseen in the future of our atomic world?

Moral regeneration or Armageddon.

Note.—"The inexorable 'either-or' of the atomic bomb, upon which hangs the fate of life on this planet, leaves the pride of man no means by which to save itself. *The only alternative to Armageddon is repentance and regeneration.* . . . Atomic energy can lift the burden of poverty from the backs of countless millions. . . . Only if man has a new spirit within him can he pass over into this Promised Land. The Atomic Age is otherwise almost certain to be extremely short and extremely brutish! . . . Unless men everywhere are moved to confess their own inadequacy, and seek to follow God's will rather than their own, no other strategy can save us. . . . *The conversion of man . . . has suddenly become a life-and-death issue,* not merely for individuals, but for the race."—Richard M. Fagley, secretary of the peace commission of the Federal Council of Churches, in *The Chaplain,* November, 1945, pp. 5-7.

Both the President and General MacArthur said, in connection with the statements quoted in the preceding reading (page 320), that the problem of avoiding destruction was the spiritual one of human moral improvement. "If men and nations," said the President, "would but live by the precepts of the ancient prophets and the teachings of the Sermon on the Mount, problems which now seem so difficult would soon disappear. . . . Unless it is done, we are headed for the disaster we would deserve."—Federal Council of Churches, *Biennial Report,* 1946, p. 109.

"As a scientist, I tell you: *there must never be another war.*"—Harold C. Urey, "I'm a Frightened Man," *The Saturday Review of Literature,* Aug. 7, 1948. (See also *One World or None,* by seventeen contributors and the Federation of American [Atomic] Scientists [McGraw-Hill Book Co., Inc., 1946].)

What did Jesus say of conditions preceding His coming?

"As it was in the days of Noe, so shall it be also in the days of the Son of man." Luke 17:26. (See also verses 27-30, and Matthew 24:37-39.)

In the days of Noah, "God saw that *the wickedness of man*

was great in the earth, and that *every imagination of the thoughts of his heart was only evil continually."* "And *the earth was filled with violence."* Genesis 6:5, 11.

Note.—Men everywhere recognize the prevailing wickedness of our times. Drunkenness, vice, crime, and debauchery have increased alarmingly. Selfishness and pride fill the hearts of men to the exclusion of righteousness. Civilization today is repeating the sins of the days of Noah.

According to the parable of the wheat and the tares, how long are the good and bad to remain together?

"The field is the world; the good seed are the children of the kingdom; but the tares are the children of the wicked one; the enemy that sowed them is the devil." *"Let both grow together until the harvest:* and in the time of harvest I will say to the reapers, Gather ye together first the tares, and bind them in bundles to burn them." Matthew 13:38, 39, 30.

"The harvest is *the end of the world."* Verse 39.

Note.—Thus it is plain that the wicked (the tares) live with the righteous (the wheat) till the end of the world. There is, then, no time before Christ's coming for a sinless state, in which all men will be converted and turn to God.

Did Christ say that worldwide preaching of the gospel will result in world conversion?

"And this gospel of the kingdom shall be preached in all the world *for a witness unto all nations;* and then shall the end come." Matthew 24:14.

Note.—He did not say that all would receive the gospel, but that the gospel was to be *preached* in all the world *for a witness* unto all nations, and that *then* the end would come.

"They [Jesus and the New Testament writers] anticipate no full victory for the Gospel within history. Jesus frankly declares that the large majority of mankind go on to destruction. He speaks of the end of the age and in his description of it there is tragedy, with the separation of the good from the evil and with weeping and fire for the latter. The wheat and the tares, he declares, are to be together until the harvest. . . . The nature of each becomes more obvious as the harvest approaches. . . . Good and evil would go on together until, by His intervention, God judged and triumphed."—Kenneth Scott Latourette, *The Christian Outlook* (Harper, 1948 ed.), pp. 188, 189.

"Far from mentioning anything like the progressive improvement of the world, Jesus, on the contrary, foresees *the end of it*, preceded by an aggravation of evil which is to be a sign announcing the return of Christ. And this is the veritable object of the Christian hope which runs through all the pages of the New Testament and which the Apocalypse sets forth in a grandiose fresco."—Translated from HENRI D'ESPINE, a Protestant professor of Geneva, reported in *Gazette de Lausanne,* Feb. 18, 1944, p. 3.

How did Paul characterize the last days?

"In the last days *perilous* times shall come." 2 Timothy 3:1. (See page 319.)

"Evil men and seducers shall wax worse and worse, deceiving and being deceived." Verse 13.

NOTE.—Commenting on the invention of the atomic bomb, E. A. Hooton, Harvard University anthropologist, said: "The present level of human behavior is so low that man is more likely to use control of unlimited natural forces for destruction rather than constructive purposes. . . . Gadgets and machines are getting better and better, and man is getting worse and worse."—UP dispatch in the Washington *Times-Herald,* Aug. 10, 1945.

"Modern man—the end product of all the humanizing influences of sixty centuries" sees in the looking-glass "the image, not of a being grown kindly and tolerant with the years, but of one whose primitive emotions lie just below the surface, and who is easily capable of discarding the principles wrought out on Sinai and the Areopagus whenever they stand in his way. J. A. Hobson's characterization of twentieth-century man appears at first glance not too inaccurate: 'A naked Polynesian, parading in top hat and spats.'"—RAYMOND B. FOSDICK, *The New York Times Magazine,* Dec. 30, 1945, p. 27.

PEACE AND SAFETY

What message indicates the state of international affairs?

"Proclaim ye this among the nations; *prepare war, stir up the mighty men; let all the men of war draw near, let them come up. Beat your plowshares into swords, and your pruninghooks into spears: let the weak say, I am strong."* Joel 3:9, 10, A.R.V.

What declaration by Jeremiah concerning the state of affairs in his day is also true in our time?

"They have healed also the hurt of the daughter of my people slightly, *saying, Peace, peace; when there is no peace."* Jeremiah 6:14.

Note.—It is one of the anomalies of our time that men have been *talking* peace and at the same time preparing for war. In spite of a series of treaties of disarmament and renunciation of war, the great powers went into the most destructive conflict of all time. Less than a year after that was ended, it could be said that the assumption that the nations would remain "united for all time to uphold a single world order of peace—is manifesting itself to be an illusion. The chances that the one-world conception can be rescued from utter disintegration are growing smaller, smaller, smaller."—Editorial, *The Christian Century*, May 29, 1946, p. 679.

How stood the prospects for international atomic control after three years? "The plain fact is that we're now worse off as a world than we were three years ago. Worse off *because we've stopped thinking about the whole problem.* Because some of the imaginary deadlines posted back in 1945 have been passed and nothing has happened, people—some people—are beginning to say this man-made earthquake isn't so bad after all. Believe me, *it is.*"—David Lilienthal, Chairman, U.S. Atomic Energy Commission, quoted in *Life*, Sept. 27, 1948, p. 115.

Will talking of world peace create a false security?

"There shall come in the last days scoffers, walking after their own lusts, and saying, *Where is the promise of his coming?* for since the fathers fell asleep, all things continue as they were from the beginning of the creation." 2 Peter 3:3, 4.

"For yourselves know perfectly that the day of the Lord so cometh *as a thief in the night.* For *when they shall say, Peace and safety;* then sudden destruction cometh upon them. . . . But *ye, brethren, are not in darkness,* that that day should overtake you as a thief." 1 Thessalonians 5:2-4.

Note.—Those in darkness are looking for a time of peace and safety, and those not in darkness are looking for the day of the Lord—a day of destruction—the end of the world and the coming of Christ. (See Jeremiah 7:1-19; Daniel 12:1; Joel 2:1-11; Zephaniah 1; Matthew 25:31-46; Galatians 5:16-21.)

All heedless of the signs of the times and the warnings of the word of God and of world events, the world will come up to the day of the Lord unprepared. As a thief in the night this day will take unawares all who are not looking, watching, and waiting for their Lord's return. Instead of looking for the world's conversion, we should be looking for Christ's coming.

"If, as many Christians believe, our Lord's return is imminent," says Latourette, "the time is short in which to prepare their fellows for that event."—*The Christian Outlook*, p. 200.

What admonition by the prophet Isaiah to the faithful in his day should also be the Christian's reaction to last-day conditions?

"Neither fear ye their fear, nor be afraid." Isaiah 8:12. (See 1 Peter 3:14.)

"When these things begin to come to pass, then look up, and lift up your heads; for your redemption draweth nigh." Luke 21:28.

NOTE.—The first-century Christians, says Wesner Fallaw, expected the end of the world in their day. They "were in training for life in a new world. Joy in the Lord of heaven and earth quite overcame anxiety about the cessation of one kind of life and the beginning of another.

"The fact that these Christians were mistaken in their belief that some among them would still be alive when all things were finished is unimportant. What is of primary importance for us is the fact that they so strengthened each other in the faith that they could rejoice over the certainty they had that the world was about to end. And no less important for us is the cue which their conduct provides. Awaiting the end which they deemed a new beginning, they were constructively active serving their fellows, putting human need foremost and thrusting property far down the scale in value. . . .

"The Christian is not anxious about tomorrow—the scientist's likely day of world's end; rather, the Christian is joyful over the prospect of God's new era wherein more justice will be realized than the most loving of men are able to achieve."—*The Christian Century*, Sept. 25, 1946. Used by permission.

O BLESSED Christ! my Strength, my King,
   He is my comfort and my stay;
In Him I hope, of Him I sing,
   While toiling o'er life's rugged way.
Chiefest among ten thousand He,
For Christ, my King, is all to me.

—MRS. L. D. AVERY-STUTTLE

Christ's Second Coming

Christ Foretells His Return

What promise did Christ make concerning His coming?

"Let not your heart be troubled: ye believe in God, believe also in me. In my Father's house are many mansions: if it were not so, I would have told you. I go to prepare a place for you. And if I go and prepare a place for you, *I will come again,* and receive you unto myself; that where I am, there ye may be also." John 14:1-3.

What follows the signs of Christ's coming?

"And then shall they see *the Son of man coming in a cloud with power and great glory.*" Luke 21:27.

Angels and Apostles Proclaim It

At His ascension, how was Christ's return promised?

"And while they looked stedfastly toward heaven as he went up, behold, two men stood by them in white apparel; which also said, Ye men of Galilee, why stand ye gazing up into heaven? *this same Jesus, which is taken up from you into heaven, shall so come in like manner as ye have seen him go into heaven.*" Acts 1:10, 11.

How does Paul give expression to this hope?

"Looking for that blessed hope, and the glorious appearing of the great God and our Saviour Jesus Christ." Titus 2:13.

What is Peter's testimony regarding it?

"We have not followed cunningly devised fables, when we made known unto you the power and coming of our Lord Jesus Christ, but were eyewitnesses of his majesty." 2 Peter 1:16.

The Unprepared

Will the inhabitants of the earth as a whole be prepared to meet Him?

"Then shall appear the sign of the Son of man in heaven: and *then shall all the tribes of the earth mourn,* and they shall see the Son of man coming in the clouds of heaven with power and great glory." Matthew 24:30. "Behold, he cometh with clouds; and every eye shall see him, and they also which pierced him: and *all kindreds of the earth shall wail because of him."* Revelation 1:7.

Why will many not be prepared for this event?

"But and if that evil servant shall say in his heart, *My lord delayeth his coming;* and shall begin to smite his fellowservants, and to eat and drink with the drunken; the lord of that servant shall come in a day when he looketh not for him, and in an hour that he is not aware of, and shall cut him asunder, and appoint him his portion with the hypocrites: there shall be weeping and gnashing of teeth." Matthew 24:48-51.

What will the world be doing when Christ comes?

"But as the days of Noe were, so shall also the coming of the Son of man be. For as in the days that were before the flood *they were eating and drinking, marrying and giving in marriage,* until the day that Noe entered into the ark, and knew not until the flood came, and took them all away; so shall also the coming of the Son of man be." Verses 37-39. "Likewise also as it was in the days of Lot; *they did eat, they drank, they bought, they sold, they planted, they builded;* but the same day that Lot went out of Sodom it rained fire and brimstone from heaven, and destroyed them all. Even thus shall it be in the day when the Son of man is revealed." Luke 17:28-30.

NOTE.—These texts do not teach that it is wrong in itself to eat, drink, marry, buy, sell, plant, or build, but that men's minds will be so taken up with these things that they will give little or no thought to the future life, and make no plans or preparation to meet Jesus when He comes.

Who is it that blinds men to the gospel of Christ?

"In whom *the god of this world* [Satan] hath blinded the minds of them which believe not, lest the light of the glorious gospel of Christ, who is the image of God, should shine unto them." 2 Corinthians 4:4.

NOTE.—"To my mind this precious doctrine—for such I must call

COPYRIGHT, 1949, BY REVIEW AND HERALD

VERNON NYE, ARTIST

CHRIST ANSWERING HIS DISCIPLES' QUESTIONS

"In my Father's house are many mansions: if it were not so, I would have told you. I go to prepare a place for you. And if I go and prepare a place for you, I will come again,

it—of the return of the Lord to this earth is taught in the New Testament as clearly as any other doctrine in it; yet I was in the Church fifteen or sixteen years before I ever heard a sermon on it. There is hardly any church that doesn't make a great deal of baptism, but in all of Paul's epistles I believe baptism is only spoken of thirteen times, while it speaks about the return of our Lord fifty times; and yet the Church has had very little to say about it. Now, I can see a reason for this; the devil does not want us to see this truth, for nothing would wake up the Church so much. The moment a man takes hold of the truth that Jesus Christ is coming back again to receive His followers to Himself, this world loses its hold upon him. Gas stocks and water stocks and stocks in banks and railroads are of very much less consequence to him then. His heart is free, and he looks for the blessed appearing of his Lord, who, at His coming, will take him into His blessed Kingdom."—D. L. MOODY, *The Second Coming of Christ* (Revell), pp. 6, 7.

" 'This same Jesus, which is taken up from you into heaven, *shall so come in like manner as ye have seen him go into heaven,*' is the parting promise of Jesus to his disciples, communicated through the two men in white apparel, as a cloud received him out of their sight. When after more than fifty years in glory he breaks the silence and speaks once more in the Revelation which he gave to his servant John, the post-ascension Gospel which he sends opens with, *'Behold, He cometh with clouds,'* and closes with *'Surely I come quickly.'* Considering the solemn emphasis thus laid upon this doctrine, and considering the great prominence given to it throughout the teaching of our Lord and of his apostles, how was it that for the first five years of my pastoral life it had absolutely no place in my preaching? Undoubtedly the reason lay in the lack of early instruction. Of all the sermons heard from childhood on, I do not remember listening to a single one upon this subject."—A. J. GORDON, *How Christ Came to Church*, pp. 44, 45.

PREPARED FOR HIS COMING

When are the saved to be like Jesus?

"Beloved, now are we the sons of God, and it doth not yet appear what we shall be: but we know that, *when he shall appear, we shall be like him;* for we shall see him as he is." 1 John 3:2.

Will Christ's coming be a time of reward?

"For the Son of man shall come in the glory of his Father with his angels; and *then he shall reward every man according to his works.*" Matthew 16:27. "And, behold, I come quickly; *and my reward is with me,* to give every man according as his work shall be." Revelation 22:12.

To whom is salvation promised at Christ's appearing?

"So Christ was once offered to bear the sins of many; and *unto them that look for him* shall he appear the second time without sin unto salvation." Hebrews 9:28.

What influence has this hope upon the life?

"We know that, when he shall appear, we shall be like him; for we shall see him as he is. And *every man that hath this hope in him purifieth himself, even as he is pure."* 1 John 3:2, 3.

To whom is a crown of righteousness promised?

"For I am now ready to be offered, and the time of my departure is at hand. I have fought a good fight, I have finished my course, I have kept the faith: henceforth there is laid up for me a crown of righteousness, which the Lord, the righteous judge, shall give me at that day: and not to me only, but *unto all them also that love his appearing."* 2 Timothy 4:6-8.

What will the waiting ones say when Jesus comes?

"And it shall be said in that day, Lo, this is our God; we have waited for him, and he will save us: this is the Lord; we have waited for him, we will be glad and rejoice in his salvation." Isaiah 25:9.

Has the exact time of Christ's coming been revealed?

"But of that day and hour *knoweth no man,* no, not the angels of heaven, but my Father only." Matthew 24:36.

In view of this fact, what does Christ tell us to do?

"Watch therefore: for ye know not what hour your Lord doth come." Verse 42.

Note.—"To the secure and careless He will come as a thief in the night: to His own, as their Lord."—Henry Alford, *The New Testament for English Readers,* vol. 1, part 1, p. 170.

"The proper attitude of a Christian is to be always looking for his Lord's return."—D. L. Moody, *The Second Coming of Christ* (Revell), p. 9.

What warning has Christ given that we might not be taken by surprise by this great event?

"And take heed to yourselves, lest at any time your hearts be overcharged with surfeiting, and drunkenness, and cares of this life, and so that day come upon you unawares. For as a snare shall it come on all them that dwell on the face of the whole earth. Watch ye therefore, and pray always, that ye may be accounted worthy to escape all these things that shall come to pass, and to stand before the Son of man." Luke 21:34-36.

What Christian grace are we exhorted to exercise in our expectant longing for this event?

"Be *patient* therefore, brethren, unto the coming of the Lord. Behold, the husbandman waiteth for the precious fruit of the earth, and hath long patience for it, until he receive the early and latter rain. Be ye also *patient;* stablish your hearts: for the coming of the Lord draweth nigh." James 5:7, 8.

What has been the general attitude of Christians toward the second coming of Christ?

The belief of the Christian church in the second coming of Christ appears in Christian literature from the origin of the so-called Apostles' Creed down through to very recent times.

Note.—These creeds can be found in the classic work *The Creeds of Christendom* (Harper) by the great church historian Philip Schaff. From that work we quote but two examples:

"The Nicene Creed is the first which obtained universal authority. It rests on older forms used in different churches of the East, and has undergone again some changes. . . . The original Nicene Creed dates from the first œcumenical Council, which was held at Nicaea, A.D. 325."—Volume 1, pp. 24, 25. The text from which we quote is the original text of A.D. 325:

"We believe in . . . one Lord Jesus Christ, . . . who . . . suffered, and the third day he rose again, ascended into heaven; from thence *He shall come* to judge the quick and the dead."—*Ibid.,* pp. 28, 29.

The New Hampshire Baptist Confession (1833), which is "widely accepted by Baptists, especially in the Northern and Western States" (*ibid.,* vol. 3, p. 742), says:

"We believe that the end of the world is approaching; that *at the last day Christ will descend from heaven, and raise the dead from the grave to final retribution;* that a solemn separation will then take place; that the wicked will be adjudged to endless punishment, and the righteous to endless joy; and that this judgment will fix forever the final state of men in heaven or hell, on principles of righteousness."—*Ibid.,* p. 748.

Manner of Christ's Coming

Does Christ Come at Time of Death?

Is Christ coming again?

"I will come *again*." John 14:3.

How does Paul speak of this coming?

"Unto them that look for him shall he appear *the second time* without sin unto salvation." Hebrews 9:28.

Did the early disciples think that death would be the second coming of Christ?

"Peter seeing him [John] saith to Jesus, Lord, and what shall this man do? Jesus saith unto him, If I will that he tarry *till I come*, what is that to thee? follow thou me. Then went this saying abroad among the brethren, that that disciple *should not die:* yet Jesus said not unto him, He shall not die; but, If I will that he tarry *till I come*, what is that to thee?" John 21:21-23.

Note.—From this it is evident that the early disciples regarded death and the coming of Christ as two separate events.

" 'Therefore be ye also ready: for in such an hour as ye think not the Son of man cometh.' Some people say that means death; but the Word of God does not say it means death. Death is our enemy, but our Lord hath the keys of Death; He has conquered death, hell and the grave. . . . Christ is the Prince of Life; there is no death where He is; death flees at His coming; dead bodies sprang to life when He touched them or spoke to them. His coming is not death; He is the resurrection and the life; when He sets up His kingdom there is to be no death, but life forevermore."—D. L. Moody, *The Second Coming of Christ* (Revell), pp. 10, 11.

Christ and Angels Testify

At His ascension, how did the angels say Christ would come again?

"When he had spoken these things, while they beheld, he was taken up; and *a cloud received him out of their sight*. And while they looked stedfastly toward heaven as he went up, behold, two men stood by them in white apparel; which also said, Ye men of

Galilee, why stand ye gazing up into heaven? this same Jesus, which is taken up from you into heaven, *shall so come in like manner as ye have seen him go into heaven."* Acts 1:9-11.

How did Christ Himself say He would come?

"For the Son of man shall come *in the glory of his Father with his angels."* Matthew 16:27. "Then shall all the tribes of the earth mourn, and they shall see the Son of man coming *in the clouds of heaven with power and great glory."* Matthew 24:30.

APOSTLES JOHN AND PAUL SPEAK

How many will see Him when He comes?

"Behold, he cometh with clouds; and *every eye shall see him,* and they also which pierced him." Revelation 1:7.

NOTE.—Christ's second coming will be as real as was His first, and as visible as His ascension, and far more glorious. To spiritualize our Lord's return is to pervert the obvious meaning of His promise, "I will come again," and nullify the whole plan of redemption; for the reward of the faithful of all ages is to be given at this most glorious of all events.

What demonstration will accompany His coming?

"The Lord himself shall descend from heaven *with a shout, with the voice of the archangel, and with the trump of God:* and the dead in Christ shall rise first." 1 Thessalonians 4:16.

JESUS WARNS OF DECEPTION

What warning has Christ given concerning false views?

"Then if any man shall say unto you, *Lo, here is Christ, or there; believe it not.* For there shall arise false Christs, and false prophets, and shall shew great signs and wonders; insomuch that, if it were possible, they shall deceive the very elect. Behold, I have told you before. Wherefore if they shall say unto you, Behold, he is in the *desert;* go not forth: behold, he is in the *secret chambers;* believe it not." Matthew 24:23-26.

How visible is His coming to be?

"For as the lightning cometh out of the east, and shineth even unto the west; so shall also the coming of the Son of man be." Verse 27.

Object of Christ's Coming

CHRIST COMES FOR HIS PEOPLE

For what purpose did Christ say He would come again?

"I go to prepare a place for you. And if I go and prepare a place for you, *I will come again, and receive you unto myself; that where I am, there ye may be also.*" John 14:2, 3.

What part will the angels have in this event?

"And he shall send his angels with a great sound of a trumpet, and *they shall gather together his elect* from the four winds, from one end of heaven to the other." Matthew 24:31.

THE DEAD AND THE LIVING

What takes place at the sounding of the trumpet?

"For the Lord himself shall descend from heaven with a shout, with the voice of the archangel, and with the trump of God: and *the dead in Christ shall rise first.*" 1 Thessalonians 4:16.

What will be done with the righteous living?

"Then we which are alive and remain shall be *caught up together with them in the clouds,* to meet the Lord in the air: and so shall we ever be with the Lord." Verse 17.

What change will then take place in both the living and the sleeping saints?

"We shall not all sleep, but *we shall all be changed,* in a moment, in the twinkling of an eye, at the last trump: for the trumpet shall sound, and the dead shall be raised *incorruptible,* and we shall be changed. For this corruptible must put on *incorruption,* and this mortal must put on *immortality.*" 1 Corinthians 15:51-53.

When are the saints to be like Jesus?

"But we know that, *when he shall appear, we shall be like him;* for we shall see him as he is." 1 John 3:2.

OBJECT OF CHRIST'S COMING

THE TIME OF REWARD

How many will receive a reward when Christ comes?

"For the Son of man shall come in the glory of his Father with his angels; and *then he shall reward every man according to his works.*" Matthew 16:27.

What promise is made to those who look for Him?

"So Christ was once offered to bear the sins of many; and unto them that look for him *shall he appear the second time without sin unto salvation.*" Hebrews 9:28.

When did Christ say the good would be recompensed?

"For thou shalt be recompensed *at the resurrection of the just.*" Luke 14:14.

Have the worthies of old gone to their reward?

"And these all, having obtained a good report through faith, *received not the promise:* God having provided some better thing for us, *that they without us should not be made perfect.*" Hebrews 11:39, 40.

When did Paul expect to receive his crown?

"Henceforth there is laid up for me a crown of righteousness, which the Lord, the righteous judge, shall give me *at that day:* and not to me only, but unto all them also that love his appearing." 2 Timothy 4:8.

A TIME OF JUDGMENT

Will this be a time of judgment?

"And Enoch also, the seventh from Adam, prophesied of these, saying, Behold, *the Lord cometh with ten thousands of his saints, to execute judgment upon all.*" Jude 14, 15.

How did David express himself on this point?

"*For he cometh, for he cometh to judge the earth:* he shall judge the world with righteousness, and the people with his truth." Psalm 96:13.

When did Paul say Christ would judge the living and the dead?

"I charge thee therefore before God, and the Lord Jesus

Christ, *who shall judge the quick and the dead at his appearing and his kingdom.*" 2 Timothy 4:1.

What great separation will then take place?

"When the Son of man shall come in his glory, and all the holy angels with him, then shall he sit upon the throne of his glory: and before him shall be gathered all nations: and *he shall separate them one from another, as a shepherd divideth his sheep from the goats.*" Matthew 25:31, 32.

What will He say to those on His right hand?

"Then shall the King say unto them on his right hand, *Come, ye blessed of my Father, inherit the kingdom prepared for you from the foundation of the world.*" Verse 34.

What will He say to those on the left?

"Then shall He say also unto them on the left hand, *Depart from me, ye cursed, into everlasting fire, prepared for the devil and his angels.*" Verse 41.

When Thou, My Righteous Judge

When Thou, my righteous Judge, shalt come,
To call Thy ransomed people home,
Shall I among them stand?
Shall such a worthless worm as I,
Who sometimes am afraid to die,
Be found at Thy right hand?

. . . . .

Let me among Thy saints be found,
Whene'er the Archangel's trump shall sound,
To see Thy smiling face;
Then joyfully Thy praise I'll sing,
While heaven's resounding mansions ring
With shouts of endless grace.

—Selina, Countess of Huntingdon

The Resurrection of the Just

THE ANCIENT HOPE OF RESURRECTION

What question does Job ask and answer?

"*If a man die, shall he live again?* all the days of my appointed time will I wait, till my change come. *Thou shalt call, and I will answer thee:* thou wilt have a desire to the work of thine hands." Job 14:14, 15.

Why did Job wish that his words were written in a book, graven with an iron pen in the rock forever?

"*For I know that my redeemer liveth,* and that he shall stand at the latter day upon the earth: and though after my skin worms destroy this body, yet *in my flesh shall I see God.*" Job 19:25, 26.

When did David say he would be satisfied?

"As for me, I will behold thy face in righteousness: I shall be satisfied, *when I awake, with thy likeness.*" Psalm 17:15.

What comforting promise has God made concerning the sleeping saints?

"I will *ransom them from the power of the grave;* I will *redeem them from death:* O death, I will be thy plagues; O grave, I will be thy destruction." Hosea 13:14.

CHRIST AND THE RESURRECTION HOPE

What does Christ proclaim Himself to be?

"*I am the resurrection, and the life:* he that believeth in me, though he were dead, yet shall he live: and whosoever liveth and believeth in me shall never die." John 11:25, 26. "*I am he that liveth, and was dead;* and, behold, *I am alive for evermore,* Amen; *and have the keys of hell and of death.*" Revelation 1:18.

NOTE.—Christ looked upon death as a *sleep*. Absolute death knows no waking; but through Christ all who have fallen under the power of death will be raised, some to a life unending, some to everlasting death.

Concerning what did Christ tell us not to marvel?

"Marvel not at this: for *the hour is coming, in the which all that are in the graves shall hear his voice, and shall come forth;* they that have done good, unto the resurrection of life; and they that have done evil, unto the resurrection of damnation." John 5:28, 29.

Upon what one fact does Paul base the Christian hope?

"Now if Christ be preached that he rose from the dead, how say some among you that there is no resurrection of the dead? But *if there be no resurrection of the dead, then is Christ not risen: and if Christ be not risen, then is our preaching vain, and your faith is also vain.* Yea, and we are found false witnesses of God; because we have testified of God that *he raised up Christ:* whom he raised not up, if so be that the dead rise not. For *if the dead rise not, then is not Christ raised: and if Christ be not raised, your faith is vain; ye are yet in your sins.* Then they also which are fallen asleep in Christ are *perished.* If in this life only we have hope in Christ, we are of all men most miserable." 1 Corinthians 15:12-19.

What positive declaration does the apostle then make?

"But now is Christ risen from the dead, and become the firstfruits of them that slept. For since by man came death, by man came also the resurrection of the dead. For as in Adam all die, even so in Christ shall all be made alive." Verses 20-22.

NOTE.—The resurrection of Christ is in many respects the most significant fact in history. It is the great and impregnable foundation and hope of the Christian church. Every fundamental truth of Christianity is involved in the resurrection of Christ. If this could be overthrown, every essential doctrine of Christianity would be invalidated. The resurrection of Christ is the pledge of our resurrection and future life.

FACTS ABOUT THE FIRST RESURRECTION

Concerning what should we not be ignorant?

"But I would not have you to be ignorant, brethren, *concerning them which are asleep,* that ye sorrow not, even as others which have no hope." 1 Thessalonians 4:13.

What is set forth as the basis for hope and comfort?

THE RESURRECTION OF THE JUST

"For if we believe that Jesus died and rose again, *even so them also which sleep in Jesus will God bring with him.*" Verse 14.

What is said of those embraced in the first resurrection?

"Blessed and holy is he that hath part in the first resurrection: on such the second death hath no power, but they shall be priests of God and of Christ, and shall reign with him a thousand years." Revelation 20:6.

When will this resurrection of the saints take place?

"For this we say unto you by the word of the Lord, that we which are alive and remain unto *the coming of the Lord* shall not prevent [precede] them which are asleep. *For the Lord himself shall descend from heaven* with a shout, with the voice of the archangel, and with the trump of God: *and the dead in Christ shall rise first.*" 1 Thessalonians 4:15, 16.

What will then take place?

"Then we which are alive and remain shall be caught up together with them in the clouds, to meet the Lord in the air: and so shall we ever be with the Lord." Verse 17.

How does Paul say the saints will be raised?

"Behold, I shew you a mystery; We shall not all sleep, but we shall all be changed, in a moment, in the twinkling of an eye, at the last trump: for the trumpet shall sound, and *the dead shall be raised incorruptible.*" 1 Corinthians 15:51, 52.

What great change will then take place in their bodies?

"So also is the resurrection of the dead. It is *sown in corruption; it is raised in incorruption: it is sown in dishonour; it is raised in glory: it is sown in weakness; it is raised in power: it is sown a natural body; it is raised a spiritual body.*" Verses 42-44.

What else has He promised to do?

"And God *shall wipe away all tears* from their eyes; and there shall be no more death, neither sorrow, nor crying, neither shall there be any more pain: for the former things are passed away." Revelation 21:4. (See pages 738-757.)

The Gathering of Israel

The Scattering of Israel

Because of disobedience, what experience came to Israel?

"I will make you to be removed into all the kingdoms of the earth." Jeremiah 34:17. (See Jeremiah 25:8-11.)

How had Moses spoken of the dispersion of Israel?

"The Lord shall bring a nation against thee from far, from the end of the earth.... And he shall besiege thee in all thy gates, until thy high and fenced walls come down, wherein thou trustedst." "And the Lord shall scatter thee among all people, from the one end of the earth even unto the other." Deuteronomy 28:49-52, 64.

Under what striking symbol was all this foretold?

"Thus saith the Lord, Go and get *a potter's earthen bottle, and*" "break the bottle ... and ... say unto them, Thus saith the Lord of hosts; *Even so will I break this people and this city, as one breaketh a potter's vessel, that cannot be made whole again.*" Jeremiah 19:1, 10, 11.

In what words does Daniel refer to the Babylonian captivity as a fulfillment of these warnings?

"Yea, all Israel have transgressed thy law, even by departing, that they might not obey thy voice; *therefore the curse is poured upon us, and the oath that is written in the law of Moses* the servant of God, because we have sinned against him. And *he hath confirmed his words, which he spake against us,* and against our judges that judged us, *by bringing upon us a great evil:* for under the whole heaven hath not been done as hath been done upon Jerusalem." Daniel 9:11, 12.

What prophecy spoke of their return from captivity?

"For I know the thoughts that I think toward you, saith the Lord, thoughts of peace, and not of evil, to give you an expected end.... And ye shall seek me, and find me, when ye shall search for me with all your heart. And I will be found of you, saith the

THE GATHERING OF ISRAEL

Lord: and *I will turn away your captivity, and I will gather you from all the nations, and from all the places whither I have driven you,* saith the Lord; and I will bring you again into the place whence I caused you to be carried away captive." Jeremiah 29:11-14. (See also Jeremiah 23:3.)

NOTE.—The first dispersion of the Jews occurred under Nebuchadnezzar, king of Babylon. Under Cyrus and Artaxerxes, Persian kings, large numbers of Jews returned to Palestine, their homeland.

After the restoration of Jerusalem and the coming of the Messiah what further desolation of the city was to take place?

"And after threescore and two weeks shall Messiah be cut off, but not for himself: and *the people of the prince that shall come shall destroy the city and the sanctuary.*" Daniel 9:26.

What warning did our Lord give of a second "captivity," or dispersion, and a second desolation of Jerusalem?

"And they shall fall by the edge of the sword, and shall be led away captive into all nations: and Jerusalem shall be trodden down of the Gentiles, *until the times of the Gentiles be fulfilled.*" Luke 21:24. Compare Matthew 24:15-20.

NOTE.—When Jesus stood on the Mount of Olives, weeping over Jerusalem with the sad lament, "How often would I have gathered thee," He said, "Behold, your house is left unto you desolate." In A.D. 70, about thirty-nine years later, occurred the destruction of Jerusalem by the Roman armies under Titus, and the scattering of the Jews into all the world. The gospel was first preached in Jerusalem and Judea, but soon thereafter the Christians were scattered by persecution and went everywhere preaching the word. (Acts 8:4.) Paul and Barnabas later said to the Jews at Antioch, "It was necessary that the word of God should first have been spoken to you: but seeing ye put it from you, and judge yourselves unworthy of everlasting life, lo, we turn to the Gentiles." Acts 13:46. By the crucifixion of the Saviour and the persecution of His disciples, the Jews as a nation filled up the cup of their iniquity. The death of the martyr Stephen marked the culmination of the period allotted to the Jewish nation, and the beginning of the times of the Gentiles. (See pages 230, 232.)

What will terminate the "times" allotted to the Gentiles?

"This gospel of the kingdom shall be preached in all the world for a witness unto all nations, and *then shall the end come.*" Matthew 24:14.

Why was the gospel to be preached to the Gentiles?

"Simeon hath declared how God at the first did visit the Gentiles, *to take out of them a people for his name.*" Acts 15:14.

TRUE ISRAEL IN GOD'S SIGHT

What promise did God once make to Abraham?

"The promise, that he should be the heir of the world." Romans 4:13.

In view of the fact that this promise was never fulfilled to Abraham, and that his descendants are now scattered among all nations, how shall we understand God's promise to Abraham?

"To Abraham and his seed were the promises made. He saith not, And to seeds, as of many; but as of one, And to thy seed, which is Christ." Galatians 3:16.

Who are included with Christ in this promise, as being of Abraham's seed?

"If ye be Christ's, then are ye Abraham's seed, and heirs according to the promise." Verse 29. See also Romans 2:28, 29.

NOTE.—Here, then, is the key that unlocks, not merely one, but many otherwise mysterious passages of the Sacred Scriptures. The gathering of Israel to their own land is not a regathering of Abraham's literal descendants to Old Jerusalem "in unbelief," but a gathering in faith of the spiritual seed to the New Jerusalem, the city for which Abraham looked, "whose builder and maker is God." (See Hebrews 11:8-10.) (See reading on page 740.)

When will this promise to Abraham's seed be fulfilled?

"When the Son of man shall come in his glory, and all the holy angels with him, then shall he sit upon the throne of his glory: and before him shall be gathered all nations: and he shall separate them one from another, as a shepherd divideth his sheep from the goats: and he shall set the sheep on his right hand, but the goats on the left. Then shall the King say unto them on his right hand, Come, ye blessed of my Father, inherit the kingdom prepared for you from the foundation of the world." Matthew 25:31-34.

The Millennium

THE MILLENNIUM AND JUDGMENT

WHAT text definitely brings the millennium to view?

"And I saw thrones, and they sat upon them, and *judgment was given unto them:* ... and *they lived and reigned with Christ a thousand years.*" Revelation 20:4.

NOTE.—The Greek may also be rendered, "they came to life and reigned."

Whom does Paul say the saints are to judge?

"Dare any of you, having a matter against another, go to law before the unjust, and not before the saints? *Do ye not know that the saints shall judge the world?* ... *Know ye not that we shall judge angels?*" 1 Corinthians 6:1-3.

NOTE.—From this and the preceding text of Scripture it is plain that the saints of all ages are to be engaged with Christ in a work of "judgment" during the millennium, or the period of one thousand years.

THE MILLENNIUM BEGINS

How many resurrections are there to be?

"Marvel not at this: for the hour is coming, in the which all that are in the graves shall hear his voice, and shall come forth; they that have done good, unto *the resurrection of life;* and they that have done evil, unto *the resurrection of damnation.*" John 5:28, 29.

What class only have part in the first resurrection?

"*Blessed and holy* is he that hath part in the first resurrection: on such the second death hath no power." Revelation 20:6.

What will Christ do with the saints when He comes?

"I will come again, and *receive you unto myself;* that where I am, there ye may be also." John 14:3.

NOTE.—In other words, Christ will take them to heaven, there to live and reign with Him during the one thousand years.

THE MILLENNIUM

1000 YEARS BETWEEN RESURRECTIONS
ON EARTH—SATAN ALONE, AND WICKED DEAD
IN HEAVEN—SAINTS ASSIST IN JUDGMENT OF WICKED

Left side (First Resurrection):
1. END OF SEVEN LAST PLAGUES
2. CHRIST'S 2ND COMING
3. RIGHTEOUS DEAD RAISED
4. WICKED PERISH — SATAN BOUND
5. RIGHTEOUS ASCEND TO HEAVEN

END OF THE WORLD

Right side (Second Resurrection):
1. CHRIST AND SAINTS DESCEND
2. HOLY CITY DESCENDS
3. WICKED DEAD RAISED
4. SATAN LOOSED
5. WICKED DESTROYED

NEW EARTH AND ETERNITY

The millennium is the closing period of God's great week of time—a great sabbath of rest to the earth and to the people of God.

It follows the close of the gospel age, and precedes the setting up of the everlasting kingdom of God on earth.

It comprehends what in the Scriptures is frequently spoken of as "the day of the Lord."

It is bounded at each end by a resurrection.

Its beginning is marked by the pouring out of the seven last plagues, the second coming of Christ, the resurrection of the righteous dead, the binding of Satan, and the translation of the saints to heaven; and its close, by the descent of the New Jerusalem, with Christ and the saints, from heaven, the resurrection of the wicked dead, the loosing of Satan, and the final destruction of the wicked.

During the one thousand years the earth lies desolate; Satan and his angels are confined here; and the saints, with Christ, sit in judgment on the wicked, preparatory to their final punishment.

The wicked dead are then raised; Satan is loosed for a little season, and he and the host of the wicked encompass the camp of the saints and the Holy City. Then fire comes down from God out of heaven and devours them. The earth is cleansed by the same fire that destroys the wicked, and, renewed, becomes the eternal abode of the saints.

The millennium is one of "the ages to come." Its close will mark the beginning of the new-earth state.

THE MILLENNIUM

Where did John, in vision, see the saints?

"After this I beheld, and, lo, a great multitude, which no man could number, of all nations, and kindreds, and people, and tongues, *stood before the throne, and before the Lamb,* clothed with white robes, and palms in their hands." Revelation 7:9.

NOTE.—This scripture shows plainly that the righteous are all taken to heaven immediately after the first resurrection. See also 1 Thessalonians 4:16-18. This accords with the words of Christ in John 14:1-3, where He says, "I go to prepare a place for you. And if I go and prepare a place for you, I will come again, and *receive you unto myself; that where I am, there ye may be also.*" Peter desired to accompany Christ to those mansions; but Jesus answered, "Thou canst not follow me now; *but thou shalt follow me afterwards.*" John 13:36. This makes it clear that when Christ returns to earth to receive His people, He takes them to the Father's house in heaven.

What becomes of the living wicked when Christ comes?

"*As it was in the days of Noe,* so shall it be also in the days of the Son of man. They did eat, they drank, they married wives, they were given in marriage, until the day that Noe entered into the ark, and *the flood came, and destroyed them all. Likewise also as it was in the days of Lot;* . . . the same day that Lot went out of Sodom it rained fire and brimstone from heaven, and *destroyed them all. Even thus shall it be in the day when the Son of man is revealed.*" Luke 17:26-30.

What does the apostle Paul say concerning this?

"When they shall say, Peace and safety; *then sudden destruction cometh upon them,* . . . and they shall not escape." 1 Thessalonians 5:3.

NOTE.—When Christ comes, the righteous will be delivered and taken to heaven, and all the living wicked will be suddenly destroyed, as they were at the time of the Flood. For further proof see 2 Thessalonians 1:7-9; Revelation 6:14-17; 19:11-21; Jeremiah 25:30-33. There will be no general resurrection of the wicked until the end of the one thousand years. See also Revelation 20:5. This will leave the earth desolate and without human inhabitant during this period.

How long is Satan to be imprisoned on this earth?

"I saw an angel come down from heaven, having the key of the bottomless pit and a great chain in his hand. And he laid hold on the dragon, that old serpent, which is the Devil, and Satan, and *bound him a thousand years,* and cast him into the bottomless pit, and shut him up, and set a seal upon him, that he should deceive the nations no more, till the thousand years should be fulfilled." Revelation 20:1-3.

Note.—The word rendered "bottomless pit" in this text is *abussos,* the Greek term employed by the Septuagint in Genesis 1:2, as the equivalent of the Hebrew word rendered "deep" in our English versions. A more literal translation would be "abyss." It is a term applied to the earth in its desolate, waste, chaotic, dark, uninhabited condition. In this condition it will remain during the one thousand years. It will be the dreary prison house of Satan during this period. Here, in the midst of the moldering bones of wicked dead, slain at Christ's coming, the broken-down cities, and the wreck and ruin of all the pomp and power of this world, Satan will have opportunity to reflect upon the results of his rebellion against God.

Close of the Millennium

The righteous dead are raised at Christ's second coming. When will the rest of the dead, the wicked, be raised?

"The rest of the dead lived not again *until the thousand years were finished."* Verse 5.

Note.—From this we see that the beginning and the close of the millennium, or one thousand years, are marked by the two resurrections.

The word *millennium* is from two Latin words, *mille,* meaning "thousand," and *annus,* "year"—a thousand years. It covers the time during which Satan is to be bound and wicked men and angels are to be judged. This period is bounded by distinct events. Its beginning is marked by the close of probation, the pouring out of the seven last plagues, the second coming of Christ, and the resurrection of the righteous dead. It closes with the resurrection of the wicked, and their final destruction in the lake of fire. (See diagram on page 346.)

What change is made in Satan's condition at the close of the one thousand years?

"After that *he must be loosed a little season."* Verse 3.

Note.—At the close of the one thousand years, Christ, accompanied by the saints, comes to the earth again, to execute judgment upon the wicked, and to prepare the earth, by a re-creation, for the eternal abode of the righteous. At this time, in answer to the summons of Christ, the wicked dead of all ages awake to life. This is the second resurrection, the resurrection unto damnation. The wicked come forth with the same rebellious spirit which possessed them in this life. Then Satan is loosed from his long period of captivity and inactivity.

As soon as the wicked are raised, what does Satan at once proceed to do?

"When the thousand years are expired, Satan shall be loosed out of his prison, and shall go out to *deceive the nations* which are in the four quarters of the earth, Gog and Magog, *to gather them together to battle:* the number of whom is as the sand of the sea." Verses 7, 8.

Against whom do the wicked go to make war, and what is the outcome?

"They went up on the breadth of the earth, and *compassed the camp of the saints about, and the beloved city;* and *fire came down from God out of heaven, and devoured them."* Verse 9.

NOTE.—This is the last act in the great controversy between Christ and Satan. The whole human race meet here for the first and last time. The eternal separation of the righteous from the wicked here takes place. At this time the judgment of God is executed upon the wicked in the lake of fire. This is the second death. This ends the great rebellion against God and His government. Now is heard the voice of God as He sits upon His throne, speaking to the saints, and saying, "Behold, I make all things new"; and out of the burning ruins of the old earth there springs forth before the admiring gaze of the millions of the redeemed, "a new heaven and a new earth," in which they shall find an everlasting inheritance and dwelling place.

The Day of the Lord

The Description

WHAT is the character of "the day of the Lord"?

"*As a destruction* from the Almighty." Joel 1:15.

"A day of darkness and of gloominess, a day of clouds and of thick darkness." Joel 2:2.

"For the day of the Lord is great and very terrible." Verse 11.

"The great and the terrible day of the Lord." Verse 31.

"That day is a day of wrath, a day of trouble and distress, a day of wasteness and desolation, . . . a day of the trumpet and alarm against the fenced cities, and against the high towers." Zephaniah 1:15, 16. (See also Jeremiah 30:7; Isaiah 13:6-13.)

The Warning

How solemn is the warning concerning "the day of the Lord"?

"Woe unto you that desire the day of the Lord! to what end is it for you? the day of the Lord is darkness, and not light." Amos 5:18. (See also Joel 1:14, 15; 2:1; 3:14.)

The Time

Does the Bible give any idea as to the time of "the day of the Lord"?

"Howl ye; for the day of the Lord is *at hand;* it shall come as a destruction from the Almighty." "For the *stars* of heaven and the constellations thereof shall not give their light: *the sun* shall be darkened in his going forth, and *the moon* shall not cause her light to shine." Isaiah 13:6, 10.

"And I will shew wonders in the heavens and in the earth, blood, and fire, and pillars of smoke. *The sun* shall be turned into darkness, and *the moon* into blood, *before* the great and the terrible day of the Lord come." Joel 2:30, 31. (See also Joel 2:10, 11; 3:14-16; Zephaniah 1:14; Matthew 24:29.)

"And I beheld when he had opened the sixth seal, and, lo, there was a *great earthquake;* and *the sun* became black . . . ,

THE DAY OF THE LORD

and *the moon* became as blood; ... and *the stars* of heaven fell." Revelation 6:12, 13.

The People's Reaction

How do the people react to "the day of the Lord"?

"For the great day of his wrath is come; and *who shall be able to stand?*" Revelation 6:17.

"For the day of the Lord is great and very terrible; and *who can abide it?*" Joel 2:11.

Note.—One class of people—the unprepared—cry out "to the mountains and rocks, Fall on us, and hide us from the face of him that sitteth on the throne, and from the wrath of the Lamb." Revelation 6:15, 16. (See also Zephaniah 1:14.)

Another class of people—the prepared—in that day will say, "Lo, this is our God; we have waited for him, and he will save us: this is the Lord; we have waited for him, we will be glad and rejoice in his salvation." Isaiah 25:9.

God's Admonition

To whom should we turn for help in "the day of the Lord"?

"Seek ye the Lord, all ye meek of the earth, ... seek righteousness, seek meekness: it may be ye shall be hid in the day of the Lord's anger." Zephaniah 2:3.

"Trust ye in the Lord for ever: for in the Lord JEHOVAH is everlasting strength." Isaiah 26:4. (See also Joel 2:12, 13, 32; 3:16, 17; Isaiah 26:20.)

What is God's personal appeal to us?

"Seeing then that all these things shall be dissolved, what manner of persons ought ye to be in all holy conversation and godliness, looking for and hasting unto the coming of the day of God, wherein the heavens being on fire shall be dissolved, and the elements shall melt with fervent heat? Nevertheless we, according to his promise, look for new heavens and a new earth, wherein dwelleth righteousness. Wherefore, beloved, seeing that ye look for such things, be diligent that ye may be found of him in peace, without spot, and blameless." 2 Peter 3:11-14.

Elijah the Prophet

WHAT does God promise concerning Elijah?

"Behold, I will send you Elijah the prophet before the coming of the great and dreadful day of the Lord." Malachi 4:5.

What will this prophet do when he comes?

"And he shall *turn the heart of the fathers to the children, and the heart of the children to their fathers.*" Verse 6.

JOHN THE BAPTIST AND ELIJAH

Whom did Christ indicate as fulfilling this prophecy?

"Jesus answered and said unto them, Elias truly shall first come, and restore all things. But I say unto you, That *Elias is come already,* and they knew him not, but have done unto him whatsoever they listed. Likewise shall also the Son of man suffer of them. Then the disciples understood that he spake unto them of *John the Baptist.*" Matthew 17:11-13.

When asked if he were Elijah, what did John say?

"And he saith, *I am not.*" John 1:21. "He said, *I am the voice of one crying in the wilderness,* Make straight the way of the Lord, as said the prophet Esaias." Verse 23.

In what sense was John the Baptist Elijah?

"Many of the children of Israel shall he turn to the Lord their God. And he shall go before him [Christ] *in the spirit and power of Elias,* to turn the hearts of the fathers to the children, and the disobedient to the wisdom of the just; to make ready a people prepared for the Lord." Luke 1:16, 17.

NOTE.—John went forth *"in the spirit and power of Elias,"* and, in preparing a people for Christ's first coming, did a work similar to that done by Elijah the prophet in Israel centuries before. (See 1 Kings 17 and 18.) In this sense, and in this sense only, he was the Elijah of Malachi 4:5.

How did Elijah answer King Ahab's accusation?

"And it came to pass, when Ahab saw Elijah, that Ahab said

unto him, *Art thou he that troubleth Israel? And he answered, I have not troubled Israel; but thou, and thy father's house, in that ye have forsaken the commandments of the Lord, and thou hast followed Baalim.*" 1 Kings 18:17, 18.

NOTE.—Israel had forsaken God and gone off into idolatry. Jezebel, Ahab's wicked and idolatrous wife, who supported the prophets of Baal, had "cut off the prophets of the Lord" (verse 4), and was seeking to slay Elijah. Elijah called for a famine on the land, and said to Ahab, "As the Lord God of Israel liveth, before whom I stand, there shall not be dew nor rain these years, but according to my word." 1 Kings 17:1. This interview came near the end of the famine. Elijah's message was a call to repentance and obedience to God's commandments.

What plain proposition did he submit to all Israel?

"And Elijah came unto all the people, and said, *How long halt ye between two opinions? if the Lord be God, follow him: but if Baal, then follow him.*" 1 Kings 18:21.

NOTE.—As a result of the test by fire which followed on Mount Carmel (read the remainder of this chapter), there was a great turning to God, the people saying, "The Lord, he is the God." Verse 39.

What was the burden of the message of John the Baptist?

"*Repent ye:* for the kingdom of heaven is at hand." "Bring forth therefore *fruits* meet for repentance." Matthew 3:2, 8.

What was the result of this message?

"Then went out to him Jerusalem, and all Judaea, and all the region round about Jordan, and *were baptized of him in Jordan, confessing their sins.*" Verses 5, 6.

NOTE.—There was a genuine work of repentance and reform. John was not satisfied with a mere profession of religion. He told the Pharisees and Sadducees who came to his baptism, to "bring forth fruits" answerable to an "amendment of life." He wished to see religion in the life, the heart, the home. Thus he prepared a people for Christ's first coming.

THE ELIJAH MESSAGE TODAY

When did the prophecy say Elijah was to come?

"Before the coming of the great and dreadful day of the Lord." Malachi 4:5.

How is this great and dreadful day described?

"For, behold, the day cometh, that shall burn as an oven; and all the proud, yea, and all that do wickedly, shall be stubble: and the day that cometh shall burn them up, saith the Lord of hosts, that it shall leave them neither root nor branch." Verse 1.

Note.—This day is yet future. Therefore, the work done by John the Baptist at Christ's first advent cannot be all that was contemplated in the prophecy concerning the sending of Elijah the prophet. There must be another and greater fulfillment of it, to precede Christ's *Second Advent,* and to prepare, or "make ready," a people for that great event.

What is the threefold message of Revelation 14:6-10?

"Fear God, and give glory to him; for the hour of his judgment is come: and worship him that made heaven, and earth, and the sea, and the fountains of waters. . . . Babylon is fallen, is fallen, that great city, because she made all nations drink of the wine of the wrath of her fornication. . . . If any man worship the beast and his image, and receive his mark in his forehead, or in his hand, the same shall drink of the wine of the wrath of God, which is poured out without mixture into the cup of his indignation." Revelation 14:7-10.

Note.—Like the messages of Elijah and John, this is a call to repentance and reform—to forsake false, idolatrous worship, and to turn to God, and worship Him alone. The first part of this threefold message points out the true God, the Creator, in language similar to that in the fourth, or Sabbath, commandment. This message, now due the world, is today being proclaimed to the world. (See readings on pages 245-260.) Those who proclaim these messages constitute the Elijah for this time, as John did at the time of Christ's first coming.

The People of the Message

How are the people described who are developed by the threefold message here referred to?

"Here is the patience of the saints: here are they that keep the commandments of God, and the faith of Jesus." Verse 12.

Part Eight

The Law of God

	PAGE
The Law of God	357
The Perpetuity of the Law	363
Why Was the Law Given at Sinai?	368
Penalty for Transgression	373
The Law of God in the Patriarchal Age	375
The Law of God in the New Testament	378
The Moral and Ceremonial Laws	381
The Two Covenants	387
What Was Abolished by Christ?	394
The Law and the Gospel	398

COPYRIGHT, 1949, BY REVIEW AND HERALD

FREDERIC R. GRUGER, ARTIST

GOD WRITES HIS LAW

"He declared unto you his covenant, which he commanded you to perform, even ten commandments; and wrote them upon two tables of stone." Deuteronomy 4:

The Law of God

How did God proclaim His law to His people?

"And the Lord spake unto you out of the midst of the fire: ye heard the voice of the words, but saw no similitude; only ye heard a voice. And *he declared unto you his covenant, which he commanded you to perform, even ten commandments; and he wrote them upon two tables of stone.*" Deuteronomy 4:12, 13. (See also Nehemiah 9:13, 14. For the Ten Commandments see Exodus 20:2-17.)

NATURE OF GOD'S LAW

What is the nature of God's law?

"Wherefore the law is *holy,* and the commandment *holy,* and *just,* and *good.*" "For we know that *the law is spiritual:* but I am carnal, sold under sin." Romans 7:12, 14.

NOTE.—In His comments on the sixth and seventh commandments (Matthew 5:21-28) Christ demonstrated the spiritual nature of the law, showing that it relates not merely to outward actions, but also to the thoughts and intents of the heart. (See Hebrews 4:12.) The tenth commandment forbids lust, or all unlawful desire. (Romans 7:7.) Obedience to this law, therefore, requires not merely an outward compliance but genuine heart service. This can be rendered only by a regenerated soul.

"The law of the Lord is perfect, converting the soul." Psalm 19:7. "Is there such a thing as a perfect law? Everything that comes from God is perfect. The law of which we are thinking came from Him. It becomes sullied in our hands. We take from it and try to add to it, and in that way it becomes less than perfect. In a very real sense the law of God is the manifestation of the nature of the Lord. It could no more be imperfect than He is."—*The Augsburg Sunday School Teacher* (Lutheran), August, 1937, vol. 63, no. 8, p. 483, on the Sunday school lesson for August 15.

How comprehensive are these commandments?

"Fear God, and keep his commandments: for *this is the whole duty of man.*" Ecclesiastes 12:13.

NOTE.—"No human lawgiver could have given forth such a law

as that which we find in the decalogue. It is a perfect law; for all human laws that are right are to be found in that brief compendium and epitome of all that is good and excellent toward God, or between man and man."—C. H. Spurgeon, *Sermons*, series 2 (1857), p. 280.

What is the essential principle of the law of God?

"Love worketh no ill to his neighbour: therefore *love* is the fulfilling of the law." Romans 13:10.

What two commandments sum up the law of God?

"Thou shalt love the Lord thy God with all thy heart, and with all thy soul, and with all thy mind. This is the first and great commandment. And the second is like unto it, Thou shalt love thy neighbour as thyself. On these two commandments hang all the law and the prophets." Matthew 22:37-40.

Note.—If you love God with all your heart, you will keep the first table; if you love your neighbor as yourself, you will keep the second.

Purpose of Law

Why should we fear God and keep His commandments?

"Fear God, and keep his commandments: for this is the whole duty of man. *For God shall bring every work into judgment,* with every secret thing, whether it be good, or whether it be evil." Ecclesiastes 12:13, 14.

What will be the standard in the judgment?

"So speak ye, and so do, as they that shall be *judged by the law of liberty.*" James 2:12.

What is sin declared to be?

"Whosoever committeth sin transgresseth also the law: for *sin is the transgression of the law.*" 1 John 3:4.

Disobedience to Law

How many of the commandments is it necessary to break in order to become a transgressor of the law?

"For *whosoever shall keep the whole law, and yet offend in one point, he is guilty of all.* For he that said, Do not commit adultery, said also, Do not kill. Now if thou commit no adultery, yet if thou kill, thou art become a transgressor of the law." James 2:10, 11.

NOTE.—"The ten commandments are not ten different laws; they are one law. If I am being held up in the air by a chain with ten links and I break one of them, down I come, just as surely as if I break the whole ten. If I am forbidden to go out of an enclosure, it makes no difference at what point I break through."—D. L. MOODY, *Weighed and Wanting* (1898 ed.), p. 119.

"The ten words of Sinai were not ten separate commandments," said G. Campbell Morgan, "but ten sides of the one law of God."—*The Ten Commandments* (Revell, 1901 ed.), p. 11.

"As he [a Methodist] loves God, so he keeps his commandments; not only some, or most of them, but all, from the least to the greatest. He is not content to 'keep the whole law, and offend in one point;' but has, in all points, 'a conscience void of offence towards God and towards man.'"—JOHN WESLEY, *The Character of a Methodist,* in *Works,* vol. 8 (1830 ed.), p. 344.

For what did Christ reprove the Pharisees?

"'Why do you, too,' He retorted, 'transgress God's commands for the sake of your tradition? God said, "Honour thy father and thy mother" (Exod. xx. 12); and "Let him who reviles father or mother be put to death" (Exod. xxi. 17); but you say: "If a man says to his father or mother, 'This thing is consecrated, otherwise you should have received it from me,' he shall be absolved from honouring his father"; and so you have rendered futile God's word for the sake of your tradition.'" Matthew 15: 3-6, Weymouth.

Consequently, how did Christ value their worship?

"But *in vain they do worship me,* teaching for doctrines the commandments of men." Verse 9, A.V.

Can one know God and not keep His commandments?

"He that saith, I know him, and keepeth not his commandments, is *a liar,* and *the truth is not in him."* 1 John 2:4.

NECESSITY OF OBEDIENCE

What was Christ's attitude toward God's will, or law?

"Then said I, Lo, I come: in the volume of the book it is written of me, *I delight to do thy will, O my God: yea, thy law is within my heart."* Psalm 40:7, 8. (See Hebrews 10:5, 7.)

Who did He say would enter the kingdom of heaven?

"Not every one that saith unto me, Lord, Lord, shall enter into the kingdom of heaven; but *he that doeth the will of my Father which is in heaven.*" Matthew 7:21.

How will men be rated in relation to God's commandments?

"Whosoever therefore shall break one of these least commandments, and shall teach men so, *he shall be called the least in the kingdom of heaven:* but *whosoever shall do and teach them,* the same shall be called great in the kingdom of heaven." Matthew 5:19.

NOTE.—"The Ten Commandments constitute a summary of the duties God requires of men. These commandments are the foundation which lies beneath the ethical life of humanity. They are as binding upon Christians today as they were upon the Hebrews who first received them."—*The Snowden-Douglass Sunday School Lessons* for 1946, p. 17. Copyright, 1945, by The Macmillan Company and used by permission.

How Can Man Obey?

Why is the carnal mind enmity against God?

"The carnal mind is enmity against God: *for it is not subject to the law of God, neither indeed can be.*" Romans 8:7.

Can man of himself, unaided by Christ, keep the law?

"I am the vine, ye are the branches: he that abideth in me, and I in him, the same bringeth forth much fruit: for *without me ye can do nothing.*" John 15:5. (See Romans 7:14-19.)

What provision has been made by which we are enabled to keep God's law?

"For what the law could not do, in that it was weak through the flesh, God sending his own Son in the likeness of sinful flesh, and for sin, condemned sin in the flesh: that the righteousness of the law might be fulfilled in us, who walk not after the flesh, but after the Spirit." Romans 8:3, 4.

How does the renewed heart regard God's law?

"For this is the love of God, that we keep his commandments: and *his commandments are not grievous.*" 1 John 5:3.

THE LAW OF GOD

BLESSINGS OF WILLING OBEDIENCE

What blessing attends those who keep God's commandments?

"Moreover by them is thy servant warned: and *in keeping of them there is great reward.*" Psalm 19:11.

What would obedience have ensured to ancient Israel?

"O that thou hadst hearkened to my commandments! *then had thy peace been as a river, and thy righteousness as the waves of the sea.*" Isaiah 48:18.

What other blessing attends commandment keeping?

"The fear of the Lord is the beginning of wisdom: *a good understanding have all they that do his commandments.*" Psalm 111:10.

What promise is made to the willing and obedient?

"If ye be willing and obedient, *ye shall eat the good of the land.*" Isaiah 1:19.

THE BETTER OF TWO

To obey is better than sacrifice, the Lord hath said;
To hearken when He commandeth, than an offering made.

All ye who say, "There is naught to do since Christ doth save,"
Remember what He commands you in the Book He gave.

Remember only the doers of the word are blest;
'Tis well to hear and believe it, but to do is best.

—F. E. BELDEN

GOD'S TEN COMMANDMENT LAW

I

Thou shalt have no other gods before me.

II

Thou shalt not make unto thee any graven image, or any likeness of any thing that is in heaven above, or that is in the earth beneath, or that is in the water under the earth: thou shalt not bow down thyself to them, nor serve them: for I the Lord thy God am a jealous God, visiting the iniquity of the fathers upon the children unto the third and fourth generation of them that hate me; and shewing mercy unto thousands of them that love me, and keep my commandments.

III

Thou shalt not take the name of the Lord thy God in vain; for the Lord will not hold him guiltless that taketh his name in vain.

IV

Remember the sabbath day, to keep it holy. Six days shalt thou labour, and do all thy work: but the seventh day is the sabbath of the Lord thy God: in it thou shalt not do any work, thou, nor thy son, nor thy daughter, thy manservant, nor thy maidservant, nor thy cattle, nor thy stranger that is within thy gates: for in six days the Lord made heaven and earth, the sea, and all that in them is, and rested the seventh day: wherefore the Lord blessed the sabbath day, and hallowed it.

V

Honour thy father and thy mother: that thy days may be long upon the land which the Lord thy God giveth thee.

VI

Thou shalt not kill.

VII

Thou shalt not commit adultery.

VIII

Thou shalt not steal.

IX

Thou shalt not bear false witness against thy neighbour.

X

Thou shalt not covet thy neighbour's house, thou shalt not covet thy neighbour's wife, nor his manservant, nor his maidservant, nor his ox, nor his ass, nor any thing that is thy neighbour's. Exodus 20:3-17.

The Perpetuity of the Law

THE GIVER OF THE LAW

How many lawgivers are there?

"There is *one lawgiver,* who is able to save and to destroy." James 4:12.

What is said of the stability of God's character?

"For I am the Lord, *I change not.*" Malachi 3:6.

How enduring are God's moral precepts?

"The works of his hands are verity and judgment; *all his commandments are sure. They stand fast for ever and ever,* and are done in truth and uprightness." Psalm 111:7, 8.

NOTE.—"This rule is unchangeable because it is in harmony with the unchangeable nature of God. . . . The rule of God among men is an expression of His holiness. It must be eternally what it has ever been."—O. C. S. WALLACE, *What Baptists Believe,* p. 81. Copyright, 1934, by the Sunday School Board of the Southern Baptist Convention. Used by permission.

CHRIST FULFILLS THE LAW

Did Christ come to abolish or to destroy the law?

"Think not that I am come to destroy the law, or the prophets: *I am not come to destroy, but to fulfil.*" Matthew 5:17.

NOTE.—"As the word 'law' is used in various senses in the Bible we may well begin our study with a brief examination of its meaning. . . .

"The word *torah* is there used [that is, in the Old Testament] for the laws revealed through Moses, but these were of a threefold character.

"(a) The civil law was strictly applicable only to the chosen people, and was adapted to their peculiar circumstances both in the wilderness and in Canaan, but it has ever since formed the pattern for the legislation of all civilized countries.

"(b) The ceremonial law was also only for Israel and proselytes from heathendom, and it was preparatory and temporary (Gal. 4:3, 9; Col. 2:16, 17, 20, 21; Heb. 7:18, 19; 9:10; 10:1); yet it not only typified the gospel dispensation, but illustrated the perpetual principles of acceptable worship.

"(c) The moral law was given to Israel in trust for all mankind. It contains the elementary rules of moral and religious duty, and embodies the eternal principles of right and wrong. It has never been abrogated but is as unchangeable as its author, being based on our essential relationships to Him and our fellow men, and it is of perpetual and universal obligation (Matt. 5:17-20). Hence the Seventh Article of the Church of England states: 'Although the law given from God by Moses as touching ceremonies and rites, does not bind Christian men, nor the civil precepts thereof ought of necessity to be received in any commonwealth, yet, notwithstanding, no Christian man whatsoever is free from the obedience of the commandments which are called moral.' . . .

"Confining our attention now to the moral law, let us consider its essential character and its original proclamation.

"1. It may be regarded as the expression of the divine mind and will, universal in its scope, but individual in its application, for it addresses us in the singular number.

"2. It is strikingly compact, but singularly complete; covering every relationship in which we stand both to God and man, and embracing alike our religious and social duties.

"It deals not only with our open words and actions, but with our hidden thoughts and motives; the first, second, and tenth commandments regulating our desires, the third and ninth our words, and the remainder our deeds. The commands imply a prohibition of the opposite conduct, and the negative involves the contrary positive duties as we see from the summary of both 'tables' in Leviticus 19:18; Deuteronomy 6:5; 10:12."—WILLIAM C. PROCTER in *Moody Bible Institute Monthly* (Copyrighted), October, 1933, p. 49. Used by permission.

"These laws are what we might call *universal*. . . . These Ten Commandments are only the codification of what man's own moral nature approves as right; and they are right, and true, and abiding in every age for every race."—*Peloubet's Select Notes* (on the International Sunday School lesson for Jan. 20, 1946), p. 35. These notes, a yearly commentary on the International Bible Lessons for Christian Teaching, are edited by Wilbur M. Smith and published by W. A. Wilde Company, Boston.

"The moral law, contained in the Ten Commandments, and enforced by the Prophets, he did not take away. It was not the design of his coming to revoke any part of this. . . . Every part of this law must remain in force upon all mankind, and in all ages; as not depending either on time or place, or any other circumstances liable to change, but on the nature of God, and the nature of man, and their unchangeable relation to each other."—JOHN WESLEY, "Upon Our Lord's Sermon on the Mount," Discourse 5, in *Works,* vol. 5 (1829 ed.), pp. 311, 312.

What does "fulfil" mean when used with reference to law?

Perform, keep, or act in accordance with; as, "Bear ye one another's burdens, and so fulfil the law of Christ." Galatians 6:2. (See Matthew 3:15; James 2:8, 9.)

How did Christ treat His Father's commandments?

"I have *kept* my Father's commandments, and abide in his love." John 15:10.

If one professes to abide in Christ, how ought he to walk?

"He that saith he abideth in him *ought himself also so to walk, even as he walked.*" 1 John 2:6.

SIN AND THE LAW

What is sin?

"Whosoever committeth sin transgresseth also the law: for *sin is the transgression of the law.*" 1 John 3:4.

NOTE.—This text says that sin *is,* not *was,* the transgression of the law, thus showing that the law is still in force in the gospel dispensation. "Whosoever" likewise shows the universality of its binding claims. Everyone who commits sin transgresses the law.

In what condition are all men?

"For *all have sinned,* and come short of the glory of God." Romans 3:23. "We have before proved *both Jews and Gentiles,* that *they are all under sin.*" Verse 9.

By what are all men proved guilty?

"Now we know that *what things soever the law saith,* it saith to them who are under the law: *that every mouth may be stopped, and all the world may become guilty before God.*" Verse 19.

NOTE.—It is what the law says, and not what one may interpret it to mean, that proves the sinner guilty, and *all* are guilty before God.

Faith, Love, and the Law

Does faith in God make void the law?

"Do we then make void the law through faith? *God forbid: yea, we establish the law.*" Verse 31.

What, more than all else, proves the perpetuity and immutability of the law of God?

"For *God so loved the world, that he gave his only begotten Son,* that whosoever believeth in him should not perish, but have everlasting life." John 3:16. "Christ died for our sins." 1 Corinthians 15:3.

NOTE.—Could the law have been abolished, and sin been disposed of in this way, Christ need not have come and died for our sins. The gift of Christ, therefore, more than all else, proves the immutability of the law of God. Christ must come and die, and satisfy the claims of the law, or the world must perish. The law could not give way. The fact that the law is to be the standard in the judgment is another proof of its enduring nature. (See Ecclesiastes 12:13, 14; James 2:8-12.)

Who has the promise of being blessed in his doing?

"But he that looketh into the perfect law, the law of liberty, and so continueth, being not a hearer that forgetteth, but *a doer that worketh,* this man shall be blessed in his doing." James 1:25, R.V.

How may we know that we have passed from death to life?

"We know that we have passed from death unto life, *because we love the brethren.*" 1 John 3:14.

And how may we know that we love the brethren?

"By this we know that we love the children of God, *when we love God, and keep his commandments.*" 1 John 5:2.

What is the love of God?

"For this is the love of God, *that we keep his commandments.*" Verse 3.

NOTE.—"In the moral government of the universe God acts in harmony with a rule. . . . Not only is it unchangeable with respect to places and races, to days and seasons, to conditions and circumstances, but also to ages. It has been unchangeable. It will be unchangeable.

"We cannot conceive of an age when the moral government of the universe shall be changed, because we cannot conceive of God becoming different morally from what he is now and ever has been.... This Law of God is holy as he himself is holy.... It is a universal law.... The Law of God is just and cannot be unjust—Its justice is universal.... It is more than just; it is gracious.... It results in welfare, in happiness, in blessedness. It is more than negative, prohibiting wrong-doing. It is more than positive, requiring right-doing. It is linked with all the outgoing of God's life towards man; and this means that it is linked with his great compassionate love. The Law of God is full of the love of God."—O. C. S. WALLACE, *What Baptists Believe* (Southern Baptist Sunday School Workers' Training Course textbook), pp. 80-83. Copyright, 1934, by the Sunday School Board of the Southern Baptist Convention. Used by permission.

How are those described who will prepare for the coming of Christ?

"Here is the patience of the saints: here are they that keep the commandments of God, and the faith of Jesus." Revelation 14:12.

> JUDGE not the Lord by feeble sense,
> But trust Him for His grace;
> Behind a frowning providence
> He hides a smiling face.
>
> Deep in unfathomable mines
> Of never-failing skill,
> He treasures up His bright designs,
> And works His sovereign will.
>
> —WILLIAM COWPER

Why Was the Law Given at Sinai?

How does Nehemiah describe the giving of the law at Sinai?

"Thou camest down also upon mount Sinai, and spakest with them from heaven, and gavest them right judgments, and true laws, good statutes and commandments: and madest known unto them thy holy sabbath, and commandedst them precepts, statutes, and laws, by the hand of Moses." Nehemiah 9:13, 14.

What is the chief advantage possessed by the Jews?

"What advantage then hath the Jew? . . . *chiefly, because that unto them were committed the oracles of God.*" Romans 3:1, 2.

Note.—The law was not spoken at this time exclusively for the Hebrews. God honored them by making them the guardians and keepers of His law, to be held by them as a sacred trust for the whole world. The precepts of the Decalogue are adapted to all mankind, and they were given for the instruction and government of all.

"We have already seen that, unlike the ceremonial and civil codes which were given to Israel as the chosen people and holy nation, the moral law is intended for all mankind, and it has never been abrogated nor repealed."—William C. Procter, *Moody Bible Institute Monthly* (Copyrighted), December, 1933, p. 160. Used by permission.

The Moral Law Before Sinai

Before receiving the law at Sinai, how did Moses judge?

"When they have a matter, they come unto me; and I judge between one and another, and *I do make them know the statutes of God, and his laws.*" Exodus 18:16.

In the wilderness, before Israel reached Sinai, how did Moses explain the absence of manna on the seventh day?

"He said unto them, This is that which the Lord hath said, *To morrow is the rest of the holy sabbath unto the Lord.* . . .

WHY WAS THE LAW GIVEN AT SINAI?

Six days ye shall gather it; but on the seventh day, *which is the sabbath,* in it there shall be none." Exodus 16:23-26.

When some went out to gather manna on the seventh day, what did the Lord say to Moses?

"And the Lord said unto Moses, *How long refuse ye to keep my commandments and my laws?*" Verse 28.

NOTE.—It is evident therefore that the Sabbath and the law of God existed before the law was given at Sinai. (See reading on page 375.)

What further evidence have we that the moral law existed prior to its proclamation at Mount Sinai?

"By one man's disobedience many were made sinners." Romans 5:19.

"Whosoever committeth sin transgresseth also the law: for sin is the transgression of the law." 1 John 3:4.

NOTE.—The one man through whom sin entered into this world was Adam. Since sin is the transgression of the law, it follows that the law existed in Eden, else there would have been no transgression, no sin.

"26. *How had God revealed this law?*

"In the creation He wrote it in men's hearts, and hence it is called the Law of nature. Rom. 2:15. . . .

"27. *Has not God revealed the Law in any other Way?*

"Yes, He gave it on Mount Sinai, written on two tables of stone."
—*Epitome of Pontoppidan's Explanation of Martin Luther's Small Catechism,* translated from the Norwegian by Edmund Belfour (1935), p. 7.

TEN COMMANDMENTS AT SINAI

How was the ten-commandment law first given at Sinai?

"God spake all these words, saying, . . . Thou shalt have no other gods before me." Exodus 20:1-3.

How did God present the law to Israel in permanent form?

"He gave unto Moses, when he had made an end of communing with him upon mount Sinai, two tables of testimony, tables of stone, written with the finger of God." Exodus 31:18.

NOTE.—The law of God, as well as the knowledge of creation, the plan of redemption, and the experiences of the early patriarchs, had been handed down from father to son until this time, but not in written form. He wrote the Ten Commandments upon two tables of stone with His own finger.

How did Moses show that the children of Israel had broken their covenant with God?

"It came to pass, as soon as he came nigh unto the camp, that he saw the [golden] calf, and the dancing: and Moses' anger waxed hot, and he cast the tables out of his hands, and brake them beneath the mount." Exodus 32:19.

With what exactness did the Lord write the law again?

"He wrote on the tables, *according to the first writing,* the ten commandments, *which the Lord spake unto you in the mount* out of the midst of the fire in the day of the assembly: and the Lord gave them unto me." Deuteronomy 10:4.

Where did Moses place these two tables of stone?

"I . . . *put the tables in the ark* which I had made; and there they be, as the Lord commanded me." Verse 5.

What other law was given at this time?

"When Moses had made an end of writing the words of *this law in a book,* until they were finished." Deuteronomy 31:24.

NOTE.—Besides the ten-commandment law, the Lord gave to Moses instruction concerning the sanctuary service, which was ceremonial, and certain civil laws regulating the subjects of the nation. These laws were written by Moses *in a book,* and are called the law of Moses, whereas the other law was written on tables of stone with the finger of God. For a further study of these laws, see the reading on page 381.

OBEDIENCE TO LAW

Why did the Lord take His people out of Egypt?

"He brought forth his people with joy, and his chosen with gladness: . . . that they might observe his statutes, and keep his laws." Psalm 105:43-45.

How were they to teach the law to their children?

"Thou shalt teach them diligently unto thy children, and shalt talk of them when thou sittest in thine house, and when thou walkest by the way, and when thou liest down, and when thou risest up." Deuteronomy 6:7.

WHY WAS THE LAW GIVEN AT SINAI?

What promise to Israel hinged on keeping the instructions He gave them?

"Now therefore, if ye will obey my voice indeed, and keep my covenant, then ye shall be a peculiar treasure unto me above all people: for all the earth is mine: and ye shall be unto me a kingdom of priests, and an holy nation." Exodus 19:5, 6.

Was this promise made to the Jews alone?

"Now the Lord had said unto Abram, Get thee out of thy country, and from thy kindred, and from thy father's house, unto a land that I will shew thee: and I will make of thee a great nation, and I will bless thee, and make thy name great; and thou shalt be a blessing: and I will bless them that bless thee, and curse him that curseth thee: and in thee shall *all families of the earth be blessed.*" Genesis 12:1-3.

"If ye be Christ's, then are ye Abraham's seed, and heirs according to the promise." Galatians 3:29.

NOTE.—From these texts it will be readily seen that God had not one provision of grace and one law for the Jew and another means of salvation and another law for the Gentile; but the plan was that through Abraham's seed all the families of the earth should be recipients of divine grace and should receive the blessing through obedience.

THE CHRISTIAN AND THE LAW

What shows that the ten-commandment law, spoken and written at Mount Sinai, is the law for the Christian?

"Whosoever shall keep the whole law, and yet offend in one point, he is guilty of all. For he that said, Do not commit adultery, said also, Do not kill. Now if thou commit no adultery, yet if thou kill, thou art become a transgressor of the law. So speak ye, and so do, as they that shall be judged by the law of liberty." James 2:10-12.

NOTE.—James, years after the Christian Era began, emphasizes the obligation of the Christian to keep the law of ten commandments, not merely one precept, but all, and sets forth this law as the standard by which men will be judged in the great day of God. To us, as Christians, God has committed the blessed law in writing, as He did to ancient Israel. This law points out sin to us, that we may confess it and find forgiveness. And when this law is written in our hearts in the new-covenant experience (Hebrews 8:10) it also becomes to us the law of life.

JUDGMENT IS SURE

"So speak ye, and so do, as they that shall be judged by the law of liberty." James 2:12.

R. M. ELDRIDGE, ARTIST

Penalty for Transgression

What is the wages of sin?

"The wages of sin is *death*." Romans 6:23. "In the day that thou eatest thereof *thou shalt surely die*." Genesis 2:17. "The soul that sinneth, *it shall die*." Ezekiel 18:4.

How did death enter the world?

"Wherefore, as by one man sin entered into the world, and *death by sin;* and so death passed upon all men, for that all have sinned." Romans 5:12.

Problem of Willful Sin

God is merciful, but does this clear the guilty?

"The Lord is longsuffering, and of great mercy, forgiving iniquity and transgression, and *by no means clearing the guilty*." Numbers 14:18. (See Exodus 34:5-7.)

What is the result of willful sin?

"If we sin wilfully after that we have received the knowledge of the truth, *there remaineth no more sacrifice for sins,* but a certain fearful looking for of judgment and fiery indignation, which shall devour the adversaries. He that despised Moses' law *died without mercy* under two or three witnesses. *Of how much sorer punishment,* suppose ye, *shall he be thought worthy, who hath trodden under foot the Son of God,* and hath counted the blood of the covenant, wherewith he was sanctified, an unholy thing, and hath done despite unto the Spirit of grace?" Hebrews 10:26-29.

To whom has execution of judgment been committed?

"Vengeance is mine; I will repay, saith the Lord." Romans 12:19.

"The Father hath . . . *given to the Son* . . . authority to execute judgment also." John 5:26, 27. (See Jude 14, 15.)

What presumptuous course do many pursue?

"Because sentence against an evil work is not executed

speedily, *therefore the heart of the sons of men is fully set in them to do evil."* Ecclesiastes 8:11.

What message has God sent by His ministers?

"Say ye to the righteous, that *it shall be well with him:* for they shall eat the fruit of their doings. *Woe unto the wicked! it shall be ill with him:* for the reward of his hands shall be given him." Isaiah 3:10, 11. *"We are ambassadors for Christ,* as though God did beseech you by us." 2 Corinthians 5:20. (See 2 Timothy 2:24-26.)

To whom is this gift given?

"For God so loved the world, that he gave his only begotten Son, that *whosoever* believeth in him should not perish, but have everlasting life." John 3:16.

How is the gift received?

"He that *believeth* on him is not condemned: but he that believeth not is condemned already, because he hath not believed in the name of the only begotten Son of God." John 3:18.

"But as many as received him, to them gave he power to become the sons of God, even to them that *believe* on his name." John 1:12.

How can man escape this penalty?

"The wages of sin is death; but *the gift of God is eternal life through Jesus Christ our Lord."* Romans 6:23.

Note.—"God threatens to punish all who transgress these Commandments: we should, therefore, fear his anger, and do nothing against such Commandments. But he promises grace and every blessing to all who keep them: we should, therefore, love and trust in him, and gladly obey his Commandments."—*Luther's Small Catechism* in Philip Schaff, *The Creeds of Christendom* (Harper), vol. 3, p. 77.

"Through the atonement of Christ more honor is done to the law, and consequently the law is more established, than if the law had been literally executed, and all mankind had been condemned." —Jonathan Edwards (Congregationalist), *Works* (1842 ed.), vol. 2, p. 369.

The Law of God in the Patriarchal Age

Adam and His Sons

When did sin and death enter the world?

"Wherefore, as *by one man [Adam] sin entered into the world,* and death by sin; and so death passed upon all men, for that all have sinned." Romans 5:12.

What shows that God imputed sin to Cain?

"If thou doest well, shalt thou not be accepted? and if thou doest not well, *sin lieth at the door....* And he [God] said, What hast thou done? the voice of thy brother's blood crieth unto me from the ground. And *now art thou cursed from the earth.*" Genesis 4:7-11.

What was the difference between Cain and Abel?

"Not as Cain, who was of that wicked one, and slew his brother. And wherefore slew he him? *Because his own works were evil, and his brother's righteous.*" 1 John 3:12.

Note.—It is the law of God that distinguishes between right and wrong. Hence the law of God must have existed at that time.

"I. God gave to Adam a law, as a covenant of works, by which he bound him and all his posterity to personal, entire, exact, and perpetual obedience; promised life upon the fulfilling, and threatened death upon the breach of it; and endued him with power and ability to keep it.

"II. This law, after his fall, continued to be a perfect rule of righteousness; and, as such, was delivered by God upon mount Sinai in ten commandments, and written in two tables; the first four commandments containing our duty towards God, and the other six our duty to man."—Westminster Confession of Faith, chap. 19, in Philip Schaff, *The Creeds of Christendom* (Harper), vol. 3, p. 640.

The Days of Noah

What situation prevailing upon the earth led God to destroy it by a Flood?

"And God said unto Noah, The end of all flesh is come before me; for the *earth is filled with violence* through them; and, behold, *I will destroy them with the earth.*" Genesis 6:13.

What is Noah called?

"And spared not the old world, but saved Noah the eighth person, *a preacher of righteousness.*" 2 Peter 2:5.

Note.—Noah must have preached repentance and that obedience of faith which brings the life into harmony with the law of God.

The Time of Lot and Abraham

Why did God make His promise to the seed of Abraham?

"Because that Abraham obeyed my voice, and kept my charge, my commandments, my statutes, and my laws." Genesis 26:5.

Note.—Then God's laws existed in Abraham's time.

Why did the Lord destroy Sodom?

"The men of Sodom were *wicked* and *sinners* before the Lord *exceedingly.*" Genesis 13:13.

What was the character of their deeds?

"And delivered just Lot, vexed with the filthy conversation of the wicked: (for that righteous man dwelling among them, in seeing and hearing, vexed his righteous soul from day to day with their *unlawful deeds*)." 2 Peter 2:7, 8.

Note.—Their deeds would not have been *unlawful* had there been no law then in existence. *Unlawful* means "contrary to law."

What did God say concerning the Amorites?

"The iniquity of the Amorites is not yet full." Genesis 15:16.

Note.—Ahab "did very abominably in *following idols, according to all things as did the Amorites,* whom the Lord cast out before the children of Israel." 1 Kings 21:26. "The nation, which I cast out before you . . . *committed all these things,* and therefore I abhorred them." Leviticus 20:23.

The statement that "they committed all these things" refers to what had been previously forbidden to the Israelites. Among these things was idolatrous worship (Leviticus 20:1-5), showing that the Gentiles, as well as the Jews, were amenable to the law of God, and were abhorred of God for violating it.

Joseph and Moses

What did Joseph, in Egypt, say when tempted to sin?

"How then can I do this great wickedness, and *sin against God?*" Genesis 39:9.

Before giving the law at Sinai, how did God rebuke the people for going out to gather manna on the seventh day?

"And the Lord said unto Moses, *How long refuse ye to keep my commandments and my laws?*" Exodus 16:28.

Had the Lord previously spoken of the Sabbath?

"This is that which the Lord hath said, To morrow is the rest of the holy sabbath." Verse 23.

Before the encampment at Sinai, what had Moses taught Israel?

"When they have a matter, they come unto me; and I judge between one and another, and *I do make them know the statutes of God and his laws.*" Exodus 18:16.

NOTE.—All this shows that the law of God existed from the beginning, and was known and taught in the world before it was proclaimed at Sinai.

"We should not suppose that the Ten Commandments were entirely new enactments when they were proclaimed from Sinai, for the Hebrew word *torah* is used in such previous passages of the Old Testament as Genesis 26:5; Exodus 12:49; Genesis 35:2 and 13:9; 16:4, 28; 18:16, 20. [Genesis 4:26; 14:22; 31:53 are cited for the principle of the third; Genesis 2:3 and Exodus 16:22-30 for the fourth; Genesis 9:6, for the sixth; and Genesis 2:24, for the seventh.] The decalogue may therefore be regarded as the full and solemn declaration of duties which had been more or less revealed previously, and this public enunciation took place under absolutely unique circumstances. We are told that 'the ten words' were spoken by God's own voice (Exod. 20:1; Deut. 5:4, 22-26); and twice afterwards 'written on tables of stone with the finger of God' (Exod. 24:12; 31:18; 32:16; 34:1, 28; Deut. 4:13; 5:22; 9:10; 10:1-4), thus appealing alike to the ear and eye, and emphasizing both their supreme importance and permanent obligation."—WILLIAM C. PROCTER, *Moody Bible Institute Monthly* (Copyrighted), October, 1933, p. 49. Used by permission.

The Law of God in the New Testament

Jesus and the Law

What did Jesus say of His attitude toward the law?

"Think not that I am come to destroy the law, or the prophets: *I am not come to destroy, but to fulfil.*" Matthew 5:17.

NOTE.—"The law" includes the five books of Moses; and "the prophets," the writings of the prophets. Christ did not come to set aside, but to fulfill, both. The ceremonial types and shadows contained in the books of Moses He fulfilled as their great Antitype. The moral law, the basic fabric underlying all Moses' writings, Christ fulfilled by perfect obedience. The prophets He fulfilled in His advent as the foretold Messiah, Prophet, Teacher, and Saviour.

What did He teach concerning the stability of the law?

"For verily I say unto you, Till heaven and earth pass, one jot or one tittle shall in no wise pass from the law, till all be fulfilled." Verse 18.

NOTE.—"We must understand that the Ten Commandments are just as binding upon Christian people as they were upon the Children of Israel. . . .

"The Moral Law is a part of the natural law of the universe. . . . Just as a natural law broken in the material world brings its inevitable consequences, so the Moral Law broken brings its inevitable consequences in the spiritual and mental worlds.

"The Lord Jesus knew this. He knew it much better than anyone else who ever lived. Therefore He built His Gospel upon a firm foundation of Moral Law, knowing that such a foundation can never be upset. . . .

"Christ's teaching goes beyond the Ten Commandments, but does not thereby make the Commandments of non-effect. Quite the contrary! Christianity strengthens the authority of the Commandments."—*The Episcopal Church Sunday School Magazine,* June-July, 1942, vol. 105, no. 6, pp. 183, 184, Sunday school lesson for June 28.

"The basic laws of morality, and particularly the Ten Command-

THE LAW OF GOD IN THE NEW TESTAMENT

ments, remain until the end of time as the moral and spiritual foundation upon which the New Testament religion is built."—*The Snowden-Douglass Sunday School Lessons* for 1946, p. 279. Copyright, 1945, by The Macmillan Company; used by their permission.

How did He stress the importance of keeping the law?

"Whosoever therefore shall break one of these least commandments, and shall teach men so, he shall be called the least in the kingdom of heaven: but whosoever shall do and teach them, the same shall be called great." Verse 19.

NOTE.—"Our King has not come to abrogate the law, but to confirm and reassert it. His commands are eternal; and if any of the teachers of it should through error break His law, and teach that its least command is nullified, they will lose rank, and subside into the lowest place. The peerage of His kingdom is ordered according to obedience."—CHARLES H. SPURGEON, *The Gospel of the Kingdom* (1893 ed.), p. 48.

What did Christ tell the rich young man to do in order to enter into life?

"If thou wilt enter into life, *keep the commandments.*" Matthew 19:17.

When asked which commandments, what did Jesus say?

"Jesus said, Thou shalt do no murder, Thou shalt not commit adultery, Thou shalt not steal, Thou shalt not bear false witness, Honour thy father and thy mother: and, Thou shalt love thy neighbour as thyself." Verses 18, 19.

NOTE.—While not quoting all ten commandments, Jesus quoted sufficient to identify the moral law. The second great commandment called attention to the principle underlying the second table of the law—love to one's neighbor—which the rich young man was not keeping.

SIN AND THE WHOLE LAW

What proves that the law is an undivided whole?

"*For whosoever shall keep the whole law, and yet offend in one point, he is guilty of all.* For he that said, Do not commit adultery, said also, Do not kill. Now if thou commit no adultery, yet if thou kill, thou art become a transgressor of the law. So speak ye, and so do, as they that shall be judged by the law of liberty." James 2:10-12.

How is sin defined?

"Whosoever committeth sin transgresseth also the law: for *sin is the transgression of the law.*" 1 John 3:4.

Does faith render the law void?

"Do we then make void the law through faith? *God forbid: yea, we establish the law.*" Romans 3:31.

How Can Man Fulfill the Law?

What is more important than any outward ceremony?

"Circumcision is nothing, and uncircumcision is nothing, but *the keeping of the commandments of God.*" 1 Corinthians 7:19.

What kind of mind is not subject to the law of God?

"*The carnal mind* is enmity against God: for it is not subject to the law of God, neither indeed can be." Romans 8:7.

How is the law fulfilled?

"Owe no man any thing, but to love one another: for *he that loveth another hath fulfilled the law*. For this, Thou shalt not commit adultery, Thou shalt not kill, Thou shalt not steal, Thou shalt not bear false witness, Thou shalt not covet; and if there be any other commandment [touching our duty to man], it is briefly comprehended in this saying, namely, Thou shalt love thy neighbour as thyself. Love worketh no ill to his neighbour: therefore *love is the fulfilling of the law.*" Romans 13:8-10.

How may we know that we love the children of God?

"By this we know that we love the children of God, *when we love God, and keep his commandments.*" 1 John 5:2.

What is the love of God declared to be?

"For *this is the love of God, that we keep his commandments:* and his commandments are not grievous." Verse 3.

How is the church of the last days described?

"The dragon was wroth with the woman, and went to make war with the remnant of her seed, *which keep the commandments of God, and have the testimony of Jesus Christ.*" "Here is the patience of the saints: *here are they that keep the commandments of God, and the faith of Jesus.*" Revelation 12:17; 14:12.

The Moral and Ceremonial Laws

THE ROYAL MORAL LAW

What title of distinction is given the law of God?

"If ye fulfil *the royal law* according to the scripture, Thou shalt love thy neighbour as thyself, ye do well." James 2:8.

By what law is the knowledge of sin?

"I had not known sin, but by the law: for I had not known lust, except the law had said, Thou shalt not covet." Romans 7:7.

Note.—The law which says this is the Ten Commandments.

By what are all men to be finally judged?

"Let us hear the conclusion of the whole matter: Fear God, and *keep his commandments:* for this is the whole duty of man. For God shall bring every work into judgment, with every secret thing, whether it be good, or whether it be evil." Ecclesiastes 12:13, 14. "So speak ye, and so do, as they that shall be judged by *the law of liberty.*" James 2:12.

Note.—"The law of liberty," which says, "Do not commit adultery" and "Do not kill" (verse 11), and is styled "the royal law" (verse 8), that is, the kingly law, is the law by which men are to be judged.

THE CEREMONIAL LAW AND SYSTEM

What system was introduced following man's transgression?

The sacrificial system, with its rites pointing to Christ.

How early was this sacrificial system known?

"By faith *Abel* offered unto God a more excellent sacrifice than Cain." Hebrews 11:4. (See Genesis 4:3-5; 8:20.)

Note.—The patriarch Job offered sacrifices. (See Job 1:4, 5.)

THE MORAL LAW STANDS FOREVER

THE CEREMONIAL LAW ENDED AT THE CROSS

R. M. ELDRIDGE, ARTIST

COPYRIGHT, 1942, BY REVIEW AND HERALD

MORAL AND CEREMONIAL COMPARED

By whom was the ten-commandment law proclaimed?

"And *the Lord spake unto you out of the midst of the fire:* ye heard the voice of the words, but saw no similitude; only ye heard a voice. And *he declared unto you his covenant, which he commanded you to perform, even ten commandments;* and he wrote them upon two tables of stone." Deuteronomy 4:12, 13.

How was the ceremonial law made known to Israel?

"And the Lord called unto Moses, . . . saying, *Speak unto the children of Israel, and say unto them,* If any man of you bring *an offering,*" etc. Leviticus 1:1, 2. *"This is the law of the burnt offering, of the meat offering, and of the sin offering, and of the trespass offering, and of the consecrations, and of the sacrifice of the peace offering;* which the Lord commanded Moses in mount Sinai, in the day that he commanded the children of Israel to offer their oblations unto the Lord." Leviticus 7:37, 38.

NOTE.—"III. Beside this law, commonly called moral, God was pleased to give to the people of Israel, as a Church under age, ceremonial laws, containing several typical ordinances, partly of worship, prefiguring Christ, his graces, actions, sufferings, and benefits; and partly holding forth divers instructions of moral duties. All which ceremonial laws are now abrogated under the New Testament.

"IV. To them also, as a body politic, he gave sundry judicial laws, which expired together with the state of that people, not obliging any other, now, further than the general equity thereof may require."—Westminster Confession of Faith, chap. 19, in PHILIP SCHAFF, *The Creeds of Christendom* (Harper), vol. 3, pp. 640, 641.

On what did God write the Ten Commandments?

"And he declared unto you his covenant, which he commanded you to perform, even ten commandments; and *he wrote them upon two tables of stone.*" Deuteronomy 4:13.

In what were the laws of sacrifices written?

"And they removed the burnt offerings, that they might . . . offer unto the Lord, as it is written in *the book of Moses.*" 2 Chronicles 35:12.

Where were the Ten Commandments placed?

"He . . . put the testimony *into the ark.*" Exodus 40:20.

Where did Moses direct his law book to be placed?

"Take this book of the law, and *put it in the side of the ark* of the covenant of the Lord your God." Deuteronomy 31:25, 26.

What is the nature of God's precepts?

"We know that the law is *spiritual.*" Romans 7:14.

NOTE.—"The law of God is a divine law, holy, heavenly, perfect. Those who find fault with the law, or in the least degree depreciate it, do not understand its design, and have no right idea of the law itself. Paul says, 'The law is holy, but I am carnal; sold under sin.' In all we ever say concerning justification by faith, we never intend to lower the opinion which our hearers have of the law, for the law is one of the most sublime of God's works. There is not a commandment too many; there is not one too few; but it is so *incomparable,* that its *perfection* is a proof of its divinity."—C. H. SPURGEON, *Sermons,* 2d series (1857), p. 280.

Could offerings make perfect the believer's conscience?

"Gifts and sacrifices, *that could not make him that did the service perfect, as pertaining to the conscience.*" Hebrews 9:9.

Until what time was the ceremonial law imposed?

"Meats and drinks, and divers washings, and carnal ordinances, *imposed on them until the time of reformation.*" Verse 10.

When was this time of reformation?

"But *Christ being come* an high priest of good things to come, by a greater and more perfect tabernacle, not made with hands, . . . having obtained eternal redemption for us." Verses 11, 12.

How did Christ's death affect the ceremonial law?

"Having *abolished* in his flesh the enmity, even *the law of commandments contained in ordinances.*" Ephesians 2:15.

What signified that the sacrificial system was ended?

"Jesus, when he had cried again with a loud voice, yielded up the ghost. And, behold, *the veil of the temple was rent in twain* from the top to the bottom." Matthew 27:50, 51.

In what words had the prophet Daniel foretold the end of the Jewish sacrificial system?

THE MORAL AND CEREMONIAL LAWS

"And he shall confirm the covenant with many for one week: and *in the midst of the week he shall cause the sacrifice and the oblation to cease.*" Daniel 9:27.

Why was the ceremonial law taken away?

"There is a disannulling of a foregoing commandment because of its weakness and unprofitableness (for the law made nothing perfect), and a *bringing in thereupon of a better hope,* through which we draw nigh unto God." Hebrews 7:18, 19, R.V.

PROTESTANT CREEDS ON THE LAW

(Page numbers refer to Philip Schaff, *The Creeds of Christendom* [Harper], vol. 3.)

LUTHERAN—Formula of Concord, article 6: "Although they who truly believe in Christ, and are sincerely converted to God, are through Christ set free from the curse and constraint of the Law, they are not, nevertheless, on that account without Law, inasmuch as the Son of God redeemed them for the very reason that they might meditate on the Law of God day and night, and continually exercise themselves in the keeping thereof."—Page 131.

REFORMED—Second Helvetic Confession, chapter 12: "We teach that the will of God is set down unto us in the law of God; to wit, what he would have us to do, or not to do, what is good and just, or what is evil and unjust. We therefore confess that 'The law is good and holy' (Rom. vii. 12); and that this law is, by the finger of God, either 'written in the hearts of men' (Rom. ii. 15), and so is called the law of nature, or engraven in the two tables of stone, and more largely expounded in the books of Moses (Exod. xx. 1-17; Deut. v. 22). . . .

"We teach that this law was not given to men, that we should be justified by keeping it; but that, by the knowledge thereof, we might rather acknowledge our infirmity, sin, and condemnation; and so, despairing of our strength, might turn unto Christ by faith."—Page 855.

PROTESTANT EPISCOPAL—Thirty-nine Articles of Religion, article 7: "The Old Testament is not contrary to the New: for both in the Old and New Testament everlasting life is offered to Mankind by Christ, who is the only Mediator between God and Man, being both God and Man. Wherefore they are not to be heard, which feign that the old Fathers did look only for transitory promises. Although the Law given from God by Moses, as touching Ceremonies and Rites, do not bind Christian men, nor the Civil precepts thereof ought of necessity to be received in any commonwealth; yet notwithstanding, no Christian man whatsoever is free from the obedience of the commandments which are called Moral."—Pages 491, 492, col. 3.

CHURCH OF ENGLAND—Thirty-nine Articles, article 7. Same wording as the above Protestant Episcopal article 7, of which it was the source.—Pages 491, 492, cols. 1, 2.

METHODIST—Articles of Religion, article 6. Same as the above article 7 of the Protestant Episcopal Articles of Religion.—Page 808.

PRESBYTERIAN—Westminster Confession of Faith. Chapter XIX: "V. The moral law doth forever bind all, as well justified persons as others, to the obedience thereof; and that not only in regard of the matter contained in it, but also in respect of the authority of God the Creator who gave it. Neither doth Christ in the gospel any way dissolve, but much strengthen, this obligation. . . .

"VII. Neither are the forementioned uses of the law contrary to the grace of the gospel, but do sweetly comply with it: the Spirit of Christ subduing and enabling the will of man to do that freely and cheerfully which the will of God, revealed in the law, requireth to be done."—Pages 641-643.

Chapter XX: "I. The liberty which Christ hath purchased for believers under the gospel consists in their freedom from the guilt of sin, the condemning wrath of God, the curse of the moral law. . . . All which were common also to believers under the law; but under the New Testament the liberty of Christians is further enlarged in their freedom from the yoke of the ceremonial law, to which the Jewish Church was subjected."—Pages 643, 644.

CONGREGATIONAL—Savoy Declaration. Same as the above quotations from the Westminster Confession.—Page 718.

BAPTIST—Philadelphia Confession. Same as the above.—Page 738.

BAPTIST—New Hampshire Confession, article 12: "We believe that the Law of God is the eternal and unchangeable rule of his moral government; that it is holy, just, and good; and that the inability which the Scriptures ascribe to fallen men to fulfill its precepts arises entirely from their love of sin; to deliver them from which, and to restore them through a Mediator to unfeigned obedience to the holy Law, is one great end of the Gospel, and of the means of grace connected with the establishment of the visible Church."—Page 746.

The Two Covenants

What two covenants are contrasted in the Bible?

"In that he saith, A *new* covenant, he hath made the first *old*. Now that which decayeth and waxeth old is ready to vanish away." Hebrews 8:13.

By what other terms are these covenants designated?

"For if that first covenant had been faultless, then should no place have been sought for the *second*." Verse 7.

The Old or First Covenant

When was the old covenant made?

"Not according to the covenant that I made with their fathers in the day *when I took them by the hand to lead them out of the land of Egypt;* because they continued not in my covenant, and I regarded them not, saith the Lord." Verse 9. (See Exodus 19:3-8.)

When God was about to proclaim His law to Israel, of what did He tell Moses to remind them?

"Tell the children of Israel; Ye have seen what I did unto the Egyptians, and how I bare you on eagles' wings, and brought you unto myself." Exodus 19:3, 4.

What proposition did He submit to them?

"Now therefore, *if ye will obey my voice indeed, and keep my covenant, then ye shall be a peculiar treasure unto me above all people:* for all the earth is mine: and ye shall be unto me a kingdom of priests, and an holy nation." Verses 5, 6.

What response did the people make to this proposition?

"And all the people answered together, and said, *All that the Lord hath spoken we will do.*" Verse 8.

What covenant obligation was imposed upon Israel?

"Now therefore, if ye will *obey my voice* indeed, and *keep my covenant.*" Verse 5, first part.

Upon what was this covenant with God based?

"He declared unto you his covenant, which he commanded you to perform, even ten commandments; and he wrote them upon two tables of stone." Deuteronomy 4:13.

Note.—Both the old covenant and the new covenant are based upon the Ten Commandments. In proposing a covenant with Israel, God said: "If ye will obey my voice indeed, and keep my covenant." Exodus 19:5. (See Exodus 24:8.) Obedience to the Ten Commandments was the condition under the old covenant upon which God made certain promises to the people. Obedience to the same ten precepts is likewise the basis of the new covenant, for the Lord declares: "This is the covenant that I will make . . . after those days, saith the Lord; I will put my laws into their mind, and write them in their hearts: and I will be to them a God, and they shall be to me a people." Hebrews 8:10. Thus "the law is a paragraph in a Covenant of Grace."—Stewart M. Robinson in *The Presbyterian,* July 28, 1932, p. 10. Under the gospel the new covenant can be entered into only when there is a knowledge of God's law, and heartfelt obedience thereto.

After the law had been proclaimed from Sinai, what did the people again say?

"And all the people answered with one voice, and said, *All the words which the Lord hath said will we do.*" Exodus 24:3.

What did Moses do to prevent misunderstanding?

"And Moses wrote all the words of the Lord, . . . and he took the book of the covenant, and read in the audience of the people." Verses 4-7.

What did the people once again promise to do?

"And they said, *All that the Lord hath said will we do, and be obedient.*" Verse 7.

How was this covenant then confirmed and dedicated?

"He sent young men of the children of Israel, which offered burnt offerings, and sacrificed peace offerings of oxen unto the Lord. And Moses took half of the blood, and put it in basons; and half of the blood he sprinkled on the altar. And he took the book of the covenant, and read in the audience of the people: and they said, All that the Lord hath said will we do, and be obedient. And *Moses took the blood, and sprinkled it on the people, and*

THE TWO COVENANTS

said, Behold the blood of the covenant which the Lord hath made with you concerning all these words." Verses 5-8.

How does Paul describe this ratification of the covenant?

"For when Moses had spoken every precept to all the people according to the law, he took the blood of calves and of goats, with water, and scarlet wool, and hyssop, and *sprinkled both the book, and all the people,* saying, This is the blood of the testament which God hath enjoined unto you." Hebrews 9:19, 20.

NOTE.—We here have the account of the making of the first, or old, covenant. God promised to make Israel His peculiar people on condition that they would keep His commandments. Again they promised to obey. The agreement was then ratified, or sealed, with blood.

Less than forty days after making this covenant, while Moses tarried on the mount, what did Israel say to Aaron?

"Up, make us gods, which shall go before us; for as for this Moses, the man that brought us up out of the land of Egypt, we wot not what is become of him." Exodus 32:1.

When Moses came down from Sinai, what did he see?

"He saw *the calf,* and *the dancing:* and Moses' anger waxed hot, and he cast the tables out of his hands, and brake them beneath the mount." Verse 19.

NOTE.—The great object and secret of the old covenant is revealed here. The people did not realize the weakness and sinfulness of their own hearts, or their need of divine grace and help to keep the law; and so, in their ignorance, they readily pledged obedience. But almost immediately they began to commit idolatry, and thus to break the law of God, or the very conditions laid down as their part of the covenant. In themselves the conditions were good; but in their own strength the people were unable to fulfill them. This covenant was designed, like the law itself, over which it was made, to make sure to them the provisions of the new, or everlasting, covenant of grace and lead them to Christ. Only in Christ is there remission of sins or power to keep from sinning.

THE NEW OR SECOND COVENANT

Wherein does the new covenant differ from the old?

"But now hath he obtained a more excellent ministry, by

how much also he is the mediator of *a better covenant,* which was established upon *better promises."* Hebrews 8:6.

What promise did God make concerning the new covenant?

"This shall be the covenant that I will make with the house of Israel; After those days, saith the Lord, *I will put my law in their inward parts, and write it in their hearts; . . . I will forgive their iniquity, and I will remember their sin no more."* Jeremiah 31:33, 34. (See Hebrews 8:8-12.)

NOTE.—The same commandments which God wrote on tables of stone He also writes in the heart. "I will put my spirit within you, and cause you to walk in my statutes, and ye shall keep my judgments, and do them." Ezekiel 36:27. Jesus likewise said, "Except a man be born of water and of the Spirit, he cannot enter into the kingdom of God." John 3:5. This is the essence of the gospel. It is God's new covenant with spiritual Israel, and it embraces both forgiveness of sins and obedience to every one of God's ten precepts through the power of the Holy Spirit in the heart.

"The moral law, contained in the Ten Commandments, and enforced by the Prophets, . . . never can be broken, which 'stands fast as the faithful witness in heaven.' The moral stands on an entirely different foundation from the ceremonial or ritual law, which was only designed for a temporary restraint upon a disobedient and stiffnecked people; whereas this was from the beginning of the world, being 'written not on tables of stone,' but on the hearts of all the children of men, when they came out of the hands of the Creator." —JOHN WESLEY, "Upon Our Lord's Sermon on the Mount," Discourse 5, in *Works,* vol. 5 (1829 ed.), p. 311.

How was Christ promised as soon as sin entered?

"And the Lord God said unto the serpent, . . . I will put enmity between thee and the woman, and between thy seed and *her seed;* it shall bruise thy head, and thou shalt bruise his heel." Genesis 3:14, 15.

NOTE.—The covenant of grace, with its provisions of pardon and peace, dates from the foundation of the world.

To whom was this covenant-promise later renewed?

"God said unto *Abraham,"* "Sarah thy wife shall bear thee a son indeed; and thou shalt call his name Isaac: and I will establish my covenant with him for an everlasting covenant, and with *his seed* after him." "I will make thy seed to multiply as the stars, ... and in *thy seed* shall all the nations of the earth be blessed." Genesis 17:15, 19; 26:4.

Who was the seed here referred to?

"Now to Abraham and his seed were the promises made. He saith not, And to seeds, as of many; but as of one, And to thy seed, *which is Christ.*" Galatians 3:16.

NOTE.—To be sure, Isaac was the promised seed. But the Holy Spirit led Paul to see that the complete fulfillment of this promise was realized only in Christ.

What shows that the new, or second, covenant and the Abrahamic covenant are virtually the same?

"And if ye be Christ's, then are ye Abraham's seed, and heirs according to the promise." Verse 29.

NOTE.—No one should be confused by the terms *first covenant* and *second covenant*. While the one made at Sinai is called the first covenant, it is by no means the first covenant that God ever made with man. Long before this He made a covenant with Abraham; He also made a covenant with Noah, and with Adam. Neither must it be supposed that the first, or old, covenant existed for a time as the *only* covenant with mankind, and that this must serve its purpose and pass away before anyone could share in the promised blessings of the second or new covenant. In that case, during that time there would have been no pardon for anyone. What is called the new, or second, covenant virtually existed before the covenant made at Sinai; for the covenant with Abraham was confirmed in Christ (Galatians 3:17), and only through Christ is there any value to the new, or second, covenant. There is no blessing that can be gained by virtue of the new covenant that was not promised to Abraham. The second covenant existed in every essential feature, except its ratification, long before the first, even from the days of Adam. It is called second because its ratification occurred after the covenant made and ratified at Sinai.

What is necessary where there is a covenant?

"For where a will is involved, *the death of the one who made it must be established*. For a will takes effect only at death, since it is not in force as long as the one who made it is alive." Hebrews 9:16, 17, R.S.V.

With whose blood was the new covenant dedicated?

"And [He took] the cup in like manner after supper, saying,

This cup is the new covenant in *my blood,* even that which is poured out for you." Luke 22:20, R.V.

What power is there in the blood of this covenant?

"Now the God of peace, that brought again from the dead our Lord Jesus, that great shepherd of the sheep, through the blood of the everlasting covenant, *make you perfect in every good work* to do his will." Hebrews 13:20, 21.

Through which covenant only is there remission of sins?

"How much more shall the blood of Christ, who through the eternal Spirit offered himself without blemish unto God, cleanse your conscience from dead works to serve the living God? And for this cause he is the mediator of a *new covenant,* that a death having taken place for the redemption of the transgressions that were under the first covenant, they that have been called may receive the promise of the eternal inheritance." Hebrews 9:14, 15, R.V.

NOTE.—The fact that Christ, as mediator of the second covenant, died for the remission of the transgressions that were under the first covenant shows that there was no forgiveness *by virtue* of the first covenant.

THE OLD AND NEW COMPARED

Under the old covenant, what did the people promise?

"And all the people answered with one voice, and said, *All the words which the Lord hath said will we do."* Exodus 24:3.

Under the new covenant, what does God promise to do?

"I will put my laws into their mind, and write them in their hearts." Hebrews 8:10.

NOTE.—The new covenant is an arrangement for bringing man again into harmony with the divine will, and placing him where he can keep God's law through the enabling power of God. The dissolution of the old covenant and the making of the new in no wise abrogated the law of God.

Where was God's law written under the old covenant?

"And I [Moses] made an ark of shittim wood, and hewed *two tables of stone....And he [God] wrote on the tables...the ten commandments."* Deuteronomy 10:3, 4.

THE TWO COVENANTS

Where is the law of God written under the new covenant?

"But this shall be the covenant that I will make with the house of Israel; After those days, saith the Lord, *I will put my law in their inward parts, and write it in their hearts.*" Jeremiah 31:33.

What reason is given for making the new covenant?

"For if that first covenant had been *faultless,* then should no place have been sought for the second. For *finding fault with them,* he saith, Behold, the days come, saith the Lord, when I will make a new covenant." Hebrews 8:7, 8.

NOTE.—The chief fault in connection with the old covenant lay with *the people.* They were not able, in themselves, to fulfill their part of it.

What unites all believers under the new covenant?

"Ye being in time past Gentiles in the flesh, . . . were without Christ, being aliens from the commonwealth of Israel, and strangers from the covenants of promise, having no hope, and without God in the world: *but now in Christ Jesus ye who sometimes were far off are made nigh by the blood of Christ.*" Ephesians 2:11-13.

SIMILARITIES BETWEEN THE TWO COVENANTS

1. Both are called covenants.
2. Both were ratified with blood.
3. Both were made concerning the law of God.
4. Both were made with the people of God.
5. Both were established upon promises.

DISSIMILARITIES BETWEEN THE TWO COVENANTS

OLD COVENANT	NEW COVENANT
Called the old covenant.	Called the new covenant.
Called the first covenant.	Called the second covenant.
A temporary compact.	An everlasting covenant.
Dedicated with the blood of animals.	Ratified with the blood of Christ.
Was faulty.	Is a better covenant.
Under this, the law was written on tables of stone.	Under this, the law is written in the heart.

What Was Abolished by Christ?

Prophetic Prediction on Sacrifices

How did Christ's death affect the sacrificial system?

"After threescore and two weeks shall Messiah be cut off. . . . And he shall confirm the covenant with many for one week: and *in the midst of the week he shall cause the sacrifice and the oblation to cease.*" Daniel 9:26, 27.

What Really Ended at the Cross?

What did Christ nail to His cross and thus abolish?

"Blotting out *the handwriting of ordinances* [literally, "decrees"] that was against us, which was contrary to us, and took it out of the way, *nailing it to his cross.*" Colossians 2:14. "Having abolished in his flesh the enmity, even *the law of commandments contained in ordinances* [literally, "decrees"]; for to make in himself of twain one new man, so making peace; and that he might reconcile both unto God in one body by the cross, having slain the enmity thereby." Ephesians 2:15, 16.

Note.—"By the handwriting of ordinances the apostle most evidently means the ceremonial law."—Dr. Adam Clarke, *Commentary.*

"Jesus did not give a new moral code. He was not a second lawgiver like Moses. He was far greater, and His moral teachings stand on a far higher plane than those of Moses. He was not so much concerned with laying down detailed rules for the regulation of the moral life as with enunciating eternal principles by which men should live under God and with talking about motives and purposes which should rule all our actions.

"Jesus did not give a new code, but He also did not say that the moral teachings of the Old Testament were suspended. The ceremonial and ritualistic laws of the Old Testament are abrogated for the Christian, but not the Ten Commandments."—J. Philip Hyatt, "God's Decrees for Moral Living," *The Teacher* (Baptist), October, 1943, vol. 57, no. 10, p. 5.

What aspects of the ceremonial system are particularly

WHAT WAS ABOLISHED BY CHRIST?

mentioned as foreshadowing Christ, and thus ending at the cross?

"Let no man therefore judge you in *meat,* or in *drink,* or in respect of an *holyday,* or of the *new moon,* or of the *sabbath days: which are a shadow of things to come;* but the body is of Christ." Colossians 2:16, 17.

NOTE.—The things concerning which no man is to judge us "are a shadow of things to come." The weekly Sabbath was given to man in Eden, not as a shadow of something to come, but as God's memorial of His creative work. For the Jews' shadowy sabbaths see Leviticus 23:4-44.

What was the purpose of the sacrifices of the ceremonial system?

"For the law *having a shadow of good things to come,* and not the very image of the things, can never with those *sacrifices* which they offered year by year continually make the comers thereunto perfect." Hebrews 10:1.

What occurred at the time of the crucifixion which indicated that the typical system had been taken away by Christ?

"The veil of the temple was rent in twain from the top to the bottom; and the earth did quake." Matthew 27:51.

NOTE.—By this supernatural act God declared that henceforth men might have direct access to His presence, without a mediating priesthood on earth.

In what language is this clearly stated?

"He said, *Sacrifice* and *offering* and *burnt offerings* and *offering for sin* thou wouldest not, neither hadst pleasure therein; which are offered by the law; then said he, Lo, I come to do thy will, O God. *He taketh away the first, that he may establish the second."* Hebrews 10:8, 9.

NOTE.—The *first* here refers to the typical offerings. These were taken away that the second, the all-sufficient offering, the blood of Christ, might stand forth as the true, the only sacrifice that could take away sin. To have continued the offering of animals after the cross would have been a denial that the Lamb of God, whom the offerings prefigured, had come.

How did Jesus intimate to the woman at Jacob's Well that the ceremonial system of worship would be abolished?

"Jesus saith unto her, Woman, believe me, the hour cometh, when ye shall neither in this mountain, nor yet at Jerusalem, worship the Father." John 4:21.

Note.—The Jewish worship centered in the ritual service of the Temple "at Jerusalem," but the Samaritans had instituted a rival service "in this mountain," Mount Gerizim. Jesus therefore indicated that the time was at hand when the whole typical system would pass away.

Testing the Issue

How did this question confront the apostles?

"And certain men which came down from Judaea taught the brethren, and said, *Except ye be circumcised after the manner of Moses, ye cannot be saved.*" Acts 15:1. "Certain which went out from us have troubled you with words, subverting your souls, saying, *Ye must be circumcised, and keep the law:* to whom we gave no such commandment." Verse 24.

What decision was then reached by the apostles?

"For it seemed good to the Holy Ghost, and to us, to lay upon you no greater burden than these necessary things; *that ye abstain from meats offered to idols, and from blood, and from things strangled, and from fornication:* from which if ye keep yourselves, ye shall do well. Fare ye well." Verses 28, 29.

Note.—The question before the council at Jerusalem concerned the Mosaic law. Christian Gentiles and Jews were keeping the seventh-day Sabbath, and in other matters observing the Ten Commandments, for the apostle James says pointedly, "Whosoever shall keep the whole law, and yet offend in one point, he is guilty of all." James 2:10.

Of what was Stephen accused concerning the Mosaic law?

"And set up false witnesses, which said, This man ceaseth not to speak blasphemous words against *this holy place,* and *the law:* for we have heard him say, that this Jesus of Nazareth shall destroy this place, and shall *change the customs which Moses delivered us.*" Acts 6:13, 14.

What similar charge was brought against Paul?

"This fellow persuadeth men to worship God *contrary to the law.*" Acts 18:13.

What statement did Paul make concerning his faith?

"I confess unto thee, that after the way which they call *heresy*, so worship I the God of my fathers, *believing all things which are written in the law and in the prophets*." Acts 24:14.

NOTE.—The charge against Stephen and Paul was not based upon any violation of the moral law, but upon their teaching concerning the ceremonial law; and Paul's admission that he was guilty of what they called heresy meant simply that he differed from them as to the obligation to observe any longer the ceremonial law, which was imposed upon them "until the time of reformation." The simple fact that such charges were made against these able teachers of the gospel shows that in their view the ceremonial law had been abolished by the death of Christ.

JESUS AND THE LAW

What is the office of the moral law?

"By the law is the knowledge of sin." Romans 3:20.

NOTE.—If the moral law were abolished, there would be no sin. But Christ always kept the Ten Commandments, and by His death established the moral law forever. (See Romans 3:31; 8:1-3.)

How is this same teaching expressed in another place?

"For *Christ is the end of the law for righteousness* to every one that believeth." Romans 10:4.

What did Christ say of the law and the prophets?

"Think not that I am come to destroy the law, or the prophets: I am not come to destroy, but to fulfil." Matthew 5:17.

NOTE.—"The ritual or ceremonial law, delivered by Moses to the children of Israel, containing all the injunctions and ordinances which related to the old sacrifices and service of the Temple, our Lord indeed did come to destroy. . . . But the moral law, contained in the Ten Commandments, and enforced by the Prophets, he did not take away." "In the highest rank of the enemies of the gospel of Christ, are they who openly and explicitly 'judge the law' itself, and 'speak evil of the law'; who teach men to break . . . all the commandments at a stroke; who teach, without any cover, in so many words,—'What did our Lord do with the law? He abolished it. There is but one duty, which is that of believing. All commands are unfit for our times. . . .' Father, forgive them; for they know not what they do!"—JOHN WESLEY, "Upon Our Lord's Sermon on the Mount," Discourse 5, in *Works,* vol. 5 (1829 ed.), pp. 311, 317.

The Law and the Gospel

THE PURPOSE OF THE LAW

WHAT is the purpose of the law?

"By the deeds of the law there shall no flesh be justified in his sight: for *by the law is the knowledge of sin.*" Romans 3:20.

How particular is God concerning Christian conduct?

"Whosoever shall keep the whole law, and yet offend in one point, he is guilty of all." James 2:10.

CHRIST SAVES MAN, MAGNIFIES LAW

What is the gospel declared to be?

"I am not ashamed of the gospel of Christ: for it is *the power of God unto salvation to every one that believeth.*" Romans 1:16.

What is the significance of the name Jesus?

"Thou shalt call his name *Jesus:* for *he shall save his people from their sins.*" Matthew 1:21.

In whom is this power to save from sin revealed?

"We preach . . . *Christ the power of God*, and the wisdom of God." 1 Corinthians 1:23, 24.

How was Christ's attitude toward God's law foretold?

"It is written of me, *I delight to do thy will, O my God:* yea, *thy law is within my heart.*" Psalm 40:7, 8.

What does Christ promise of the new covenant?

"But now hath he obtained a more excellent ministry, by how much also he is the *mediator* of a better covenant." "For this is the covenant that I will make with the house of Israel after those days, saith the Lord; *I will put my laws into their mind, and write them in their hearts.*" Hebrews 8:6, 10.

What must we do in order to benefit by Christ's work?

"With the heart man *believeth* unto righteousness; and with the mouth *confession* is made unto salvation." Romans 10:10.

For what did the apostle Paul trust Christ?

"I count all things but loss . . . that I may win Christ, and be found in him, not having mine own righteousness, which is of the law, but that which is through the faith of Christ, *the righteousness which is of God by faith*." Philippians 3:8, 9.

Does the faith which brings righteousness abolish the law?

"Do we then make void the law through faith? God forbid: yea, *we establish the law*." Romans 3:31.

Note.—In the gospel, the law, first written in the heart of Christ, is transferred to the heart of the believer, where Christ dwells by faith. Thus the new covenant promise is fulfilled. This is righteousness by faith—a righteousness which is witnessed by the law, and revealed in the life in harmony with the law. Such faith, instead of making void the law, establishes it in the heart of the believer.

"The law demands obedience, but cannot produce it; it is holy in itself, but it cannot make us holy; it convinces of sin, but it cannot cure it; it reveals the disease, but it cannot provide the remedy; while the gospel both requires and enables, saves and sanctifies (Rom. 3:19-22; 4:15; 5:20, 21; 7:7-13; II Cor. 3:7-9; Gal. 3:21-24; I Tim. 1:8-11). . . .

"While it is in the very nature of all law to provoke opposition to itself in our wayward minds and wilful hearts, it is the essence of the gospel to appeal to the two strongest motives that actuate men and women—gratitude and love (contrast Rom. 7:5, 7-11; with 6:1-15; II Cor. 5:14, 15). . . .

"The gospel shows us the Saviour whom we need, and declares that He has fully obeyed the precepts of the law by His spotless life as our great representative, as well as completely exhausted its penalties through His atoning death as our great substitute (II Cor. 5: 21). . . . Divine justice and righteousness have been more entirely vindicated through His work for men than they could have been by the obedience or sufferings of the whole human race!

"It is the aim alike of the law and of the gospel to secure obedience, but the law compels us to it as a duty, making it irksome and distasteful, while the gospel constrains us to it as a privilege, rendering it easy and delightful. The law sets obedience before us as a means of salvation, and makes blessing strictly conditional upon it. The gospel reveals it as the natural consequence of redemption, and enjoins obedience as the necessary result of blessing."—William C. Procter, *Moody Bible Institute Monthly* (Copyrighted), November, 1933, pp. 107, 108. Used by permission.

What did Christ take away?

"Behold the Lamb of God, which taketh away *the sin of the world.*" John 1:29.

What has Christ abolished?

"Jesus Christ, who hath *abolished death,* and hath brought life and immortality to light through the gospel." 2 Timothy 1:10.

NOTE.—"Man ... needs to be solemnly reminded that the law of the spirit of life in Christ sets him free from *the law of sin and death,* but not from the law of God."—G. CAMPBELL MORGAN, *The Ten Commandments* (Revell, 1901 ed.), p. 12.

What change is brought about through the gospel?

"But we all, with open face beholding as in a glass the glory of the Lord, are *changed into the same image* from glory to glory even as by the Spirit of the Lord." 2 Corinthians 3:18.

NOTE.—It is sometimes claimed that Christ changed, abolished, or took away the moral law, and put the gospel in its place; but this shows a misapprehension of the real work of Christ. The individual believer is changed by beholding the glory revealed in the gospel (2 Corinthians 4:4; John 1:14); death has been abolished through the death of Christ; and sin has been taken away by the great Sin Bearer; but the law of God still remains unchanged as the very foundation of His throne. (See note on page 517.)

What spiritual interpretation did Christ give to the sixth and seventh commandments?

"Ye have heard that it was said by them of old time, Thou shalt not kill; and whosoever shall kill shall be in danger of the judgment: but I say unto you, That *whosoever is angry with his brother* without a cause shall be in danger of the judgment." Matthew 5:21, 22. "Ye have heard that it was said by them of old time, Thou shalt not commit adultery: but I say unto you, That *whosoever looketh on a woman to lust after her hath committed adultery with her already in his heart.*" Verses 27, 28.

Of what prophecy was this teaching a fulfillment?

"The Lord is well pleased for his righteousness' sake; *he will magnify the law, and make it honourable.*" Isaiah 42:21.

NOTE.—Christ not only gave a spiritual interpretation to the law, and Himself thus observed it, but He showed the holiness and the immutable nature of the law by dying on the cross to pay the penalty of its transgression. In this way, above all, He magnified the law.

GRACE AND THE LAW

In what promise was the gospel preached to Abraham?

"And the scripture ... preached before *the gospel* unto Abraham, saying, *In thee shall all nations be blessed.*" Galatians 3:8.

On what basis was Abraham accounted righteous?

"For what saith the scripture? *Abraham believed God, and it was counted unto him for righteousness.*" Romans 4:3.

What scripture cuts off all hope of justification by works?

"By the deeds of the law there shall no flesh be justified in his sight: for by the law is the knowledge of sin." Romans 3:20.

In what way are all believers in Jesus justified?

"Being *justified freely by his grace* through the redemption that is in Christ Jesus." Verse 24.

Is the believer expected to go on in sin after this?

"What shall we say then? Shall we continue in sin, that grace may abound? God forbid. How shall we, that are dead to sin, live any longer therein?" Romans 6:1, 2.

What was Christ's personal attitude toward the law?

"Think not that I am come to destroy the law, or the prophets: *I am not come to destroy, but to fulfil.*" Matthew 5:17. "If ye keep my commandments, ye shall abide in my love; even as *I have kept my Father's commandments,* and abide in his love." John 15:10.

What scripture shows that God's remnant people will understand the proper relation between law and gospel?

"Here is the patience of the saints: *here are they that keep the commandments of God, and the faith of Jesus.*" Revelation 14:12.

NOTE.—"God has not left men enmeshed in their own disobedience—He has provided a way of restoration. This is not by pulling the heavenly standard down to the level of our guiltiness and weakness, but by lifting men up to the level of the eternal standard of his holiness.... This restoration is *restoration to a state of obedience to the Law*....

"The atonement of Jesus Christ ... bears an eternal relation to the Law of God, the Law which is holy, just and good.... [As the believer is] delivered by the work of Christ from the penalty of a broken law, and given a new heart by the Holy Spirit, by which he loves the way of obedience that once he shunned, the Law and the gospel are seen working in glorious harmony for the blessing of the redeemed man.

"To achieve this is *the one great purpose* of the proclamation of the gospel."—O. C. S. WALLACE, *What Baptists Believe,* pp. 83, 84. Copyright, 1934, by the Sunday School Board of the Southern Baptist Convention. Used by permission.

ALL praise to Thee, eternal Lord,
Clothed in a garb of flesh and blood;
Choosing a manger for Thy throne,
While worlds on worlds are Thine alone!
. . . . . .

A little child, Thou art our guest,
That weary ones in Thee may rest;
Forlorn and lowly is Thy birth,
That we may rise to heaven from earth.
. . . . . .

All this for us Thy love hath done,
By this to Thee our life is won;
For this we tune our cheerful lays,
And tell our thanks in songs of praise.

—MARTIN LUTHER

Part Nine

The Sabbath

	PAGE
Institution of the Sabbath	405
God's Memorial	409
Reasons for Sabbathkeeping	413
Manner of Observing the Sabbath	417
Christ and the Sabbath	423
The Sabbath in the New Testament	427
The Change of the Sabbath	430
The Seal of God and the Mark of Apostasy	442
The Lord's Day	447
The Sabbath in History	453
Sabbath Reform	460

THE FIRST SABBATH IN EDEN

"Remember the sabbath day, to keep holy." "For . . . the Lord blessed the sabbath day, and hallowed it." Exodus 20:8, 1

Institution of the Sabbath

HOW THE SABBATH WAS MADE

WHEN and by whom was the Sabbath made?

"Thus the heavens and the earth were finished, and all the host of them. And *on the seventh day God ended his work* which he had made; *and he rested on the seventh day* from all his work which he had made." Genesis 2:1, 2.

What is the reason for keeping the Sabbath day holy?

"For in six days the Lord made heaven and earth, the sea, and all that in them is, and rested the seventh day: wherefore the Lord blessed the sabbath day, and hallowed it." Exodus 20:11.

NOTE.—The Sabbath is the memorial of creation. God designed that through keeping it man should forever remember Him as the true and living God, the Creator of all things.

On the perpetuity of the Sabbath command, Wesley declared: "'Six days shalt thou do all manner of work. But the seventh day is the Sabbath of the Lord thy God.' It is not thine, but God's day. He claims it for his own. He always did claim it for his own, even from the beginning of the world. 'In six days the Lord made heaven and earth, and rested the seventh day. Therefore the Lord blessed the Sabbath-day and hallowed it.' He *hallowed* it; that is, he made it holy; He reserved it for his own service. He appointed, that as long as the sun or the moon, the heavens and the earth, should endure, the children of men should spend this day in the worship of Him who 'gave them life and breath and all things.'"—JOHN WESLEY, "A Word to a Sabbath-Breaker," in *Works,* vol. 11 (1830 ed.), pp. 164-166.

Did Christ have anything to do with creation and the making of the Sabbath?

"All things were made *by him; and without him was not any thing made that was made."* John 1:3. (See also Ephesians 3:9; Colossians 1:16; Hebrews 1:2.)

NOTE.—Christ was the active agent in creation. God rested on the seventh day from the work of creation; therefore, Christ must have rested on the seventh day with the Father. Consequently, it is His rest day as well as the Father's.

After resting on the seventh day, what did God do?

"And God *blessed the seventh day, and sanctified it:* because that in it he had rested from all his work which God created and made." Genesis 2:3.

NOTE.—By three distinct acts, then, was the Sabbath made: God *rested* on it; He *blessed* it; He *sanctified* it. *Sanctify* means "to make sacred or holy," "to consecrate," "to set apart as sacred."

MAN AND THE SABBATH

For whom did Christ say the Sabbath was made?

"And he said unto them, *The sabbath was made for man,* and not man for the sabbath." Mark 2:27.

NOTE.—*Man* here means "mankind." God instituted the Sabbath to be a source of benefit and blessing to the human family.

"Jesus says: 'The Sabbath was made for man;' and the necessary inference is that from the beginning man knew the primary uses of the day, and received the benefits which it was designed to impart. . . .

"Before the giving of the law from Sinai the obligation of the Sabbath was understood."—J. J. TAYLOR (Baptist), *The Sabbatic Question* (Revell, 1914 ed.), pp. 20-24.

Regarding the perpetuity of the Sabbath commandment, Moody wrote: "I honestly believe that this commandment is just as binding to-day as it ever was. I have talked with men who have said that it has been abrogated, but they have never been able to point to any place in the Bible where God repealed it. When Christ was on earth, He did nothing to set it aside; He freed it from the traces under which the scribes and Pharisees had put it, and gave it its true place. 'The sabbath was made for man, not man for the sabbath.' It is just as practicable and as necessary for men to-day as it ever was—in fact, more than ever, because we live in such an intense age.

"The sabbath was binding in Eden, and it has been in force ever since. This fourth commandment begins with the word 'remember,' showing that the sabbath already existed when God wrote this law on the tables of stone at Sinai. How can men claim that this one commandment has been done away with when they will admit that the other nine are still binding?"—D. L. MOODY, *Weighed and Wanting* (1898 ed.), pp. 46, 47.

When did God bless and sanctify the seventh day?

"And on the seventh day God ended his work which he had made; and he rested on the seventh day from all his work which he had made. And God blessed the seventh day, and sanctified it: *because that in it he* HAD *rested from all his work* which God created and made." Genesis 2:2, 3.

NOTE.—"If we had no other passage than this of Genesis 2:3, there would be no difficulty in deducing from it a precept for the universal observance of a Sabbath, or seventh day, to be devoted to God as holy time, by all of that race for whom the earth and its nature were specially prepared. The first men must have known it. The words 'He hallowed it' can have no meaning otherwise. They would be a blank unless in reference to some who were required to keep it holy."—JOHN PETER LANGE, *A Commentary on the Holy Scriptures,* on Genesis 2:3, vol. 1, p. 197.

THE SABBATH TEST IN ISRAEL

What does the Sabbath commandment require?

"*Remember the sabbath day, to keep it holy.* Six days shalt thou labour, and do all thy work: but the seventh day is the sabbath of the Lord thy God: *in it thou shalt not do any work,* thou, nor thy son, nor thy daughter, thy manservant, nor thy maidservant, nor thy cattle, nor thy stranger that is within thy gates." Exodus 20:8-10.

NOTE.—Luther says, on Exodus 16:4, 22-30: "Hence you can see that the Sabbath was before the law of Moses came, and has existed from the beginning of the world. Especially have the devout, who have preserved the true faith, met together and called upon God on this day."—Translated from *Auslegung des Alten Testaments* (Commentary on the Old Testament), in *Sammtliche Schriften* (Collected Writings), edited by J. G. Walch, vol. 3, col. 950.

How did God prove Israel in the wilderness?

"*I will rain bread from heaven for you;* and the people shall go out and gather a certain rate every day, *that I may prove them, whether they will walk in my law, or no.*" Exodus 16:4.

On which day was a double portion of manna gathered?

"And it came to pass, that *on the sixth day they gathered twice as much bread,* two omers for one man." Verse 22.

What did Moses say to the rulers?

"*This is that which the Lord hath said, To morrow is the rest of the holy sabbath* unto the Lord." Verse 23.

Note.—"2. The Sabbath is indispensable to man, being promotive of his highest good, physically, intellectually, socially, spiritually, and eternally. Hence its observance is connected with the best of promises, and its violation with the severest penalties. Exod. xxiii, 12; xxxi, 12-18; Neh. xiii, 15-22; Isa. lvi, 2-7; lviii, 13-14; Jer. xvii, 21-27; Ezek. xx, 12, 13; xxii, 26-31. Its sanctity was very distinctly marked in the gathering of the manna. Exod. xvi, 22-30.

"3. The original law of the Sabbath was renewed and made a prominent part of the moral law, or ten commandments, given through Moses at Sinai. Exod. xx, 8-11."—AMOS BINNEY AND DANIEL STEELE, *Binney's Theological Compend Improved* (1902 ed.), p. 170.

What did some of the people do on the seventh day?

"It came to pass, that *there went out some of the people on the seventh day for to gather,* and they found none." Verse 27.

How did God reprove their disobedience?

"And the Lord said unto Moses, *How long refuse ye to keep my commandments and my laws?*" Verse 28.

Why was twice as much manna given on the sixth day?

"See, *for that the Lord hath given you the sabbath, therefore he giveth you on the sixth day the bread of two days;* abide ye every man in his place, let no man go out of his place on the seventh day." Verse 29.

How, then, did the Lord test the people?

Over the keeping of the Sabbath.

Note.—Thus we see that the Sabbath commandment was a part of God's law before this law was spoken from Sinai, for this incident occurred before Israel came to Sinai.

"As presented to us in the Scriptures the Sabbath was not the invention of any religious founder. It was not at first part of any system of religion, but an entirely independent institution. Very definitely it is presented in Genesis as the very first institution, inaugurated by the Creator himself. It was purely religious, wholly moral, wholly spiritual. It had no prescribed ceremonies, no sacramentarian significance. It required no priest, no liturgy. It was for man as God's creature, steward and friend."—W. O. CARVER, *Sabbath Observance,* p. 41. Copyright, 1940, by the Sunday School Board of the Southern Baptist Convention. Used by permission.

God's Memorial

EXAMPLES OF MEMORIALS

What was the monument erected by Joshua declared to be?

"And *these stones shall be for a memorial* unto the children of Israel for ever." Joshua 4:7.

What were these stones to commemorate?

"And he spake unto the children of Israel, saying, When your children shall ask their fathers in time to come, saying, What mean these stones? then *ye shall let your children know, saying, Israel came over this Jordan on dry land*." Verses 21, 22.

NOTE.—These stones were to be a standing memorial, or reminder, of Israel's coming dry shod over the Jordan.

What was the Passover called?

"And *this day shall be unto you for a memorial;* and ye shall keep it a feast to the Lord throughout your generations; ye shall keep it a feast by an ordinance for ever." Exodus 12:14.

NOTE.—This, the Passover, was a *periodical* memorial, to be observed on the fourteenth day of the first month of each year, the day on which the Israelites were delivered from Egyptian bondage, and its celebration was to be, with the seven days' feast of unleavened bread following and connected with it, in commemoration of that event. (See Exodus 13:3-9.)

GOD'S CREATION AND MEMORIAL

What has God commanded men to observe in memory of His work of creation?

"Remember the sabbath day, to keep it holy. . . . For in six days the Lord made heaven and earth, the sea, and all that in them is, and rested the seventh day: wherefore the Lord blessed the sabbath day, and hallowed it." Exodus 20:8-11.

Of what was this memorial to be a sign?

"And hallow my sabbaths; and they shall be *a sign* between

me and you, *that ye may know that I am the Lord your God."* Ezekiel 20:20.

How long was the Sabbath to be a sign of the true God?

"It is a sign between me and the children of Israel for ever: for in six days the Lord made heaven and earth, and on the seventh day he rested, and was refreshed." Exodus 31:17.

Note.—It is manifest that if the object of the Sabbath was to remember God as the Creator, and the day had been faithfully kept from the first, there would not now be a heathen or an idolater on the face of the earth.

Memorial of Deliverance and Redemption

What besides creation were Israel to remember when they kept the Sabbath?

"And remember that thou wast a servant in the land of Egypt, and that the Lord thy God brought thee out thence through a mighty hand and by a stretched out arm: therefore the Lord thy God commanded thee to keep the sabbath day." Deuteronomy 5:15.

Note.—The recollection of their bondage and oppressed condition in Egypt was to be to the Israelites an additional incentive for keeping the Sabbath in the land of freedom. The Sabbath, therefore, besides being a memorial of creation, was to be to them a memorial of their deliverance from bondage, and of the great power of God as manifested in this deliverance. And as Egypt stands as a symbol of the condition of everyone in the world under the slavery of sin, so the Sabbath is to be kept by every saved soul as a memorial of the deliverance from this slavery by the mighty power of God through Christ.

Of what else does God say He gave the Sabbath to His people to be a sign, or reminder?

"Moreover also I gave them my sabbaths, to be *a sign* between me and them, *that they might know that I am the Lord that sanctify them."* Ezekiel 20:12.

Note.—Sanctification is a work of redemption—of making holy sinful or unholy beings. Like the work of creation itself, this requires creative power. (See Psalm 51:10; John 3:3, 6; Ephesians 2:10.) And as the Sabbath is the appropriate sign, or memorial, of the creative power of God, so it is also of God's re-creative power. This will be one great reason for the saints' keeping it throughout eternity. It will remind them not only of their own creation and the creation of the universe but also of their redemption.

Through whom do we have sanctification?

"But of him are ye in *Christ Jesus,* who of God is made unto us wisdom, and righteousness, and *sanctification,* and redemption." 1 Corinthians 1:30.

NOTE.—Then, as the Sabbath is a sign, or memorial, that it is Jehovah who sanctifies us, and as Christ is the one through whom the work of sanctification is accomplished, the Sabbath is a sign, or memorial, that the believer is united with Christ. Through the Sabbath, therefore, God designed that the believer and Christ should be very closely linked together.

GOD'S MEMORIAL IN THE HEREAFTER

How often will the redeemed congregate to worship the Lord?

"For as the new heavens and the new earth, which I will make, shall remain before me, saith the Lord, so shall your seed and your name remain. And it shall come to pass, that *from one new moon to another,* and *from one sabbath to another,* shall all flesh come to worship before me, saith the Lord." Isaiah 66: 22, 23.

NOTE.—The Sabbath, which is the memorial of God's creative power, will never cease to exist. When this sinful state of things shall give way to the sinless new earth, the fact upon which the Sabbath institution is based will still remain; and those who shall be permitted to live in the new earth will still commemorate the creative power of God, while singing the song of Moses and the Lamb. (Revelation 15:3. See Revelation 22:1, 2.)

H. M. LAMBERT

SABBATH MORNING

"Remember the sabbath day, keep it holy." Exodus 20

Reasons for Sabbathkeeping

The Sabbath and the True God

How is the true God distinguished from all false gods?

"The Lord is the true God, he is the living God, and an everlasting king. . . . *The gods that have not made the heavens and the earth,* even they shall perish from the earth, and from under these heavens. *He hath made the earth by his power,* he hath established the world by his wisdom, and hath stretched out the heavens by his discretion." Jeremiah 10:10-12.

How did Paul describe God to the idolatrous Athenians?

"Whom therefore ye ignorantly worship, him declare I unto you. *God that made the world and all things therein.*" Acts 17: 23, 24.

What did the apostles say to the idolaters at Lystra?

"Turn from these vanities unto *the living God, which made heaven, and earth, and the sea, and all things that are therein.*" Acts 14:15. (See also Revelation 10:6; 14:6, 7.)

What reason is given in the fourth commandment for keeping the Sabbath day holy?

"For in six days the Lord made heaven and earth, the sea, and all that in them is, and rested the seventh day." Exodus 20:11.

Note.—The Sabbath is the great memorial of the creative power of the true and living God. God's design in making the Sabbath was that man might never forget Him, the Creator of all things.

"The week, with its Sabbath, is an artificial device. The reason for it is found only in the Old Testament Scriptures. Here it is always associated with revelation from God. . . .

"Religious ideas and practices among all peoples, in varying degree, have been associated with all the time divisions which men have adopted. But in connection only with the week is religion obviously the explanation of its origin, and the week only is uniformly attributed to command of God. The week exists because of the Sabbath. It is historically and scientifically true that the Sabbath was made by God."—W. O. Carver, *Sabbath Observance,* pp. 34, 35.

Copyright, 1940, by the Sunday School Board of the Southern Baptist Convention. Used by permission.

When we remember that millions of the world's inhabitants today are idolaters, and that since the Fall, idolatry, with its train of resultant evils, has ever been a prevailing sin, and then think that the observance of the Sabbath, as God ordained it, would have prevented all this, we can better appreciate the value of the Sabbath institution, and of Sabbathkeeping.

THE SABBATH AND KNOWING GOD

What is the Sabbath to those who keep it holy?

"And hallow my sabbaths; and *they shall be a sign between me and you, that ye may know that I am the Lord your God.*" Ezekiel 20:20.

NOTE.—"The observance of the Sabbath connects man with the origin of his race, with the six days' creation, and with the Creator Himself. . . . The Sabbath thus becomes a sign by which the believers in a historical Revelation are distinguished from those who have allowed these great facts to fade from their remembrance (Exodus 31:13). . . . The observance of the Sabbath, then, becomes the characteristic of those who cherish the recollections of the origin of their race, and who worship God not merely as Elohim, the Everlasting Almighty, but as Jehovah, the historical God, the Creator, who has revealed Himself to man from the dawn of his existence as the God of love, and afterwards of mercy and grace, of promise and performance."—JAMES G. MURPHY, *Commentary on the Book of Exodus,* pp. 143, 144.

How important is it that we know God?

"And *this is life eternal,* that they might know thee the only true God, and Jesus Christ, whom thou hast sent." John 17:3.

Is there any danger of God's people forgetting Him?

"*Beware that thou forget not the Lord thy God,* in not keeping his commandments, and his judgments, and his statutes." Deuteronomy 8:11.

SANCTIFICATION AND DELIVERANCE

What other reason is given for keeping the Sabbath?

"Verily my sabbaths ye shall keep: *for it is a sign between me and you* throughout your generations; *that ye may know that I am the Lord that doth sanctify you.*" Exodus 31:13.

NOTE.—To sanctify is to make holy, or to set apart for a holy use. The sanctification, or making holy, of sinful beings can be wrought only by the creative power of God through Christ by the Holy Spirit. In 1 Corinthians 1:30 we are told that Christ is made unto us "sanctification"; and in Ephesians 2:10 it is said that "we are his workmanship, *created* in Christ Jesus unto good works." The Sabbath, therefore, is a sign of what Christ is to the believer, because it is a reminder of the creative power of God as manifested in the work of regeneration. It is the sign of the power of God, therefore, in both creation and redemption. To the believer it is the evidence, or sign, that he knows the true God, who, through Christ, created all things, and who, through Christ, redeems the sinner and makes him whole.

What special reason did Israel have for Sabbathkeeping?

"And remember that thou wast a servant in the land of Egypt, and that the Lord thy God brought thee out thence through a mighty hand and by a stretched out arm: therefore the Lord thy God commanded thee to keep the sabbath day." Deuteronomy 5:15.

NOTE.—In their bondage the Israelites had to some extent lost the knowledge of God, and departed from His precepts. In consequence of the oppression, especially the rigorous exactions made upon them by the Pharaoh of the Exodus, Sabbath observance was doubtless extremely difficult if not entirely impossible. Deliverance from this oppression was therefore an additional reason for their keeping the Sabbath. Since Egyptian bondage is illustrative of the bondage of sin, everyone who has been delivered from sin may regard himself as having the same reason for keeping the Sabbath as had the Israelites who were released from Egyptian bondage.

What does the psalmist say was the reason why God brought His people out of Egypt and placed them in Canaan?

"He brought forth his people . . . : and gave them the lands of the heathen . . . ; *that they might observe his statutes, and keep his laws."* Psalm 105:43-45.

NOTE.—Their deliverance from Egyptian bondage was a reason for the keeping not only of the fourth commandment but of every precept of God's law. This is indicated by the preamble to the law as given on Sinai: "I am the Lord thy God, which have brought thee out of the land of Egypt, out of the house of bondage," prefacing "Thou shalt have no other gods before me." Exodus 20:2, 3. (See also Leviticus 19:35-37; Deuteronomy 10:19; 15:12-15; 24:17, 18.) Likewise, God calls everyone who, through Christ, has been delivered from the bondage of sin, to keep not only the Sabbath but every precept of His holy law. "Blessed is the man that doeth this, and the son of man that layeth hold on it; that *keepeth the sabbath* from polluting it, and keepeth his hand from doing *any* evil." Isaiah 56:2.

Personal Rest and Public Worship

What is the meaning of the word "sabbath"?

Rest.

NOTE.—Previous to the Fall, God designed that man's time should be occupied with pleasant, invigorating labor. (Genesis 2:15.) Wearisome toil came in consequence of sin. (Genesis 3:17-19.) Since the Fall the Sabbath may bring physical rest to both man and beast of burden (Exodus 23:12), but physical rest was not its original and primary design or purpose. Cessation from the ordinary labors of the week was ordained, not because these are sinful in themselves, but that man might have a frequently recurring period for the contemplation of the Creator and His works.

Was the Sabbath intended as a day for public worship?

"Six days shall work be done: but the seventh day is the sabbath of rest, *an holy convocation*." Leviticus 23:3.

NOTE.—A convocation is an assembly of people.

What warning concerning neglect of assembly is given in the New Testament?

"Let us consider one another to provoke unto love and to good works: *not forsaking the assembling of ourselves together,* as the manner of some is; but exhorting one another: and so much the more, as ye see the day approaching." Hebrews 10:24, 25.

Will the Sabbath be observed as a day of worship in the new earth?

"For as the new heavens and the new earth, which I will make, shall remain before me, saith the Lord, so shall your seed and your name remain. And it shall come to pass, that from one new moon to another, and *from one sabbath to another, shall all flesh come to worship before me, saith the Lord*." Isaiah 66:22, 23.

Manner of Observing the Sabbath

KEEPING HOLY WHAT GOD MADE HOLY

What is first commanded in the Sabbath commandment?

"*Remember* the sabbath *day*." Exodus 20:8.

Which day is the Sabbath?

"*The seventh day* is the sabbath." Verse 10.

For what purpose are we to remember the Sabbath day?

"Remember the sabbath day, *to keep it holy*." Verse 8.

NOTE.—All through the week we are to "remember the sabbath day, to keep it holy." This means that all our plans are to be laid and all our business adjusted with reference to the Sabbath, the object of which is to remind us that God is the Creator of all things. This is just as essential to spiritual growth during the six working days as upon the Sabbath itself. We are to remember that day, also, that when it comes we may not be tempted by circumstances of our own creating to treat it, or any part of it, as secular, or common, time. Thus the Sabbath commandment is to be obeyed every day, though the Sabbath itself can be kept, or observed, only upon the seventh day, for "the seventh day is the sabbath."

Who made the Sabbath day holy?

"Wherefore the *Lord* blessed the sabbath day, and *hallowed it*." Verse 11.

NOTE.—God made the Sabbath day holy; we are to keep it holy.

When, according to the Bible, does the Sabbath begin?

"And the *evening* and the morning were the first day." "And the *evening* and the morning were the second day," etc. (See Genesis 1:5, 8, 13, 19, 23, 31.) "From even unto even, shall ye celebrate your sabbath." Leviticus 23:32.

NOTE.—The reference in Leviticus is to the Day of Atonement (see chap. 23:27); however, a comparison with Mark 1:32 shows that

GATHERING THE MANNA

"On the sixth day they gathered twice as much bread.... B on the seventh day ... there shall be none." Exodus 16:22-2

the same regulation was followed with respect to the seventh-day Sabbath.

One advantage of keeping the Sabbath according to the Bible method of reckoning the day from sunset to sunset, rather than the Roman reckoning, from midnight to midnight, is that by the former, one is awake to welcome and to bid adieu to the day when it comes and goes, whereas by the latter, he is asleep when the day begins and ends. Sunset is a great natural sign for marking the division of time into days.

PHYSICAL AND SPIRITUAL REST

What kind of labor is to be done through the week?

"Six days shalt thou labour, and do all *thy work*." Exodus 20:9.

Is any of this kind of work to be done on the Sabbath?

"In it thou shalt not do *any work*." Verse 10.

NOTE.—If the Sabbath is to be kept "holy," mere physical rest one day in seven cannot be the great object of the Sabbath institution.

How does the Lord, through the prophet Isaiah, indicate what is true Sabbathkeeping?

"If thou *turn away thy foot from the sabbath,* from doing *thy pleasure* on my holy day; and *call the sabbath a delight, the holy of the Lord, honourable;* and shalt *honour him, not doing thine own ways, nor finding thine own pleasure, nor speaking thine own words:* then shalt thou *delight thyself in the Lord;* and I will cause thee to ride upon the high places of the earth, and feed thee with the heritage of Jacob thy father: for the mouth of the Lord hath spoken it." Isaiah 58:13, 14.

NOTE.—"As the Jews departed from God, and failed to make the righteousness of Christ their own by faith, the Sabbath lost its significance to them. Satan was seeking to exalt himself and to draw men away from Christ, and he worked to pervert the Sabbath, because it is the sign of the power of Christ. The Jewish leaders accomplished the will of Satan by surrounding God's rest day with burdensome requirements. In the days of Christ the Sabbath had become so perverted that its observance reflected the character of selfish and arbitrary men rather than the character of the loving heavenly Father. The rabbis virtually represented God as giving laws which it was impossible for men to obey. They led the people to look upon God as a tyrant, and to think that the observance of the Sabbath, as He required it, made men hardhearted and cruel. It was the work of Christ to clear away these misconceptions. Although the rabbis followed Him with merciless hostility, He did not even appear to conform to their requirements, but went straight forward, keeping the Sabbath according to the law of God."—ELLEN G. WHITE, *The Desire of Ages,* pp. 283, 284.

What is the character of God, and how only can He be truly worshiped?

"*God is a Spirit:* and they that worship him must worship him *in spirit and in truth.*" John 4:24.

NOTE.—This is one reason why the attempt to produce Sabbathkeeping by human Sabbath laws is altogether out of place. Such laws can never produce true Sabbathkeeping, for that is *spiritual,* and must be of the *mind* and from the *heart,* and not *perfunctory, mechanical,* or *of force.*

What is one thing of which the Sabbath is a sign?

That it is God who *sanctifies* His people, or makes them *holy.* (See Exodus 31:13; Ezekiel 20:12; and page 411.)

What does the psalm for "the sabbath day" suggest as proper themes for Sabbath thought and action?

"It is a good thing to *give thanks unto the Lord,* and to *sing praises unto thy name, O most High: to shew forth thy lovingkindness* in the morning, and *thy faithfulness* every night, *upon an instrument of ten strings,* and upon the *psaltery;* upon the *harp* with a solemn sound. For thou, Lord, hast made me glad *through thy work:* I will triumph in *the works of thy hands.* O Lord, *how great are thy works!* and *thy thoughts are very deep.*" Psalm 92:1-5.

What do the works of God declare?

"The heavens declare *the glory of God;* and the firmament sheweth *his handywork.* Day unto day uttereth *speech,* and night unto night *sheweth knowledge.* There is no speech nor language, where *their voice* is not heard." Psalm 19:1-3. (See margin.)

NOTE.—God designed that the Sabbath should direct the minds of men to His created works, and through these to Him, the Creator. Nature itself speaks to our senses, telling us that there is a God, the Creator and Supreme Ruler of the universe. The Sabbath was designed to keep the Creator constantly in mind.

What evidence is there that the Sabbath was designed to be a day for public worship?

"Six days shall work be done: but the seventh day is the sabbath of rest, *an holy convocation.*" Leviticus 23:3.

Note.—*Convocation* means "a calling together," a meeting.

What was Christ's custom on the Sabbath day?

"And as his custom was, *he went into the synagogue on the sabbath day, and stood up for to read.*" Luke 4:16.

What else did Jesus do on the Sabbath?

"And it was the sabbath day when Jesus *made the clay, and opened his eyes.*" John 9:14.

Note.—A large share of Christ's ministry consisted of miracles and acts of mercy performed for the relief of suffering humanity; and not a few of these were done on the Sabbath. See next reading.

In what words did He justify acts of mercy on the Sabbath?

"Wherefore it is *lawful* to do well on the sabbath days." Matthew 12:12.

Preparing for the Sabbath

What is the day on which to prepare for the Sabbath?

"And that day [the sixth day] was *the preparation,* and the sabbath drew on." Luke 23:54. (See also Exodus 16:22, 23.)

Note.—In order to keep the Sabbath day holy, it must be remembered all through the week; and on the sixth day, or the day just before the Sabbath, special preparation should be made *to be ready* to welcome and observe the day when it comes.

How did the Israelites in the wilderness on the sixth day prepare for the Sabbath?

"*On the sixth day they gathered twice as much.*" Exodus 16:22.

Note.—The Sabbath should be the happiest day of all the week. "The Sabbath is not intended to be a period of useless inactivity. The law forbids secular labor on the rest day of the Lord; the toil that gains a livelihood must cease; no labor for worldly pleasure or profit is lawful upon that day; but as God ceased His labor of creating, and rested upon the Sabbath and blessed it, so man is to leave the occupations of his daily life, and devote those sacred hours to healthful rest, to worship, and to holy deeds."—Ellen G. White, *The Desire of Ages,* p. 207.

HEALING THE BLIND MAN ON THE SABBATH

"Therefore did the Jews persecute Jesus, a sought to slay him, because he had do these things on the sabbath day." John 5:1

Christ and the Sabbath

Maker and Keeper of the Sabbath

Of what did Christ say the Son of man is Lord?

"The Son of man is Lord even *of the sabbath day*." Matthew 12:8. (See also Mark 2:28.)

Who made the Sabbath?

"All things were made *by him* [*Christ, the Word*]." John 1:3.

Note.—Christ was the creative agent. (See page 405.)

Did Christ, while on earth, keep the Sabbath?

"*As his custom was, he went into the synagogue on the sabbath day, and stood up for to read.*" Luke 4:16.

Debate on How to Keep the Sabbath

Although Lord, Maker, and an observer of the Sabbath, how was He watched and spied upon on this day?

"And the scribes and Pharisees watched him, *whether he would heal on the sabbath day;* that they might find an accusation against him." Luke 6:7.

How did Christ meet their false ideas of Sabbathkeeping?

"Then said Jesus, . . . *Is it lawful on the sabbath days to do good, or to do evil? to save life, or to destroy it?*" Verse 9.

How did they manifest their displeasure at His healing the man with the withered hand on the Sabbath?

"And they were *filled with madness;* and *communed one with another what they might do to Jesus.*" Verse 11. "And the Pharisees went forth, and straightway *took counsel . . . , how they might destroy him.*" Mark 3:6.

Note.—Although the miracle Christ performed had given evidence that He was from God, they were angry because He had shown *their views of Sabbathkeeping* to be *wrong*. Wounded pride, obstinacy, and malice, therefore, combined to fill them with *madness;* and they went out immediately and held counsel with the

Herodians—their political enemies—for the purpose of accomplishing His death.

Because Jesus healed a man on the Sabbath day, and told him to take up his bed and walk, what did the Jews do?

"Therefore did the Jews *persecute Jesus,* and *sought to slay him,* because he had done these things on the sabbath day." John 5:16.

NOTE.—It is noteworthy that not the least of the malice that finally caused His crucifixion was engendered over this very question of Sabbath observance. Christ did not keep the Sabbath according to their ideas, and so they sought to kill Him. Many today cherish this same spirit. Because some do not agree with their ideas of the Sabbath, or Sabbath observance, they seek to persecute and oppress them—seek laws, and alliances with political powers, to compel respect for their own views.

How did Jesus answer them?

"But Jesus answered them, *My Father worketh hitherto, and I work.*" Verse 17.

NOTE.—The ordinary operations of nature, as manifested in God's almighty, upholding, beneficent, and healing power, go on on the Sabbath. To cooperate with God and nature in the work of healing on the Sabbath cannot, therefore, be out of harmony with God's Sabbath law.

What effect did this answer have upon the Jews?

"Therefore the Jews *sought the more to kill him.*" Verse 18.

Because the disciples plucked a few heads of grain on the Sabbath day to satisfy hunger, what did the Pharisees say?

"And the Pharisees said unto him, *Behold, why do they on the sabbath day that which is not lawful?*" Mark 2:24.

What was Christ's reply?

"And he said unto them, Have ye never read what David did, when he had need, and was an hungred, he, and they that were with him? how he . . . did eat the shewbread, which is not lawful to eat but for the priests, and gave also to them which were with him? And he said unto them, *The sabbath was made for man, and not man for the sabbath.*" Verses 25-27.

What was said of Christ's healing a woman one Sabbath?

CHRIST AND THE SABBATH

"The ruler of the synagogue answered, . . . *There are six days in which men ought to work: in them therefore come and be healed, and not on the sabbath day."* Luke 13:14.

What was Christ's answer?

"Thou hypocrite, doth not each one of you on the sabbath loose his ox or his ass from the stall, and lead him away to watering? and ought not this woman, being a daughter of Abraham, whom Satan hath bound, lo, these eighteen years, be loosed from this bond on the sabbath day?" Verses 15, 16.

What effect did Christ's answers have upon the people?

"All his adversaries were ashamed: and all the people rejoiced for all the glorious things that were done by him." Verse 17.

How did Christ justify acts of mercy on the Sabbath?

"What man shall there be among you, that shall have one sheep, and if it fall into a pit on the sabbath day, will he not lay hold on it, and lift it out? How much then is a man better than a sheep? Wherefore it is lawful to do well on the sabbath days." Matthew 12:11, 12. (See also Luke 14:5, 6.)

NOTE.—"Jesus observed the Sabbath Day of his own people. It was his custom to worship in the synagogues on the Sabbath Day. After he entered upon his own ministry, he and his followers continued to recognize and use the Sabbath Day, but according to his own individual and spiritual insight and interpretation. Even when Sabbath observance was made one of the chief grounds of bitter antagonism to him by the Pharisees he continued his recognition of the Sabbath and uttered no word that can properly be construed as lacking in deep reverence. Apparently, he expected that his followers would continue to hold and inculcate the spirit of the historic Sabbath."—W. O. CARVER, *Sabbath Observance,* p. 25. Copyright, 1940, by the Sunday School Board of the Southern Baptist Convention. Used by permission.

What dispute did Christ's miracles cause?

"Therefore said some of the Pharisees, *This man is not of God, because he keepeth not the sabbath day.* Others said, *How can a man that is a sinner do such miracles?"* John 9:16.

NOTE.—By these miracles God was setting the seal of His approval to Christ's views and teachings respecting the Sabbath, and to His manner of observing it, and thus condemning the narrow and false views of the Pharisees. Hence the division.

Jesus Magnifies the Sabbath

According to Isaiah, what was Christ to do with the law?

"He will *magnify* the law, and *make it honourable.*" Isaiah 42:21.

Note.—In nothing, perhaps, was this more strikingly fulfilled than in the matter of Sabbath observance. By their numerous traditional regulations and senseless restrictions the Jews had made the Sabbath a burden, and anything but a delight. Christ removed all these, and by His life and teachings restored the Sabbath to its proper place as a day of worship, of contemplation of God, a day for doing acts of charity and mercy. Thus He magnified it and made it honorable. One of the most prominent features of Christ's ministry was this work of *Sabbath reform.* Christ did not *abolish* or *change* the Sabbath; but He did rescue it from the rubbish of tradition, false ideas, and superstitions by which it had been degraded. The Pharisees had placed the institution *above* man, and *against* man. Christ reversed the order, and said, "The sabbath was made *for man,* and not man *for the sabbath.*" He showed that it was to minister to the happiness and well-being of both man and beast.

In view of the coming destruction and desolation of the city of Jerusalem, for what did Christ tell His disciples to pray?

"But pray ye that your flight be not in the winter, *neither on the sabbath day.*" Matthew 24:20.

Note.—"Christ is here speaking of the flight of the apostles and other Christians out of Jerusalem and Judea, just before their final destruction, as is manifest by the whole context, and especially by the 16th verse: 'Then let them which be in Judea flee into the mountains.' But the final destruction of Jerusalem was after the dissolution of the Jewish constitution, and after the Christian dispensation was fully set up. Yet it is plainly implied in these words of the Lord, that even then Christians were bound to a strict observation of the Sabbath."—Jonathan Edwards, *Works* (reprint of Worcester ed., 1844-1848), vol. 4, pp. 621, 622.

"The Great Teacher never intimated that the Sabbath was a ceremonial ordinance to cease with the Mosaic ritual. . . . Instead of anticipating its extinction along with the ceremonial law, He speaks of its existence after the downfall of Jerusalem. [See Matthew 24:20.]" —W. D. Killen (Irish Presbyterian), *The Ancient Church* (1883 ed.), p. 188.

The Sabbath in the New Testament

THE SABBATH AND THE CROSS

What day immediately precedes the first day of the week?

"In the end of *the sabbath,* as it began to dawn toward the first day of the week." Matthew 28:1.

NOTE.—According to the New Testament, therefore, the Sabbath had passed when the first day of the week began.

After the crucifixion, what day was kept by the women who followed Jesus?

"They returned, and prepared spices and ointments; and *rested the sabbath day according to the commandment."* Luke 23:56.

What day of the week is the Sabbath, "according to the commandment"?

"But *the seventh day is the sabbath* of the Lord thy God." Exodus 20:10.

JESUS AND THE SABBATH

What was Christ's custom respecting the Sabbath?

"And he came to Nazareth, where he had been brought up: and, as his custom was, *he went into the synagogue on the sabbath day,* and stood up for to read." Luke 4:16.

In what instruction to His disciples did Christ recognize the existence of the Sabbath long after His ascension?

"But pray ye that your flight be not in the winter, *neither on the sabbath day."* Matthew 24:20.

NOTE.—The flight of the Christians took place late in October, A.D. 66, three and one-half years before the fall of Jerusalem. (See page 303.) For Jesus' attitude toward the Sabbath, see the preceding reading.

Paul and the Sabbath

On what day did Paul and Barnabas preach at Antioch?

"They came to Antioch in Pisidia, and went into the synagogue on *the sabbath day*." Acts 13:14.

When did the Gentiles ask Paul to repeat his sermon?

"And when the Jews were gone out of the synagogue, the Gentiles besought that these words might be preached to them *the next sabbath*." Verse 42.

On what day did Paul preach to the women at Philippi?

"And *on the sabbath* we went out of the city by a river side, where prayer was wont to be made; and we sat down, and spake unto the women which resorted thither." Acts 16:13.

On what day did Paul preach to the Jews at Thessalonica?

"They came to Thessalonica, where was a synagogue of the Jews: and Paul, *as his manner was, went in unto them, and three sabbath days reasoned with them out of the scriptures*." Acts 17:1, 2.

How did the apostle spend the working days of the week when at Corinth, and what did he do on the Sabbath?

"Because he was of the same craft, he abode with them, and *wrought:* for by their occupation they were *tentmakers*." Acts 18:3. (See Ezekiel 46:1.) "And *he reasoned in the synagogue every sabbath*, and persuaded the Jews and the Greeks." Verse 4.

John and the Lord's Day

On what day was John in the Spirit?

"I was in the Spirit *on the Lord's day*." Revelation 1:10.

Who is Lord of the Sabbath?

"The Son of man is Lord also of the sabbath." Mark 2:28.

What, through Isaiah, does the Lord call the Sabbath?

"If thou turn away thy foot from the sabbath, from doing thy pleasure on *my holy day*." Isaiah 58:13.

Why does the Lord call the Sabbath His day?

"For in six days the Lord made heaven and earth, the sea, and all that in them is, and *rested the seventh day:* wherefore the Lord *blessed* the sabbath day, and *hallowed* it." Exodus 20:11.

Through whom did God create the world?

"God . . . hath in these last days spoken unto us by *his son, . . . by whom also he made the worlds."* Hebrews 1:1, 2.

NOTE.—The Bible recognizes but one weekly Sabbath—the day upon which God rested in the beginning; which was made known to Israel at Sinai (Nehemiah 9:13, 14); was observed by Christ and His apostles; and is to be kept by the redeemed in the new earth (Isaiah 66:22, 23).

The terms *Sabbath, Sabbaths,* and *Sabbath days* occur sixty times in the New Testament, and in every case but one refer to the seventh day. In Colossians 2:16, 17, reference is made to the annual sabbaths connected with the three annual feasts observed by Israel before the first coming of Christ.

"The sacred name of the seventh day is Sabbath. This fact is too clear to require argument. The truth is stated in concise terms: 'The seventh day is the Sabbath of the Lord thy God.' This utterance is repeated in Exodus 16:26, 23:12, 31:15, 35:2, Leviticus 23:3, and Deuteronomy 5:14. On this point the plain teaching of the word has been admitted in all ages. Except to certain special sabbaths appointed in Levitical law, and these invariably governed by the month rather than the week, the Bible in all its utterances never, no, not once, applies the name Sabbath to any other day."—J. J. TAYLOR, *The Sabbatic Question* (Revell), pp. 16, 17.

The first day of the week is mentioned but eight times in the New Testament, six of which are found in the four Gospels, and refer to the day on which Christ arose from the dead. (See Matthew 28:1; Mark 16:2, 9; Luke 24:1; John 20:1, 19.) The other two (Acts 20:7; 1 Corinthians 16:2) refer to the only religious meeting held on the first day of the week after the ascension, in apostolic times, recorded in the New Testament, and to a systematic accounting and laying by in store at home on that day for the poor saints in Judea and Jerusalem.

It is evident, therefore, that the Sabbath of the New Testament is the same as the Sabbath of the Old Testament, and that there is nothing in the New Testament setting aside the seventh-day Sabbath, and putting the first day of the week in its place.

The Change of the Sabbath

THE SABBATH AND THE LAW

Of what is the Sabbath commandment a part?

The law of God. (See Exodus 20:8-11.)

In His most famous sermon, what did Christ say of the law?

"Think not that I am come to destroy the law, or the prophets: I am not come to destroy, but to fulfil." Matthew 5:17.

NOTE.—"He [Christ] fulfilled the moral law by obeying, by bringing out its fulness of meaning, by showing its intense spirituality, and He established it on a surer basis than ever as the eternal law of righteousness. He fulfilled the ceremonial and typical law, not only by conforming to its requirements, but by realizing its spiritual significance. He filled up the shadowy outlines of the types, and, thus fulfilled, they pass away, and it is no longer necessary for us to observe the Passover or slay the daily lamb: we have the substance in Christ."—*The International Standard Bible Encyclopaedia,* vol. 3, p. 1847.

How enduring did He say the law is?

"Till heaven and earth pass, one jot or one tittle shall in no wise pass from the law, till all be fulfilled." Verse 18.

What did He say of those who should break one of the least of God's commandments, and teach men so to do?

"Whosoever therefore shall break one of these least commandments, and shall teach men so, *he shall be called the least in the kingdom of heaven.*" Verse 19.

NOTE.—From this it is evident that all ten commandments are binding in the Christian dispensation, and that Christ had no thought of changing any of them. (See readings on pages 363, 394.) One of these commands the observance of the seventh day as the Sabbath. But most Christians keep the first day of the week instead.

"It is a remarkable and regrettable fact that while most Christians regard the decalogue as a whole as being of personal and perpetual obligation, so many should make the fourth commandment an exception. It is the most complete and comprehensive of them all, and,

THE LAW OF GOD

AS GIVEN BY JEHOVAH

I
Thou shalt have no other gods before me.

II
Thou shalt not make unto thee any graven image, or any likeness of any thing that is in heaven above, or that is in the earth beneath, or that is in the water under the earth: thou shalt not bow down thyself to them, nor serve them: for I the Lord thy God am a jealous God, visiting the iniquity of the fathers upon the children unto the third and fourth generation of them that hate me; and shewing mercy unto thousands of them that love me, and keep my commandments.

III
Thou shalt not take the name of the Lord thy God in vain; for the Lord will not hold him guiltless that taketh his name in vain.

IV
Remember the sabbath day, to keep it holy. Six days shalt thou labour, and do all thy work: but the seventh day is the sabbath of the Lord thy God: in it thou shalt not do any work, thou, nor thy son, nor thy daughter, thy manservant, nor thy maidservant, nor thy cattle, nor thy stranger that is within thy gates: for in six days the Lord made heaven and earth, the sea, and all that in them is, and rested the seventh day: wherefore the Lord blessed the sabbath day, and hallowed it.

V
Honour thy father and thy mother: that thy days may be long upon the land which the Lord thy God giveth thee.

VI
Thou shalt not kill.

VII
Thou shalt not commit adultery.

VIII
Thou shalt not steal.

IX
Thou shalt not bear false witness against thy neighbour.

X
Thou shalt not covet thy neighbour's house, thou shalt not covet thy neighbour's wife, nor his manservant, nor his maidservant, nor his ox, nor his ass, nor any thing that is thy neighbour's.

(Ex. 20:3-17.)

AS CHANGED BY MAN

I
I am the Lord thy God; thou shalt not have strange gods before me.

II
Thou shalt not take the name of the Lord thy God in vain.

III
Remember thou keep holy the Sabbath day.

IV
Honor thy father and thy mother.

V
Thou shalt not kill.

VI
Thou shalt not commit adultery.

VII
Thou shalt not steal.

VIII
Thou shalt not bear false witness against thy neighbor.

IX
Thou shalt not covet thy neighbor's wife.

X
Thou shalt not covet thy neighbor's goods.

(PETER GEIERMANN, *The Convert's Catechism of Catholic Doctrine* [1946 ed.], pp. 37, 38.)

unlike the rest, is expressed both positively and negatively."—W. C. PROCTER in *Moody Bible Institute Monthly*, December, 1933, p. 160.

Many believe that Christ changed the Sabbath. But, from His own words, we see that He came for no such purpose. The responsibility for this change must therefore be looked for elsewhere.

Those who believe that Jesus changed the Sabbath base it only on a supposition:

"Jesus, after his resurrection, changed the Sabbath from the seventh to the first day of the week; thus showing his authority as Lord even of the Sabbath. . . .

"When Jesus gave instructions for this change we are not told, but very likely during the time when he spake to his apostles of the things pertaining to his kingdom. Acts i, 3. This is probably one of the many unrecorded things which Jesus did. John xx, 30; xxi, 25."—AMOS BINNEY AND DANIEL STEELE (Methodist), *Binney's Theological Compend Improved*, p. 171.

BIBLE PREDICTS ATTEMPTED CHANGE

What did God, through the prophet Daniel, say the power represented by the "little horn" would think to do?

"He shall speak words against the Most High, and shall wear out the saints of the Most High; and *shall think to change the times and the law.*" Daniel 7:25, R.S.V.

NOTE.—For an explanation of this symbolism, see reading on page 211.

What did the apostle Paul say the "man of sin" would do?

"For that day shall not come, except there come a falling away first, and that man of sin be revealed, the son of perdition; *who opposeth and exalteth himself above all that is called God, or that is worshipped.*" 2 Thessalonians 2:3, 4.

NOTE.—An effective way by which a power could exalt itself above God would be by assuming to change the law of God, and by requiring obedience to its own law instead of God's law.

PAPAL POWER ACKNOWLEDGES THIS ACT

What power has claimed authority to change God's law?

The papacy.

NOTE.—"The pope is of so great authority and power that he can modify, explain, or interpret even divine laws. . . . The pope can modify divine law, since his power is not of man, but of God, and he acts as vicegerent of God upon earth."—Translated from Lucius Ferraris, *Prompta Bibliotheca* (Ready Library), "Papa," art. 2.

What part of the law of God has the papacy thought to change?

The fourth commandment.

Note.—"They [the Catholics] allege the change of the Sabbath into the Lord's day, contrary, as it seemeth, to the Decalogue; and they have no example more in their mouths than the change of the Sabbath. They will needs have the Church's power to be very great, because it hath dispensed with a precept of the Decalogue."—The Augsburg Confession (Lutheran), part 2, art. 7, in Philip Schaff, *The Creeds of Christendom* (Harper), vol. 3, p. 64.

"It [the Roman Catholic Church] *reversed* the Fourth Commandment by doing away with the Sabbath of God's word, and instituting Sunday as a holiday."—N. Summerbell, *History of the Christian Church* (1873), p. 415.

Why did God command Israel to hallow the Sabbath?

"For in six days the Lord made heaven and earth, the sea, and all that in them is, and rested the seventh day: wherefore the Lord blessed the sabbath day, and hallowed it." Exodus 20:11.

Note.—As the Sabbath was given that man might keep God in mind as Creator, it can be readily seen that a power endeavoring to exalt itself above God could do this in no other way so effectually as by setting aside God's memorial—the seventh-day Sabbath. To this work of the papacy Daniel had reference when he said, "And he shall . . . think to change *times* and *laws*." Daniel 7:25.

Does the papacy acknowledge changing the Sabbath?

It does.

Note.—The *Catechismus Romanus* was commanded by the Council of Trent and published by the Vatican Press, by order of Pope Pius V, in 1566. This catechism for priests says: "It pleased the church of God, that the religious celebration of the Sabbath day should be transferred to 'the Lord's day.'"—*Catechism of the Council of Trent* (Donovan's translation, 1867), part 3, chap. 4, p. 345. The same, in slightly different wording, is in the McHugh and Callan translation (1937 ed.), p. 402.

"*Ques.*—How prove you that the Church hath power to command feasts and holydays?

*"Ans.—*By the very act of changing the Sabbath into *Sunday,* which Protestants allow of; and therefore they fondly contradict themselves, by keeping *Sunday* strictly, and breaking most other feasts commanded by the same Church."—Henry Tuberville, *An Abridgment of the Christian Doctrine* (1833 approbation), p. 58. (Same statement in *Manual of Christian Doctrine*, ed. by Daniel Ferris [1916 ed.], p. 67.)

*"Ques.—*Have you any other way of proving that the Church has power to institute festivals of precept?

*"Ans.—*Had she not such power, she could not have done that in which all modern religionists agree with her;—she could not have substituted the observance of Sunday the first day of the week, for the observance of Saturday the seventh day, a change for which there is no Scriptural authority."—Stephen Keenan, *A Doctrinal Catechism* (3d ed.), p. 174.

"The Catholic Church, . . . by virtue of her divine mission, changed the day from Saturday to Sunday."—*The Catholic Mirror,* official organ of Cardinal Gibbons, Sept. 23, 1893.

"1. Is Saturday the 7th day according to the Bible & the 10 Commandments.

"I answer *yes*.

"2. Is Sunday the first day of the week & did the Church change the 7th day—Saturday—for Sunday, the 1st. day:

"I answer yes.

"3. Did Christ change the day?

"I answer no! Faithfully yours,

"J. Card. Gibbons"

—Gibbons' autograph letter

*"Ques.—*Which is the Sabbath day?

*"Ans.—*Saturday is the Sabbath day.

*"Ques.—*Why do we observe Sunday instead of Saturday?

*"Ans.—*We observe Sunday instead of Saturday because the Catholic Church transferred the solemnity from Saturday to Sunday."—Peter Geiermann, *The Convert's Catechism of Catholic Doctrine* (1946 ed.), p. 50. Geiermann received the "apostolic blessing" of Pope Pius X on his labors, Jan. 25, 1910.

Do Catholic authorities acknowledge that there is no command in the Bible for the sanctification of Sunday?

They do.

Note.—"You may read the Bible from Genesis to Revelation, and you will not find a single line authorizing the sanctification of Sunday. The Scriptures enforce the religious observance of Saturday, a day which we never sanctify."—JAMES CARDINAL GIBBONS, *The Faith of Our Fathers* (1917 ed.), pp. 72, 73.

"Nowhere in the Bible is it stated that worship should be changed from Saturday to Sunday. The fact is that the Church was in existence for several centuries before the Bible was given to the world. The Church made the Bible, the Bible did not make the Church.

"Now the Church . . . instituted, by God's authority, Sunday as the day of worship. This same Church, by the same divine authority, taught the doctrine of Purgatory long before the Bible was made. We have, therefore, the same authority for Purgatory as we have for Sunday."—MARTIN J. SCOTT, *Things Catholics Are Asked About* (1927 ed.), p. 136.

"If we consulted the Bible only, we should still have to keep holy the Sabbath Day, that is, Saturday."—JOHN LAUX, *A Course in Religion for Catholic High Schools and Academies,* vol. 1 (1936 ed.), p. 51. Quoted by permission of Benziger Brothers, Inc., proprietors of the copyright.

"Some theologians have held that God likewise directly determined the Sunday as the day of worship in the New Law, that He Himself has explicitly substituted the Sunday for the Sabbath. But this theory is now entirely abandoned. It is now commonly held that God simply gave His Church the power to set aside whatever day or days, she would deem suitable as Holy Days. The Church chose Sunday, the first day of the week, and in the course of time added other days, as holy days."—VINCENT J. KELLY (Catholic), *Forbidden Sunday and Feast-Day Occupations* (1943 ed.), p. 2.

PROTESTANTS AGREE NO BIBLE COMMAND

Do Protestant writers acknowledge the same?

They do.

NOTE.—"The Lord's day was merely of ecclesiastical institution. It was not introduced by virtue of the fourth commandment."—JEREMY TAYLOR (Church of England), *Ductor Dubitantium,* part 1, book 2, chap. 2, rule 6, secs. 51, 59 (1850 ed.), vol. 9, pp. 458, 464.

"The Lord's Day is not sanctified by any specific command or by any inevitable inference. In all the New Testament there is no hint or suggestion of a legal obligation binding any man, whether saint or sinner, to observe the Day. Its sanctity arises only out of what it means to the true believer."—J. J. TAYLOR (Baptist), *The Sabbatic Question,* p. 72.

"Because it was requisite to appoint a certain day, that the people might know when they ought to come together, it appears that the [Christian] Church did for that purpose appoint the Lord's day."—

THE LAW OF GOD

I
Thou shalt have no other gods before Me.

II
Thou shalt not make unto thee any graven image, or any likeness of anything that is in heaven above, or that is in the earth beneath, or that is in the water under the earth: thou shalt not bow down thyself to them, nor serve them: for I the Lord thy God am a jealous God, visiting the iniquity of the fathers upon the children unto the third and fourth generation of them that hate Me; and showing mercy unto thousands of them that love Me, and keep My commandments.

III
Thou shalt not take the name of the Lord thy God in vain; for the Lord will not hold him guiltless that taketh His name in vain.

IV
Remember the Sabbath day, to keep it holy. Six days shalt thou labor, and do all thy work: but the seventh day is the Sabbath of the Lord thy God: in it thou shalt not do any work, thou, nor thy son, nor thy daughter, thy manservant, nor thy maidservant, nor thy cattle, nor thy stranger that is within thy gates: for in six days the Lord made heaven and earth, the sea, and all that in them is, and rested the seventh day: wherefore the Lord blessed the Sabbath day, and hallowed it.

V
Honor thy father and thy mother: that thy days may be long upon the land which the Lord thy God giveth thee.

VI
Thou shalt not kill.

VII
Thou shalt not commit adultery.

VIII
Thou shalt not steal

IX
Thou shalt not bear false witness against thy neighbor.

Thou shalt

COPYRIGHT, 1949, BY REVIEW AND HERALD

VERNON NYE, ARTIST

CHRIST AND THE LAW   "Think not that I am come to destroy the law." Matthew 5:

THE CHANGE OF THE SABBATH

Augsburg Confession, part 2, art. 7, in PHILIP SCHAFF, *The Creeds of Christendom* (Harper), vol. 3, p. 69.

For additional testimonies, see reading on pages 450, 451.

"And where are we told in the Scriptures that we are to keep the first day at all? We are commanded to keep the seventh; but we are nowhere commanded to keep the first day. . . . The reasons why we keep the first day of the week holy instead of the seventh is for the same reason that we observe many other things, not because the Bible, but because the church, has enjoined it."—ISAAC WILLIAMS (Anglican), *Plain Sermons on the Catechism*, vol. 1, pp. 334, 336.

A GRADUAL CHANGE

How did this change in observance of days come about?

Through a *gradual* transference.

NOTE.—"The Christian Church made no formal, but a *gradual* and almost unconscious, transference of the one day to the other."—F. W. FARRAR, *The Voice From Sinai*, p. 167. This of itself is evidence that there was no divine command for the change of the Sabbath.

For how long a time was the seventh-day Sabbath observed in the Christian church?

For many centuries. In fact, its observance has never wholly ceased in the Christian church.

NOTE.—Mr. Morer, a learned clergyman of the Church of England, says: "The *Primitive Christians* had a great veneration for the *Sabbath*, and spent the *Day* in Devotion and Sermons. And 'tis not to be doubted but they derived this Practice from the *Apostles* themselves."—*A Discourse in Six Dialogues on the Name, Notion, and Observation of the Lord's Day*, p. 189.

"A history of the problem shows that in some places, it was really only after some centuries that the Sabbath rest really was entirely abolished, and by that time the practice of observing a bodily rest on the Sunday had taken its place."—VINCENT J. KELLY, *Forbidden Sunday and Feast-Day Occupations*, p. 15.

Lyman Coleman says: "Down even to the fifth century the observance of the Jewish Sabbath was continued in the Christian church, but with a rigor and a solemnity gradually diminishing until it was wholly discontinued."—*Ancient Christianity Exemplified*, chap. 26, sec. 2.

The church historian Socrates, who wrote in the fifth century, says: "Almost all the churches throughout the world celebrate the sacred mysteries on the Sabbath of every week, yet the Christians of

Alexandria and at Rome, on account of some ancient tradition, have ceased to do this."—*Ecclesiastical History,* book 5, chap. 22, in *A Select Library of Nicene and Post-Nicene Fathers,* 2d series, vol. 2, p. 132.

Sozomen, another historian of the same period, writes: "The people of Constantinople, and almost everywhere, assemble together on the Sabbath, as well as on the first day of the week, which custom is never observed at Rome or at Alexandria."—*Ecclesiastical History,* book 7, chap. 19, in the same volume as the above quotation.

All this would have been inconceivable had there been a divine command given for the change of the Sabbath. The last two quotations also show that Rome led in the apostasy and in the change of the Sabbath.

Sunday Observance

How did Sunday observance originate?

As a voluntary celebration of the resurrection, a custom without pretense of divine authority.

Note.—"Opposition to Judaism introduced the particular festival of Sunday very early, indeed, into the place of the Sabbath. . . . The festival of Sunday, like all other festivals, was always only a human ordinance, and it was far from the intentions of the apostles to establish a Divine command in this respect, far from them, and from the early apostolic Church, to transfer the laws of the Sabbath to Sunday. Perhaps, at the end of the second century a false application of this kind had begun to take place; for men appear by that time to have considered labouring on Sunday as a sin."—Augustus Neander, *The History of the Christian Religion and Church* (Rose's translation from the 1st German ed.), p. 186.

" 'The observance of the Sunday was at first supplemental to that of the Sabbath, but in proportion as the gulf between the Church and the Synagogue widened, the Sabbath became less and less important and ended at length in being entirely neglected.' "—L. Duchesne, *Christian Worship: Its Origin and Evolution* (tr. from the 4th French ed. by M. L. McClure, London, 1910), p. 47.

Who first enjoined Sundaykeeping by law?

Constantine the Great.

Note.—"(1) That the Sunday was in the beginning not looked on as a day of bodily repose; nor was an analogy drawn between the Jewish Sabbath and the Christian Sunday, except as days of worship. . . .

"(3) The keeping of the Sunday rest arose from the custom of the people and the constitution of the Church. . . .

"(5) Tertullian was probably the first to refer to a cessation of worldly affairs on the Sunday; the Council of Laodicea issued the first conciliar legislation for that day; Constantine I issued the first civil legislation; St. Martin of Braga was probably the first to use the term 'servile work' in its present theological sense."—VINCENT J. KELLY, *Forbidden Sunday and Feast-Day Occupations*, p. 203.

"The earliest recognition of the observance of Sunday as a legal duty is a constitution of Constantine in 321 A.D., enacting that all courts of justice, inhabitants of towns, and workshops were to be at rest on Sunday (*venerabili die solis*), with an exception in favor of those engaged in agricultural labor."—*Encyclopaedia Britannica*, 11th ed., art. "Sunday." (See page 484.)

"On the venerable Day of the Sun let the magistrates and people residing in cities rest, and let all workshops be closed. In the country, however, persons engaged in agriculture may freely and lawfully continue their pursuits; because it often happens that another day is not so suitable for grain-sowing or for vine planting; lest by neglecting the proper moment for such operations the bounty of heaven should be lost. (Given the 7th day of March, Crispus and Constantine being consuls each of them for the second time.)"—*Codex Justinianus*, lib. 3, tit. 12, 3; translated in *History of the Christian Church*, by Philip Schaff (Scribners, 1902 ed.), vol. 3, p. 380.

This edict, issued by Constantine, who first opened the way for the union of church and state in the Roman Empire, in a manner supplied the lack of a divine command for Sunday observance. It was one of the important steps in bringing about and establishing the change of the Sabbath.

What testimony does Eusebius bear on this subject?

"All things whatsoever that it was duty to do on the Sabbath, these *we* [the church] have transferred to the Lord's day."—Translated from EUSEBIUS, *Commentary on the Psalms*, in Migne, *Patrologia Graeca*, vol. 23, cols. 1171, 1172.

NOTE.—The change of the Sabbath was the result of the combined efforts of church and state, and it took centuries to accomplish it. Eusebius of Caesarea (270-338) was a noted bishop of the church, biographer and flatterer of Constantine, and the reputed father of ecclesiastical history.

By what church council was the observance of the seventh day forbidden and Sunday observance enjoined?

The Council of Laodicea, in Asia Minor, fourth century.

NOTE.—Canon 29 reads: "Christians shall not Judaize and be idle on Saturday [*sabbato,* the Sabbath], but shall work on that day; but the Lord's day they shall especially honour, and, as being Christians, shall, if possible, do no work on that day. If, however, they are found Judaizing, they shall be shut out [*anathema*] from Christ."—CHARLES JOSEPH HEFELE, *A History of the Councils of the Church,* vol. 2 (1896 English ed.), p. 316.

The Puritan William Prynne said (1655) that "the Council of Laodicea . . . first set[t]led the observation of the Lords-day, and prohibited . . . the keeping of the Jewish Sabbath under an Anathema."—*A Briefe Polemicall Dissertation Concerning . . . the Lords-day-Sabbath,* p. 44.

What was done at the Council of Laodicea was but one of the steps by which the change of the Sabbath was effected. It was looked back upon as the first church council to forbid Sabbath observance and enjoin Sunday rest as far as possible, but it was not so strict as later decrees. Different writers give conflicting dates for this council of Laodicea. The exact date is unknown, but may be placed "generally somewhere between the years 343 and 381." (Hefele, vol. 2, p. 298.)

What do Catholics say of Protestant Sundaykeepers?

They are obeying the authority of the Catholic Church.

NOTE.—"For ages all Christian nations looked to the Catholic Church, and, as we have seen, the various states enforced by law her ordinances as to worship and cessation of Labor on Sunday. Protestantism, in discarding the authority of the church, has no good reason for its Sunday theory, and ought logically, to keep Saturday as the Sabbath."

"The State, in passing laws for the due Sanctification of Sunday, is unwittingly acknowledging the authority of the Catholic Church, and carrying out more or less faithfully its prescriptions.

"The Sunday, as a day of the week set apart for the obligatory public worship of Almighty God, to be sanctified by a suspension of all servile labor, trade, and worldly avocations and by exercises of devotion, *is purely a creation of the Catholic Church.*"—*The American Catholic Quarterly Review,* January, 1883, pp. 152, 139.

"If protestants would follow the Bible, they should worship God on the Sabbath Day. In keeping the Sunday they are following a law of the Catholic Church."—ALBERT SMITH, Chancellor of the Archdiocese of Baltimore, replying for the Cardinal in a letter of Feb. 10, 1920. (See also the quotation from Monsignor Segur on page 446.)

Choice of Service and Worship

What determines whose servants we are?

"Know ye not, that to whom ye yield yourselves servants to obey, *his servants ye are to whom ye obey?*" Romans 6:16.

When asked to bow to Satan, how did Christ reply?

"It is written, Thou shalt worship the Lord thy God, and *him only shalt thou serve.*" Matthew 4:10.

What kind of worship does the Saviour call that which is not according to God's commandments?

"But *in vain they do worship me,* teaching for doctrines *the commandments of men.*" Matthew 15:9.

What appeal did Elijah make to apostate Israel?

"How long halt ye between two opinions? *if the Lord be God, follow him: but if Baal, then follow him.*" 1 Kings 18:21.

Note.—In times of ignorance God winks at that which otherwise would be sin; but when light comes He commands men everywhere to repent. (Acts 17:30.) The period during which the saints, times, and the law of God were to be in the hands of the papacy has expired (Daniel 7:25); the true light on the Sabbath question is now shining; and God is sending a message to the world, calling upon men to fear and worship Him, and to return to the observance of His holy rest day, the seventh-day Sabbath. (Revelation 14:6-12.) (See pages 257, 442, 460, 540.)

> Before the heavens were spread abroad,
> From everlasting was the Word;
> With God He was, the Word was God!
> And must divinely be adored.
>
> —Isaac Watts

The Seal of God and the Mark of Apostasy

SIGNIFICANCE OF A SEAL

What is the purpose of a sign, or seal?

"Now, O king, *establish* the decree, and *sign the writing, that it be not changed.*" Daniel 6:8.

NOTE.—That is, affix the signature of royalty, that it may have the proper authority. Anciently kings used a seal ring, containing the name, initials, or monogram, for this purpose. Jezebel, the wife of Ahab, "wrote letters in Ahab's *name,* and sealed them with his *seal.*" 1 Kings 21:8. Of a Persian decree it is said that "in the *name* of King Ahasuerus was it written, and sealed with the king's *ring.*" Esther 3:12.

What are the three essentials of an official seal?

The seal of a lawgiver must show three things: (1) his name; (2) his official position, title, or authority, and so his right to rule; and (3) the extent of his dominion and jurisdiction.

GOD'S SEAL

What was the prophet commanded to seal?

"Bind up the testimony, *seal the law among my disciples.*" Isaiah 8:16.

Which commandment alone of the Decalogue reveals the *name, authority,* and *dominion* of the Author of this law?

"Remember the sabbath day, to keep it holy. Six days shalt thou labour, and do all thy work: but the seventh day is the sabbath of the Lord thy God: in it thou shalt not do any work, thou, nor thy son, nor thy daughter, thy manservant, nor thy maidservant, nor thy cattle, nor thy stranger that is within thy gates: for in six days *the Lord made heaven and earth, the sea, and all that in them is,* and rested the seventh day: wherefore the Lord blessed the sabbath day, and hallowed it." Exodus 20:8-11.

NOTE.—In six days, (1) the *Lord* (name); (2) *made* (office,

THE SEAL OF GOD AND THE MARK OF APOSTASY

Creator); (3) *heaven and earth* (dominion). This commandment alone, therefore, contains "the *seal* of the living God." This commandment shows God's authority to enact all the commandments, and shows all other gods to be false gods. The Sabbath commandment, therefore, contains the seal of God; and the Sabbath itself, which is enjoined by the commandment, is inseparably connected with this seal; it is to be kept in memory of God's creation of all things; and it is itself called a "sign" of the knowledge of this great truth. (Exodus 31:17; Ezekiel 20:20.)

Why is the Sabbath a sign between God and His people?

"It is *a sign* between me and the children of Israel for ever: *for in six days the Lord made heaven and earth, and on the seventh day he rested, and was refreshed."* Exodus 31:17.

NOTE.—The Sabbath is the sign, or mark, or seal, of the Creator.

In what two ways does God say the Sabbath is a sign?

1. "And hallow my sabbaths; and they shall be *a sign* between me and you, *that ye may know that I am the Lord your God."* Ezekiel 20:20.

2. "Verily my sabbaths ye shall keep: for it is *a sign* between me and you throughout your generations; *that ye may know that I am the Lord that doth sanctify you."* Exodus 31:13.

NOTE.—The Sabbath is the sign of God's creative power, whether manifested in creation or redemption; for redemption is creation— *re*-creation. It requires the same power to *redeem* that it does to *create.* "*Create* in me a clean heart." Psalm 51:10. "We are . . . *created* in Christ Jesus unto good works." Ephesians 2:10. God designs that each Sabbath shall call Him to mind as the One who created us, and whose grace and sanctifying power are working in us to fit us for His eternal kingdom.

SPECIAL SEALING WORK PREDICTED

What special sealing work is to take place just before the letting loose of the winds of destruction upon the earth?

"And I saw another angel ascending from the east, *having the seal of the living God:* and he cried with a loud voice to the four angels, . . . saying, *Hurt not the earth, neither the sea, nor the trees, till we have sealed the servants of our God in their foreheads."* Revelation 7:2, 3. (See Ezekiel 9:1-6.)

How is this same company described a little later?

"And I looked, and, lo, a Lamb stood *on the mount Sion,* and with him an hundred forty and four thousand, *having his Father's name written in their foreheads."* Revelation 14:1.

NOTE.—The name of the Father is expressive of His character. When Moses asked to see the glory of God, the Lord passed by and proclaimed His *name*—"The Lord, the Lord God, *merciful* and *gracious, longsuffering,* and abundant in goodness and truth." (Exodus 33:18, 19; 34:6.) God's law is the transcript of that character, and the name referred to in Revelation 14:1 may be thought of as equivalent to the law of God. This is in harmony with the work of the new covenant, under which the law is written in the mind. (Hebrews 8:10.) Since the law is written in the mind, the seal of the law is there also.

What is said of the character of these sealed ones?

"And in their mouth was found no guile: for *they are without fault before the throne of God."* Verse 5.

How is the remnant church described?

"And the dragon was wroth with the woman, and went to make war with the remnant of her seed, which keep the commandments of God, and have the testimony of Jesus Christ." Revelation 12:17.

GOD'S SPECIAL WARNING

What threefold warning does the third angel give?

"And the third angel followed them, saying with a loud voice, If any man *worship the beast and his image, and receive his mark in his forehead, or in his hand,* the same shall drink of the wine of the wrath of God." Revelation 14:9, 10.

NOTE.—The beast represents the papacy; the image to the beast represents another ecclesiastical body dominating the civil power. (See readings on pages 266, 271.) And over against the seal of God stands the mark of the beast, the mark of apostasy. Against this false and idolatrous worship and the reception of this mark, God sends this solemn warning.

By contrast with the worshipers of the beast, how are the worshipers of God described?

"Here is the patience of the saints: here are they that *keep the commandments of God, and the faith of Jesus."* Verse 12.

NOTE.—The keeping of the commandments by the worshipers of God and the violation of these commandments by the worshipers of the beast will constitute the distinction between these two classes of worshipers.

What power is to enforce a certain mark?

"And *he* [the two-horned beast] causeth all, both small and great, rich and poor, free and bond, to receive *a mark* in their right hand, or in their foreheads." Revelation 13:16.

NOTE.—The two-horned beast is understood to represent the United States of America. (See reading on page 271.) As this nation repudiates her principles of civil and religious liberty and becomes a persecuting power, other nations will follow her example in oppressing those who refuse to yield their allegiance to God.

THE MARK OF APOSTASY

What is the papacy's mark, or sign, of authority?

"*Ques.*—How prove you that the Church hath power to command feasts and holydays?

"*Ans.—By the very act of changing the Sabbath into Sunday,* which Protestants allow of."—HENRY TUBERVILLE, *An Abridgment of the Christian Doctrine* (1833 approbation), p. 58.

NOTE.—In a letter written on February 8, 1898, Mr. H. F. Thomas, chancellor to Cardinal Gibbons, replying to an inquiry addressed to the cardinal, said:

"If Protestants observe the first day of the week are they in that act recognizing the authority of the Catholic Church? . . . It looks that way: Since the custom they observe is of the Church and from the Church."

The official newspaper of the Cleveland Diocese says:

"By what authority did the Church change the observance of the Sabbath from Saturday to Sunday?

"The Church changed the observance of the Sabbath to Sunday by right of the divine, infallible authority given to her by her Founder, Jesus Christ. The Protestant, claiming the Bible to be the only guide of faith, has no warrant for observing Sunday. In this matter the Seventh Day Adventist is the only consistent Protestant. Sunday as the day of rest to honor our Lord's Resurrection dates to Apostolic times and was so established, among other reasons, to mark off the Jew from the Christian. St. Justin the Martyr, speaks of it in his Apologies."—*The Catholic Universe Bulletin*, Aug. 14, 1942, p. 4.

The true Sabbath being a sign of loyalty to the true God, it is but natural that the false sabbath should be regarded as a sign of allegiance to the apostate church. Such we find to be the case. For other statements concerning Sunday, see pages 433, 434, 439, 460, 461.

What do Catholics say of Protestant Sundaykeepers?

"The observance of *Sunday* by the Protestants is an homage they pay, in spite of themselves, to the authority of the [Catholic] church."—Monsignor Louis Segur, *Plain Talk About the Protestantism of Today* (1868), p. 213.

Note.—A full realization of this fact will lead those who honestly, but ignorantly, have been observing Sunday as the Sabbath, to refuse longer to pay homage to apostasy, and return to the observance of that which is the sign of loyalty to Heaven—the only weekly day of rest which God, in His Word, has commanded men to keep holy, the seventh day.

Persecution of Commandment Keepers

How will the dragon treat God's remnant people?

"And the dragon *was wroth with the woman, and went to make war with the remnant of her seed*, which keep the commandments of God, and have the testimony of Jesus Christ." Revelation 12:17.

How far will the enforcement of this mark be urged?

"That the image of the beast should both speak, and cause that as many as would not worship the image of the beast *should be killed*. And he causeth all, both small and great, rich and poor, free and bond, to receive *a mark* in their right hand, or in their foreheads: and *that no man might buy or sell, save he that had the mark*." Revelation 13:15-17. (See pages 278, 279.)

Over what do the people of God finally gain the victory?

"And I saw . . . them that had gotten the victory *over the beast, and over his image, and over his mark, and over the number of his name*, stand on the sea of glass, having the harps of God." Revelation 15:2.

The Lord's Day

CHRIST, AGENT OF CREATION

FROM what time was Christ associated with the Father?

"*In the beginning* was the Word, and the Word was with God, and the Word was God. The same was in the beginning with God." John 1:1, 2. (Compare verse 14.)

By whom were all things created?

"God, *who created all things by Jesus Christ.*" Ephesians 3:9. "God . . . hath in these last days spoken unto us by *his Son, . . . by whom also he made the worlds.*" Hebrews 1:1, 2. "For *by him were all things created,* that are in heaven, and that are in earth, . . . *all things were created by him,* . . . and by him all things consist." Colossians 1:16, 17.

Was there anything made without Christ?

"Without him was not any thing made that was made." John 1:3.

CHRIST MAKES THE SABBATH

Was the Sabbath "made"?

"The sabbath was *made* for man." Mark 2:27.

Then by whom was the Sabbath made?

By Christ.

NOTE.—This conclusion is inevitable. If all things were made by Christ, and the Sabbath was one of the things that were made, then it follows that the Sabbath must have been made by Christ. This being so, the Sabbath must be *the Lord's day.*

What did God do in the beginning on the seventh day?

"*He rested on the seventh day* from all his work which he had made. And God *blessed the seventh day, and sanctified it: because that in it he had rested* from all his work." Genesis 2:2, 3.

NOTE.—If all things were made by Jesus Christ, then He, with the Father, rested on the first seventh day from His work of creation, blessed the day, and sanctified it.

How much honor is due to Christ?

"All men should honour the Son, *even as they honour the Father.*" John 5:23. "I and my Father are *one.*" John 10:30.

NOTE.—Sabbathkeeping, then, honors Christ equally with the Father.

CHRIST KEEPS THE SABBATH

Did Christ keep the Sabbath?

"*As his custom was,* he went *into the synagogue on the sabbath day,* and stood up for to read." Luke 4:16. "*I have kept* my Father's commandments." John 15:10.

Did Christ's followers keep the Sabbath after His death?

"They returned, and prepared spices and ointments; *and rested the sabbath day according to the commandment.*" Luke 23:56.

THE LORD'S DAY

On what day does John say he was in the Spirit?

"I was in the Spirit on *the Lord's day.*" Revelation 1:10.

What day does the commandment say is the Lord's?

"*The seventh day* is the sabbath of the Lord." Exodus 20:10.

What does the prophet Isaiah, speaking for God, call the seventh-day Sabbath?

"My holy day." Isaiah 58:13.

NOTE.—We do not need to speculate as to what is the Lord's, if we will but take the word of God for our guide.

On what day must John have been in the Spirit?

The *seventh,* if he referred to a day of the week at all.

NOTE.—*No other day of the week in all the Bible is claimed by God as His day.* During the early centuries of the Christian Era, apostasy came. Men, without any command of Scripture, thinking to honor Christ and spite the Jews, who crucified Christ, began to neglect the Sabbath of the commandment and to honor the first day of the week, on which Christ rose from the dead, and called it "the Lord's day." Finally the Sabbath was almost lost sight of, and the Sunday generally replaced it. But there was no warrant for this change in the divine and unchangeable law of God. The Bible knows but one God, one Lawgiver, one Mediator between God and man, one Lord and Saviour Jesus Christ, one Spirit, one faith, one baptism, and *one Sabbath*. (See Jeremiah 10:10-12; Revelation 14:6, 7; 1 Timothy 2:5; Ephesians 4:4-6; Exodus 20:8-11.) (See readings on pages 405, 423.)

Why have not scholars and churchmen found that there is no Bible authority for first-day sacredness?

The answer is, They have found and declared it so.

What influence do the Bible and history show working in the church immediately after apostolic days?

"Also of your own selves shall men arise, speaking perverse things, to draw away disciples after them." Acts 20:30.

NOTE.—"Between the days of the apostles and the conversion of Constantine, the Christian commonwealth changed its aspect. . . . Rites and ceremonies, of which neither Paul nor Peter ever heard, crept silently into use, and then claimed the rank of divine institutions."—W. D. KILLEN (Presbyterian), *The Ancient Church*, Preface, pp. xv, xvi.

What did Christ say of worship based on tradition?

"In vain they do worship me, teaching for doctrines the commandments of men." Matthew 15:9.

NOTE.—"Protestants often deride the authority of Church tradition, and claim to be directed by the Bible only; yet they, too, have been guided by customs of the ancient Church, which find no warrant in the Bible, but rest on Church tradition only! . . . The Bible, which Protestants claim to obey exclusively, gives no authorisation for the substitution of the first day of the week for the seventh. On what authority, therefore, have they done so? Plainly on the authority of that very Catholic Church which they abandoned, and whose traditions they condemn."—JOHN L. STODDARD, *Rebuilding a Lost Faith* (1826 ed.), p. 80.

What will be done with every plant not planted by God?

"Every plant, which my heavenly Father hath not planted, *shall be rooted up.*" Verse 13.

In all matters of religion, whose commands should we obey?

"We ought to obey God rather than men." Acts 5:29.

NOTE.—In all matters of religion we as Christians must walk as Christ walked, think as Christ thought, talk as Christ talked. To His disciples He said, "Go ye therefore, and make Christians of all nations [margin], . . . teaching them to observe all things whatsoever I have commanded you." Matthew 28:19, 20.

Testimony of Eminent Men

The extracts that follow are from noted clergymen, scholars, and eminent writers, all of whom doubtless kept the Sunday as a matter of church custom. But they nevertheless bear witness that there is no Bible command for it.

William E. Gladstone, England's great prime minister, in his *Later Gleanings* (1898 ed.), makes these observations:

"The Seventh day of the week has been deposed from its title to obligatory religious observance, and its prerogative has been carried over to the first; under no direct precept of Scripture."—Page 342.

Canon Knox Little, replying to those who quote the example of Christ against the High-Church ritualism, says:

"It is certain that our Lord when on earth *did* observe Saturday, and did *not* observe Sunday." "If they are consistent, as I have said, they must keep Saturday, not Sunday, as the day of rest."—*Sacerdotalism* (1894 ed.), pp. 71, 89.

Timothy Dwight's *Theology* (American Congregationalist) says: "The Christian Sabbath [Sunday] is not in the Scripture, and was not by the primitive church called the Sabbath."—Sermon 107 (1818 ed.), vol. 4, p. 49.

Dr. R. W. Dale (British Congregationalist): "It is quite clear that, however rigidly or devoutly we may spend Sunday, we are not keeping the Sabbath. . . . The Sabbath was founded on a specific, Divine command. We can plead no such command for the obligation to observe Sunday. . . . There is not a single sentence in the New Testament to suggest that we incur any penalty by violating the supposed sanctity of Sunday."—*The Ten Commandments*, pp. 127-129.

Dr. Edward T. Hiscox (Baptist): "There was and is a commandment to keep holy the Sabbath day, but that Sabbath day was not Sunday. It will, however, be readily said, and with some show of triumph, that the Sabbath was transferred from the Seventh to the First day of the week. . . . Where can the record of such a transaction be found? Not in the New Testament,—absolutely not."—Paper read Aug. 20, 1893, at a Baptist ministers' meeting at Saratoga, New York.

Alexander Campbell (founder of Disciples of Christ): " 'But,' say some, 'it was changed from the seventh to the first day.' Where? when? and by whom? No man can tell. No; it never was changed, nor could it be, unless creation was to be gone through again: for the *reason assigned must be changed* before the observance, or respect to the reason, can be changed!! It is all old wives' fables to talk of the change of the sabbath from the seventh to the first day. If it be changed, it was that august personage changed it who changes times and laws *ex officio*—I think his name is DOCTOR ANTI-CHRIST."—*The Christian Baptist,* Feb. 2, 1824, vol. 1, no. 7.

Cardinal Gibbons (Roman Catholic): "You may read the Bible from Genesis to Revelation, and you will not find a single line authorizing the sanctification of Sunday."—*Faith of Our Fathers* (1917 ed.), pp. 72, 73.

Prize Book of American Sunday-School Union: "Up to the time of Christ's death, no change had been made in the day. . . . So far as the record shows, they [the apostles] did not, however, give any explicit command enjoining the abandonment of the seventh-day Sabbath, and its observance on the first day of the week."—A. E. WAFFLE, *The Lord's Day,* pp. 186-188.

"We have seen how gradually the impression of the Jewish sabbath faded from the mind of the Christian Church, and how completely the newer thought underlying the observance of the first day took possession of the church. We have seen that the Christians of the first three centuries never confused one with the other, but for a time celebrated both."—*The Sunday Problem* (1923 ed.), a study book of the United Lutheran Church, p. 36.

Encyclopedias and Church Literature

A Dictionary of Christian Antiquities: "The notion of a formal substitution by apostolic authority of the Lord's Day [meaning Sunday] for the Jewish Sabbath, and the transference to it, perhaps in a spiritualized form, of the Sabbatical obligation established by the promulgation of the Fourth Commandment, has no basis whatever, either in Holy Scripture or in Christian antiquity."—SMITH AND CHEETHAM, art. "Sabbath."

Cyclopaedia of Biblical, Theological, and Ecclesiastical Literature: "It must be confessed that there is no law in the New Test. concerning the first day."—M'CLINTOCK AND STRONG, vol. 9, p. 196, art. "Sabbath, Christian."

Methodist Episcopal *Theological Compend,* by Amos Binney: "It is true there is no positive command for infant baptism. . . . Nor is there any for keeping holy the first day of the week."—Pages 180, 181.

Dr. William Gildea, in article "Paschale Gaudium," states: "She [the church] took the pagan Sunday and made it the Christian Sunday. . . . And thus the pagan Sunday, dedicated to Balder [a sun god] became the Christian Sunday, sacred to Jesus."—*Catholic World,* March, 1894, p. 809.

JESUS TEACHING IN THE SYNAGOGUE AT NAZARETH

"And, as his custom was, he went into the synagogue the sabbath day, and stood up for to read." Luke 4:

The Sabbath in History

WHEN and by what act was the Sabbath made?

"And on *the seventh day* God ended his work which he had made; and he *rested* on the seventh day from all his work which he had made. And God *blessed* the seventh day, and *sanctified* it: because that in it he had rested from all his work which God created and made." Genesis 2:2, 3.

THE SEVEN-DAY WEEK

What division of time is marked off by the Sabbath?

The week.

NOTE.—The week is a "time unit that, unlike all others, has proceeded in absolutely invariable manner since what may be called the dawn of history."—*Nature*, June 6, 1931.

In the official League of Nations *Report on the Reform of the Calendar*, published at Geneva, August 17, 1926, are statements from astronomers:

"The week . . . has been followed for thousands of years, and therefore has been hallowed by immemorial use."—M. ANDERS DONNER, formerly professor of astronomy at the University of Helsingfors, quoted on p. 51.

"I have always hesitated to suggest breaking the continuity of the week, which is without a doubt the most ancient scientific institution bequeathed to us by antiquity."—M. EDOUARD BAILLAND, director of the Paris Observatory, quoted on p. 52.

"So far as our knowledge goes the week was used only by the progenitors of the Hebrews, by them and related Semetic [Semitic] peoples, and where their influence extended. Since Jesus the extension of Christianity, especially in the last two centuries, has carried with it increasingly the use of the week for time reckoning."—W. O. CARVER (Baptist), *Sabbath Observance*, p. 34. Copyright, 1940, by the Sunday School Board of the Southern Baptist Convention. Used by permission.

SABBATH IN OLD TESTAMENT TIMES

Why did God set apart the seventh day as holy?

"For in six days the Lord made heaven and earth, the sea,

and all that in them is, and rested the seventh day." Exodus 20:11.

What promise did God make to Israel, through Jeremiah, if they would keep the Sabbath?

"If ye diligently hearken unto me, saith the Lord, to bring in no burden through the gates of this city on the sabbath day, but hallow the sabbath day, to do no work therein; *then shall there enter into the gates of this city kings and princes sitting upon the throne of David, . . . and this city shall remain for ever."* Jeremiah 17:24, 25.

What would happen if they did not hallow the Sabbath?

"But *if ye will not hearken unto me to hallow the sabbath day,* and not to bear a burden, even entering in at the gates of Jerusalem on the sabbath day; *then will I kindle a fire in the gates thereof, and it shall devour the palaces of Jerusalem, and it shall not be quenched."* Verse 27.

What befell Jerusalem in fulfillment of this when it was captured by Nebuchadnezzar, king of Babylon?

"And all the vessels of the house of God . . . he brought to Babylon. And *they burnt the house of God, and brake down the wall of Jerusalem, and burnt all the palaces thereof with fire."* "To fulfil the word of the Lord by the mouth of Jeremiah, until the land had enjoyed her sabbaths: for as long as she lay desolate she kept sabbath." 2 Chronicles 36:18, 19, 21.

After Israel's restoration from the Babylonian captivity, what did Nehemiah say was the reason for their punishment?

"What evil thing is this that ye do, and *profane the sabbath day? Did not your fathers thus, and did not our God bring all this evil upon us, and upon this city?* yet ye bring more wrath upon Israel *by profaning the sabbath."* Nehemiah 13:17, 18.

How does he speak of God's giving the Sabbath to Israel?

"Thou camest down also upon mount Sinai, and spakest with them from heaven, and *gavest them right judgments, and true laws, good statutes and commandments: and madest known unto them thy holy sabbath."* Nehemiah 9:13, 14.

NOTE.—Let it be noted that this text does not say that God *made* the Sabbath then, but simply that He made it *known* to Israel then. They had largely forgotten it while in Egypt. (See pages 410, 415.)

Sabbath in New Testament Times and Later

How did Christ, while on earth, regard the Sabbath?

"As his custom was, he went into the synagogue on the sabbath day, and stood up for to read." Luke 4:16.

In what words did Christ recognize the Sabbath law?

"And he said unto them, ... It is *lawful* to do well on the sabbath days." Matthew 12:11, 12.

NOTE.—"The fact, however, that Christ until His death, and His Apostles at least for a time after Christ's Ascension, observed the Sabbath is evidence enough that our Lord Himself did not substitute the Lord's day for the Sabbath, during His lifetime on earth."—VINCENT J. KELLY (Catholic), *Forbidden Sunday and Feast-Day Occupations* (1943 ed.), pp. 19, 20.

William Prynne says: "It is certain, that Christ himself, his Apostles, and the Primitive Christians, for some good space of time did constantly observe the seventh day Sabbath."—*A Briefe Polemicall Dissertation, Concerning ... the Lordsday-Sabbath*, p. 33.

"There was never any formal or authoritative change from the Jewish Seventh Day Sabbath to the Christian First Day observance. The early Christians leave no evidence that they thought of their day of worship as a substitution for the pre-Christian Sabbath, or as continuing that Sabbath. Jewish Christians at first seem to have continued to observe the Sabbath as Jews. As their independent Christian consciousness grew and incorporated the whole of their religious experience, life and program, under their own ideals and forms, they more and more left the Jewish Sabbath out of their thought....

"There are in the New Testament no commands, no prescriptions, no rules, no liturgies applying to the observance of the Lord's Day [Sunday]."—W. O. CARVER, *Sabbath Observance*, pp. 49-54. Copyright, 1940, by the Sunday School Board of the Southern Baptist Convention. Used by permission.

What was one of the first efforts of the Roman Church in behalf of the recognition of Sunday?

About A.D. 196, Victor, bishop of Rome, attempted to impose on all the churches the Roman custom of having the Passover, or Easter, as it is commonly called, celebrated every year on Sunday, and presumed to excommunicate the churches of Asia Minor because they observed it annually, regardless of the day of the week.

NOTE.—Dr. Bower, in his *History of the Popes,* volume 1, page 18, styles this "the first essay of papal usurpation."

What was one of the principal questions settled at the Council of Nice (Nicaea), A.D. 325?

"The question relating to the observance of Easter, which was agitated in the time of Anicetus and Polycarp, and afterwards in that of Victor, was still undecided. It was one of the principal reasons for convoking the council of Nice, being the most important subject to be considered after the Arian controversy."—ISAAC BOYLE, *Historical View of the Council of Nice* (1836 ed.), p. 23.

NOTE.—The council fixed Easter on the Sunday immediately following the full moon which was nearest after the vernal equinox.

In urging the observance of this decree on the churches, what reason did Constantine assign for it?

"Let us then, have nothing in common with the detestable Jewish crowd."—EUSEBIUS, *The Life of Constantine,* book 3, chap. 8.

What had Constantine already done, in A.D. 321, to help forward Sunday to a place of prominence?

He issued an edict requiring "the magistrates and people residing in the cities" to rest on "the venerable day of the sun" and calling for all workshops to be closed. (See page 438.)

Who did Eusebius, bishop of Caesarea, and one of Constantine's most ardent supporters, say had transferred the obligations of the Sabbath to Sunday?

"All things whatsoever that it was duty to do on the Sabbath, these *we* [the church] have transferred to the Lord's day."—Translated from EUSEBIUS, *Commentary on the Psalms,* in Migne, *Patrologia Graeca,* vol. 23, cols. 1171, 1172.

What did Sylvester, bishop of Rome (A.D. 314 to 337), do for the Sunday institution by his "apostolic authority"?

He officially changed the title of the first day, calling it the LORD'S DAY. (See the Venerable Bede, *De Ratione Computi,* in Migne, *Patrologia Graeca,* vol. 90, col. 584.)

What did the Council of Laodicea decree?

Canon 29. "Christians shall not Judaize and be idle on

Saturday [*sabbato*, the Sabbath], but shall work on that day; but the Lord's day they shall especially honour."—CHARLES JOSEPH HEFELE, *A History of the Councils of the Church*, vol. 2 (1896 English ed.), p. 316.

How late did Christians keep the Sabbath?

Public worship on both Sabbath and Sunday can be traced down to the fifth century.

NOTE.—"Down even to the fifth century the observance of the Jewish Sabbath was continued in the Christian church."—LYMAN COLEMAN, *Ancient Christianity Exemplified*, chap. 26, sec. 2.

Various writers who kept Sunday, and who were not interested in Sabbath observance, nevertheless mention the fact that it was being observed. (See Justin Martyr, *Dialogue With Trypho*, chap. 47; Tertullian, *On Prayer*, chap. 23; Origen, *Homily on Numbers 23*, sec. 4; the anonymous *Constitutions of the Holy Apostles*, book 2, sec. 4, chap. 36; book 2, sec. 7, chap. 59; book 7, sec. 3, chap. 36; book 8, sec. 4, chap. 33; Cassian, *Institutes*, book 3, chap. 12; book 5, chap. 26.)

How general was this practice in the middle of the fifth century?

"Although almost all the churches throughout the world celebrate the sacred mysteries on the Sabbath of every week, yet the Christians of Alexandria and at Rome, on account of some ancient tradition, have ceased to do this."—SOCRATES, *Ecclesiastical History*, book 5, chap. 22, in *A Select Library of Nicene and Post-Nicene Fathers*, 2d Series, vol. 2, p. 32.

How late was Sabbathkeeping preached in Rome?

In the time of Pope Gregory I (590-604).

NOTE.—Gregory denounced as "preachers of Antichrist" those who in Rome "forbid anything to be done on the Sabbath." (See his epistle to the Roman citizens, book 13, no. 1, in *Nicene and Post-Nicene Fathers*, 2d series, vol. 13 [1898], p. 92.)

Did observance of the seventh-day Sabbath survive later?

Traces can be found in modified form or in scattered places through the centuries.

NOTE.—"Traces of seventh-day keepers are found in the times of Gregory I, Gregory VII, and in the twelfth century in Lombardy."—

M'Clintock and Strong, *Cyclopaedia of Biblical, Theological, and Ecclesiastical Literature*, vol. 1, p. 660.

The Eastern Church through many centuries held church services on both Sabbath and Sunday, and refused to follow the Roman method of disparaging the Sabbath by fasting on it. For example:

Syria: "They keep Saturday holy, nor esteem Saturday fast lawful but on Easter Even. They have solemn service on Saturdays, eat flesh, and feast it bravely like the Jews."—Samuel Purchas, *Purchas His Pilgrimes* (London, 1625 ed.), part 2, book 8, chap. 6, p. 1269.

Ethiopia (1534): "It is not, therefore, in imitation of the Jews, but in obedience to Christ and His holy apostles, that we observe that day [the Sabbath]."—Michael Geddes, *Church History of Ethiopia* (London, 1696), pp. 87, 88.

Celtic Church of Scotland: "The Celts used a Latin Bible unlike the Vulgate, and kept Saturday as a day of rest, with special religious services on Sunday."—A. C. Flick, *The Rise of the Mediaeval Church* (Putnam, 1909), p. 237.

Waldenses: Some of the Waldenses were observers of the Sabbath. We have no evidence of this practice in the main body represented by the modern inhabitants of the Waldensian valleys of the Italian Alps, yet among the widespread groups embraced under the term *Waldenses* in the broad sense, there were Sabbathkeepers. The Passagii, or Passaginians, classified by Perrin as a branch of the Waldenses, kept the seventh day. (See Jean Perrin, *History of the Vaudois*, book 1, chap. 3.) Also the "Waldensian Picards"—Bohemian Brethren, who had procured ordination from a Waldensian bishop—are described thus in a Catholic manuscript:

"They do not hear the masses of Christians [i.e. Catholics] . . . they flee the image of the Crucifix as the devil, they do not celebrate the feasts of the divine Virgin Mary and of the Apostles; certain ones the Lord's day only. *Some indeed celebrate the Sabbath with the Jews.*"—Translated from the Latin text printed by J. J. I. von Döllinger, *Beiträge zur Sektengeschichte des Mittelalters*, vol. 2, no. 61, p. 662.

Who among the early Reformers raised this question of Sabbath observance?

Carlstadt, a colleague of Luther.

Note.—Carlstadt held to the divine authority of the Sabbath from the Old Testament, but he was uncertain about which day ought to be kept. He wrote: "Concerning Sunday one is uneasy that men have instituted it. Concerning Saturday, it is still under dispute. It is clear, however, that you should celebrate the seventh day and

allow your servants to do so as often as they have worked six days."
—Translated from his *Von dem Sabbat und gebotten feyer-tagen* (1524), chap. [10].

What development took place in post-Reformation England?

The hybrid "Puritan Sabbath" (Sunday).

NOTE.—In the English Reformation, "Sundays and holydays stood much on the same footing as days on which no work except for good cause was to be performed," but later "the more scrupulous party, while they slighted the Church-festivals as of human appointment, prescribed a stricter observance of the Lord's day."—HENRY HALLAM, *The Constitutional History of England* (New York, 1873), p. 227.

"The use of the word Sabbath instead of Sunday became in that age a distinctive mark of the Puritan party."—*Ibid.,* p. 229.

Was the seventh-day Sabbath observed at this time?

During this battle between the Reformation Sunday and the "Sabbatarian" Sunday, the observers of the seventh day increased.

NOTE.—On the Continent and in England many found the truth of the Bible Sabbath, and persecutions resulted.

What claim is made by the Roman Church concerning the change of the Sabbath to Sunday?

"*Ques.*—Have you any other way of proving that the Church has power to institute festivals of precept?

"*Ans.*—Had she not such power, she could not have done that in which all modern religionists agree with her;—she could not have substituted the observance of Sunday the first day of the week, for the observance of Saturday the seventh day, a change for which there is no Scriptural authority."—STEPHEN KEENAN, *A Doctrinal Catechism,* p. 174.

NOTE.—Through want of sufficient light and investigation, and because of the efforts of some who opposed the Sabbath during the Reformation, Sunday was brought from Catholicism into Protestantism, and is now cherished as an institution of the Lord. It is clear, however, that it is none of His planting, but rather the work and result of apostasy. But a message is now going forth to revive the truth on this point, and calling for a genuine reformation upon it. (See pages 245-260, and next reading.)

Sabbath Reform

UNACCEPTABLE WORSHIP

What kind of worship does Christ say results from doctrines based on the commandments of men?

"But in vain they do worship me, teaching for doctrines the commandments of men." Matthew 15:9.

What commandment had the Pharisees made void?

"God said, 'Honour thy father and thy mother'; . . . but you say; 'If a man says to his father or mother, "This thing is consecrated, otherwise you should have received it from me," he shall be absolved from honouring his father'; and so you have rendered futile God's word for the sake of your tradition." Matthew 15:4-6, Weymouth.

NOTE.—They taught that by a gift of property to the Temple service a man might be freed from the duties enjoined by the fifth commandment.

When asked, "Knowest thou that the Pharisees were offended?" what answer did the Saviour make?

"But he answered and said, *Every plant, which my heavenly Father hath not planted, shall be rooted up.*" Verse 13.

NOTE.—What is true of the fifth commandment is true of every other commandment. If through tradition men set aside any other of God's commandments, those words are equally applicable to them. They are guilty of making void the commandment of God.

TWO PLANTS IN THE CHURCH GARDEN

When and by whom was the Sabbath "planted"?

"For in six days *the Lord* made heaven and earth, the sea, and all that in them is, and *rested the seventh day: wherefore the Lord blessed the sabbath day, and hallowed it.*" Exodus 20:11.

Who claims to have planted the Sunday institution?

"*Q.*—Has the [Catholic] Church a power to make any alterations in the commandments of God?

"A.— . . . Instead of the seventh day, and other festivals appointed by the old law, the Church has prescribed the Sundays and holydays to be set apart for God's worship; and these we are now obliged to keep in consequence of God's commandment, instead of the ancient Sabbath."—RICHARD CHALLONER, *The Catholic Christian Instructed* (1853), p. 204.

NOTE.—"We Catholics, then, have precisely the same authority for keeping Sunday holy instead of Saturday as we have for every other article of our creed, namely, the authority of *'the Church* of the living God, the pillar and ground of the truth' (1 Tim. iii. 15); whereas you who are Protestants have really no authority for it whatever; for *there is no authority for it in the Bible,* and you will not allow that there *can be* authority for it anywhere else. Both you and we do, in fact, follow *tradition* in this matter; but *we* follow it, believing it to be a part of God's word, and the Church to be its divinely-appointed guardian and interpreter; *you* follow it, denouncing it all the time as a fallible and treacherous guide, which often 'makes the commandment of God of none effect.' "—*Clifton Tracts,* vol. 4, art. "A Question for All Bible Christians," p. 15.

For further quotations on this subject, see pages 433-441, 450, 451.

A Special Message of Reform

When God's salvation is "near to come," upon whom does He pronounce a blessing?

"Thus saith the Lord, Keep ye judgment, and do justice: for my salvation is near to come, and my righteousness to be revealed. *Blessed is the man that doeth this, and the son of man that layeth hold on it; that keepeth the sabbath from polluting it, and keepeth his hand from doing any evil.*" Isaiah 56:1, 2.

Is this promised blessing confined to any one class?

"*Also the sons of the stranger,* that join themselves to the Lord, to serve him, and to love the name of the Lord, to be his servants, *every one that keepeth the sabbath from polluting it,* and taketh hold of my covenant; *even them will I bring to my holy mountain, and make them joyful in my house of prayer.*" Verses 6, 7.

What message of Sabbath reform does He send?

"If thou *turn away thy foot from the sabbath, from doing*

thy pleasure on my holy day; and call the sabbath a delight, the holy of the Lord, honourable; and shalt honour him, not doing thine own ways, nor finding thine own pleasure, nor speaking thine own words: then shalt thou delight thyself in the Lord; and I will cause thee to ride upon the high places of the earth, and feed thee with the heritage of Jacob thy father: for the mouth of the Lord hath spoken it." Verses 13, 14.

NOTE.—The Sabbath of Jehovah is not now, by the majority even of professed Christians, called holy and honorable. By many it is stigmatized as "Jewish." The Lord foresaw how this would be in this age, and inspired the prophet to write as he did. *"If thou turn away thy foot from the sabbath."* This is a strong expression, indicating that many would be trampling upon God's day and doing their own pleasure upon it, instead of seeking God and honoring Him by keeping the Sabbath holy.

What will those be called who engage in this reformation?

"And thou shalt be called, *The repairer of the breach, The restorer of paths to dwell in."* Verse 12.

During the closing scenes of earth's history, what message is God sending to the world to turn men from false worship to the worship of the true and living God?

"Fear God, and give glory to him; for the hour of his judgment is come: and worship him that made heaven, and earth, and the sea, and the fountains of waters. . . . Babylon is fallen, is fallen, that great city, because she made all nations drink of the wine of the wrath of her fornication. . . . If any man worship the beast and his image, and receive his mark in his forehead, or in his hand, the same shall drink of the wine of the wrath of God, which is poured out without mixture into the cup of his indignation." Revelation 14:7-10.

NOTE.—This is the last gospel message to be sent to the world before the Lord comes. Under it will be developed two classes of people, one having the mark of the beast (the papacy), and the other keeping the commandments of God, and having His seal, the Sabbath of the fourth commandment. (See pages 257, 442.)

How does the Bible describe those who accept this message?

"Here is the patience of the saints: here are they that *keep the commandments of God, and the faith of Jesus."* Revelation 14:12.

Part Ten

Christian Liberty

	PAGE
The Author of Liberty	465
The Powers That Be	469
Individual Accountability	475
Union of Church and State	477
Sabbath Legislation	483
Who Persecute and Why	487

COPYRIGHT, 1949, BY REVIEW AND HERALD

VERNON NYE, ARTIST

CHRIST AND THE TRIBUTE MONEY

"Render to Caesar the things that are Caesar's, and

The Author of Liberty

Out of Egyptian Bondage

How is the bondage of Israel in Egypt described?

"And the children of Israel *sighed* by reason of the bondage, and they *cried*, and their cry came up unto God by reason of the bondage." Exodus 2:23. Compare with James 5:1-4.

Who heard their groaning?

"*God* heard their groaning, and God remembered his covenant with Abraham, with Isaac, and with Jacob." Exodus 2:24.

What did God say to Moses?

"Now therefore, behold, the cry of the children of Israel is come unto me: and I have also seen the oppression wherewith the Egyptians oppress them. Come now therefore, and I will send thee unto Pharaoh, that thou mayest bring forth my people the children of Israel out of Egypt." Exodus 3:9, 10.

In giving Israel His law, how did God describe Himself?

"I am the Lord thy God, which have *brought thee out of* the land of Egypt, out of *the house of bondage.*" Exodus 20:2.

Protection Against Permanent Bondage

How did God protect Israel against slavery?

"And if thy brother, an Hebrew man, or an Hebrew woman, be sold unto thee, and serve thee six years; then *in the seventh year thou shalt let him go free* from thee. And when thou sendest him out free from thee, *thou shalt not let him go away empty:* thou shalt furnish him liberally out of thy flock, and out of thy floor, and out of thy winepress: of that wherewith the Lord thy God hath blessed thee thou shalt give unto him. And *thou shalt remember that thou wast a bondman in the land of Egypt,* and the Lord thy God redeemed thee: therefore I command thee this thing to day." Deuteronomy 15:12-15. *"Thou shalt neither vex a stranger, nor oppress him:* for ye were strangers in the land of Egypt." Exodus 22:21. (See 2 Corinthians 1:3, 4.)

What was one reason why Israel should keep the Sabbath?

"And *remember that thou wast a servant in the land of Egypt,* and that the Lord thy God brought thee out thence through a mighty hand and by a stretched out arm: *therefore the Lord thy God commanded thee to keep the sabbath day.*" Deuteronomy 5:15.

What was to be proclaimed in Israel every fifty years?

"And ye shall hallow the fiftieth year, and *proclaim liberty throughout all the land unto all the inhabitants thereof:* it shall be a jubile unto you; and ye shall return every man unto his possession, and ye shall return every man unto his family." Leviticus 25:10.

Because Israel failed to do this, became oppressive, and disregarded and misused the Sabbath, what did God do?

"Therefore thus saith the Lord; Ye have not hearkened unto me, in proclaiming liberty, every one to his brother, and every man to his neighbour: behold, I proclaim a liberty for you, saith the Lord, to the *sword,* to the *pestilence,* and to the *famine; and I will make you to be removed into all the kingdoms of the earth.*" Jeremiah 34:17. (See also Jeremiah 17:24-27; 2 Chronicles 36:19-21.)

What fault did God find with Israel's fasts?

"Behold, in the day of your fast ye *find pleasure,* and *exact all your labours.* Behold, ye fast for *strife* and *debate,* and to *smite with the fist of wickedness.*" Isaiah 58:3, 4.

What does God set forth as the acceptable fast to Him?

"Is not this the fast that I have chosen? to *loose the bands of wickedness,* to *undo the heavy burdens,* and to *let the oppressed go free,* and that ye *break every yoke?* Is it not to *deal thy bread to the hungry,* and that thou *bring the poor that are cast out to thy house?* when thou seest the naked, that thou *cover him;* and that thou hide not thyself from thine own flesh?" Verses 6, 7.

NOTE.—All this shows that God loves liberty and hates bondage.

CHRIST'S MISSION OF DELIVERANCE
What was Christ's mission to this world?

"The Spirit of the Lord is upon me, because he hath anointed

THE AUTHOR OF LIBERTY

me *to preach the gospel* to the poor; he hath sent me *to heal* the brokenhearted, *to preach deliverance* to the captives, and recovering of sight to the blind, *to set at liberty* them that are bruised." Luke 4:18.

NOTE.—The Gospels show that a large part of Christ's time even on the Sabbath was devoted to relieving the oppressed and distressed.

In what condition are those who commit sin?

"Whosoever committeth sin is *the servant of sin*." John 8:34.

NOTE.—*Servant* may here be rendered *slave*.

Why was Christ's name to be called Jesus?

"And thou shalt call his name Jesus: *for he shall save his people from their sins*." Matthew 1:21.

What lies at the root of all sin?

"When *lust* hath conceived, it bringeth forth sin." James 1:15. "I had not known *lust,* except the law had said, Thou shalt not *covet*." Romans 7:7.

NOTE.—Lust, covetousness, and unlawful desire are only different names for *selfishness*. Selfishness lies at the root of all sin; and selfishness is simply the love of self to the disregard of the equal rights of others.

By what scripture is the equality of rights clearly shown?

"Thou shalt love thy neighbour *as thyself*." Leviticus 19:18.

What rule has Christ laid down in harmony with this?

"Whatsoever ye would that men should do to you, do ye even so to them." Matthew 7:12.

NOTE.—Selfishness, then, must be uprooted from men's hearts before they will recognize the equal rights of their fellow men.

Who alone can cleanse men's hearts from selfishness?

"Neither is there salvation in any other: for there is none other name under heaven given among men, whereby we must be saved." Acts 4:12. (See also 1 John 1:9.)

Who alone, then, can give men real freedom?

"If *the Son* therefore shall make you free, ye shall be *free indeed*." John 8:36.

Tolerance and True Worship

What was Christ's attitude toward unbelievers?

"If any man hear my words, and believe not, *I judge him not:* for I came not to *judge* the world, but to *save* the world." John 12:47.

What spirit did Christ say should control His disciples?

"But Jesus . . . saith unto them, Ye know that they which are accounted to rule over the Gentiles exercise *lordship* over them; and their great ones exercise *authority* upon them. But *so shall it not be among you:* but whosoever will be great among you, shall be your *minister:* and whosoever of you will be the chiefest, shall be *servant of all*. For even the Son of man came not to be ministered unto, but to minister, and to give his life a ransom for many." Mark 10:42-45.

What is present where the Spirit of the Lord is?

"Now the Lord is that Spirit: and where the Spirit of the Lord is, there is *liberty*." 2 Corinthians 3:17.

What kind of worship only is acceptable to God?

"But the hour cometh, and now is, when the true worshippers shall worship the Father *in spirit and in truth:* for the Father seeketh such to worship him. God is a Spirit: and they that worship him must worship him in spirit and in truth." John 4:23, 24.

"Freedom and reason make brave men;
Take these away, what are they then?—
Mere groveling brutes, and just as well
The beasts may think of heaven or hell.

"Know, then, that every soul is free
To choose his life, and what he'll be;
For this eternal truth is given:
That God will force no man to heaven.

"He'll call, persuade, direct him right,
Bless him with wisdom, love, and light,
In nameless ways be good and kind,
But never force the human mind."

The Powers That Be

The Realm of Civil Power

Who should be subject to civil government?

"Let *every soul* be subject unto the higher powers. For there is no power but of God." Romans 13:1.

By whom are the powers that be ordained?

"The powers that be are ordained of *God*." Same verse.

What does one resist who resists civil authority?

"Whosoever therefore resisteth the power, resisteth *the ordinance of God:* and they that resist shall receive to themselves damnation." Verse 2.

Note.—"That is, they who rise up against *government itself;* who seek anarchy and confusion; who oppose the regular execution of the laws. It is implied, however, that those laws shall not be such as to violate the rights of conscience, or oppose the laws of God."—Albert Barnes, on Rom. 13:2.

What are the proper sphere and work of civil authority?

"For rulers are not a terror to good works, but to the *evil*. . . . If thou do that which is *evil,* be afraid; for he beareth not the sword in vain: for he is the minister of God, *a revenger to execute wrath upon him that doeth evil.*" Verses 3, 4.

For whom is law made?

"Knowing this, that the law is not made for a righteous man, but *for the lawless and disobedient.*" 1 Timothy 1:9.

How are Christians admonished to respect civil authority?

"Put them in mind to be subject to principalities and powers, to obey magistrates, to be ready to every good work." Titus 3:1. "Submit yourselves to every ordinance of man for the Lord's sake: whether it be to the king, as supreme; or unto governors, as unto them that are sent by him for the punishment of evildoers, and for the praise of them that do well. . . . Honour all men. Love the brotherhood. Fear God. Honour the king." 1 Peter 2:13-17. "For for this cause pay ye tribute also: for they are God's ministers, attending continually upon this very thing. Render therefore to all their dues: tribute to whom tribute is due; custom to whom custom; fear to whom fear; honour to whom honour." Romans 13:6, 7.

THE SPECIAL SPIRITUAL REALM

In what words does Christ show that there is another realm outside of Caesar's, or civil government?

"Render therefore unto Caesar the things which are Caesar's; *and unto God the things that are God's.*" Matthew 22:21.

To whom alone did He say worship is to be rendered?

"Thou shalt worship *the Lord thy God, and him only shalt thou serve.*" Matthew 4:10.

CIVIL POWER INVADES GOD'S REALM

What decree did King Nebuchadnezzar once make?

"That at what time ye hear the sound of the cornet, flute, harp, sackbut, psaltery, dulcimer, and all kinds of musick, ye *fall down and worship the golden image* that Nebuchadnezzar the king hath set up: and whoso falleth not down and worshippeth shall the same hour be cast into the midst of a burning fiery furnace." Daniel 3:5, 6.

NOTE.—This decree was in direct conflict with the second commandment of God's law, which forbids making, bowing down to, and serving images. It was religious, idolatrous, and persecuting in character.

What answer did the three Hebrew captives give?

"O Nebuchadnezzar, we are not careful to answer thee in this matter. If it be so, our God whom we serve is able to deliver us from the burning fiery furnace, and he will deliver us. . . . But if not, . . . *we will not serve thy gods, nor worship the golden image which thou hast set up.*" Verses 16-18.

What did Nebuchadnezzar then do?

"He commanded the most mighty men that were in his army to bind Shadrach, Meshach, and Abed-nego, and to *cast them into the burning fiery furnace.*" Verse 20.

After their miraculous deliverance, what did Nebuchadnezzar say?

"Blessed be the God of Shadrach, Meshach, and Abed-nego, who hath sent his angel, and delivered his servants that trusted in him, and have changed the king's word, and yielded their bodies, that they might not serve nor worship any god, except their own God." Verse 28.

Note.—By preserving these men in the fire, God was demonstrating before all the world, through this great kingdom, that religion is a realm outside the legitimate sphere of civil authority; and that every individual should be left free to worship, or not to worship, according to the dictates of his own conscience.

How only could the envious princes complain of Daniel?

"We shall not find any occasion against this Daniel, except we find it against him *concerning the law of his God.*" Daniel 6:5.

What decree did they prevail upon the king to make?

"That whosoever shall ask a petition of any God or man for thirty days, save of thee, O king, he shall be cast into the den of lions." Verse 7.

Note.—Unlike the decree of Nebuchadnezzar, this decree forbade the worship of the true God, and was in direct conflict with the first commandment of the Decalogue, which forbids the worship of any other god.

How did Daniel regard this decree?

"He went into his house; and his windows being open in his chamber toward Jerusalem, *he kneeled upon his knees three times a day, and prayed, and gave thanks before his God, as he did aforetime.*" Verse 10.

What was finally done with Daniel?

"Then the king commanded, and they brought Daniel, and *cast him into the den of lions.*" Verse 16.

What did Darius say when he came to the lions' den?

"O Daniel, servant of the living God, is thy God, whom thou servest continually, able to deliver thee from the lions?" Verse 20.

What was Daniel's reply?

"O king, live for ever. My God hath sent his angel, and hath shut the lions' mouths, that they have not hurt me: forasmuch as before him innocency was found in me; and also before thee, O king, have I done no hurt." Verses 21, 22.

Note.—Here again was demonstrated by a miracle, wrought in the face of this great nation, that with the directing, prescribing, proscribing, or interfering with religion or its free exercise, civil governments can of right have nothing whatever to do.

God's Commands vs. Man's

What parting command did Christ give His disciples?

"Go ye into all the world, and preach the gospel to every creature." Mark 16:15.

What countercommand did the Jews soon give them?

"And they called them, and commanded them not to speak at all nor teach in the name of Jesus." Acts 4:18.

What reply did Peter and John make?

"Whether it be right in the sight of God to hearken unto you more than unto God, judge ye. For we cannot but speak the things which we have seen and heard." Verses 19, 20.

For continuing to preach, what befell the apostles?

"Then the high priest rose up, and all they that were with him, (which is the sect of the Sadducees,) and were filled with indignation, and *laid their hands on the apostles, and put them in the common prison."* Acts 5:17, 18.

What did an angel of God then do?

"But the angel of the Lord by night *opened the prison doors, and brought them forth,* and said, *Go, stand and speak in the temple to the people all the words of this life."* Verses 19, 20.

Note.—Here once again is demonstrated the fact that men have no right to interfere with the free exercise of religion, and that when the laws of men conflict with the law and word of God, we are to obey the latter, whatever the consequences may be.

When the apostles were called before the council again, what question did the high priest ask them?

THE POWERS THAT BE

"Did not we straitly command you that ye should not teach in this name? and, behold, ye have filled Jerusalem with your doctrine, and intend to bring this man's blood upon us." Verse 28.

What reply did the apostles make?

"We ought to obey God rather than men." Verse 29.

NOTE.—"Obedience is to be rendered to all human governments, in subordination to the will of God. These governments are a recognized necessity, in the nature of the case, and their existence is manifestly in accordance with the divine will. Hence the presumption is always in favor of the authority of civil law; and any refusal to obey, must be based on the moral proof that obedience will be sin. . . . It is too obvious to need discussion, that the law of God, the great principle of benevolence, is supreme, and that 'we ought to obey God, rather than men,' in any case of conflict between human law and the divine."—JAMES H. FAIRCHILD, *Moral Philosophy* (1869 ed.), pp. 178-181.

Who is higher than the "higher powers"?

"If thou seest the oppression of the poor, and violent perverting of judgment and justice in a province, marvel not at the matter: for *he that is higher than the highest* regardeth; and *there be higher than they."* Ecclesiastes 5:8.

NOTE.—In attempting to defend the right of civil government to enforce religious observances by law, some still ask, "Shall we not obey the powers that be?" We answer, "Yes, when they are in harmony with the higher powers that be. God made His law for all the universe. He is to be recognized, His law honored, before all the great men and the highest earthly powers."

Because Mordecai refused to bow down to Haman, what decree did Haman succeed in having the king issue?

"And the letters were sent by posts into all the king's provinces, *to destroy, to kill, and to cause to perish, all Jews, both young and old, little children and women, in one day,* even upon the thirteenth day of the twelfth month, which is the month Adar, and to take the spoil of them for a prey." Esther 3:13.

NOTE.—God has placed the sword (civil authority) in the hands of Caesar (civil government) for the punishment of evildoers; but when the sword is raised to slay the *innocent,* as in the case of the children of Bethlehem (Matthew 2:16); or to *enforce idolatrous worship,* as in the case of the three Hebrews (Daniel 3); or to *prohibit the worship of the true God,* as in the case of Daniel (Daniel 6); or to slay *all God's people,* as in the time of Esther; or to *enforce the observance of a false sabbath,* as in the case of all Sunday laws, it is an *abuse* of civil authority, and not a proper or justifiable use of it; and God honors those who, under such circumstances, in the face of persecution, oppression, and death, remain loyal and true to Him.

"Government is never the gainer in the execution of a law that is manifestly unjust. . . . Conscientious men are not the enemies, but the friends, of any government but a tyranny. They are its strength, and not its weakness. Daniel, in Babylon, praying, contrary to the law, was the true friend and supporter of the government; while those who, in their pretended zeal for the law and the constitution, would strike down the good man, were its real enemies. It is only when government transcends its spheres that it comes in conflict with the consciences of men. . . .

"It should always be remembered, that the great end of government is human well-being—that law and authority are nothing in themselves, and that all their sacredness arises from the uses which they serve. The machinery of government is valuable, only for the work it does; in itself, it has no value. . . . The most grievous of all imperfections in government, is the failure to secure the just and good result."—JAMES H. FAIRCHILD, *Moral Philosophy,* pp. 184-186.

God is above all earthly rulers, and His law above all human laws. He made us, and we therefore owe allegiance to Him before any earthly power, potentate, or tribunal.

THERE's never a night but is followed by day,
   And the darkest to dawn must give place:
There's never a sorrow that crosses our way
   But is sent with a message of grace.
It comes to the peasant, it comes to the king,
   It comes in our pleasures and pain;
It comes from the Father of mercies, to bring
   To His fold His own stray ones again.
O soul! is thy burden too heavy to bear?
   Does the load seem too weighty for one?
There's a Helper at hand all thy sorrows to share,
   'Tis thy Father's own well-beloved Son.
Then cast every burden on Jesus thy Lord,
   And thy troubles will quickly depart;
Make every sweet promise in His precious Word
   An entrance to His loving heart.

—JOHN WILLIAMS

Individual Accountability

PERSONAL RESPONSIBILITY TO GOD ALONE

What is religion?

"The recognition of God as an object of worship, love, and obedience."—WEBSTER. Other definitions equally good are: "The duty which we owe to our Creator, and the manner of discharging it." "Man's personal relation of faith and obedience to God."

In religious things, whom alone should we call Father?

"And call no man your father upon the earth: *for one is your Father, which is in heaven.* Matthew 23:9.

When tempted to bow to Satan, what did Christ reply?

"Then saith Jesus unto him, Get thee hence, Satan: for it is written, *Thou shalt worship the Lord thy God, and him only shalt thou serve.*" Matthew 4:10. (See Deuteronomy 6:13; 10:30.)

To whom alone, then, is each one accountable in religion?

"So then every one of us shall give account of himself *to God.*" Romans 14:12.

NOTE.—With this agree the words of Washington in his reply to the Virginia Baptists, in 1789: "Every man, conducting himself as a good citizen, and being accountable to God alone for his religious opinions, ought to be protected in worshipping the Deity according to the dictates of his own conscience."—*Writings of George Washington* (J. C. Fitzpatrick, ed.), vol. 30, p. 321.

HUMAN USURPERS

What do those do, therefore, who make men accountable to them in religious affairs?

They put themselves in the place of God. (See 2 Thessalonians 2:3, 4.)

Why, in religious matters, did Christ say men should not be called masters?

"Neither be ye called masters: *for one is your Master, even Christ.*" Matthew 23:10.

Note.—Everyone, therefore, who acts as master in Christ's church, or lords it over God's heritage (1 Peter 5:3), puts himself in the place of Christ.

To whom, then, as servants, are we responsible in matters of faith and worship?

"Who art thou that judgest another man's servant? *to his own master he standeth or falleth.*" Romans 14:4.

Whose servants are we not to be?

"Ye are bought with a price; *be not ye the servants of men.*" 1 Corinthians 7:23.

Note.—"Satan's methods ever tend to one end—to make men the slaves of men," and thus separate them from God, destroy faith in God, and so expose men to temptation and sin. Christ's work is to set men free, to renew faith, and to lead to willing and loyal obedience to God. Says Luther:

"Concerning God's Word and eternal matters God does not permit such a submission of one man to another ... because faith, submission, and humility is the real worship which ... should not be rendered to any creature, ... since to trust any creature in things pertaining to eternal life means the same as giving honor to a created being, an honor which belongs to God alone."—Translated from Martin Luther, Letter to the Emperor Charles V, April 28, 1521, in his *Sämmtliche Schriften* (Walch ed.), vol. 15, col. 1897.

At the Judgment Seat

Where must all finally appear to render their account?

"For we must all appear *before the judgment seat of Christ;* that every one may receive the things done in his body, according to that he hath done, whether it be good or bad." 2 Corinthians 5:10.

Note.—Inasmuch, then, as religion is an individual matter, and each individual must give account of himself to God, it follows that there should be no human constraint nor compulsion in religious affairs.

Dare to be a Daniel,
  Dare to stand alone!
Dare to have a purpose firm!
Dare to make it known!

—P. P. Bliss

Union of Church and State

What was already at work in the church in Paul's day?

"*The mystery of iniquity* doth already work." 2 Thessalonians 2:7.

What class of men did he say would arise in the church?

"For I know this, that after my departing shall *grievous wolves* enter in among you, not sparing the flock. *Also of your own selves shall men arise, speaking perverse things, to draw away disciples after them.*" Acts 20:29, 30.

What was to develop in the church before Christ's second coming?

"*That day shall not come, except there come a falling away first, and that man of sin be revealed*, the son of perdition." 2 Thessalonians 2:3.

How was this "falling away" from the truth shown?

By the adoption of heathen rites and customs in the church.

NOTE.—Tertullian, about A.D. 200, mentions many admittedly nonscriptural practices as already traditional in his day, such as immersing thrice in baptism, thus "making a somewhat ampler pledge than the Lord has appointed in the Gospel"; offerings for the dead as birthday honors; the prohibition of "fasting or kneeling in worship on the Lord's day, . . . also from Easter to Whitsunday"; a special reverence for bread and wine; and the tracing of the sign of the cross on the forehead "at every forward step and movement, at every going in and out, when we put on our clothes and shoes, when we bathe, when we sit at table, when we light the lamps, on couch, on seat, in all the ordinary actions of daily life."—*De Corona*, chaps. 3, 4, in *The Ante-Nicene Fathers*, vol. 3 (1918 ed.), pp. 94, 95.

"We are told in various ways by Eusebius," says Cardinal Newman, "that Constantine, in order to recommend the new religion to the heathen, transferred into it the outward ornaments to which they had been accustomed in their own," such as incense, candles, votive offerings, holy water, images, and similar things. Newman's full list is quoted in the reading on page 250.

Union of Church and State Begins

What came to be the character and work of many bishops?

"*Worldly-minded bishops,* instead of caring for the salvation of their flocks, were often but too much inclined to travel about, and *entangle themselves in worldly concerns.*"—Neander, *General History of the Christian Religion and Church* (Torrey's translation), vol. 2, p. 16.

What did the bishops determine to do?

"This theocratical theory was already the prevailing one in the time of Constantine; and . . . the bishops voluntarily made themselves dependent on him by their disputes, *and by their determination to make use of the power of the state for the furtherance of their aims.*"—*Ibid.,* p. 132.

Note.—The "theocratical theory," that of a government administered by God through the bishops, was confronted by the actuality of the pagan system under which the emperor had been Pontifex Maximus, or chief priest, of the pagan state religion, in consequence of which Constantine, after his recognition of Christianity, regarded himself as a sort of bishop of the external affairs of the church, and the church as a sort of department of the government. The ideal of the bishops, that of a government guided by God through the church, was pursued with variable but increasing success in Western Europe in the development of the bishop of Rome as the pope.

What has been one great characteristic of the papacy?

A union of church and state, or the religious power dominating the civil power to further its ends.

When was the union of church and state formed from which the papacy grew?

The foundation was laid for it during the reign of Constantine, A.D. 313-337, and it developed under his successors.

Note.—Constantine's granting first liberty and then preference to the recently persecuted Christians *"opened the door to the elevation of Christianity,* and specifically of Catholic hierarchical Christianity, with its exclusiveness towards heretical and schismatic sects, to be the religion of the state. For, once put on an equal footing with heathenism, it must soon, in spite of numerical minority, bear away the victory from a religion which had already inwardly outlived itself. From this time Constantine decidedly favored the church,

UNION OF CHURCH AND STATE

though without persecuting or forbidding the pagan religions."—PHILIP SCHAFF, *History of the Christian Church* (Scribners, 1902 ed.), vol. 3, pp. 30, 31.

Under Constantine's successors official paganism was abolished, and Christianity made the only legal religion of the state.

STATE SUPPORT

How did this elevation of the church begin?

Through the *patronage* and *religious legislation* of Constantine.

NOTE.—Authorities differ as to when—or whether—Constantine was converted to Christianity, and whether he favored the church more from religious or political motives. The outline of events follows:

A.D. 306—Constantine's accession as one of four rulers of the empire, with jurisdiction over the Prefecture of Gaul.

312—His victory over Maxentius, which made him sole ruler of the West, and which he attributed to the aid of the God of the Christians, whom he had invoked after a supposed vision of a cross in the sky.

313—The so-called Edict of Milan, issued jointly with his colleague Licinius, granting religious liberty to all, of whatever religious belief, and particularly mentioning the Christians. Hereafter Constantine surrounded himself with bishops, gave preference to the Christians, and issued legislation in their favor, without renouncing or persecuting paganism.

321—His famous Sunday law, which served to unite his Christian and pagan subjects in the observance of "the venerable day of the Sun."

323 or 324—His attainment of sole rule of the whole empire by the defeat of his last rival, the pagan Licinius, who had resumed persecution of Christians in the East; his open espousal and promotion of Christianity about this time, and the subsequent disappearance of the sun-god and other pagan symbols from his coinage.

325—His convening of the Council of Nicaea, which he dominated, in order to secure unity in the church; subsequently, his enforcement of that unity against heretical Christians in favor of the Catholic Church.

337—His long-deferred baptism during his last illness.

For the principal facts about Constantine, see Philip Schaff, *History of the Christian Church,* vol. 3, pp. 12-36; for shorter treatment see A. C. Flick, *The Rise of the Mediaeval Church,* pp. 115-122; A. E. R. Boak, *A History of Rome to 565 A.D.,* pp. 347-350.

What form did this government patronage take under Constantine and later rulers?

Immunities, privileges, and certain judicial functions for the clergy, and gifts, endowments, and financial support for the church; first on a basis of equality with the priesthood and temples of paganism, then on a preferred basis, and finally to the exclusion of all except Catholic orthodoxy.

What kinds of religious legislation united church and state?

Laws granting privileges and patronage, and those enforcing church dogmas, practices, or disciplinary decrees, or suppressing paganism and heresy.

NOTE.—Constantine's earliest Christian legislation "exempted the Christian clergy from military and municipal duty (March, 313); abolished various customs and ordinances offensive to the Christians (315); facilitated the emancipation of Christian slaves (before 316); legalized bequests to catholic churches (321); enjoined the civil observance of Sunday, though not as dies Domini [Lord's day], but as dies Solis [the Sun's day], . . . and in company with an ordinance for the regular consulting of the haruspex [soothsayer] (321)."— PHILIP SCHAFF, *History of the Christian Church* (Scribners, 1902 ed.), vol. 3, p. 31. For Sunday legislation see the following reading.

STATE SUPERVISION

How did Constantine initiate state supervision of the church?

Having achieved political unity in the empire, he sought to gain church unity through church councils.

NOTE.—The first ecumenical, or general, council at Nicaea, in 325, was called and presided over by Constantine. "The ecumenical councils," says Schaff, "have not only an ecclesiastical significance, but bear also a *political* or state-church character. The very name refers to . . . the empire. . . . The Christian Graeco-Roman *emperor* is indispensable to an ecumenical council in the ancient sense of the term; its temporal head and its legislative strength. . . . Upon this Byzantine precedent, and upon the example of the kings of Israel, the Russian Czars and the Protestant princes of Germany, Scandinavia, and England—be it just or unjustly—build their claim to a similar and still more extended supervision of the church in their dominions."—*Ibid.*, pp. 334, 335.

UNION OF CHURCH AND STATE

What were the principal questions discussed at Nicaea?

First the Arian controversy; next, the date of Easter.

Note.—"It appears that the churches of Syria and Mesopotamia continued to follow the custom of the Jews, and celebrated Easter on *the fourteenth day of the moon,* whether falling on Sunday or not. All the other churches observed that solemnity *on Sunday only,* viz: those of Rome, Italy, Africa, Lydia, Egypt, Spain, Gaul and Britain; and all Greece, Asia, and Pontus."—Isaac Boyle, *Historical View of the Council of Nice* (1836 ed.), p. 23.

By this council *Easter was fixed on the Sunday* immediately following the full moon which was nearest after the vernal equinox.

What does Neander say of the securing of religious laws?

"In this way, the church received help from the state for the furtherance of her ends."—*General History of the Christian Religion and Church* (Torrey translation, 1852 ed.) vol. 2, p. 301.

Note.—In this way church and state were united. In this way the church gained control of the civil power, which she later used as a means of carrying on most bitter and extensive persecutions. In this way she denied Christ and the power of godliness, and demanded that the civil power should be exerted to compel men to serve God as the church should dictate.

What did Augustine, the father of the Christian theocratic, or church-and-state theory, teach concerning it?

"'Who doubts but what it is better to be led to God by instruction, than by fear of punishment or affliction? But because the former, who will be guided only by instruction, are better, the others are still not to be neglected. . . . Many, like bad servants, must often be reclaimed to their master by the rod of temporal suffering, ere they can attain to this highest state of religious development.'"—*Ibid.,* pp. 214, 215.

CONSTANTINE ISSUES THE FIRST SUNDAY LAW

"Constantine the Great made a law for the whole empire (321 A.D.) that Sunday should be kept as a day of rest."—*Encyclopedia Americana*, article "Sabbath"

Sabbath Legislation

GOD, MAN, AND THE SABBATH

Who made the Sabbath?

"In six days *the Lord* made heaven and earth, the sea, and all that in them is, and *rested the seventh day:* wherefore *the Lord blessed the sabbath day, and hallowed it."* Exodus 20:11.

To whom does the Sabbath belong?

"The seventh day is the sabbath of *the Lord thy God."* Verse 10.

To whom, then, should its observance be rendered?

"Render to Caesar the things that are Caesar's, and *to God the things that are God's."* Mark 12:17.

NOTE.—When men make Sabbath laws, therefore, they require Sabbath observance to be rendered to the *government,* or, presumably, to God *through the government,* which amounts to the same thing.

In religious things, to whom alone are we accountable?

"So then every one of us shall give account of himself *to God."* Romans 14:12.

NOTE.—But when men make compulsory Sabbath laws, they make men accountable to the *government* for Sabbath observance.

THE NATURE OF SABBATH LAWS

How does God show the holiness of the Sabbath day?

"Remember the sabbath day, to *keep it holy."* Exodus 20:8. "The seventh day is the sabbath of rest, *an holy convocation."* Leviticus 23:3.

Since the Sabbath is *holy,* is to be *kept holy,* and is a day for *holy convocations,* it must be *religious.*

What, then, must be the nature of all Sabbath legislation?

It is *religious legislation.*

When the State Enacts Religious Laws

What has generally been the result of religious legislation, or a union of church and state?

Religious intolerance and persecution.

What was the first Sunday law?

Constantine's Sunday law of March 7, 321.

NOTE.—"On the venerable Day of the Sun let the magistrates and people residing in cities rest, and let all workshops be closed. In the country, however, persons engaged in agriculture may freely and lawfully continue their pursuits; because it often happens that another day is not so suitable for grain-sowing or for vine-planting; lest by neglecting the proper moment for such operations the bounty of heaven should be lost. (Given the 7th day of March, Crispus and Constantine being consuls each of them for the second time.)"—*Codex Justinianus*, lib. 3, tit. 12, 3; translated by Philip Schaff, *History of the Christian Church*, vol. 3 (1902), p. 380, note.

What church council required Sunday observance and forbade Sabbath observance?

The Council of Laodicea decreed that Christians should keep the Sunday, and that if they persisted in resting on the Sabbath, "They shall be shut out from Christ." (See Hefele, *A History of the Councils of the Church*, vol. 2, p. 316.)

Was there further imperial Sunday legislation?

Constantine's decrees marked the beginning of a long, though intermittent series of imperial decrees in support of Sunday rest.

NOTE.—"By a law of the year 386 [in the reign of Theodosius I], those older changes effected by the emperor Constantine were more rigorously enforced, and, in general, civil transactions of every kind on Sunday were strictly forbidden. . . .

"In the year 425 [in the reign of Theodosius the Younger], the exhibition of spectacles on Sunday, and on the principal feast-days of the Christians, was forbidden, in order that the devotion of the faithful might be free from all disturbance. . . .

"*In this way, the church received help from the state for the furtherance of her ends.* . . . But had it not been for that confusion of spiritual and secular interests, had it not been for the vast number of mere *outward conversions* thus brought about, she would have needed no such help."—NEANDER, *General History of the Christian Religion and Church,* vol. 2 (1852 ed.), pp. 300, 301.

The decrees of later emperors between 364 and 467 added other prohibitions and exemptions from time to time. Justinian's code collected the laws of the empire on the subject, and from the time when Charlemagne, king of the Franks, was crowned emperor (800), this code was in effect all over what later became the "Holy Roman Empire." The medieval decrees and canons of popes and councils concerning Sunday observance were enforced by the civil power. (See *The New Schaff-Herzog Encyclopedia of Religious Knowledge,* vol. 11, p. 147.)

Later the church councils had an influence to some extent throughout the former Roman Empire, for the church maintained a large degree of unity. The Council of Laodicea (fourth century) ordered men to work on the Sabbath and rest if possible on Sunday. "The Council of Orleans (538), while protesting against excessive Sabbatarianism, forbade all field work under pain of censure; and the Council of Macon (585) laid down that the Lord's Day 'is the day of perpetual rest, which is suggested to us by the type of the seventh day in the law and the prophets,' and ordered a complete cessation of all kinds of business. How far the movement had gone by the end of the 6th cent. is shown by a letter of Gregory the Great (pope 590-604) protesting against prohibition of baths on Sunday."—HASTINGS, *Encyclopaedia of Religion and Ethics,* vol. 12, pp. 105, 106, art. "Decrees of Church Councils."

Law of Charlemagne 789: "And, we decree according to what the Lord commanded also in the law, that servile work shall not be done on the Lord's days, and just as my father of blessed memory commanded in his synodal edicts, that is, that men shall not carry on rural work, neither in cultivating the vine, nor in plowing in the fields [etc.]. . . . Likewise the women shall not do weaving [etc.] . . . in order that in every way the honor and rest of the Lord's day may be kept. But let them come together from everywhere to the church to the celebration of the mass, and praise God in all the good things which He has done for us on that day."—Translated from CHARLEMAGNE, *Admonitio Generalis,* in *Monumenta Germaniae Historica, Leges,* sect. 2, tom. 1, p. 61, par. 81.

In England, according to Lord Mansfield (Swann vs. Browne, 3 Burrow, 1599), William the Conqueror and Henry II declared the codes of Justinian on Sunday observance to be the law of England. A succession of Parliamentary acts regulated Sunday observance in England. (See *The New Schaff-Herzog Encyclopedia of Religious Knowledge,* vol. 11, pp. 147, 148.)

The first Sunday law promulgated in America, Virginia, 1610:

"Every man and woman shall repair in the morning to the divine service, and sermons preached upon the Sabbath day, and in the afternoon to divine service, and catechizing, upon pain for the first fault to *lose their provision and the allowance for the whole week following,* for the second to *lose the said allowance and also be whipped,* and for the third to *suffer death."*—For the Colony in Virginea Britannia, Lavves, Morall and Martiall, & c, in PETER FORCE, *Tracts Relating to the Colonies in North America* (Washington, 1844), vol. 3, no. 2, p. 10.

Law of Charles II, 29th year, 1676-77: "Be it enacted . . . that all and every Person and Persons whatsoever, shall on every Lord's Day apply themselves to the Observation of the same, by exercising themselves thereon in the Duties of Piety and true Religion, publickly and privately; and that no . . . Person whatsoever, shall do or exercise any worldly Labour, Business, or Work of their ordinary Callings, upon the Lord's Day, or any Part thereof (Works of Necessity and Charity only excepted;) . . . and that no Person or Persons whatsoever, shall publickly cry, shew forth, or expose to Sale, any Wares, Merchandizes," etc.—*British Statutes at Large,* 29th year of Charles II, chap. 7.

Modeled somewhat after the Puritan laws of 1644 to 1658, but much shorter and milder, it further forbids travel, but does not mention sports and pastimes, and makes the same exception for food and milk.

The importance of this act is that it stood, with modifications, as the basic Sunday law of England for nearly two hundred years (see *Encyclopaedia Britannica* [1945 ed.], vol. 21, p. 565), and was followed as a model for many of the subsequent Sunday laws in various American colonies, and thus somewhat set the pattern for our State laws.

"WICKED spirits gather round thee,
  Legions of those foes to God—
Principalities most mighty—
  Walk unseen the earth abroad;
They are gathering to the battle,
  Strengthened for the last deep strife;
Christian, arm! be watchful, ready,
  Struggle manfully for life."

Who Persecute and Why

Evil Men Persecute Righteous

Because Jesus had not kept the Sabbath according to their ideas, what did the Jews do?

"*Therefore did the Jews persecute Jesus, and sought to slay him,* because he had done these things on the Sabbath day." John 5:16.

What kind of fast is most acceptable to God?

"Is not this the fast that I have chosen? *to loose the bands of wickedness, to undo the heavy burdens, and to let the oppressed go free, and that ye break every yoke?*" Isaiah 58:6.

Note.—This is what Jesus did. He, the Author and Lord of the Sabbath, in addition to attending and taking part in religious services (Luke 4:16), went about doing good, healing the sick, relieving the oppressed, and restoring the impotent, lame, and blind, on the Sabbath day. But this, while in perfect accord with the law of God, the great law of love, was contrary to the traditions and perverted ideas of the Jews respecting the Sabbath. Hence they persecuted Him, and sought to slay Him.

Why did Cain kill Abel?

"For this is the message that ye heard from the beginning, that we should love one another. Not as Cain, who was of that wicked one, and slew his brother. And wherefore slew he him? *Because his own works were evil, and his brother's righteous.*" 1 John 3:11, 12.

Note.—If you will read the word of God, you will find that from the beginning all good people were persecuted because they were good. Abel was slain by his brother because he was good, and Cain could not endure the sight of him.

Commenting upon the treatment of Isaac, the son of Sarah, by Ishmael, the son of the bondwoman, what principle does the apostle Paul lay down?

"But as then *he that was born after the flesh persecuted him that was born after the Spirit, even so it is now.*" Galatians 4:29.

Note.—Other instances of persecution mentioned in the Bible are:

a. Esau, who sold his birthright, persecuted Jacob. Genesis 25:29-34; 27:41.

b. The wayward and envious sons of Jacob persecuted Joseph. Genesis 37; Acts 7:9.

c. The idolatrous Egyptians persecuted the Hebrews. Exodus 1 and 5.

d. The Hebrew who did his neighbor wrong thrust Moses, as mediator, aside. Exodus 2:13, 14; Acts 7:26, 27.

e. Saul, who disobeyed God, persecuted David, who feared God. 1 Samuel 15, 19, 24.

f. Israel, in their apostasy, persecuted Elijah and Jeremiah, who were prophets of God. 1 Kings 19:9, 10; Jeremiah 36:20-23; 38:1-6.

g. Nebuchadnezzar, while an idolater, persecuted the three Hebrew captives for refusing to worship idols. Daniel 3.

h. The envious and idolatrous princes under Darius persecuted Daniel for daring to pray to the God of heaven. Daniel 6.

i. The murderers of Christ persecuted the apostles for preaching Christ. Acts 4 and 5.

j. Paul, before his conversion, persecuted the church of God. Acts 8:1; 9:1, 2; 22:4, 5, 20; 26:9-11; Galatians 1:13; 1 Timothy 1:12, 13.

The history of all the religious persecutions since Bible times is but a repetition of this same story—the wicked persecute the righteous. And thus it will continue to be until the conflict between good and evil is ended. (See Psalm 37:12, 14, 32.)

Who does Paul say shall suffer persecution?

"Yea, and *all that will live godly in Christ Jesus shall suffer persecution.*" 2 Timothy 3:12.

What is essential to extensive religious persecution?

Ecclesiastical control of the civil power, or a union of church and state.

Since persecution is invariably wrong, what must be true of persecuting governments?

They likewise must be in the wrong.

Note.—"There are many who do not seem to be sensible that all violence in religion is irreligious, and that whoever is wrong, the persecutor cannot be right."—Thomas Clarke, *History of Intolerance* (1819 ed.), vol. 1, p. 3.

"Have not almost all the governments in the world always been in the wrong on religious subjects?"—Macaulay, Essay on "Gladstone on Church and State," in his *Critical and Historical Essays* (1865 ed.), vol. 2, p. 60.

God never forces the will or the conscience; but, in order to bring men under sin, Satan resorts to force. To accomplish his purpose, he works through religious and secular rulers, influencing them to enact and enforce human laws in defiance of the law of God.

Under what terrible deception did Christ say men would persecute His followers?

"They shall put you out of the synagogues: yea, the time cometh, *that whosoever killeth you will think that he doeth God service.*" John 16:1, 2.

Who is the original murderer?

"Ye are of your father *the devil,* and the lusts of your father ye will do. *He was a murderer from the beginning.*" John 8:44.

When James and John wished to call down fire from heaven to consume the Samaritans who did not receive Christ, what did Christ say to them?

"He turned, and rebuked them, and said, *Ye know not what manner of spirit ye are of. For the Son of man is not come to destroy men's lives but to save them.*" Luke 9:55, 56.

Some Who Would Justify Persecution

Has the papacy ever claimed authority to persecute?

Yes.

NOTE.—"That the Church of Rome has shed more innocent blood than any other institution that has ever existed among mankind, will be questioned by no Protestant who has a competent knowledge of history. The memorials, indeed, of many of her persecutions are now so scanty that it is impossible to form a complete conception of the multitude of her victims, and it is quite certain that no powers of imagination can adequately realize their sufferings."—W. E. H. LECKY in *History of the Rise and Influence of the Spirit of Rationalism in Europe* (1910 ed.), vol. 2, p. 32.

"This claim to exercise coercive jurisdiction has, as might be expected, been denied by various heterodox writers. Thus Marsilius Patavinus (Defensor Pacis, II, iv), Antonius de Dominis (De rep. eccl., IV, vi, vii, ix), Richer (De eccl. et pol. Potestate, xi-xii), and later the Synod of Pistoia, all alike maintained that coercive jurisdiction of every kind belongs to the civil power alone, and sought to restrict the Church to the use of moral means. This error has always been condemned by the Holy See. Thus, in the Bull 'Auctorem Fidei', Pius VI makes the following pronouncement regarding one of the Pistoian propositions: '[The aforesaid proposition] in respect of its insinuation that the Church does not possess authority to exact subjection to her decrees otherwise than by means dependent on persuasion: so far as this signifies that the Church "has not received from God power, not merely to direct by counsel and persuasion, but further to command by laws, and to coerce and compel the delinquent and contumacious by external and salutary penalties" [from the brief "Ad assiduas" (1755) of Benedict XIV], leads to a system already condemned as heretical.' Nor may it be held that the pope's laws must exclusively concern spiritual objects, and their penalties be exclusively of a spiritual character. The Church is a perfect society (see Church, XIII). She is not dependent on the permission of the State for her existence, but holds her charter from God. As a perfect society she has a right to all those means which are necessary for the attaining of her end. These, however, will include far more than spiritual objects and penalties alone: for the Church requires certain material possessions, such, for example, as churches, schools, seminaries, together with the endowments necessary for their sustentation. The administration and the due protection of these goods will require legislation other than what is limited to the spiritual sphere. A large body of canon law must inevitably be formed to determine the conditions of their management. Indeed, there is a fallacy in the assertion that the Church is a spiritual society; it is spiritual as regards the ultimate end to which all its activities are directed, but not as regards its present constitution nor as regards the means at its disposal. The question has been raised whether it be lawful for the Church, not merely to sentence a delinquent to physical penalties, but itself to inflict these penalties. As to this, it is sufficient to note that the right of the Church to invoke the aid of the civil power for her sentences to execute her sentences is expressly asserted by Boniface VIII in the Bull 'Unam Sanctam.' This declaration, even if it be not one of those portions of the Bull in which the pope is defining a point of faith, is so clearly connected with the parts expressly stated to possess such character that it is held by theologians to be theologically certain (Palmieri, 'De Romano Pontifice', thes. xxi). The question is of theoretical, rather than of practical importance, since civil Governments have long ceased to own the obligation of enforcing the decisions of any ecclesiastical authority. This indeed became inevitable when large sections of the population ceased to be Catholic. The state of things supposed could only exist when a whole nation was thoroughly Catholic in spirit, and the force of papal decisions was recognized by all as binding in conscience."—*The Catholic Encyclopedia*, vol. 12, p. 266, art. "Pope." New York: The Gilmary Society, A Membership Corporation. Used by permission.

"The Roman Catholic Church, convinced, through its divine prerogatives, of being the only true church, must demand the right to freedom for herself alone, because such a right can only be possessed by truth, never by error. As to other religions, the church will certainly never draw the sword, but she will require that by legitimate means they shall not be allowed to propagate false doctrine. Consequently, in a state where the majority of the people are Catholic, the church will require that legal existence be denied to error, and that if religious minorities actually exist, they shall have only a *de facto* existence without opportunity to spread their beliefs. If, however, actual circumstances, either due to government hostility or the strength of the dissenting groups, makes the complete application of this principle impossible, then the [Catholic] church will require for herself all possible concessions, limiting herself to accept, as a minor evil, the *de jure* toleration of other forms of worship. In some countries, Catholics will be obliged to ask full religious freedom for all, resigned at being forced to cohabitate where they alone should rightfully be allowed to live. . . . We ask Protestants to understand that the Catholic Church would betray her trust if she were to proclaim, theoretically and practically, that error can have the same rights as truth, especially where the supreme duties and interest of man are at stake. The church cannot blush for her own want of tolerance, as she asserts it in principle and applies it in practice."—F. CAVALLI, S.J., in *La Civilta Cattolica* (a Jesuit organ published at Rome), April, 1948, quoted in an editorial in *The Christian Century*, June 23, 1948, p. 623. Used by permission.

"There is reason to believe, accordingly," says Paul Hutchinson, speaking of modern political developments, "that the old issue of church and state, or of church against state, will soon be upon us in a fury unknown for a thousand years. Are we ready to face that storm? Do we comprehend from how many quarters it is likely to blow?"—*The New Leviathan* (1946 ed.), p. 19.

WISER MEN CONDEMN PERSECUTION

This erroneous position has been well refuted by Lord Macaulay in the following words: "The doctrine which, from the very first origin of religious dissensions, has been held by all bigots of all sects, when condensed into a few words, and stripped of rhetorical disguise, is simply this: I am in the right, and you are in the wrong. When you are the stronger, you ought to tolerate me; for it is your duty to tolerate truth. But when I am the stronger, I shall persecute you; for it is my duty to persecute error."—Essay on "Sir James Mackintosh" in *Critical and Historical Essays* (1865 ed.), vol. 1, pp. 333, 334.

Benjamin Franklin: "When a religion is good, I conceive that it will support itself; and, when it cannot support itself, and God does not take care to support, so that its professors are obliged to call for the help of the civil power, it is a sign, I apprehend, of its being a bad one."—Letter to Dr. Price, Oct. 9, 1780, in *The Writings of Benjamin Franklin,* edited by Albert Henry Smyth, vol. 8, p. 154.

John Wesley gave the following Christian advice: "Condemn no man for not thinking as you think: Let every one enjoy the full and free liberty of thinking for himself: Let every man use his own judgment, since every man must give an account of himself to God. Abhor every approach, in any kind or degree, to the spirit of persecution. If you cannot reason or persuade a man into the truth, never attempt to force him into it. If love will not compel him to come, leave him to God, the Judge of all."—"Advice to the People Called Methodists" in his *Works,* vol. 8 (1830 ed.), p. 357.

THE DIVINE CURE FOR THE BIGOT

What divine precepts received and obeyed would do away with all oppression and persecution?

"Thou shalt love thy neighbour as thyself." Matthew 22:39. "All things whatsoever ye would that men should do to you, do ye even so to them." Matthew 7:12.

What does love not do?

"Love worketh no ill to his neighbour: therefore love is the fulfilling of the law." Romans 13:10.

How does Christ bless those who are persecuted?

"Blessed are they which are persecuted for righteousness' sake: for their's is the kingdom of heaven. Blessed are ye, when men shall revile you, and persecute you, and shall say all manner of evil against you falsely, for my sake. Rejoice, and be exceeding glad: for great is your reward in heaven: for so persecuted they the prophets which were before you." Matthew 5:10-12. (See Revelation 2:10; 6:9-11.)

Part Eleven

Life Only in Christ

	PAGE
Origin, History, and Destiny of Satan	495
What Is Man?	500
Life Only in Christ	505
The Intermediate State	506
The Two Resurrections	509
Fate of the Transgressor	514
The Ministration of Good Angels	518
The Dark Ministry of Evil Angels	524
Spiritualism	527

THE PRIDE OF LUCIFER

"I will exalt my throne above the stars of God: . . . I will be like the most High." Isaiah 14:13, 1

Origin, History, and Destiny of Satan

HAVE any others than the human family sinned?

"God spared not *the angels that sinned.*" 2 Peter 2:4.

What is the one who led the angels to sin called?

"Depart from me, ye cursed, into everlasting fire, prepared for *the devil* and his angels." Matthew 25:41.

NOTE.—He is also called "the great dragon," "that old serpent," "Satan," "Lucifer." (Revelation 12:9; Isaiah 14:12.)

What was Satan's condition when created?

"Thou wast perfect in thy ways from the day that thou wast created, till iniquity was found in thee." Ezekiel 28:15.

NOTE.—Under the figure of the king of Tyrus the prophet Ezekiel describes him thus: *"Thou sealest up the sum, full of wisdom, and perfect in beauty.* Thou hast been in Eden the garden of God; every precious stone was thy covering, . . . the workmanship of thy tabrets and of thy pipes was prepared in thee in the day that thou wast created. Thou art the anointed cherub that covereth; and I have set thee so: thou wast upon the holy mountain of God; thou hast walked up and down in the midst of the stones of fire." Ezekiel 28:12-14.

Thus it is evident that Satan was a high and exalted angel before he fell, a masterpiece of wisdom and beauty. The reference to his "tabrets" and "pipes" probably means that he led the angelic host in song. In the earthly sanctuary the covering cherubim overshadowed the mercy seat. (Exodus 25:16-22; Hebrews 9:3-5; Psalm 99:1.)

CAUSE OF SATAN'S FALL

What unholy, ambitious spirit led to Satan's fall?

"Thou hast said in thine heart, I will ascend into heaven, I will exalt my throne above the stars of God: I will sit also upon the mount of the congregation, in the sides of the north: I will ascend above the heights of the clouds; I will be like the most High." Isaiah 14:13, 14. *"Thine heart was lifted up because of thy beauty,* thou hast corrupted thy wisdom by reason of thy *brightness.*" Ezekiel 28:17.

What does Solomon say precedes destruction and a fall?

"*Pride* goeth before destruction, and *an haughty spirit* before a fall." Proverbs 16:18.

Under the figure of the king of Babylon, how does the prophet Isaiah describe Satan's fall?

"How art thou fallen from heaven, O Lucifer, son of the morning! how art thou cut down to the ground, which didst weaken the nations!" Isaiah 14:12.

Why was Satan cast from his high position?

"*Thou hast sinned:* therefore I will cast thee as profane out of the mountain of God: and I will destroy thee, O covering cherub, from the midst of the stones of fire." Ezekiel 28:16.

Satan Cast Out

How is the conflict elsewhere described?

"And there was war in heaven: Michael [Christ] and his angels fought against the dragon; and the dragon fought and his angels, and prevailed not; neither was their place found any more in heaven. And the great dragon was *cast out,* that old serpent, called the Devil, and Satan, which deceiveth the whole world: he was *cast out into the earth,* and his angels were cast out with him." Revelation 12:7-9.

In what terms did Christ refer to Satan's fall?

"I beheld Satan as lightning fall from heaven." Luke 10:18.

In what figurative terms did Peter describe the fate of the rebellious angels?

"God spared not the angels that sinned, but *cast them down to hell, and delivered them into chains of darkness,* to be reserved unto judgment." 2 Peter 2:4.

Satan Since the Fall

What has been the character of Satan since his fall?

"The devil sinneth from the beginning." 1 John 3:8.

ORIGIN, HISTORY, AND DESTINY OF SATAN

Was he ever in the truth?

"He was a murderer from the beginning, and *abode not in the truth,* because there is no truth in him." John 8:44.

NOTE.—This implies that Satan, once *in* the truth, did not *remain* there.

What besides a *murderer* did Christ say Satan is?

"He is a liar, and the father of it." Same verse.

What did God tell Adam and Eve would be the result if they transgressed by partaking of the forbidden fruit?

"Thou shalt *surely die.*" Genesis 2:17.

What did Satan say to Eve through the serpent?

"Ye shall NOT *surely die."* Genesis 3:4.

NOTE.—This, as far as the record shows, was *the first lie*—a direct denial of the word of God. By persuading Eve to accept and believe it, Satan led our first parents to *commit sin;* and, as "the wages of sin is *death,*" by it, also, he caused their *death,* and so became, in reality, *the first murderer.* A lie, therefore, is a twin brother to murder, and one of the most hateful things to God, the God of *truth.* (See Proverbs 6:16-19; 12:19.) "All liars shall have their part in the lake which burneth with fire and brimstone." Revelation 21:8. (See also Revelation 21:27; 22:15.)

What has been the result of sin's entrance into the world?

"By one man sin entered into the world, and *death by sin*"; "by one man's disobedience *many were made sinners.*" Romans 5:12, 19. *"The whole world lieth in wickedness."* 1 John 5:19. "In Adam *all die."* 1 Corinthians 15:22.

When Christ came to redeem man, what did Satan do?

"He was there in the wilderness forty days, *tempted of Satan.*" Mark 1:13. (See also Matthew 4:1-11.)

How severely was Christ during His earthly life tempted of Satan?

"[He was] touched with the feeling of our infirmities; but was *in all points tempted like as we are,* yet without sin." Hebrews 4:15.

What has the church suffered since the days of Christ?

"And when the dragon [Satan] saw that he was cast unto the earth, *he persecuted the woman* [*the church*]." Revelation 12:13.

NOTE.—Untold millions of the people of God have been put to death under pagan and papal persecutions, all of which have been instigated by Satan. (See readings on pages 219, 261, 266, 487.)

Is the remnant church to feel his wrath, and why?

"And the dragon was wroth with the woman, and went to make war with the remnant of her seed, which keep the commandments of God, and have the testimony of Jesus Christ." Verse 17.

Through what agency will Satan cause deception in the last days?

"And I beheld another beast coming up out of the earth; and he ... deceiveth them that dwell on the earth *by means of those miracles which he had power to do in the sight of the beast.*" Revelation 13:11-14.

NOTE.—This, we understand, refers to spiritualistic manifestations and miracles to be wrought to fasten men in error and deception. (See readings on pages 524, 527.)

What will influence the nations to gather for the battle of the day of God?

"They are *the spirits of devils,* working miracles, which go forth unto the kings of the earth and of the whole world, *to gather them to the battle of that great day of God Almighty.*" Revelation 16:14.

SATAN'S MILLENNIUM AND DOOM

For how long is Satan to be bound at the Second Advent?

"An angel ... laid hold on the dragon, that old serpent, which is the Devil, and Satan, and *bound him a thousand years.*" Revelation 20:1, 2.

What is to take place at the close of the thousand years?

"And when the thousand years are expired, *Satan shall be loosed out of his prison,* and shall *go out to deceive the nations* which are in the four quarters of the earth, Gog and Magog, *to gather them together to battle.*" Verses 7, 8.

NOTE.—Satan's evil career began in rebellion against God in heaven, and ends in rebellion against Him on earth.

What is the final fate of Satan and his host?

"They . . . compassed the camp of the saints about, and the beloved city: and *fire came down from God out of heaven, and devoured them.*" Verse 9.

Personal Defeat or Victory

How are Christians warned against Satan's hatred?

"Be sober, be vigilant; because your adversary the devil, as a roaring lion, walketh about, seeking whom he may devour: whom *resist stedfast in the faith."* 1 Peter 5:8, 9. *"Resist the devil,* and he will flee from you." James 4:7.

Why will men be allowed to fall under the delusion of Satan?

"Because they received not the love of the truth, that they might be saved. *And for this cause God shall send them strong delusion, that they should believe a lie:* that they all might be damned who believed not the truth, but had pleasure in unrighteousness." 2 Thessalonians 2:10-12.

Why did Christ partake of our nature?

"Forasmuch then as the children are partakers of flesh and blood, he also himself likewise took part of the same; *that through death he might destroy him that had the power of death, that is, the devil."* Hebrews 2:14.

What was Christ's weapon against Satan?

The word of God. *"It is written."* (See Matthew 4:4-10.)

NOTE.—The word of God is the "sword of the Spirit." (Ephesians 6:17.) If Christ met and vanquished the enemy with this, so also may we.

> 'Tis by the faith of joys to come
>   We walk through deserts dark as night;
> Till we arrive at heaven, our home,
>   Truth is our guide, and faith our light.
>
> —Isaac Watts

What Is Man?

Man's Creation and Nature

Of what was man formed in the beginning?

"God formed man *of the dust of the ground*." Genesis 2:7.

What act made him a living soul?

"And [God] *breathed into his nostrils the breath of life;* and man became a living soul." Same verse, last part.

Note.—The living soul was not put *into* the man; but the breath of *life* which was put into man made *him*—the man, formed of the earth—a *living* soul, or creature. "Man became a living being," says the Smith-Goodspeed American translation. (University of Chicago Press.)

The Hebrew words translated "living soul" in this text are *nephesh chayyah*, the same expression used in Genesis 1:24, translated "living creature."

The word *nephesh* occurs 755 times in the Hebrew Old Testament. In the King James Version the word is translated: 428 times as "soul." For example: Genesis 2:7; 12:5; Numbers 9:13; Psalm 6:3; Isaiah 1:14.

119 times, life (life's, lives). For example: Genesis 1:20, 30; 9:4; 1 Kings 19:14; Job 6:11; Psalm 38:12.

29 times, person. For example: Numbers 31:19; 35:11, 15, 30; Deuteronomy 27:25; Joshua 20:3, 9; 1 Samuel 22:22.

15 times, mind. For example: Deuteronomy 18:6; Jeremiah 15:1.

15 times, heart. For example: Exodus 23:9; Proverbs 23:7.

9 times, creature. Genesis 1:21, 24; 2:19; 9:10, 12, 15, 16; Leviticus 11:46.

7 times, body (or, dead body). Leviticus 21:11; Numbers 6:6; 9:6, 7, 10; 19:13; Haggai 2:13.

5 times, dead. Leviticus 19:28; 21:1; 22:4; Numbers 5:2; 6:11.

3 times, man. Exodus 12:16; 2 Kings 12:4; 1 Chronicles 5:21.

3 times, me. Numbers 23:10; Judges 16:30; 1 Kings 20:32.

3 times, beast. Leviticus 24:18.

2 times, ghost. Job 11:20; Jeremiah 15:9.

1 time, fish. Isaiah 19:10.

One or more times as various forms of the personal pronouns. (These figures are from Young's *Analytical Concordance*.)

WHAT IS MAN?

Are other creatures besides man called "living souls"?

"And God created great whales, and every living creature that moveth, which the waters brought forth abundantly." Genesis 1:21. "And out of the ground the Lord God formed every beast of the field, and every fowl of the air; and brought them unto Adam to see what he would call them: and whatsoever Adam called every living creature, that was the name thereof." Genesis 2:19.

NOTE.—Look up the nine instances of *nephesh,* "soul," translated as "creature," and you will see that they all refer to animals as "living creatures," or, as the words might have been translated, "living souls." On the phrase *nephesh chayyah,* living soul or creature, in Genesis 1:24, Adam Clarke says: "A general term to express all creatures endued with animal life, in any of its infinitely varied gradations, from the half-reasoning *elephant* down to the stupid *potto,* or lower still, to the *polype,* which seems equally to share the vegetable and animal life."

An examination of the various occurrences of *nephesh* in the Old Testament shows that *nephesh* describes the individual rather than being a constituent part of the individual. It would be more correct, therefore, to say that a man *is* a *nephesh,* or "soul," than that he *has* a *nephesh,* or "soul." True, the expressions "my soul," "thy soul," "his soul," etc., occur frequently, but in most instances these are simply idiomatic expressions meaning "myself," "thyself," "himself," etc. Translators recognizing this have at times substituted the personal pronoun. For examples see Psalm 35:25; Proverbs 6:16; 16:26; Isaiah 5:14. In other instances *nephesh* means "life." Where such is its meaning "my soul" would mean "my life," "thy soul," "thy life," etc. See 2 Samuel 1:9; Jeremiah 4:30; etc.

In the New Testament the word translated "soul" is the Greek *psuchē.* This is the word which in the Septuagint, the Greek translation of the Hebrew Old Testament, translates the Hebrew word *nephesh.* New Testament writers used *psuchē* as the equivalent of *nephesh,* and did not attach to *psuchē* the pagan Greek concept of the allegedly immortal part of man as opposed to his body or perishable part. *Psuchē* is rendered by the following words in our King James Version:

58 times, soul.

40 times, life. For example: Mark 3:4; 10:45; Luke 6:9; 9:56; John 13:37; Romans 11:3; Revelation 8:9; 12:11.

3 times, mind. Acts 14:2; Philippians 1:27; Hebrews 12:3.

1 time, heart. Ephesians 6:6.

1 time, heartily (literally, from the soul). Colossians 3:23.

Puschē is also used once in John 10:24 and in 2 Corinthians 12:15, in idiomatic phrases that are properly translated by the personal pronoun.

Do others besides man have the "breath of life"?

"And all flesh died that moved upon the earth, both of *fowl,* and of *cattle,* and of *beast,* and of *every creeping thing* that creepeth upon the earth, and every man: *all in whose nostrils was the breath of life."* Genesis 7:21, 22.

When man gives up this spirit, what becomes of it?

"Then shall the dust return to the earth as it was: and *the spirit shall return unto God who gave it."* Ecclesiastes 12:7.

NOTE.—The word translated "breath" is *ruach,* which is defined in Gesenius' Lexicon as *"Ruach:* (1) Spirit, breath. (*a*) Breath of the mouth. . . . Hence used of anything quickly perishing. . . . Often used of the vital spirit. . . . (*b*) Breath of the nostrils, snuffing, snorting. . . . Hence anger. . . . (*c*) Breath of air, air in motion, i.e., breeze. . . .

"(2) Psuche anima, breath, life, the vital principle, which shows itself in the breathing of the mouth and nostrils (see No. 1, *a, b*), whether of men or of beasts, Ecclesiastes 3:21; 8:8; 12:7; . . .

"(3) The rational mind or spirit. (*a*) As the seat of the senses, affections, and emotions of various kinds. . . . (*b*) As to the mode of thinking and acting. . . . (*c*) Of will and counsel. . . . More rarely (*d*) it is applied to the intellect. . . .

"(4) The Spirit of God."—TREGELLES' translation (1875 ed.).

The word *spirit* in the Old Testament is always from *ruach,* except twice (Job 26:4 and Proverbs 20:27 from *neshamah*). Ruach, besides being rendered 232 times as "spirit," is also translated:

90 times, wind. (Wind in the Old Testament is always a translation of *ruach.*)

28 times, breath. For example: Genesis 6:17; 7:15, 22; Job 12:10; Psalms 104:29; 146:4; Ecclesiastes 3:19.

8 times, mind. Genesis 26:35; Proverbs 29:11; Ezekiel 11:5; 20:32; Daniel 5:20; Habakkuk 1:11.

4 times, blast. Exodus 15:8; 2 Kings 19:7; Isaiah 25:4; 37:7.

Also translated one or more times by the following words: anger, air, tempest, vain.

At death the spirit goes back to the great Author of life. Having come from Him, it belongs to God, and man can have it eternally only as a gift from God, through Jesus Christ. (Romans 6:23.) When the spirit goes back to God, the dust, from which man's body was formed, goes back *as it was,* to the earth, and the individual no longer exists as a living, conscious, thinking being.

"Our personal identity is preserved in the resurrection, though not the same particles of matter or material substance as went into the grave. The wondrous works of God are a mystery to man. The spirit, the character of man, is returned to God, there to be preserved. In the resurrection every man will have his own character. God in His own time will call forth the dead, giving again the breath of life, and bidding the dry bones live. The same form will come forth, but it will be free from disease and every defect. It lives again bearing the same individuality of features, so that friend will recognize friend. There is no law of God in nature which shows that God gives back the same identical particles of matter which composed the body before death. God shall give the righteous dead a body that will please Him."
—ELLEN G. WHITE in *SDA Bible Commentary*, vol. 6, p. 1093.

FROM WRATH AND DEATH TO LIFE

Who only have hold of the life eternal?

"He that hath the Son hath life; and he that hath not the Son of God hath not life." 1 John 5:12.

NOTE.—The veriest sinner has this temporal life; but when he yields up this life, he has no prospect or promise of the life eternal. That can be received only through Christ.

Why was Adam driven from Eden and the tree of life?

"And now, lest he put forth his hand, and take also of the tree of life, and eat, and *live for ever*." Genesis 3:22.

What was done to keep man away from the tree of life?

"So he [the Lord God] drove out the man; and he placed at the east of the garden of Eden Cherubims, and a flaming sword which turned every way, to keep the way of the tree of life." Verse 24.

How are all men in the natural state regarded?

"We all . . . were by nature *the children of wrath*, even as others." Ephesians 2:3.

If the wrath of God *abides* on us, of what are we deprived?

"He that believeth not the Son *shall not see life;* but the wrath of God abideth on him." John 3:36.

Through whom can we be saved from wrath and given immortality?

"Much more then, being now justified by his blood, we shall be saved from wrath *through him.*" Romans 5:9. *"Our Saviour Jesus Christ, who hath abolished death, and hath brought life and immortality to light through the gospel."* 2 Timothy 1:10.

Who only possesses inherent immortality?

"The blessed and only Potentate, the King of kings, and Lord of lords; *who only hath immortality.*" 1 Timothy 6:15, 16.

Note.—God is the only being who possesses original life or immortality in Himself. All others must receive it from God. (See John 5:26; 6:27; 10:10, 27, 28; Romans 6:23; 1 John 5:11.)

To whom is eternal life promised?

"To them who by patient continuance in well doing *seek for glory and honour and immortality,* eternal life." Romans 2:7.

Note.—One does not need to seek for a thing which he already possesses. The fact that we are to seek for immortality is proof in itself that we do not now possess it.

When will the faithful be changed to immortality?

"We shall not all sleep, but *we shall all be changed,* in a moment, in the twinkling of an eye, *at the last trump:* for the trumpet shall sound, and the dead shall be raised incorruptible, and we shall be changed." 1 Corinthians 15:51, 52.

What is then to be swallowed up?

"So when this corruptible shall have put on incorruption, and this mortal shall have put on immortality, then shall be brought to pass the saying that is written, *Death is swallowed up in victory.*" Verse 54. (See verse 57.)

I count this thing to be grandly true:
    That a noble deed is a step toward God,
    Lifting the soul from the common clod
To a purer air and a broader view.

We rise by the things that are under our feet;
    By what we have mastered of good and gain;
    By the pride deposed and the passion slain,
And the vanquished ills that we hourly meet.

—J. G. Holland

Life Only in Christ

What is the wages of sin?

"The wages of sin is *death*." Romans 6:23.

Through whom only is there salvation from sin?

"Neither is there salvation in any other: for there is none other name under heaven given among men, whereby we must be saved." Acts 4:12.

Why did God send His only-begotten Son to this world?

"That whosoever believeth in him should not *perish*, but have *everlasting life*." John 3:16.

What does Christ declare Himself to be?

"I am the way, the truth, and *the life*." John 14:6.

What does He say He gives to those who follow Him?

"My sheep hear my voice, and I know them, and they follow me: and *I give unto them eternal life;* and they shall never perish, neither shall any man pluck them out of my hand." John 10: 27, 28.

Conditions of Receiving Life

Upon what is the possession of this life conditioned?

"Except ye *eat the flesh of the Son of man, and drink his blood,* ye have no life in you." John 6:53.

In whom is the life eternal?

"And this is the record, that God hath given to us eternal life, *and this life is in his Son*." 1 John 5:11.

Who only have this life?

"He that hath the Son hath life; and he that hath not the Son of God hath not life." Verse 12. *"He that heareth my word, and believeth on him that sent me, hath everlasting life,* and shall not come into condemnation; but is passed from death unto life." John 5:24.

The Intermediate State

What Death Is Like

By what figure does the Bible represent death?

"But I would not have you to be ignorant, brethren, concerning them which are *asleep,* that ye sorrow not, even as others which have no hope." 1 Thessalonians 4:13. (See also 1 Corinthians 15:18, 20; John 11:11-14.)

Note.—In sound sleep one is wholly lost to consciousness; time goes by unmeasured; and mental activity is suspended for the time being.

Where does Daniel represent the dead as sleeping?

"And many of them that *sleep in the dust of the earth* shall awake." Daniel 12:2. (See also Ecclesiastes 3:20; 9:10.)

Thoughts and Feelings of the Dead

What does one in this condition know about his family?

"His sons come to honour, and *he knoweth it not;* and they are brought low, but *he perceiveth it not of them."* Job 14:21.

What becomes of man's thoughts at death?

"His breath goeth forth, he returneth to his earth; *in that very day his thoughts perish."* Psalm 146:4.

Do the dead know *anything?*

"For the living know that they shall die: *but the dead know not any thing."* Ecclesiastes 9:5.

Do they take any part in earthly things?

"Also their *love,* and their *hatred,* and their *envy,* is now perished; neither have they any more a portion for ever in any thing that is done under the sun." Verse 6.

Note.—If one remained conscious after death, he would know of the promotion or dishonor of his sons; but in death one loses all the attributes of mind—love, hatred, envy, etc. Thus it is plain that his thoughts have perished, and that he can have nothing more to do with the things of this world. But if, as taught by some, man's powers of thought continue after death, he *lives;* and if he lives, he must be *somewhere.* Where is he? Is he in heaven, or in hell? If he goes to either place at death, what then is the need of a future judgment, or of a resurrection, or of the second coming of Christ? If men go to their reward at death, before the judgment takes place, then their *rewards* precede their *awards.*

How much does one know of God when dead?

"For in death *there is no remembrance of thee."* Psalm 6:5.

NOTE.—As already seen, the Bible everywhere represents the dead as *asleep,* with not even a remembrance of God. If they were in heaven or hell, would Jesus have said, "Our friend Lazarus *sleepeth"*? John 11:11. If so, calling him to life was really robbing him of the bliss of heaven that rightly belonged to him. The parable of the rich man and Lazarus (Luke 16) teaches not consciousness in death but that riches will avail nothing in the judgment and that poverty will not keep one out of heaven.

WHERE ARE THE DEAD?

Are not the righteous dead in heaven praising God?

"For *David is not ascended into the heavens."* Acts 2:34. *"The dead praise not the Lord,* neither any that go down into silence." Psalm 115:17.

Where did Job say he would await his final change?

"If a man die, shall he live again? all the days of my appointed time will I wait, *till my change come."* Job 14:14. *"If I wait, the grave is mine house:* I have made my bed in the darkness." Job 17:13.

NOTE.—The Hebrew for "grave" in this verse is *she'ol,* meaning among other things a dark, hollow, subterranean place, used simply in reference to the abode of the dead in general, without distinguishing between the good and the bad. (Young's *Analytical Concordance.*)

The same word is also translated "pit" 3 times (Numbers 16:30, 33; Job 17:16), and "hell" 31 times (every occurrence of the word "hell" in the King James Version of the Old Testament). The translation of *she'ol* as "grave" 31 times bears witness to the unsuitability of the present English word *hell* to the idea of *she'ol,* especially in reference to Jacob (Genesis 37:35; 42:38), Job (Job 14:13), the psalmist (Psalm 30:3), and even Christ (Psalm 16:10; cf. Acts 2:27, 31). The American Revised Version avoids choosing between "hell" and "grave" by retaining *she'ol* as an untranslated place name, just as it does the corresponding Greek word *hadēs* in the New Testament (see page 515). It should be remembered that "hell" in the Old Testament always means *she'ol*, the figurative abode of the dead, a place of darkness and silence, *not* a place of fiery torment.

When the Dead Rise Again

What must take place before the dead can praise God?

"Thy dead men shall live, together with my dead body shall they arise. *Awake and sing, ye that dwell in dust:* for . . . the earth shall cast out the dead." Isaiah 26:19.

When did the psalmist say he would be satisfied?

"As for me, I will behold thy face in righteousness: I shall be satisfied, *when I awake, with thy likeness.*" Psalm 17:15.

Were there to be no resurrection of the dead, what would be the condition of those fallen asleep in Christ?

"For if the dead rise not, then is not Christ raised. . . . *Then they also which are fallen asleep in Christ are perished.*" 1 Corinthians 15:16-18.

When is the resurrection of the righteous to take place?

"For *the Lord himself shall descend from heaven* with a shout, with the voice of the archangel, and with the trump of God: *and the dead in Christ shall rise first.*" 1 Thessalonians 4:16.

Note.—If, as stated in Ecclesiastes 9:5, the dead know not anything, then they have no knowledge of the lapse of time; it will seem to them when they awake that absolutely no time has elapsed. "Six thousand years in the grave to a dead man is no more than a wink of the eye to the living."

It ought also to be a comforting thought to those whose lives have been filled with anxiety and grief for deceased loved ones who persisted in sin, to know that they are not now suffering in torments, but, with all the rest of the dead, are quietly sleeping in their graves.

Again, it would mar the felicity of one's employment in heaven could he look upon earth and see his friends and relatives suffering from persecution, want, cold, or hunger, or sorrowing for the dead. God's way is best—that all sentient life, animation, activity, thought, and consciousness should cease at death, and that all should wait till the resurrection for their eternal reward. (See Hebrews 11:39, 40.)

The Two Resurrections

SIN, DEATH, AND THE GRAVE

WHAT comes to all men as the result of the Fall?

"In Adam *all die.*" 1 Corinthians 15:22. (See also Romans 5:12.)

In what condition is man while in death?

"Whatsoever thy hand findeth to do, do it with thy might; for *there is no work, nor device, nor knowledge, nor wisdom, in the grave, whither thou goest.*" Ecclesiastes 9:10.

NOTE.—That is, man, when dead, has no use of the powers of mind or body. He cannot, therefore, while in the grave, praise God, or even think of Him (Psalm 6:5); for in the day he dies his thoughts perish. Psalm 146:2-4. (See preceding reading.)

RANSOMED FROM THE GRAVE

What has been promised in order that man may be redeemed from this condition?

"*I will ransom them from the power of the grave; I will redeem them from death:* O death, I will be thy plagues; O grave, I will be thy destruction." Hosea 13:14.

Through whom will come this redemption from the grave?

"For since by man came death, by man came also the resurrection of the dead. For as in Adam all die, *even so in Christ shall all be made alive.*" 1 Corinthians 15:21, 22.

What would have been the result to the dead had not Christ procured their release from the grave?

"For if the dead rise not, then is not Christ raised: and if Christ be not raised, your faith is vain; ye are yet in your sins. Then *they also which are fallen asleep in Christ are perished.*" Verses 16-18.

Why did God give His only-begotten Son to the world?

"For God so loved the world, that he gave his only begotten

THE RESURRECTION OF THE JUST

"Marvel not at this: for the hour is coming, in the which all that are in the graves shall hear his voice, and shall come forth." John 5:28.

THE TWO RESURRECTIONS

Son, *that whosoever believeth in him should not perish,* but have everlasting life." John 3:16.

What did the Sadducees in Christ's time deny?

"Then came to him certain of the Sadducees, *which deny that there is any resurrection."* Luke 20:27.

How did Christ, from the Old Testament Scriptures, prove the resurrection?

"Now that the dead are raised, even Moses shewed at the bush, when he calleth the Lord the God of Abraham, and the God of Isaac, and the God of Jacob. For he is not a God of the dead, but of the living: for all live unto him." Verses 37, 38.

NOTE.—That is, in view of the resurrection—of the fact that there is to be a resurrection—all live unto God. In His purpose, all are alive.

Under what illustration from nature are the resurrection and the final salvation of the righteous taught?

"That which thou sowest is not quickened, except it die." 1 Corinthians 15:36. "Verily, verily, I say unto you, *Except a corn of wheat fall into the ground and die,* it abideth alone: but if it die, it bringeth forth much fruit." John 12:24.

NOTE.—The seed dies to spring forth into new life. In this we are taught the lesson of the resurrection. All who love God will spring forth to life, and live again through endless ages in the earth made new.

Whose voice raises the dead?

"Marvel not at this: for the hour is coming, in the which all that are *in the graves* shall hear *his voice,* and shall come forth." John 5:28, 29.

TWO DISTINCT RESURRECTIONS

How many distinct classes will have a resurrection?

"There shall be a resurrection of the dead, both of the *just* and *unjust."* Acts 24:15.

By what terms did Christ refer to the two resurrections?

"All that are in the graves shall hear his voice, and shall come forth; they that have done good, unto *the resurrection of life;*

and they that have done evil, unto *the resurrection of damnation.*" John 5:28, 29.

When will the resurrection of the just occur?

"For *the Lord himself shall descend from heaven with a shout,* with the voice of the archangel, and with the trump of God: *and the dead in Christ shall rise first."* 1 Thessalonians 4:16. (See also 1 Corinthians 15:23.)

When are the righteous to be recompensed?

"For thou shalt be recompensed *at the resurrection of the just."* Luke 14:14.

In what condition did the psalmist expect to rise?

"As for me, I will behold thy face in righteousness: I shall be satisfied, *when I awake, with thy likeness."* Psalm 17:15.

What great contrast will be seen between the present body and the one to be put on in the resurrection?

"So also is the resurrection of the dead. It is sown in *corruption;* it is raised in *incorruption:* it is sown in *dishonour;* it is raised in *glory:* it is sown in weakness; it is raised in *power:* it is sown a *natural body;* it is raised a *spiritual body."* 1 Corinthians 15:42-44.

After whose body will these resurrected ones be fashioned?

"We look for the Saviour, the Lord Jesus Christ: who shall change our vile body, that it may be fashioned *like unto his glorious body."* Philippians 3:20, 21.

In what words is the ultimate triumph over death and the grave expressed?

"O death, where is thy sting? O grave, where is thy victory?" 1 Corinthians 15:55.

How long will the righteous live?

"Neither can they die any more: for they are equal unto the angels; and are the children of God, being the children of the resurrection." Luke 20:36.

How long do the other class wait after the first resurrection before they are raised?

"And they [the righteous] lived and reigned with Christ a thousand years. *But the rest of the dead lived not again until the thousand years were finished.*" Revelation 20:4, 5.

What is to be their fate?

"And fire came down from God out of heaven, and devoured them." Verse 9.

Who are to share this fate?

"But the *fearful,* and *unbelieving,* and the *abominable,* and *murderers,* and *whoremongers,* and *sorcerers,* and *idolaters,* and *all liars,* shall have their part in the lake which burneth with fire and brimstone: which is the second death." Revelation 21:8.

What is the last enemy to be destroyed?

"The last enemy that shall be destroyed is *death.*" 1 Corinthians 15:26. (See Revelation 20:13, 14.)

How will the righteous ever afterward appear?

"Then shall the righteous *shine forth as the sun* in the kingdom of their Father. Who hath ears to hear, let him hear." Matthew 13:43.

"Like wand'ring sheep o'er mountains cold,
  Since all have gone astray;
To life and peace within the fold,
  How may I find the way?

"To Christ the Way, the Truth, the Life,
  I come, no more to roam;
He'll guide me to my Father's house,
  To my eternal home."

Fate of the Transgressor

Cause of the Sinner's Destruction

What question does the apostle Peter ask regarding the wicked?

"What shall the end be of them that obey not the gospel of God?" 1 Peter 4:17.

What does the Bible say is the wages of sin? What is to be the fate of one who persists in sin?

"For the wages of sin is *death*." Romans 6:23. "The soul that sinneth, it shall *die*." Ezekiel 18:4.

Completeness of the Destruction

What will be the character of this death?

"Who shall be punished with *everlasting destruction*." 2 Thessalonians 1:9.

What will befall those who do not repent?

"Except ye repent, ye shall all likewise *perish*." Luke 13:3. "But these, as natural brute beasts, made to be taken and destroyed, speak evil of the things that they understand not; and *shall utterly perish in their own corruption*." 2 Peter 2:12.

How does John the Baptist describe the destruction of the wicked?

"He will . . . gather his wheat into the garner; but *he will burn up the chaff with unquenchable fire*." Matthew 3:11, 12.

For whom was this fire originally prepared?

"Then shall he say also unto them on the left hand, Depart from me, ye cursed, into everlasting fire, *prepared for the devil and his angels*." Matthew 25:41.

NOTE.—This fire is called "everlasting" (Greek, *aionion,* "age lasting") because of the character of the *work* it does; just as it is called "unquenchable" (Greek, *asbestos,* "unquenchable," "unquenched") because it cannot be *put* out, and not because it will not *go* out when it has done its work. "Eternal fire" reduced Sodom and Gomorrah to ashes. (Jude 9; 2 Peter 2:6.)

FATE OF THE TRANSGRESSOR

Will any part of the wicked be left?

"For, behold, the day cometh, that shall burn as an oven; and all the proud, yea, and *all* that do wickedly, shall be stubble: and the day that cometh shall *burn them up,* saith the Lord of hosts, that *it shall leave them neither root nor branch.*" Malachi 4:1.

How completely will man be destroyed in hell?

"Fear him which is able to *destroy both soul and body in hell.*" Matthew 10:28.

Note.—This scripture proves that the soul is neither immortal nor indestructible.

The everlasting punishment—"destruction"—of the wicked is this destruction of soul and body in hell (Greek, *Geenna* [Gehenna]).

"Hell" in the New Testament is from three Greek words:

Hadēs, 10 times. Matthew 11:23; 16:18; Luke 10:15; 16:23; Acts 2:27, 31; Revelation 1:18; 6:8; 20:13, 14. (*Hadēs* is also translated "grave" once, 1 Corinthians 15:55.)

Geenna (Gehenna), 12 times. Matthew 5:22, 29, 30; 10:28; 18:9; 23:15, 33; Mark 9:43, 45, 47; Luke 12:5; James 3:6.

Tartaroō, 1 time (the only occurrence in the Bible). 2 Peter 2:4.

Hadēs (the lower world, place of the dead, the grave) is the equivalent of *she'ol* (see pages 507, 508). *Tartaroō,* describing the fall of Satan's rebel angels, is a verb, meaning "to cast down to Tartarus." This is a striking figure of speech, alluding to the Tartarus of Greek mythology, an abyss deeper than Hades, the prison of the Titans, who fought against the gods.

Gehenna, the only other word for hell, is the Valley of Hinnom, used symbolically of the fires of the last great day of judgment. This is the word that is used in Matthew 10:28 to describe the place where the wicked will be destroyed, body and soul.

Where, When, and How

When will the wicked be punished?

"But the heavens and the earth, which are now, by the same word are kept in store, *reserved unto fire against the day of judgment and perdition of ungodly men.*" 2 Peter 3:7.

Note.—The present heavens and earth and sinners await the fires of the last day. The Greek for "perdition" is *apoleia,* "loss," "destruction."

What will be the result of the fires of the last day?

"Looking for and hasting unto the coming of the day of God, wherein *the heavens being on fire shall be dissolved, and the elements shall melt with fervent heat.*" "*The earth also and the works that are therein shall be burned up.*" Verses 12, 10.

How does Christ say sin and sinners will be eliminated?

"His angels . . . *shall gather out of his kingdom all things that offend, and them which do iniquity; and shall cast them into a furnace of fire.*" Matthew 13:41, 42.

When are the wicked dead to be raised to receive this final punishment?

"But the rest of the dead lived not again *until the thousand years were finished.*" Revelation 20:5.

Whence will come the fire that will destroy them?

"And they went up on the breadth of the earth, and compassed the camp of the saints about, and the beloved city: *and fire came down from God out of heaven, and devoured them.*" Verse 9.

NOTE.—This may be called God's "strange act" and His "strange work"—the work of destruction. (Isaiah 28:21.) But by this means God will once and forever cleanse the universe of sin and all its sad results. Death itself will then be at an end—cast into the lake of fire. (Revelation 20:14.)

By what figure does Malachi describe the destruction of the wicked?

"And ye shall tread down the wicked; for *they shall be ashes under the soles of your feet.*" Malachi 4:3.

NOTE.—The wicked are to be utterly destroyed. Through sin they have forfeited the right to life and an immortal existence, and chosen the way of death and destruction. By their choice they have proved themselves worthless, like chaff, briers, thorns, etc. They will themselves have lost their opportunity to obtain eternal life, by the way in which they used their probationary time. Their destruction will, in fact, be an act of love and mercy on the part of God; for to perpetuate their lives would only be to perpetuate sin, sorrow, suffering, and misery. Terrible, therefore, as this judgment will be, there will, in consequence of it, be nothing of value lost—nothing lost worth saving. The experiment of sin will be over, and God's original plan of peopling the earth with a race of holy, happy beings will be carried out. (2 Peter 3:13.)

FATE OF THE TRANSGRESSOR

What is this final destruction of the wicked called?

"This is *the second death.*" Revelation 20:14.

After the burning day, what will appear?

"We, according to his promise, look for *new heavens and a new earth,* wherein dwelleth righteousness." 2 Peter 3:13.

How will the righteous be recompensed in the earth?

"Blessed are the meek: for *they shall inherit the earth.*" Matthew 5:5. "Then shall the righteous shine forth as the sun *in the kingdom of their Father.*" Matthew 13:43.

NOTE.—Satan and the wicked now have this world as their "place." In due time Christ will have it. He will cleanse it from sin and sinners, and restore it, that He may give it to the saints of the Most High for an everlasting possession. (See Daniel 7:18, 22, 27.)

THE STATUE OF THE GREEK SLAVE GIRL

A beautiful statue once stood in the market place of an Italian city. It was the statue of a Greek slave girl. It represented the slave as tidy and well dressed. A ragged, uncombed little street child, coming across the statue in her play one day, stopped and gazed at it in admiration. She was captivated by it. She gazed long and lovingly. Moved by a sudden impulse, she went home and washed her face and combed her hair. Another day she stopped again before the statue and admired it, and got a new idea. Next day her tattered clothes were washed and mended. Each time she looked at the statue she found something in its beauties to admire and copy, until she was a transformed child.

The Ministration of Good Angels

GOD'S FAMILY

Of what family does Paul speak in Ephesians?

"For this cause I bow my knees unto the Father of our Lord Jesus Christ, of whom *the whole family in heaven and earth* is named." Ephesians 3:14, 15.

By what name are the members of this family called?

"Now there was a day when *the sons of God* came to present themselves before the Lord." Job 1:6. "Behold, what manner of love the Father hath bestowed upon us, that we should be called *the sons of God.*" 1 John 3:1.

By what name do we know the family in heaven?

"And I beheld, and I heard the voice of *many angels* round about the throne . . . : and the number of them was *ten thousand times ten thousand, and thousands of thousands.*" Revelation 5:11.

Did angels exist before the death of any of the human family?

"So he drove out the man; and he placed at the east of the garden of Eden *Cherubims.*" Genesis 3:24.

NOTE.—*"The morning stars* sang together, and all *the sons of God* shouted for joy" at the foundation of the earth. Job 38:6, 7.

What does Paul say of their number?

"But ye are come unto mount Sion, and unto the city of the living God, the heavenly Jerusalem, and to *an innumerable company of angels.*" Hebrews 12:22. (See also Daniel 7:10.)

Are angels of a higher order of beings than man?

"Thou hast made him *a little lower than the angels.*" Psalm 8:5.

THE MINISTRATION OF GOOD ANGELS

Is Christ ever called an angel?

"Behold, I send *an Angel* before thee, to keep thee in the way, and to bring thee into the place which I have prepared." Exodus 23:20. (See verse 23; Acts 7:38.) *"The angel of his presence* saved them." Isaiah 63:9. "Michael *the archangel."* Jude 9. (See also Daniel 12:1; 1 Thessalonians 4:16.)

NOTE.—Angel means *messenger.* In Malachi 3:1, Christ is called "the *messenger* of the covenant."

To whose authority are the angels subject?

"Jesus Christ: who is gone into heaven, and is on the right hand of God; *angels and authorities and powers being made subject unto him."* 1 Peter 3:21, 22.

In what form did Gabriel appear to Daniel?

"His body also was like the *beryl,* and his face as the appearance of *lightning,* and his eyes as *lamps of fire,* and his arms and his feet like in colour to *polished brass,* and the voice of his words *like the voice of a multitude."* Daniel 10:6.

NOTE.—The form in which other celestial beings revealed themselves in vision is similar. See, for example, the description of God, the "Ancient of days," in Daniel 7:9; and of Christ, "the Son of man," in Revelation 1:13-15. The angel that rolled away the stone from Christ's sepulcher is thus described: "His countenance was *like lightning,* and his raiment *white as snow."* Matthew 28:3.

Why does Paul encourage us to entertain strangers?

"Be not forgetful to entertain strangers: *for thereby some have entertained angels unawares."* Hebrews 13:2.

CHARACTER, POWER, AND WORK OF ANGELS

What is said of the strength and character of the angels?

"His angels, *that excel in strength, that do his commandments,* hearkening unto the voice of his word." Psalm 103:20.

In what work are angels engaged?

"Are they not all *ministering spirits,* sent forth to minister for them who shall be heirs of salvation?" Hebrews 1:14.

In his dream at Bethel, what did Jacob see?

"And he dreamed, and behold *a ladder* set up on the earth,

THE GUARDIAN ANGEL "He shall give his angels charge over thee." Psalm 91:

and the top of it reached to heaven: *and behold the angels of God ascending and descending on it."* Genesis 28:12.

What scripture indicates that each child of God has an accompanying angel?

"Take heed that ye despise not one of these little ones; for I say unto you, That in heaven *their angels* do always behold the face of my Father which is in heaven." Matthew 18:10.

NOTE.—Another has said: "Christians who live in the light of God's countenance are always accompanied by unseen angels, and these holy beings leave behind them a blessing in our homes."

How is their watchcare over God's people expressed?

"The angel of the Lord *encampeth round about them that fear him, and delivereth them."* Psalm 34:7.

When surrounded by the Syrians, what did Elisha do?

"And he answered, *Fear not: for they that be with us are more than they that be with them.* And Elisha prayed, and said, Lord, I pray thee, *open his eyes, that he may see.* And the Lord opened the eyes of the young man; *and he saw: and, behold, the mountain was full of horses and chariots of fire round about Elisha."* 2 Kings 6:16, 17.

What does the psalmist say of the chariots of God?

"The chariots of God are twenty thousand, even *thousands of angels."* Psalm 68:17.

By what means were the apostles delivered from prison?

"The angel of the Lord by night *opened the prison doors,* and brought them forth." Acts 5:19.

How was Peter delivered later?

"The angel of the Lord came upon him, and a light shined in the prison: and he smote Peter on the side, and raised him up, saying, Arise up quickly. And his chains fell off from his hands. . . . And he saith unto him, Cast thy garment about thee, and follow me. . . . They came unto the iron gate that leadeth unto the city; which opened to them of his own accord: and they went out, and passed on through one street; and forthwith the angel departed from him." Acts 12:7-10.

NOTE.—"What we call physical law is no obstruction to angelic ministrations. Bolts and bars and prison gates disappear at their volition, and dungeons like palaces shine in their presence. No place can be so dismal, no cavern so deep and dark, no Inquisition cell so hidden and fetid, no fortress so strongly guarded, that they cannot find quick and easy access, if a child of God is there."—E. A. STOCKMAN, *Footprints of Angels in Fields of Revelation*, pp. 74, 75.

How was Elijah strengthened for a forty days' journey?

"*The angel of the Lord came again the second time, and touched him, and said, Arise and eat.* . . . He arose, and did eat and drink, and went in the strength of that meat forty days and forty nights unto Horeb the mount of God." 1 Kings 19:7, 8.

After His forty days' temptation, how was Christ strengthened?

"Behold, *angels came and ministered unto him.*" Matthew 4:11.

How was Christ strengthened in Gethsemane?

"And *there appeared an angel unto him from heaven, strengthening him.*" Luke 22:43.

Are the angels interested in the plan of salvation?

"Which things *the angels desire to look into.*" 1 Peter 1:12. "Likewise, I say unto you, *there is joy in the presence of the angels of God over one sinner that repenteth.*" Luke 15:10.

For what must men give account in the judgment?

"But I say unto you, That *every idle word* that men shall speak, they shall give account thereof in the day of judgment." Matthew 12:36. (See also Ecclesiastes 12:13, 14.)

Out of what will men be judged before God's throne?

"And I saw the dead, small and great, stand before God; and the books were opened: and another book was opened, which is the book of life: and the dead were judged *out of those things which were written in the books,* according to their works." Revelation 20:12.

In the judgment how many angels minister before God?

"*Thousand thousands ministered unto him, and ten thousand times ten thousand stood before him:* the judgment was set, and the books were opened." Daniel 7:10.

THE MINISTRATION OF GOOD ANGELS

What does Christ promise overcomers?

"He that overcometh, ... I will not blot out his name out of the book of life, but *I will confess his name before my Father, and before his angels.*" Revelation 3:5.

What protection has God promised His people in time of trouble?

"There shall no evil befall thee, neither shall any plague come nigh thy dwelling. For *he shall give his angels charge over thee, to keep thee in all thy ways. They shall bear thee up in their hands, lest thou dash thy foot against a stone.*" Psalm 91:10-12.

Who will come with Christ, and what will they do?

"For the Son of man shall come in the glory of his Father *with his angels.*" "And *they shall gather together his elect* from the four winds, from one end of heaven to the other." Matthew 16:27; 24:31.

Where will all the saints then go?

"Then we which are alive and remain shall be caught up together with them in the clouds, to meet the Lord in the air: and *so shall we ever be with the Lord.*" 1 Thessalonians 4:17.

Down at the cross where my Saviour died,
Down where for cleansing from sin I cried,
There to my heart was the blood applied,
  Glory to His name.
—E. A. HOFFMAN

The Dark Ministry of Evil Angels

THIS WORLD A PLACE OF CONFLICT

AGAINST whom do we wrestle?

"For we wrestle not against flesh and blood, but *against principalities, against powers, against the rulers of the darkness of this world, against spiritual wickedness* ["the spiritual hosts of wickedness," R.S.V.] in high places." Ephesians 6:12.

To what place were the angels that sinned cast? For what purpose?

"For if God spared not the angels that sinned, but *cast them down to hell*, and delivered them into *chains of darkness*, to be reserved unto judgment." 2 Peter 2:4.

What is Satan himself called?

"The *god of this world*." 2 Corinthians 4:4. "The *prince of this world*." John 14:30. "The *prince of the power of the air*." Ephesians 2:2.

TEMPTATION AND DECEPTION

What is the chief occupation of Satan and his angels? To what is Satan compared?

"And he [Jesus] was there in the wilderness forty days, *tempted of Satan*." Mark 1:13. "Be sober, be vigilant; because your adversary the devil, as a roaring lion, walketh about, *seeking whom he may devour*." 1 Peter 5:8. (See Revelation 12:9, 12; 16:14.)

NOTE.—"Angels of God will preserve His people while they walk in the path of duty, but there is no assurance of such protection for those who deliberately venture upon Satan's ground. An agent of the great deceiver will say and do anything to gain his object. It matters little whether he calls himself a spiritualist, an 'electric physician,' or a 'magnetic healer.' By specious pretenses he wins the confidence of the unwary. He pretends to read the life history and to understand

THE DARK MINISTRY OF EVIL ANGELS

all the difficulties and afflictions of those who resort to him. Disguising himself as an angel of light, while the blackness of the pit is in his heart, he manifests great interest in women who seek his counsel. He tells them that all their troubles are due to an unhappy marriage. This may be too true, but such a counselor does not better their condition. He tells them that they need love and sympathy. Pretending great interest in their welfare, he casts a spell over his unsuspecting victims, charming them as the serpent charms the trembling bird. Soon they are completely in his power; sin, disgrace, and ruin are the terrible sequel.

"These workers of iniquity are not few. Their path is marked by desolated homes, blasted reputations, and broken hearts. But of all this the world knows little; still they go on making fresh victims, and Satan exults in the ruin he has wrought.

"The visible and the invisible world are in close contact. Could the veil be lifted, we would see evil angels pressing their darkness around us and working with all their power to deceive and destroy. Wicked men are surrounded, influenced, and aided by evil spirits. The man of faith and prayer has yielded his soul to divine guidance, and angels of God bring to him light and strength from heaven."—ELLEN G. WHITE, *Testimonies,* vol. 5, pp. 198, 199.

What are we admonished not to do?

"Be ye angry, and sin not: let not the sun go down upon your wrath: *neither give place to the devil.*" Ephesians 4:26, 27.

NOTE.—Those who give vent to anger or retain old grudges, who parley with temptation or tamper with vice, who indulge in intemperance, pride, foolishness, or levity, or give way to any other weakness, give place to the devil; that is, they give the devil an opportunity to work through them—give him an advantage over them. We should therefore close every avenue to Satan and his angels. We should suppress anger, be sober and watchful, and nip in the bud every prompting to sin.

THE LAST DAYS OF DEVILS

As we near the closing scenes of human probation, why may we expect an increase in demoniacal manifestations?

"Woe to the inhabiters of the earth and of the sea! *for the devil is come down unto you, having great wrath, because he knoweth that he hath but a short time.*" Revelation 12:12.

NOTE.—As enemies of God, Satan and his angels pervert the truth and disseminate error as far as possible. Far better, also, than the inhabitants of the world, do they know that the end of all things is fast approaching, and that their time to work is short.

Concerning what have we been definitely informed?

"Now the Spirit speaketh expressly, that *in the latter times some shall depart from the faith, giving heed to seducing spirits, and doctrines of devils.*" 1 Timothy 4:1.

NOTE.—Realizing that the Bible condemns spiritualism, Sir William F. Barrett says of mediumship:

"These practices were condemned in unmeasured terms by the Hebrew prophets, and this irrespective of any question as to whether the phenomena were genuine or merely the product of trickery and superstition. . . .

"The Apostle [Paul] saw clearly, as every Christian sees, that the foundation of religious life, which consisted of *faith* in a risen Lord, is seriously imperiled when the seen is substituted for the unseen, the phantasms of the Spiritualistic seance for the realities of the Kingdom of Heaven, which cometh not with observation.

"The same peril exists to-day, and always will exist. This, every thoughtful and reverent mind must admit, and it is a distinct warning against making a religion of Spiritualism."—*On the Threshold of the Unseen* (1927 ed.), pp. 30-34. Copyright, 1918. New York: E. P. Dutton & Co., Inc.

What will be the final doom of Satan, his angels, and all the wicked?

"Then shall he say also unto them on the left hand, Depart from me, ye cursed, into everlasting fire, *prepared for the devil and his angels.*" Matthew 25:41. "And the day that cometh shall *burn them up,* saith the Lord of hosts, that it shall leave them neither *root* nor *branch.*" Malachi 4:1. (See Revelation 20:9.)

Spiritualism

WHAT is spiritualism defined to be?

"A belief that departed spirits hold intercourse with mortals by means of physical phenomena, as by rapping, or during abnormal mental states, as in trances, or the like, commonly manifested through a medium; spiritism."—WEBSTER.

Spiritism: "The theory that mediumistic phenomena are caused by spirits of the dead."—WEBSTER.

NOTE.—The word *spiritualism* (or *spiritism*) is not found in the Bible, but there is general accord that *spiritualism* is based upon the belief in the natural immortality of man, and that the spirit which leaves the fleshly body at death can and does return to communicate with the living through "the medium" and "the control."

SPIRITISM IN BIBLE TIMES

Did this belief exist in ancient times?

"Regard not them that have *familiar spirits,* neither seek after *wizards,* to be defiled by them: I am the Lord your God." Leviticus 19:31. (See also 1 Chronicles 10:13, 14.)

NOTE.—"Rudyard Kipling, with his robust common sense, has warned intruders who seek to establish a traffic with discarnate beings that they are entering on a dangerous path.

> "'Oh the road to En-dor is the oldest road
> And the craziest road of all.
> Straight it runs to the Witch's abode,
> As it did in the days of Saul.
> And nothing has changed of the sorrow in store
> For such as go down on the road to En-dor!'

"That old road has never been more crowded than it is to-day."— JANE T. STODDARD, *The Case Against Spiritualism* (Hodder and Stoughton, 1919 ed.), Preface. (The extract from the poem "En-dor" from *The Years Between,* by Rudyard Kipling is used by permission of Mrs. George Bambridge, owner of the copyright.)

How does God regard sorcerers?

"And I will come near to you to judgment; and *I will be a swift witness against the sorcerers.*" Malachi 3:5.

Note.—"Modern Spiritualism has its roots in necromancy, a practice hated in all ages by sober and reverent minds. It was only the worst type of sorcerer, according to Mr. Waite, who attempted to communicate with the spirits of departed men and women."—*Ibid.*, p. 31.

"Sir Arthur Conan Doyle, in 'The New Revelation,' admits that the opponents of spiritualism are guided in part by that strange instinct which warns men and women to keep off forbidden ground. The man who would violate a grave is naturally regarded with loathing."—*Ibid.*, p. 34.

What does He say of the teachings of enchanters and sorcerers?

"Therefore hearken not ye to . . . your enchanters, nor to your sorcerers, . . . for *they prophesy a lie unto you,* to remove you far from your land." Jeremiah 27:9, 10.

Before their entrance into Canaan, what instruction did Moses give Israel concerning these things?

"There shall not be found among you any one that maketh his son or his daughter to pass through the fire, or that useth divination, or an observer of times, or an enchanter, or a witch, or a charmer, or a consulter with familiar spirits, or a wizard, or a necromancer. For all that do these things are an abomination unto the Lord: and because of these abominations the Lord thy God doth drive them out from before thee. Thou shalt be perfect with the Lord thy God." Deuteronomy 18:10-13.

Note.—Whoever consults or has to do with mediums or any who profess to receive instruction or communications from the spirits of the dead, disregards this plain instruction, and places himself upon the enemy's ground. Ever since Satan told that first lie in Eden, when he denied that *death* would be the result of *sin,* in the very face of death itself, he, working upon man's natural dread of death and upon his distress at the thought of being separated from loved ones, has been endeavoring to persuade men to believe that the dead are not dead, and that men do not die. Idolatry, heathenism, spiritualism, occultism, and the whole brood of false isms of this kind, it will be noticed, deal very largely with *death*. This, of itself, indicates their origin, and should be a warning to all to let them alone—to have nothing whatever to do with them. They are from beneath, and not from above. However promising or pleasing they may be at first, they are downward and destructive in their tendency, and ultimately lead away from God, into unbelief of His word and into sin.

"Warning—It may be well to give a word of warning to those who find that they possess any unusual power in the psychic direction, and to counsel regulated moderation in its use. Every power can be abused, and even the simple faculty of automatic writing can with the best intentions be misapplied. Self-control is more important than any other form of control, and whoever possesses the power of receiving communications in any form should see to it that he remains master of the situation. To give up your own judgment and depend solely on adventitious aid is a grave blunder, and may in the long run have disastrous consequences. Moderation and common sense are required in those who try to utilise powers which neither they nor any fully understand, and a dominating occupation in mundane affairs is a wholesome safeguard."—Sir Oliver Lodge, *Raymond or Life and Death* (Hodder and Stoughton, 1916 ed.), p. 225. Used by permission of the executors of Sir Oliver Lodge's estate.

"It may be asked, do I recommend all bereaved persons to devote the time and attentions which I have done to getting communications and recording them? *Most certainly I do not.*"—*Ibid.*, p. 342.

Under the theocracy of Israel, what was the law concerning witches and those who had familiar spirits?

"Thou shalt not suffer a witch to live." Exodus 22:18. "A man also or woman that hath a familiar spirit, or that is a wizard, shall surely be put to death." Leviticus 20:27.

With what is witchcraft classed by Paul, and what does he say to those who are guilty of such things?

"Idolatry, witchcraft, hatred, variance, emulations, wrath, strife, seditions, heresies, . . . I have also told you in time past, that they which do such things shall not inherit the kingdom of God." Galatians 5:20-23.

What should one do if asked to inquire of a familiar spirit?

"And when they shall say unto you, Seek unto them that have familiar spirits, and unto wizards that peep, and that mutter: *should not a people seek unto their God?* for the *living* to the *dead?*" Isaiah 8:19.

Note.—Giving the sense of this passage, Dr. Adam Clarke says: "Should not a nation seek unto its God? Why should you seek unto the dead concerning the living?" But this is exactly what spiritualism teaches men to do—to seek unto the *dead* concerning the *living*.

Should we allow ourselves to be influenced by signs or

wonders performed by those who would try to lead us away from God and His law?

"If there arise among you a prophet, or a dreamer of dreams, and giveth thee a sign or a wonder, and the sign or the wonder come to pass, whereof he spake unto thee, saying, Let us go after other gods, which thou hast not known, and let us serve them; *thou shalt not hearken unto the words of that prophet, or that dreamer of dreams:* for the Lord your God proveth you, to know whether ye love the Lord your God with all your heart and with all your soul. Ye shall walk after the Lord your God, and fear him, and keep his commandments, and obey his voice." Deuteronomy 13:1-4.

COMMUNICATION WITH THE DEAD

How much do the dead know of what is going on among men?

"Thou changest his countenance, and sendest him away. His sons come to honour, and *he knoweth it not;* and they are brought low, but *he perceiveth it not of them.*" Job 14:20, 21.

Do the dead know *anything*?

"For the living know that they shall die: but *the dead know not any thing.*" Ecclesiastes 9:5. "His breath goeth forth, he returneth to his earth; *in that very day his thoughts perish.*" Psalm 146:4.

What scripture forever precludes the idea that the dead come back to earth to communicate with the living?

"Also their love, and their hatred, and their envy, is now perished; *neither have they any more a portion for ever in any thing that is done under the sun.*" Ecclesiastes 9:6.

DECEPTION IN THE LAST DAYS

What will be one characteristic of last-day apostasies?

"Now the Spirit speaketh expressly, that in the latter times some shall depart from the faith, *giving heed to seducing spirits, and doctrines of devils.*" 1 Timothy 4:1.

NOTE.—The following items illustrate a condition widely prevalent:

"'A lawyer with a national reputation, well known to me,' said

J. L. Hall, of New York, 'never begins the preparation of a difficult case without getting "advice from the other side," as he describes the search. . . . Another distinguished man of New York City once asserted to me that he had his familiar spirit with which he talked as freely as with a human companion.' "—Washington *Herald*, May 8, 1911.

How does Satan deceive the people?

"And no marvel; for Satan himself is *transformed into an angel of light*." 2 Corinthians 11:14.

What role do his agents assume?

"Therefore it is no great thing if his ministers also be *transformed as the ministers of righteousness*." Verse 15.

Will Satan and his agents attempt to counterfeit the coming of Christ, and work signs and wonders to confirm their pretentious claims?

"Then if any man shall say unto you, *Lo, here is Christ*, or there; believe it not. For there shall arise false Christs, and false prophets, *and shall shew great signs and wonders;* insomuch that, if it were possible, they shall deceive the very elect." Matthew 24:23, 24.

NOTE.—"As the crowning act in the great drama of deception, Satan himself will personate Christ. The church has long professed to look to the Saviour's advent as the consummation of her hopes. Now the great deceiver will make it appear that Christ has come. In different parts of the earth, Satan will manifest himself among men as a majestic being of dazzling brightness, resembling the description of the Son of God given by John in the Revelation. The glory that surrounds him is unsurpassed by anything that mortal eyes have yet beheld. The shout of triumph rings out upon the air, 'Christ has come! Christ has come!' The people prostrate themselves in adoration before him, while he lifts up his hands, and pronounces a blessing upon them, as Christ blessed His disciples when He was upon the earth. His voice is soft and subdued, yet full of melody. In gentle, compassionate tones he presents some of the same gracious, heavenly truths which the Saviour uttered. . . .

"But the people of God will not be misled. The teachings of this false christ are not in accordance with the Scriptures. . . .

"And, furthermore, Satan is not permitted to counterfeit the manner of Christ's advent. The Saviour has warned His people against deception upon this point, and has clearly foretold the manner of His second coming. 'There shall arise false christs, and false prophets, and shall show great signs and wonders; insomuch that, if it were possible, they shall deceive the very elect. . . . Wherefore if they shall say unto you, Behold, He is in the desert; go not forth: behold, He is in the secret chambers; believe it not. For as the lightning cometh out of the east, and shineth even unto the west; so shall also the coming of the Son of man be.' This coming, there is no possibility of counterfeiting. It will be universally known—witnessed by the whole world."—ELLEN G. WHITE, *The Great Controversy*, pp. 624, 625.

What will be one of the last great signs performed by this means, to fasten men in deception?

"And he doeth great wonders, so that *he maketh fire come down from heaven on the earth in the sight of men,* and deceiveth them that dwell on the earth by means of those miracles which he had power to do in the sight of the beast; saying to them that dwell on the earth, that they should make an image to the beast, which had the wound by a sword, and did live." Revelation 13:13, 14.

What scripture shows that Satan is to work with special power and deceptive wonders just before Christ's second coming?

"Whose coming is *after the working of Satan with all power and signs and lying wonders,* and with all deceivableness of unrighteousness in them that perish." 2 Thessalonians 2:9, 10. (See also Revelation 12:12.)

While many will be deceived by these wonders, and accept of the false christs that appear, what will those say who have maintained their love for the truth, and patiently waited for Christ's return?

"And it shall be said in that day, *Lo,* THIS *is our God; we have waited for him, and he will save us:* THIS *is the Lord; we have waited for him, we will be glad and rejoice in his salvation."* Isaiah 25:9.

What warning has been given us through the apostle Peter?

"Be sober, be vigilant; because your adversary the devil, as a roaring lion, walketh about, seeking whom he may devour." 1 Peter 5:8.

Part Twelve

Christian Growth and Experience

	PAGE
Growth in Grace	535
The Christian Armor	537
Walking in the Light	540
Saving Faith	543
Trials and Their Object	547
Overcoming	550
The Ministry of Sorrow	552
Comfort in Affliction	555
Trusting in Jesus	560
Patient Endurance	562
Contentment	564
Cheerfulness	567
Christian Courtesy	570
Confessing Faults and Forgiving One Another	571
The Duty of Encouragement	575
Unity of Believers	577
Meekness and Humility	580
Sobriety and Dignity	583
True Wisdom	585
Diligence in Labor	589
Perfection of Character	592
Sowing and Reaping	593

CHRIST OR DIANA?

"Be thou faithful unto death, and I will give th[ee] a crown of life." Revelation 2:10. (See page 53

Growth in Grace

GRACE MULTIPLIED

How does the apostle Peter close his second epistle?

"But *grow in grace*, and in the knowledge of our Lord and Saviour Jesus Christ." 2 Peter 3:18.

How may grace and peace be multiplied in believers?

"Grace and peace be multiplied unto you *through the knowledge of God, and of Jesus our Lord*." 2 Peter 1:2.

What is implied in a knowledge of God and Jesus Christ?

"And *this is life eternal*, that they might know thee the only true God, and Jesus Christ, whom thou hast sent." John 17:3.

By what may we be partakers of the divine nature?

"Whereby are given unto us *exceeding great and precious promises:* that by these ye might be partakers of the divine nature, having escaped the corruption that is in the world through lust." 2 Peter 1:4.

GRACE BY ADDITION

What graces are we to add in our character building?

"Add to your faith *virtue;* and to virtue *knowledge;* and to knowledge *temperance* [*self-control*]; and to temperance *patience;* and to patience *godliness;* and to godliness *brotherly kindness;* and to brotherly kindness *charity*." Verses 5-7.

NOTE.—*Faith* is the first round in the Christian ladder, the first step Godward. "He that cometh to God must *believe*." Hebrews 11:6.
But an inoperative faith is useless. "Faith without *works* is dead." James 2:20. To be of value, there must be coupled with faith *virtue*, or *moral excellence*.

To moral excellence there needs to be added *knowledge;* otherwise, like the stumbling Jews, one may have a zeal, "but *not according to knowledge*." Romans 10:2. Fanaticism is the result of such zeal. Knowledge, therefore, is an essential to healthy Christian growth.

To knowledge there needs to be added *temperance*, or *self-control*

—self-government. To know to do good, and not do it, is as useless as is faith without works. (See James 4:17.)

Patience, or *steadfast endurance,* naturally follows *temperance,* or *self-control.* It is well-nigh impossible for an intemperate person to be *patient.*

Having gained control of oneself, and become patient, one is in a condition to manifest *godliness,* or *Godlikeness.*

Kindness toward the brethren, or *brotherly kindness,* naturally follows godliness.

Charity, or love for *all,* even our *enemies,* is the crowning grace, the highest step, the eighth round, in the Christian ladder.

The arrangement in this enumeration of graces is by no means accidental or haphazard, but logical and sequential, each following the other in natural, necessary order. The finger of Inspiration is seen here.

What is said of charity in the Scriptures?

"Charity *suffereth long, and is kind; . . . thinketh no evil; rejoiceth not in iniquity,* but *rejoiceth in the truth; beareth all things, believeth all things, hopeth all things, endureth all things.*" 1 Corinthians 13:4-7. "And above all things have fervent charity among yourselves: for *charity shall cover the multitude of sins.*" 1 Peter 4:8.

NOTE.—*Charity* and *love* are translations of the same Greek word. Instead of *charity* most versions read *love.*

What is charity called?

"And above all these things put on charity, which is *the bond of perfectness.*" Colossians 3:14.

What is the result of cultivating these eight graces?

"For if these things be in you, and abound, *they make you that ye shall neither be barren nor unfruitful in the knowledge of our Lord Jesus Christ.*" 2 Peter 1:8.

What is the condition of one who lacks these graces?

"But he that lacketh these things *is blind, and cannot see afar off, and hath forgotten that he was purged from his old sins.*" Verse 9.

What is promised those who add grace to grace?

"If ye do these things, *ye shall never fall.*" Verse 10.

The Christian Armor

WHAT power was to make war upon the remnant church prior to the Second Advent?

"And *the dragon* [*Satan*] was wroth with the woman, and went to make war with the remnant of her seed, which keep the commandments of God, and have the testimony of Jesus Christ." Revelation 12:17.

What reward is promised to the overcomer?

"To him that overcometh will I give *to eat of the tree of life,* which is in the midst of the paradise of God." Revelation 2:7. (See also Revelation 2:11, 17, 26-28; 3:5, 12, 21.) "He that overcometh shall inherit *all things.*" Revelation 21:7.

THE CONQUERING LEADER

Through whom are we able to conquer?

"Nay, in all these things we are more than conquerors *through him that loved us.*" Romans 8:37.

Who was the invisible leader of the armies of Israel?

"Behold, there stood a man over against him with his sword drawn in his hand: and Joshua went unto him, and said unto him, Art thou for us, or for our adversaries? And he said, Nay; but as *captain of the host of the Lord* am I now come." Joshua 5:13, 14. (See also 1 Corinthians 10:1-4.)

WEAPONS FOR WARFARE

What is the character of the Christian's weapons of warfare?

"For the weapons of our warfare are *not carnal, but mighty through God to the pulling down of strong holds.*" 2 Corinthians 10:4.

What are these weapons able to conquer?

"Casting down *imaginations,* and *every high thing that exalteth itself against the knowledge of God,* and bringing into captivity *every thought* to the obedience of Christ." Verse 5.

What are we to put on?

"*Put on the whole armour of God*, that ye may be able to stand against the wiles of the devil." Ephesians 6:11.

With what kind of forces do we have to contend?

"For we wrestle not against flesh and blood, but against *principalities*, against *powers*, against *the rulers of the darkness of this world*, against *spiritual wickedness in high places*." Verse 12.

Note.—"Spiritual wickedness in high places" is more accurately rendered, "wicked spirits in heavenly places."

What are the first essentials of the needed armor?

"Stand therefore, having your *loins girt about with truth*, and having on *the breastplate of righteousness*." Verse 14.

With what are the feet to be shod?

"And your feet shod with *the preparation of the gospel of peace*." Verse 15. (See also Ephesians 2:14; James 3:18.)

What piece of armor is next mentioned as necessary?

"Above all, taking *the shield of faith*, wherewith ye shall be able to quench all the fiery darts of the wicked." Ephesians 6:16. (See 1 John 5:4; Hebrews 11:6.)

What armor is the Christian to put on as protection to his head?

"And take *the helmet of salvation*." Ephesians 6:17.

Note.—In 1 Thessalonians 5:8 the helmet is called "the *hope* of salvation." The helmet was worn to protect the head. So the hope of salvation will preserve the courage, and thus aid in protecting the spiritual life of the Christian pilgrim when beset by the enemy of righteousness.

With what sword is the Christian soldier to be armed?

"*The sword of the Spirit*, which is *the word of God*." Ephesians 6:17.

Note.—By this Christ defeated the enemy. (See Matthew 4:1-11; Luke 4:1-13.) But no one can *use this sword* who does not *know* it. Hence, the importance of studying and knowing for oneself what the Bible teaches.

THE CHRISTIAN ARMOR

FAITHFULNESS AND VICTORY

In what words are the courage, faithfulness, and loyalty of the church expressed?

"And they overcame him by the blood of the Lamb, and by the word of their testimony; and *they loved not their lives unto the death.*" Revelation 12:11.

Will Christ's loyal soldiers be victorious under Him?

"And I saw as it were a sea of glass mingled with fire: and them that had *gotten the victory* over the beast, and over his image, and over his mark, and over the number of his name, stand on the sea of glass, having the harps of God." Revelation 15:2.

CHRIST OR DIANA?

(See page 534)

The artist has here represented a scene from the early days of the Christian faith. In the background rise the circular walls of an amphitheater. To the Christian maiden is being read the pagan decree which commits her to the lions in the arena if she will not offer incense to Diana. On the altar before the image of that goddess the fire is burning; in her lover's outstretched hand is the incense which he begs her to place upon the flame in order to save her life. The priest of Diana, standing beside the shrine of the goddess, the choir of maidens, ready to join in a hymn of praise, and even the soldiers— all are absorbed in watching her, and show on their faces the impression she is making upon them. Her uplifted eyes look away toward her invisible Lord; and the expression of faith and courage upon her countenance clearly indicates what her noble decision is to be.

The picture is an inspiring one. It succeeds in conveying the very spirit of the great apostle's immortal declaration: "I am persuaded, that neither death, nor life, nor angels, nor principalities, nor powers, nor things present, nor things to come, nor height, nor depth, nor any other creature, shall be able to separate us from the love of God, which is in Christ Jesus our Lord." Romans 8:38, 39.

Walking in the Light

How important is it that we walk in the light when it comes to us?

"Walk while ye have the light, *lest darkness come upon you:* for he that walketh in darkness knoweth not whither he goeth." John 12:35.

NOTE.—It is important to settle a plain question of duty at once, and not delay obedience under the excuse of waiting for more light. To do as did Balaam—ask God again concerning that which He has plainly and expressly spoken—is dangerous. Nor should we, like the unbelieving Jews, seek a sign from Heaven to convince us that we ought to obey the written word. Has God spoken? Is it His word? Then obey. Do not insult Heaven with the question whether it is right to obey. (See 1 Kings 22:1-36; Ezekiel 14:1-5.)

Upon what condition are we promised cleansing from sin?

"*But if we walk in the light, as he is in the light,* we have fellowship one with another, and the blood of Jesus Christ his Son cleanseth us from all sin." 1 John 1:7.

SOURCES OF LIGHT

Who is the light of the world?

"*I am the light of the world:* he that followeth me shall not walk in darkness, but shall have the light of life." John 8:12.

How are we to walk in Christ?

"*As ye have therefore received Christ Jesus the Lord,* so walk ye in him." Colossians 2:6.

What has God given to guide our feet aright in the path of truth and duty?

"*Thy word is a lamp* unto my feet, and *a light* unto my path." Psalm 119:105. (See Proverbs 6:23.)

What does the entrance of God's word give?

"The entrance of thy words *giveth light;* it giveth understanding unto the simple." Psalm 119:130.

Who does Christ say will be blessed through the prophecies of the book of Revelation?

"Blessed *is he that readeth,* and *they that hear* the words of this prophecy, *and keep those things which are written therein.*" Revelation 1:3.

Note.—We are in the last days, in the generation that is to hear the final warning message contained in this book. (See Revelation 14:6-10; 18:1-5.)

More Light for the Righteous

How long may the just expect increased light to shine upon their pathway?

"But the path of the just is as the shining light, *that shineth more and more unto the perfect day."* Proverbs 4:18.

Note.—The more earnestly one desires to know the will of God, while living up to all the light he has, the more light and truth from God will shine upon his pathway. If light is sown for the righteous, such are the very ones who may expect advanced light to come to them, and to see new duties presented to them from a study of the word of God.

How did God respond to Cornelius' sincerity of worship?

"He saw in a vision evidently about the ninth hour of the day *an angel of God coming in to him, and saying unto him, Cornelius.* And when he looked on him, he was afraid, and said, What is it, Lord? And he said unto him, Thy prayers and thine alms are come up for a memorial before God." Acts 10:3, 4.

Because God acknowledged Cornelius' worship, was this evidence that he had nothing more to learn or do?

"And now send men to Joppa, and call for one Simon, whose surname is Peter: he lodgeth with one Simon a tanner, whose house is by the sea side: *he shall tell thee what thou oughtest to do."* Verses 5, 6.

Note.—The reason the Lord favored Cornelius with a visit from one of His angels was not that Cornelius knew the way of salvation perfectly, but that the Lord saw in him a sincere desire for more light, and a willing mind to comply with every known requirement. That spirit was pleasing to God. All may now receive advanced light if, like Cornelius, they seek it and are willing to walk in it when it comes to them. If it is neglected, they are guilty before God, and will be left to the buffetings of the enemy.

Results of Our Choice

What will become of the light that one has if he fails to walk in it?

"The light of the body is the eye: therefore when thine eye is single, thy whole body also is full of light; but when thine eye is evil, thy body also is full of darkness. *Take heed therefore that the light which is in thee be not darkness."* Luke 11:34, 35.

Why did the sin of those who rejected Christ remain?

"Jesus said unto them, If ye were blind, ye should have no sin: but now ye say, *We see;* therefore your sin remaineth." John 9:41. (See also John 15:22.)

Note.—With advanced light comes increased responsibility. Duty is always in proportion to one's light and privileges. Present truth always brings with it present duty. (See reading on "Present Truth," page 127.)

Why are those condemned who do not come to the light?

"And this is the condemnation, that light is come into the world, and *men loved darkness rather than light, because their deeds were evil."* John 3:19.

If one is really seeking for truth, what will he do?

"But he that doeth truth *cometh to the light,* that his deeds may be made manifest, that they are wrought in God." Verse 21.

What will those who reject light and truth finally be led to believe?

"And for this cause God shall send them strong delusion, *that they should believe a lie:* that they all might be damned who believed not the truth, but had pleasure in unrighteousness." 2 Thessalonians 2:11, 12.

Note.—The opposite of light is darkness; the opposite of truth is a lie. For those who reject light and truth, only darkness and error remain. God is sometimes in the Scriptures represented as sending that which He permits to come.

Upon what condition only may we be made partakers of Christ?

"For we are made partakers of Christ, *if we hold the beginning of our confidence stedfast unto the end."* Hebrews 3:14.

Saving Faith

WHAT is faith?

"Faith is the *substance* [or, *"ground," "confidence"*] of things hoped for, the *evidence* of things not seen." Hebrews 11:1.

How important is faith? What must one believe about God?

"Without faith it is impossible to please him: for he that cometh to God *must believe that he is,* and that he is a rewarder of them that diligently seek him." Verse 6.

CHRIST AND SAVING FAITH

How only can we truly know God?

"Neither knoweth any man the Father, save the Son, *and he to whomsoever the Son will reveal him."* Matthew 11:27.

In whom must we believe in order to be saved?

"For God so loved the world, that he gave *his only begotten Son,* that whosoever believeth in *him* should not perish, but have everlasting life." John 3:16.

How only can a man be justified? Since the law cannot justify a sinner is it thereby rendered without value?

"Therefore being justified *by faith,* we have peace with God through our Lord Jesus Christ." Romans 5:1. "Therefore *by the deeds of the law there shall no flesh be justified* in his sight: for by the law is the knowledge of sin." Romans 3:20.

What will be the experience of those who walk after the Spirit?

"That *the righteousness of the law might be fulfilled in us,* who walk not after the flesh, but after the Spirit. . . . Because the carnal mind is enmity against God: for it is not subject to the law of God, neither indeed can be." Romans 8:4-7. "For *sin shall not have dominion over you:* for ye are not under the law, but under grace." Romans 6:14.

Genuine Faith and Its Fruits

What challenge does the apostle James make as to the evidence that one has genuine faith?

"Shew me thy faith *without* thy works, and I will shew thee my faith *by* my works." James 2:18.

How did Abraham show that he had perfect faith in God?

"Was not Abraham our father justified by works, *when he had offered Isaac his son upon the altar?* Seest thou how faith wrought with his works, and *by works was faith made perfect?*" Verses 21, 22.

By what practical example does the apostle illustrate the difference between genuine, living faith and a dead faith?

"If a brother or sister be naked, and destitute of daily food, and one of you say unto them, Depart in peace, be ye warmed and filled; notwithstanding ye give them not those things which are needful to the body; what doth it profit?" Verses 15, 16.

How necessary are works in maintaining living faith?

"But wilt thou know, O vain man, that *faith without works is dead?* . . . For *as the body without the spirit* [margin, *"breath"*] *is dead, so faith without works is dead also."* Verses 20-26.

Note.—The apostle was not here arguing for justification or salvation by faith *and* works, but for a living faith—a faith *that* works.

"There are two errors against which the children of God—particularly those who have just come to trust in His grace—especially need to guard. The first . . . is that of looking to their own works, trusting to anything they can do, to bring themselves into harmony with God. He who is trying to become holy by his own works in keeping the law, is attempting an impossibility. All that man can do without Christ is polluted with selfishness and sin. It is the grace of Christ alone, through faith, that can make us holy. The opposite and no less dangerous error is, that belief in Christ releases men from keeping the law of God; that since by faith alone we become partakers of the grace of Christ, our works have nothing to do with our redemption. . . . Obedience—the service and allegiance of love—is the true sign of discipleship. . . . Instead of releasing man from obedience, it is faith, and faith only, that makes us partakers of the grace of Christ, which enables us to render obedience. We do not

SAVING FAITH

earn salvation by our obedience; for salvation is the free gift of God, to be received by faith. But obedience is the fruit of faith. . . . That so-called faith in Christ which professes to release men from the obligation of obedience to God, is not faith, but presumption."—*Steps to Christ,* pp. 64-66.

Says Luther: "If it is He alone that taketh away our sins, it cannot be ourselves and our own works. But good works follow redemption, as the fruit grows on the tree."—Quoted in J. H. MERLE D'AUBIGNE, *History of the Reformation of the Sixteenth Century,* book 2, chap. 6.

What does the hope of salvation lead one to do?

"And every man that hath this hope in him *purifieth himself,* even as he is pure." 1 John 3:3.

Upon what condition are we made partakers of Christ?

"For we are made partakers of Christ, *if we hold the beginning of our confidence stedfast unto the end."* Hebrews 3:14.

FAITH OR FEELING

Upon what conditions has God promised us cleansing and the forgiveness of our sins?

"But *if we walk in the light,* as he is in the light, we have fellowship one with another, and the blood of Jesus Christ his Son cleanseth us from all sin. . . . *If we confess our sins,* he is faithful and just to forgive us our sins, and to cleanse us from all unrighteousness." 1 John 1:7-9.

NOTE.—Intelligent faith as to what God will do for us touching any matter must be gained by what God's word says concerning that point. No one can consistently hope for that which God has not promised. To expect that God will do that which He has never promised to do is only presumption. Faith is distinct from presumption. To have abiding confidence in the promise of God is faith; but presumption may rest entirely on feeling or desire. Feeling cannot therefore be relied on in the matter of faith. Faith is a pure belief, a confiding trust, in the promises of God, irrespective of feeling. This perfect trust enables one to surmount difficulties under the most trying circumstances, even when the feelings are depressed or wellnigh crushed.

Upon what, then, is genuine, saving faith based?

"Faith cometh by hearing, and hearing by *the word of God."* Romans 10:17.

What was the cause of Peter's sinking after he had started to meet the Saviour on the stormy sea?

"And immediately Jesus stretched forth his hand, and caught him, and said unto him, *O thou of little faith, wherefore didst thou doubt?*" Matthew 14:31.

Note.—Peter's fear of the boisterous sea caused him to doubt the strength of Christ's word, "Come."

With what is it our privilege to be filled?

"Now the God of hope *fill you with all joy and peace in believing,* that ye may abound in hope, through the power of the Holy Ghost." Romans 15:13.

Everyday Faith

Faith may be strengthened by daily exercise. It is not some great thing, done once for all, that gives an individual faith; but an everyday, simple, childlike trust in God, and an implicit obedience to His word. Some make faith a more difficult matter than God would have them, because they try to embrace too much at one time. They take on the burdens of tomorrow or next week, when the Lord supplies strength only for TODAY. *When tomorrow comes, grapple with its duties, but not until it does come. We should remember the precious promise, "As thy days, so shall thy strength be." Deuteronomy 33:25.*

Away, my unbelieving fear!
   Fear shall in me no more have place:
My Saviour doth not yet appear,
   He hides the brightness of His face;
But shall I therefore let Him go,
   And basely to the tempter yield?—
No, in the strength of Jesus, no;
   I never will give up my shield.

—Charles Wesley

Trials and Their Object

VALUE AND GLORY OF TRIALS

WHAT does the apostle Peter say concerning the trials through which every believer must pass?

"Beloved, *think it not strange concerning the fiery trial which is to try you,* as though some strange thing happened unto you: but rejoice, inasmuch as ye are partakers of Christ's sufferings; that, when his glory shall be revealed, ye may be glad also with exceeding joy." 1 Peter 4:12, 13.

How important is the trial of our faith?

"That the trial of your faith, *being much more precious than of gold that perisheth,* though it be tried with fire, might be found unto praise and honour and glory at the appearing of Jesus Christ." 1 Peter 1:7.

NOTE.—"When David was fleeing through the wilderness, pursued by his own son, he was being prepared to become the sweet singer of Israel. The pit and the dungeon were the best schools at which Joseph ever graduated. The hurricane that upset the tent and killed Job's children prepared the man of Uz to write the magnificent poem that has astounded the ages. There is no way to get the wheat out of the straw, but to thresh it. There is no way to purify the gold, but to burn it."—T. DE WITT TALMAGE, *One Thousand Gems* (1873 ed.), pp. 93, 94.

What reason did Paul give for glorying in tribulations?

"We glory in tribulations also: *knowing that tribulation worketh patience; and patience, experience; and experience, hope: and hope maketh not ashamed;* because the love of God is shed abroad in our hearts by the Holy Ghost which is given unto us." Romans 5:3-5.

PROPHECY OF TRIALS

What, according to the prophecy of Daniel, was to befall the people of God down through the ages?

"And they that understand among the people shall instruct

many: *yet they shall fall by the sword, and by flame, by captivity, and by spoil, many days.*" Daniel 11:33.

Why was this to be?

"And some of them of understanding shall fall, *to try them, and to purge, and to make them white,* even to the time of the end." Verse 35.

Looking forward to the conflicts through which His followers must pass, what cheering message did Christ send them through the revelator?

"*Fear none of those things which thou shalt suffer:* behold, the devil shall cast some of you into prison, *that ye may be tried;* . . . *be thou faithful unto death, and I will give thee a crown of life.* . . . *He that overcometh shall not be hurt of the second death.*" Revelation 2:10, 11. (See notes on pages 284, 304.)

How many does Paul say will suffer persecution?

"Yea, and *all that will live godly in Christ Jesus shall suffer persecution.*" 2 Timothy 3:12.

Trials in Ancient Times

What description does Paul give of the sufferings endured by some of God's people in former ages?

"Others were *tortured*, not accepting deliverance; that they might obtain a better resurrection: and others had trial of *cruel mockings* and *scourgings*, yea, moreover of *bonds* and *imprisonment:* they were *stoned*, they were *sawn asunder*, were *tempted*, were *slain with the sword:* they wandered about in sheepskins and goatskins; being destitute, afflicted, tormented; (of whom the world was not worthy:) *they wandered in deserts, and in mountains, and in dens and caves of the earth.*" Hebrews 11:35-38.

Chastening and the Crown

Does God willingly afflict the children of men?

"For the Lord will not cast off for ever: but though he cause grief, yet will he have compassion according to the multitude of his mercies. *For he doth not afflict willingly nor grieve the children of men.*" Lamentations 3:31-33.

Why does God permit the chastening rod to fall?

"For they [parents] verily for a few days chastened us after their own pleasure; but he *for our profit, that we might be partakers of his holiness."* Hebrews 12:10.

Referring to Peter's coming sore trial, for what did Christ say He had prayed?

"Satan hath desired to have you, that he may sift you as wheat: but I have prayed for thee, *that thy faith fail not."* Luke 22:31, 32.

What cheering promise is made to those who endure the trials and temptations of this life?

"Blessed is the man that endureth temptation: for when he is tried, *he shall receive the crown of life,* which the Lord hath promised to them that love him." James 1:12.

NOTE.—Says a Christian writer: "Our sorrows do not spring out of the ground. God 'doth not afflict willingly nor grieve the children of men.' When He permits trials and afflictions, it is 'for our profit, that we might be partakers of His holiness.' If received in faith, the trial that seems so bitter and hard to bear will prove a blessing. The cruel blow that blights the joys of earth will be the means of turning our eyes to heaven. How many there are who would never have known Jesus had not sorrow led them to seek comfort in Him! The trials of life are God's workmen, to remove the impurities and roughness from our character. Their hewing, squaring, and chiseling, their burnishing and polishing, is a painful process; it is hard to be pressed down to the grinding wheel. But the stone is brought forth prepared to fill its place in the heavenly temple."

Overcoming

WHAT overcomes the world?

"For *whatsoever is born of God* overcometh the world." 1 John 5:4, first part.

In whose victory may the Christian ever rejoice and take courage?

"These things I have spoken unto you, that in me ye might have peace. In the world ye shall have tribulation: but be of good cheer; *I have overcome the world.*" John 16:33.

Who alone overcomes?

"Who is he that overcometh the world, but *he that believeth that Jesus is the Son of God?*" 1 John 5:5.

Through what, then, is the victory gained in the work of overcoming?

"And this is the victory that overcometh the world, even *our faith.*" Verse 4, last part.

Through whom do we obtain the victory?

"But thanks be to God, which giveth us the victory *through our Lord Jesus Christ.*" 1 Corinthians 15:57. "Nay, in all these things we are more than conquerors *through him that loved us.*" Romans 8:37.

How did Christ overcome when tempted?

By the word of God. (See Matthew 4:1-11.)

How do the Scriptures say the saints overcame the enemy?

"And they overcame him *by the blood of the Lamb, and by the word of their testimony;* and they loved not their lives unto the death." Revelation 12:11.

With what does the apostle Paul tell us to overcome evil?

"Be not overcome of evil, but *overcome evil with good.*" Romans 12:21.

Why was the patriarch Jacob's name changed to Israel?

"And he said, Thy name shall be called no more Jacob, but Israel: *for as a prince hast thou power with God and with men, and hast prevailed."* Genesis 32:28.

Exceeding Great and Precious Promises

"To him that overcometh will I give to eat of the tree of life, which is in the midst of the paradise of God." Revelation 2:7.

"He that overcometh shall not be hurt of the second death." Verse 11.

"To him that overcometh will I give to eat of the hidden manna." Verse 17.

"He that overcometh, and keepeth my works unto the end, to him will I give power over the nations." Verse 26.

"He that overcometh, the same shall be clothed in white raiment; and I will not blot out his name out of the book of life, but I will confess his name before my Father, and before his angels." Revelation 3:5.

"Him that overcometh will I make a pillar in the temple of my God." Verse 12.

"To him that overcometh will I grant to sit with me in my throne, even as I also overcame, and am set down with my Father in his throne." Verse 21.

"He that overcometh shall inherit *all things;* and I will be his God, and he shall be my son." Revelation 21:7.

The Way to Win

"The victory is not won without much earnest prayer, without the humbling of self at every step. Our will is not to be forced into cooperation with divine agencies, but it must be voluntarily submitted. Were it possible to force upon you with a hundredfold greater intensity the influence of the Spirit of God, it would not make you a Christian, a fit subject for heaven. The stronghold of Satan would not be broken. The will must be placed on the side of God's will. You are not able, of yourself, to bring your purposes and desires and inclinations into submission to the will of God; but if you are 'willing to be made willing,' God will accomplish the work for you."—Ellen G. White, *Thoughts From the Mount of Blessing* (1956 ed.), p. 142.

The Ministry of Sorrow

SENSING THE LIMITS OF LIFE

WHY is it better to go to the house of mourning than to the house of feasting?

"It is better to go to the house of mourning, than to go to the house of feasting: *for that is the end of all men; and the living will lay it to his heart.*" Ecclesiastes 7:2.

What did the psalmist ask God to teach him?

"Lord, *make me to know mine end,* and the measure of my days, what it is; *that I may know how frail I am.*" Psalm 39:4. (See also Psalm 90:12.)

SORROW'S POSSIBILITIES

Why is sorrow better than laughter?

"Sorrow is better than laughter: *for by the sadness of the countenance the heart is made better.*" Ecclesiastes 7:3.

NOTE.—"Many of the loveliest songs of peace and trust and hope which God's children sing in this world have been taught in the hushed and darkened chambers of sorrow. . . . Afflictions, sanctified, soften the asperities of life. They tame the wildness of nature. They temper human ambitions. They burn out the dross of selfishness and worldliness. They humble pride. They quell fierce passions. They reveal to men their own hearts, their own weaknesses, faults, blemishes, and perils. They teach patience and submission. They discipline unruly spirits. They deepen and enrich our experiences."—J. R. MILLER, *Week-Day Religion,* pp. 90, 91.

Are the righteous freed from afflictions in this world?

"*Many are the afflictions of the righteous:* but the Lord delivereth him out of them all." Psalm 34:19.

Does God delight to afflict any?

"For the Lord will not cast off for ever: but though he cause grief, yet will he have compassion according to the multitude of his mercies. *For he doth not afflict willingly nor grieve the children of men.*" Lamentations 3:31-33.

Does He afflict to leave the one chastened in despair?

"Behold, happy is the man whom God correcteth: therefore despise not thou the chastening of the Almighty: *for he maketh sore, and bindeth up: he woundeth, and his hands make whole.*" Job 5:17, 18.

In what language is the same truth again expressed?

"Come, and let us return unto the Lord: for *he hath torn, and he will heal us; he hath smitten, and he will bind us up.*" Hosea 6:1. (See also Isaiah 61:1-3.)

Whom does the Lord chasten?

"For *whom the Lord loveth he chasteneth*, and scourgeth every son whom he receiveth." Hebrews 12:6.

Is this, for the time being, a source of pleasure?

"Now *no chastening for the present seemeth to be joyous, but grievous:* nevertheless afterward it yieldeth the peaceable fruit of righteousness unto them which are exercised thereby." Verse 11.

Note.—"Many of the sweetest joys of Christian hearts are songs which have been learned in the bitterness of trial." "Many a cold, icy nature is made warm and tender by the grief that crushes it."—J. R. Miller, *Week-Day Religion*, pp. 89, 91.

What, aside from sin, causes more sorrow than all else?

Death, or the loss of loved ones.

Does death bring to Christians unassuaged sorrow?

"I would not have you to be ignorant, brethren, concerning them which are asleep, *that ye sorrow not, even as others which have no hope.*" 1 Thessalonians 4:13.

Note.—The loss of loved ones is sometimes the means of conversion, and of severing the ties which bind to earth. Persecution; sickness; the loss of sight, hearing, or limb; the loss of property; or other calamities may likewise be instrumental in drawing us nearer to God. (See Psalm 119:71; Isaiah 26:9.)

Who is the author of disease and death?

"And ought not this woman, being a daughter of Abraham, *whom Satan hath bound,* lo, these eighteen years, be loosed from this bond on the sabbath day?" Luke 13:16.

"And lest I should be exalted above measure through the abundance of the revelations, there was given to me a thorn in the flesh, *the messenger of Satan to buffet me,* lest I should be exalted above measure." 2 Corinthians 12:7.

"That through death he [Christ] might destroy him that *had the power of death, that is, the devil.*" Hebrews 2:14.

NOTE.—It should be remembered that suffering and death come from Satan, the one who "sowed tares among the wheat" (Matthew 13:25). But God overrules the devices of the enemy for the good of those who put their trust in Him. He worketh all things for good to them that love Him (Romans 8:28).

What do our transient afflictions do for us?

"For our light affliction, which is but for a moment, *worketh for us a far more exceeding and eternal weight of glory.*" 2 Corinthians 4:17. (See Romans 8:28.)

EVEN JESUS

As a Saviour of man, even Jesus was perfected for His work through suffering. He suffered hunger, reproach, temptation in all points, and death. All this that He "might be a merciful and faithful high priest," "touched with the feeling of our infirmities." Hebrews 2:10-18; 4:15.

"WHEN things don't go to suit you,
  And the world seems upside down,
Don't waste your time in fretting,
  But drive away that frown;
Since life is oft perplexing,
  'Tis much the wisest plan
To bear all trials bravely,
  And smile whene'er you can."

Comfort in Affliction

God and Affliction

Are God's people free from affliction?

"Many are the afflictions of the righteous: but the Lord delivereth him out of them all." Psalm 34:19.

How does God regard the afflicted?

"He *heareth the cry* of the afflicted." Job 34:28.

What has He promised to be to those in trouble?

"God is our refuge and strength, *a very present help in trouble.*" Psalm 46:1.

With what feelings does the Lord look upon His children?

"Like as a father pitieth his children, so the Lord pitieth them that fear him." Psalm 103:13.

What does He know and remember?

"For he knoweth *our frame;* he remembereth *that we are dust."* Verse 14.

What has the Lord promised to be to the oppressed?

"The Lord also will be *a refuge for the oppressed, a refuge in times of trouble."* Psalm 9:9.

What has God promised His children when they pass through trials and afflictions?

"When thou passest through the waters, *I will be with thee;* and through the rivers, *they shall not overflow thee:* when thou walkest through the fire, *thou shalt not be burned; neither shall the flame kindle upon thee."* Isaiah 43:2.

Learning Lessons Through Affliction

What did the psalmist say with reference to his being afflicted?

"It is good for me that I have been afflicted; that I might learn thy statutes." Psalm 119:71.

When afflicted, for what did he pray?

"Look upon mine affliction and my pain; and *forgive all my sins.*" Psalm 25:18.

Before he was afflicted, what did he do?

"*Before I was afflicted I went astray:* but now have I kept thy word." Psalm 119:67.

What did Christ learn through suffering?

"Though he were a Son, yet *learned he obedience by the things which he suffered.*" Hebrews 5:8.

In the perfecting of character, what must come to all? What attitude should we take when chastened by God?

"And ye have forgotten the exhortation which speaketh unto you as unto children, My son, despise not thou *the chastening of the Lord,* nor faint when thou art rebuked of him: *for whom the Lord loveth he chasteneth, and scourgeth every son whom he receiveth.*" Hebrews 12:5, 6.

Is this chastening a pleasant experience?

"Now *no chastening for the present seemeth to be joyous, but grievous:* nevertheless afterward it yieldeth the peaceable fruit of righteousness unto them which are exercised thereby." Verse 11.

What courage and strength, therefore, should come to us even in the hour of affliction?

"Wherefore *lift up the hands which hang down, and the feeble knees.*" Verse 12. (See also Job 4:3, 4; Isaiah 35:3.)

What did Job say in the midst of his afflictions?

"Though he slay me, yet will I trust in him." Job 13:15.

Receiving and Giving Comfort

What is God called in the Scriptures?

"The God of all comfort." 2 Corinthians 1:3.

Whom does God comfort?

"God, that comforteth *those that are cast down.*" 2 Corinthians 7:6.

COMFORT IN AFFLICTION

What promise is made to those that mourn?

"Blessed are they that mourn: for *they shall be comforted."* Matthew 5:4.

Why does God comfort us in tribulation?

"Who comforteth us in all our tribulation, *that we may be able to comfort them which are in any trouble, by the comfort wherewith we ourselves are comforted of God."* 2 Corinthians 1:4.

NOTE.—One who has passed through trouble and affliction himself, and received comfort from God, is better able to minister comfort to others.

How should we sympathize with others when they experience sorrow?

"Weep with them that weep." Romans 12:15. "To him that is afflicted *pity should be shewed from his friend."* Job 6:14.

Does Jesus sympathize with us in our afflictions?

"For we have not an high priest which cannot be *touched with the feeling of our infirmities;* but was in all points tempted like as we are." Hebrews 4:15.

How did He manifest His sympathy in the case of Mary and her friends weeping over the death of Lazarus?

"When Jesus therefore saw her weeping, and the Jews also weeping which came with her, *he groaned in the spirit, and was troubled,* and said, Where have ye laid him? They said unto him, Lord, come and see. *Jesus wept."* John 11:33-35.

NOTE.—Not alone for Mary and her friends did Jesus weep. Looking down through the ages, He saw the tears and the heartaches that death would bring to mankind in this sin-stricken world. His heart was touched with human woe, and He wept with those who wept.

Whatever may come, what blessed assurance has everyone who loves God?

"And we know that *all things work together for good to them that love God."* Romans 8:28.

NOTE.—If one loves God, he may rest assured that out of every trial and affliction good will come.

BLACK & WHITE PICTURES © RAPHAEL TUCK AND CO.

AFTER HAROLD COPPING, ARTIST

CHRIST THE CONSOLER

"Blessed are they that mourn: for they shall be comforted." Matthew 5

COMFORT IN AFFLICTION

From Tears to Eternal Joy

In bereavement, like whom should we not sorrow?

"As others which have no hope." 1 Thessalonians 4:13.

When our friends fall asleep in death, with what words are we told to comfort one another?

"For if we believe that Jesus died and rose again, even so them also which sleep in Jesus will God bring with him.... For the Lord himself shall descend from heaven with a shout, with the voice of the archangel, and with the trump of God: and the dead in Christ shall rise first: then we which are alive and remain shall be caught up together with them in the clouds, to meet the Lord in the air: and so shall we ever be with the Lord. *Wherefore comfort one another with these words.*" Verses 14-18.

What did Christ say would be the experience of His people in this world?

"*In the world ye shall have tribulation:* but be of good cheer; I have overcome the world." "*Ye shall weep and lament*, but the world shall rejoice: and *ye shall be sorrowful*, but your sorrow shall be turned into joy." John 16:33, 20.

In what respect is the reaping of God's people to differ from their sowing?

"*They that sow in tears shall reap in joy.* He that goeth forth and *weepeth*, bearing precious seed, shall doubtless come again with *rejoicing*, bringing his sheaves with him." Psalm 126:5, 6.

Be of good cheer! I know sometime
Life's song will run in perfect rhyme.
Somewhere, I know, all things will be
Attuned to perfect harmony.
Sometime, somewhere, each sad refrain
Shall be its own surcease of pain.
The compensation love will send
Will be in bringing friend to friend;
And all the heartaches that we bore,
In God's good time will be no more.

—Robert Lee Walden

Trusting in Jesus

THE CALL TO CONFIDENCE

WHAT did the prophet Isaiah predict of Christ?

"And in that day there shall be a root of Jesse, which shall stand for an ensign of the people; *to it shall the Gentiles seek: and his rest shall be glorious.*" Isaiah 11:10.

NOTE.—Paul renders this, "In him shall the Gentiles *trust.*" Romans 15:12.

Why does God wish us to trust in Jesus?

"That we should be *to the praise of his glory,* who first trusted in Christ." Ephesians 1:12.

DRAWING BACK FROM THE CALL

How does God regard one who abandons his faith?

"Now the just shall live by faith: but *if any man draw back, my soul shall have no pleasure in him.*" Hebrews 10:38.

Is there danger of believers losing their hold on Christ?

"And because iniquity shall abound, *the love of many shall wax cold.*" Matthew 24:12.

ANSWERING THE CALL

What did the Ephesians do upon hearing the gospel?

"*In whom ye also trusted,* after that ye heard the word of truth, the gospel of your salvation." Ephesians 1:13, first part.

What experience followed this trust in Jesus?

"In whom also after that ye believed, *ye were sealed with that holy Spirit of promise.*" Verse 13, last part.

NOTE.—To trust in Jesus is to believe in Him, to have abiding and unbounded confidence in Him. When such trust exists, we are sealed by the Holy Spirit of promise.

What is the gospel to every one that believes?

"I am not ashamed of the gospel of Christ: for *it is the power of God unto salvation to every one that believeth.*" Romans 1:16.

By what does one gain the victory over the world?

"This is the victory that overcometh the world, *even our faith.*" 1 John 5:4.

What encouragement does Jesus give us to meet cheerfully the troubles and trials of life?

"These things I have spoken unto you, that in me ye might have peace. In the world ye shall have tribulation: but *be of good cheer; I have overcome the world.*" John 16:33.

What has this firm trust in Jesus led many to do?

"And they overcame him by the blood of the Lamb, and by the word of their testimony; and *they loved not their lives unto the death.*" Revelation 12:11. "And others had trial of cruel mockings and scourgings, yea, moreover of bonds and imprisonment: they were stoned, they were sawn asunder, were tempted, were slain with the sword: they wandered about in sheepskins and goatskins; being destitute, afflicted, tormented; (of whom the world was not worthy)." Hebrews 11:36-38.

What did it lead Moses to do?

"By faith Moses, when he was come to years, *refused to be called the son of Pharaoh's daughter; choosing rather to suffer affliction with the people of God, than to enjoy the pleasures of sin for a season;* esteeming the reproach of Christ greater riches than the treasures in Egypt: for he had respect unto the recompence of the reward." Verses 24-26.

What is promised those who trust in Jesus?

"There is no man that hath left house, or brethren, or sisters, or father, or mother, or wife, or children, or lands, for my sake, and the gospel's, but *he shall receive an hundredfold now in this time, houses, and brethren, and sisters, and mothers, and children, and lands,* with persecutions; and *in the world to come eternal life.*" Mark 10:29, 30.

What is Jesus able to do?

"Now unto him that is *able to keep you from falling, and to present you faultless before the presence of his glory.*" Jude 24.

Patient Endurance

PATIENCE TAUGHT AND EXEMPLIFIED

WHAT has the Bible to say concerning patience?

"The *patient in spirit* is better than the *proud in spirit*." Ecclesiastes 7:8. "Be patient *toward all men*." 1 Thessalonians 5:14. "In your patience *possess ye your souls*." Luke 21:19.

What contrast is drawn between the patient and the hasty in spirit?

"He that is slow to wrath is of *great understanding:* but he that is hasty of spirit *exalteth folly*." Proverbs 14:29.

Who are cited as examples of patience?

"Take, my brethren, *the prophets,* . . . for an example of suffering affliction, and of *patience.* . . . Ye have heard of the patience of *Job*." James 5:10, 11.

DEVELOPMENT OF PATIENCE

What does the trying of faith work?

"Knowing this, that the trying of your faith *worketh patience*." James 1:3. "Not only so, but we glory in tribulations also: knowing that tribulation *worketh patience*." Romans 5:3.

What grace is to be added to temperance, or self-control?

"And to temperance *patience*." 2 Peter 1:6.

NOTE.—Patience, or steadfast endurance, naturally follows temperance. Hence the importance of right living—of gaining control over the appetites and passions.

Why are we exhorted to patience?

"But let patience have her perfect work, *that ye may be perfect and entire, wanting nothing*." James 1:4.

What important test of perfection of character is given?

"*If any man offend not in word,* the same is a perfect man, and able also to bridle the whole body." James 3:2.

Winning the Race

How are we exhorted to run the Christian race?

"Let us *run with patience* the race that is set before us, looking unto Jesus the author and finisher of our faith." Hebrews 12:1, 2.

What is said of those who endure?

"Behold, *we count them happy which endure.*" James 5:11. "*Blessed* is the man that endureth temptation." James 1:12. "He that endureth to the end *shall be saved.*" Matthew 10:22.

For what glorious event are we bidden patiently to wait?

"And the Lord direct your hearts into the love of God, and into *the patient waiting for Christ.*" 2 Thessalonians 3:5. "Be *patient* therefore, brethren, *unto the coming of the Lord.* . . . Be ye also *patient;* stablish your hearts: for *the coming of the Lord draweth nigh.*" James 5:7, 8.

What will be one characteristic of the remnant church?

"Here is the *patience* of the saints: here are they that keep the commandments of God, and the faith of Jesus." Revelation 14:12.

What should be the language of every heart?

"*I wait for the Lord, my soul doth wait,* and in his word do I hope." Psalm 130:5.

When Christ comes, what will His people say?

"And it shall be said in that day, Lo, this is our God; *we have waited for him,* and he will save us: this is the Lord; *we have waited for him,* we will be glad and rejoice in his salvation." Isaiah 25:9.

> The home where changes never come,
>   Nor pain nor sorrow, toil nor care;
> Yes! 'tis a bright and blessed home;
>   Who would not fain be resting there?
> Yet when bowed down beneath the load
>   By heaven allowed, thine earthly lot;
> Thou yearnst to reach that blest abode,
>   Wait, meekly wait, and murmur not.
>
> —W. H. Bellamy

Contentment

WHAT does the apostle say is great gain?

"But *godliness with contentment* is great gain. For we brought nothing into this world, and it is certain we can carry nothing out." 1 Timothy 6:6, 7.

With what are we exhorted to be content?

"Let your conversation be without covetousness; and *be content with such things as ye have:* for he hath said, I will never leave thee, nor forsake thee." Hebrews 13:5. "And *having food and raiment* let us be therewith content." 1 Timothy 6:8.

Concerning what does Christ tell us not to be anxious?

"Be not therefore anxious, saying, *What shall we eat?* or, *What shall we drink?* or, *Wherewithal shall we be clothed?* For after all these things do the Gentiles seek; for your heavenly Father knoweth that ye have need of all these things." Matthew 6:31, 32, R.V.

NOTE.—"Live not in *careful suspense.*" Luke 12:29, margin.

What evils befall those who are determined to be rich?

"But they that will be rich *fall into temptation and a snare, and into many foolish and hurtful lusts,* which drown men in destruction and perdition. For the love of money is the root of all evil: which while some coveted after, they have *erred from the faith, and pierced themselves through with many sorrows.*" 1 Timothy 6:9, 10.

By what illustrations did Christ teach contentment?

"*Consider the ravens:* for they neither sow nor reap; which neither have storehouse nor barn; and God feedeth them: how much more are ye better than the fowls? . . . *Consider the lilies* how they grow: they toil not, they spin not; and yet I say unto you, that Solomon in all his glory was not arrayed like one of these. If then God so clothe the grass, which is to day in the field, and to morrow is cast into the oven; how much more will he clothe you, O ye of little faith?" Luke 12:24-28.

What lesson in contentment did Paul say he had learned?

"I have learned, *in whatsoever state I am, therewith to be content.*" Philippians 4:11.

What ancient promise should lead to contentment?

"While the earth remaineth, seedtime and harvest, and cold and heat, and summer and winter, and day and night shall not cease." Genesis 8:22.

Upon whom should we cast all our care?

"Casting all your care upon *him* [God]; for he careth for you." 1 Peter 5:7.

The Philosopher's Stone

A contented mind sees something good in everything—fair weather in every wind, blessings in every storm.

"If we cannot get what we like, we should try to like what we get."

"A contented mind is a continual feast."

"Fortify yourself with contentment, for this is an impregnable fortress."—Epictetus.

"Content is the Philosopher's Stone, that turns all it touches into gold."—Benjamin Franklin.

"Content is wealth, the riches of the mind;
And happy he who can such riches find."—John Dryden.

"God holds the future in His hand,
  O heart of mine, be still!
His love will plan the best for thee,
The best, or light or dark it be:
  Then rest ye in His will.

"God holds the future in His hand,
  Why should I shrink or fear?
Through every dark and cloudy day—
Yea, all along my pilgrim way—
  His love will bless and cheer.

"God holds the future in His hand,
  And I can trust His love.
The past declares His faithfulness;
His eye will guide, His heart will bless,
  Till I am safe above."

A HAPPY FAMILY

"A merry heart doeth good like a medicine." Proverbs 17:22.

Cheerfulness

BEFORE leaving His disciples, what did Jesus say to them?

"These things I have spoken unto you, that in me ye might have peace. In the world ye shall have tribulation: but *be of good cheer;* I have overcome the world." John 16:33.

What were some of the cheering words He said to them?

"Let not your heart be troubled: ye believe in God, believe also in me. In my Father's house are many mansions: if it were not so, I would have told you. *I go to prepare a place for you. And if I go and prepare a place for you, I will come again and receive you unto myself; that where I am, there ye may be also.*" John 14:1-3.

In what spirit should we serve the Lord?

"Serve the Lord with *gladness:* come before his presence with *singing.*" Psalm 100:2.

What is sown for the upright in heart?

"Light is sown for the righteous, and *gladness* for the upright in heart." Psalm 97:11.

GOOD AND BAD MEDICINE

What effect has a merry heart?

"A merry heart *doeth good like a medicine:* but a broken spirit drieth the bones." Proverbs 17:22.

NOTE.—From this we may learn the influence which the mind has over the body. Cheerfulness is conducive to life and health; sorrow, care, anxiety, and worry tend to disease and death.

What effect do helpful, cheerful words have upon the heart?

"Heaviness in the heart of man maketh it stoop: but *a good word maketh it glad.*" Proverbs 12:25.

By what temporal blessings does God fill men's hearts with gladness?

"Nevertheless he left not himself without witness, in that he did good, and *gave us rain from heaven, and fruitful seasons, filling our hearts with food and gladness.*" Acts 14:17.

Why and for what may every child of God rejoice?

"I will greatly rejoice in the Lord, my soul shall be joyful in my God; for *he hath clothed me with the garments of salvation, he hath covered me with the robe of righteousness.*" Isaiah 61:10.

Against what are Christians warned? What fate once overtook the children of Israel when they murmured?

"*Neither murmur ye, as some of them also murmured,* and were destroyed of the destroyer." 1 Corinthians 10:10.

Note.—"There are those who take to gloom as a bat to darkness or as a vulture to carrion. They would rather nurse a misery than cherish a joy. They always find the dark side of everything, if there is a dark side to be found. They appear to be conscientious grumblers, as if it were their duty to extract some essence of misery from every circumstance. . . . On the other hand, there are rare spirits who always take cheerful views of life. They look at the bright side. They find some joy and beauty everywhere. . . . In the most faulty picture they see some bit of beauty which charms them. In the most disagreeable person they discover some kindly trait or some bud of promise. In the most disheartening circumstances they find something for which to be thankful, some gleam of cheer breaking in through the thick gloom.

"When a ray of sunlight streamed through a crack in the shutter and made a bright patch on the floor in the darkened room, the little dog rose from his dark corner and went and lay down in the one sunny spot; and these people live in the same philosophical way. If there be one beam of cheer or hope anywhere in their lot, they will find it. . . . We have no right to project the gloom of our discontent over any other life. Our ministry is to be ever toward joy. There is nothing so depressing in its effect upon others as morbidness. . . . Discontent helps nothing. . . . One never feels better for complaining."—J. R. Miller, *Week-Day Religion*, pp. 234-239.

"How many people," says Jeremy Taylor, "are busy in the world gathering together a handful of thorns to sit upon."

"As a little girl was eating, the sun dashed upon her spoon; and she cried, 'O mamma, I have swallowed a spoonful of sunshine!' Would God that we might all indulge in the same beverage!"— T. De Witt Talmage, *One Thousand Gems* (1873 ed.), p. 59.

REJOICING ALWAYS

Even when persecuted, what are we told to do, and why?

"Rejoice ye in that day, and leap for joy: for, behold, your reward is great in heaven." Luke 6:23.

When beaten by the Jewish rulers for preaching Christ, what did the apostles do?

"And they departed from the presence of the council, *rejoicing that they were counted worthy to suffer shame for his name,*" Acts 5:41.

After receiving "many stripes," and with their feet made fast in the stocks, what did Paul and Silas do while in prison?

"And at midnight Paul and Silas *prayed, and sang praises unto God:* and the prisoners heard them." Acts 16:25.

What assurance is given that the child of God may bravely endure every trial and hardship of life?

"And we know that *all things work together for good to them that love God,* to them who are the called according to his purpose." Romans 8:28.

How constant should our rejoicing be?

"Rejoice in the Lord *alway:* and again I say, *Rejoice.*" Philippians 4:4.

THE HALLMARK OF A HEALTHY SOUL

One writer says that "good cheer is the hallmark of a brave and healthy soul. To give way to gloomy thoughts, otherwise the 'blues,' is a sign of weakness. This isn't asserting that no one but weaklings is attacked by the blues; but it is one thing to be attacked and another to rout the disturber. And that is what the brave soul does. There may be a very real and tangible reason why the heart faints and halts, for life is serious, and the world full of unexpected trials; but to sit and brood over a trouble only makes it look larger and larger until it finally obscures the horizon line, and darkness descends upon the soul. Wherefore, the thing to do is to cast aside all thoughts of worry for a moment,—just say to yourself, It is only for a moment,—and when you return to it again you will be surprised to find it has lessened in size and importance."

Christian Courtesy

WHAT should be our conduct one toward another?

"Love as brethren, be pitiful, *be courteous.*" 1 Peter 3:8.

How many should we honor?

"Honour *all* men. Love the brotherhood." 1 Peter 2:17.

Whom should we salute?

"If ye salute your brethren only, what do ye more than others? do not even the publicans so?" Matthew 5:47.

What respect should be shown the aged?

"Thou shalt *rise up* before the hoary head, and *honour* the face of the old man." Leviticus 19:32. (See 2 Kings 2:23, 24.)

Whom especially should children honor?

"Honour thy *father* and thy *mother*." Exodus 20:12.

How should faithful Christian leaders be regarded?

"Let the elders that rule well be counted worthy of *double honour.*" 1 Timothy 5:17.

What is the basis of true Christian courtesy?

"Charity [love] . . . is kind; . . . charity vaunteth not itself, is not puffed up, doth not behave itself unseemly, seeketh not her own." 1 Corinthians 13:4, 5.

Note.—Genuine Christian courtesy is the outgrowth of love, and manifests itself in thoughtful consideration for others.

Two Compared

Self rushes for a seat. Courtesy says, "You take it." Self elbows to the counter. Courtesy says, "This lady was before me." Self presses hard and long on the auto horn. Courtesy sounds, "Please, and Thank you!" Self always chooses the end seat of the row in church. Courtesy sits in the center. Self reveals the ugly scars of others. Courtesy covers them. Self salutes its friends. Courtesy salutes all men. Self loves self. Courtesy regards others. Self will be shut out of heaven. Courtesy will reign forever.

Confessing Faults and Forgiving One Another

CONFESSION OF SINS TO GOD

What has God promised to do when, in sincerity, we confess our sins?

"If we confess our sins, *he is faithful and just to forgive us our sins,* and to cleanse us from all unrighteousness." 1 John 1:9.

How has it been made possible for sins to be forgiven?

"If any man sin, we have an advocate with the Father, Jesus Christ the righteous: and *he is the propitiation for our sins.*" 1 John 2:1, 2.

To whom should sins be confessed, and why?

"*Against thee, thee only, have I sinned,* and done this evil in thy sight." Psalm 51:4. (See Genesis 39:9.)

When we do wrong, what is the natural thing for us to do?

Excuse it, seek to hide it, or blame someone else for it. (See Genesis 3:12, 13; 4:9.)

After David's great sin had been pointed out to him, what did he say?

"I have sinned." 2 Samuel 12:13. "I acknowledge my transgressions." Psalm 51:3.

When David in contrition of heart confessed his sin, what was God's word to him by Nathan, the prophet?

"And David said unto Nathan, I have sinned against the Lord. And Nathan said unto David, *The Lord also hath put away thy sin;* thou shalt not die." 2 Samuel 12:13.

NOTE.—This scripture is especially encouraging. God hates sin. He wants us likewise to hate it and shun it, because it invariably gets us into trouble, causes sorrow of heart, and in the end brings death. But when involved in it, as was David, as soon as we sincerely repent and confess our sin, *that very moment it is forgiven.*

Pointing Out a Brother's Fault

Is it ever right to tell a brother of his faults?

"If thy brother shall trespass against thee, *go and tell him his fault between thee and him alone:* if he shall hear thee, thou hast gained thy brother." Matthew 18:15. "Thou shalt not hate thy brother in thine heart: *thou shalt in any wise rebuke thy neighbour, and not suffer sin upon him.*" Leviticus 19:17.

One writer aptly says: "Confess your sins to God, who only can forgive them, and your faults to one another. If you have given offense to your friend or neighbor, you are to acknowledge your wrong, and it is his duty freely to forgive you. Then you are to seek the forgiveness of God, because the brother you have wounded is the property of God, and in injuring him you sinned against his Creator and Redeemer."

To confess one's faults is not an easy thing to do; in fact, it is one of the hardest lessons to learn, for it requires the grace of humility as well as that of sorrow and true repentance. It has been said that the four hardest words to pronounce in the English language are, "I made a mistake." Frederick the Great wrote to the Prussian senate, "I have just lost a battle, and it is my own fault." Concerning this Goldsmith says, "His confession shows more greatness than his victories."

The confession should not only be complete, but it should be as broad and as public as was the offense. Private offenses should be confessed in private.

In what spirit should this kind of work be done?

"Brethren, if a man be overtaken in a fault, ye which are spiritual, restore such an one *in the spirit of meekness;* considering thyself, lest thou also be tempted." Galatians 6:1.

Note.—It is much easier to tell *someone else* of a brother's faults than it is to tell *him* of them *yourself;* but this is not the Christian way to proceed. The first efforts should be made with the offender *in person,* and *alone.* But it is easier even to tell *a brother* of *his* faults than it is to confess to him *our own.* This, again, let it be noted, is the one difficult lesson to learn, the one Christian duty difficult to perform. Only humility and the grace of God will enable one to do it.

Forgiving Others

When we pray, what does Christ tell us to do, and why?

"And when ye stand praying, *forgive,* if ye have ought against any: *that your Father* also which is in heaven *may forgive you your trespasses."* Mark 11:25.

If we do not forgive others, what will God not do?

"But if ye do not forgive, *neither will your Father which is in heaven forgive your trespasses."* Verse 26. (See, for illustration, Christ's parable recorded in Matthew 18:23-35.)

What words of Joseph to his brethren show that he forgave them for selling him into Egypt?

"Now therefore *be not grieved, nor angry with yourselves, that ye sold me hither:* for God did send me before you to preserve life. . . . *So now it was not you that sent me hither, but God."* Genesis 45:5-8.

What was Christ's reply to Peter's question as to the number of times we should forgive one another?

"Then came Peter to him, and said, Lord, how oft shall my brother sin against me, and I forgive him? till seven times? Jesus saith unto him, *I say not unto thee, Until seven times: but, Until seventy times seven."* Matthew 18:21, 22.

Note.—That is, an unlimited number. We must pardon offenses against us though ever so often done; we must forgive to the end.

What spirit did Jesus manifest toward those who nailed Him to the cross?

"Then said Jesus, *Father, forgive them; for they know not what they do."* Luke 23:34.

How did Stephen manifest the same spirit toward those who stoned him?

"And they stoned Stephen, calling upon God. . . . And he kneeled down, and cried with a loud voice, *Lord, lay not this sin to their charge."* Acts 7:59, 60. (See 1 Peter 4:8.)

BE NOT DISMAYED   "Be strong and of a good courage." Joshua

The Duty of Encouragement

THE EFFECT OF AN EVIL REPORT

WHEN the ten spies brought back an evil report from the land of Canaan, what did Caleb say?

"And Caleb stilled the people before Moses, and said, *Let us go up at once, and possess it; for we are well able to overcome it.*" Numbers 13:30.

What did the ten spies say?

"But the men that went up with him said, *We be not able to go up against the people; for they are stronger than we.*" Verse 31.

What effect did this evil report have upon the people?

"And all the congregation lifted up their voice, and *cried;* and the people *wept* that night. And all the children of Israel *murmured* against Moses and against Aaron: and the whole congregation said unto them, *Would God that we had died in the land of Egypt! or would God we had died in this wilderness!* ... And they said one to another, *Let us make a captain, and let us return into Egypt.*" Numbers 14:1-4.

A NEW LEADER IS ENCOURAGED

With what words did Moses seek to encourage Joshua?

"And Moses called unto Joshua, and said unto him in the sight of all Israel, *Be strong and of a good courage.* ... The Lord, he it is that doth go before thee; he will be with thee, he will not fail thee, neither forsake thee: *fear not, neither be dismayed.*" Deuteronomy 31:7, 8.

In his final charge to Joshua, what did Moses, speaking for God, say to him?

"And he gave Joshua the son of Nun a charge, and said, *Be strong and of a good courage:* for thou shalt bring the children of Israel into the land which I sware unto them: and I will be with thee." Verse 23.

After Moses' death, how did the Lord encourage Joshua?

"There shall not any man be able to stand before thee all the days of thy life: as I was with Moses, so I will be with thee: I will not fail thee, nor forsake thee. *Be strong and of a good courage.*" Joshua 1:1-6.

Leaders Encourage the People

When Sennacherib, king of Assyria, came against Jerusalem, what did King Hezekiah say to Israel?

"Be strong and courageous, be not afraid nor dismayed for the king of Assyria, nor for all the multitude that is with him: for there be more with us than with him: with him is an arm of flesh; but with us is the Lord our God to help us, and to fight our battles." 2 Chronicles 32:7, 8, first part.

What effect did these words have upon the people?

"And *the people rested themselves upon the words of Hezekiah* king of Judah." Verse 8, last part.

How did Josiah seek to promote the worship of God?

"And he set the priests in their charges, and *encouraged them to the service of the house of the Lord.*" 2 Chronicles 35:2.

Heaven Encourages All

By what message, through the prophet Haggai, did God seek to encourage the people to rebuild the Temple?

"Be strong, O Zerubbabel, saith the Lord; and *be strong, O Joshua,* son of Josedech, the high priest; and *be strong, all ye people of the land,* saith the Lord, *and work: for I am with you, saith the Lord of hosts.*" Haggai 2:4.

What encouraging message has Christ left us?

"Be of good cheer; I have overcome the world." John 16:33.

Note.—A discouraged man, like a dispirited horse, is powerless to perform his task.

"What men need most in this world's struggle and strife is not usually direct help, but cheer. . . . Many men have fainted and succumbed in the great struggles whom one word of cheer would have made strong to overcome. We should never, then, lose an opportunity to say an inspiring word. We know not how much it is needed or how great and far-reaching its consequences may be."— J. R. Miller, *Week-Day Religion,* p. 170.

Unity of Believers

BASIS OF UNITY IN HEAVEN

What relation do the Father and the Son sustain to each other?

"I and my Father *are one.*" John 10:30.

In what does this oneness consist?

"I seek not mine own will, but *the will of the Father* which hath sent me." John 5:30.

Note.—Their oneness, therefore, consists in their having the same mind, will, and purpose.

DESIRE FOR UNITY ON EARTH

What did Christ pray the Father in behalf of His disciples?

"That they may be one, even as we are one." John 17:22. (See also verses 11 and 23.)

Why did Christ desire this oneness, or unity, to exist among His followers?

"That they all may be one; as thou, Father, art in me, and I in thee, that they also may be one in us: *that the world may believe that thou hast sent me."* Verse 21.

By what did Christ say all men should know His disciples?

"By this shall all men know that ye are my disciples, *if ye have love one to another."* John 13:35.

Note.—"God has united believers in church capacity in order that one may strengthen another in good and righteous endeavor. The church on earth would indeed be a symbol of the church in heaven if the members were of one mind and of one faith. It is those who are not moved by the Holy Spirit that mar God's plan. Another spirit takes possession of them, and they help to strengthen the forces of darkness. Those who are sanctified by the precious blood of Christ will not become the means of counterworking the great plan which God has devised. They will not bring human depravity into things small or great. They will do nothing to perpetuate division in the church."—ELLEN G. WHITE, *Testimonies*, pp. 238, 239.

When there is disunion among believers, the world concludes that they cannot be the people of God because they are working against one another. When believers are one with Christ, they will be united among themselves.

How did Paul show his concern in this matter?

"Now I beseech you, brethren, by the name of our Lord Jesus Christ, *that ye all speak the same thing,* and *that there be no divisions among you;* but *that ye be perfectly joined together in the same mind and in the same judgment.*" 1 Corinthians 1:10.

DIVISION FORETOLD

What was a prominent cause of division in the early church?

"For I know this, that after my departing shall grievous wolves enter in among you, not sparing the flock. Also of *your own selves shall men arise, speaking perverse things, to draw away disciples after them.*" Acts 20:29, 30.

What was already at work in the church in Paul's day?

"For *the mystery of iniquity doth already work:* only he who now letteth [hindereth] will let, until he be taken out of the way." 2 Thessalonians 2:7.

Before Christ should come, what did Paul say was to take place?

"Let no man deceive you by any means: for that day shall not come, except there come *a falling away* first, and *that man of sin be revealed, the son of perdition;* who opposeth and exalteth himself above all that is called God, or that is worshipped; so that he as God sitteth in the temple of God, shewing himself that he is God." Verses 3, 4.

NOTE.—The huge system of error now fostered in the papal church is the result of the falling away here referred to. (See readings on pages 211, 266.)

UNITY ILLUSTRATED AND PREDICTED

Together, what do believers in Christ form?

"Now *ye are the body of Christ,* and members in particular." 1 Corinthians 12:27.

Being members of Christ's body, of what else do we become members?

"So we, being many, are one body in Christ, and *every one members one of another.*" Romans 12:5.

As members of one another, what is the duty of each?

"That there should be no schism in the body; but that *the members should have the same care one for another.*" 1 Corinthians 12:25.

What should they endeavor to keep?

"I therefore, the prisoner of the Lord, beseech you that ye walk worthy of the vocation wherewith ye are called, with all lowliness and meekness, with longsuffering, forbearing one another in love; *endeavouring to keep the unity of the Spirit in the bond of peace.*" Ephesians 4:1-3.

What solemn message, just before the Lord's coming, will unite God's people in bonds of faith and love?

"Fear God, and give glory to him; for the hour of his judgment is come: and worship him that made heaven, and earth, and the sea, and the fountains of waters. . . . Babylon is fallen, is fallen, that great city, because she made all nations drink of the wine of the wrath of her fornication. . . . If any man worship the beast and his image, and receive his mark in his forehead, or in his hand, the same shall drink of the wine of the wrath of God." Revelation 14:7-10. (See Revelation 18:1-5.)

How are those who receive this message described?

"Here is the patience of the saints: here are they that keep the commandments of God, and the faith of Jesus." Verse 12.

When the Lord comes, what will be the united cry of God's people?

"And it shall be said in that day, Lo, this is our God; we have waited for him, and he will save us: this is the Lord; we have waited for him, we will be glad and rejoice in his salvation." Isaiah 25:9.

"How blest the sacred tie that binds
In sweet communion kindred minds!
How swift the heavenly course they run,
Whose hearts, whose faith, whose hopes, are one!"

Meekness and Humility

THE NATURE AND SOURCE OF MEEKNESS

WHAT promise is made to the meek?

"Blessed are the meek: for *they shall inherit the earth.*" Matthew 5:5.

NOTE.—*Meek:* The Greek word thus translated means "gentle," "humble," "considerate."

What did Christ say of His own character?

"Take my yoke upon you, and learn of me; for *I am meek and lowly in heart:* and ye shall find rest unto your souls." Matthew 11:29.

What is said of the character of Moses?

"Now *the man Moses was very meek,* above all the men which were upon the face of the earth." Numbers 12:3.

Of what is meekness a fruit?

"But *the fruit of the Spirit is* love, joy, peace, longsuffering, gentleness, goodness, faith, *meekness,* temperance: against such there is no law." Galatians 5:22, 23.

GOD'S FELLOWSHIP WITH THE MEEK

With whom does God dwell?

"I dwell in the high and holy place, *with him also that is of a contrite and humble spirit,* to revive the spirit of the humble, and to revive the heart of the contrite ones." Isaiah 57:15.

Whom has God promised to guide in judgment?

"*The meek* will he guide in judgment: and *the meek* will he teach his way." Psalm 25:9.

MEEKNESS AND EXALTATION CONTRASTED

What does Christ say of those who exalt themselves?

"For whosoever exalteth himself *shall be abased;* and he that humbleth himself shall be exalted." Luke 14:11.

MEEKNESS AND HUMILITY

NOTE.—The spirit of self-exaltation is of Satan. (See Isaiah 14:12-14; Ezekiel 28:17.) Christ humbled Himself, made Himself of no reputation, and became obedient even to the death on the cross. (See Philippians 2:5-8.)

By what means did Jesus illustrate true humility?

"And Jesus called *a little child* unto him, and set him in the midst of them, and said, . . . *Whosoever therefore shall humble himself as this little child, the same is greatest in the kingdom of heaven.*" Matthew 18:2-4.

NOTE.—Humility is "freedom from pride and arrogance; lowliness of mind; a modest estimate of one's own worth." It implies a sense of one's own unworthiness through imperfection and sinfulness, and consists in rating our *claims* low, in being willing to *waive our rights,* and to *take a lower place than might be our due.* It does not require that we underrate ourselves or our lifework. The humility of Christ was perfect, yet He had a true sense of the importance of His life and mission.

"Humility is like a tree, whose root, when it sets deepest in the earth, rises higher, and spreads fairer, and stands surer, and lasts longer, and every step of its descent is like a rib of iron."—BISHOP TAYLOR.

MEEKNESS IN ACTION

How will humility lead us to esteem others?

"Let nothing be done through strife or vainglory; but in lowliness of mind *let each esteem other better than themselves.*" Philippians 2:3.

When asked a reason for our hope, in what spirit should we answer?

"But sanctify the Lord God in your hearts: and be ready always to give an answer to every man that asketh you a reason of the hope that is in you *with meekness and fear.*" 1 Peter 3:15.

Who should labor for one overtaken in a fault, and in what spirit?

"Brethren, if a man be overtaken in a fault, *ye which are spiritual,* restore such an one *in the spirit of meekness;* considering thyself, lest thou also be tempted." Galatians 6:1.

With what should Christian women adorn themselves?

"Whose adorning let it not be that outward adorning of

plaiting the hair, and of wearing of gold, or of putting on of apparel; but let it be the hidden man of the heart, in that which is not corruptible, even *the ornament of a meek and quiet spirit,* which is in the sight of God of great price." 1 Peter 3:3, 4.

Note.—The instruction given here, *in principle* applies with equal force to men professing godliness. It is the needless display of apparel and outward adornment that is here condemned. God desires the ornaments *within,* displayed in the heart and life, rather than those *without,* simply to be seen of men. Needless outward adornment, therefore, may generally be taken as an indication that the inward adornment, so precious in the sight of God, is lacking. Neatness in dress is not here discouraged.

What are the meek exhorted to seek?

"Seek ye the Lord, all ye meek of the earth, which have wrought his judgment; seek righteousness, *seek meekness:* it may be ye shall be hid in the day of the Lord's anger." Zephaniah 2:3.

Note.—The fact that the meek are exhorted to seek meekness is evidence that the meek themselves should cherish and cultivate meekness, and that sanctification, or the development of a perfect character, is a progressive work.

The Reward of the Meek

Why are we exhorted to humble ourselves?

"Humble yourselves therefore under the mighty hand of God, *that he may exalt you in due time."* 1 Peter 5:6.

Note.—"The higher a man is in grace, the lower he will be in his own esteem."—Spurgeon.

With what has the Lord promised to beautify the meek?

"For the Lord taketh pleasure in his people: *he will beautify the meek with salvation."* Psalm 149:4.

What inheritance is promised the meek?

"For yet a little while, and the wicked shall not be: yea, thou shalt diligently consider his place, and it shall not be. But *the meek shall inherit the earth; and shall delight themselves in the abundance of peace."* Psalm 37:10, 11.

Sobriety and Dignity

SOLOMON'S SCHOOL OF EXPERIENCE

To what extent did Solomon test the pleasures of this world?

"*Whatsoever mine eyes desired* I kept not from them, I withheld not my heart from *any joy.*" "I said in mine heart, Go to now, I will prove thee with *mirth,* therefore enjoy *pleasure.*" Ecclesiastes 2:10, 1.

How much true enjoyment did such a course afford?

"Behold, *all was vanity and vexation of spirit.*" Verse 11.

Of what does Solomon bid the young, in the buoyancy of youth, to be mindful?

"Rejoice, O young man, in thy youth; and let thy heart cheer thee in the days of thy youth, and walk in the ways of thine heart, and in the sight of thine eyes: *but know thou, that for all these things God will bring thee into judgment.*" Ecclesiastes 11:9.

GRACE GIVES SOBER COUNSEL

How does the grace of God teach us that we should live?

"For the grace of God that bringeth salvation hath appeared to all men, teaching us that, denying ungodliness and worldly lusts, we should *live soberly, righteously, and godly, in this present world.*" Titus 2:11, 12.

What classes of individuals are admonished to be sober?

"That the *aged men* be sober, grave, temperate, sound in faith, in charity, in patience. The *aged women* likewise, that they be in behaviour as becometh holiness, . . . that they may teach the *young women* to be sober. . . . *Young men* likewise exhort to be sober minded." Verses 2-6.

NOTE.—These four classes include all. All should be sober.

What similar advice is given in the epistle to the Romans?

"Let us walk honestly, as in the day; not in rioting and

drunkenness, not in chambering and wantonness, not in strife and envying." Romans 13:13.

Foolishness, Sin, and Satan

Why are foolish talking and jesting to be avoided?

"Neither filthiness, nor foolish talking, nor jesting, *which are not convenient.*" Ephesians 5:4.

Note.—To indulge in such things is not becoming a Christian. Life, with all its responsibilities and great issues at stake, is too serious a matter to be spent in such vanities. Levity, foolishness, light and loose talking, throw us off our guard, and open the way to temptation and sin. To avoid sin, we must be sober and constantly on guard.

Why are sobriety and vigilance especially necessary?

"Be sober, be vigilant; *because your adversary the devil, as a roaring lion, walketh about, seeking whom he may devour.*" 1 Peter 5:8.

Sobriety and Christ's Second Coming

What testimony does the apostle Peter bear on this point?

"Wherefore gird up the loins of your mind, *be sober,* and hope to the end for the grace that is to be brought unto you at the revelation of Jesus Christ." 1 Peter 1:13.

What other consideration should lead us to sobriety and watchfulness?

"But *the end of all things is at hand:* be ye therefore sober, and watch unto prayer." 1 Peter 4:7.

> How vain are all things here below!
> How false, and yet how fair!
> Each pleasure hath its poison too,
>   And every sweet a snare.
>
> —Isaac Watts

True Wisdom

THE VALUE OF WISDOM

WHY are we told to get wisdom?

"Wisdom is the principal thing; therefore get wisdom." Proverbs 4:7.

NOTE.—Wisdom implies the ability to judge soundly and deal sagaciously. It is knowledge, with the capacity to make due use of it. One may have abundance of *knowledge* and at the same time possess little *wisdom*.

Of how much value is wisdom?

"She is more precious than rubies: and all the things thou canst desire are not to be compared unto her." Proverbs 3:15.

THE SOURCE OF WISDOM

Who gives wisdom?

"For the Lord giveth wisdom." Proverbs 2:6.

How may it be obtained?

"If any of you lack wisdom, *let him ask of God*, that giveth to all men liberally, and upbraideth not; *and it shall be given him.*" James 1:5.

When Solomon became king, what did he ask the Lord to give him?

"Give me now *wisdom and knowledge.*" 2 Chronicles 1:10.

How did the Lord regard this request?

"And *the speech pleased the Lord,* that Solomon had asked this thing." 1 Kings 3:10.

How was Solomon's prayer answered?

"And God said unto him, Because thou hast asked this thing, and hast not asked for thyself long life; neither hast asked riches for thyself, nor hast asked the life of thine enemies; . . . *behold, I have done according to thy words: lo, I have given thee a wise and an understanding heart. . . . And I have also given thee that which thou hast not asked, both riches, and honour."* Verses 11-13.

What is the beginning of wisdom?

"*The fear of the Lord* is the beginning of wisdom: a good understanding have all they that do his commandments." Psalm 111:10.

By what means was the psalmist made wiser than his enemies?

"Thou *through thy commandments* hast made me wiser than mine enemies: for they are ever with me." Psalm 119:98.

Why did his understanding excel that of his teachers?

"I have more understanding than all my teachers: *for thy testimonies are my meditation."* Verse 99.

THE EFFECTS OF WISDOM

What blessings follow the acquisition of wisdom?

"Exalt her, and she shall *promote thee:* she shall *bring thee to honour,* when thou dost embrace her. She shall give to thine head *an ornament of grace: a crown of glory shall she deliver to thee."* Proverbs 4:8, 9.

What effect does wisdom have upon the countenance?

"A man's wisdom maketh his face to *shine."* Ecclesiastes 8:1.

Are great men always wise?

"*Great men are not always wise:* neither do the aged understand judgment." Job 32:9.

TWO KINDS OF WISDOM

In what did Christ say the children of this world excel the children of light?

"For the children of this world are in their generation *wiser* than the children of light." Luke 16:8.

NOTE.—That is, they show more prudence, more cunning, and more intelligence about their business than do Christians concerning the things of God's kingdom. "They show more skill, study more plans, contrive more ways, to provide for themselves than the children of light do to promote the interests of religion."—ALBERT BARNES.

In what did the apostle say he would have us wise, and in what simple?

"I would have you *wise unto that which is good,* and *simple* concerning evil." Romans 16:19.

How many kinds of wisdom are there?

"Howbeit we speak wisdom among them that are perfect: yet not *the wisdom of this world,* . . . but we speak *the wisdom of God* in a mystery, even *the hidden wisdom, which God ordained before the world unto our glory.*" 1 Corinthians 2:6, 7.

How is worldly wisdom regarded by God?

"For the wisdom of this world is *foolishness* with God." 1 Corinthians 3:19.

What is the character of that wisdom which comes from God?

"But the wisdom that is from above is first *pure,* then *peaceable, gentle,* and *easy to be intreated, full of mercy and good fruits, without partiality, and without hypocrisy.*" James 3:17.

What wisdom are the Scriptures able to give?

"And that from a child thou hast known the holy scriptures, which are able to make thee *wise unto salvation* through faith which is in Christ Jesus." 2 Timothy 3:15.

> BROAD is the road that leads to death,
>   And thousands walk together there;
> But wisdom shows a narrow path,
>   With here and there a traveler.
>
> Deny thyself, and take thy cross,
>   Is thy Redeemer's great command;
> Nature must count her gold but dross,
>   If she would gain that heavenly land.
>
> The fearful soul that tries and faints,
>   And walks the ways of God no more,
> Is but esteemed almost a saint,
>   And makes his own destruction sure.
>   —ISAAC WATTS

A. DEVANEY

DILIGENCE IS THE ENEMY OF POVERTY

"He that tilleth his land shall have plenty of bread." Proverbs 28:19

Diligence in Labor

WHAT general command has God given concerning labor?

"Six days shalt thou labour, and do all thy work." Exodus 20:9.

What are men instructed to do instead of living upon the earnings of others?

"Let him that stole steal no more: but rather *let him labour, working with his hands* the thing which is good, that he may have to give to him that needeth." Ephesians 4:28.

What general rule does Paul lay down upon this subject?

"For even when we were with you, this we commanded you, that *if any would not work, neither should he eat.*" 2 Thessalonians 3:10.

In what language does he condemn idleness?

"For we hear that there are some which walk among you disorderly, *working not at all,* but are busybodies. Now them that are such *we command and exhort* by our Lord Jesus Christ, *that with quietness they work, and eat their own bread.*" Verses 11, 12.

What example did the apostle himself set in this matter?

"Neither did we eat any man's bread for nought; but *wrought with labour and travail night and day,* that we might not be chargeable to any of you." Verse 8.

What labor was appointed man in consequence of the Fall?

"*In the sweat of thy face shalt thou eat bread,* till thou return unto the ground." Genesis 3:19.

NOTE.—A life of laborious and perpetual toil, in a world cursed with weeds, thorns, and thistles, was appointed to man in consequence of the entrance of sin. This was a part of the curse. And yet even this was appointed in love, and, under existing circumstances, is a blessing in disguise.

Solomon Speaks on Industry

What are some of the results of industry?

"He that tilleth his land *shall have plenty of bread.*" Proverbs 28:19. "The hand of the diligent *maketh rich.*" Proverbs 10:4.

What does Solomon say concerning diligence in business?

"Whatsoever thy hand findeth to do, do it with thy might." Ecclesiastes 9:10.

What does Solomon say of the industrious woman?

"She looketh well to the ways of her household, and eateth not the bread of idleness. Her children arise up, and call her blessed; her husband also, and he praiseth her." Proverbs 31: 27, 28.

Indolence in Bible Light

What results from slackness and indolence in business?

"He *becometh poor* that dealeth with a slack hand." Proverbs 10:4. "The soul of the sluggard desireth, and *hath nothing.*" Proverbs 13:4.

Note.—In temporal matters the difference between a prosperous man and a sluggard lies principally in the improvement of opportunities.

What picture has Solomon given of the slothful man?

"I went by the field of the slothful, and by the vineyard of the man void of understanding; and, lo, it was all grown over with thorns, and nettles had covered the face thereof, and the stone wall thereof was broken down." Proverbs 24:30, 31.

What has Paul said of the professed Christian who does not provide for his own family?

"But if any provide not for his own, and specially for those of his own house, *he hath denied the faith, and is worse than an infidel.*" 1 Timothy 5:8.

Diligence in Spiritual Things

In spiritual matters, what is also necessary?

"And beside this, *giving all diligence,* add to your faith virtue; and to virtue knowledge. . . . Give *diligence* to make your calling and election sure." 2 Peter 1:5-10.

Perfection of Character

THE CALL TO PERFECTION

Why are we exhorted to patience?

"But let patience have her perfect work, *that ye may be perfect and entire, wanting [lacking] nothing.*" James 1:4.

How perfect does Christ tell us to be?

"Be ye therefore perfect, *even as your Father which is in heaven is perfect.*" Matthew 5:48.

In whom are we complete?

"And ye are complete *in him.*" Colossians 2:10.

GROWTH AND ADVANCEMENT

After accepting Christ, what are we to do?

"Therefore leaving the principles of the doctrine of Christ, *let us go on unto perfection.*" Hebrews 6:1.

In what is the Christian to grow?

"But grow in *grace,* and in *the knowledge of our Lord and Saviour Jesus Christ.*" 2 Peter 3:18.

How may one grow in grace?

"Giving all diligence, *add to your faith virtue;* . . . *knowledge;* . . . *temperance;* . . . *patience;* . . . *godliness;* . . . *brotherly kindness;* . . . *charity.*" 2 Peter 1:5-7.

Why does Christ desire this growth in His followers?

"That he might present it to himself *a glorious church,* not having *spot,* or *wrinkle,* or *any such thing;* but that it should be *holy* and *without blemish.*" Ephesians 5:27.

SOURCES OF SPIRITUAL NOURISHMENT

What will cause the Christian to grow?

"As newborn babes, desire *the sincere milk of the word,* that ye may grow thereby." 1 Peter 2:2.

In order to grow by the word of God, what must one do?

"Thy words were found, and I did *eat* them." Jeremiah 15:16. "Thy word have I *hid in mine heart.*" Psalm 119:11. (See Colossians 3:16.)

What does God's word then become to the believer?

"Thy word was unto me *the joy and rejoicing of mine heart.*" Jeremiah 15:16, last part.

Why are the Scriptures given?

"All scripture is given by inspiration of God, and is profitable for doctrine, for reproof, for correction, for instruction in righteousness: *that the man of God may be perfect,* throughly furnished unto all good works." 2 Timothy 3:16, 17.

How may the lack of wisdom be supplied?

"If any of you lack wisdom, *let him ask of God,* that giveth to all men liberally, and upbraideth not; *and it shall be given him.*" James 1:5.

In how many things may we ask help from God?

"Be careful for nothing; but *in every thing* by prayer and supplication with thanksgiving *let your requests be made known unto God.*" Philippians 4:6.

EVIDENCES AND FULLNESS OF PERFECTION

What is an evidence of perfection?

"*If any man offend not in word, the same is a perfect man,* and able also to bridle the whole body." James 3:2.

What is the bond of perfection?

"And above all these things put on *charity,* which is the bond of perfectness." Colossians 3:14. (See Philippians 3:13, 14; Hebrews 12:14.)

How perfect would God have us become?

"And the very God of peace *sanctify you wholly;* and I pray God *your whole spirit and soul and body be preserved blameless* unto the coming of our Lord Jesus Christ." 1 Thessalonians 5:23.

Sowing and Reaping

THE LAW THAT GOVERNS

WHAT does Paul say regarding sowing and reaping?

"Be not deceived; God is not mocked: for *whatsoever a man soweth, that shall he also reap.*" Galatians 6:7.

How is a similar law expressed by Christ?

"Judge not, and ye shall not be judged: condemn not, and ye shall not be condemned: forgive, and ye shall be forgiven: give, and it shall be given unto you; good measure, pressed down, and shaken together, and running over, shall men give into your bosom. *For with the same measure that ye mete withal it shall be measured to you again.*" Luke 6:37, 38.

NOTE.—A man's deeds, good or evil, usually return to bless or curse him. A farmer who sold butter to a village storekeeper and took sugar in exchange complained that he was getting short weight. "Look here," said he to the merchant, "it seems to me you're giving me short weight sugar." "No," replied the storekeeper, "that cannot be, for in measuring out that sugar of yours I always use a pound of your butter as a weight."

"Good and evil come back.... God made the universe on the plan of the circle. Isaiah 40:22.... We ourselves start the circle of good or bad actions, and it will surely come around again to us unless by divine intervention it be hindered. Those bad or good actions may make the circuit of many years; but come back to us they will as certainly as that God sits on the circle of the earth.... What a stupendous thought that the good and the evil we start come back to us! Do you know that the judgment-day will be only the point at which the circle joins, the good and the bad we have done coming back to us, unless divine intervention hinders,—coming back to us, welcome of delight or curse of condemnation?"—T. DE WITT TALMAGE.

THE LAW APPLIED TO THE WICKED

How does the psalmist apply the law to the wicked?

"As he loved *cursing,* so let it come unto him: as he delighted not in *blessing,* so let it be far from him." Psalm 109:17.

According to what was judgment called upon Babylon?

"Recompense her according to her work; according to all that she hath done, do unto her." Jeremiah 50:29.

Why did Christ tell Peter to put up his sword?

"Put up again thy sword into his place: *for all they that take the sword shall perish with the sword.*" Matthew 26:52.

Why was the power represented by the beast to go into captivity?

"He that leadeth into captivity shall go into captivity: he that killeth with the sword must be killed with the sword." Revelation 13:10.

What is to be the punishment of spiritual Babylon?

"Reward her even as she rewarded you, and double unto her double according to her works." Revelation 18:6.

What does the psalmist say will come to the persecutor?

"His mischief shall return upon his own head, and his violent dealing shall come down upon his own pate." Psalm 7:16.

Note.—In his letter addressed to the Jews, dated November 16, 1905, President Theodore Roosevelt said: "I feel very strongly that if any people are oppressed anywhere, the wrong inevitably reacts in the end on those who oppress them; for it is an immutable law in the spiritual world that no one can wrong others and yet in the end himself escape unhurt."

What befell Haman, who sought to slay all the Jews?

"So they hanged Haman on the gallows that he had prepared for Mordecai." Esther 7:10. (See Psalm 9:15.)

THE RULE WORKS WITH THE RIGHTEOUS

On what condition does Christ say God will forgive us?

"For *if ye forgive men their trespasses,* your heavenly Father will also forgive you: but if ye forgive not men their trespasses, neither will your Father forgive your trespasses." Matthew 6:14, 15. (See also Matthew 18:23-35.)

Part Thirteen

Prayer and Public Worship

	PAGE
Importance of Prayer	597
Meditation and Prayer	601
Watching Unto Prayer	604
Answers to Prayer	606
Public Worship	609
Reverence for the House of God	613
Christian Communion	617
Praise and Thanksgiving	619
The Value of Song	621

COURTESY, HAMMOND INSTRUMENT CO.

IN THE HOUSE OF PRAYER AND PRAISE

"Enter into his gates with thanksgiving, and into his courts with

Importance of Prayer

God's Promises Regarding Prayer

By what title does the psalmist address God?

"*O thou that hearest prayer,* unto thee shall all flesh come." Psalm 65:2.

Of whom does the Bible teach that God is a rewarder?

"A rewarder *of them that diligently seek him.*" Hebrews 11:6.

How willing is God to hear and answer prayer?

"If ye then, being evil, know how to give good gifts unto your children, *how much more shall your Father which is in heaven give good things to them that ask him?*" Matthew 7:11.

What above all else shows God's willingness to do this?

"He that spared not his own Son, but delivered him up for us all, how shall he not with him also freely give us all things?" Romans 8:32.

The First Step in Prayer

Upon what conditions are we promised needed blessings?

"*Ask,* and it shall be given you; *seek,* and ye shall find; *knock,* and it shall be opened unto you: for every one that asketh receiveth; and he that seeketh findeth; and to him that knocketh it shall be opened." Matthew 7:7, 8.

Note.—"Prayer is the opening of the heart to God as to a friend."—Ellen G. White, *Steps to Christ* (pocket ed.), p. 93. Prayer does not change God; but it does change *us* and our *relation* to God. It places us in the channel of blessings, and in that frame of mind in which God can consistently and safely grant our requests.

"How shall we pray so as to be heard and to receive help? For one thing, there must be a real desire in our hearts. Forms of words do not make prayer: we must want something, and must realize our dependence upon God for it."—J. R. Miller.

From whom do all good and perfect gifts come?

"Every good gift and every perfect gift is from above, and

cometh down from *the Father of lights,* with whom is no variableness, neither shadow of turning." James 1:17.

If one lacks wisdom, what is he told to do?

"If any of you lack wisdom, *let him ask of God,* that giveth to all men liberally, and upbraideth not; and it shall be given him." Verse 5.

Three Conditions to Answered Prayer

How must one ask in order to receive?

"But let him *ask in faith, nothing wavering.* For he that wavereth is like a wave of the sea driven with the wind and tossed. For let not that man think that he shall receive any thing of the Lord." Verses 6, 7. (See Mark 11:24.)

Note.—"Prayer is the key in the hand of faith to unlock heaven's storehouse, where are treasured the boundless resources of Omnipotence."—Ellen G. White, *Steps to Christ* (pocket ed.), pp. 94, 95.

Under what condition does the psalmist say the Lord will not hear prayer?

"If I regard iniquity in my heart, the Lord will not hear me." Psalm 66:18. (See Isaiah 59:1, 2; James 4:3.)

Whose prayers does Solomon say are an abomination?

"He that turneth away his ear from hearing the law, even his prayer shall be abomination." Proverbs 28:9.

Note.—Contention and discord quench the spirit of prayer. (1 Peter 3:1-7.) Many grieve the Spirit and drive Christ from their homes by giving way to impatience and passion. Angels of God flee from homes where there are unkind words, contention, and strife.

For whom did Christ teach us to pray?

"But I say unto you, Love your enemies, bless them that curse you, do good to them that hate you, and *pray for them which despitefully use you, and persecute you."* Matthew 5:44.

Note.—We cannot hate those for whom we pray sincerely.

When praying, what must we do in order to be forgiven?

"And when ye stand praying, *forgive, if ye have ought against any:* that your Father also which is in heaven may forgive you your trespasses." Mark 11:25.

IMPORTANCE OF PRAYER

TIME, PLACE, AND CONTENT OF PRAYER

What did Christ say concerning secret prayer?

"But thou, when thou prayest, *enter into thy closet,* and when thou hast shut thy door, *pray to thy Father which is in secret;* and thy Father which seeth in secret shall reward thee openly." Matthew 6:6.

To what place did Jesus retire for secret devotion?

"And when he had sent the multitudes away, *he went up into a mountain apart to pray:* and when the evening was come, he was there alone." Matthew 14:23.

With what should our prayers be mingled?

"Be careful for nothing; but in every thing by prayer and supplication *with thanksgiving* let your requests be made known unto God." Philippians 4:6.

How often should we pray?

"Praying always with all prayer and supplication in the Spirit." Ephesians 6:18. *"Pray without ceasing."* 1 Thessalonians 5:17. *"Every day will I bless thee;* and I will praise thy name for ever and ever." Psalm 145:2.

How often did the psalmist say he would pray?

"Evening, and *morning,* and at *noon,* will I pray, and cry aloud: and he shall hear my voice." Psalm 55:17. (See Daniel 6:10.)

In whose name did Christ teach us to pray?

"And whatsoever ye shall ask in *my name,* that will I do." John 14:13.

Why did the unjust judge answer the widow's prayer?

"Though I fear not God, nor regard man; yet *because this widow troubleth me,* I will avenge her, *lest by her continual coming she weary me."* Luke 18:4, 5.

NOTE.—The lesson of the parable is that "men ought always to pray, and not to faint." Verse 1. If this woman, by her persistence in asking, obtained her request from such a man, surely God, who is just, will answer the earnest, persistent prayers of His people, though the answer may be long delayed.

THE LORD'S PRAYER

~~~

Our father which art in heaven, hallowed be thy name. ∞ Thy kingdom come. Thy will be done in earth, as it is in heaven. ∞ Give us this day our daily bread. ∞ And forgive us our debts, as we forgive our debtors. ∞ And lead us not into temptation, but deliver us from evil: for thine is the kingdom, and the power, and the glory, for ever. Amen.

Meditation and Prayer

SUBJECTS OF MEDITATION

WHAT was one of Paul's injunctions to Timothy?

"*Meditate upon these things;* give thyself wholly to them." 1 Timothy 4:15.

NOTE.—Meditation is to the soul what digestion is to the body. It assimilates, appropriates, and makes personal and practical that which has been seen, heard, or read.

When did the psalmist say he would praise God with joyful lips?

"*When I remember thee* upon my bed, *and meditate on thee* in the night watches." Psalm 63:6.

How will such meditation be to one who loves God?

"My meditation of him shall be *sweet*." Psalm 104:34.

In what does the psalmist say the man who is blessed delights and meditates?

"His delight is in *the law of the Lord;* and in *his law* doth he meditate day and night." Psalm 1:2.

TEMPTATION AND MEDITATION

With what adversary do we constantly have to contend?

"Be sober, be vigilant; because *your adversary the devil,* as a roaring lion, walketh about, seeking whom he may devour." 1 Peter 5:8.

When is a man tempted?

"But every man is tempted, when *he is drawn away of his own lust, and enticed.*" James 1:14.

That we may not be overcome, what are we told to do?

"*Watch and pray, that ye enter not into temptation:* the spirit indeed is willing, but the flesh is weak." Matthew 26:41.

LIGHT FROM THE SACRED PAGE

"Thy word is a lamp unto my feet, and

J. BYRON LOGAN

MEDITATION AND PRAYER

Necessity of Constant Prayer Attitude

How constantly should we pray?

"Pray *without ceasing*." 1 Thessalonians 5:17. "Continuing *instant* in prayer." Romans 12:12.

Note.—This does not mean that we should be constantly bowed before God in prayer, but that we should not *neglect* prayer, and that we should *ever be in a prayerful frame of mind,* even when walking by the way or engaged in the duties of life—ever ready to send up our petitions to heaven for help in time of need.

Preparation for Christ's Return

That we might be prepared for His coming, what admonition did Christ give?

"*Take ye heed, watch and pray:* for ye know not when the time is. . . . And what I say unto you I say unto all, *Watch*." Mark 13:33-37. (See also Luke 21:36.)

Why are watchfulness and prayer especially imperative in the last days?

"Woe to the inhabiters of the earth and of the sea! for the devil is come down unto you, having great wrath, because he knoweth that he hath but a short time." Revelation 12:12.

> Lord, what a change within us one short hour
>   Spent in Thy presence will prevail to make!
>   What heavy burdens from our bosoms take!
> What parched grounds refresh, as with a shower!
> We kneel, and all around us seems to lower!
>   We rise, and all, the distant and the near,
>   Stands forth in sunny outline, brave and clear.
> We kneel, how weak! we rise, how full of power!
> Why, therefore, should we do ourselves this wrong,
>   Or others, that we are not always strong,
> That we are ever overborne with care,
>   That we should ever weak or heartless be,
> Anxious or troubled, when with us is prayer,
>   And joy and strength and courage are with Thee?
>
>   —Archbishop Trench

Watching Unto Prayer

THE COMMAND TO WATCH

UNTO what are we exhorted to watch?

"But the end of all things is at hand: be ye therefore sober, and *watch unto prayer*." 1 Peter 4:7.

How general is the command to watch?

"And what I say unto *you* I say unto *all*, Watch." Mark 13:37.

TEMPTATION AND WATCHING

What is one of the petitions of the Lord's Prayer?

"Lead us not into *temptation*." Matthew 6:13.

By what means can we escape temptation?

"*Watch and pray*, that ye enter not into temptation: the spirit indeed is willing, but the flesh is weak." Matthew 26:41.

NOTE.—To couple with our prayers a spirit of watchful cooperation with God in answering them is watching unto prayer.

How is this duty again expressed?

"Continue in prayer, and *watch in the same* with thanksgiving." Colossians 4:2.

How faithful should we be in this matter?

"Praying always with all prayer and supplication in the spirit, and *watching thereunto with all perseverance* and supplication for all saints." Ephesians 6:18.

EXAMPLES OF FAITHFUL WATCHING

When did Israel prevail in battle?

"And it came to pass, *when Moses held up his hand, that Israel prevailed:* and when he let down his hand, Amalek prevailed." Exodus 17:11.

What experience came to the householder as a result of failing to watch?

"But know this, that if the goodman of the house had known in what watch the thief would come, he would have *watched,* and would not have suffered his house to be *broken up."* Matthew 24:43.

What experience comes to those who wait upon the Lord?

"But *they that wait upon the Lord shall renew their strength;* they shall mount up with wings as eagles; they shall run, and not be weary; and they shall walk, and not faint." Isaiah 40:31.

For what did Habakkuk say he would watch?

"I will stand upon my watch, and set me upon the tower, and *will watch to see what he will say unto me."* Habakkuk 2:1.

Note.—Some are very anxious that God should hear them when they pray, but are quite indifferent as to what He says in reply.

Success or Failure

How may we escape the evils coming on the world?

"Watch ye therefore, and pray always, that ye may be accounted worthy to escape all these things that shall come to pass, and to stand before the Son of man." Luke 21:36.

Note.—Vigilance as well as prayer is necessary if we would escape the evils, delusions, and calamities of the last days.

What will be the result of not watching?

"But and if that servant say in his heart, My lord delayeth his coming; and shall begin to beat the menservants and maidens, and to eat and drink, and to be drunken; *the lord of that servant will come in a day when he looketh not for him, and at an hour when he is not aware, and will cut him in sunder, and will appoint him his portion with the unbelievers."* Luke 12:45, 46.

What will Christ's servants be doing when He comes?

"Let your loins be girded about, and your lights burning; and ye yourselves like unto men that wait for their lord, when he will return from the wedding; that when he cometh and knocketh, they may open unto him immediately. Blessed are those servants, whom the lord when he cometh shall find *watching."* Verses 35-37.

Answers to Prayer

GOD'S UNLIMITED ABILITY

How does God anticipate the needs of His children?

"And it shall come to pass, that *before they call, I will answer;* and while they are yet speaking, I will hear." Isaiah 65:24.

Is there any limit to God's ability to help?

"Now unto him that is *able to do exceeding abundantly above all that we ask or think.*" Ephesians 3:20.

How fully has God promised to supply our needs?

"My God shall supply all your need according to his riches in glory by Christ Jesus." Philippians 4:19.

MAN'S LIMITED UNDERSTANDING

Do we always know what to pray for?

"Likewise the Spirit also helpeth our infirmities: *for we know not what we should pray for as we ought.*" Romans 8:26.

Does God always see fit to grant our petitions?

"For this thing I besought the Lord thrice, that it might depart from me. And he said unto me, My grace is sufficient for thee: for my strength is made perfect in weakness." 2 Corinthians 12:8, 9.

NOTE.—Paul's affliction, some have thought, was impaired sight. (Acts 9:8, 9, 18; 22:11-13.) The retaining of such an imperfection would be a constant reminder to him of his conversion, and hence a blessing in disguise.

PATIENCE AND PERSEVERANCE

If an answer does not come at once, what should we do?

"Rest in the Lord, and *wait patiently for him.*" Psalm 37:7.

Why was the parable of the importunate widow given?

"And he spake a parable unto them to this end, *that men ought always to pray, and not to faint.*" Luke 18:1.

NOTE.—The request of the importunate widow was granted because of her persistency. God wants us to *seek* Him, and to seek Him *earnestly,* when we pray. He is a rewarder of them that *diligently* seek Him. (Hebrews 11:6.)

How did Elijah pray before obtaining his request?

"Elias was a man subject to like passions as we are, and *he prayed earnestly* that it might not rain: and it rained not on the earth by the space of three years and six months. And he prayed again, and the heaven gave rain, and the earth brought forth her fruit." James 5:17, 18. (See Revelation 11:3-6.)

Two Fundamental Conditions

Upon what condition does Christ say we shall receive?

"Therefore I say unto you, What things soever ye desire, when ye pray, *believe that ye receive them, and ye shall have them."* Mark 11:24.

Without this faith, will God answer prayer?

"But let him ask in faith, nothing wavering. For he that wavereth is like a wave of the sea driven with the wind and tossed. For *let not that man think that he shall receive any thing of the Lord."* James 1:6, 7.

What petitions may we confidently expect God to hear?

"And this is the confidence that we have in him, that, *if we ask any thing according to his will,* he heareth us: and if we know that he hear us, whatsoever we ask, we know that we have the petitions that we desired of him." 1 John 5:14, 15.

NOTE.—God's will is expressed in His law, His promises, and His word. (Psalm 40:8; Romans 2:17, 18; 1 Peter 1:4.)

Examples of Answered Prayer

When Daniel and his fellows were about to be slain because the wise men of Babylon could not reveal to Nebuchadnezzar his dream, how did God answer their united prayers?

"Then was the secret revealed unto Daniel in a night vision. Then Daniel blessed the God of heaven." Daniel 2:19.

NOTE.—In 1839 the sultan of Turkey decreed that not a representative of the Christian religion should remain in the empire.

Learning of this, Dr. William Goodell, an American missionary to Turkey, came home to his friend and colleague, Dr. Cyrus Hamlin, the first president of Robert College, Constantinople, with the sad news: "It is all over with us; we have to leave. The American consul and the British ambassador say it is no use to meet with antagonism this violent and vindictive monarch." To this Dr. Hamlin replied: "The Sultan of the universe can, in answer to prayer, change the decree of the sultan of Turkey." They gave themselves to prayer. The next day the sultan died, and the decree was never executed. (See Daniel 4:17, 24, 25.)

When Peter was imprisoned and about to be executed by Herod, what did the church do?

"Peter therefore was kept in prison: but *prayer was made without ceasing of the church unto God for him.*" Acts 12:5.

How were their prayers answered?

"Behold, the angel of the Lord came upon him, . . . and he saith unto him, Cast thy garment about thee, and follow me. . . . And they went out, and passed on through one street; and forthwith the angel departed from him." Verses 7-10.

Because Solomon asked for wisdom rather than for long life and riches, what besides wisdom did God give him?

"I have also given thee that which thou hast not asked, *both riches, and honour.*" 1 Kings 3:11-13.

NOTE.—The following are some things we are taught in the Scriptures to pray for:

(1) For daily bread. Matthew 6:11. (2) For the forgiveness of sin. 2 Chronicles 7:14; Psalm 32:5, 6; 1 John 1:9; 5:16. (3) For the Holy Spirit. Luke 11:13; Zechariah 10:1; John 14:16. (4) For deliverance in the hour of temptation and danger. Matthew 6:13; John 17:11, 15; Proverbs 3:26; Psalm 91; Matthew 24:20. (5) For wisdom and understanding. James 1:5; 1 Kings 3:9; Daniel 2:17-19. (6) For peaceable and quiet lives. 1 Timothy 2:1, 2. (7) For the healing of the sick. James 5:14, 15; 2 Kings 20:1-11. (8) For the prosperity of the ministers of God and the gospel. Ephesians 6:18, 19; Colossians 4:3; 2 Thessalonians 3:1. (9) For those who suffer for the truth's sake. Hebrews 13:3; Acts 12:5. (10) For kings, rulers, and all in authority. 1 Timothy 2:1, 2; Ezra 6:10. (11) For temporal prosperity. 2 Corinthians 9:10; James 5:17, 18. (12) For our enemies. Matthew 5:44. (13) For the coming of Christ and of God's kingdom. Matthew 6:10; Revelation 22:20.

Public Worship

THE SPIRIT OF TRUE WORSHIP

How only can God be truly worshiped?

"God is a Spirit: and *they that worship him must worship him in spirit and in truth.*" John 4:24.

How are we instructed to worship the Lord?

"Give unto the Lord the glory due unto his name; *worship the Lord in the beauty of holiness.*" Psalm 29:2.

What attitude is indicative of a spirit of humility and of true reverence in worship?

"O come, let us worship and *bow down:* let us *kneel* before the Lord our maker." Psalm 95:6.

Is singing a part of divine worship?

"Enter into his gates with thanksgiving, and into his courts with praise." "Come before his presence with *singing.*" Psalm 100:4, 2.

Does the Bible approve the use of musical instruments in the worship of God?

"Praise him with the sound of the *trumpet:* praise him with the *psaltery* and *harp.* Praise him with the *timbrel* and *dance* [margin, *"pipe"*]: praise him with *stringed instruments* and *organs.* Praise him upon the *loud cymbals:* praise him upon the *high sounding cymbals.*" Psalm 150:3-5. (See also Psalm 92:1-3.)

What gracious promise is made to those who wait upon the Lord?

"They that wait upon the Lord shall *renew their strength;* they shall *mount up with wings as eagles;* they shall *run, and not be weary;* and they shall *walk, and not faint.*" Isaiah 40:31.

Is Christ's presence limited to large congregations?

"Where *two or three* are gathered together in my name, there am I in the midst of them." Matthew 18:20.

Value and Joy of Public Worship

What were the psalmist's feelings concerning public worship?

"I was *glad* when they said unto me, Let us go into the house of the Lord." "My soul *longeth,* yea, even *fainteth* for the courts of the Lord: my heart and my flesh *crieth out* for the living God." *"For a day in thy courts is better than a thousand.* I had rather be a *doorkeeper* in the house of my God, than to dwell in the tents of wickedness." Psalms 122:1; 84:2, 10.

What admonition has Paul given concerning assembling for public worship?

"Not forsaking the assembling of ourselves together, as the manner of some is; but exhorting one another: and so much the more, as ye see the day approaching." Hebrews 10:25.

Does God take account of the associations of His people?

"Then they that feared the Lord spake often one to another: *and the Lord hearkened, and heard it,* and a book of remembrance was written before him for them that feared the Lord, and that thought upon his name. And they shall be mine, saith the Lord of hosts, in that day when I make up my jewels [margin, "special treasure"]; and I will spare them, as a man spareth his own son that serveth him." Malachi 3:16, 17.

What caution is given regarding behavior in God's house?

"Keep thy foot when thou goest to the house of God, and be more ready to hear, than to give the sacrifice of fools: for they consider not that they do evil." Ecclesiastes 5:1. (See 1 Timothy 3:15.)

Are offerings an appropriate part of divine worship?

"Give unto the Lord the glory due unto his name: *bring an offering,* and come into his courts." "Vow, and pay unto the Lord your God: let all that be round about him *bring presents unto him* that ought to be feared." Psalms 96:8; 76:11.

God's Appointed Time

What day has God specially designed for public worship?

"The seventh day is the sabbath of rest, *an holy convocation."* Leviticus 23:3.

How has God commanded us to keep this day?

"Remember the sabbath day, to *keep it holy*. . . . In it thou shalt not do any work." Exodus 20:8-10. (See Isaiah 58:13, 14.)

Will there be public worship in the new creation?

"As the new heavens and the new earth, which I will make, shall remain before me, saith the Lord, so shall your seed and your name remain. *And it shall come to pass, that from one new moon to another, and from one sabbath to another, shall all flesh come to worship before me,* saith the Lord." Isaiah 66:22, 23.

Rules on Going to Church

1. Go early to church. Not only be punctual, but be in your place before the hour announced for the service to begin.

2. Go in a reverent spirit. On the way remember whither you go. Avoid lightness of manner and conversation on worldly topics.

3. Before you enter and as you enter the church breathe a silent prayer of invocation for the influence of the Holy Spirit.

4. As you take your place, bow your head reverently in prayer for yourself and for all others who enter the sanctuary.

5. Resolve that you will foster no thought, fix your eyes on no object, utter no word, that will tend to divert your mind from the holy purpose for which you have come into this place.

6. As the minister enters the pulpit, offer an earnest silent prayer in his behalf.

7. In all the service take an active part, as hearer, as worshiper.

8. At the close of the service, after a moment of prayerful silence, greet with cheerfulness and good will all whom you happen to meet, remembering that Christian fellowship is a part of Christian worship.
—Bishop Vincent.

Note.—An excellent suggestion is contained in the notice posted at the doorway of many churches: "Whosoever thou art that entereth this church, remember it is the house of God. Be reverent, be silent, be thoughtful. And leave it not without a prayer to God, for thyself, for him who ministers, and for those who worship here."

THE CHRIST

HEINRICH HOFMANN, ARTIST

"We have found the Messias, which is, being interpreted, the Christ." John 1:

Reverence for the House of God

Why did God instruct His people to build a sanctuary?

"And let them make me a sanctuary; *that I may dwell among them.*" Exodus 25:8.

How did He tell them to regard this dwelling place of God?

"Ye shall keep my sabbaths, and *reverence my sanctuary:* I am the Lord." Leviticus 19:30.

What does the Lord say of things dedicated to His service?

"Every devoted thing is *most holy* unto the Lord." Leviticus 27:28.

When God met Moses at the burning bush, why did He tell him to take off his shoes?

"And he said, Draw not nigh hither: put off thy shoes from off thy feet, *for the place whereon thou standest is holy ground.*" Exodus 3:5. (See also Joshua 5:15.)

NOTE.—The presence of God made the place holy. Wherever God meets with His people, that place is holy.

When the tabernacle was reared anciently, what occurred?

"Then a cloud covered the tent of the congregation, and *the glory of the Lord filled the tabernacle.*" Exodus 40:34. (See 2 Chronicles 5:13, 14.)

Why should all show respect for the house of worship?

"*The Lord is in his holy temple:* let all the earth keep silence before him." Habakkuk 2:20.

NOTE.—A failure to recognize this fact leads many to treat the house of worship without due respect. Nothing seems more appropriate to divine worship than that a sense of awe and silence should pervade the place of worship, and that only the sound of prayer, praise, and thanksgiving to God should be heard within its walls. Both upon entering and just before leaving the house of God it is highly appropriate and a most excellent practice for each worshiper to bow the head for a few moments in silent prayer.

God's Frown Upon Irreverence

How did Christ manifest His regard for the sanctity of God's house?

"And they come to Jerusalem: and Jesus went into the temple, and began to cast out them that sold and bought in the temple, and overthrew the tables of the moneychangers, and the seats of them that sold doves; and would not suffer that any man should carry any vessel through the temple. And he taught, saying unto them, Is it not written, My house shall be called of all nations the house of prayer? but ye have made it a den of thieves." Mark 11:15-17.

NOTE.—This cleansing occurred at the close of Christ's public ministry. There was a similar cleansing also at the beginning of His ministry. (See John 2:13-17.)

What punishment did God bring upon Nadab and Abihu for offering strange, or common, fire in the tabernacle service?

"And Nadab and Abihu, the sons of Aaron, took either of them his censer, and put fire therein, and put incense thereon, and offered strange fire before the Lord, which he commanded them not. *And there went out fire from the Lord, and devoured them, and they died before the Lord.*" Leviticus 10:1, 2.

NOTE.—This, like the two cleansings of the Temple by Christ at the beginning and close of His ministry (John 2:13-17; Matthew 21:12-16), shows that God is particular in regard to the worship and conduct of the worshipers in His house. No performance or exercise should be permitted in any church or building especially dedicated to God's service which is not in keeping with its sacred character, or conducive to reverence for God and for holy things. It should not be made a place for feasting, visiting, or worldly entertainment and amusement.

Reverence and Godly Fear

For what purpose are we exhorted to have grace?

"Wherefore we receiving a kingdom which cannot be moved, let us have grace, *whereby we may serve God acceptably with reverence and godly fear:* for our God is a consuming fire." Hebrews 12:28, 29.

In what spirit did the psalmist say he would worship?

"But as for me, I will come into thy house in the multitude of thy mercy: and *in thy fear will I worship toward thy holy temple.*" Psalm 5:7.

What instruction has Solomon given respecting our conduct in the house of God?

"Keep thy foot when thou goest to the house of God, and be more ready to hear, than to give the sacrifice of fools: for they consider not that they do evil." Ecclesiastes 5:1.

Who is present in all assemblies met in Christ's name?

"For where two or three are gathered together in my name, *there am I in the midst of them.*" Matthew 18:20.

> THE spacious firmament on high,
> With all the blue, ethereal sky,
> And spangled heavens, a shining frame,
> Their great Original proclaim.
> The unwearied sun from day to day
> Does his Creator's power display,
> And publishes to every land
> The work of an almighty hand.
>
> Soon as the evening shades prevail,
> The moon takes up the wondrous tale;
> And nightly to the listening earth
> Repeats the story of her birth;
> While all the stars that round her burn,
> And all the planets in their turn,
> Confirm the tidings as they roll,
> And spread the truth from pole to pole.
>
> What though in solemn silence all
> Move round the dark terrestrial ball?
> What though no real voice nor sound
> Amid their radiant orbs be found?
> In reason's ear they all rejoice
> And utter forth a glorious voice,
> Forever singing as they shine,
> "The hand that made us is divine."
>
> —JOSEPH ADDISON

THE LORD'S SUPPER

E. ZIMMERMAN, ARTIST

"As often as ye eat this bread, and drink this cup, ye do

Christian Communion

Ordinances in Old Testament Times

What was connected with the worship of God before the First Advent?

"Then verily the first covenant had also *ordinances of divine service,* and a worldly sanctuary." Hebrews 9:1.

To whom did the sacrificial offerings point forward?

"And walk in love, as *Christ* also hath loved us, and *hath given himself for us an offering and a sacrifice to God* for a sweetsmelling savour." Ephesians 5:2.

Note.—Through the provisions of the sacrificial law, the repentant sinner showed his faith in the coming Redeemer, who was to shed His blood for the sins of mankind. These sacrificial offerings pointed forward to the work of Christ, which they typified. Since the crucifixion, the ordinances of the Christian church point backward, and are designed to show faith in the work of Christ already accomplished.

New Testament Ordinances

What does the Lord desire us to keep in mind?

"*Keep in memory* what I preached unto you, . . . *how that Christ died for our sins* according to the scriptures; and that he was *buried,* and that he *rose again* the third day according to the scriptures." 1 Corinthians 15:2-4.

What ordinance commemorates Christ's burial and resurrection?

"Buried with him in *baptism,* wherein also ye are risen with him through the faith of the operation of God, who hath raised him from the dead." Colossians 2:12.

For what purpose was the Lord's Supper instituted?

"*The Lord Jesus the same night in which he was betrayed took bread:* and when he had given thanks, he brake it, and said, Take, eat: *this is my body,* which is broken for you: *this do in remembrance of me.*" 1 Corinthians 11:23, 24.

What is signified by the wine?

"In the same way also the cup, after supper, saying, 'This cup is *the new covenant in my blood*. Do this, as often as you drink it, in remembrance of me.' " Verse 25, R.S.V.

What do both the bread and the wine commemorate?

"For as often as ye eat this bread, and drink this cup, ye do shew *the Lord's death* till he come." Verse 26.

What caution is given concerning engaging in this ordinance unworthily?

"Whosoever shall eat this bread, and drink this cup of the Lord, unworthily, shall be *guilty of the body and blood of the Lord*. . . . He that eateth and drinketh unworthily, eateth and drinketh damnation to himself, *not discerning the Lord's body*." Verses 27-29.

NOTE.—The last expression shows what is meant by eating and drinking unworthily. It is not the one who has a deep sense of his sinfulness and of his unworthiness of God's mercy and grace, but he who does not discern that Christ died for his sins—who is not penitent—who eats and drinks unworthily.

What preparation should be made for this service?

"Let a man *examine himself*, and so let him eat of that bread, and drink of that cup." Verse 28.

PRIVILEGE AND ESSENTIAL OF FELLOWSHIP

What is essential to Christian fellowship and cleansing from sin?

"*If we walk in the light, as he is in the light*, we have fellowship one with another, and the blood of Jesus Christ his Son cleanseth us from all sin." 1 John 1:7.

What still higher fellowship does the Christian enjoy?

"And truly our fellowship is *with the Father, and with his Son Jesus Christ*." Verse 3.

Praise and Thanksgiving

ALWAYS AND IN EVERYTHING

WHEN did the psalmist say he would bless the Lord?

"I will bless the Lord *at all times:* his praise shall *continually be in my mouth.*" "*Every day* will I bless thee; and I will praise thy name *for ever and ever.*" Psalms 34:1; 145:2.

In how many things should we give thanks?

"*In every thing give thanks:* for this is the will of God in Christ Jesus concerning you." 1 Thessalonians 5:18.

How often, and for how much, should we render thanks?

"Giving thanks *always for all things* unto God and the Father in the name of our Lord Jesus Christ." Ephesians 5:20.

Into what condition did those lapse anciently who failed to glorify God and to be thankful?

"Because that, when they knew God, they glorified him not as God, neither were thankful; but *became vain in their imaginations, and their foolish heart was darkened.*" Romans 1:21.

What element should enter into all our worship?

"Be careful for nothing; but in every thing by prayer and supplication *with thanksgiving* let your requests be made known unto God." Philippians 4:6. (See Colossians 4:2.)

EXALTING GOD'S NAME

What do those do who offer praise?

"Whoso offereth praise *glorifieth me.*" Psalm 50:23.

What does the psalmist exhort all to do?

"O magnify the Lord with me, and *let us exalt his name together.*" Psalm 34:3.

Where does he say he will praise God?

"My praise shall be of thee *in the great congregation:* I will pay my vows before them that fear him." Psalm 22:25.

Personal Testimony

What personal experience does he say he will declare in the hearing of all who fear God?

"Come and hear, all ye that fear God, and *I will declare what he hath done for my soul.*" Psalm 66:16.

What effect do such testimonies have upon the humble?

"My soul shall make her boast in the Lord: *the humble shall hear thereof, and be glad.*" Psalm 34:2.

The Psalmist's Final Exhortation

With what exhortation does the psalmist close his songs of praise?

"Praise ye the Lord. Praise God in his sanctuary: praise him in the firmament of his power. Praise him for his mighty acts: praise him according to his excellent greatness. Praise him with the sound of the trumpet: praise him with the psaltery and harp. Praise him with the timbrel and dance: praise him with stringed instruments and organs. Praise him upon the loud cymbals: praise him upon the high sounding cymbals. Let every thing that hath breath praise the Lord. Praise ye the Lord." Psalm 150.

O worship the Lord in the beauty of holiness,
  Bow down before Him, His glory proclaim;
With gold of obedience, and incense of lowliness,
  Kneel and adore Him; the Lord is His name.

Low at His feet lay thy burden of carefulness;
  High on His heart He will bear it for thee,
Comfort thy sorrows, and answer thy prayerfulness,
  Guiding thy steps as may best for thee be.

Fear not to enter His courts in the slenderness
  Of the poor wealth thou wouldst reckon as thine.
Truth in its beauty and love in its tenderness,
  These are the offerings to lay on His shrine.

These, though we bring them in trembling and fearfulness,
  He will accept for the Name that is dear;
Mornings of joy give for evenings of tearfulness,
  Trust for our trembling, and hope for our fear.

—J. S. B. Monsell

The Value of Song

SONGS OF LONG AGO

How early in the world's history do we read of singing?

"Where wast thou when I laid the foundations of the earth? ... *when the morning stars sang together, and all the sons of God shouted for joy?*" Job 38:4-7.

What did Israel do when delivered from Egypt?

"Then sang Moses and the children of Israel this song unto the Lord, ... The Lord is my strength and song, and he is become my salvation: ... and I will exalt him." Exodus 15:1, 2.

How did the angels manifest their joy at Christ's birth?

"And suddenly there was with the angel a multitude of the heavenly host praising God, and saying, Glory to God in the highest, and on earth peace, good will toward men." Luke 2:13, 14.

COUNSEL ON ACCEPTABLE SINGING

How are we told to come before the Lord?

"Serve the Lord with gladness: *come before his presence with singing.*" Psalm 100:2. (See 2 Chronicles 29:30.)

How does the psalmist say such service is regarded by God?

"I will praise the name of God with *a song,* and will magnify him with *thanksgiving. This also shall please the Lord better than an ox or bullock that hath horns and hoofs.*" Psalm 69:30, 31.

What instruction did Paul give concerning singing?

"Let the word of Christ dwell in you richly in all wisdom; teaching and admonishing one another in *psalms* and *hymns* and *spiritual songs, singing with grace in your hearts to the Lord.*" Colossians 3:16. (See also Ephesians 5:19; James 5:13; Psalm 149:5, 6.)

NOTE.—Music, like poetry and flowers, is elevating and refining in its nature, and should therefore have its place in the worship of

God, and in the life and experience of God's people. It is adapted to every mood and feeling of the human soul, and many times has reached hearts when other means have failed. Next to prayer, music seems best adapted to worship.

"The history of the songs of the Bible is full of suggestion as to the uses and benefits of music and song. Music is often perverted to serve purposes of evil, and it thus becomes one of the most alluring agencies of temptation. But, rightly employed, it is a precious gift of God, designed to uplift the thoughts to high and noble themes, to inspire and elevate the soul. As the children of Israel, journeying through the wilderness, cheered their way by the music of sacred song, so God bids His children today gladden their pilgrim life. There are few means more effective for fixing His words in the memory than repeating them in song. And such song has wonderful power. It has power to subdue rude and uncultivated natures; power to quicken thought and to awaken sympathy, to promote harmony of action, and to banish the gloom and foreboding that destroy courage and weaken effort."—ELLEN G. WHITE, *Education,* pp. 167, 168.

"O that we might sing evening and morning, and let song touch song all the way through! O that we could put songs under our burden! O that we could extract the sense of sorrow by song! Then sad things would not poison so much. Sing in the house; teach your children to sing. When troubles come, go at them with song. When griefs arise, sing them down. Lift the voice of praise against cares. Praise God by singing; that will lift you above trials of every sort. Attempt it. They sing in heaven, and among God's people on earth song is the appropriate language of Christian feeling."—HENRY WARD BEECHER.

MUSIC OF THE FUTURE

In vision, what instrument did John see the saints have?

"I saw . . . them . . . *having the harps of God."* Revelation 15:2.

And what song are they to sing?

"And they sing *the song of Moses* the servant of God, *and the song of the Lamb,* saying, Great and marvellous are thy works, Lord God Almighty; just and true are thy ways, thou King of saints." Verse 3. (See Psalm 87:7.)

Part Fourteen

Christian Service

	PAGE
The Gift of Giving	624
The Shepherd and His Work	627
Preaching the Gospel	629
Missionary Work	632
The Poor, and Our Duty Toward Them	635
Christian Help Work	637
Visiting the Sick	641
Healing the Sick	643
Order and Organization	646
Support of the Ministry	649
Freewill Offerings	651
Who Is the Greatest?	654

The Gift of Giving

HEAVEN'S EXAMPLE

What example of giving has God given to the world?

"God so loved the world, that *he gave his only begotten Son,* that whosoever believeth in him should not perish, but have everlasting life." John 3:16.

What did Christ do to redeem us?

"Who *gave himself* for our sins." Galatians 1:4. (See also Titus 2:14; 1 Timothy 2:6.)

Why did He lay aside His riches and become poor?

"For ye know the grace of our Lord Jesus Christ, that, though he was rich, yet *for your sakes he became poor, that ye through his poverty might be rich.*" 2 Corinthians 8:9.

ABRAHAM'S CHARGE AND TEST

After Abraham was blessed, what was he to be?

"I will bless thee, . . . *and thou shalt be a blessing.*" Genesis 12:2.

By what were Abraham's faith and devotion tested?

"By faith Abraham, when he was tried, *offered up Isaac;* and he that had received the promises *offered up his only begotten son.*" Hebrews 11:17.

THE MORE BLESSED WAY

As Christ sent His disciples out to preach, to heal the sick, and to raise the dead, what did He say to them?

"Freely ye have received, *freely give.*" Matthew 10:8.

Why does God comfort us in our troubles?

"Who comforteth us in all our tribulation, *that we may be able to comfort them which are in any trouble, by the comfort wherewith we ourselves are comforted of God.*" 2 Corinthians 1:4.

THE GIFT OF GIVING

Note.—All who accept the gospel take upon themselves the obligation to pass its blessings on to others. In this way the work of salvation is extended. God expects every soul reclaimed from sin to join in the same work for others that lifted him up and placed his feet upon the Rock. The good things of God are not to be selfishly kept to ourselves. We receive to give. Says Whittier, "The soul is lost that's saved alone." And as love prompted God's great gift, so His love in our hearts will prompt us to give, to minister, and to engage in loving service for the welfare and the happiness of others.

What did Christ say of the blessedness of giving?

"I have shewed you all things, how that so labouring ye ought to support the weak, and to remember the words of the Lord Jesus, how he said, *It is more blessed to give than to receive.*" Acts 20:35.

Note.—The government of God is founded on the principle of benevolence, or the desire to bless others. Our richest blessings come as the result of the good things we have passed on to our fellow men.

The Ministry of the Spirit

For what was Christ anointed by the Holy Spirit?

"The Spirit of the Lord God is upon me; because the Lord hath anointed me *to preach good tidings unto the meek; he hath sent me to bind up the brokenhearted, to proclaim liberty to the captives, and the opening of the prison to them that are bound.*" Isaiah 61:1. (See Luke 4:18.)

Note.—The Holy Spirit is given to fit God's children for service.

After being thus anointed, what did Jesus do?

"Who went about *doing good.*" Acts 10:38.

> Have you had a kindness shown?
> Pass it on;
> 'Twas not given for you alone,
> Pass it on;
> Let it travel down the years,
> Let it wipe another's tears,
> Till in heaven the deed appears—
> Pass it on.
>
> —Henry K. Burton

THE GOOD SHEPHERD

"Feed the flock of God which is among y taking the oversight thereof." 1 Peter

The Shepherd and His Work

The Chief Shepherd

Who did Christ say is the good shepherd?

"I am the good shepherd." John 10:11.

What is Christ elsewhere called?

"The Shepherd and *Bishop of your souls.*" "The *chief Shepherd.*" 1 Peter 2:25; 5:4.

Undershepherds

What does the expression "the *chief* Shepherd" imply?

That there are *under*shepherds.

How does the good shepherd manifest his love and care for the sheep?

"The good shepherd *giveth his life for the sheep.*" John 10:11.

What does the hireling, or false shepherd, do, and why?

"The hireling *fleeth, because he is an hireling,* and *careth not for the sheep.*" Verse 13.

What example will the true shepherd set before his flock?

"In all things shewing thyself *a pattern of good works.*" Titus 2:7.

What is the special work of the gospel shepherd?

"Take heed therefore unto yourselves, and to all the flock, over the which the Holy Ghost hath made you overseers, *to feed the church of God,* which he hath purchased with his own blood." Acts 20:28. *"Feed the flock of God* which is among you, *taking the oversight thereof.*" 1 Peter 5:2. (See also John 21: 15-17.)

With what kind of food will the true shepherd feed the flock?

"I charge thee therefore before God, and the Lord Jesus

Christ, who shall judge the quick and the dead at his appearing and his kingdom; *Preach the word*." 2 Timothy 4:1, 2. "O son of man, I have set thee a watchman unto the house of Israel; therefore *thou shalt hear the word at my mouth, and warn them from me*." Ezekiel 33:7. (See Ezekiel 3:17-21.)

When Sheep Desire False Shepherds

Was there to come a time when people would not listen to plain Bible truth?

"*For the time will come when they will not endure sound doctrine;* but after their own lusts shall they heap to themselves teachers, having itching ears; and they shall turn away their ears from the *truth*, and shall be *turned unto fables*." 2 Timothy 4:3, 4.

Instead of the straight testimony, what kind of preaching will such demand?

"Prophesy not unto us right things, *speak unto us smooth things, prophesy deceits*." Isaiah 30:10.

What will those servants be doing upon whom Christ pronounces a blessing when He comes?

"Who then is a faithful and wise servant, whom his lord hath made ruler over his household, to *give them meat in due season?* Blessed is that servant, whom his lord when he cometh shall find so doing. Verily I say unto you, That he shall make him ruler over all his goods." Matthew 24:45-47.

How faithfully will the true shepherd watch the flock?

"They watch for your souls, *as they that must give account*." Hebrews 13:17.

Note.—Mark Guy Pearse once said to Mr. Spurgeon: "When I was a young fellow in London, I used to sit right over there and hear you preach, and you will never know how much good you did me. You used to wind me up like an eight-day clock. I was bound to go right for a week after hearing you."

If God's watchmen fail to warn the wicked, what terrible responsibility will be charged to their account?

"If thou dost not speak to warn the wicked from his way, that wicked man shall die in his iniquity; but *his blood will I require at thine hand*." Ezekiel 33:8. (See Isaiah 3:10, 11.)

Preaching the Gospel

THE GREAT COMMISSION

Before leaving His disciples, what great commission did Christ give them?

"And he said unto them, *Go ye into all the world, and preach the gospel to every creature.*" Mark 16:15.

Note.—The word translated *gospel* means "good news," or "glad tidings."

What is the gospel of Christ declared to be?

"I am not ashamed of the gospel of Christ: for *it is the power of God unto salvation to every one that believeth.*" Romans 1:16.

How extensively and for how long did Christ say the gospel should be preached?

"And this gospel of the kingdom shall be preached *in all the world* for a witness unto all nations; and *then shall the end come.*" Matthew 24:14.

THE GOSPEL TO THE GENTILES

What was the object of Christ's ministry?

"I the Lord have called thee in righteousness, and will hold thine hand, and will keep thee, and give thee for a covenant of the people, for a light of the Gentiles; *to open the blind eyes, to bring out the prisoners from the prison, and them that sit in darkness out of the prison house.*" Isaiah 42:6, 7.

For what purpose did Christ select the apostle Paul, and send him to the Gentiles?

"And he said, . . . I have appeared unto thee for this purpose, *to make thee a minister and a witness . . . , to open their eyes, and to turn them from darkness to light, and from the power of Satan unto God,* that they may receive forgiveness of sins, and inheritance among them which are sanctified by faith that is in me." Acts 26:15-18.

Why was the gospel to be preached to the Gentiles?

"Simeon hath declared how God at the first did visit the Gentiles, *to take out of them a people for his name.*" Acts 15:14.

The Mission of the Minister

How are those who preach the gospel described?

"How beautiful upon the mountains are the feet of him that bringeth good tidings, that publisheth peace; that bringeth good tidings of good, that publisheth salvation; that saith unto Zion, Thy God reigneth!" Isaiah 52:7.

What is the Christian minister commanded to preach?

"Preach *the word.*" 2 Timothy 4:2.

Of what did Christ say the Scriptures testify?

"They are they which testify of *me.*" John 5:39.

Note.—Everyone, therefore, who preaches the word aright will preach Christ. Paul, who faithfully preached God's word, said he was determined not to know anything "save Jesus Christ, and him crucified." 1 Corinthians 2:2. Jonathan Edwards, it is said, was once asked by a young minister what he thought of a sermon he had just preached. "It was a very poor sermon, indeed," said Mr. Edwards. "Why?" asked the young minister. "Because," said Mr. Edwards, "there was no *Christ* in it." All the great truths of the Scriptures center in Christ. Rightly understood, all lead to Him. Christ, therefore, should be presented in every discourse as the alpha and omega, the beginning and the end, of the great plan of salvation.

How did Christ present the truth to the people?

"And with many such parables spake he the word unto them, *as they were able to hear it.*" Mark 4:33.

Note.—Ministers should learn to adapt their labors to those for whom they labor—to meet the people where they are.

How should the servant of God labor?

"And the servant of the Lord must not strive; but be gentle unto all men, apt to teach, patient, in meekness instructing those that oppose themselves; if God peradventure will give them repentance to the acknowledging of the truth." 2 Timothy 2: 24, 25.

Note.—While the claims of the law of God are presented to the sinner, ministers should never forget that love—the love of God—is the only power that can soften the heart and lead to repentance and obedience, and that to *save* men is their great work.

Preparation to Preach With Power

In preparing the disciples for their work, what did Christ do?

"Then *opened he their understanding,* that they might understand the scriptures." Luke 24:45.

For what did He tell them to tarry in Jerusalem?

"But tarry ye in the city of Jerusalem, *until ye be endued with power from on high.*" Verse 49.

How did the apostles preach the gospel?

"With the Holy Ghost sent down from heaven." 1 Peter 1:12.

What was the result of this preaching?

"Many of them which heard the word *believed."* "And the word of God *increased;* and *the number of the disciples multiplied* in Jerusalem *greatly;* and a great company of the *priests* were obedient to the faith." Acts 4:4; 6:7.

What promise is made to the faithful gospel minister?

"He that goeth forth and weepeth, bearing precious seed, *shall doubtless come again with rejoicing, bringing his sheaves with him.*" Psalm 126:6.

"To every clime, where lost by sin,
  The grace of Christ a soul may win,
  From here Thy messengers go forth
  From east to west, from south to north.

"Perchance, in heaven one day to me
    Some blessed soul may come and say,
  All hail, beloved! But for thee
    My soul to death had been a prey.
  Ah, then what sweetness in the thought
  One soul to glory to have brought!"

Missionary Work

SERVANTS, THEIR WORK AND TALENTS

WHAT has been given to every man?

"For the Son of man is as a man taking a far journey, who left his house, and gave authority to his servants, and *to every man his work.*" Mark 13:34.

Besides work, what else has been given to every man?

"And unto one he gave five *talents,* to another two, and to another one; *to every man according to his several ability.*" Matthew 25:15.

What are those called to whom this work is committed?

"For the kingdom of heaven is as a man travelling into a far country, who called his own *servants,* and delivered unto them his goods." Verse 14.

RIGHT AND WRONG USE OF TALENTS

What use did these servants make of their talents?

"Then he that had received the five talents *went and traded with the same,* and made them other five talents. . . . But he that had received one went and digged in the earth, and hid his lord's money." Verses 16-18.

What excuse did the one who hid his talent make?

"*I was afraid,* and went and hid thy talent in the earth: lo, there thou hast that is thine." Verse 25.

What did his master say to him?

"His lord answered and said unto him, *Thou wicked and slothful servant.*" Verse 26.

What did he say the servant should have done?

"Thou oughtest therefore to have *put my money to the exchangers,* and then at my coming I should have received mine own with usury." Verse 27.

MISSIONARY WORK

What is characteristic of slothful persons?

"The slothful man saith, There is a lion without, I shall be slain in the streets." Proverbs 22:13.

NOTE.—That is, they see great obstacles before them, and are always ready with excuses.

What was the fate of the slothful servant?

"And *cast ye the unprofitable servant into outer darkness:* there shall be weeping and gnashing of teeth." Matthew 25:30.

What was said to the servant who improved his talents?

"His lord said unto him, *Well done, thou good and faithful servant:* thou hast been faithful over a few things, I will make thee ruler over many things: *enter thou into the joy of thy lord.*" Verse 21.

THE JOY OF SERVICE

Why did Christ endure the cruel death on the cross?

"Looking unto Jesus the author and finisher of our faith; *who for the joy that was set before him endured the cross, despising the shame,* and is set down at the right hand of the throne of God." Hebrews 12:2.

What will bring to the Lord this satisfaction and joy?

"He shall *see of the travail of his soul,* and shall be satisfied." Isaiah 53:11.

What did Paul set forth as his crown of rejoicing?

"For what is our hope, or joy, or crown of rejoicing? *Are not even ye in the presence of our Lord Jesus Christ at his coming?* For ye are our glory and joy." 1 Thessalonians 2:19, 20.

Since this joy comes to Christ only through His self-denial and suffering for others, in what way must all others partake of that joy?

"It is a faithful saying: For if we be dead with him, we shall also live with him: *if we suffer, we shall also reign with him:* if we deny him, he also will deny us." 2 Timothy 2:11, 12.

What motive should prompt to soul-saving labor?

"For *the love of Christ constraineth us.*" 2 Corinthians 5:14.

AMBASSADORS FOR CHRIST

Whom does every faithful Christian worker represent?

"Now then we are *ambassadors for Christ, as though God did beseech you by us:* we pray you in Christ's stead, be ye reconciled to God." Verse 20.

What does God do with the unfruitful members?

"*Every branch in me that beareth not fruit he taketh away:* and every branch that beareth fruit, he purgeth it, that it may bring forth more fruit." John 15:2.

Can one occupy a mere neutral position toward Christ?

"He that is not with me is *against* me: and he that gathereth not with me *scattereth.*" Luke 11:23.

For what does the Lord tell us to pray?

"The harvest truly is great, but the labourers are few: *pray ye therefore the Lord of the harvest, that he would send forth labourers into his harvest.*" Luke 10:2.

How are we cautioned against delaying the work?

"Say not ye, There are yet four months, and then cometh harvest? behold, I say unto you, Lift up your eyes, and look on the fields; for they are white already to harvest." John 4:35.

What promise is made to those who sow the gospel seed?

"They that sow in tears *shall reap in joy.* He that goeth forth and weepeth, bearing precious seed, *shall doubtless come again with rejoicing, bringing his sheaves with him.*" Psalm 126:5, 6.

What promise is made to soul winners?

"And they that be wise shall *shine as the brightness of the firmament;* and they that turn many to righteousness *as the stars for ever and ever.*" Daniel 12:3.

The Poor, and Our Duty Toward Them

THE RIGHT ATTITUDE TOWARD THE POOR

What is God's attitude toward the poor?

"He shall *deliver* the needy when he crieth; the poor also, and him that hath no helper." Psalm 72:12.

For what purpose did Christ say God had anointed Him?

"He hath anointed me *to preach the gospel to the poor.*" Luke 4:18.

When did He say we could minister to the poor?

"Whensoever ye will ye may do them good." Mark 14:7.

What classes are we especially enjoined to help?

"Learn to do well; seek judgment, *relieve the oppressed, judge the fatherless, plead for the widow.*" Isaiah 1:17.

How did the patriarch Job treat the poor?

"I was a *father* to the poor: and *the cause which I knew not I searched out.*" Job 29:16.

THE RELATION OF TRUE RELIGION TO CHARITY

What is pure and undefiled religion declared to be?

"Pure religion and undefiled before God and the Father is this, *To visit the fatherless and widows in their affliction,* and to keep himself unspotted from the world." James 1:27.

What kind of fast is most acceptable to God?

"Is not this the fast that I have chosen? . . . Is it not to *deal thy bread to the hungry,* and that thou *bring the poor that are cast out to thy house?* when thou seest *the naked, that thou cover him;* and that *thou hide not thyself from thine own flesh?*" Isaiah 58:6, 7.

How does the Lord regard kindness shown to the poor?

"He that hath pity upon the poor *lendeth unto the Lord;* and that which he hath given *will he pay him again.*" Proverbs 19:17. "For *God is not unrighteous to forget your work and labour of love,* which ye have shewed toward his name, in that ye have ministered to the saints, and do minister." Hebrews 6:10.

FATE AND REWARD

What fate awaits those who turn a deaf ear to the poor?

"Whoso stoppeth his ears at the cry of the poor, *he also shall cry himself, but shall not be heard.*" Proverbs 21:13.

What promises are made to those who consider the poor?

"Blessed is he that considereth the poor: the Lord will deliver him in time of trouble. The Lord will preserve him, and keep him alive; and he shall be blessed upon the earth: and thou wilt not deliver him unto the will of his enemies. The Lord will strengthen him upon the bed of languishing: thou wilt make all his bed in his sickness." Psalm 41:1-3.

What is promised those who do this work?

"Then shalt thou call, and the Lord shall answer; thou shalt cry and he shall say, Here I am. . . . And if thou draw out thy soul to the hungry, and satisfy the afflicted soul; then shall thy light rise in obscurity, and thy darkness be as the noon day: and the Lord shall guide thee continually, and satisfy thy soul in drought, and make fat thy bones: and thou shalt be like a watered garden, and like a spring of water, whose waters fail not." Isaiah 58:9-11.

What did Christ tell the rich young man to do?

"Jesus said unto him, If thou wilt be perfect, *go and sell that thou hast, and give to the poor,* and thou shalt have treasure in heaven: and come and follow me." Matthew 19:21.

NOTE.—From Matthew 25:31-45 we learn that Christ identifies Himself with needy, suffering humanity; and that any neglect shown them He regards as done unto Himself, and any service rendered to them as though done for Him. We are not saved because we help the needy; but if we experience the salvation of Christ, we will love the unfortunate. This is a test of the genuineness of our profession.

Christian Help Work

The Good, the Rich, and the Poor

What was the character of Christ's work among men?

"Who went about *doing good*." Acts 10:38.

What will His true followers do?

"He that saith he abideth in him ought himself also so *to walk, even as he walked*." 1 John 2:6.

In ministering to the needy, whom are we really serving?

"Inasmuch as ye have done it unto one of the least of these my brethren, *ye have done it unto me*." Matthew 25:40.

How long will there be poor in the world?

"Ye have the poor *always with you*." Matthew 26:11.

What relation do all sustain to God?

"The rich and poor *meet together*: the Lord is *the maker* of them all." Proverbs 22:2.

Whom to Help and How

What classes are subjects for Christian help work?

"Pure religion and undefiled before God and the Father is this, To visit the *fatherless* and *widows* in their affliction, and to keep himself unspotted from the world." James 1:27.

How did Job learn of the needs of the poor?

"The cause of him that I knew not *I searched out* [or, "*investigated*"]." Job 29:16, R.V.

What parable illustrates practical Christian help work?

The parable of the good Samaritan. Luke 10:30-37.

When Christ sent out the Seventy, what did He tell them to do in the cities whither they went?

"And *heal the sick* that are therein, and say unto them, The kingdom of God is come nigh unto you." Verse 9.

THE GOOD SAMARITAN

"He had compassion on him, ... and bound up his wou
... and set him on his own beast." Luke 10:33,

What incentive have Christians for doing prison work?

"*I was in prison*, and ye came unto me." Matthew 25:36.

Who notes the groans of the prisoner?

"From heaven did *the Lord* behold the earth; *to hear the groaning of the prisoner.*" Psalm 102:19, 20.

Is it our duty always to give what is expected or asked?

"Then Peter said, Silver and gold have I none; but *such as I have give I thee:* In the name of Jesus Christ of Nazareth rise up and walk." Acts 3:6. (See 2 Corinthians 12:8.)

What is sometimes of greater value even than money to discouraged souls?

"*I smiled on them* when they had no confidence." Job 29:24, R.S.V.

EVIDENCES AND FRUITS OF TRUE SALVATION

What is one good evidence of genuine repentance?

"Break off thy sins by righteousness, and thine iniquities by *shewing mercy to the poor.*" Daniel 4:27.

What is one evidence that one has a knowledge of God?

"He *judged the cause of the poor and needy;* then it was well with him: was not this to *know me?* saith the Lord." Jeremiah 22:16.

What divine law of retroaction attends giving?

"*Give, and it shall be given unto you;* good measure, pressed down, and shaken together, and running over, shall men give into your bosom. For *with the same measure that ye mete withal it shall be measured to you again.*" Luke 6:38. (See Psalms 18:25, 26; 109:17; Galatians 6:7.)

What is promised those who give to the poor?

"He that hath pity upon the poor lendeth unto the Lord; and *that which he hath given will he pay him again.*" Proverbs 19:17. "He that giveth unto the poor *shall not lack.*" Proverbs 28:27.

What work constitutes the fast most acceptable to God?

"Is not this the fast that I have chosen? to loose the bands of wickedness, to undo the heavy burdens, and to let the oppressed go free, and that ye break every yoke? Is it not to deal thy bread to the hungry, and that thou bring the poor that are cast out to thy house? when thou seest the naked, that thou cover him." Isaiah 58:6, 7.

What promises are made to those who thus minister to the wants and distresses of others?

"If thou draw out thy soul to the hungry, and satisfy the afflicted soul; then shall thy light rise in obscurity, and thy darkness be as the noon day: and the Lord shall guide thee continually, and satisfy thy soul in drought, and make fat thy bones: and thou shalt be like a watered garden, and like a spring of water, whose waters fail not." Verses 10, 11.

Somebody near you is struggling alone
    Over life's desert sand.
Faith, hope, and courage together are gone:
    Reach him a helping hand,
Turn on his darkness a beam of your light;
Kindle, to guide him, a beacon-fire bright;
Cheer his discouragement; soothe his affright;
    Lovingly help him to stand.

Somebody near you is hungry and cold;
    Send him some aid today.
Somebody near you is feeble and old,
    Left without human stay.
Under his burdens put hands kind and strong;
Speak to him tenderly, sing him a song;
Haste to do something to help him along
    Over his weary way.

—Mrs. E. E. Williams

Visiting the Sick

For what will Christ finally commend the righteous?

"I was sick, and *ye visited me*." Matthew 25:36.

With what is Christ touched?

"With the feeling of our infirmities." Hebrews 4:15.

What relief did He bring to Peter's household?

"And when Jesus was come into Peter's house, he saw his wife's mother laid, and sick of a fever. *And he touched her hand, and the fever left her:* and she arose, and ministered unto them." Matthew 8:14, 15.

How did Peter summarize Christ's ministry?

"Who *went about doing good,* and *healing all that were oppressed of the devil;* for God was with him." Acts 10:38.

What should we not forget in our ministry for the sick?

"*Pray one for another, that ye may be healed.* The effectual fervent prayer of a righteous man availeth much." James 5:16.

Wise Counsel on Visiting the Sick

"It is misdirected kindness, a false idea of courtesy, that leads to much visiting of the sick. Those who are very ill should not have visitors. The excitement connected with receiving callers wearies the patient at a time when he is in the greatest need of quiet, undisturbed rest.

"To a convalescent or a patient suffering from chronic disease, it is often a pleasure and a benefit to know that he is kindly remembered; but this assurance conveyed by a message of sympathy or by some little gift will often serve a better purpose than a personal visit, and without danger of harm."—The Ministry of Healing, p. 222.

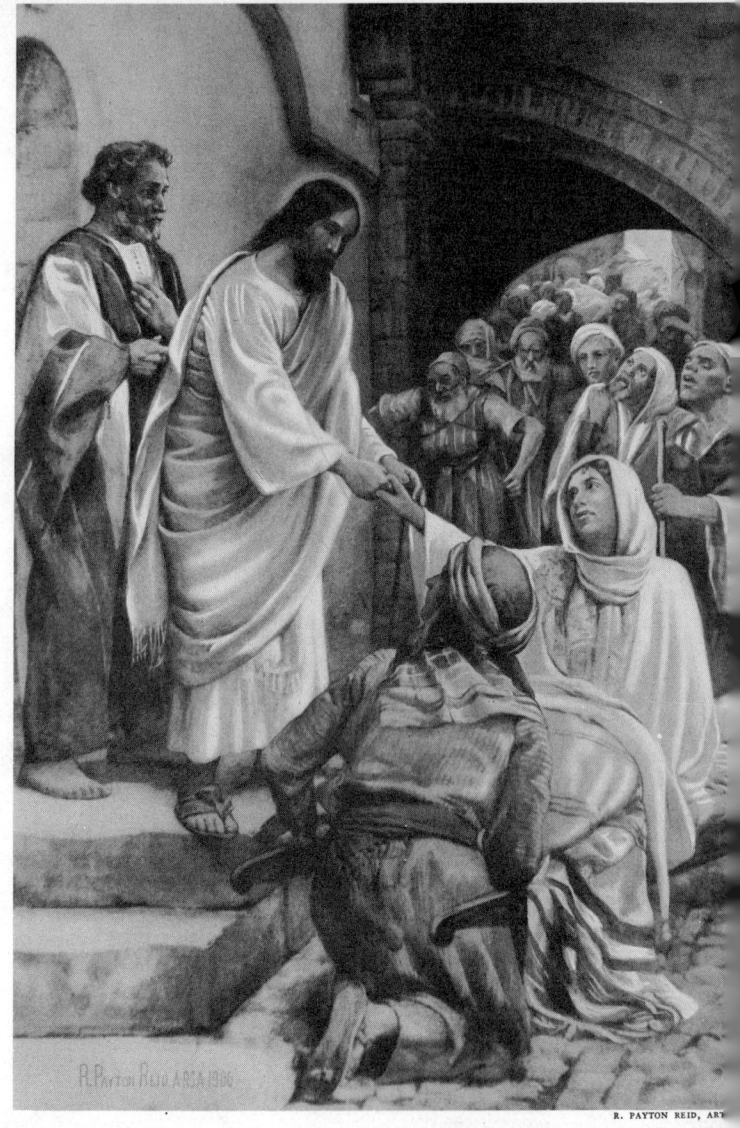

THE GREAT PHYSICIAN

"Who forgiveth all thine iniquities; healeth all thy diseases." Psalm 10

Healing the Sick

GOD'S ABILITY TO HEAL

WHAT does the Lord declare Himself to be?

"I am the Lord that *healeth* thee." Exodus 15:26. "Who forgiveth all thine iniquities; *who healeth all thy diseases.*" Psalm 103:3.

What was promised Israel on condition of obedience?

"Thou shalt therefore keep the commandments, . . . and *the Lord will take away from thee all sickness.*" Deuteronomy 7:11-15.

OLD TESTAMENT EXPERIENCES OF HEALING

When through disobedience Jeroboam's hand was withered, by what means was it restored?

"And the king answered and said unto the man of God, Intreat now the face of the Lord thy God, and *pray for me, that my hand may be restored me again. And the man of God besought the Lord, and the king's hand was restored him again, and became as it was before.*" 1 Kings 13:6.

When Miriam was stricken with leprosy, how was she healed?

"And *Moses cried unto the Lord,* saying, Heal her now, O God, I beseech thee." Numbers 12:13.

What mistake did Asa make in his severe affliction?

"And Asa in the thirty and ninth year of his reign was diseased in his feet, until his disease was exceeding great: yet in his disease *he sought not to the Lord, but to the physicians.*" 2 Chronicles 16:12.

How was a child restored to life by Elijah?

"And he stretched himself upon the child three times, and *cried unto the Lord,* and said, O Lord my God, I pray thee, let this child's soul come into him again. And the Lord heard the voice of Elijah; *and the soul of the child came into him again, and he revived.*" 1 Kings 17:21, 22.

How was Hezekiah's prayer for restoration from sickness answered?

"Thus saith the Lord, the God of David thy father, *I have heard thy prayer, I have seen thy tears: behold, I will add unto thy days fifteen years.*" Isaiah 38:5.

CHRIST'S WORK AND PROPHECY THEREOF

What constituted a large part of Christ's ministry?

"And Jesus went about all Galilee, teaching in their synagogues, and preaching the gospel of the kingdom, and *healing all manner of sickness and all manner of disease among the people.*" Matthew 4:23.

In doing this, what prophecy was fulfilled?

"He cast out the spirits with his word, and healed all that were sick: that it might be fulfilled which was spoken by Esaias the prophet, saying, *Himself took our infirmities, and bare our sicknesses.*" Matthew 8:16, 17.

In the case of the woman healed of an infirmity, what gave effect to her touch of Christ's garment?

"And he said unto her, Daughter, be of good comfort: *thy faith hath made thee whole;* go in peace." Luke 8:48.

Before sending out the Twelve, what power did Christ give them?

"Then he called his twelve disciples together, and gave them power and authority over all devils, and *to cure diseases.* And he sent them to preach the kingdom of God, and *to heal the sick.*" Luke 9:1, 2. (See Matthew 10:1, 7, 8; Luke 10:1, 9.)

HEALING IN APOSTOLIC TIMES

What notable miracle was performed by the apostles shortly after the day of Pentecost?

"Then Peter said [to the lame man], Silver and gold have I none; but such as I have give I thee: In the name of Jesus Christ of Nazareth rise up and walk. And he took him by the right hand, and lifted him up: and *immediately his feet and ankle bones received strength*. And he leaping up stood and walked, and entered with them into the temple, walking, and leaping, and praising God." Acts 3:6-8.

Among others, what gift has God set in the church?

"And God hath set some in the church, first apostles, secondarily prophets, thirdly teachers, after that miracles, then *gifts of healings,* helps, governments, diversities of tongues." 1 Corinthians 12:28.

BIBLE COUNSEL TO THE SICK

In sickness, what is every child of God privileged to do?

"Is any sick among you? *let him call for the elders of the church; and let them pray over him,* anointing him with oil in the name of the Lord." James 5:14.

What assurance of blessing is given to those who ask according to God's will?

"The prayer of faith shall save the sick, and the Lord shall raise him up; and if he have committed sins, they shall be forgiven him." Verse 15.

NOTE.—Physical healing may not always be for our good or to the glory of God. Hence we must be ready to pray with Jesus, "Nevertheless not my will, but thine, be done." Luke 22:42. Paul was denied the removal of infirmity, but the Lord assured him, "My grace is sufficient for thee." 2 Corinthians 12:9. It is not a denial of faith to make use of the simple remedial means that God has given, or those ordinary essentials upon which He makes life dependent, as proper food, pure air, rest, exercise, and sunshine. Medical care may be used of God in restoring health.

> "THE quality of mercy is not strain'd,
> It droppeth as the gentle rain from heaven
> Upon the place beneath. It is twice bless'd:
> It blesseth him that gives and him that takes."

Order and Organization

IMPORTANCE OF ORDER AND SYSTEM

Of what is God the author?

"For God is not the author of confusion, but of *peace,* as in all churches of the saints." 1 Corinthians 14:33.

Why did Paul give instruction to Timothy concerning the duties and qualifications of bishops and deacons?

"These things write I unto thee, . . . *that thou mayest know how thou oughtest to behave thyself in the house of God,* which is the church of the living God, the pillar and ground of the truth." 1 Timothy 3:14, 15.

How should everything pertaining to God's work be done?

"Let all things be done *decently and in order*." 1 Corinthians 14:40.

NOTE.—"Order is Heaven's first law."—POPE. In the Scriptures Christians are likened to soldiers, and their work to that of a warrior (2 Timothy 2:3, 4; 1 Timothy 1:18; Revelation 6:2.) As order, organization, direction, and discipline are necessary in an army, so are they also in the church. The weapons used and the object sought are different in each case (Romans 13:4; 2 Corinthians 10:3, 4); but the necessity for order and organization are the same in both.

DIVISION OF RESPONSIBILITY

That the burden of judging and looking after the affairs of Israel might not all rest on Moses, what instruction did Jethro, his father-in-law, give him?

"Moreover thou shalt provide out of all the people able men, such as fear God, men of truth, hating covetousness; and place such over them, to be rulers of thousands, and rulers of hundreds, rulers of fifties, and rulers of tens: and let them judge the people at all seasons: and it shall be, that every great matter they shall bring unto thee, but every small matter they shall judge: so shall it be easier for thyself, and they shall bear the burden with thee." Exodus 18:21, 22.

ORDER AND ORGANIZATION

How many apostles did Christ at first ordain to preach the gospel?

"And *he ordained twelve,* that they should be with him, and that he might send them forth to preach." Mark 3:14.

How many did He later appoint to this work?

"After these things the Lord appointed *other seventy also,* and sent them two and two before his face into every city and place, whither he himself would come." Luke 10:1.

When the number of the disciples multiplied, what instruction did the apostles give the believers, that none might be neglected in the daily ministration of temporal necessities?

"Wherefore, brethren, look ye out among you seven men of honest report, full of the Holy Ghost and wisdom, whom we may appoint over this business." Acts 6:3.

NOTE.—The men thus selected were known as deacons. The lesson to be learned from this is that leaders and people should unite in planning and providing for the necessary organization and officering of the church according to its growth and needs. This cooperation is again shown in the words of Paul, "Whomsoever ye shall approve by your letters, them will I send." 1 Corinthians 16:3. (See also Acts 15:22.)

What word came through the Spirit to the ministering prophets and teachers laboring at Antioch?

"As they ministered to the Lord, and fasted, the Holy Ghost said, *Separate me Barnabas and Saul for the work whereunto I have called them.* And when they had fasted and prayed, and laid their hands on them, they sent them away." Acts 13:2, 3.

What is one of the gifts which God has set in the church?

"And God hath set some in the church, first apostles, secondarily prophets, thirdly teachers, after that . . . helps, *governments.*" 1 Corinthians 12:28.

NOTE.—The word here rendered *governments* implies the work or office of "steering, piloting, directing."

For the direction of matters in each local church, what instruction did the apostle Paul give Titus?

"For this cause left I thee in Crete, that thou shouldest set in order the things that are wanting, and *ordain elders in every city,* as I had appointed thee." Titus 1:5.

Relationship of Members and Leaders

What instruction did he give to the members of the church as to their relationship to those thus appointed?

"Obey them that have the rule [margin, *"guide"*] *over you, and submit yourselves:* for they watch for your souls, as they that must give account, that they may do it with joy, and not with grief." Hebrews 13:17. (See 1 Peter 5:5; Mark 10:42-45.)

What instruction and caution are given to elders?

"The elders which are among you I exhort, who am also an elder, . . . *Feed the flock of God* which is among you, *taking the oversight thereof,* not by constraint, but willingly; not for filthy lucre, but of a ready mind; *neither as being lords over God's heritage,* but being ensamples to the flock." 1 Peter 5:1-3.

Note.—For the qualifications and duties of elders, see 1 Timothy 3:1-3; Titus 1:6-9; Acts 20:28-31; and the scripture just quoted. How God regards rebellion against divinely appointed authority and leadership is illustrated in the expulsion of Satan and his angels from heaven, and in the fate of Korah, Dathan, and Abiram. (See Revelation 12:7-9; Numbers 16.) The unity and harmony which should exist among believers is described in John 13:34, 35; 17:20-23; and Ephesians 4:1-6. The evil of place seeking in the church is shown in Mark 10:35-45 and Luke 14:7-11; and of ecclesiastical tyranny, in Daniel 7:25; 8:24, 25; 2 Thessalonians 2:3, 4; and John 16:2. The course to be pursued toward offending members, and in cases where differences arise, is pointed out in Matthew 18:15-18; 5:23, 24; Galatians 6:1; 1 Timothy 5:19, 20; Titus 3:10, 11; 1 Corinthians 5; and Acts 15. And the guidebook in all matters of both doctrine and discipline should be the Bible. (Isaiah 8:20; 2 Timothy 3:16, 17; 4:1, 2.)

"Has someone seen Christ in you today?
Christian, look to your heart, I pray;
The little things you have done or said—
Did they accord with the way you prayed?
Have your thoughts been pure and words been kind?
Have you sought to have the Saviour's mind?
The world with a criticizing view
Has watched; but did it see Christ in you?"

Support of the Ministry

God's Portion and Its Purpose

What is one way in which we are commanded to honor God?

"Honour the Lord *with thy substance,* and *with the firstfruits of all thine increase.*" Proverbs 3:9.

What part of one's income has the Lord especially claimed as His?

"And *all the tithe* [tenth] *of the land,* whether of the seed of the land, or of the fruit of the tree, *is the Lord's: it is holy unto the Lord.*" Leviticus 27:30.

For whose support and for what work was the tithe devoted in Israel?

"Behold, I have given *the children of Levi* all the tenth in Israel for an inheritance, *for their service which they serve, even the service of the tabernacle of the congregation.*" Numbers 18:21.

How does Paul say the gospel ministry is to be supported?

"If we have sown unto you spiritual things, is it a great thing if we shall reap your carnal things? ... Do ye not know that they which minister about holy things live of the things of the temple? and they which wait at the altar are partakers with the altar? *Even so hath the Lord ordained that they which preach the gospel should live of the gospel.*" 1 Corinthians 9:11-14.

Fundamental Basis of Tithe Paying

Upon what fundamental basis does the requirement of tithe paying rest?

"*The earth is the Lord's,* and the fulness thereof; the world, and they that dwell therein." Psalm 24:1.

Who gives man power to get wealth?

"But thou shalt remember the Lord thy God: for *it is he that giveth thee power to get wealth.*" Deuteronomy 8:18.

What statement of Christ shows that man is not an original owner, but a steward of God's goods?

"For the kingdom of heaven is as a man travelling into a far country, who called his own servants, and *delivered unto them his goods.*" Matthew 25:14. (See 1 Corinthians 4:7.)

History of Tithe Paying

How early in the history of the world do we read of tithe paying?

"For this Melchisedec, king of Salem, priest of the most high God, who met Abraham returning from the slaughter of the kings, and blessed him; to whom also *Abraham gave a tenth part of all.*" Hebrews 7:1, 2. (See Genesis 14:17-20.)

What vow did Jacob make at Bethel?

"And Jacob vowed a vow, saying, If God will be with me, and will keep me in this way that I go, and will give me bread to eat, and raiment to put on, so that I come again to my father's house in peace; then shall the Lord be my God: . . . and *of all that thou shalt give me I will surely give the tenth unto thee.*" Genesis 28:20-22.

Curse or Blessing

Of what is one guilty who withholds the tithe and freewill offerings?

"Will a man rob God? Yet *ye have robbed me.* But ye say, Wherein have we robbed thee? *In tithes and offerings.*" Malachi 3:8.

Concerning what does the Lord ask us to prove Him, and upon what conditions does He promise great blessings?

"*Bring ye all the tithes into the storehouse,* that there may be meat in mine house, and *prove me now herewith,* saith the Lord of hosts, if I will not open you the windows of heaven, and pour you out a blessing, that there shall not be room enough to receive it. And I will rebuke the devourer for your sakes, and he shall not destroy the fruits of your ground; neither shall your vine cast her fruit before the time in the field, saith the Lord of hosts." Verses 10, 11.

Freewill Offerings

A Distinction in Tithes and Offerings

By what has God ordained that His work be sustained?

"Tithes and offerings." Malachi 3:8.

How are we told to come into His courts?

"Bring an offering, and come into his courts." Psalm 96:8.

NOTE.—Various offerings are mentioned in the Bible, such as thank offerings, peace offerings, sin offerings, and trespass offerings.

Concerning the celebration of the three annual feasts, what instruction did God give to His people anciently?

"Three times thou shalt keep a feast unto me in the year.... And *none shall appear before me empty."* Exodus 23:14, 15.

Acceptable Offerings

With what spirit would God have us give?

"Every man according as he purposeth in his heart, so let him give; not grudgingly, or of necessity: for *God loveth a cheerful giver."* 2 Corinthians 9:7.

What has Christ said regarding giving?

"It is *more blessed to give than to receive."* Acts 20:35.

According to what rule were the Israelites commanded to give?

"Every man shall give as he is able, according to the blessing of the Lord thy God which he hath given thee." Deuteronomy 16:17. Compare 1 Corinthians 16:2.

Upon what basis are gifts acceptable to God?

"For if there be first a willing mind, *it is accepted according to that a man hath,* and not according to that he hath not." 2 Corinthians 8:12.

What charge was Timothy instructed to give the rich?

"Charge them that are rich in this world, that they be not

HUGO MIETH, ARTIST

THE WIDOW'S TWO MITES

"This poor widow hath cast in more than they all." Luke 21:3.

highminded, nor trust in uncertain riches, but in the living God, who giveth us richly all things to enjoy; *that they do good, that they be rich in good works, ready to distribute, willing to communicate;* laying up in store for themselves a good foundation against the time to come, that they may lay hold on eternal life." 1 Timothy 6:17-19.

How does God regard such a course?

"But to do good and to communicate ["share what you have," R.S.V.] forget not: for *with such sacrifices God is well pleased.*" Hebrews 13:16.

THE CASE OF THE COVETOUS MAN

How does God regard the covetous man?

"The wicked boasteth of his heart's desire, and blesseth the covetous, *whom the Lord abhorreth.*" Psalm 10:3. (See Exodus 18:21.)

What warning did Christ give against covetousness?

"Take heed, and *beware of covetousness:* for a man's life consisteth not in the abundance of the things which he possesseth." Luke 12:15.

How, in the parable, did God regard the selfish rich man?

"But God said unto him, *Thou fool,* this night thy soul shall be required of thee: then whose shall those things be, which thou hast provided?" Verse 20.

What application does Christ make of this parable?

"So is he that layeth up treasure for himself, and is not rich toward God." Verse 21. (See 1 Timothy 6:7.)

TREASURES IN HEAVEN

By what means can men lay up treasure in heaven?

"Sell that ye have, and give alms; provide yourselves bags which wax not old, a treasure in the heavens that faileth not, where no thief approacheth, neither moth corrupteth." Luke 12:33. (See 1 Timothy 6:7.)

What indicates where our hearts are?

"For *where your treasure is,* there will your heart be also." Luke 12:34.

Who Is the Greatest?

A New Idea on Greatness

At the last Passover, what did Christ say to His disciples?

"And he said unto them, With desire I have desired to eat this passover with you before I suffer: for I say unto you, I will not any more eat thereof, until it be fulfilled in the kingdom of God." Luke 22:15, 16.

Concerning what had there been a strife among the disciples?

"And there was also a strife among them, *which of them should be accounted the greatest.*" Verse 24.

How did Christ rebuke this spirit?

"And he said unto them, The kings of the Gentiles exercise lordship over them; and they that exercise authority upon them are called benefactors. But ye shall not be so: but *he that is greatest among you, let him be as the younger; and he that is chief, as he that doth serve.*" Verses 25, 26. (See Mark 10:42-45.)

The Saviour Sets an Example

What did the Saviour say of His own position?

"For whether is greater, he that sitteth at meat, or he that serveth? is not he that sitteth at meat? but *I am among you as he that serveth.*" Verse 27.

Notwithstanding that He was their Lord and Master, what example of humility and willing service did Christ give?

"He riseth from supper, and laid aside his garments; and took a towel, and girded himself. After that *he poureth water into a bason, and began to wash the disciples' feet, and to wipe them with the towel wherewith he was girded.*" John 13:4, 5.

What was the custom anciently respecting foot washing?

"Let a little water, I pray you, be fetched, and *wash your feet.*" "And he said, Behold now, my lords, turn in, I pray you,

WHO IS THE GREATEST?

into your servant's house, and tarry all night, and *wash your feet.*" "And the man brought the men into Joseph's house, and *gave them water, and they washed their feet.*" Genesis 18:4; 19:2; 43:24. (See also Judges 19:21; 2 Samuel 11:8.)

How did Christ reprove Simon for misjudging Him in permitting a woman who was a sinner to wash His feet?

"And he turned to the woman and said unto Simon, Seest thou this woman? I entered into thine house, *thou gavest me no water for my feet:* but she hath washed my feet with tears, and wiped them with the hairs of her head." Luke 7:44.

Note.—From the scriptures just cited, it appears that the usual custom in Christ's time was for the guests to wash their own feet.

"As sandals were ineffectual against the dust and heat of an Eastern climate, washing the feet on entering a house was an act both of respect to the company, and of refreshment to the traveller."— *Smith's Comprehensive Dictionary of the Bible* (1884 ed.), edited by Barnum, art. "Washing the Hands and Feet."

At a feast it was an Oriental custom for servants or slaves to wash the feet of guests. (See 1 Samuel 25:40, 41.) It was not the custom, however, of *equals* to wash the feet of *equals,* much less for *superiors* to wash the feet of *inferiors.* But this is the very thing that Christ did when He washed the disciples' feet, and instituted the ordinance of foot washing. In this lies the lesson of humility and willingness to serve which He designed to teach.

What question did Peter ask concerning this proffered service?

"Then cometh he to Simon Peter: and Peter saith unto him, *Lord, dost thou wash my feet?*" John 13:6.

What answer did Jesus make?

"Jesus answered and said unto him, *What I do thou knowest not now; but thou shalt know hereafter.*" Verse 7.

How did Peter feel about the Saviour's washing his feet?

"Peter saith unto him, *Thou shalt never wash my feet.*" Verse 8, first part.

The Significance of the Service

What was the Master's reply to Peter?

"Jesus answered him, *If I wash thee not, thou hast no part with me.*" Verse 8, last part.

Note.—This ordinance is a type of a higher cleansing—the cleansing of the heart from the stain of sin. It is a rebuke to all selfishness and seeking of place and preferment among Christ's professed followers, and a witness to the fact that, in God's sight, it is true humility and loving service which constitute real greatness.

Learning that union with Christ depended on this service, what did Peter say?

"Simon Peter saith unto him, Lord, *not my feet only, but also my hands and my head.*" Verse 9. (See verse 10.)

After having washed their feet, what did Christ say?

"*I have given you an example,* that ye should do as I have done to you." Verse 15.

What did He say about their washing one another's feet?

"Ye call me Master and Lord: and ye say well; for so I am. If I then, your Lord and Master, have washed your feet; *ye also ought to wash one another's feet.*" Verses 13, 14.

What did Christ say would be their experience in obeying His instruction?

"If ye know these things, *happy are ye if ye do them.*" Verse 17.

How does Christ regard an act performed toward the humblest of His disciples?

"Inasmuch as ye have done it unto one of the least of these my brethren, *ye have done it unto me.*" Matthew 25:40.

Note.—The great lesson intended to be taught by the instituting of this ordinance evidently was such humility as would lead to willing service for others. The ordinance itself has been practiced here and there by devout followers of Christ during the Christian Era, and is still observed by some. Kitto, in his *Cyclopaedia of Biblical Literature,* says foot washing became "a part of the observances practised in the early Christian church," and that "traces of the practise abound in ecclesiastical history."

"I will never, never leave thee,
I will never thee forsake;
I will guide, and save, and keep thee,
For My name and mercy's sake:
Fear no evil,
Only all My counsel take."

Part Fifteen

Admonitions and Warnings

	PAGE
Sinful Pride	659
Selfishness	660
Covetousness	661
Danger of Debt	666
Respect of Persons	669
Backsliding	672
Unbelief and Doubt	675
Judging and Criticizing	678
Gossiping and Backbiting	681
Hypocrisy and Dissimulation	685
The Just Recompense	687

THE CHASE OF FORTUNE "What is a man profited, if he shall gain the whole world, and lose his own soul?" Matthew 16:26.

Sinful Pride

God's Estimate of Pride

How does the Lord regard pride?

"Six things doth the Lord *hate:* . . . *a proud look,*" etc. Proverbs 6:16-19.

What is God's attitude toward the proud?

"God *resisteth* the proud." James 4:6. (See Psalms 40:4; 101:5; 138:6; 1 Timothy 6:4.)

What Pride Is

Why should we not indulge in pride?

"An high look, and a proud heart, . . . is *sin*." Proverbs 21:4.

What is to be one of the sins of the last days?

"Men shall be . . . *proud*." 2 Timothy 3:2.

The Results of Pride

Of what is pride a forerunner?

"Pride goeth before *destruction,* and an haughty spirit before *a fall.*" Proverbs 16:18. (See Proverbs 29:23.)

What was the cause of Satan's downfall?

"Thine heart was *lifted up because of thy beauty*." Ezekiel 28:17.

How are the proud now generally regarded?

"Now we call the proud *happy*." Malachi 3:15.

What is to be the fate of the proud?

"All the proud . . . shall be stubble: and *the day that cometh shall burn them up*." Malachi 4:1.

Selfishness

THE COMMANDMENTS AND SELFISHNESS

What great commandment excludes selfishness?

"Thou shalt love thy neighbour as thyself." Matthew 22:39.

What sin is forbidden by the tenth commandment?

"Thou shalt not *covet*." Exodus 20:17.

How are we admonished with regard to selfishness?

"Let no man *seek his own*." 1 Corinthians 10:24. "Look not every man *on his own things,* but every man also *on the things of others*." Philippians 2:4. "Even as I please all men in all things, *not seeking mine own profit*, but the profit of many, that they may be saved." 1 Corinthians 10:33. "Let every one of us *please his neighbour* for his good to edification." Romans 15:2.

SELF-SEEKING YESTERDAY AND TODAY

How prevalent is the sin of self-seeking?

"For *all seek their own,* not the things which are Jesus Christ's." Philippians 2:21.

What sins are to characterize the last days?

"Men shall be *lovers of their own selves, covetous*." 2 Timothy 3:2.

THE CURE FOR SELFISHNESS

What does charity not do?

"Charity . . . *seeketh not her own*." 1 Corinthians 13:4, 5.

What example of unselfishness did Christ leave us?

"For your sakes *he became poor*." 2 Corinthians 8:9. "Even Christ *pleased not himself*." Romans 15:3. (See 1 John 3:17.)

Covetousness

THE NATURE OF COVETOUSNESS

WHAT warning did Christ give concerning covetousness?

"And he said unto them, *Take heed, and beware of covetousness:* for a man's life consisteth not in the abundance of the things which he possesseth." Luke 12:15.

What commandment forbids this sin?

"Thou shalt not covet." Exodus 20:17.

What does Paul call covetousness?

"Mortify therefore your members which are upon the earth; fornication, uncleanness, inordinate affection, evil concupiscence, and *covetousness, which is idolatry.*" Colossians 3:5.

What do these sins bring upon mankind?

"For which things' sake *the wrath of God* cometh on the children of disobedience." Verse 6.

What double service did Christ say is impossible?

"Ye cannot serve *God* and *mammon.*" Luke 16:13.

BIBLE EXAMPLES OF THE COVETOUS

What showed this principle to have been strong in the rich man who already had abundance?

"And he said, This will I do: *I will pull down my barns, and build greater;* and there will I bestow all my fruits and my goods. And I will say to my soul, *Soul, thou hast much goods laid up for many years; take thine ease, eat, drink, and be merry.*" Luke 12:18, 19.

What did God say to him?

"But God said unto him, *Thou fool, this night thy soul shall be required of thee: then whose shall those things be, which thou hast provided?*" Verse 20.

What application of this parable did the Saviour make?

"So is he that layeth up *treasure for himself*, and is *not rich toward God*." Verse 21.

Of what sin were the Pharisees guilty?

"And the Pharisees also, *who were covetous*, heard all these things: and they derided him." Luke 16:14.

What reply did Christ make?

"And he said unto them, Ye are they which justify yourselves before men; but God knoweth your hearts: for *that which is highly esteemed among men is abomination in the sight of God*." Verse 15.

What did this sin lead Achan to do?

"When I saw among the spoils a goodly Babylonish garment, and two hundred shekels of silver, and a wedge of gold . . . *I coveted them, and took them*." Joshua 7:21.

What did covetousness lead Judas to do?

"And Judas Iscariot, one of the twelve, went unto the chief priests, *to betray him* unto them. And when they heard it they were glad, and *promised to give him money*. And he sought how he might conveniently *betray him*." Mark 14:10, 11.

How does the Lord regard the covetous?

"For the wicked boasteth of his heart's desire, and blesseth the covetous, *whom the Lord abhorreth*." Psalm 10:3.

False and True Ideas of Wealth

What parable did Christ give to correct the false idea of the Pharisees that wealth was a sign of special favor with God?

The parable of the rich man and Lazarus. (Luke 16:19-31.)

What did He point out as one of the dangers of the possession of wealth?

"And Jesus looked round about, and saith unto his disciples, *How hardly shall they that have riches enter into the kingdom of God!* . . . Jesus answereth again, and saith unto them, Children, *how hard is it for them that trust in riches to enter into the kingdom of God!*" Mark 10:23, 24.

Note.—And how hard it is for those who have riches not to trust in them!

COVETOUSNESS

As a rule, what class generally accept the gospel?

"Hearken, my beloved brethren, Hath not God chosen *the poor of this world* rich in faith, and heirs of the kingdom which he hath promised to them that love him?" James 2:5.

How difficult did Christ say it is for a rich man to enter the kingdom of God?

"It is easier for a camel to go through the eye of a needle, than for a rich man to enter into the kingdom of God." Mark 10:25.

Why was the rich young man desiring salvation unwilling to sell what he had and give alms, as Christ told him to do?

"But when the young man heard that saying, *he went away sorrowful: for he had great possessions.*" Matthew 19:22.

What is the love of money declared to be?

"For the *love* of money is *the root of all evil.*" 1 Timothy 6:10.

What evils befall those who are determined to be rich?

"But they that will be rich *fall into temptation and a snare, and into many foolish and hurtful lusts, which drown men in destruction and perdition.*" Verse 9.

Who gives man the power to get wealth?

"But thou shalt remember the Lord thy God: for *it is he that giveth thee power to get wealth.*" Deuteronomy 8:18.

How may all, rich and poor, honor God?

"Honour the Lord *with thy substance,* and *with the firstfruits of all thine increase.*" Proverbs 3:9.

What caution is given concerning riches?

"If riches increase, *set not your heart upon them.*" Psalm 62:10.

Can riches be retained to men's hurt?

"There is a sore evil which I have seen under the sun, namely, *riches kept for the owners thereof to their hurt.*" Ecclesiastes 5:13.

What charge is given to the rich?

"Charge them that are rich in this world, *that they be not highminded, nor trust in uncertain riches, but in the living God,* who giveth us richly all things to enjoy; that they *do good,* that they be *rich in good works, ready to distribute, willing to communicate;* laying up in store for themselves a good foundation against the time to come, that they may lay hold on eternal life." 1 Timothy 6:17-19.

What makes rich without adding sorrow?

"The blessing of the Lord, it maketh rich, and he addeth no sorrow with it." Proverbs 10:22.

How are true riches obtained?

"By *humility* and the *fear of the Lord* are riches, and honour, and life." Proverbs 22:4.

How did Moses esteem the reproach of Christ?

"Esteeming the reproach of Christ *greater riches than the treasures in Egypt:* for he had respect unto the recompence of the reward." Hebrews 11:26.

What two classes of rich men are mentioned in the Bible?

"There is that maketh himself *rich,* yet *hath nothing:* there is that maketh himself *poor,* yet *hath great riches."* Proverbs 13:7.

Note.—In Luke 12:16-20 is an example of the first class; in Acts 4:34-37 are examples of the second.

Man's Last Golden Opportunity

Why are the last days to be perilous?

"This know also, that in the last days perilous times shall come. For men shall be *lovers of their own selves, covetous,* boasters, proud, blasphemers." 2 Timothy 3:1, 2.

What solemn warning is addressed to the rich who, in the last days, have heaped up treasure and oppressed the poor?

"Go to now, ye rich men, *weep and howl for your miseries that shall come upon you.* Your riches are corrupted, and your garments are motheaten. Your gold and silver is cankered; and *the rust of them shall be a witness against you, and shall eat your flesh as it were fire.* Ye have heaped treasure together for the last days. Behold, the hire of the labourers who have reaped down your fields, which is of you kept back by fraud, crieth: and the cries of them which have reaped are entered into the ears of the Lord of sabaoth. Ye have lived in pleasure on the earth, and been wanton; ye have nourished your hearts, as in a day of slaughter." James 5:1-5.

Will silver or gold be able to deliver in the day of wrath?

"Neither their silver nor their gold shall be able to deliver them in the day of the Lord's wrath." Zephaniah 1:18. (See also Proverbs 11:4.)

What will the rich men do with their money then?

"They shall cast their silver in the streets, and their gold shall be removed: their silver and their gold shall not be able to deliver them in the day of the wrath of the Lord: they shall not satisfy their souls, neither fill their bowels: because it is the stumblingblock of their iniquity." Ezekiel 7:19.

NOTE.—The story is told that when the steamer *Central America,* with nearly six hundred passengers aboard, was wrecked off Cape Hatteras, September 12, 1857, in a fearful storm, many of the passengers who were returning miners from the gold mines of California divested themselves of their treasure belts and scattered the gold upon the cabin floors, telling those to take it who would, lest its weight about their persons should carry them to their death. Full purses, containing in some instances thousands of dollars, lay around untouched. Carpetbags were opened, and the shining metal was poured out on the floor with the prodigality of death's despair. One of the passengers opened a bag and dashed about the cabin twenty thousand dollars in gold dust, and told him who wanted to gratify his greed for gold to take it. But it was passed by untouched, as the veriest dross.

It is said that when the steamship *Arctic* was lost from a collision in mid-ocean, September 20, 1854, one passenger offered thirty thousand pounds sterling, or one hundred and fifty thousand dollars, if the lifeboats would put back to save him. They turned to do so, but he sank before they reached him.

As stewards of God's gifts, what are we told to do?

"And I say unto you, *Make to yourselves friends of the mammon of unrighteousness;* that, when ye fail, they may receive you into everlasting habitations." Luke 16:9. "As every man hath received the gift, *even so minister the same one to another,* as good stewards of the manifold grace of God." 1 Peter 4:10.

Danger of Debt

BONDAGE OF THE DEBTOR

What general rule is laid down in the Bible respecting the meeting of obligations?

"Render therefore to all their dues: tribute to whom tribute is due; custom to whom custom. . . . *Owe no man any thing, but to love one another."* Romans 13:7, 8.

In what condition is one who borrows?

"The borrower is *servant to the lender."* Proverbs 22:7.

To what extent is one responsible for that borrowed?

"And if a man borrow ought of his neighbour, and it be hurt, or die, . . . *he shall surely make it good."* Exodus 22:14.

Why did the young man in Elisha's time feel so concerned about the loss of an axhead?

"But as one was felling a beam, the axe head fell into the water: and he cried, and said, Alas, master! for *it was borrowed."* 2 Kings 6:5.

What miracle was wrought by Elisha for its restoration?

"And he cut down a stick, and cast it in thither; *and the iron did swim."* Verse 6.

NOTE.—From this we may learn God's willingness to help those who honestly seek to meet their obligations.

BUSINESS DISCRETION

How does the good man guide his affairs?

"A good man sheweth favour, and lendeth: he will guide his affairs *with discretion."* Psalm 112:5.

To what should those listen who lack business discretion?

"Poverty and shame shall be to him that refuseth *instruction:* but he that regardeth *reproof* shall be honoured." Proverbs 13:18.

NOTE.—It is wise for those who, from lack of natural business ability, find themselves constantly running into debt, to seek advice and counsel from those endowed with more wisdom in such matters.

Which of Christ's parables teaches business discretion?

"For which of you, intending to build a tower, sitteth not down first, and *counteth the cost, whether he have sufficient to finish it?* Lest haply, after he hath laid the foundation, and is not able to finish it, all that behold it begin to mock him, saying, This man began to build, and was not able to finish." Luke 14: 28-30.

How were means provided for building the tabernacle?

"And Moses spake unto all the congregation of the children of Israel, saying, This is the thing which the Lord commanded, saying, Take ye from among you *an offering* unto the Lord: whosoever is of a willing heart, let him bring it, an offering of the Lord; gold, and silver, and brass," etc. Exodus 35:4-9.

What provision did David make for building the Temple?

"I have prepared with all my might for the house of my God." 1 Chronicles 29:2.

How did the people respond to his call for contributions?

"Then the chief of the fathers and princes . . . *offered willingly*. . . . Then the people rejoiced, for that *they offered willingly*, because with perfect heart *they offered willingly* to the Lord: and David the king also rejoiced with great joy." Verses 6-9.

When King Jehoash wished to repair the Temple, what provision did he make for raising the necessary means?

"And Jehoash said to the priests, All the money of the dedicated things that is brought into the house of the Lord, . . . and all the money that cometh into any man's heart to bring into the house of the Lord, let the priests take it to them, every man of his acquaintance: and let them repair the breaches of the house, wheresoever any breach shall be found." 2 Kings 12:4, 5.

When, after sixteen years, it was found that these repairs had not yet been made, what was done?

"Jehoiada the priest *took a chest, and bored a hole in the lid of it, and set it beside the altar, on the right side as one cometh into the house of the Lord:* and the priests that kept the door put therein all the money that was brought into the house of the Lord." Verse 9.

What was done with the money thus raised?

"They gave the money . . . into the hands of them that did the work, . . . and they laid it out to the carpenters and builders, that wrought upon the house of the Lord." Verse 11.

Note.—These examples furnish good lessons on financing gospel enterprises. In each instance, it will be noticed, the means were provided before the work of building was begun. No debt, therefore, was created. In all business transactions this plan is an excellent one to follow.

Wise Words on Dubious Debt

The following paragraph is credited to T. De Witt Talmage:

"Debt! There is no worse demoralizer of character. The sad records of defaulting, embezzling, and dishonest failure which we meet with so constantly in the daily press are often, indeed most frequently, the result of the demoralization of debt, and the consequent desperate efforts of extraction. The financial props have given way. . . . Debt ruins as many households and destroys as many fine characters as rum; it is the devil's mortgage on the soul, and he is always ready to foreclose. Pay all your bills. Look every man in the face, conscious that you owe the world no more than it owes you. Be indebted for nothing but love, and even that be sure you pay in kind, and that payments are frequent."

"This running into debt is a great cause of dishonesty. . . . Young men are growing quite shameless about being in debt; and the immorality extends throughout society. Tastes are becoming more extravagant and luxurious, without the corresponding increase of means to enable them to be gratified. But they are gratified, nevertheless; and debts are incurred, which afterwards weigh like a millstone round the neck. . . . The safest plan is, to run up no bills, and never to get into debt; and the next is, if one does get into debt, to get out of it again as quickly as possible. A man in debt is not his own master: he is at the mercy of the tradesmen he employs. . . . No man can be free who is in debt. The inevitable effect of debt is not only to injure personal independence, but, in the long run, to inflict moral degradation. The debtor is exposed to constant humiliations."—Samuel Smiles, *Thrift,* pp. 243-247.

Respect of Persons

GOD'S STRICT IMPARTIALITY

Of what has God made all nations?

"And hath made *of one blood* [or, *"of one,"* that is, Adam] all nations of men for to dwell on all the face of the earth, and hath determined the times before appointed, and the bounds of their habitation." Acts 17:26.

To how many is God good?

"The Lord is *good to all:* and his tender mercies are over all his works." Psalm 145:9.

Is God a respecter of persons?

"Neither doth God respect any person." 2 Samuel 14:14.

Who is accepted with God?

"Then Peter opened his mouth, and said, Of a truth I perceive that God is no respecter of persons: but in every nation *he that feareth him, and worketh righteousness, is accepted with him.*" Acts 10:34, 35.

MAN'S RESPONSIBILITY TO BE FAIR

What prohibitions are given in the Scriptures against having respect of persons?

"Ye shall not respect persons *in judgment;* but ye shall hear the *small* as well as the *great;* ye shall not be afraid of the face of man." Deuteronomy 1:17. "Ye shall do no unrighteousness in judgment: thou shalt not respect the person of the *poor,* nor honour the person of the *mighty:* but in righteousness shalt thou judge thy neighbour." Leviticus 19:15. "Blessed is that man that . . . respecteth not the *proud,* nor such as turn aside to *lies.*" Psalm 40:4.

Of what are those guilty who respect persons?

"If ye have respect to persons, *ye commit sin,* and are convinced of the law as *transgressors.*" James 2:9. "He that despiseth his neighbour *sinneth.*" Proverbs 14:21.

"COME UNTO ME"

COPYRIGHT, 1949, BY REVIEW AND HERALD

PAUL REMMEY, ARTIST

"There is neither bond nor free, . . . for y are all one in Christ Jesus." Galatians 3:2

By what illustration is this sin made plain?

"My brethren, have not the faith of our Lord Jesus Christ, the Lord of glory, with respect of persons. For if there come unto your assembly a man with a gold ring, in goodly apparel, and there come in also a poor man in vile raiment; and ye have respect to him that weareth the gay clothing, and say unto him, Sit thou here in a good place; and say to the poor, Stand thou there, or sit here under my footstool: are ye not then partial in yourselves, and are become judges of evil thoughts?" James 2:1-4.

What led to the appointment of deacons in the early Christian church?

"And in those days, when the number of the disciples was multiplied, *there arose a murmuring of the Grecians against the Hebrews, because their widows were neglected in the daily ministration.*" Acts 6:1.

What mistake did Peter and others make some years later in their conduct?

"But when Peter was come to Antioch, I withstood him to the face, because he was to be blamed. For before that certain came from James, he did eat with the Gentiles: *but when they were come, he withdrew and separated himself, fearing them which were of the circumcision.* And the other Jews dissembled likewise with him; insomuch that Barnabas also was carried away with their dissimulation." Galatians 2:11-13.

SUBLIME UNITY IN CHRIST

How are all national, unholy, and unjust distinctions among men swept away in Christ?

"For as many of you as have been baptized into Christ have put on Christ. *There is neither Jew nor Greek, there is neither bond nor free, there is neither male nor female: for ye are all one in Christ Jesus.*" Galatians 3:27, 28. (See also Colossians 3:11.)

Backsliding

NATURE OF, AND TENDENCY TO, BACKSLIDING

How does God regard backsliding?

"Thy backslidings shall reprove thee: . . . *it is an evil thing and bitter, that thou hast forsaken the Lord thy God,* and that my fear is not in thee, saith the Lord God of hosts." Jeremiah 2:19. "If any man draw back, *my soul shall have no pleasure in him.*" Hebrews 10:38.

What persistent tendency did the Israelites display?

"My people are *bent to backsliding from me.*" Hosea 11:7.

To what is backsliding likened?

"Surely *as a wife treacherously departeth from her husband,* so have ye dealt treacherously with me, O house of Israel, saith the Lord." Jeremiah 3:20.

CAUSES AND CHARACTERISTICS OF BACKSLIDING

What inevitably leads to departure from God?

"Take heed, brethren, lest there be in any of you *an evil heart of unbelief,* in departing from the living God." Hebrews 3:12.

In what ways did the constant backsliding of the people of Jerusalem manifest itself?

"Why then is this people of Jerusalem slidden back by a perpetual backsliding? *they hold fast deceit, they refuse to return.* I hearkened and heard, but *they spake not aright: no man repented him of his wickedness,* saying, What have I done? *every one turned to his course,* as the horse rusheth into the battle." Jeremiah 8:5, 6.

What is one characteristic of backsliding?

"Even from the days of your fathers *ye are gone away from mine ordinances, and have not kept them.* Return unto me, and I will return unto you, saith the Lord of hosts. But ye said, Wherein shall we return?" Malachi 3:7.

BACKSLIDING

In response, what neglected ordinance does God cite?

"Will a man rob God? Yet ye have robbed me. But ye say, Wherein have we robbed thee? In tithes and offerings." Verse 8.

What remedy is indicated?

"Bring ye all the tithes into the storehouse, that there may be meat in mine house, and prove me now herewith, saith the Lord of hosts, if I will not open you the windows of heaven, and pour you out a blessing, that there shall not be room enough to receive it." Verse 10.

Because of Christ's plain teachings, what did some of His disciples do?

"From that time many of his disciples *went back, and walked no more with him."* John 6:66.

BACKSLIDER'S WAY BACK TO GOD

On what condition does God promise His abundant mercy to sinners?

"Let the wicked forsake his way, and the unrighteous man his thoughts: and let him return unto the Lord, and he will have mercy upon him, and to our God, for he will abundantly pardon." Isaiah 55:7.

Why must the wicked forsake their thoughts and ways in order to find salvation?

"For my thoughts are not your thoughts, neither are your ways my ways, saith the Lord." Verse 8.

Note.—God desires that we shall think His thoughts, which are right thoughts, pure thoughts, everlasting thoughts. He desires also that we shall take on His ways, which are ways of pleasantness, and walk in His paths, which are paths of peace.

What is especially necessary to prevent backsliding?

"Watch ye and pray, lest ye enter into temptation. The spirit truly is ready, but the flesh is weak." Mark 14:38.

What are believers exhorted to do?

"Examine yourselves, whether ye be in the faith; prove your own selves. Know ye not your own selves, how that Jesus Christ is in you, except ye be reprobates?" 2 Corinthians 13:5.

If one has God's law in the heart, what will not occur?

"The law of his God is in his heart; *none of his steps shall slide.*" Psalm 37:31.

When the backslider repents, what does God do?

"Take with you words, and turn to the Lord: say unto him, Take away all iniquity, and receive us graciously: so will we render the calves of our lips. . . . *I will heal their backsliding, I will love them freely:* for mine anger is turned away from him." Hosea 14:2-4.

Last-Day Backsliding

Will there be special danger of backsliding in the last days?

"And because iniquity shall abound, the love of many shall wax cold." Matthew 24:12.

What are some of the evils against which we are specially warned at this time?

"And take heed to yourselves, lest at any time your hearts be overcharged with *surfeiting,* and *drunkenness,* and *cares of this life,* and so that day come upon you unawares." Luke 21:34.

In view of the perils surrounding us, what are we told to do?

"*Watch ye therefore, and pray always,* that ye may be accounted worthy to escape all these things that shall come to pass, and to stand before the Son of man." Verse 36.

> O, FOR a closer walk with God!
> A calm and heavenly frame,
> A light to shine upon the road
> That leads me to the Lamb.
>
> —William Cowper

Unbelief and Doubt

God's Attitude Toward Unbelief

What warning is given in the Bible concerning unbelief?

"Take heed, brethren, lest there be in any of you an *evil heart of unbelief, in departing from the living God.*" Hebrews 3:12.

In whom does the Lord have no pleasure?

"But if any man *draw back*, my soul shall have no pleasure in him." Hebrews 10:38.

Against what are we warned when rebuked of God?

"My son, despise not thou the chastening of the Lord, *nor faint when thou art rebuked of him.*" Hebrews 12:5.

Whom does the Lord chasten?

"*For whom the Lord loveth he chasteneth*, and scourgeth every son whom he receiveth." Verse 6.

Examples of, and Lessons From, Unbelief

What kind of report did the ten spies bring back concerning the Promised Land?

"They brought up *an evil report* of the land which they had searched." Numbers 13:32.

What did Caleb say of the ability of Israel to take it?

"Let us go up at once, and possess it; for *we are well able to overcome it.*" Verse 30.

What did the ten spies say?

"But the men that went up with him said, *We be not able to go up against the people; for they are stronger than we.*" Verse 31.

Why did many fail to enter into God's rest anciently?

"And to whom sware he that they should not enter into his rest, but to them that *believed not*? So we see that *they could not enter in because of unbelief.*" Hebrews 3:18, 19.

How does the apostle Paul speak of the unbelieving ones who failed to enter Canaan?

"But with whom was he grieved forty years? was it not with *them that had sinned*, whose carcases fell in the wilderness?" Verse 17.

What practical lesson should we learn from their perverse course?

"Let us therefore fear, lest, a promise being left us of entering into his rest, any of you should seem to come short of it." Hebrews 4:1.

Note.—God does not change. If He was grieved at the unbelief of the Israelites, and refused them admittance to Canaan in consequence, He cannot permit us to enter the heavenly rest as long as we indulge in unbelief.

What should all labor to do?

"Let us labour therefore *to enter into that rest,* lest any man fall after the same example of unbelief." Verse 11.

When told of the disciples' failure to heal an afflicted son, what did Christ say of that generation?

"He answereth him, and saith, *O faithless generation,* how long shall I be with you? how long shall I suffer you? bring him unto me." Mark 9:19.

What did Christ say to Thomas because he did not believe the testimony of his brethren concerning His resurrection?

"Reach hither thy finger, and behold my hands; and reach hither thy hand, and thrust it into my side: and *be not faithless, but believing."* John 20:27.

Note.—The Lord rebuked Thomas for his unbelief, because he would not accept the testimony of so many credible witnesses who had seen Him. How much more reprehensible is that unbelief which holds out against the present "cloud of witnesses" of prophecy fulfilled and fulfilling!

Faith and Justification

Without faith, what is impossible?

"Without faith it is impossible *to please him."* Hebrews 11:6.

UNBELIEF AND DOUBT

How only can we be justified?

"Being justified *by faith*, we have peace with God through our Lord Jesus Christ." Romans 5:1.

By what do the just live?

"Now the just shall live *by faith*." Hebrews 10:38.

Faith, Righteousness, and Victory

Why did not Israel attain to the standard of righteousness?

"But Israel, which followed after the law of righteousness, hath not attained to the law of righteousness. Wherefore? *Because they sought it not by faith*." Romans 9:31, 32.

When God made a promise to Abraham that seemed impossible of fulfillment, how did the patriarch receive it?

"He staggered not at the promise of God through unbelief; but was *strong in faith*, giving glory to God." Romans 4:20.

For what was Abraham's faith counted?

"For what saith the scripture? Abraham believed God, and *it was counted unto him for righteousness*." Verse 3.

When troubled with doubts, how should we pray?

"Lord, I believe; *help thou mine unbelief*." Mark 9:24.

What is promised those who believe when they pray?

"Therefore I say unto you, What things soever ye desire, when ye pray, believe that ye receive them, and *ye shall have them*." Mark 11:24.

After speaking of the numerous examples of faith presented in Hebrews 11, what does Paul exhort us to do?

"Wherefore seeing we also are compassed about with so great a cloud of witnesses, let us *lay aside every weight, and the sin which doth so easily beset us*, and let us run with patience the race that is set before us." Hebrews 12:1.

Judging and Criticizing

The Note of Warning

What warning does Christ give concerning judging?

"Judge not, that ye be not judged." Matthew 7:1.

What is Satan called in the Scriptures?

"The accuser of our brethren . . . which accused them before our God day and night." Revelation 12:10.

Note.—Then when we judge, accuse, and condemn one another, we are doing the work of Satan.

If we bite and devour one another, what may we expect?

"But if ye bite and devour one another, *take heed that ye be not consumed one of another.*" Galatians 5:15.

Of what are those generally guilty who judge others?

"Therefore thou art inexcusable, O man, whosoever thou art that judgest: for wherein thou judgest another, thou condemnest thyself; *for thou that judgest doest the same things.*" Romans 2:1.

What instruction does James give regarding judging?

"Speak not evil one of another, brethren. He that speaketh evil of his brother, and judgeth his brother, speaketh evil of the law and judgeth the law: but if thou judge the law, thou art not a doer of the law, but a judge." James 4:11. (See Titus 3:2.)

Why is it safer not to judge and condemn others?

"Judge not, and ye shall not be judged: condemn not, and ye shall not be condemned." Luke 6:37. *"For with what judgment ye judge, ye shall be judged: and with what measure ye mete, it shall be measured to you again."* Matthew 7:2. (See Psalm 18:25, 26.)

Difficulty in Judging Correctly

Wherein do man's judging and God's judging differ?

"For the Lord seeth not as man seeth; for *man looketh on the outward appearance, but the Lord looketh on the heart."* 1 Samuel 16:7. "Ye are they which justify yourselves before men; but *God knoweth your hearts:* for *that which is highly esteemed among men is abomination in the sight of God."* Luke 16:15.

How does Christ tell us to judge?

"Judge *not according to the appearance,* but *judge righteous judgment."* John 7:24.

A Safe Way for Man

Before attempting to judge, criticize, or correct others, what should we first do?

"And why beholdest thou the mote that is in thy brother's eye, but considerest not the beam that is in thine own eye? Or how wilt thou say to thy brother, Let me pull out the mote out of thine eye; and, behold, a beam is in thine own eye? Thou hypocrite, *first cast out the beam out of thine own eye;* and then shalt thou see clearly to cast out the mote out of thy brother's eye." Matthew 7:3-5.

Whom are we not likely to judge and condemn?

"For if we would judge *ourselves* we should not be judged." 1 Corinthians 11:31.

What did Christ say He did not come to do?

"If any man hear my words, and believe not, I judge him not: for *I came not to judge the world,* but to save the world." "For God sent not his Son into the world to *condemn* the world; but that the world through him might be *saved."* John 12:47; 3:17.

How, by whom, and in what spirit should those having committed faults be dealt with?

"Brethren, if a man be overtaken in a fault, *ye which are spiritual, restore such an one in the spirit of meekness; considering thyself, lest thou also be tempted."* Galatians 6:1.

What exhortation, therefore, does the apostle give?

"Let us not therefore judge one another any more: but judge this rather, that no man put a stumblingblock or an occasion to fall in his brother's way." Romans 14:13.

Trusting Matters to God

What question does Paul ask concerning judging?

"*Who art thou that judgest another man's servant?* to his own master he standeth or falleth." Romans 14:4.

To whom are all to give account?

"So then every one of us shall give account of himself *to God.*" Verse 12.

Instead of railing on His enemies, what did Christ do?

"Who, when he was reviled, reviled not again; when he suffered, he threatened not; but *committed himself to him that judgeth righteously.*" 1 Peter 2:23.

To what time are we exhorted to defer judgment?

"Therefore judge nothing before the time, *until the Lord come,* who both will bring to light the hidden things of darkness, and will make manifest the counsels of the hearts." 1 Corinthians 4:5.

JUDGE not; the workings of his brain
  And of his heart thou canst not see;
What looks to thy dim eyes a stain,
  In God's pure light may only be
A scar, brought from some well-won field,
Where thou wouldst only faint and yield.

The look, the air, that frets thy sight
  May be a token that below
The soul has closed in deadly fight
  With some infernal fiery foe,
Whose glance would scorch thy smiling grace,
And cast thee shuddering on thy face!

And judge none lost; but wait and see,
  With hopeful pity, not disdain;
The depth of that abyss may be
  The measure of the height of pain
And love and glory that may raise
This soul to God in after days!

—ADELAIDE ANNE PROCTER

Gossiping and Backbiting

THE TONGUE AND THE HEART

WHAT does the ninth commandment forbid?

"Thou shalt not bear *false witness* against thy neighbour." Exodus 20:16.

NOTE.—The evident object of this commandment is to guard the rights, interests, and reputation of our neighbor by guarding our conversation and confining our words to that which is strictly true.

What instruction did John the Baptist give the soldiers who asked of him advice regarding the way of life?

"And he said unto them, Do violence to no man, *neither accuse any falsely;* and be content with your wages." Luke 3:14.

What is one test of a perfect man?

"If any man *offend not in word,* the same is *a perfect man,* and able also to bridle the whole body." James 3:2.

How did Christ teach the importance of guarding our speech?

"But I say unto you, That *every idle word* that men shall speak, they shall give account thereof in the day of judgment. For by thy *words* thou shalt be justified, and by thy *words* thou shalt be condemned." Matthew 12:36, 37.

To whom are our words all known?

"For there is not a word in my tongue, but, lo, *O Lord, thou knowest it altogether.*" Psalm 139:4.

Of what are one's words an index?

"Out of the abundance of *the heart* the mouth speaketh." Matthew 12:34.

THE TALEBEARER

What conduct is condemned by the Scriptures?

"Thou shalt not go up and down *as a talebearer among thy people:* neither shalt thou stand against the blood of thy neighbour: I am the Lord." Leviticus 19:16.

CHARLES CAREY

MARK YOUR WORDS

"By thy words thou shalt be justified, and by thy words thou shalt be condemned." Matthew 12:37

To what are the words of a talebearer compared?

"The words of a talebearer are *as wounds*." Proverbs 26:22.

What is their effect?

"He that covereth a transgression seeketh love; but *he that repeateth a matter separateth very friends*." Proverbs 17:9.

What would follow if there were no talebearers?

"Where no wood is, there the fire goeth out: so *where there is no talebearer, the strife ceaseth*." Proverbs 26:20.

BACKBITING

Among other things, what did Paul fear he would find in the Corinthian church?

"For I fear, lest, when I come, I shall not find you such as I would, and that I shall be found unto you such as ye would not: lest there be debates, envyings, wraths, strifes, *backbitings*, whisperings, swellings, tumults." 2 Corinthians 12:20.

What result follows backbiting and like evils?

"For all the law is fulfilled in one word, even in this; Thou shalt love thy neighbour as thyself. But *if ye bite and devour one another, take heed that ye be not consumed one of another*." Galatians 5:14, 15.

To whom is the promise made of abiding in the tabernacle of the Lord and dwelling in His holy hill?

"He that walketh uprightly, and worketh righteousness, and speaketh the truth in his heart. *He that backbiteth not with his tongue, nor doeth evil to his neighbour, nor taketh up a reproach against his neighbour*." Psalm 15:2, 3.

Note.—Kirkle is quoted as saying, "Never carry a sword in your tongue to wound the reputation of any man." Noah Webster laid down this rule: "We should say nothing of a person in his absence that we should be unwilling to say if he were present." How few govern their conversation according to this rule! (See Proverbs 31: 10, 26.)

What caution is given in regard to receiving an accusation against an elder?

"Against an elder receive not an accusation, *but before two or three witnesses.*" 1 Timothy 5:19.

NOTE.—"Many who listen to the preaching of the word of God make it the subject of criticism at home. They sit in judgment on the sermon as they would on the words of a lecturer or a political speaker. The message that should be regarded as the word of the Lord to them is dwelt upon with trifling or sarcastic comment. The minister's character, motives, and actions, and the conduct of fellow members of the church, are freely discussed. Severe judgment is pronounced, gossip or slander repeated, and this in the hearing of the unconverted. Often these things are spoken by parents in the hearing of their own children. Thus are destroyed respect for God's messengers, and reverence for their message."—ELLEN G. WHITE, *Christ's Object Lessons* (1941 ed.), pp. 45, 46.

TAMING THE TONGUE

Can man, unrenewed by grace, control his tongue?

"For every kind of beasts, and of birds, and of serpents, and of things in the sea, is tamed, and hath been tamed of mankind: *but the tongue can no man tame; it is an unruly evil, full of deadly poison.*" James 3:7, 8.

As a guard against the misuse of the power of speech, therefore, for what should we pray?

"Set a *watch*, O Lord, before my mouth; keep the *door* of my lips." Psalm 141:3.

What vow did the psalmist take against offenses of the tongue?

"I said, *I will take heed to my ways,* that I sin not with my *tongue: I will keep my mouth with a bridle,* while the wicked is before me." Psalm 39:1.

What is a sure cure for backbiting?

"Thou shalt love thy neighbour as thyself." Matthew 22:39. "Whatsoever ye would that men should do to you, do ye even so to them." Matthew 7:12. "Speak evil of no man." Titus 3:2. (See also James 4:11.)

What are those words like which are fitly spoken?

"A word fitly spoken is *like apples of gold in pictures of silver.*" Proverbs 25:11.

Hypocrisy and Dissimulation

THE PHARISEES AND HYPOCRISY

Of what sin were the Pharisees guilty?

"Beware ye of the leaven of the Pharisees, which is *hypocrisy*." Luke 12:1.

NOTE.—Hypocrisy is a feigning to be what one is not; dissimulation; a concealment of one's real character or motives; especially, the assuming of a false appearance of virtue or religion.

How did the Pharisees show themselves to be hypocrites?

"Ye hypocrites, well did Esaias prophesy of you, saying, This people *draweth nigh unto me with their mouth, and honoureth me with their lips; but their heart is far from me*." Matthew 15:7, 8.

How did they make void one of God's commandments?

"For God commanded, saying, Honour thy father and mother. . . . But ye say, Whosoever shall say to his father or his mother, It is a gift, by whatsoever thou mightest be profited by me; and honour not his father or his mother, he shall be free. *Thus have ye made the commandment of God of none effect by your tradition*." Verses 4-6.

How did Christ say hypocrites pray?

"And when thou prayest, thou shalt not be as the hypocrites are: for *they love to pray standing in the synagogues and in the corners of the streets, that they may be seen of men*. Verily I say unto you, They have their reward." Matthew 6:5.

THE HYPOCRITE AND HIS NEIGHBOR

What does Christ call one who readily sees the faults of others, but does not see nor correct his own?

"*Thou hypocrite*, first cast out the beam out of thine own eye; and then shalt thou see clearly to cast out the mote out of thy brother's eye." Matthew 7:5.

How does a hypocrite treat his neighbor?

"An hypocrite with his mouth *destroyeth his neighbour*." "For as he thinketh in his heart, so is he: *Eat and drink, saith he to thee; but his heart is not with thee*." Proverbs 11:9; 23:7.

HYPOCRITICAL TENDENCIES IN GOOD MEN

Which of the apostles was once guilty of dissimulation?

"And the other Jews dissembled likewise with him [Peter]; insomuch that Barnabas also was carried away with their dissimulation." Galatians 2:13.

Why did Paul say he opposed Peter in this matter?

"But when Peter was come to Antioch, I withstood him to the face, *because he was to be blamed*." Verse 11.

What did the psalmist say he would not do?

"I have not sat with vain persons, *neither will I go in with dissemblers*." Psalm 26:4.

THE HYPOCRITE'S FATE AND LOVE'S WAY

What will become of the hypocrite's hope?

"So are the paths of all that forget God; and *the hypocrite's hope shall perish*." Job 8:13.

What is to be the fate of that servant who, while professing to love the Lord, shows by his actions that he is worldly, and is not looking nor longing for His coming?

"The Lord of that servant shall come in a day when he looketh not for him, and in an hour that he is not aware of, and shall cut him asunder, and *appoint him his portion with the hypocrites:* there shall be weeping and gnashing of teeth." Matthew 24:50, 51. "The sinners in Zion are afraid; fearfulness hath surprised the hypocrites." Isaiah 33:14.

How pure should be our love?

"Let love be *without dissimulation*." Romans 12:9.

What is characteristic of heavenly wisdom?

"The wisdom that is from above is first pure, then peaceable, gentle, and easy to be intreated, full of mercy and good fruits, without partiality, and *without hypocrisy*." James 3:17.

The Just Recompense

GOD'S JUST WAY

How has God recompensed men in the past?

"For if the word spoken by angels was stedfast, and every transgression and disobedience received *a just recompence of reward;* how shall we escape, if we neglect so great salvation?" Hebrews 2:2, 3.

How are all to be rewarded in the judgment?

"For we must all appear before the judgment seat of Christ; that every one may receive the things done in his body, *according to that he hath done, whether it be good or bad.*" 2 Corinthians 5:10. "Who will render to every man *according to his deeds:* . . . for there is no respect of persons with God." Romans 2:6-11. "Be not deceived; God is not mocked: for *whatsoever a man soweth, that shall he also reap.*" Galatians 6:7.

What will be the reward of the wrongdoer?

"For he that soweth to his flesh shall of the flesh reap *corruption.*" Verse 8. "*Tribulation* and *anguish,* upon every soul of man that *doeth evil.*" Romans 2:9.

What will be the recompense of the righteous?

"But he that soweth to the Spirit shall of the Spirit reap *life everlasting.*" Galatians 6:8. "But *glory, honour, and peace,* to every man that worketh good." Romans 2:10.

GOD USES MAN'S MEASURING STICK

What general rule of recompense is laid down in the Bible?

"Judge not, that ye be not judged. For *with what judgment ye judge, ye shall be judged: and with what measure ye mete, it shall be measured to you again.*" Matthew 7:1, 2. "With the *merciful* thou wilt shew thyself *merciful;* with an *upright* man thou wilt shew thyself *upright;* with the *pure* thou wilt shew thyself *pure;* and with the *froward* thou wilt shew thyself *froward.*" Psalm 18:25, 26.

In view of this, what are we warned not to do?

"Recompense to no man *evil for evil.*" Romans 12:17. "Not rendering *evil for evil,* or *railing for railing:* but contrariwise blessing." 1 Peter 3:9.

What is said of those who render evil for good?

"Whoso rewardeth evil for good, *evil shall not depart from his house.*" Proverbs 17:13.

Justice and Final Awards

What principle of justice should govern us in our dealings?

"Withhold not good from them *to whom it is due,* when it is in the power of thine hand to do it." Proverbs 3:27.

In meting out the final awards, what may we be sure God will do?

"Shall not the Judge of all the earth *do right?*" Genesis 18:25. "*Justice* and *judgment* are the habitation of thy throne: *mercy* and *truth* shall go before thy face." Psalm 89:14.

O that the Lord would guide my ways
  To keep His statutes still!
O that my God would grant me grace
  To know and do His will!

. . . . .

Order my footsteps by Thy word,
  And make my heart sincere;
Let sin have no dominion, Lord,
  But keep my conscience clear.

Make me to walk in Thy commands,
  'Tis a delightful road;
Nor let my head, nor heart, nor hands
  Offend against my God.

—Isaac Watts

Part Sixteen

The Home

	PAGE
The Marriage Institution	691
A Happy Home	695
Religion in the Home	699
Honor Due to Parents	703
Child Training	706
Promises for the Children	709
Teaching the Children	711
The Mother	715
Evils of City Life	717
Purity of Heart	720

H. A. ROBERTS

MARRIAGE IS HONORABLE

"Whoso findeth a wife findeth a good thing, a obtaineth favour of the Lord." Proverbs 18:

The Marriage Institution

A Woman for the Man

After creating man, what did God say?

"And the Lord God said, *It is not good that the man should be alone.*" Genesis 2:18.

What, therefore, did God say He would make?

"I will make him *an help* meet for him." Same verse.

Note.—Not a *helpmeet* nor a *helpmate,* but—two words—a help *meet* for him; that is, *fit* or *suitable* for him. Man's companion, or help, was to correspond to him. Each was to be suited to the other's needs.

Could such a help be found among the creatures which God had already made?

"And Adam gave names to all cattle, and to the fowl of the air, and to every beast of the field; *but for Adam there was not found an help meet for him.*" Verse 20.

A Woman From the Man

What, therefore, did God do?

"And the Lord God caused a deep sleep to fall upon Adam, and he slept: and he took one of his ribs, and closed up the flesh instead thereof; and the rib, which the Lord God had taken from man, *made he a woman, and brought her unto the man.*" Verses 21, 22.

Note.—How beautiful, in its fullness of meaning, is this simple but suggestive story, at which skeptics sneer. God did not make man after the order of the lower animals, but "in his own image." Neither did He choose man's companion, or "help," from some other order of beings, but made her from man—of the same substance. And He took this substance, not from man's *feet,* that he might have an excuse to degrade, enslave, or trample upon her; nor from man's *head,* that woman might assume authority over man; but from man's *side,* from over his *heart,* the *seat of affections,* that woman might stand at his side as *man's equal.* Together, under God, they are to work out the purpose and destiny of the race—man, the strong, the noble, the dignified; woman, the weaker, the sympathetic, the loving. How much more exalted and inspiring is this view than the theory that man developed from the lower order of animals.

What did Adam say as he received his wife from God?

"And Adam said, *This is now bone of my bones, and flesh of my flesh:* she shall be called *Woman,* because she was taken out of *Man.*" Verse 23.

THE TWO BECOME ONE

What great truth was then stated?

"Therefore shall a man leave his father and his mother, and shall cleave unto his wife: and *they shall be one flesh.*" Verse 24.

In what words does Christ recognize marriage as of God?

"Wherefore they are no more twain, but one flesh. *What therefore God hath joined together,* let not man put asunder." Matthew 19:6.

NOTE.—Thus was the marriage institution ordained of God in Eden, before man sinned. Like the Sabbath, it has come down to us with the Edenic dews of divine blessing still upon it. It was ordained not only for the purpose of peopling the earth and perpetuating the race, but to promote social order and human happiness; to prevent irregular affection; and, through well-regulated families, to transmit truth, purity, and holiness from age to age. Around it cluster all the purest and truest joys of home and the race. When the divine origin of marriage is recognized, and the divine principles controlling it are obeyed, marriage is indeed a blessing; but when these are disregarded, untold evils are sure to follow. That which, rightly used, is of greatest blessing, when abused becomes the greatest curse.

By what commands has God guarded the marriage relation?

"Thou shalt not commit adultery." "Thou shalt not covet thy neighbour's wife." Exodus 20:14, 17.

What New Testament injunction is given respecting marriage?

"*Let marriage be held in honor among all,* and let the marriage bed be undefiled; for God will judge the immoral and adulterous." Hebrews 13:4, R.S.V.

NOTE.—By many, marriage is lightly regarded—is often made

even a subject of jest. Its divine origin, its great object, and its possibilities and influences for good or evil are little thought of, and hence it is often entered into with little idea of its responsibilities or its sacred obligations. The marriage relationship is frequently used in the Scriptures as a symbol of the relationship existing between God and His people. (See Romans 7:1-4; 2 Corinthians 11:2; Hosea 2:19, 20; Revelation 19:7.)

Marriage With Unbelievers

After the Fall, what sort of marriages were introduced by men, which were productive of great evil?

"And it came to pass, when men began to multiply on the face of the earth, and daughters were born unto them, that *the sons of God saw the daughters of men* that they were fair; *and they took them wives of all which they chose."* Genesis 6:1, 2.

Note.—The "sons of God," descending from Seth, married the "daughters of men," the descendants from the idolatrous line of Cain. As a result the barriers against evil were broken down, the whole race was soon corrupted, violence filled the earth, and the Flood followed.

What prohibition did God give His chosen people against intermarrying with the heathen nations about them, and why?

"Neither shalt thou make marriages with them; thy daughter thou shalt not give unto his son, nor his daughter shalt thou take unto thy son. *For they will turn away thy son from following me, that they may serve other gods:* so will the anger of the Lord be kindled against you, and destroy thee suddenly." Deuteronomy 7:3, 4.

Note.—Intermarriage with the ungodly was the mistake made by the professed people of God before the Flood, and God did not wish Israel to repeat that folly.

What instruction is given in the New Testament regarding partnership with unbelievers?

"Be ye not unequally yoked together with unbelievers: for what fellowship hath righteousness with unrighteousness? and what communion hath light with darkness? and what concord hath Christ with Belial? or what part hath he that believeth with an infidel? and what agreement hath the temple of God with idols? for ye are the temple of the living God." 2 Corinthians 6:14-16.

NOTE.—This instruction forbids all compromising partnerships. Marriage of believers with unbelievers has ever been a snare by which Satan has captured many earnest souls who thought they could win the unbelieving, but in most cases have themselves drifted away from the moorings of faith into doubt, backsliding, and loss of religion. It was one of Israel's constant dangers, against which God warned them repeatedly. "Give not your daughters unto their sons, neither take their daughters unto your sons, nor seek their peace [by such compromise] or their wealth for ever." Ezra 9:12. (See also Exodus 34:14-16; Judges 14:1-3; Ezra 9 and 10; Nehemiah 13:23-27.) Even Solomon fell before the influence of heathen wives. Concerning him the inspired word has left this melancholy record: "His wives turned away his heart after other gods." 1 Kings 11:4. No Christian can marry an unbeliever without running serious risk, and placing himself upon the enemy's ground. The Scriptures do not advocate separation after the union has been formed (see 1 Corinthians 7: 2-16), but good sense should teach us that faith can best be maintained, and domestic happiness best ensured, where both husband and wife are believers, and of the same faith. Ministers and parents, therefore, should warn the young against all improper marriages.

What instruction did Abraham give his servant Eliezer when sending him to select a wife for his son Isaac?

"Thou shalt take a wife for my son *of my kindred, and of my father's house.*" Genesis 24:40.

NOTE.—This passage indicates that in early Bible times parents generally had more to do in the selection of life companions for their children than they commonly have now. Young people who are wise will seek the advice and counsel of their parents, and above all, will seek to know the will of God, before entering upon this important relationship, with its grave responsibilities and its momentous consequences.

MARRIAGE AND DIVORCE

For how long does marriage bind the contracting parties?

"For the woman which hath an husband is bound by the law to her husband *so long as he liveth.*" Romans 7:2. (See 1 Corinthians 7:39.)

What only does Christ recognize as proper ground for dissolving the marriage relationship?

"Whosoever shall put away his wife, *except it be for fornication,* and shall marry another, committeth adultery." Matthew 19:9.

A Happy Home

THE COMPLETE HOME

Where and by whom were the foundations of the home laid?

"And *the Lord God* planted a garden eastward *in Eden;* and *there* he put the man whom he had formed." Genesis 2:8.

In making this home, what besides man was needed?

"And the Lord God said, It is not good that the man should be alone; I will make him *an help meet* [one *adapted,* or *suitable*] *for him.*" Verse 18.

After creating Adam and Eve, what did God say to them?

"And God blessed them, and God said unto them, *Be fruitful, and multiply, and replenish the earth.*" Genesis 1:28.

To what are the wife and children of the man who fears the Lord likened?

"Happy shalt thou be, and it shall be well with thee. Thy wife shall be *as a fruitful vine* by the sides of thine house: thy children *like olive plants* round about thy table." Psalm 128:2, 3.

What are children declared to be?

"Lo, children are *an heritage of the Lord.*" Psalm 127:3. "Children's children are *the crown of old men;* and the glory of children are their fathers." Proverbs 17:6.

RELATIONSHIP OF HUSBAND AND WIFE

How should the wife relate herself to her husband?

"Wives, *submit yourselves unto your own husbands, as unto the Lord*. For the husband is the head of the wife, even as Christ is the head of the church." Ephesians 5:22, 23.

And how should husbands regard their wives?

"Husbands, *love your wives, even as Christ also loved the church,* and gave himself for it. . . . So ought men to *love their wives as their own bodies. He that loveth his wife loveth himself.*

H. M. LAMBERT

THE HOME CIRCLE "Happy the home when God is there, and love fills every brea

... Let every one of you in particular *so love his wife even as himself;* and the wife see that she reverence her husband." Verses 25-33.

Against what are husbands cautioned?

"Husbands, love your wives, and *be not bitter against them."* Colossians 3:19.

Why should wives be in subjection to their husbands?

"Likewise, ye wives, be in subjection to your own husbands; *that, if any obey not the word, they also may without the word be won by the conversation* [manner of life] *of the wives."* 1 Peter 3:1.

Why should husbands be considerate of their wives?

"Likewise, ye husbands, dwell with them according to knowledge, giving honour unto the wife, as unto the weaker vessel, and as being heirs together of the grace of life; *that your prayers be not hindered."* Verse 7.

Parents and Children

Why should children obey their parents?

"Children, obey your parents in the Lord: *for this is right."* Ephesians 6:1.

How should parents bring up their children?

"And, ye fathers, provoke not your children to wrath: but *bring them up in the nurture and admonition of the Lord."* Verse 4.

Why should fathers not provoke their children to anger?

"Fathers, provoke not your children to anger, *lest they be discouraged."* Colossians 3:21.

By what means may the mother bind the hearts of the loved ones at home together?

"She openeth her mouth with wisdom; and in her tongue is the *law of kindness."* Proverbs 31:26.

Note.—"We want to get into the hearts of our children if we hold them, and help them, and bless them, and take them to heaven with us."—Frances Murphy.

How will such a mother be regarded?

"Her children arise up, and *call her blessed;* her husband also, and *he praiseth her."* Verse 28.

NOTE.—"Show me a loving husband, a worthy wife, and good children, and no pair of horses that ever flew along the road could take me in a year where I could see a more pleasing sight. Home is the grandest of all institutions."—SPURGEON.

How faithfully should parents teach the precepts and commandments of God to their children?

"And thou shalt *teach them diligently* unto thy children, and shalt talk of them *when thou sittest in thine house, and when thou walkest by the way, and when thou liest down, and when thou risest up."* Deuteronomy 6:7.

NOTE.—"The home is the child's first school, and it is here that the foundation should be laid for a life of service. Its principles are to be taught not merely in theory. They are to shape the whole life training. . . .

"Such an education must be based upon the word of God. Here only are its principles given in their fullness. The Bible should be made the foundation of study and of teaching. The essential knowledge is a knowledge of God and of Him whom He has sent."—ELLEN G. WHITE, *Your Home and Health,* pp. 72-75.

"Continue thou in the things which thou hast learned and hast been assured of, knowing of whom thou hast learned them; and that from a child thou hast known the holy scriptures, which are able to make thee wise unto salvation through faith which is in Christ Jesus." 2 Timothy 3:14, 15.

"A church within a church, a republic within a republic, a world within a world, is spelled by four letters—home! If things go right there, they go right everywhere; if things go wrong there, they go wrong everywhere. The door-sill of the dwelling-house is the foundation of church and state. . . . In other words, domestic life overarches and undergirds all other life. . . . First, last, and all the time, have Christ in your home."—TALMAGE.

What is the great secret of a happy home?

"Better is a dinner of herbs where *love* is, than a stalled ox and hatred therewith." Proverbs 15:17.

Religion in the Home

SENSING THE GAZE OF GOD

How well acquainted is God with each individual's life?

"Thou knowest my downsitting and mine uprising, thou understandest my thought afar off. Thou compassest my path and my lying down, and art acquainted with all my ways. For there is not a word in my tongue, but, lo, O Lord, thou knowest it altogether." Psalm 139:2-4.

What is the beginning of wisdom?

"*The fear of the Lord* is the beginning of wisdom: a good understanding have all they that do his commandments." Psalm 111:10.

INSTRUCTING CHILDREN

How are parents instructed to bring up their children?

"And, ye fathers, provoke not your children to wrath: but *bring them up in the nurture and admonition of the Lord.*" Ephesians 6:4.

NOTE.—"Religion is love, and a religious home is one in which love reigns. There must be love in action, love that flows out in all the home intercourse, showing itself in a thousand little expressions of thoughtfulness, kindness, unselfishness and gentle courtesy."—J. R. MILLER, *Week-Day Religion* (1880), p. 81.

How faithfully should parents teach their children the word of God?

"And these words, which I command thee this day, shall be in thine heart: and *thou shalt teach them diligently unto thy children,* and shalt talk of them when thou sittest in thine house, and when thou walkest by the way, and when thou liest down, and when thou risest up." Deuteronomy 6:6, 7.

What is the value of proper early instruction?

"Train up a child in the way he should go: and *when he is old, he will not depart from it.*" Proverbs 22:6.

NOTE.—No man ever said that he began the service of God too

young. No parent ever regretted bringing up his children to love, fear, honor, and obey God.

How early were the Scriptures taught to Timothy?

"And that *from a child thou hast known the holy scriptures,* which are able to make thee wise unto salvation through faith which is in Christ Jesus." 2 Timothy 3:15.

Note.—Timothy's father was a Greek, and his mother a Jewess. From a child he had been taught the Scriptures. The faith of his mother and of his grandmother in the word of God had early been implanted in him through their faithful instruction. (2 Timothy 1:5.) The piety which he saw in his home life had a molding influence upon his own life. This, with his knowledge of the Scriptures, qualified him to bear responsibilities and to render faithful service later in the cause of Christ. His home instructors had cooperated with God in preparing him for a life of usefulness. Thus it should be in every home.

Why did God confide in Abraham, and commit sacred trusts to him?

"For I know him, *that he will command his children and his household after him,* and they shall keep the way of the Lord, to do justice and judgment." Genesis 18:19.

The Altar of Prayer

Wherever Abraham went, what was his practice?

"And there he builded an altar unto the Lord, and called upon the name of the Lord." Genesis 12:8. (See also Genesis 13:4; 21:33.)

Note.—"The manner in which the family worship is conducted is very important. It should be made so pleasant as to be looked forward to with gladness even by the youngest children. Too often it is made tedious, monotonous or burdensome.... To make it dull and irksome is treason to true religion.... A few minutes given every day to preparation for family worship will serve to make it, as it should be, the most pleasant and attractive incident of the day."—J. R. Miller, *Week-Day Religion,* pp. 79-81.

What instruction suggests the giving of thanks for daily food?

"*In everything give thanks:* for this is the will of God in Christ Jesus concerning you." 1 Thessalonians 5:18.

Note.—As a rule, children will reflect the life and principles manifested in their parents. The reason so many children are irreverent, irreligious, and disobedient today is that their parents are so. Like parent, like child. If parents would see a different state of things, they must themselves reform. They must bring God into their homes, and make His word their counselor and guide. They must teach their children the fear of God, and that His word is the voice of God addressed to them, and that it is to be implicitly obeyed. "In too many households, prayer is neglected. . . . If ever there was a time when every house should be a house of prayer, it is now. Fathers and mothers should often lift up their hearts to God in humble supplication for themselves and their children. Let the father, as priest of the household, lay upon the altar of God the morning and evening sacrifice, while the wife and children unite in prayer and praise. In such a household Jesus will love to tarry."—Ellen G. White, *Patriarchs and Prophets*, p. 144.

Are all the children in? The night is falling,
    And storm-clouds gather in the threatening west;
The lowing cattle seek a friendly shelter;
    The bird hies to her nest.
The thunder crashes; wilder grows the tempest,
    And darkness settles o'er the fearful din;
Come, shut the door and gather round the hearthstone.
    Are all the children in?

Are all the children in? The night is falling,
    When gilded sin doth walk about the streets.
O, "at the last it biteth like a serpent!"
    Poisoned are stolen sweets.
O mothers, guard the feet of inexperience,
    Too prone to wander in the paths of sin!
O, shut the door of love against temptation!
    Are all the children in?

Are all the children in? The night is falling,
    The night of death is hastening on apace;
The Lord is calling, "Enter thou thy chamber,
    And tarry there a space."
And when He comes, the King in all His glory,
    Who died the shameful death our hearts to win,
O, may the gates of heaven shut about us,
    With all the children in!

—Elizabeth Rosser

JESUS AND HIS MOTHER

B. PLOCKHORST, ARTIST

"Blessed art thou among women." Luke 1:2

Honor Due to Parents

THE RESPONSIBILITY OF CHILDREN

By what is every child known?

"Even a child is known *by his doings,* whether his work be pure, and whether it be right." Proverbs 20:11.

What is the duty of every child?

"My son, *hear the instruction of thy father,* and *forsake not the law of thy mother."* Proverbs 1:8.

What does the fifth commandment require of children?

"Honour thy father and thy mother: that thy days may be long upon the land which the Lord thy God giveth thee." Exodus 20:12.

NOTE.—To the child too young to know God, the earthly parent takes the place of God. Learning to honor, respect, and obey his earthly parents is the child's first and most important lesson in learning to honor, respect, and obey God, his heavenly Parent. Benjamin Franklin well said: "Let thy child's first lesson be obedience, and the second will be what thou wilt."

For how long a time should one honor his parents?

"Hearken unto thy father that begat thee, and despise not thy mother *when she is old."* Proverbs 23:22.

NOTE.—As long as parents live, they should be honored and respected by their children. The duty enjoined in the fifth commandment does not cease at maturity, nor when the child leaves the parental roof.

DISOBEDIENT, DISHONORABLE OFFSPRING

What is the character of a child who will not listen to his father's instruction?

"A fool despiseth his father's instruction: but he that regardeth reproof is prudent." Proverbs 15:5.

What is one way in which a child may dishonor his parents?

"He that is *a companion of riotous men* shameth his father." Proverbs 28:7.

What is said of one who robs his father or his mother?

"Whoso robbeth his father or his mother, and saith, It is no transgression; *the same is the companion of a destroyer.*" Verse 24.

How did the Jewish leaders in the days of Christ, for the sake of gain, make void the fifth commandment?

"But ye say, Whosoever shall say to his father or his mother, It is a gift, by whatsoever thou mightest be profited by me; and honour not his father or his mother, he shall be free. Thus have ye made the commandment of God of none effect by your tradition." Matthew 15:5, 6.

Note.—The word translated "gift" in this text means a thing dedicated to the service of God in the Temple. In this way the Jewish teachers, by their traditional law, taught children that by saying that their property was thus dedicated to the Temple or to religious purposes, they were free from the obligation to honor and support their parents, thus making void one of the commandments of God. This Christ condemned.

In what other way do some dishonor their father and mother?

"There is a generation that *curseth their father,* and *doth not bless their mother.*" Proverbs 30:11.

The Spirit of Honor and Obedience

What course on the part of children is well pleasing to the Lord?

"Children, *obey your parents in all things:* for this is well pleasing unto the Lord." Colossians 3:20.

In what spirit should children obey their parents?

"Children, obey your parents *in the Lord:* for this is right." Ephesians 6:1.

How did Jesus honor His parents?

"He went down with them, and came to Nazareth, and *was subject unto them.*" Luke 2:51.

HONOR DUE TO PARENTS

What did the wise man say will be the fate of the one who curseth his father or his mother?

"Whoso curseth his father or his mother, *his lamp shall be put out in obscure darkness.*" "The eye that mocketh at his father, and despiseth to obey his mother, *the ravens of the valley shall pick it out, and the young eagles shall eat it.*" Proverbs 20:20; 30:17.

What will be the reward of those who honor their parents?

"Honour thy father and thy mother: *that thy days may be long upon the land which the Lord thy God giveth thee.*" Exodus 20:12.

NOTE.—The fullness of this promise will be realized in the life to come when the earth, restored to its Edenic beauty, will become the eternal home of all those who have truly honored their parents and kept all God's commandments.

What comment has the apostle Paul made upon this commandment?

"Honour thy father and mother; *which is the first commandment with promise; that it may be well with thee, and thou mayest live long on the earth.*" Ephesians 6:2, 3.

THE MODERN TREND

In what age of the world is disobedience to parents to be especially manifest?

"This know also, that *in the last days* perilous times shall come. For men shall be lovers of their own selves, covetous, boasters, proud, blasphemers, *disobedient to parents,* unthankful, unholy." 2 Timothy 3:1, 2.

NOTE.—Disobedience to parents is a marked characteristic of the present generation. Never before was it so common or so widespread. The root of the evil, however, lies not so much in the children as in the parents. Many of the latter are disobedient to God, their Father in heaven, and so have failed to bring up their children in the fear of God and in the ways of righteousness. Bible instruction, lessons of faith, and prayer must not be neglected in the home if we would see obedient, God-fearing children growing up in the world.

Child Training

What to Teach Children

How should parents train their children?

"Train up a child *in the way he should go:* and when he is old, he will not depart from it." Proverbs 22:6. "And, ye fathers, provoke not your children to wrath: but *bring them up in the nurture and admonition of the Lord.*" Ephesians 6:4.

How diligently should parents teach children God's word?

"These words, which I command thee this day, shall be in thine heart: and *thou shalt teach them diligently unto thy children.*" "Ye shall teach them your children, *speaking of them when thou sittest in thine house, and when thou walkest by the way, when thou liest down, and when thou risest up.*" Deuteronomy 6:6, 7; 11:19.

What high ideal should be placed before the young?

"Let no man despise thy youth; but *be thou an example of the believers,* in word, in conversation, in charity, in spirit, in faith, in purity." 1 Timothy 4:12.

What duty does God require of children?

"Honour thy father and thy mother." Exodus 20:12.

Correcting Children—Caution to Parents

How should the youth be taught to regard the aged?

"Thou shalt *rise up before the hoary head,* and *honour the face of the old man,* and fear thy God: I am the Lord." Leviticus 19:32.

What are some good fruits of proper child training?

"Correct thy son, and *he shall give thee rest; yea, he shall give delight unto thy soul.*" Proverbs 29:17.

What will result if correction is withheld?

"The rod and reproof give wisdom: but *a child left to him-*

self bringeth his mother to shame." Verse 15. (See Proverbs 22:15.)

Is there danger of delaying correction too long?

"Chasten thy son while there is hope, and let not thy soul spare for his crying." Proverbs 19:18. (See Proverbs 23:13, 14.)

Does proper correction evidence a want of parental love?

"He that spareth his rod hateth his son: but *he that loveth him chasteneth him betimes."* Proverbs 13:24.

NOTE.—One Christian mother writes thus concerning the importance of child training: "Children who are allowed to come up to manhood or womanhood with the will undisciplined and the passions uncontrolled, will generally in after-life pursue a course which God condemns. The neglect of parents to properly discipline their children has been a fruitful source of evil in many families. The youth have not been restrained as they should have been. Parents have neglected to follow the directions of the Word of God in this matter, and the children have taken the reins of government into their own hands. The consequence has been that they have generally succeeded in ruling their parents, instead of being under their authority. False ideas and a foolish, misdirected affection have nurtured traits which have made the children unlovely and unhappy, have embittered the lives of the parents, and have extended their baleful influence from generation to generation. Any child that is permitted to have his own way will dishonor God and bring his father and mother to shame."

Whom does the Lord chasten?

"For whom the Lord *loveth* he chasteneth, and scourgeth every son whom he receiveth." Hebrews 12:6.

NOTE.—From this we may learn that all child training should be done in love, and that proper child training is an evidence of true love.

Against what evil should fathers guard?

"Fathers, *provoke not your children to anger,* lest they be discouraged." Colossians 3:21.

NOTE.—Correction should never be given in anger, for anger in the parents stirs up anger in the child. It is well to pray with a child before correcting him, and frequently mild but faithful instruction, admonition, and prayer are all the training necessary—are, in fact, the best training that can be given. But in any case of perverseness, stubbornness, or willful disobedience the correction, whatever it may be, should be persisted in until the child yields submissively to the will and wishes of the parent. It is best, generally, that correction should be done in private, as this tends to preserve the self-respect of the child, a very important element in character building. No correction or training should be violent or abusive, or given for the purpose of breaking the will of the child, but rather to direct the will, bring it into proper subjection, and the child to a realizing sense of what is right and duty.

How are the present effects and future results of God's chastisement contrasted?

"Now no chastening for the present seemeth to be joyous, but *grievous:* nevertheless afterward *it yieldeth the peaceable fruit of righteousness* unto them which are exercised thereby." Hebrews 12:11.

ANCIENT AND MODERN FAILURES

Why did God reprove Eli?

"In that day I will perform against Eli all things which I have spoken concerning his house: when I begin, I will also make an end. For I have told him that I will judge his house for ever for the iniquity which he knoweth; *because his sons made themselves vile, and he restrained them not.*" 1 Samuel 3:12, 13.

What is to be one of the prominent sins of the last days?

"For men shall be lovers of their own selves, covetous, boasters, proud, blasphemers, *disobedient to parents,* unthankful, unholy." 2 Timothy 3:2.

"BE kind to thy father, for when thou wert young,
    Who loved thee so fondly as he?
He caught the first accents that fell from thy tongue,
    And joined in thy innocent glee.

"Be kind to thy mother, for lo! on her brow
    May traces of sorrow be seen;
O well may'st thou cherish and comfort her now,
    For loving and kind hath she been."

Promises for the Children

HONOR AND ITS REWARD

WHAT is said of the fifth commandment?

"Honour thy father and mother; which is *the first commandment with promise.*" Ephesians 6:2.

What is promised those who honor their father and their mother?

"Honour thy father and thy mother: *that thy days may be long upon the land which the Lord thy God giveth thee.*" Exodus 20:12.

TRUE WISDOM

What is the fear of the Lord declared to be?

"The fear of the Lord is *the beginning of wisdom:* a good understanding have all they that do his commandments." Psalm 111:10.

What is said of the poor but wise child?

"*Better* is a poor and a wise child *than an old and foolish king,* who will no more be admonished." Ecclesiastes 4:13.

JESUS AND THE CHILDREN

How did Christ show His tender regard for children?

"*Suffer little children, and forbid them not, to come unto me:* for of such is the kingdom of heaven." Matthew 19:14.

How did He show that He loved them?

"And he took them up in his arms, put his hands upon them, and blessed them." Mark 10:16.

UNITY AND HAPPINESS

With what promise do the Old Testament Scriptures close?

"Behold, I will send you Elijah the prophet before the coming of the great and dreadful day of the Lord: and *he shall turn the heart of the fathers to the children, and the heart of the children to their fathers,* lest I come and smite the earth with a curse." Malachi 4:5, 6.

Note.—From this we learn that while disobedience to parents and the breaking up of home ties will characterize the last days (2 Timothy 3:1-3; Matthew 24:37-39; Genesis 6:1, 2), God's message for the last days will strengthen the cords of love and affection and bind the hearts of parents and children together.

How does Isaiah describe the happy conditions in the "new heavens" and the "new earth"?

"They shall not labour in vain, *nor bring forth for trouble;* for they are the seed of the blessed of the Lord, and *their offspring with them." "The sucking child shall play on the hole of the asp, and the weaned child shall put his hand on the cockatrice' den.* They shall not hurt nor destroy in all my holy mountain: for the earth shall be full of the knowledge of the Lord, as the waters cover the sea." Isaiah 65:23; 11:8, 9.

~~~~~~~

"A pair of very chubby legs
    Incased in scarlet hose,
A pair of little stubby boots
    With rather doubtful toes,
A little kilt, a little coat,
    Cut as a mother can—
And, lo! before us strides in state
    The future's 'coming man.'

"Ah! blessings on those little hands,
    Whose work is yet undone,
And blessings on those little feet,
    Whose race is yet unrun.
And blessings on the little brain,
    That has not learned to plan.
Whate'er the future holds in store,
    God bless the 'coming man.'"

Teaching the Children

OLD TESTAMENT ADMONITION

What should be the prayer of every parent?

"O my Lord, ... teach us what we shall do unto the child that shall be born." Judges 13:8.

NOTE.—This is a part of the prayer of Manoah, the father of Samson.

How should our children be taught?

"All thy children shall be *taught of the Lord;* and great shall be the peace of thy children." Isaiah 54:13.

What will happen if a child is not properly instructed?

"A child left to himself *bringeth his mother to shame.*" Proverbs 29:15.

How earnestly should parents teach their children the things of God?

"Thou shalt teach them *diligently* unto thy children." "Ye shall teach them your children, speaking of them *when thou sittest in thine house,* and *when thou walkest by the way, when thou liest down,* and *when thou risest up.*" Deuteronomy 6:7; 11:19.

OLD TESTAMENT EXAMPLES

How did Solomon's parents regard him as a child?

"I was my father's *son, tender and only beloved* in the sight of my mother." Proverbs 4:3.

What does Solomon say his father did for him as a child?

"He *taught me also,* and said unto me, *Let thine heart retain my words: keep my commandments, and live.*" Verse 4.

From what time does the psalmist say he was taught?

"O God, thou hast taught me *from my youth.*" Psalm 71:17.

How was Moses taught during the days of his early childhood?

By faith, under the instruction of a devoted mother. (See Hebrews 11:23; Exodus 2:1-10.)

Note.—The hiding of Moses was at the time when Pharaoh, king of Egypt, had issued a decree that every Hebrew male child should be killed as soon as he was born, to prevent too rapid an increase of the Hebrews. The second chapter of Exodus tells the story of the finding of Moses by the king's daughter, and his being brought up by his own mother employed as a nurse. She was a woman of faith, and her teaching of Moses was such that after he had been at the Egyptian court till he "was come to years," he chose to suffer affliction with God's people rather than to enjoy the honor of succeeding to the throne of Egypt as the adopted heir. He became the leader of God's people when they escaped from the Egyptian bondage, and after he died, he was raised to life and taken to heaven. (See Hebrews 11:24; Jude 9; Matthew 17:1-3.)

How was Joseph regarded by his father?

"Israel *loved Joseph* more than all his children, because he was the son of his old age." Genesis 37:3.

Note.—The record of Joseph's life, found in Genesis 37-50, shows that he lived intimately with his father till he was seventeen years of age. He must have been carefully taught of God also, for in all his marvelous experience as slave, prisoner, and premier of Egypt, he remained true to his heavenly Father, not a single sin being recorded of him to the day of his death.

New Testament Instruction and Example

How should all Christian parents bring up their children?

"Fathers, provoke not your children to wrath: but bring them up *in the nurture and admonition of the Lord.*" Ephesians 6:4.

How early does Paul say Timothy was instructed?

"From a child thou hast known the holy scriptures, which are able to make thee wise unto salvation." 2 Timothy 3:15.

Reward and Blessing

What reward in this life is promised the faithful mother?

"Her children arise up, and call her blessed; her husband also, and he praiseth her." Proverbs 31:28.

TEACHING THE CHILDREN

What beautiful picture of home life is drawn by the psalmist for the father who fears the Lord?

"Thy wife shall be as a fruitful vine by the sides of thine house: thy children like olive plants round about thy table. Behold, that thus shall the man be blessed that feareth the Lord." Psalm 128:3, 4.

What motive will inspire all true parents to faithfulness in teaching their children?

"That our sons may be as plants grown up in their youth; that our daughters may be as corner stones, polished after the similitude of a palace." Psalm 144:12.

NOTE.—We often hear the saying, "The hand that rocks the cradle is the hand that rules the world." This agrees with the saying of the wise man, "Train up a child in the way he should go: and when he is old, he will not depart from it." Proverbs 22:6. No father or mother knows the future of the little child prattling about the home circle. But God knows, as He did in the cases of Moses and Esther and Timothy. Whether it is His purpose for some of our children to rule the world, as did Joseph and Daniel virtually, as prime ministers, or for some of them to "stand before kings," as did Moses and Esther and Daniel, or for some of them to serve and suffer for the name of Christ, as did Peter and John and Paul, it is our sacred privilege to teach the children faithfully and diligently during their tender years.

"HAPPY the home when God is there,
    And love fills every breast;
When one their wish, and one their prayer,
    And one their heavenly rest.

"Happy the home where Jesus' name
    Is sweet to every ear;
Where children early lisp His fame,
    And parents hold Him dear.

"Happy the home where prayer is heard,
    And praise is wont to rise;
Where parents love the Sacred Word,
    And live but for the skies."

H. M. LAMBERT

THE FIRST TEACHER

"Bring them up in the nurture and admonition of the Lord." Ephesians

The Mother

THE WORD "MOTHER"

Why did Adam call his wife's name Eve?

"And Adam called his wife's name Eve; *because she was the mother of all living.*" Genesis 3:20.

NOTE.—It is said that the three sweetest words in any language are *mother, home,* and *heaven.*

What did God say to Abraham concerning his wife, Sarah?

"And I will bless her, and give thee a son also of her: yea, I will bless her, and *she shall be a mother of nations;* kings of people shall be of her." Genesis 17:16.

HONOR DUE TO MOTHERS

What commandment guards the honor of the mother?

"Honour thy father and thy *mother.*" Exodus 20:12.

What tender, filial regard did Christ manifest for His mother in the hour of His death?

"When Jesus therefore saw his mother, and the disciple standing by, whom he loved [John], he saith unto his mother, *Woman, behold thy son!* Then saith he to the disciple, *Behold thy mother!* And from that hour that disciple took her unto his own home." John 19:26, 27.

THE MOTHER'S INFLUENCE ON CHILDREN

What did Hannah promise to do if the Lord should grant her a man child?

"And she vowed a vow, and said, O Lord of hosts, if thou wilt indeed . . . give unto thine handmaid a man child, then I will give him unto the Lord all the days of his life." 1 Samuel 1:11.

To whom did God commit the care and early training of His only-begotten Son?

"And when they were come into the house, they saw the young child with *Mary his mother,* and fell down, and worshipped him." Matthew 2:11.

What is said of the child life of Jesus under the influence of His mother's tender care and faithful instruction?

"And the child grew, and waxed strong in spirit, filled with wisdom: and the grace of God was upon him." "And Jesus increased in wisdom and stature, and in favour with God and man." Luke 2:40, 52.

Note.—"The hand that rocks the cradle is the hand that rules the world."

A Christian mother, above all others, can deeply implant and faithfully cherish the seeds of truth in the young and tender heart. More even than the father, the mother molds the life, character, and destiny of man. Every stage and phase of life is touched and influenced by her. Infancy, childhood, youth, manhood, and old age alike look to her for inspiration; thus she is both the morning and the evening star of life.

How early did Timothy know the Scriptures?

"And that *from a child* thou hast known the holy scriptures." 2 Timothy 3:15.

What is said of his mother and grandmother?

"When I call to remembrance *the unfeigned faith* that is in thee, *which dwelt first in thy grandmother Lois, and thy mother Eunice."* 2 Timothy 1:5.

Note.—No position in life is superior to that of the mother, no influence more potent for good or evil. "All that I am or hope to be, I owe to my mother," said Abraham Lincoln. "All that I have ever accomplished in life, I owe to my mother," declared D. L. Moody. "A kiss from my mother," said Benjamin West, "made me a painter." "My mother was the making of me," declared the noted inventor, Thomas A. Edison. And Andrew Carnegie, the millionaire, who gave his mother his earnings when a boy, said, "I am deeply touched by the remembrance of one to whom I owe everything that a wise mother ever gave to a son who adored her." It has been truly said that the home is the primeval school, the best, the most hallowed, and the most potential of all academies, and that the mother is the first, the most influential, and therefore the most important of all teachers.

Evils of City Life

Lot's Choice

When Abraham told Lot to choose that part of the country which he preferred, what choice did Lot make?

"And Lot lifted up his eyes, and beheld all the plain of Jordan, that it was well watered every where, before the Lord destroyed Sodom and Gomorrah, even as the garden of the Lord. . . . *Then Lot chose him all the plain of Jordan.*" Genesis 13:10, 11.

Where did Lot dwell?

"Abram dwelled in the land of Canaan, and *Lot dwelled in the cities of the plain, and pitched his tent toward Sodom.*" Verse 12.

Sodom and Its Citizens

What was the character of the inhabitants of Sodom?

"But the men of Sodom were *wicked and sinners before the Lord exceedingly.*" Verse 13.

What further description is given of this city?

"Behold, this was the iniquity of thy sister Sodom, *pride, fulness of bread,* and *abundance of idleness* was in her and in her daughters, *neither did she strengthen the hand of the poor and needy.* And they were *haughty,* and *committed abomination* before me: therefore I took them away as I saw good." Ezekiel 16:49, 50. (See Genesis 19:1-9.)

How did their conduct affect Lot?

"And delivered just Lot, *vexed with the filthy conversation of the wicked:* (for that righteous man dwelling among them, in seeing and hearing, *vexed his righteous soul from day to day with their unlawful deeds*)." 2 Peter 2:7, 8.

The Warning of Angels

Before destroying Sodom and Gomorrah, whom did the Lord send to deliver Lot and his family?

"And there came *two angels* to Sodom at even." "And the men [angels] said unto Lot, Hast thou here any besides? son in law, and thy sons, and thy daughters, and whatsoever thou hast in the city, bring them out of this place: for we will destroy this place, because the cry of them is waxen great before the face of the Lord; and the Lord hath sent us to destroy it." Genesis 19:1, 12, 13.

What did Lot do, and how were his efforts rewarded?

"And Lot went out, and *spake unto his sons in law,* which married his daughters, and said, *Up, get you out of this place;* for the Lord will destroy this city. *But he seemed as one that mocked unto his sons in law."* Verse 14.

What did the angels say to Lot the next morning?

"Arise, take thy wife, and thy two daughters, which are here; lest thou be consumed in the iniquity of the city.... *Escape for thy life; look not behind thee,* neither stay thou in all the plain; *escape to the mountain,* lest thou be consumed." Verses 15-17.

What then took place?

"Then the Lord rained upon Sodom and upon Gomorrah brimstone and fire from the Lord out of heaven; and he overthrew those cities, and all the plain, and all the inhabitants of the cities, and that which grew upon the ground." Verses 24, 25.

Because she disregarded the instruction given by the angels, what became of Lot's wife?

"But his wife looked back from behind him, and *she became a pillar of salt."* Verse 26.

NOTE.—As a result of choosing a city life, Lot lost nearly all his family.

LESSONS FOR OUR DAY

Foretelling the condition of the world previous to His Second Advent, to what did Christ liken it?

"Likewise also *as it was in the days of Lot;* they did eat, they drank, they bought, they sold, they planted, they builded; but the same day that Lot went out of Sodom it rained fire and brimstone from heaven, and destroyed them all. *Even thus shall it be in the day when the Son of man is revealed."* Luke 17:28-30.

NOTE.—The cities of today are like Sodom and Gomorrah—centers and sinkholes of vice, pride, violence, confusion, and crime. The cities of the United States furnish most of the nation's crime. The numerous holidays, the whirl of excitement, pleasure, and sports, theatergoing, gambling, liquor drinking, and reveling in the cities, attract thousands from the sober duties of life, and stimulate every evil passion to activity. What a poor place, therefore, are the cities of today in which to rear a family! Too many, like Lot, have pitched their tent toward Sodom.

Of what is the destruction of Sodom and Gomorrah a type?

"And turning the cities of Sodom and Gomorrah into ashes condemned them with an overthrow, *making them an ensample unto those that after should live ungodly.*" 2 Peter 2:6.

NOTE.—The destruction of such cities as Sodom and Gomorrah, Babylon, and Jerusalem is set forth as a type of the destruction awaiting the world. Says one writer: "The time is near when the large cities will be visited by the judgments of God. In a little while, these cities will be terribly shaken. No matter how large or strong their buildings, no matter how many safeguards against fire may have been provided, let God touch these buildings, and in a few minutes or in a few hours they will be in ruins. The ungodly cities of our world are to be swept away by the besom of destruction. In the calamities that are now befalling immense buildings and large portions of the cities, God is showing us what will come upon the whole earth."

"Improved atomic bombs" will be "ideally suited to sudden unannounced attacks in which a country's major cities might be destroyed overnight by an ostensibly friendly power."—GENERAL H. H. ARNOLD, quoted in *Questions and Answers About Atomic Energy*, p. 4.

Terrible as the atomic bomb was to contemplate when it was first produced, it is small by comparison with the hydrogen bomb. It has been estimated that the explosion of only 250 such bombs strategically placed could blot out all life on the earth and make it uninhabitable for years to come.

What is to take place under the seventh plague?

"And the seventh angel poured out his vial into the air; . . . and there was *a great earthquake,* such as was not since men were upon the earth, so mighty an earthquake, and so great. . . . *And the cities of the nations fell.*" Revelation 16:17-19.

Purity of Heart

GETTING THE HEART RIGHT

WHAT did Christ say of the pure in heart?

"Blessed are the pure in heart: for they shall see God." Matthew 5:8.

What did He declare to be a violation of the seventh commandment?

"Ye have heard that it was said by them of old time, Thou shalt not commit adultery: but I say unto you, That *whosoever looketh on a woman to lust after her hath committed adultery with her already in his heart.*" Verses 27, 28.

ANCIENT LUSTFUL INCLINATIONS

What sins brought on the Deluge?

"And it came to pass, when men began to multiply on the face of the earth, and daughters were born unto them, that the sons of God saw the daughters of men that they were fair; and *they took them wives of all which they chose.* . . . And God saw that the wickedness of man was great in the earth, and that *every imagination of the thoughts of his heart was only evil continually.* . . . And the Lord said, I will destroy man whom I have created from the face of the earth. . . . The earth also was *corrupt* before God, and the earth was filled with violence." Genesis 6:1-11.

What was the character of the inhabitants of Sodom?

"But the men of Sodom were *wicked and sinners* before the Lord *exceedingly.*" Genesis 13:13. "And they were *haughty,* and *committed abomination* before me: therefore I took them away as I saw good." Ezekiel 16:50. (See also verse 49.)

NOTE.—Genesis 19:1-9 and 2 Peter 2:6-8 show that they were exceedingly corrupt in morals.

When tempted to sin, what noble example did Joseph set?

"How then can I do this great wickedness, and sin against God?" Genesis 39:9.

PAUL AND CHRIST SPEAK

Against what are the people of God warned?

"But *fornication*, and *all uncleanness*, or *covetousness, let it not be once named among you*, as becometh saints; *neither filthiness*, nor *foolish talking*, nor *jesting*, which are not convenient: but rather giving of thanks." Ephesians 5:3, 4.

What are mentioned as works of the flesh?

"Now the works of the flesh are manifest, which are these; *Adultery, fornication, uncleanness, lasciviousness*." Galatians 5:19.

What is said of those who do such things?

"They which do such things *shall not inherit the kingdom of God*." Verse 21.

What did Christ say would be the condition of the world at His Second Advent?

"*As it was in the days of Noe*, so shall it be also in the days of the Son of man. . . . Likewise also *as it was in the days of Lot;* . . . even thus shall it be in the day when the Son of man is revealed." Luke 17:26-30.

ASSOCIATION AND CONVERSATION

We are warned against keeping company with whom?

"But now I have written unto you not to keep company, if any man that is called a brother be *a fornicator*." 1 Corinthians 5:11.

Why are evil associations to be avoided?

"Do not be deceived: 'Bad company ruins good morals.'" 1 Corinthians 15:33, R.S.V.

What inexorable law is laid down in the Scriptures?

"Be not deceived; God is not mocked: for *whatsoever a man soweth, that shall he also reap*. For he that soweth to his flesh shall of the flesh reap corruption; but he that soweth to the Spirit shall of the Spirit reap life everlasting." Galatians 6:7, 8.

Instead of sanctioning evil, what should we do?

"And have no fellowship with the unfruitful works of darkness, but rather *reprove them*." Ephesians 5:11.

What exhortations did the apostle Paul give Timothy?

"Flee also youthful lusts." 2 Timothy 2:22. "Keep thyself pure." 1 Timothy 5:22.

How should we guard our conversation?

"Let no corrupt communication proceed out of your mouth," but that which is good to the use of edifying, that it may minister grace unto the hearers." Ephesians 4:29.

THE HIGH CALL TO HOLINESS

To whom are all things pure?

"Unto the pure all things are pure: but unto them that are defiled and unbelieving is nothing pure; but even their mind and conscience is defiled." Titus 1:15.

What does the Lord call upon the wicked man to do?

"Let the wicked *forsake his way,* and the unrighteous man his *thoughts:* and let him return unto the Lord, and he will have mercy upon him; and to our God, for he will abundantly pardon." Isaiah 55:7.

What are the proper things to engage one's mind?

"Finally, brethren, whatsoever things are *true,* whatsoever things are *honest,* whatsoever things are *just,* whatsoever things are *pure,* whatsoever things are *lovely,* whatsoever things are of *good report;* if there be any *virtue,* and if there be any *praise, think on these things.*" Philippians 4:8.

NOTE.—The greatest foes to social purity are immoral associates, impure literature, improper dress, idleness, intemperance, theater-going, and viewing questionable television shows. For this reason parents should look well to their children's home life; their companions; the books, papers, and magazines they read; how their time is occupied; what they eat, drink, and wear; where they spend their nights; and the character of their amusements.

Part Seventeen

Health and Temperance

	PAGE
Good Health	725
Christian Temperance	727
Evils of Intemperance	729
Sacred Admonitions	734
True Temperance Reform	735

IN THE OUT-OF-DOORS

"I wish above all things that thou mayest prosper and be in health." 3 John

Good Health

What did the apostle John wish concerning Gaius?

"Beloved, I wish above all things *that thou mayest prosper and be in health,* even as thy soul prospereth." 3 John 2.

What did God promise His people anciently?

"And ye shall serve the Lord your God, and he shall bless thy bread, and thy water; and *I will take sickness away from the midst of thee."* Exodus 23:25.

Upon what conditions was freedom from disease promised?

"If thou wilt diligently hearken to the voice of the Lord thy God, and wilt do that which is right in his sight, and wilt give ear to his commandments, and keep all his statutes, I will put none of these diseases upon thee, which I have brought upon the Egyptians: for I am the Lord that healeth thee." Exodus 15:26.

What does the psalmist say the Lord does for His people?

"Who forgiveth all thine iniquities; *who healeth all thy diseases."* Psalm 103:3.

What constituted a large part of Christ's ministry?

"Who went about doing good, and *healing all that were oppressed of the devil."* Acts 10:38. (See Luke 13:16.) "And Jesus went about all Galilee, . . . *healing all manner of sickness and all manner of disease among the people."* Matthew 4:23.

The Bible Speaks of Our Bodies

Why should the health of the body be preserved?

"For ye are bought with a price: therefore *glorify God in your body,* and in your spirit, which are God's." 1 Corinthians 6:20.

What is the body of the believer said to be?

"What? know ye not that *your body is the temple of the Holy Ghost* which is in you, which ye have of God, and ye are not your own?" Verse 19.

Food Principles—Not Food Fads

What example did Daniel set in this matter?

"But Daniel purposed in his heart *that he would not defile himself with the portion of the king's meat, nor with the wine which he drank.*" Daniel 1:8.

With what food did he ask to be provided?

"Prove thy servants, I beseech thee, ten days; and *let them give us pulse to eat, and water to drink.*" Verse 12.

What was the original diet prescribed for man?

"And God said, Behold, I have given you *every herb bearing seed,* which is upon the face of all the earth, and *every tree, in the which is the fruit of a tree yielding seed;* to you it shall be for meat." Genesis 1:29.

Why did the Lord restrict the Hebrews in their diet?

"For *thou art an holy people unto the Lord thy God, and the Lord has chosen thee to be a peculiar people unto himself,* above all the nations that are upon the earth. Thou shalt not eat any abominable thing." Deuteronomy 14:2, 3.

NOTE.—Both mind and body are affected by the food we eat.

Rest, Cheer, and High Purpose

What effect does cheerfulness have upon the health?

"A merry heart *doeth good* like a medicine." Proverbs 17:22.

How did the Saviour provide rest for His disciples?

"And he said unto them, Come ye yourselves apart into a desert place, and *rest a while.*" Mark 6:31.

How are we exhorted to present our bodies to God?

"I beseech you . . . that *ye present your bodies a living sacrifice, holy, acceptable unto God.*" Romans 12:1.

What high purpose should control our habits of life?

"Whether therefore ye eat, or drink, or whatsoever ye do, *do all to the glory of God.*" 1 Corinthians 10:31.

Christian Temperance

THE BODY AND SELF-CONTROL

In running the Christian race, what did Paul say he did?

"But *I keep under my body, and bring it into subjection:* lest that by any means, when I have preached to others, I myself should be a castaway." Verse 27.

Why are kings and rulers admonished to be temperate?

"It is not for kings to drink wine; nor for princes strong drink: lest they drink, and *forget the law, and pervert the judgment of any of the afflicted."* Proverbs 31:4, 5.

Why were priests forbidden to use intoxicating drink while engaged in the sanctuary service?

"And the Lord spake unto Aaron, saying, Do not drink wine nor strong drink, thou, nor thy sons with thee, when ye go into the tabernacle . . . *that ye may put difference between holy and unholy, and between unclean and clean."* Leviticus 10:8-10.

Why is indulgence in strong drink dangerous?

"And be not drunk with wine, *wherein is excess;* but be filled with the Spirit." Ephesians 5:18.

For what should men eat and drink?

"Blessed art thou, O land, when thy king is the son of nobles, and thy princes eat in due season, *for strength,* and not for drunkenness!" Ecclesiastes 10:17.

FOUR FEARLESS YOUTH TEST TEMPERANCE

Why did Daniel refuse the food and wine of the king?

"But Daniel purposed in his heart *that he would not defile himself* with the portion of the king's meat, nor with the wine which he drank." Daniel 1:8. (See Judges 13:4.)

Instead of these, what did he request?

"Prove thy servants, I beseech thee, ten days; and let them give us *pulse to eat,* and *water to drink."* Verse 12.

At the end of ten days' test, how did he and his companions appear?

"And at the end of ten days their countenances appeared *fairer and fatter in flesh than all the children which did eat the portion of the king's meat.*" Verse 15.

At the end of their three years' course in the school of Babylon, how did the wisdom of Daniel and his companions compare with that of others?

"Now at the end of the days . . . the king communed with them; *and among them all was found none like Daniel, Hananiah, Mishael, and Azariah:* . . . and in all matters of wisdom and understanding, that the king enquired of them, *he found them ten times better* than all the magicians and astrologers that were in all his realm." Verses 18-20.

BEGINNING AND END OF DRUNKARDS

What warning is given against leading others into intemperance?

"Woe unto him that giveth his neighbour drink, that puttest thy bottle to him, and makest him drunken." Habakkuk 2:15.

What kind of professed Christians are not fellowshiped?

"But now I have written unto you not to keep company, if any man that is called a brother be a fornicator, or covetous, or an idolater, or a railer, or a *drunkard*." 1 Corinthians 5:11.

Can drunkards enter the kingdom of God?

"Neither fornicators, nor idolaters, . . . nor thieves, nor covetous, nor *drunkards,* nor revilers, nor extortioners, shall inherit the kingdom of God." 1 Corinthians 6:9, 10. (See Revelation 21:27.)

For what perfection of character did the apostle pray?

"And the very God of peace sanctify you wholly; and I pray God *your whole spirit and soul and body be preserved blameless* unto the coming of our Lord Jesus Christ." 1 Thessalonians 5:23.

NOTE.—For examples of total abstinence in the Bible, see the wife of Manoah, the mother of Samson (Judges 13:4, 12-14); Hannah, the mother of Samuel (1 Samuel 1:15); the Rechabites (Jeremiah 35:1-10); and John the Baptist (Luke 1:13-15).

Evils of Intemperance

EVIL EFFECTS OF ALCOHOL

WHAT do the Scriptures say of wine?

"Wine is a *mocker,* strong drink is *raging:* and whosoever is *deceived* thereby is not wise." Proverbs 20:1.

NOTE.—All intoxicating drinks are deceptive. They seem to give strength, but in reality cause weakness; they seem to create heat, but in fact lower the general temperature; they seem to impart vitality, but really destroy life; they seem to promote happiness, but cause the greatest unhappiness and misery. To intemperance may be attributed much of the world's sorrow.

"Had this been all—could this today be all—the story of alcohol would be differently told. If from the beginning of its use each drinker could have known the swift comfort of his cups and wrapped the curse of its fulfillment as cerements to be buried with him forever, we would be living in a more content world and the vast problem of human misery and unhappiness would exist only as a fraction. Wars might never have been fought, countless murders never committed, domestic tragedies would have been minimized, Bedlams today be far less numerous, and crime divided by three. We cannot forego the temptation to quote with partial acceptance the words of the lawgiver, '. . . visiting the iniquity of the fathers upon the children unto the third and fourth generation.' "—ROBERT S. CARROLL, *What Price Alcohol?* (1941 ed.), p. 8.

With what sins is drunkenness classed?

"Adultery, fornication, uncleanness, lasciviousness, idolatry, witchcraft, hatred, variance, emulations, wrath, strife, seditions, heresies, envyings, murders, *drunkenness,* revelings, and such like." Galatians 5:19-22.

What is one of the evil results of intemperance?

"Be not among winebibbers; among riotous eaters of flesh: for the drunkard and the glutton shall come to *poverty.*" Proverbs 23:20, 21.

What are other evil effects of intemperance?

"Whoredom and wine and new wine *take away the heart.*"

DEATH ON THE HIGHWAY

Some drinkers realize too late that even moderate drinking is on the wrong side of the road.

EVILS OF INTEMPERANCE

Hosea 4:11. "They also have *erred* through wine, and through strong drink are out of the way; . . . they err in *vision*, they stumble in *judgment*." Isaiah 28:7.

What are common accompaniments of intemperance?

"Who hath *woe*? who hath *sorrow*? who hath *contentions*? who hath *babbling*? who hath *wounds* without cause? who hath *redness of eyes*? They that tarry long at the wine; they that go to seek mixed wine." Proverbs 23:29, 30.

How do intoxicants serve one in the end?

"Look not thou upon the wine when it is red, when it giveth his colour in the cup, when it moveth itself aright. *At the last it biteth like a serpent, and stingeth like an adder.*" Verses 31, 32.

NOTE.—The effects of alcoholic liquors do not decrease with the passing of the years. These effects are well described in the *American Prohibition Year Book of 1912*.

"*On the Individual.* Alcoholic liquors, whether fermented, brewed, or distilled, are poisonous, increasing greatly the liability to fatal termination of diseases, weakening and deranging the intellect, polluting the affections, hardening the heart, and corrupting the morals, 'bequeathing to posterity' a degeneration of physical and moral character.

"*On the Family.* A disturber and destroyer of its peace, prosperity, and happiness, and thus removing the sure foundation for good government, national prosperity and welfare.

"*On the Community.* Producing demoralization, vice, and wickedness, counteracting the efficacy of religious efforts and of all means for the intellectual elevation, moral purity, social happiness, and eternal good of mankind.

"*On the State.* Promoting crime and pauperism, paralyzing thrift and industry, corrupting politics, legislation, and the execution of laws."—Pages 26, 27.

"We have condensed the substance of thousands of pages into a few paragraphs in outlining the pernicious influence of alcohol upon the various organs of the body. . . . Our interest from first to last centers about the unquestioned ill-effects of this drug upon nervous tissue, not its hurt to the body, ever its injury to the brain. This discounting, discrediting, destroying agent while often associated with a lowering of general health is the sole cause of alterations in conduct, scaling the gamut from mild euphoria to wild insanity, on to driveling dementia."—ROBERT S. CARROLL, *What Price Alcohol?* p. 106.

"The scientific study of alcohol—intensive, increasingly intelligent, and eminently fair these latter years—has little good to say for it. . . . Frankly, we cannot think of this drug longer as being on trial. It has already been condemned."—*Ibid.*, p. 99.

To what extent is intemperance the cause of crime?

"Philip L. Griffin, chief probation officer of the Municipal Court of Minneapolis, says, 'Practically 90 per cent of the cases that come through the court, . . . are as a result of drinking.' "—*Listen*, October-December, 1948, p. 34.

NATURE AND EFFECT OF TOBACCO

What may be said of the use of tobacco?

Being a rank poison, tobacco is highly injurious.

NOTE.—"Tobacco is the most subtle poison known to chemists, except the deadly prussic acid."—M. ORFILA, a former president of the Paris Medical Academy.

"Tobacco slows up reflexes, lowers morale; any advertisement that says smoking helps an athlete is a falsehood and a fraud."—KNUTE ROCKNE.

Ty Cobb, for many years one of the highest-paid ball players in the world, said: "Cigarette-smoking stupefies the brain, saps vitality, undermines health, and lessens the moral fiber of the man. No boy who hopes to be successful in any line can afford to contract a habit that is so detrimental to his physical and moral development."

" 'I have never used any strong alcoholic beverages. Certainly drinking of this type has no place in the life of any person who wants to keep himself physically fit.

" 'I have never smoked. I feel that temperance in such things leads to more healthful living, and I would not change my habits even if I were to close my athletic career. Most of the Olympic trackmen were nonsmokers.' "—MEL PATTON, winner of the 200-meter dash, quoted in *Listen*, January-March, 1949, p. 5.

"It's over thirteen years since I retired from the Heavyweight Championship. But here's a challenge: If Joe Louis will start smoking, and promise to inhale a couple of packages of cigarettes every day for six months, I'll engage to lick him in fifteen rounds! Of course, Joe wouldn't be foolish enough to meet my terms. No boxer, no athlete in training smokes. He knows that whenever nerves, muscles, heart and brain are called upon for a supreme effort, the tobacco-user is the first to fold."—GENE TUNNEY, *Reader's Digest*, December, 1941, p. 21.

"Men who smoke one cigar a day cannot be trusted with some of my most delicate work. These men, while able to do the rough work of farming, call budding and other delicate work 'puttering,' and have to give it up owing to an inability to concentrate their nerve force. Cigarettes are even more damaging than cigars, and their use by young boys is little short of criminal, and will produce in them the same results that sand placed in a watch will produce—destruction."—LUTHER BURBANK.

INNOCENT BEGINNING AND SAD ENDING

Where does intemperance often begin?

Intemperance often begins in the home.

NOTE.—"The quick pick-me-ups of sweets in childhood, the dependence of many youths on the influence of caffein in tea, coffee, and chocolate, reinforced today from puberty on by increasingly concentrated absorption of nicotin, early result in the acquiring of an hourly need for drugged foods. From these milder drug-helps it is an easy step to light drinks, then to the essence of false help—hard liquor."—ROBERT S. CARROLL, *What Price Alcohol?* pp. 278, 279.

What will drunkards, with other workers of iniquity, never inherit?

"Neither fornicators, nor idolaters, . . . nor thieves, nor covetous, nor *drunkards,* . . . shall inherit *the kingdom of God."* 1 Corinthians 6:9, 10.

CHRIST'S WARNING AND PROPHECY

What admonition against intemperance did Christ give that is especially applicable at the present time?

"And take heed to yourselves, lest at any time your hearts be overcharged with *surfeiting,* and *drunkenness,* and cares of this life, and so that day come upon you unawares." Luke 21:34.

THOUGHTS TO THINK

"Grape-juice has killed more people than grape-shot."—SPURGEON.

"O that men should put an enemy in their mouths, to steal away their brains!"—SHAKESPEARE.

"The liquor traffic is the most degrading and ruinous of all human pursuits."—WILLIAM MCKINLEY.

"In every community three things always work together—the grog-shop, the jail, and the gallows—an infernal trinity."—HENRY WARD BEECHER.

Sacred Admonitions

A Responsive Reading

"And the Lord spake unto Aaron, saying, Do not drink wine nor strong drink, thou, nor thy sons with thee." Leviticus 10:8, 9.

"They shall not drink wine with a song; strong drink shall be bitter to them that drink it." Isaiah 24:9.

"He that loveth pleasure shall be a poor man: he that loveth wine and oil shall not be rich." Proverbs 21:17.

"For the drunkard and the glutton shall come to poverty: and drowsiness shall clothe a man with rags." Proverbs 23:21.

"Woe unto him that giveth his neighbour drink, that puttest thy bottle to him, and makest him drunken also." Habakkuk 2:15.

"Woe unto them that are mighty to drink wine, and men of strength to mingle strong drink." Isaiah 5:22.

"Be not drunk with wine, wherein is excess; but be filled with the Spirit." Ephesians 5:18.

"Wine is a mocker, strong drink is raging: and whosoever is deceived thereby is not wise." Proverbs 20:1.

"Who hath woe? who hath sorrow? who hath contentions? who hath babbling? who hath wounds without cause? who hath redness of eyes?" Proverbs 23:29.

"They that tarry long at the wine; they that go to seek mixed wine." Verse 30.

"Look not thou upon the wine when it is red, when it giveth his colour in the cup, when it moveth itself aright." Verse 31.

"At the last it biteth like a serpent, and stingeth like an adder." Verse 32.

"Be not deceived: neither fornicators, nor idolaters, nor adulterers, . . . nor thieves, nor covetous, nor drunkards, nor revilers, nor extortioners, shall inherit the kingdom of God." 1 Corinthians 6:9, 10.

"Now therefore beware, I pray thee, and drink not wine nor strong drink, and eat not any unclean thing." Judges 13:4.

"Know ye not that your body is the temple of the Holy Ghost which is in you, which ye have of God, and ye are not your own?" 1 Corinthians 6:19.

"For ye are bought with a price: therefore glorify God in your body, and in your spirit, which are God's." Verse 20.

"Whether therefore ye eat, or drink, or whatsoever ye do, do all to the glory of God." 1 Corinthians 10:31.

True Temperance Reform

God's Early Instruction on Diet

What was the original food provided for man?

"And God said, Behold, I have given you every *herb bearing seed,* which is upon the face of all the earth, and every tree, in the which is *the fruit of a tree* yielding *seed;* to you it shall be for meat." Genesis 1:29.

Note.—In other words, vegetables, grains, fruits, and nuts.

After the Flood what other food was indicated as permissible?

"Every moving thing that liveth shall be meat for you; even as the green herb have I given you all things." Genesis 9:3.

Note.—From this it is evident that flesh food was not included in the original diet provided for man, but that because of the changed conditions resulting from the Fall and the Flood, its use was permitted. However, Noah understood the difference between the clean and the unclean animals, and a larger number of the clean beasts were housed safely in the ark. See Genesis 7:2.

Specific Written Instruction to Israel

When God chose Israel for His people, what kinds of flesh food were excluded from their diet by written instruction?

Those called unclean. (See Leviticus 11 and Deuteronomy 14.)

What special food did God provide for the children of Israel during their forty years' wandering in the wilderness?

"Then said the Lord unto Moses, Behold, I will rain *bread from heaven* for you." "And the children of Israel did eat *manna* forty years, until they came to a land inhabited." Exodus 16:4, 35.

At the same time what did God promise to do for them?

"I will take *sickness* away from the midst of thee." Exodus 23:25.

What testimony does the psalmist bear regarding their physical condition?

"There was not one feeble person among their tribes." Psalm 105:37.

Note.—When they complained at God's dealings with them, and longed for the food of Egypt, God gave them their desires, but sent "leanness into their soul." (See Numbers 11; Psalm 106:13-15; 1 Corinthians 10:6.) Like many today, they were not content with a simple but wholesome and nourishing diet.

Three Important Questions

Where, above all, should true temperance reform begin?

In the home.

Note.—Unless fathers and mothers practice temperance, they cannot expect their children to do so.

What classes of men especially should be strictly temperate?

"Be thou an *example* of the believers." 1 Timothy 4:12.

Note.—Of all men in the world, ministers and physicians should lead strictly temperate lives. The welfare of society demands this of them, for their influence is constantly telling for or against moral reform and the improvement of society. By precept and example they can do much toward bringing about the much-needed reform.

Can the fact that the liquor traffic brings in a large revenue to the state justify men in licensing it?

"Woe to him that buildeth a town with *blood*, and stablisheth a city by *iniquity!*" Habakkuk 2:12.

Note.—In all the walks and relationships of life, whether in the home, the medical profession, the pulpit, or the legislative assembly, men should stand for temperance. To license the liquor traffic is to legalize and foster it. It cannot exist or thrive without the patronage of each rising generation, a large number of whom it must necessarily ruin, body, soul, and spirit. For the state to receive money from such a source, therefore, must be highly reprehensible. The practice has fittingly been likened to a father catching sharks, and baiting his hook with his own children.

Part Eighteen

The Kingdom Restored

	PAGE
Promises to the Overcomer	738
The Subjects of the Kingdom	740
Eternal Life	744
The Home of the Saved	747
The New Jerusalem	752
The Conflict Ended	755

Promises to the Overcomer

The Things to Be Overcome

What are we admonished to overcome?

"Be not overcome of evil, but *overcome evil* with good." Romans 12:21.

Note.—In 1 John 5:4 that which we are to overcome is called "the world"; and in 1 John 2:15-17 the things of which "the world" consists are described as "the lust of the flesh, and the lust of the eyes, and the pride of life."

How to Overcome

What only can overcome the world?

"For *whatsoever is born of God* overcometh the world." 1 John 5:4.

What gives us the victory in our conflict with the world?

"And this is the victory that overcometh the world, *even our faith*." Same verse.

Promises to the Overcomer

What promises are made by Christ to the overcomer?

1. "To him that overcometh will I give *to eat of the tree of life,* which is in the midst of the paradise of God." Revelation 2:7.

2. "He that overcometh *shall not be hurt of the second death*." Verse 11.

3. "To him that overcometh will I give *to eat of the hidden manna,* and will give him a white stone, and in the stone a new name written, which no man knoweth saving he that receiveth it." Verse 17.

4. "He that overcometh, and keepeth my works unto the end, to him will I give *power over the nations:* and he shall rule them with a rod of iron; as the vessels of a potter shall they be broken to shivers: even as I received of my Father. And I will give him *the morning star.*" Verses 26-28.

5. "He that overcometh, the same shall be *clothed in white*

raiment; and *I will not blot out his name out of the book of life, but I will confess his name before my Father, and before his angels."* Revelation 3:5.

6. "Him that overcometh will I *make a pillar in the temple of my God,* and he shall go no more out: and I will *write upon him the name of my God, and the name of the city of my God,* which is new Jerusalem, which cometh down out of heaven from my God: and I will write upon him *my new name."* Verse 12.

7. "To him that overcometh will I grant *to sit with me in my throne,* even as I also overcame, and am set down with my Father in his throne." Verse 21.

In what one promise are all these promises summed up?

"He that overcometh shall inherit all things; and I will be his God, and he shall be my son." Revelation 21:7.

NOTE.—The exceeding great and precious promises to the overcomer embrace everything—eternal life, health, happiness, and an everlasting home. What more could be asked?

"IN heaven there will be no parting, no pain to bear;
No care-worn brow, no sigh, no silvery hair;
No death to snatch our loved ones from our side,
No angry waves, no sea, no treacherous tide.

"In heaven there'll be no thirst, no cry for bread;
No soul who knows not where to lay his head;
No one to feel the winter's chilling blast,
For there the piercing storms will all be past.

"In heaven there'll be no toil without repay;
No building for a brief, ephemeral day;
For all the joys that prophets old have told
'Twill take the endless ages to unfold.

"In heaven there'll be no weary pilgrim band;
No seekers for a better, fairer land;
For all who reach that blissful, happy shore,
Will never cry nor sigh, nor wish for more."

The Subjects of the Kingdom

THE LITERAL ISRAELITES

Upon whom was the name Israel first bestowed?

"And he said, Thy name shall be called no more *Jacob,* but *Israel:* for as a prince hast thou power with God and with men, and hast prevailed." Genesis 32:28.

Afterward who came to be called by this title?

"Now these are the names of *the children of Israel,* which came into Egypt; . . . Reuben, Simeon, Levi, and Judah, Issachar, Zebulun, and Benjamin, Dan, and Naphtali, Gad, and Asher. . . . Joseph." Exodus 1:1-5.

Note.—In other words, the descendants of Jacob, the grandson of Abraham, were known as the twelve tribes of Israel.

What special blessings were conferred on the Israelites?

"Who are Israelites; to whom pertaineth the *adoption,* and the *glory,* and the *covenants,* and the *giving of the law,* and the *service of God,* and the *promises;* whose are the fathers, and of whom as concerning the flesh *Christ came,* who is over all." Romans 9:4, 5.

THE TRUE, SPIRITUAL ISRAEL

Who constitute the true Israel, or seed of Abraham?

"They are not all Israel, which are of Israel: neither, because they are the seed of Abraham, are they all children: but, In Isaac shall thy seed be called. That is, They which are the children of the flesh, these are not the children of God: but *the children of the promise are counted for the seed."* Verses 6-8.

What did John the Baptist say to the Pharisees and Sadducees who came to his baptism?

"And think not to say within yourselves, We have Abraham to our father: for I say unto you, that *God is able of these stones to raise up children unto Abraham."* Matthew 3:9.

THE SUBJECTS OF THE KINGDOM

What determines whether one is a child of Abraham?

"Know ye therefore that *they which are of faith, the same are the children of Abraham.*" Galatians 3:7.

To whom must one belong in order to be Abraham's seed?

"*And if ye be Christ's,* then are ye Abraham's seed, and heirs according to the promise." Verse 29.

In what scripture are Christians recognized as Israel?

"And as many as walk according to this rule, peace be on them, and mercy, and upon *the Israel of God.*" Galatians 6:16.

To whom is the gospel the power of God unto salvation?

"For I am not ashamed of the gospel of Christ: for it is the power of God unto salvation *to every one that believeth;* to the Jew first, and also to the Greek." Romans 1:16.

Christ's Earthly Ministry to Literal Israel

To whom did Jesus first send the twelve disciples?

"These twelve Jesus sent forth, and commanded them, saying, Go not into the way of the Gentiles, and into any city of the Samaritans enter ye not: but go rather to *the lost sheep of the house of Israel.*" Matthew 10:5, 6.

When the woman of Canaan came to Christ, beseeching Him to heal her daughter, what did He say?

"But he answered and said, *I am not sent but unto the lost sheep of the house of Israel.*" Matthew 15:24.

When she persisted in her request, and fell down to worship Him, what did He say?

"But he answered and said, *It is not meet to take the children's bread, and to cast it to dogs.*" Verse 26.

Note.—By her persistent faith, this woman, although a Canaanite, showed that she was really a true child of Abraham.

While dining with Zacchaeus, what did Christ say?

"This day is salvation come to this house, *forsomuch as he also is a son of Abraham.*" Luke 19:9.

What did He say to the woman of Samaria as to the source of salvation?

"Ye worship ye know not what: we know what we worship: for *salvation is of the Jews.*" John 4:22.

Gentiles Become Spiritual Israelites

When the Jews rejected Paul's preaching of the gospel, what did Paul and Barnabas say?

"Then Paul and Barnabas waxed bold, and said, It was necessary that the word of God should first have been spoken to you: but seeing ye put it from you, and judge yourselves unworthy of everlasting life, *lo, we turn to the Gentiles.*" Acts 13:46.

NOTE.—From all this it is plain that had not the Jews as a nation rejected Christ, they would still have maintained the pre-eminence as the children of God, and as God's light bearers to the world. But because of this rejection, they were rejected as God's peculiar people, and others took their place, and now bear the name of *Israel* in common with those who were first called by that name.

Under what figure are the Gentile believers represented who have become a part of the true Israel of God?

"And if some of the branches be broken off, and thou, being *a wild olive tree,* wert graffed in among them, and with them partakest of the root and fatness of the olive tree; boast not against the branches." Romans 11:17, 18.

Lest the Gentile grafts should boast, saying that the Jews were broken off to let them come in, what warning is given them?

"Well; because of unbelief they were broken off, and thou standest by faith. *Be not highminded, but fear:* for if God spared not the natural branches, *take heed lest he also spare not thee.*" Verses 20, 21.

What encouragement is held out concerning the branches that have been broken off?

"And they also, if they abide not still in unbelief, *shall be graffed in:* for God is able to graff them in again." Verse 23.

Before the Gentiles become Israelites, in what condition are they?

"Wherefore remember, that ye being in time past Gentiles . . . at that time ye were *without Christ, being aliens from the*

THE SUBJECTS OF THE KINGDOM

commonwealth of Israel, and strangers from the covenants of promise, having no hope, and without God in the world." Ephesians 2:11, 12.

GOD'S LAST-DAY REMNANT PEOPLE

How are God's remnant people described?

"Here is the patience of the saints: here are they that *keep the commandments of God, and the faith of Jesus.*" Revelation 14:12.

Whose names are in the foundations of the Holy City?

"And the wall of the city had twelve foundations, and in them *the names of the twelve apostles of the Lamb.*" Revelation 21:14.

Whose names are on the twelve gates of the city?

"And [the wall] had twelve gates, and at the gates twelve angels, and names written thereon, which are *the names of the twelve tribes of the children of Israel.*" Verse 12.

Who will walk in the light of the city?

"And *the nations of them which are saved* shall walk in the light of it: and *the kings of the earth* do bring their glory and honour into it." Verse 24.

> "Has someone seen Christ in you today?
> Christian, look to your life, I pray;
> There are aching hearts and blighted souls
> Being lost on sin's destructive shoals,
> And perhaps of Christ their only view
> May be what they see of Him in you.
> Will they see enough to bring hope and cheer?
> Look to your light! Does it shine out clear?"

Eternal Life

Eternal Life and How to Obtain It

What precious promise has God made to His children?

"And this is the promise that he hath promised us, even *eternal life*." 1 John 2:25.

How may we obtain eternal life?

For God so loved the world, that he gave his only begotten Son, *that whosoever believeth in him should not perish, but have everlasting life."* John 3:16.

Who has everlasting life?

"*He that believeth on the Son* hath everlasting life." Verse 36.

Where is this everlasting or eternal life?

"And this is the record, that God hath given to us eternal life, and *this life is in his son."* 1 John 5:11.

What therefore follows?

"*He that hath the Son hath life;* and he that hath not the Son of God hath not life." Verse 12.

What does Christ give His followers?

"I give unto them *eternal life;* and they shall never perish." John 10:28.

The Tree of Life, Past and Future

Why, after the Fall, was man shut away from the tree of life?

"*Lest he* put forth his hand, and *take also of the tree of life, and eat, and live for ever."* Genesis 3:22.

What has Christ promised the overcomer?

"To him that overcometh will I give *to eat of the tree of life,* which is in the midst of the paradise of God." Revelation 2:7.

When Saints Become Immortal

When will immortality be conferred upon the saints?

"We shall not all sleep, but we shall all be changed, in a moment, in the twinkling of an eye, at the last trump: for the trumpet shall sound, and the dead shall be raised incorruptible, and we shall be changed. For this corruptible must put on incorruption, and this mortal must put on immortality." 1 Corinthians 15:51-53.

Note.—In accepting Christ the believer receives "that eternal life, which was with the Father," and this eternal life he retains as long as Christ dwells in the heart by faith. This wondrous gift may be lost by failure to maintain the faith which holds Christ fast. At the resurrection, immortality is conferred upon those who have fallen asleep in Christ, and thus the possession of eternal life becomes a permanent experience.

> Toil on a little longer here,
>   For thy reward awaits above,
> Nor droop in sadness or in fear
>   Beneath the rod that's sent in love;
> The deeper wound our spirits feel,
> The sweeter heaven's balm to heal.
>
> Faith lifts the veil before our eyes,
>   And bids us view a happier clime,
> Where verdant fields in beauty rise,
>   Beyond the withering blasts of time;
> And brings the blissful moment near,
> When we in glory shall appear.
>
> . . . . .
>
> Then let us hope; 'tis not in vain;
>   Though moistened by our grief the soil,
> The harvest brings us joy for pain,
>   The rest repays the weary toil;
> For they shall reap who sow in tears,
> Rich gladness through eternal years.
>
> —Annie R. Smith

COPYRIGHT, 1949, BY REVIEW AND HERALD

FRANKLIN BOOTH, ARTIST

"A LITTLE CHILD SHALL LEAD THEM"

"They shall not hurt nor destroy in all my holy mountain: for the earth shall be

The Home of the Saved

GOD'S PURPOSE IN CREATION

For what purpose was the earth created?

"For thus saith the Lord that created the heavens; God himself that formed the earth and made it; he hath established it, he created it not in vain, *he formed it to be inhabited*." Isaiah 45:18.

To whom has God given the earth?

"The heaven, even the heavens, are the Lord's: but *the earth hath he given to the children of men*." Psalm 115:16.

For what purpose was man made?

"Thou madest him *to have dominion over the works of thy hands;* thou hast put all things under his feet." Psalm 8:6.

SATAN, AND MAN'S LOST DOMINION

How did man lose his dominion?

Through sin. Romans 5:12; 6:23.

When man lost his dominion, to whom did he yield it?

"For of whom a man is overcome, of the same is he brought in bondage." 2 Peter 2:19.

NOTE.—Man was overcome by Satan in the Garden of Eden, and there yielded himself and his possessions into the hands of his captor.

In tempting Christ, what ownership did Satan claim?

"And the devil, taking him up into an high mountain, shewed unto him all the kingdoms of the world in a moment of time. And the devil said unto him, All this power will I give thee, and the glory of them: *for that is delivered unto me; and to whomsoever I will I give it.*" Luke 4:5, 6.

THE RESTORED DOMINION

What promise of restoration did the Lord make through Micah?

HOME AT LAST

COPYRIGHT, 1942, BY REVIEW AND HERALD

R. M. ELDRIDGE, ARTIST

"They shall build houses, and inhabit them; and they shall

THE HOME OF THE SAVED

"And thou, *O tower of the flock, the strong hold of the daughter of Zion, unto thee shall it come, even the first dominion;* the kingdom shall come to the daughter of Jerusalem." Micah 4:8.

Why did Christ say the meek are blessed?

"Blessed are the meek: *for they shall inherit the earth.*" Matthew 5:5.

Note.—This inheritance cannot be realized in this life, for here the truly meek generally have little of earth's good things.

Who does the psalmist say have most now?

"For I was envious at *the foolish,* when I saw the prosperity of *the wicked.* . . . Their eyes stand out with fatness: *they have more than heart could wish.*" Psalm 73:3-7.

What promise was made to Abraham concerning the land?

"And the Lord said unto Abram, after that Lot was separated from him, Lift up now thine eyes, and look from the place where thou art northward, and southward, and eastward, and westward: for *all the land which thou seest, to thee will I give it, and to thy* SEED *for ever.*" Genesis 13:14, 15.

How much did this promise comprehend?

"*For the promise, that he should be the heir of the world,* was not to Abraham, or to his seed, through the law, but through the righteousness of faith." Romans 4:13.

How much of the land of Canaan did Abraham own in his lifetime?

"*And he gave him none inheritance in it, no, not so much as to set his foot on:* yet he promised that he would give it to him for a possession, and to his seed after him, when as yet he had no child." Acts 7:5. (See Hebrews 11:13.)

How much of the promised possession did Abraham expect during his lifetime?

"By faith Abraham, when he was called to go out into a place which he should after receive for an inheritance, obeyed; and he went out, not knowing whither he went. By faith *he sojourned in the land of promise, as in a strange country,* dwelling in tabernacles with Isaac and Jacob, the heirs with him of the same promise: *for he looked for a city which hath foundations, whose builder and maker is God."* Hebrews 11:8-10.

In a special sense, who is the seed to whom this promise was made?

"Now to Abraham and his seed were the promises made. He saith not, And to seeds, as of many; but as of one, *And to thy seed, which is Christ."* Galatians 3:16.

Who are heirs of the promise?

"And *if ye be Christ's, then are ye Abraham's seed, and heirs according to the promise."* Verse 29.

Why did not these ancient worthies receive the promise?

"And these all, having obtained a good report through faith, received not the promise: God having provided some better thing for us, *that they without us should not be made perfect."* Hebrews 11:39, 40.

When This Earth Is Made New

What is to become of our earth in the day of the Lord?

"But the day of the Lord will come as a thief in the night; in the which the heavens shall pass away with a great noise, and *the elements shall melt with fervent heat, the earth also and the works that are therein shall be burned up."* 2 Peter 3:10.

What will follow this great conflagration?

"Nevertheless we, according to his promise, *look for new heavens and a new earth,* wherein dwelleth righteousness." Verse 13.

Note.—As shown in the reading on "The Millennium," page 345, at the coming of Christ the living wicked will die, and the saints will be taken to heaven to dwell with Christ a thousand years, or until the wicked of all ages are judged and the time comes for their destruction and the purification of the earth by the fires of the last day. Following this, the earth will be formed anew, and man, redeemed from sin, will be restored to his original dominion.

To what Old Testament promise did Peter evidently refer?

"For, behold, I create new heavens and a new earth: and the former shall not be remembered, nor come into mind." Isaiah 65:17.

THE HOME OF THE SAVED

What was shown the apostle John in vision?

"And I saw *a new heaven and a new earth:* for the first heaven and the first earth were passed away; and there was no more sea." Revelation 21:1.

How did Isaiah describe conditions on the "new earth"?

"And they shall build houses, and inhabit them; and they shall plant vineyards, and eat the fruit of them. They shall not build, and another inhabit; they shall not plant, and another eat: for as the days of a tree are the days of my people, and mine elect shall long enjoy the work of their hands. They shall not labour in vain, nor bring forth for trouble; for they are the seed of the blessed of the Lord, and their offspring with them." Isaiah 65:21-23.

How readily will their wants be supplied?

"And it shall come to pass, that before they call, I will answer; and while they are yet speaking, I will hear." Verse 24.

What peaceful condition will reign throughout the earth then?

"The wolf and the lamb shall feed together, and the lion shall eat straw like the bullock: and dust shall be the serpent's meat. They shall not hurt nor destroy in all my holy mountain, saith the Lord." Verse 25.

What seasons of worship will be observed in the new earth?

"For as the new heavens and the new earth, which I will make, shall remain before me, saith the Lord, so shall your seed and your name remain. And it shall come to pass, that *from one new moon to another, and from one sabbath to another,* shall all flesh come to worship before me, saith the Lord." Isaiah 66:22, 23.

What will the ransomed of the Lord then do?

"And the ransomed of the Lord shall return, and come to Zion with songs and everlasting joy upon their heads: they shall obtain joy and gladness, and sorrow and sighing shall flee away." Isaiah 35:10.

The New Jerusalem

WHAT was one of Christ's parting promises to His disciples?

"In my Father's house are many mansions: if it were not so, I would have told you. *I go to prepare a place for you.*" John 14:2.

What does Paul say God has prepared for His people?

"But now they desire a better country, that is, an heavenly: wherefore God is not ashamed to be called their God: for *he hath prepared for them a city.*" Hebrews 11:16.

Where is this city, and what is it called?

"But *Jerusalem which is above* is free, which is the mother of us all." Galatians 4:26.

For what did Abraham look?

"For *he looked for a city* which hath foundations, whose builder and maker is God." Hebrews 11:10.

What assurance has God given to believers?

"God is not ashamed to be called their God: for he hath prepared for them a city." Hebrews 11:16.

Saint John Describes the City

What did John see concerning this city?

"And *I John saw the holy city, new Jerusalem, coming down from God out of heaven*, prepared as a bride adorned for her husband." Revelation 21:2.

How many foundations has this city?

"And the wall of the city had *twelve foundations,* and in them the names of the twelve apostles of the Lamb." Verse 14.

What is the measurement of the city?

"And the city lieth foursquare, and the length is as large as the breadth: and *he measured the city with the reed, twelve thousand furlongs.*" Verse 16.

What is the height of the wall?

"And he measured the wall thereof, *an hundred and forty and four cubits.*" Verse 17.

NOTE.—One hundred and forty-four cubits are estimated at 216 feet in our measure.

Of what material is the wall constructed?

"And the building of *the wall of it was of jasper:* and the city was pure gold, like unto clear glass." Verse 18.

With what are the twelve foundations adorned?

"And the foundations of the wall of the city were garnished with all manner of precious stones. The first foundation was *jasper;* the second, *sapphire;* the third, a *chalcedony;* the fourth, an *emerald;* the fifth, *sardonyx;* the sixth, *sardius;* the seventh, *chrysolyte;* the eighth, *beryl;* the ninth, a *topaz;* the tenth, a *chrysoprasus;* the eleventh, a *jacinth;* the twelfth, an *amethyst.*" Verses 19, 20. (See Exodus 28:15-21; Isaiah 54:11, 12.)

Of what are the twelve gates composed?

"And the twelve gates were *twelve pearls:* every several gate was of one pearl." Revelation 21:21.

What is written on these gates?

"The names of the twelve tribes of the children of Israel." Verse 12.

Of what does John say the streets of the city are composed?

"And the street of the city was *pure gold,* as it were transparent glass." Verse 21.

Why will this city have no need of the sun or moon?

"And the city had no need of the sun, neither of the moon, to shine in it: *for the glory of God did lighten it, and the Lamb is the light thereof.* And the nations of them which are saved shall walk in the light of it: and the kings of the earth do bring their glory and honour into it." Verses 23, 24. (See Revelation 22:5; Isaiah 60:19, 20.)

Why are its gates not to be closed?

"And the gates of it shall not be shut at all by day: *for there shall be no night there.*" Revelation 21:25.

Who May, and Who May Not, Enter

What will be excluded from this city?

"And there shall in no wise enter into it *any thing that defileth, neither whatsoever worketh abomination, or maketh a lie.*" Verse 27.

Who will be permitted to enter it?

"*Blessed are they that do his commandments,* that they may have right to the tree of life, and may enter in through the gates into the city." Revelation 22:14.

Note.—The late English and American revisions render this, "Blessed are they that wash their robes," etc. The result is the same, for those who wash their robes cease to sin, and hence do God's commandments.

When this city becomes the metropolis of the new earth, what will be the condition of God's people?

"And God shall wipe away all tears from their eyes; and there shall be no more death, neither sorrow, nor crying, neither shall there be any more pain: for the former things are passed away." Revelation 21:4.

Everlasting Life and Glorious Privilege

What will flow through the city?

"And he shewed me *a pure river of water of life,* clear as crystal, proceeding out of the throne of God and of the Lamb." Revelation 22:1.

What stands on either side of the river?

"In the midst of the street of it, and on either side of the river, was there *the tree of life,* which bare twelve manner of fruits, and yielded her fruit every month: and the leaves of the tree were for the healing of the nations." Verse 2.

Note.—The tree of life, which Adam lost through transgression, is to be restored by Christ. Access to this is one of the promises to the overcomer. (Revelation 2:7.) Its bearing twelve kinds of fruit, a new kind each month, suggests a reason why in the new earth "from one *new moon* to another," as well as "from one sabbath to another," all flesh is to come before God to worship, as stated in Isaiah 66:22, 23.

The Conflict Ended

Four Steps of a Completed Work

In the narration of the work of creation, what statement is made concerning its completion?

"Thus the heavens and the earth were *finished,* and all the host of them. And on the seventh day God *ended* his work which he had made." Genesis 2:1, 2.

Note.—God's work here referred to was "very good." Genesis 1:31. Had it not been for sin, this first plan of God would not have been followed by the three steps we shall now study.

When expiring on the cross, what did Christ say?

"When Jesus therefore had received the vinegar, he said, *It is finished:* and he bowed his head, and gave up the ghost." John 19:30.

Note.—Christ came into the world to save sinners. Costly though the price was, He paid it. Bitter as was the cup, He drank its last dregs. In that final moment He said, "It is finished."

At the pouring out of the seventh plague, what announcement will be made?

"And the seventh angel poured out his vial into the air; and there came a great voice out of the temple of heaven, from the throne, saying, *It is done.*" Revelation 16:17.

Note.—This outpouring of God's wrath is upon the rejecters of Heaven's mercy. Human probation has closed, and when the great voice cries, "It is done," Christ starts on His way to earth the second time.

And when the new heavens and the new earth have appeared, and the Holy City, New Jerusalem, has descended from God and become the metropolis of the new creation, what announcement will then be made?

"And he that sat upon the throne said, Behold, I make all things new. And he said unto me, Write: for these words are true and faithful. And he said unto me, *It is done.* I am Alpha and Omega, the beginning and the end." Revelation 21:5, 6.

Pleasures Forevermore

In the new earth, what will be no more?

"And God shall wipe away all *tears* from their eyes; and there shall be no more *death*, neither *sorrow*, nor *crying*, neither shall there be any more *pain:* for the former things are passed away." Verse 4. "And there shall be no more *curse*." Revelation 22:3.

How does Isaiah describe the condition of all the earth?

"The wolf also shall dwell with the lamb, and the leopard shall lie down with the kid; and the calf and the young lion and the fatling together; and a little child shall lead them. And the cow and the bear shall feed; their young ones shall lie down together: and the lion shall eat straw like the ox. And the sucking child shall play on the hole of the asp, and the weaned child shall put his hand on the cockatrice' den. They shall not hurt nor destroy in all my holy mountain: for the earth shall be full of the knowledge of the Lord, as the waters cover the sea." Isaiah 11:6-9.

Seeing Him as He Is

What will finally be the privilege of God's children?

"And they shall *see his face*." Revelation 22:4.

How perfect will be their knowledge of God?

"For now we see through a glass, darkly; but then face to face: now I know in part; but *then shall I know even as also I am known*." 1 Corinthians 13:12.

Whom will they be like?

"Beloved, now are we the sons of God, and it doth not yet appear what we shall be: but we know that, when he shall appear, *we shall be like him;* for we shall see him as he is." 1 John 3:2.

From what ills will the saints be forever delivered?

"And God shall wipe away all *tears* from their eyes; and there shall be no more *death*, neither *sorrow*, nor *crying*, neither shall there be any more *pain:* for the former things are passed away." Revelation 21:4.

THE CONFLICT ENDED

Who will dwell with the redeemed?

"*He* will dwell with them, and they shall be his people, and *God himself shall be with them, and be their God.*" Verse 3.

How long will they possess the future kingdom?

"But the saints of the most High shall take the kingdom, and possess the kingdom *for ever, even for ever and ever.*" Daniel 7:18.

How long will they reign?

"And they shall reign *for ever and ever.*" Revelation 22:5.

"Out of my heart I sing a song,
  O world so great and grand!
But hearts are weak, and hands reach out
  For the touch of a kindly hand.

"O song that I sing, I pray you bring
  To some sad soul thy balm;
Fall soft, I pray, like the breath of May,
  Or the touch of a loving hand.

"I sing for hearts that ache and break,
  I sing for hearts that are true;
O world so vast, O world so wide,
  I sing my song for you!"

COPYRIGHT, 1949, BY REVIEW AND HERALD

HARRY ANDERSON, ARTIST

THE GAME OF LIFE

"For we wrestle not against flesh and blood, b[ut] against principalities, against powers, against t[he] rulers of the darkness of this world." Ephesians 6:

The Game of Life

IN THIS striking picture is an allegorical presentation of the conflict between man and the powers of darkness. A young man is playing a game for his life against the most wily of opponents —the prince of evil himself. Behind these contestants—and apparently unobserved by either—is an angel from heaven, sent by man's Creator as a personal guardian. "Are they not all ministering spirits, sent forth to minister for them who shall be heirs of salvation?" Hebrews 1:14.

In the game of life the stakes are high, for Satan is determined to get the mastery over man's soul. With desperate earnestness the man pits himself against this enemy of righteousness. As is all too frequent in human experience, Satan at the outset gains an advantage. He has taken away the symbols representing Bible reading, prayer, and church attendance. Although the young man has given up liquor, tobacco, and card playing, apparently he is still losing the game. What shall the next move be? It is a tense and anxious moment in his life. In contrast with his deep concern is the exultation of his opponent, whose face is marked with malice and cunning. Satan is confident that he has his victim started on the downward path. In deep meditation and conviction the young man hesitantly reaches for the cross, the one symbol that alone can checkmate every move of the enemy.

The tide is turned. With the cross in his hand the young man obtains the victory, not because of his skill or cleverness but because of his complete dependence on the cross of Christ. Like the apostle Paul, he is able to say, "In the cross of Christ I glory."

This is the game in which we are each engaged. What its outcome will be depends upon how we meet and fight life's battle day by day. Through Christ we may all be victorious.

So, take courage if you too are struggling against the enemy. God never forsakes one who turns to Him for help.

Authorities Quoted in Bible Readings for the Home

PROTESTANT WRITERS

Dean Henry Alford, *Church of England* 332
Dr. Albert Barnes, *Presbyterian* 176, 186, 586, 587
Henry Ward Beecher, *American Congregationalist* 622, 733
Amos Binney, *Methodist Episcopal* 451
Amos Binney and Daniel Steele, *Methodist Episcopal* 408, 432
T. R. Birks, *Church of England* 209, 214
Alexander Campbell, *Disciples of Christ* 450, 451
Carlstadt, *German Reformer* 458, 459
W. O. Carver, *Baptist* 408, 413, 425, 453, 455
J. Wilbur Chapman, *Presbyterian* 118
Dr. Adam Clarke, *Wesleyan* 207, 208, 209, 213, 214
W. F. Crafts, *Presbyterian* 277
Dr. R. W. Dale, *British Congregationalist* 450
Timothy Dwight, *American Congregationalist* 305, 306, 450
Jonathan Edwards, *Congregationalist* 374, 426
James H. Fairchild, *Congregationalist* 473, 474
F. W. Farrar, *Church of England* 144, 437
Benjamin Franklin, *Deist* 491, 492, 565
A. J. Gordon, *Baptist* 331
H. Grattan Guinness, *Independent* 266
Dr. Edward T. Hiscox, *Baptist* 450
J. Philip Hyatt, *Baptist* 394
W. D. Killen, *Irish Presbyterian* 426, 449

John Peter Lange, *German Protestant* 407
Canon Knox Little, *Church of England* 450
Martin Luther, *German Reformer* 110, 407, 476, 545
J. R. Miller, *Presbyterian* 552, 553, 568, 576, 597, 700
D. L. Moody, *Independent* 331, 332, 334, 359, 406
Thomas Morer, *Church of England* 437
G. Campbell Morgan, *English Congregationalist* 359, 400
William Prynne, *Puritan* 440, 455
Stewart M. Robinson, *Presbyterian* 388
Uriah Smith, *Seventh-day Adventist* 221, 222, 223, 282
C. H. Spurgeon, *Baptist* 357, 358, 379, 384, 698, 733
Vernon Staley, *Church of England* 121
E. A. Stockman, *Advent Christian* 520, 522
T. De Witt Talmage, *Presbyterian* 125, 271, 547, 568, 593, 668, 698
J. J. Taylor, *Baptist* 277, 406, 429, 435
Jeremy Taylor, *Church of England* 435
O. C. S. Wallace, *Baptist* 363, 367, 402
John Wesley, *Methodist* 271, 359, 364, 365, 390, 397, 405, 492
Ellen G. White, *Seventh-day Adventist* 38, 66, 88, 419, 420, 421, 503, 524, 525, 531, 532, 544, 545, 551, 577, 578, 597, 622, 641, 684, 698, 701
Isaac Williams, *Church of England* 437
and others

CATHOLIC WRITERS

Leonard Woolsey Bacon 212
Cesare Baronius 213
Robert Cardinal Bellarmine 212
Richard Challoner 461
Joseph Faa di Bruno 253
L. Duchesne 438
Lucius Ferraris 212, 215, 432, 433
Peter Geiermann 431, 434
James Cardinal Gibbons 215, 216, 434, 435, 445, 451
Dr. William Gildea 451
Gloss 212

The Great Encyclical Letters of Leo XIII 275
Pope Gregory I 457
The Decretals of Gregory IX 212
Charles Joseph Hefele 440, 456, 457, 484
Stephen Keenan 215, 434, 459
Vincent J. Kelly 435, 437, 438, 439, 455
John Laux 253, 435
J. D. Mansi 212
Cardinal John Henry Newman 251, 477
Pope Pius XII 275
John L. Stoddard 449
Henry Tuberville 216, 278, 434, 445

OTHER AUTHORITIES

General H. H. Arnold 719
M. Edouard Bailland 453
Sir William F. Barrett 526
The Venerable Bede 456
A. E. R. Boak 209, 479
A. E. R. Boak, Albert Hyma, and Preston Slosson 208, 224
Dr. Archibald Bower 456
Robert J. Burdette 733

The Cambridge Ancient History 222, 251
Charlemagne 485
Thomas Clarke 488
Agnes M. Clerke (on astronomy) 290, 306
Charles C. Coffin 18
Lyman Coleman 437, 457
Norman Cousins 311
Franz Cumont 250, 251, 252

760

AUTHORITIES QUOTED IN BIBLE READINGS

M. Anders Donner 453
Frederick Douglass 306, 307
Sir Arthur Conan Doyle 528
Carl Conrad Eckhardt 210
Eusebius 303, 439, 456
A. C. Flick 210, 250, 267, 287, 458, 479
Peter Force 277, 486
Edward Gibbon 197, 198
William E. Gladstone 450
Henry Hallam 459
Adolf Harnack 211, 267
Thomas Jefferson 272, 273
Virgil Jordan 317
Josephus 13
Justinian 217
Gordon J. Laing 251, 252
S. H. Langdon 251
Kenneth Scott Latourette 312, 317, 324, 326
W. E. H. Lecky 214, 489
Llorente 214
Sir Oliver Lodge 529
Sir Charles Lyell 289
Thomas B. Macaulay 488, 489, 491
Justin Martyr 457

William McKinley 733
Augustus Neander 276, 438, 478, 481, 484, 485
Denison Olmsted (on astronomy) 306
M. Orfila 732
Origen 457
Jean Perrin 458
Lucien Price 311
Samuel Purchas 458
Philip Schaff 213, 283, 287, 333, 374, 375, 383, 385, 433, 436, 437, 439, 478, 479, 480, 484
Louis Segur 279, 446
Socrates 437, 438, 457
Pitirim A. Sorokin 320
Sozomen 438
James S. Stewart 317, 319
Henry L. Stimson 317
N. Summerbell 433
Samuel Tenney 305
Tertullian 457, 477
Joseph Turmel 211
Henry P. Warren 17
George Washington 475
Samuel Williams 305
Charles A. Young (on astronomy) 290

There are also many quotations from periodicals published by various denominations.

ENCYCLOPEDIAS AND DICTIONARIES

The Catholic Encyclopedia 490
A Dictionary of Christian Antiquities 451
Encyclopaedia Britannica 251, 289, 486
Encyclopaedia of Religion and Ethics 485
The International Standard Bible Encyclopaedia 430
Kitto's Cyclopaedia of Biblical Literature 656
M'Clintock and Strong's Cyclopaedia of Biblical, Theological, and Ecclesiastical Literature 237, 451, 457, 458
Nelson's New Loose-Leaf Encyclopedia 289
The New Schaff-Herzog Encyclopedia of Religious Knowledge 485
Smith's Comprehensive Dictionary of the Bible 655
Webster's Dictionary 475, 527
Young's Analytical Concordance to the Bible 500

Index

ABOLISHED by Christ, what was 394
Acceptance with God 103
Accountability, individual 475
Addison, Joseph (poem) 615
Admonitions and warnings 657
Admonitions, sacred 734
Affliction, comfort in 555
Age, the atomic—what next? 316
   the law of God in the patriarchal 375
Alford, Dean 39, 332
Alford, Henry, *The New Testament for English Readers* 332
American Catholic Quarterly Review, The 440
American Prohibition Year Book of 1912 731
Angels, the dark ministries of evil 524
   the ministration of good 518
Answers to prayer 606
Antichrist, the kingdom and work of 211
Antitype, the atonement in type and 234
Armor, the Christian 537
Arnold, General H. H., in *Questions and Answers About Atomic Energy* 719
Atomic age—what next? the 316
Atonement in type and antitype, the 234
Attributes of God, the character and 59
Augsburg Confession 433, 437
Augsburg Sunday School Teacher, The 357
Auslegung des Alten Testaments (Commentary on the Old Testament) 407
Author of liberty, the 465
Avery-Stuttle, Mrs. L. D. (poem) 327

BABYLON, the fall of modern 249
Backbiting, gossiping and 681
Backsliding 672
Bacon, Leonard Woolsey, *An Inside View of the Vatican Council* 212
Bailland, Edouard, *Report on the Reform of the Calendar* 453
Baptism, Christian 97
Barber, John W., *Connecticut Historical Collections* 306
Barnes, Dr. Albert 155
   Notes on the Book of Revelation; The Cottage Bible 176, 186, 587
Baronius, Cesare, *Annales* 213
Barrett, Sir William F., *On the Threshold of the Unseen* 526
Bathurst, William H. (poem) 204
Baxter 132
Beast, making an image to the 271
Bede, Venerable 456
Beecher, Henry Ward 622, 733
Belden, F. E. (poem) 71, 361
Believers, unity of 577
Bellamy, W. H. (poem) 563
Bellarmine, Robert, *Disputationes de Controversiis* 212
"Better of Two, The" (poem) 361
Bible, Christ in all the 39
   how to understand the 28
   how to study and understand it 23
   its origin, history, and place in the world 13
   titles given to Christ in the 42

Bible, election 116
   sanctification 119
   study, the value of 19
Biennial Report 320, 323
Binney, Amos, *Theological Compend* 451
Binney, Amos and Daniel Steele, *Binney's Theological Compend Improved* 408, 432
Birks, Rev. T. R., *The Four Prophetic Empires, and the Kingdom of the Messiah* 209, 214
Birth, childhood, and early life of Christ 139
"Blind Hymn Writer, The" (poem) 280
Bliss, P. P. (poem) 476
Boak, A. E. R., *A History of Rome to 565 A.D.* 209, 479
Boak, A. E. R., Albert Hyma, and Preston Slosson, *The Growth of European Civilization* 208, 224
Book with seven seals, the 286
Bower, Dr., *History of the Popes* 456
Boyle, Isaac, *Historical View of the Council of Nice* 456, 481
Britannica, Encylopaedia 251, 286, 289, 439, 486
British Statutes at Large 486
Burbank, Luther 733
Burdette, Robert J. 733
Burton, Henry K. (poem) 625

Cambridge Ancient History, The 222, 223, 251
Campbell, Alexander, *The Christian Baptist* 450, 451
Capital and labor, conflict between 313
Carlstadt, *Von dem Sabbat und gebotten feyertagen* 458
Carroll, Robert S., *What Price Alcohol?* 729, 731, 732
Carver, W. O., *Sabbath Observance* 408, 413, 425, 453, 455
Cassian, *Institutes* 457
Catechism of the Council of Trent 433
Catholic Advocate, The 268
Catholic Encyclopedia, The 215, 490
Catholic Mirror, The 434
Catholic Universe Bulletin, The 445
Ceremonial laws, the moral and 381
Challoner, Rt. Rev. Dr., *The Catholic Christian Instructed* 461
Change of the Sabbath, the 430
Chapman, J. Wilbur 118
Character and attributes of God, the 60
Character, perfection of 591
Charlemagne, *Admonitio Generalis*, in *Monumenta Germaniae Historica, Leges* 485
Cheerfulness 567
Child training 706
Childhood of Christ, birth, and early life 139
Children, promises for the 709
   teaching the 711
Christ, and the Sabbath 423
   birth, childhood, and early life of 139
   in all the Bible 39
   life only in 493, 505
   miracles of 156
   or Diana? 539

762

INDEX

prophecies relating to 67
salvation only through 75
sufferings of 161
the deity of 64
the great Teacher 153
the resurrection of 166
the Way of life 72
the way to 77
titles given to, in the Bible 42
what was abolished by 394
Christian, armor, the 537
baptism 97
communion 617
courtesy 570
growth and experience 533
help work 637
liberty 463
service 623
temperance 723
Christian Century, The 318, 320, 321, 326, 327, 491
Christian Statesman 274, 277
Christ's, coming, manner of 334
coming, object of 336
ministry 149
second coming 328
Church and state, union of 477
Church, Satan's warfare against the 261
Churches, the seven 281
City life, evils of 717
Civilta Cattolica, La 212, 491
Clarke, Adam, *Commentary* 208, 209, 214, 394, 501, 529
Clarke, Thomas, *History of Intolerance* 488
Clerke, Agnes M., *A Popular History of Astronomy in the Nineteenth Century* 290, 306
Clifton Tracts 461
Closing gospel message, the 257
Cobb, Ty 732
Codex Justinianus 439, 484
Coffin, Charles C. 18
Coleman, Lyman, *Ancient Christianity Exemplified* 437, 455, 457
Comfort in affliction 555
Coming, Christ's second 328
Coming events and signs of the times 299
Coming, manner of Christ's 334
object of Christ's 336
Communion, Christian 617
Confessing faults and forgiving one another 571
Confession and forgiveness 88
Conflict between capital and labor 313
Conflict ended, the 755
Consecration 113
Constitutions of the Holy Apostles 457
Contentment 564
Conversion, or the new birth 93
the world's 323
Corpus Juris Canonici 212
Courtesy, Christian 570
Cousins, Norman, editorial, *The Saturday Review of Literature* 321
Modern Man Is Obsolete 311
Covenants, the two 387
Covetousness 661
Cowper, William (poem) 53, 674
Crafts, Rev. W. F., *History of the International Reform Bureau* 275
Christian Statesman 274, 277
Creation, and redemption 55
and the Creator 45
Criticizing, judging and 678

Cumont, Franz, *Astrology and Religion Among the Greeks and Romans* 250, 251, 252
The Oriental Religions in Roman Paganism 251

DALE, Dr. R. W., *The Ten Commandments* 450
Danger of debt 666
Daniel 8, the prophetic symbols of 219
Daniel, Robert T. (poem) 100
Dark ministries of evil angels, the 524
Davis, Corie (poem) 285
Davis, Helen M., editorial in *Chemistry* 318
Day of the Lord, the 350
Day, the Lord's 447
Decision of the Court of Appeals of the District of Columbia 277
Debt, danger of 666
Deity of Christ, the 64
D'Espine, Henry, in *Gazette de Lausanne*, 325
Destiny of Satan, origin, history and 495
Di Bruno, Joseph Faa, *Catholic Belief* 253
Dignity, sobriety and 583
Diligence in labor 588
Dissimulation, hypocrisy and 685
Doctrine, importance of sound 123
Doellinger, J. J. I. Von, *Beitraege zur Sektengeschichte des Mittelalters* 458
Donner, M. Anders 453
Doubt, unbelief and 675
Douglass, Frederick, *Life and Times of Frederick Douglass* 306, 307
Doyle, Sir Arthur Conan, *The New Revelation* 528
Dream, Nebuchadnezzar's 195
Dryden, John 565
Duchesne, L., *Christian Worship: Its Origin and Evolution* 438
Duty and encouragement, the 575
Duty, our, toward the poor 635
Dwight, Timothy, *Theology* 305, 450

Ecclesiastical History, An 438
Eckhardt, Carl Conrad, *The Papacy and World-Affairs* 210
Edwards, Jonathan, *Works*. Reprint of Worcester ed., 426
Works 374
Election, Bible 116
Elijah the prophet 352
Encouragement, the duty of 575
Encyclopaedia Britannica 251, 289, 439, 486
Endurance, patient 562
Epictetus 565
Episcopal Church Sunday School Magazine, The 378
Epitome of Pontoppidan's Explanation of Martin Luther's Small Catechism 369
Eternal life 744
Eusebius, *Church History* 303
Commentary on the Psalms 439
The Life of Constantine 456
Evening Star (Washington, D.C.) 275
Evil angels, the dark ministries of 524
Evil, the origin of 48
Evils, of city life 717
of intemperance 729
Experience, Christian growth and 533
Extravagantes Communes 212

BIBLE READINGS

FAGLEY, Richard M., *The Chaplain* 323
Fairchild, James H., *Moral Philosophy* 473, 474
Faith, justification by 106
  saving 543
  the obedience of 133
  victorious 79
Fall, and redemption of man, the 50
  of modern Babylon, the 249
Fallaw, Wesner, in *The Christian Century* 320, 322, 327
Farrar, Dean F. W., *The Life of Christ* 144
  The Voice From Sinai 437
Fate of the transgressor 514
Faults, confessing, and forgiving one another 571
Ferraris, Lucius, *Prompta Bibliotheca* 212, 215, 432, 433
Ferris, Daniel, *Manual of Christian Doctrine* 434
Flick, A. C., *The Rise of the Mediaeval Church* 210, 250, 267, 287, 458, 479
Force, Peter, *Tracts Relating to the Colonies in North America* 277, 486
Forgiveness, confession and 88
Forgiving one another, confessing faults and 571
Fortune 319
Fosdick, Raymond B., *The New York Times Magazine* 319, 325
Four great monarchies 205
Franklin, Benjamin 565
  Writings of Benjamin Franklin 492
Frederick the Great 572
Freewill offerings 651
Friend, our helper and 147
Fruit of the Spirit 174

GAME of life, the 759
Gathering of Israel, the 342
Geddes, Michael, *Church History of Ethiopia* 458
Geiermann, Peter, *The Convert's Catechism of Catholic Doctrine* 431, 434
Gibbon, *History of the Decline and Fall of the Roman Empire* 198
Gibbons' autograph letter 434
Gibbons, James Cardinal, *The Catholic Mirror* 434
  The Faith of Our Fathers 216, 435, 451
Gift, of giving, the 624
  of prophecy, the 179
Gifts of the Spirit 177
Gildea, Dr. William, *Catholic World* 451
Giving, gift of, 624
Gladstone, William E., *Later Gleanings* 450
Glory, the kingdom of 740
  kingdoms of grace and 200
Gloss 212
God, acceptance with 103
  hope in 82
  reconciled to 101
  reverence for the house of 613
  the character and attributes of 59
  the law of 357, 362, 363, 368, 381, 431
  the law of, in the patriarchal age 375
  the love of 61
  the mystery of, finished 298
  the seal of, and the mark of apostasy 442
Goddell, Dr. William 608

"God's Holy Word" (poem) 22
God's, judgment, the hour of 226
  memorial 409
  ten-commandment law 362
Good, angels, the ministration of 518
  health 725
Gordon, A. J., *How Christ Came to Church* 331
Gospel, preaching the 629
  the law and the 398
Gospel message, the closing 257
Gossiping and backbiting 681
Grace and glory, the kingdoms of 200
Grace, growth in 535
Great persecuting power, a 266
Greatest, who is he? 654
Gregory (Pope) I, *Nicene and Post-Nicene Fathers* 457
Gregory (Pope) VII, 213
Gregory IX, *The Decretals of* 212
Griffin, Philip L., 732
Growth and experience, Christian 533
Growth in grace 535
Guinness, H. Grattan, *Romanism and the Reformation* 266

HALLAM, Henry, *The Constitutional History of England* 459
Hamlin, Dr. Cyrus 608
Happy home 695
Harnack, Adolph, *What Is Christianity?* 211, 267
Harper's Magazine 317
Hart, Joseph (poem) 184, 244
Hartzell, Ethel M. (poem) 148
Haskins, Charlotte (poem) 126
Hastings, *Encyclopedia of Religion and Ethics* 485
Haweis, Thomas (poem) 255
Healing the sick 675
Health and temperance 723
Health, good 725
Heart, purity of 715
Hefele, Charles Joseph, *A History of the Councils of the Church* 440, 457, 484
Helper and friend, our 147
Hiscox, Dr. Edward T. 450
History of Satan, origin and destiny 495
  the Sabbath in 453
Hoffman, E. A. (poem) 523
Holland, J. G. (poem) 504
Holy Spirit and His work, the 171
Holy Spirit, the 169
Home, the 689
  a happy 695
  of the saved, the 747
  religion in the 699
Honor due to parents 703
Hooton, E. A., in *Times-Herald* (Washington, D.C.) 325
Hope in God 82
Hour of judgment, the 226
House of God, reverence for the 613
"How Readest Thou?" (poem) 297
How to understand the Bible 28
How, William Walsham (poem) 145
Hudson, Winthrop S., *The Christian Century* 321
Humility, meekness and 580
Hutchinson, Paul, *The Forum* 319
  The New Leviathan 491
Hyatt, J. Philip, *The Teacher* 394
Hypocrisy and dissimulation 685

INDEX

IMAGE to the beast, making an 271
Importance, of prayer 597
　of sound doctrine 123
Increase of knowledge 309
Independent Chronicle 290
Individual accountability 475
Institution, of the Sabbath 405
　the marriage 691
Intemperance, evils of 729
Intermediate state, the 506
International Standard Bible Encyclopaedia 430
Israel, the gathering of 342

JEFFERSON, Thomas, *Thomas Jefferson Papers* 272, 273
　The Works of Thomas Jefferson 272
Jesus, trusting in 560
Jordan, Virgil, *Manifesto for the Atomic Age* 317
Josephus, *Wars of the Jews* 13, 304
Judging and criticizing 678
Judgment, the 240
　the hour of God's 226
Judgment-hour message, the 245
Just, the resurrection of the 339
Just recompense, the 687
Justification by faith 106
Justin Martyr, *Dialogue With Trypho* 457
Justinian's Code 217

KEENAN, Rev. Stephen, *A Doctrinal Catechism* 215, 434, 459
Kelly, Vincent J., *Forbidden Sunday and Feast-Day Occupations* 435, 437, 439, 455
Killen, W. D., *The Ancient Church* 426, 449
Kingdom, and work of antichrist, the 211
　the subjects of the 740
Kingdoms of grace and glory, the 200
Kitto, *Cyclopaedia of Biblical Literature* 656
Knowledge, increase of 309
Knox, John 131

LABOR, conflict between capital and 313
　diligence in 588
Laing, Gordon J., *Survivals of Roman Religion* 251-252
Langdon, S. H., *Semitic Mythology* 251
Lange, John Peter, *The Commentary on the Holy Scriptures* 407
Latourette, Kenneth Scott, *The Christian Outlook* 312, 317, 324, 326
Laux, John, *A Course in Religion for Catholic High Schools and Academies* 253, 435
Law, and the gospel, the 398
　of God, the 355, 357, 362, 431
　of God in the New Testament, the 378
　of God in the patriarchal age, the 375
　the perpetuity of the 363
　why given at Sinai 368
Laws, the moral and ceremonial 381
Lecky, W. E. H., *History of the Rise and Influence of the Spirit of Rationalism in Europe* 214, 489
Legislation, Sabbath 483
Leo XIII, *The Great Encyclical Letters of Leo XIII* 275

Liberty, Christian 463
　the author of 465
Life, a sinless 143
　eternal 744
　evils of city 717
　of Christ, early; birth, childhood, and 139
　only in Christ 493, 505
　miracles of Christ 156
　righteousness and 111
　the game of 759
Light, walking in the 540
"Like the Pattern" (poem) 146
Lilienthal, David, in *Life* 326
Lindbergh, Charles A., in *Reader's Digest* 318
Little, Canon Knox, *Sacerdotalism* 450
Listen 732
Llorente, *The History of the Inquisition in Spain* 214
Lodge, Sir Oliver, *Raymond or Life and Death* 529
Lord, the day of the 350
Lord's Day Alliance, The 274
Lord's day, the 447
　great prophecy, our 301
　prayer, the 604
Love of God, the 61
Luther, Martin 131, 369, 545
　(poem) 142
　Sämmtliche Schriften 110, 407, 476
Luther's Small Catechism 369
Lyell, Sir Charles, *Principles of Geology* 289

MACARTHUR, Douglas A., *The New York Times* 323
Macaulay, Lord, *Critical and Historical Essays* 488-489, 491
Making an image to the beast 271
Man, the fall and redemption of 50
　what is 500
Manner, of Christ's coming 334
　of observing the Sabbath 417
Mansi, J. D., *Sacrorum Conciliorum. . . . Collectio* 212
Mark of apostasy, the seal of God and the 442
Marriage institution, the 691
Martyr, Justin 457
McAllister, David, *The National Reform Movement . . . A Manual of Christian Civil Government* 274
M'Clintock and Strong, *Cyclopaedia of Biblical, Theological, and Ecclesiastical Literature* 237, 451, 458
McKinley, William 733
Meditation and prayer 601
Meekness and humility 580
Memoirs of the American Academy of Arts and Sciences 305
Memorial, God's 409
Merle d'Aubigne, J. H., *History of the Reformation* 110, 545
Message, the closing gospel 257
　the judgment-hour 245
Migne, *Patrologia Graeca* 439, 456
Millennium, the 345
Miller, J. R., *Week-Day Religion* 552, 553, 568, 576, 597, 700
Ministration of good angels, the 518
Ministries of evil angels, the dark 524
Ministry, Christ's 149
　of sorrow, the 552
　support of the 649

Miracles, of Christ 156
Missionary work 632
Monarchies, four great 205
Monsell, J. S. B. (poem) 620
Moody, D. L., *The Second Coming of Christ* 331, 332, 334
  Weighed and Wanting 359, 406
Moral and ceremonial laws, the 381
Morer, *A Discourse in Six Dialogues on the Name, Notion, and Observation of the Lord's Day* 437
Morgan, G. Campbell, *The Ten Commandments* 359, 400
Morrison, Charles Clayton, in *The Christian Century* 320
Mother, the 715
Murphy, Frances 697
Murphy, James G., *Commentary on the Book of Exodus* 414
Mystery of God finished, the 298

NATURE 453
Neander, Augustus, *General History of the Christian Religion and Church* 276, 438, 478, 481, 485
  The History of the Christian Religion and Church 484
Nebuchadnezzar's dream 195
Nelson's New Loose-leaf Encyclopedia 289
New birth, conversion or the 93
New Jerusalem, the 752
New Schaff-Herzog Encyclopedia of Religious Knowledge, The 237, 485
New Testament, the law of God in the 378
  the Sabbath in the 427
New York Journal of Commerce 290
Newman, J. H., *An Essay on the Development of Christian Doctrine* 251, 477
Newton, Thomas, *Dissertations on the Prophecies* 282

OBEDIENCE of faith, the 133
Object of Christ's coming 336
Object, trials and their 547
Offerings, freewill 651
Olmsted, Denison, *The American Journal of Science and Arts* 306
Order and organization 646
Orfila, M. 732
Organization, order and 646
Origen, *Homily on Numbers* 457
Origin, history, and destiny of Satan 495
  of evil, the 48
Our, helper and friend 147
  Lord's great prophecy 301
  pattern 145
Outpouring of the Spirit, the 185
Overcomer, promises to the 738
Overcoming 550

PARENTS, honor due to 703
Patient endurance 562
Patriarchal age, the law of God in the 375
Pattern, our 145
Patton, Mel, in *Listen* 732
Peloubet's Select Notes 364
Penalty for transgression 373
Pennsylvania Evening Post 290
Perfection of character 591
Perpetuity of the law, the 363
Perrin, Jean, *History of the Vaudois* 458
Persecute, who, and why 487

Persecuting power, a great 266
Persons, respect of 669
Pius (Pope) XII 275
Plagues, the seven last 292
Poor, the, and our duty toward them 635
Power, a great persecuting 266
Power in the word of God 33
Powers that be, the 469
Praise and thanksgiving 619
Prayer, and public worship 595
  answers to 606
  importance of 597
  meditation and 601
  watching unto 604
Preaching the gospel 629
Present truth 127
Price, Lucien, *Religion in the Post-War World* 311
Pride, sinful 659
Procter, Adelaide A. (poem) 680
Procter, William C., in *Moody Bible Institute Monthly* 364, 368, 377, 399, 432
Promises, for the children 709
  to the overcomer 738
Prophecies relating to Christ 67
Prophecy, our Lord's great 301
  the gift of 179
  the sure word of 189
  why given 191
Prophet, Elijah the 352
Prophetic history of the church, a 281
Prophetic symbols of Daniel 8, the 219
Prynne, William, *A Briefe Polemicall Dissertation Concerning . . . the Lordsday-Sabbath* 440, 455
Public worship 609
  prayer and 595
Purchas, Samuel, *Purchas His Pilgrimes* 458
Purity of heart 720

REAPING, sowing and 593
Reasons for Sabbathkeeping 413
Recompense, the just 687
Reconciled to God 101
Redemption, creation and 55
  of man, the fall and 50
Reform, Sabbath 460
  true temperance 735
Religion in the home 699
Repentance 85
Respect of persons 669
Resurrection, of Christ, the 166
  of the just, the 339
Resurrections, the two 509
Reverence for the house of God 613
Ridley 131
Righteousness and life 111
Robinson, John 131
Robinson, Stewart M., in *The Presbyterian* 388
"Rock, The" (poem) 148
Rockne, Knute 732
Rosser, Elizabeth (poem) 701

SABBATH, the 403
  Christ and the 423
  in history, the 453
  in the New Testament, the 427
  institution of the 405
  legislation 483
  manner of observing the 417

INDEX

reform 460
  the change of the 430
Sabbathkeeping, reasons for 413
Sacred admonitions 734
Salvation only through Christ 75
Sanctification, Bible 119
San Francisco Chronicle 268
Satan, origin, history, and destiny of 495
Satan's warfare against the church 261
Saved, the home of the 747
Saving faith 543
Schaff, Philip, *Creeds of Christendom* 213, 333, 374, 375, 383, 385, 433, 437
  History of the Christian Church 283, 287, 439, 479, 480, 484
Scott, Martin J., *Things Catholics Are Asked About* 435
Scriptures, the sacred 25
Seal of God and the mark of apostasy 442
Seals, the seven 286
Second coming, Christ's 328
Segur, Louis, *Plain Talk About the Protestantism of Today* 279, 446
Selfishness 660
Selina, Countess of Huntingdon (poem) 338
Service, Christian 623
Seven, churches 281
  last plagues 292
  seals 286
Shakespeare 733
Shepherd and his work, the 627
Sick, healing the 643
  visiting the 641
Signs of the times, coming events and 299
Sin, its origin, results, and remedy 43
Sinai, why was the law given at 368
Sinful pride 659
Sinless life, a 143
Sixty-nine weeks, or 483 years, diagram of 230
Smiles, Samuel, *Thrift* 668
Smith and Cheetham, *A Dictionary of Christian Antiquities* 451
Smith, Albert 440
Smith, Annie R. (poem) 745
Smith, Harrison, editorial in *The Saturday Review of Literature* 318, 322
Smith's Comprehensive Dictionary of the Bible 655
Smith, Uriah, *The Prophecies of Daniel and the Revelation* 222, 223, 282
Snowden-Douglass Sunday School Lessons, The 360, 379
Sobriety and dignity 583
Socrates, *Ecclesiastical History*, in *A Select Library of Nicene and Post-Nicene Fathers* 437-438, 457
Song, the value of 621
Sorokin, Pitirim A., *The Crisis of Our Age* 320
Sorrow, the ministry of 552
Sound doctrine, importance of 123
Sowing and reaping 593
Sozomen, *Ecclesiastical History* 438
Spirit, fruit of the 174
  gifts of the 177
  the holy 169
  the outpouring of the 185
Spiritualism 127
Spurgeon, C. H. 582, 698, 733
  The Gospel of the Kingdom 379
  Sermons 358, 384
Staley, Rev. Vernon, *The Catholic Religion* 121

State, the intermediate 506
  union of church and 477
Stewart, James S., *Heralds of God* 317, 319
Stimson, Henry L. 317
Stockman, E. A., *Footprints of Angels in Fields of Revelation* 520, 522
Stoddard, Jane T., *The Case Against Spiritualism* 527-528
Stoddard, John L., *Rebuilding a Lost Faith* 449
Subjects of the kingdom, the 740
Sufferings of Christ 161
Summerbell, N., *History of the Christian Church* 433
Support of the ministry 649
Symbols, of Daniel 8, the prophetic 219

TALMAGE, T. De Witt 125, 271, 547, 568, 593, 668, 698
Tappan, William B. (poem) 269
Taylor, Bishop 581
Taylor, J. J., *The Sabbatic Question* 277, 406, 429, 435
Taylor, Jeremy, *Ductor Dubitantium* 435
Teacher, Christ the great 153
Teaching the children 711
Temperance, Christian 727
  health and 723
  reform, true 735
Tenney, Samuel, *Collections of the Massachusetts Historical Society* 305
Tertullian, *De Corona*, in ANF 477
  On Prayer 457
Testament, the law of God in the New 378
Thanksgiving, praise and 619
Thomas, H. F. 445
Titles given to Christ in the Bible 42
Tittle, Ernest Fremont, in *The Christian Century* 321
Transgression, penalty for 373
Transgressor, fate of the 514
Tregelles' translation 502
Trench, Archbishop (poem) 603
Trials and their object 547
Training, child 706
True, temperance reform 735
  wisdom 585
Trusting in Jesus 560
Truth, present 127
Tuberville, Rev. Henry, *An Abridgement of the Christian Doctrine* 216, 278, 434, 445
Tunney, Gene, in *Reader's Digest* 732
Turmel, Joseph, *The Latin Church in the Middle Ages* 211
Two covenants, the 387
Two resurrections, the 509
Type and antitype, the atonement in 234

UNBELIEF and doubt 675
Union of church and state 477
Unity of believers 577
Urey, Harold C., *The Saturday Review of Literature* 318, 323

VALUE of song, the 621
Van Paassen, Pierre, *Days of Our Years* 320
Victorious faith 79
Vincent, Bishop 611
Visiting the sick 641

WAFFLE, A. E., *The Lord's Day* 451
Walden, Robert Lee (poem) 559
Walking in the light 540
Wallace, O. C. S., *What Baptists Believe*, 363, 367, 402
Warnings, admonitions and 657
Warfare against the church, Satan's 261
Warren, Henry P. 17
Washington, George, *Writings of George Washington* 475
Washington Herald 531
Washington Law Reporter 277
Watching unto prayer 604
Watts, Isaac (poem) 280, 441, 499, 584, 587, 688
Way, of life, Christ the 72
  to Christ, the 77
Webster's Collegiate Dictionary 475, 527
Wesley, Charles (poem) 546
Wesley, John, *The Character of a Methodist* 359
  Explanatory Notes Upon the New Testament 271
  Works 359, 365, 390, 397, 405, 492
Wharey, James, *Sketches of Church History* 287
What is man? 500
What was abolished by Christ? 394
"When Thou, My Righteous Judge" (poem) 338
White, Mrs. E. G. 525, 578
White, E. G., *Christ's Object Lessons* 684
  The Desire of Ages 66, 421
  Education 622
  The Great Controversy 532
  Ministry of Healing 641
  Patriarchs and Prophets 701
  SDA Bible Commentary 503
  Steps to Christ 88, 545, 597
  Thoughts From the Mount of Blessing 551
  Your Home and Health 698
Who is the greatest? 654
Who persecute and why 487
Why was the law given at Sinai? 368
Williams, Mrs. E. E. (poem) 640
Williams, Isaac, *Plain Sermons on the Catechism* 437
Williams, Rev. John (poem) 474
Williams, Samuel 305
Wisdom, true 585
Word, of God, power in the 33
  of prophecy, the sure 189
  the life-giving 36
Work, Christian help 637
  missionary 632
  of antichrist, the kingdom and 211
  the shepherd and his 627
World's conversion, the 323
Worship, public 609
  prayer and 595

YOUNG, *Analytical Concordance* 500, 507
Young, Charles A., *Manual of Astronomy* 290